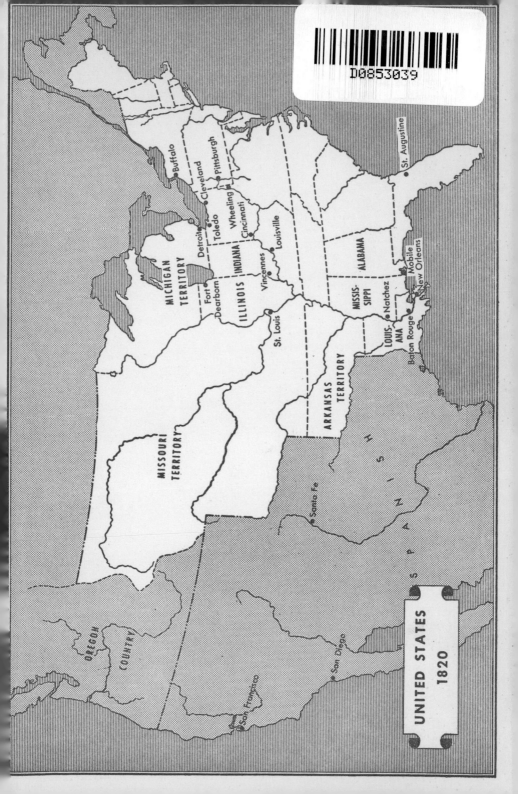

AMERICA
MOVES WEST

Third Edition

ROBERT E. RIEGEL

Dartmouth College

HOLT, RINEHART AND WINSTON, INC.

New York

27450–0216

PRINTED IN THE UNITED STATES OF AMERICA

TO

M.C.R.

PREFACE TO THIRD EDITION

A NY author feels pleased when his work remains in sufficient demand to warrant revision, and welcomes the opportunity to make the changes necessitated by the passing of the years. The present revision corrects a few errors where author, typist, or printer slipped, but more important it adds pertinent research of the past decade. There is also a new chapter on the Pacific Coast, and the reading lists have been completely redone. Many people, including particularly Professor Robert G. Athearn of the University of Colorado, have made useful suggestions, and I am only sorry that in some cases they have seemed impossible of adoption. I hope, however, that the new book will give profit and pleasure to its readers.

R. E. R.

HANOVER, N. H.
NOVEMBER 30, 1955

v

PREFACE TO SECOND EDITION

OUR understanding of American westward expansion has increased so tremendously within the past twenty years that a revised edition of *America Moves West* has seemed desirable. Major improvements have been made. Over half of the text has been rewritten completely, and the remainder has been revised thoroughly. The organization has been altered. Certain types of material, as on the railroads, have been condensed, and others expanded. A chapter on frontier theory has been introduced. The specific movements of population have been stated more accurately. The treatment of the entire trans-Mississippi West has been changed a great deal in the light of more information. In many ways the present revision is a new book.

The opportunity to make this fresh synthesis of western history is a real privilege, and thanks should go to the many teachers and students who have used the original book and hence have made the revision practical. To them I express the hope that the new book will fit their needs and desires, and also my thanks for the many kind comments they have made in the past.

My debt to other people is too great for adequate expression. Professor Fred A. Shannon of the University of Illinois has read the entire manuscript, and his many incisive and stimulating comments have been of great value. My colleague Professor Allen R. Foley has also read the entire manuscript, and has given me the benefit of his judgment. Professor George W. Pierson of Yale University has read the last chapter, with advantage to the presentation. Dozens of other people have given very useful help in personal conversations, in letters, and in their writings. Among those who have made specific suggestions of value are Professors J. C. Malin of the University of Kansas, Bayrd Still of Duke University, A. V. House, Jr., of Wilson Teachers College, T. P. Abernethy of the University of Virginia, H. E. Briggs of the University of Miami, H. J. Carman of Columbia University, R. C. Downes of the University of Toledo, W. M. Gewehr of the University of Maryland, J. D. Hicks of the University of California, W. J. Peterson of the University of Iowa, J. P. Pritchett of Queens College, R. M. Robbins of Butler University and R. H. Shryock of the University of Pennsylvania. To them, as to the many others who have given assistance, whether they realized it or not, my deepest appreciation. And I should not forget my wife, Mabel C. Riegel, whose greatest service has not been her arduous labor on the book, but her tolerance of a husband who preferred writing about mining and homesteading to obviously more interesting activities.

R. E. R.

DARTMOUTH COLLEGE
NOVEMBER 15, 1946

CONTENTS

LIST OF ILLUSTRATIONS

CHAPTER 1

THE
MOUNTAIN BARRIER

THE United States has been a frontier nation through most of its history. For over two centuries settled America could look west toward dimly known mountain ranges, vast forests, unexplored streams and immense prairies. The American West beckoned alluringly to the ambitious, the restless, the discontented, and the lawless. The whole course of American history was conditioned by the existence of a sparsely settled frontier that pushed continuously into the Indian country.

American white population moved across continental United States with ever increasing momentum. From Jamestown and Plymouth to the Appalachians required a hundred and fifty years, but the Mississippi was attained in an additional fifty, while the remaining two-thirds of the continent was spotted with white civilization in another fifty.

National boundaries seldom gave the frontier more than temporary pause. Not only were Indian claims brushed aside, but also those of Mexico, Spain, Russia, and England. Settlers poured into Florida, Louisiana, Texas, California, and Oregon before the United States obtained control. When new lands beckoned in Canada, the international boundary proved no deterrent. And when lands beyond the sea attracted American enterprise, that call was answered.

This questing of peoples for new land and opportunity, while notable in America, should not be considered as purely American, even if one includes all the Americas. European and Asiatic frontiers have existed within historic times. Some day there may be a study of frontier advance which will show the traits common to all frontiers and the ones peculiar to the United States. Even within

1

the United States there have been differences as well as similarities between various racial and national groups.

For Americans, migration to the West was but one of the possible outlets for the ambitious. The young Yankee farmer might equally well try his fortune in a factory at Boston or Fall River, at a store in Richmond or New Orleans, or on a ship trading with Calcutta or Honolulu. The movement from country to town was coexistent with the frontier, while all movement from section to section was by no means east to west. In fact many men moved from west to east, either as they failed and came back home or as they saw greater opportunities on the Atlantic seaboard.

The limits of a study of the American frontier are not easy to set — even in time. A start might be made with Columbus and the story carried to non-American countries of the present. Actually this book begins about the time of the American Revolution, when the colonies had attained some measure of independence socially and economically as well as politically, and hence when the frontier might be considered more American than European. It ends somewhere around 1900, at which time the American West was no longer distinctively a frontier region.

COLONIES AT TIME OF REVOLUTION

The American Revolution was a dramatic indication of the rapidly increasing gap between European and American conditions and points of view. Americans had been conditioned by a century and a half of contact with an untamed wilderness. They had begun to realize their own potentialities — that they could provide their own economic, social and religious necessities, for which they had depended upon Europe for so many years. The Revolution was an indication of a definite cleavage already in existence between the Old and the New World.

Self-confidence and youthful enthusiasm did not necessarily imply strength, for, when viewed realistically, the English colonies at the time of the Revolution were far from awe-inspiring as a factor in the affairs of the world. Thirteen small colonies straggling along the coast from Maine to Georgia could boast of a population of only some 2,600,000. Virginia was the most populous, and after her followed in order Massachusetts, Pennsylvania, North Carolina, and Maryland. Philadelphia was the largest colonial city, her competitors being Boston, Newport, New York, and Charleston. None of them would today be entitled to the appellation of a large city. Every important city was either on the seaboard or on some large river which afforded good communication with the sea.

Outside of the larger towns, population tended to concentrate along the rivers, so that produce could be shipped to market more easily. The inland limit of civilization was in general the Appalachians, and few people had gone that far or farther west. To the north and south settlement became more sparse and finally gave way to the wilderness. In the north a small fraction of Maine was settled; central and northern New Hampshire and Vermont were just being opened; in New York adventurous German immigrants were pushing out along the Mohawk. In the south the population of Georgia was largely prospective.

Agriculture was the predominant pursuit. Everywhere there were small farms, but south of the Potomac there were also large plantations growing tobacco, indigo, and rice, with slave labor. Slavery, however, seemed to be an uneconomic and dying institution, and many of the farseeing planters were looking forward to a not too distant day when slavery would cease to exist. North of the Potomac small farms were almost universal, with the owner, his wife and his children doing most of the work, with now and then a hired laborer to help with planting and harvesting.

Manufacturing remained largely in the home, since the mother country discouraged any competition with her new and struggling industries. Here and there iron forges, hat factories, and other small enterprises gave a faint promise of future industrialization.

Shipping was an item of major interest to the northern colonies. The Yankee shipper was a well-known figure on the seas. His business was expanding rapidly, and he was soon to talk of Canton, Singapore, Oregon, the Sandwich Islands, and other far places of the world. South of New England the ports did most of their business in foreign bottoms. The tendency of the plantation owner was to deal directly with his European connections, eliminating American middlemen.

Intercolonial business by land was small and unimportant. The first good improved road was not built until after the Revolution. People depended for the most part on rivers as their best means of communication, and in general the rivers flowed from west to east, not north and south, with the result that trade between the colonies never assumed large proportions. As late as 1803 John Quincy Adams needed twenty days to ride his horse to Washington from his home at Quincy.

The population of the seaboard area of the thirteen colonies was overwhelmingly English, although other racial stocks were represented. A landed Dutch aristocracy dominated the Hudson and Mohawk River valleys; a few Swedes were settled along the Delaware River; some French Huguenots were scattered at various places along the Atlantic Coast. In the main, however, the coast settlements were English in race and heritage.

COLONIAL FRONTIERSMEN

In the western part of the colonies were two new and growing groups, the Germans and the Scotch-Irish. Both differed so vastly from the majority of the population that such good patriots as Benjamin Franklin deplored what they held to be the new, strange and uncouth peoples. The Germans came from the Palatinate after 1710 and landed for the most part at New York and Philadelphia. The colonists encouraged them to go west, settle new land and fight the Indians — with certain obvious advantages to the easterners. In consequence there emerged such regions as the " German flats " along the Mohawk River, and the " Pennsylvania Dutch " section of Pennsylvania. The Scotch-Irish tended to enter America at Philadelphia or farther south, and went to the frontier at about the same time as the Germans. Particular regions in Pennsylvania still show the checkerboard of alternate German and Scotch-Irish settlement.

As frontiersmen the Germans and the Scotch-Irish had both desirable and undesirable traits. From the viewpoint of the earlier settlers they served as a buffer against the Indians, but the Scotch-Irish were considered turbulent and self-willed, contentious, cantankerous, belligerent; everyone was glad to see them go west, and felt sorry only because the West was not farther away. On the other hand these new entrants were an important colonial unifying force. Moving directly to the West they spread north and south in the valleys, disregarding colonial boundaries, even if they knew of them, which they probably did not. They came to think of themselves as Americans, and not as inhabitants of some particular colony.

These new groups were always in trouble with constituted authority, no matter by whom it was wielded. They wanted land and they reasoned that wild land should belong to those who were willing to work it rather than to those who merely claimed a more or less indefinite ownership. Furthermore, they wanted legislative

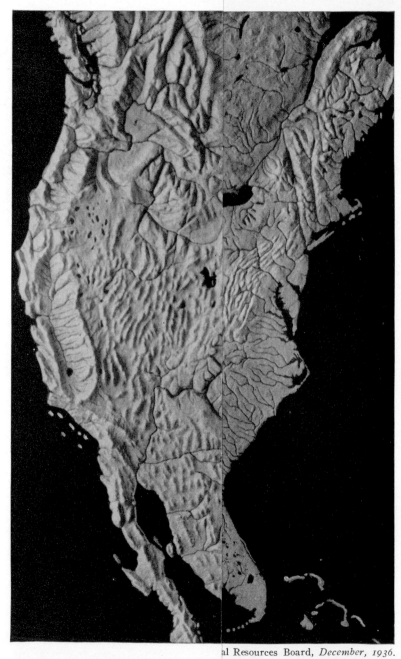

al Resources Board, *December, 1936.*

Topography and history are closely e of the physical features of the United States upon the success

representation according to their numbers. In general the East had made sure that the new western counties would be large and meagerly represented in the colonial legislatures, in order that control might remain always in the East. Surely, said the westerner, this situation was unjust — " no taxation without representation." With these views the Germans and Scotch-Irish, as representing the West, supported protest movements in New York, Pennsylvania, Virginia, North Carolina, and South Carolina just prior to the Revolution, going even so far as to wage war against the constituted authorities. But when the Revolution came, the West was just as ready to fight England as it had been willing to fight the old sources of power in the East.

West of the Scotch-Irish and Germans lay the barrier of the main ranges of the Appalachian Mountains, while still farther west were three thousand miles of wilderness — much of it as yet unknown to the white man. Well-informed persons knew the main characteristics of the country east of the Mississippi, but west of that river information was lacking. It was rumored that somewhere far in the West lay a great range of snow-capped mountains, but only a few white men had seen even small portions of the country beyond the Mississippi and north of the Red. The Spanish had occupied portions of Texas and New Mexico and were just beginning to enter the present California.

ROUTES TO THE WEST

The exploration of this vast area proceeded almost inevitably from the East, a fact of great importance in the tempo of occupation. Early exploration followed the great natural water routes, from the Atlantic Coast to the interior. Most important was the route of the St. Lawrence and the Great Lakes, which provided a variety of alternative possibilities for the traveler to proceed from the Great Lakes drainage basin to that of the Ohio-Mississippi system, with only one short portage. It was this route that the Jesuit fathers and the early French traders and trappers used to reach the heart of the continent. These early French adventurers were not much interested in establishing permanent settlements, and possibly because of this fact succeeded in living among the Indians with a minimum of friction — often intermarrying and bringing up half-breed families in the American wilds.

The second good entrance to the American continent lay in the South, for by landing almost anywhere on the Gulf Coast it was fairly easy to go inland as far as the particular explorer's strength and desire for knowledge led him. It was in this region, partly by accident, that Spain entered the continent. Starting with Columbus, numerous explorers operating under the Spanish flag came to the new land. Like the French, the Spanish were not interested primarily in settlement; precious metals and stones were more to their liking. Even the fur trade attracted no great number of Spanish adventurers. Consequently North America was less attractive to Spain than the region around the Gulf of Mexico and to the south.

Between the chief northern and southern approaches to the interior of North America were a number of routes leading more directly west. These routes were generally more difficult than those farther north or south, but became the most important in the history of westward expansion because of their use by the English colonists. Since the English were the main population element on the continent, it was their westward trek which finally conquered the wilderness.

Starting at the north, the most desirable route followed the Hudson and Mohawk rivers, and then through central New York from Ft. Stanwix through Oneida to Lake Erie, whence it was easy to follow the Great Lakes, then to ascend some river flowing into one of the lakes, and eventually to portage to the Ohio-Mississippi system. In general this is the present route of the New York Central Railroad, and excellent because of the absence of mountains. Unfortunately for the early traveler the Iroquois Indians were a more effective barrier than mountains, and before 1800 their friendship was never sufficiently assured to permit safe traveling by the Hudson-Mohawk route.

Farther south there were two routes in Pennsylvania. The first of these, the Kittanning Path, ran along the Susquehanna and Juniata rivers to the mountains, and then crossed the Appalachians to Fort Pitt (present Pittsburgh) on the Ohio River; today the Pennsylvania Railroad follows this route. In southern Pennsylvania was the Forbes Road, opened between Philadelphia and Fort Pitt in 1758; it is the general route of the present Lincoln Highway, running through Bedford, Ligonier, and Greensburg.

Along the Potomac River lay another possibility — Braddock's Road, opened in 1755, and later to become the National, or Cumberland, Road. This route followed the Potomac as far as the town of Cumberland, and then cut overland to Fort Pitt. It should be added that when the National Road was built it left the old trail west of Cumberland and had its terminus at Wheeling.

Still farther south was the Cumberland Gap — a beautiful pass through the main range of mountains in the extreme southwestern corner of present Virginia. As a pass through the mountains it was excellent and much used in Revolutionary days. Unfortunately no important settlements arose at either end of the gap, owing largely to the absence of navigable rivers and to the existence of other mountains to the east and west, so that the importance of the Cumberland Gap route tended to decrease with time.

A final important possibility for entrance to the continent lay in skirting the Appalachians to the south through Georgia. Here the mountains no longer offered a barrier to travel, but in earlier days other handicaps were just as potent. Georgia was still in the earliest stages of her development, and no considerable bodies of people were interested in going farther west. More important, powerful Indian tribes, including the Creek, lay to the west and barred travel just as effectively as did the Iroquois in New York.

Most of these routes had originally been buffalo trails, and all of them were known and used by the Indians. Before the French and Indian War they were exceedingly primitive, being only unblazed footpaths. Whenever possible they followed the uplands to avoid the spring floods. A few logs enabled the traveler to pass the worst places. Rivers were crossed on sand bars, which shifted from time to time, so that a crossing could only be made after some experimentation. During the French and Indian War Braddock's Road and Forbes Road were opened for wagons — but this merely meant that enough trees were felled and brush removed to allow the passage of crude ox carts.

Farther to the west were other trails of a similar nature — frequently well-known and much used by the Indians and by white hunters. Among them were hunting trails, penetrating farther and farther into the forest as the game was killed off; war trails; portage trails, to connect navigable bodies of water; river trails, following the streams; traders' trails, to permit travel to and from the trader's establishment. As with the trails farther east, all these paths were beaten down by countless Indian moccasins, and were usually impassable except for a man on foot. These trails were well-known to the Indians and could easily be followed by them, but to the unknowing white the wilderness seemed complete and unbroken.

COLONIAL CLASHES

While the greater part of the North American continent was unoccupied except for the native Indians, it was by no means undesired. Prior to the Revolution Spain, France, and England all had extensive claims. Conflict was inevitable, particularly between the last two powers, whose colonial empires clashed throughout the world. The American portions of this world-wide struggle for colonial domination were King William's War, Queen Anne's War, King George's War, the French and Indian War, and the American Revolution. The French and Indian War, or the Seven Years' War (1756–63), was the one which produced the map of North America which was in existence at the time of the Revolution. By the treaty of Paris, which marked the conclusion of peace, France was eliminated from the continent. England received Canada and East and West Florida, while Louisiana (including the western half of the Mississippi valley and New Orleans) went to Spain.

England, now dominant, immediately tried to settle North American affairs permanently. By the Proclamation of 1763 white settlement was limited, at least for the time being, to the region east of the Appalachians; Quebec province was given the basin of the St. Lawrence west to Lake Nipissing; East and West Florida (to the Mississippi) were given the boundary of 31° and a separate government (West Florida was later expanded as far north as the Yazoo River). A series of Indian treaties attempted to limit Indian claims and avoid conflict with the whites. Most important were the Treaty of Fort Stanwix (New York) with the Six Nations of the Iroquois confederacy, and the Treaty of Hard Labour with the Cherokee confederacy of the South; both came in 1768. A final and logical step in the development of the English policy concerning America came in 1774 when the " Old Northwest " — that is, the region between the Ohio River and the Great Lakes, and between the Mississippi River and the Appalachian Mountains — was added to the province of Quebec for administrative purposes.

These developments of English colonial administration were among the sources of irritation which eventuated in the American Revolution. Many of the colonists were interested in western land and the possibility of its settlement, and were therefore opposed to the Proclamation of 1763 and the restrictions on trade with the Indians. Many thought the Indians too well treated and the colonies given insufficient protection. Furthermore, there were stren-

HUDSON'S BAY COMPANY

SPANISH

QUEBEC

INDIAN RESERVE

GEORGIA

WEST FLORIDA

EAST FLORIDA

North America in 1774 after the "Quebec Act"

uous objections to the expansion of French Catholic Quebec to act as a barrier to the plans and ambitions of the Protestant English colonies.

INDIANS

The numerous colonial plans for expansion gave little consideration to the claims of the Indians to the land which they and their forefathers had occupied for countless generations. Indians were dismissed contemptuously as " uncivilized " since they were still in the stone age, seminomadic, and with no written language except pictographs. In fact, however, the Indian had a well-developed civilization. Unfortunately, some of his best efforts were to be eliminated in the first push of the white frontier across the Appalachians.

The Indian has been misunderstood both by his friends and by his enemies. His friends have drawn him as an impossibly noble savage, animated always by bravery, generosity, sagacity, and sensitivity; his enemies have painted him as sly, cruel, bloodthirsty, untrustworthy and depraved. Actually he was a man as other men, by turns generous and selfish, kind and cruel. He was sometimes able and sometimes stupid. Generally he was fun-loving and reasonably garrulous, with strong family devotion. His way of life was different from that of the white, but reasonably adapted to his circumstances. His cultural elimination now appears as a tragedy, even though inevitable.

Although Indian culture was finally eliminated as an independent entity, the Indian had numerous effects on his conquerors. Indian names such as Oshkosh, Winnebago and Arkansas are found throughout the United States. Indian plants such as corn, potatoes, tobacco, pumpkin, squash and tomato have in time been estimated to constitute over half of white agricultural production. Not only the plants but their methods of cultivation have been adopted, while today's methods of preparing such things as hominy, pone and succotash were originally Indian. Other white adoptions have ranged from lacrosse to scalping. Truly the effect of the Indian has been by no means negligible.

To the north, centering in present New York state, were the ten to twelve thousands of the Iroquois or Six Nations — the Mohawk, Oneida, Onondaga, Cayuga, Seneca, and Tuscarora — a confederation which represented the highest type of political organization ever developed by the North American Indians. They claimed a nominal overlordship of the tribes as far west as the Mississippi, and now and then enforced part of their claims. During the Revolution the Iroquois were powerful and important, but their power then waned so that after 1800 they were no longer significant.

The second important group of Indians between the Appalachians and the Mississippi was the tribes which occupied the region between the Ohio River and the Great Lakes. Foremost were the Shawnee in present Ohio, the Wyandot near Detroit, the Miami in present Indiana, the Illinois in present Illinois, the Sauk and Fox north of the Illinois River, and the Potawatami, Winnebago, Ottawa, and Chippewa in the upper Great Lakes region. Most of them were Algonkin, and in contrast to the Iroquois, almost always acted independently. Together they totaled possibly fifty thousand persons, but in all probability not over three thousand warriors were on the warpath at any one time.

The Indians north of the Ohio were sufficiently similar to permit of a single description. They were normally peaceful, but could on occasion be warlike and cruel. Each tribe, each group, and often each individual acted independently in case of war; each warrior sought whatever shelter he could find, did his fighting, and then went home. Pitched battles were rare. The dead were scalped, since the warrior who could show one or more scalps had proof of his own prowess in touching the enemy and of his service to the tribe. Prisoners were sometimes taken and adopted by the tribe, particularly if they were women or children; now and then a captive was tortured, but such incidents were sufficiently unusual to be worthy of particular notice.

Land ownership among the Algonkins existed only through use. Whoever planted a crop of corn had possession of that piece of land until the corn was harvested, and no longer. Agriculture was limited usually to the raising of corn, with sometimes squash and beans. More important was the fishing and hunting land, for the Indians lived mostly on fish and game. Here also was a rough ownership through use. Each tribe had vague limits to the land over which it could hunt, and invasion by other tribes might mean war. The region immediately south of the Ohio (present Kentucky) was used as a common hunting ground by both the northern and southern tribes. These tribes were not truly nomadic, but a hunting life meant much movement and consequently houses were simple wigwams — usually an oval framework, dome-shaped, and covered with bark. Here and there, at strategic points, permanent towns were constructed.

At the coming of the whites all the clothing of these Indians was of leather. The man ordinarily wore a breechcloth, moccasins, leggings, and a hunting shirt; during a war he confined his attire to a breechcloth and plenty of bright paint. The woman wore a skirt extending below her knees, and sometimes a jacket. Polygamy was usually permitted, but never was widely practiced, there being no large surplus of women. Infidelity on the part of the wife was punished by cutting off her nose or by killing her. Such punishment was meted out by the injured husband, since there was no organized system of justice and all punishments were by vengeance on the part of the injured party. A woman's life was difficult and arduous. It was she who did the planting and cultivating, gathered herbs and firewood, cooked, dressed the leather, sewed the clothes with sinew, made the utensils, constructed the wigwam, and cared for the children. The men confined their activities mainly to hunting, fishing and fighting.

Sickness was considered supernatural and due to evil spirits or to the failure to perform the proper ceremonials correctly. The " medicine man " depended heavily on elaborate rituals designed to drive out the wicked spirits. Incidentally he used simple herbs, which may have played some part in his therapeutics. Frequently the medicine man would suck the part affected, and then spit out of his mouth hair, stones, sticks, or similar material; these articles were supposed to have come from the ailing member and their absence was expected to relieve the patient. Wonderful cures were often effected, particularly with wounds, probably due to the sucking, the herbs, and the outdoor life of the patient, but functional disorders and contagious diseases were frequently fatal.

The treatment of sickness was to the Indian but one phase of the continual process of placating the innumerable spirits, both good and bad, which were thought to inhabit the world. There were hundreds of ceremonials to gratify the various Indian desires, such as getting rain, securing good hunting, curing disease, obtaining success against enemies, and producing brave warriors. Each of these ceremonies had complicated ritual, with specified ceremonial actions, decorations, fire and speeches. Usually it included some kind of instrumental music (drum or whistle), singing, and dancing. Often particular animals such as the snake and the bear were mimicked. In addition to the hundreds of small good and bad

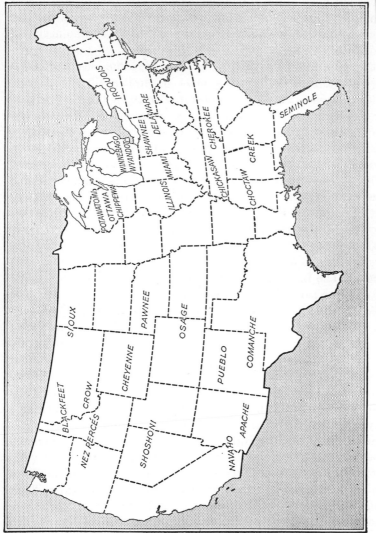

Indians of North America

spirits which had to be placated, most tribes believed in one more important good and one more important bad spirit. Usually they also believed in a future life in which the good Indian would live at his ease, with much fine hunting and fishing, and no accidents or disease.

To the south of the Ohio River were the large loose confederations of the Five Civilized Nations — Cherokee, Choctaw, Creek, Chickasaw and Seminole — whose destinies in the decade after the Revolution were controlled to some extent by the unusually able Creek half-breed Alexander McGillivray. The Cherokee, comprising about twelve thousand people, were situated in the mountainous parts of the present states of Tennessee, Alabama, Georgia, and North and South Carolina. They constituted an industrious and intelligent group, tilling the land, hunting, raising horses, dogs, and poultry, and having many picturesque dances — ceremonial, lascivious and warlike. One of their amusements was an early form of the present lacrosse. The main differences were that the field was larger, the players unlimited in number, and the game even rougher. The Indian seldom lost his temper, even though he might bet and lose his entire possessions on a game.

West of the Cherokee, and extending to the Mississippi, were the Chickasaw, about four thousand strong. They were the most warlike of the Five Nations, and usually acted together in case of trouble. South of the Chickasaw were the Choctaw, the least important of the groups. They were commonly reported as treacherous, and did not act together. East of them (in present Florida) were the Seminole, numbering between five and ten thousand; they were really a branch of the Creek.

Strongest of the Five Nations was the Creek, numbering twenty thousand and living south of the Cherokee. Not only were they the strongest, but also they were probably the most civilized of the Indians within the present boundaries of the United States. Their fields were extensive and sometimes fenced, being worked by communal effort, and producing rice, corn, tobacco, beans, and potatoes. Not only did they hunt and fish, but they also raised horses, hogs, and poultry, and sometimes owned Negro slaves. Their clothing, blankets, and wigwams were well-made and beautifully trimmed. Their pottery was of clay, and glazed to give it a hard surface.

The Creek had permanent towns. In the center of each town was an open square surrounded by four long low buildings in which the warriors were housed according to their rank. The families of the warriors lived in lodges which were built around the central square and up and down a creek or river; from fifteen to two hundred lodges constituted an ordinary village. For each town there was a head man in addition to the war chiefs, and each town sent representatives to general tribal councils. A rough confederation existed, and sometimes resulted in common action. Its greatest strength came, as mentioned before, under the leadership of Alexander McGillivray.

As with all Indians, the Creek had elaborate rituals and ceremonies. Their principal festival was the green corn dance, at which the first ear of corn was burned with intricate rites. For three days the men stayed in the square and fasted, while the women bathed frequently. The big ceremony came on the fourth day, when both sexes mingled in the open square. As was usual, such ceremonies were connected with the belief in a good and a bad spirit, and in a time of future reward or punishment.

The marital relations of the Creek had some interesting differences from those of other tribes. Courtship was carried on by a female friend of the male suitor. Both marriage and divorce were easy, either party being permitted to leave his or her mate at any time without warning. The family centered in the woman; the husband moved to his wife's home. Adultery was punished by whipping or by cutting off the hair or ears; such punishment was inflicted either by the husband or by the male relatives of the wife.

These eastern Indians were soon to feel the impact of the white frontier, as traders and trappers were followed by home seekers. Within a half century the tribes were metamorphized from vigorously independent nations to defeated and demoralized people, dependant upon white bounty for continued existence.

READINGS

COLONIES AND ROUTES: C. W. Alvord, *The Mississippi Valley in British Politics* (2 vols., 1917)—scholarly on decade before Revolution; B. W. Bond Jr., *The Foundations of Ohio* (1941), chs. 1–7; I. Bowman, *The New World* (1928)—geography and history; R. H. Brown, *Historical Geography* (1948); S. J. and E. H. Buck, *The Planting of Civilization in Western Pennsylvania* (1939), chs. 2–6—reads well; C. E. Carter, *Great Britain and the Illinois Country, 1763–1774* (1910)—scholarly; J. A. Frost, *Life on the Upper Susquehanna* (1951)—the New York frontier; C. A.

Hanna, *The Wilderness Trail* (1911); L. P. Kellogg, *The British Regime in Wisconsin and the Northwest* (1936), chs. 1–8, *The French Regime in Wisconsin and the Northwest* (1925)—scholarly; T. Roosevelt, *The Winning of the West* (5 vols., 1889–1896), vol. 1, part 1, chs. 3–5—references are to New Library Edition. INDIANS: C. H. Ambler, *A History of West Virginia* (1933), chs. 2–6; L. H. Appleton, *Indian Art* (1950)—good illustrations; P. M. Ashburn, *The Ranks of Death* (1947)—Indians and disease, largely before 1700; J. Collier, *The Indians of the Americas* (1947)—generalized, very sympathetic; R. S. Cotterill, *The Southern Indians* (1954), ch. 1—good; A. Debo, *The Rise and Fall of the Choctaw Republic* (1934), ch. 1, *The Road to Disappearance* (1941), ch. 1—very good; D. McNickle, *They Came Here First* (1949), chs. 1–17—early Indian culture; W. H. Mohr, *Federal Indian Relations, 1774–1788* (1933), ch. 1—monograph; R. H. Pearce, *The Savages of America* (1953)—white ideas about them; A. Pound and R. E. Day, *Johnson of the Mohawks* (1930) —fair; P. Radin, *The Story of the American Indian* (1927)— anthropology; F. W. Seymour, *Story of the Red Man* (1929)— popular; E. W. and A. E. Stearn, *The Effect of Smallpox on the Destiny of the Amerinds* (1945); R. M. Underhill, *Red Man's America* (1953), chs. 1–7; A. H. Verrill, *The Real Americans* (1954)—interesting, thin; C. Wissler, *The American Indian* (1917), *Indians of the United States* (1940), chs. 7–11, 13—good anthropology.

CHAPTER 2

CROSSING
THE APPALACHIANS

WESTWARD expansion of American colonies in the years immediately before the Revolution seemed unlikely — not so much because of the Proclamation of 1763 as because the thirteen sparsely settled and stubbornly separatist colonies, beset by internal problems, seemed to have neither the energy to be interested in wild western lands nor the people to occupy them. Yet in spite of these obvious and practical deterrents, the colonies felt the alluring beckoning of the West.

COLONIAL LAND SPECULATION

The expulsion of the French opened the way for the English. Traders and trappers went west of the mountains in increasing numbers, beginning in the 1760s. Colonial land speculators increased in number and in ardor. At times it seemed as though every prominent colonial, as for example Washington and Franklin, was interested in western land. Even officials sent from England contracted the prevailing fever. Lord Dunmore, governor of Virginia, carried his interests so far that he precipitated an Indian conflict (1774) which took his name. Incidentally he showed an amazing official blindness to the terms of the Proclamation of 1763.

Many of the land speculations were promoted by organized companies, since the purchase, survey, and settling of western land required large amounts of capital. Best known was the Ohio Land Company, organized as early as 1748 by men from both Virginia and England. It obtained a royal charter which granted some 200,000 acres — later increased to 500,000 — near the present site of Pittsburgh. Christopher Gist immediately opened a trail to the new land, and in 1750 built Fort Cumberland at the great bend of the Potomac River, but the company never succeeded in settling its far-flung domain.

PITTSBURGH SETTLEMENT

The Pittsburgh area, where the Monongahela and Allegheny join to form the Ohio River, was of obvious strategic importance — a fact which was apparent to others than the members of the Ohio Land Company. It was a point of English-French rivalry during the 1750s, and after varying fortunes of war ended in the possession of the British when Forbes captured it in 1758. The next year saw the beginning of the construction of Fort Pitt.

English control inevitably drew white settlers from east of the mountains, particularly since military operations entailed the opening of better roads from the East. Even Braddock's disastrous campaign produced a wagon road along the path marked earlier by Gist. The Forbes campaign opened an alternate route through southern Pennsylvania.

The first settlers at Fort Pitt were not the English, Germans and Scotch-Irish who were pushing over the Pennsylvania mountains but Virginians who advanced along the Braddock Road. By 1760 there were 150 of them, and the number increased steadily in spite of the Proclamation of 1763 and official discouragement. With the Indian treaty of Fort Stanwix in 1768 the way was opened for an even faster immigration, and by 1774 there were some 50,000 people in southwestern Pennsylvania.

Early Pittsburgh was the first permanent English settlement west of the mountains in the present United States, and assumed immediately a vital importance in business between East and West. At the head of the Ohio River, it was on the natural route of travel for all men and materials moving west, and long deserved its appellation of " the gateway of the West." In its early years it was a commercial rather than a manufacturing center, although it did some manufacturing. Until 1790 all the iron used in Pittsburgh was hauled over the mountains from the East.

WATAUGA

The next crossing of the mountains by settlers was farther south, since to the north the twin barriers of considerable amounts of open land and the still powerful Iroquois remained to be surmounted. The first settlers in present Tennessee plodded through

the mountain passes to the Watauga River in 1768. While mountain ranges were still to the west, this settlement was actually in
the Mississippi drainage system. The Watauga is a tributary of the
Holston, which empties into the Tennessee and finally reaches the
Mississippi.

The Watauga community grew but slowly. Far removed from
eastern centers of population, the connections were poor. The Indians were menacing and had to be persuaded to give up the
necessary land. No regular government existed, and in fact there
was considerable doubt as to whether the new communities were
in Virginia or North Carolina.

The settlement at Watauga was particularly notable because of
the unusual ability of some of its members; from it came the men
who were to be the leaders of further migration into Tennessee and
Kentucky. James Robertson, who arrived at Watauga in 1770, was
a dour Scotchman — somber, silent, and uneducated, but masterful
and daring — typically Scotch Presbyterian. The direct antith-
esis of Robertson was John Sevier — tall, slender, blue-eyed,
handsome, pleasure-loving, daring, elegant, well-educated, the
friend of Madison and Franklin, and probably the most cultured
man on the frontier. Sevier took his family to the Holston in 1773,
at which time he was only twenty-eight years old — three years
younger than Robertson.

Best known of all the settlers in the Watauga region was Daniel
Boone, the outstanding frontiersman of the period. Boone came
from Welsh and English stock, and was born in Berks County,
Pennsylvania, in 1734. His family wandered south in 1750–51, eventually settling on the Yadkin, which is a short distance east of
the Watauga. When Braddock led his ill-fated expedition against
the French, Boone participated as wagoner and blacksmith; in the
final debacle he jumped on one of the horses he was driving and
rode to safety. Coming back to the Yadkin, Boone spent most of
his time in hunting, going farther and farther west as the eastern
game decreased. In 1765 he made an extended trip to Florida, and
was so impressed that he bought a house and lot in Pensacola. His
wife was not equally lured by the South, and refused to move.

In the course of his many travels Boone undoubtedly heard
rumors of the new and rich country of Kentucky. He must have
been increasingly interested in these stories for, starting in 1767,
he engaged in a series of hunting trips which carried him into Kentucky. These expeditions were not notably successful. Game was

plentiful, but because of hostile Indians and long distances, very little of either meat or hides ever reached the East. Hardships were many and severe. In 1769 Boone was captured by the Shawnee, who adopted him into the tribe; eventually he escaped.

Boone's interest in Kentucky continued to increase in spite of his failure to make a profitable return from his hunting. In 1773 he started to lead five families of settlers into the new region, but this attempt failed because of the hostility of the Shawnee. At about this time Boone was at the height of his power and vigor. Only five feet eight inches tall, he was well-built, with broad shoulders, narrow hips, and slender legs. His eyes were blue, and his hair, which he wore long, was black. His ordinary dress was that of the Indians. He had practically no schooling and could write his own name only with the greatest difficulty.

While Boone was making his first sorties into Kentucky, the Watauga settlement continued to grow and prosper. Many new settlers arrived during and after 1771, which was coincident with the collapse of the Regulator Movement in North Carolina. Here in the western part of the state men were free from the undesired governmental restrictions which existed farther east. But suddenly they found themselves too free; they had no government at all, and no one realized more than they the need for government. They petitioned North Carolina to make some provision for the new community, but the colony failed to act and they were forced to work out their own salvation by organizing a government of their own. The Watauga Association (probably formed in 1772) provided the authority for making laws, negotiating with the Indians, registering deeds and wills, solemnizing marriages, and performing the other essential functions of government. It was particularly important as the first in a long series of local western efforts to solve the problem of government when the regularly constituted authorities would not act. North Carolina finally made the district into the County of Washington in 1777, continuing the old officers in power.

KENTUCKY

The growth of the settlement at Watauga encouraged many people to look farther west and, with Boone, to covet the fertile plains of the Kentucky, the Tennessee and the Cumberland. One of these visionaries was Judge Richard Henderson of North Carolina, who organized the Transylvania Company (not chartered) to buy land from the Indians and then sell it to white settlers — a procedure which was illegal under the terms of the Proclamation of 1763. Boone was sent early in 1775 to sound out the Indians on the subject. He was followed immediately by Henderson, who had among his companions Sevier and Robertson. At the Sycamore Shoals Conference (March 1775) Henderson succeeded in buying from the Cherokee the region between the Kentucky and Cumberland rivers, or what is now the greater part of the state of Kentucky and a little of Tennessee.

The Transylvania Company at once opened this huge tract of land to purchase on easy terms, and sent Boone to mark a trail from the eastern settlements through the mountains and down the Kentucky River to the Ohio. This route, as marked by Boone, came to be known as the Wilderness Trail. It was the only practicable path through the mountains in that region and was used extensively by early westbound settlers. In addition, Boone established a small fort (Boonesborough) on the Kentucky River, near the present city of Lexington. As soon as the trail was opened many settlers began to pour into the Kentucky region, going not only to Boonesborough, but also to nearby places such as Harrodsburg, Boiling Springs and St. Asaph's. Some of them held Virginia grants, since Virginia did not recognize Henderson's ownership. In consequence, Henderson received but little for his land and his settlement at Boonesborough was not very successful; his company store charged high prices and drove the settlers to other trading centers.

Just as in the case of Watauga, the Kentucky settlers grew impatient at eastern delay and established a government of their own. The constitution was accepted by popular vote, but it was written by Henderson, who gave himself most of the power. An appeal to the Continental Congress for recognition was blocked by Virginia. In 1776 the region was organized by Virginia as the county of Kentucky. Henderson, in spite of his illegal acts, was compensated for the loss of his claim by land in the Cumberland Valley.

The outbreak of the Revolution caused a temporary cessation of the movement into Kentucky. This lull was due in part to pressing eastern preoccupations, but more to an increase of Indian hostility in the West. The Shawnee and Cherokee in particular seized this opportunity to attempt to drive away or kill the most advanced of the white settlers — a procedure which seemed worthy of encouragement by British commanders in the West. The new settlers found the problem of defense exceedingly difficult because of a lack of both men and materials of war. Appeals for aid were forwarded to Virginia and North Carolina, while a local militia was organized under the leadership of George Rogers Clark, Daniel Boone, James Harrod, Benjamin Logan, and John Todd, Jr. Aid was slow in arriving and local efforts were barely sufficient to save the settlers from annihilation. Many of them returned to the East, so that by 1777 only two of the western towns remained — Boonesborough and Harrodsburg — and both were attacked unsuccessfully in that year.

During this period Daniel Boone was incessantly active and almost continually in danger. At one time his ankle was shattered by an Indian arrow and his life saved by the prompt action of Simon Kenton, who killed Boone's attacker and carried Boone into the fort. Late in 1777 Boone was captured by the Shawnee. A council was held to determine his fate, and it is related that his life was spared by the close vote of fifty-nine to sixty-one. When the Shawnee party returned from its attack on the Kentucky settlements to its home at the old Chillicothe near the present Xenia, Ohio, it took Boone alone. Here Boone commended himself by his actions, so that he was adopted as a son by Black Fish, and given the Indian name of Big Turtle. Nominally he was now a full member of the tribe, but actually he was kept under close observation to prevent his escape.

When the Indians visited Henry Hamilton, the English governor at Detroit, Boone was taken with them. Here it seems that Boone assured Hamilton of his loyalty to the English crown, and Hamilton offered to buy Boone from the Indians for a hundred dollars, which offer was refused. After the Indians returned to Chillicothe, Boone finally found an opportunity to escape. His trip on foot back to Kentucky was a marvel of speed and endurance; he covered the distance in four days with but one meal. In Kentucky he was welcomed as one returning from the dead, since he had been gone for four and a half months and had been given up as lost.

Most of the important Indian depredations on the Kentucky region were at an end by the close of the year 1778, although periodic forays still occurred. With the diminution of Indian warfare settlers again began to appear; old towns were rebuilt and new ones established. The war whoop was heard less frequently and the sound of the frontiersman's axe became more common. White civilization was arriving.

TENNESSEE

Among these settlers was the indomitable Judge Richard Henderson, who now turned his attention to the development of his grant on the Cumberland River. In 1779 an advance guard composed of James Robertson and eight others started a settlement at Nashborough (the present Nashville) by beginning the construction of houses and planting corn. Within a year five hundred settlers, including Henderson himself, had arrived and the town was becoming an important center of population. Again there was no regularly constituted government, and so on May 1, 1780, the settlers drew up their own compact; the signers guaranteed to each other the possession of their land claims and the obedience to whatever laws should be drawn up by a committee of twelve, which was apportioned according to population. North Carolina constituted the Cumberland region as Davidson County in 1783.

The many problems which confronted the early settlers in the West did not prevent them from taking an active interest in the progress of the war farther east. For the most part the westerners were strong patriots and ardent supporters of the revolutionary cause. When Cornwallis captured Charleston in 1780 and began his campaign in the interior, the frontiersmen felt that the time had come for action, and so they flocked east across the mountains to oppose the progress of the British army. These westerners made possible the American victory at the battle of King's Mountain, which played no inconsiderable part in the outcome of the war.

WEST AT CLOSE OF REVOLUTION

The close of the Revolution found an ever increasing number of settlers pouring into the West, and with the larger population the problem of government immediately become more difficult. The simple local government which had sufficed in an earlier day would not meet the needs of a larger and more intricate social group. Even the county governments established by Virginia and North Carolina did but little to alleviate the confusion. Such governments were far from their seaboard sources of power and had but little authority to solve the very definite and pressing needs of the West. Peace and order had to be produced from the very chaotic conditions in existence. Marriages, deeds, and wills had to be legalized and made uniform. Land titles needed to be made more easily obtainable and more exact, for land had been sold in the East upon

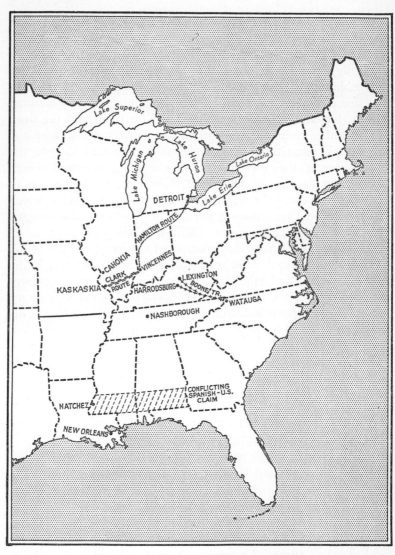

West near the End of the Revolution

the vaguest kind of identification, and consequently many of the claims overlapped. Some provision had to be made for the families which came west without land claims. Furthermore, defense against the Indians was still important, for the Indians continued to attack outlying groups and individuals from time to time. The joint action of all of the settlers in the region menaced was not a good substitute for effective action by an active government. In warfare against the Indians the best form of defense was always offense, and unorganized settlers found sustained offensive operations difficult. Another menace requiring unified action was the possibility of Spanish advance up the Mississippi Valley.

STATE OF FRANKLIN

The desirability of a more effective government in the region south of the Ohio River produced considerable discussion among the settlers in the years 1782 to 1784. Meetings were held, speeches were made, and Congress was petitioned to form the new region into a state. As it happened, Congress was in no position to act. The Articles of Confederation were still in force, and their deficiencies made it nearly impossible for Congress ever to settle any problem satisfactorily. Furthermore, Congress was especially handicapped at this time because it was urging the various states to cede their claims to western lands. Such cessions would never come from dissatisfied states, and any Congressional action which would overlook the rights and powers of such important land-claiming states as Virginia and North Carolina would hardly hasten the progress of cession. Consequently Congress did nothing.

The western movement for more effective government was strongest in the Holston River region, where North Carolina claimed control. Long debates were held in the North Carolina legislature to decide just what should be done with this western land and with these westerners who asked so much aid and protection and could pay such small taxes. The decision of the legislature, made by a close vote in 1784, was to cede the western district to Congress. While Congress was taking its time in accepting the cession, a movement in favor of independence was culminating in the Holston region. Because of this talk of independence and the failure of Congress to act, North Carolina changed her mind and repealed her cession in the same year in which it had been passed.

The movement for the independence of the Holston region had gradually been growing in strength ever since 1782. Various conventions met and discussed the whole situation, and their general trend showed an increasing sentiment for the establishment of an independent government. The most influential man in the region was John Sevier, and it was probably due in considerable part to his counsels of moderation that the freedom movement did not develop more rapidly; just what his action would be in the event of a declaration of independence was uncertain, but there were many who thought that he would throw in his fortunes with his neighbors and friends.

The freedom movement culminated in the Jonesboro Convention, which on December 14, 1784, declared the independence of the Holston region by a vote of twenty-eight to fifteen. The new state was given the name of Franklin, in honor of Benjamin Franklin, who might conceivably give aid to his infant namesake. A temporary constitution provided for a Senate and a House of Representatives, which jointly were to elect a governor. The legislature held its first meeting in March 1785, at which time John Sevier was elected to, and accepted, the office of governor. At the same time laws were passed about such matters as land titles, education, militia, county divisions, coinage, taxation, and elections.

With the adoption of a permanent constitution (November 1785) based on that of North Carolina, the new state of Franklin started to operate as an independent commonwealth. Internal affairs progressed satisfactorily, for Sevier was an able administrator. Foreign affairs of the new government, however, did not run so smoothly. The Indians were a continual source of annoyance; Sevier led a number of fairly successful expeditions against them, but the forces of the state of Franklin were never able to subdue the Indians completely. Negotiations were carried on with Spain to obtain her recognition and assistance. In this regard the state of Franklin was in an unfortunate geographical position, for it acted as a buffer between Spain and the United States at a time when friction and border collisions were not uncommon.

The foreign affairs in which the state of Franklin was most interested were its relations to the various states of the United States and to the nation as a whole. Congress was approached for recognition, and efforts were made to induce Franklin to aid his namesake. But Congress was weak and unwilling to meddle. Overtures were made to the Kentucky region to persuade it to join in the new venture. Kentucky was dilatory, but finally decided it had more to gain from Congress and from Virginia than from independence.

With Georgia the new state of Franklin had its greatest success, for Georgia recognized Franklin and was willing to cooperate in fighting the Indians. With North Carolina, its ungrateful progeny had a war of words. Efforts at recognition failed, and so the two states proceeded to issue manifesto and counter-manifesto as fast as their brains and printing presses could operate. At this time North Carolina was in no position to enforce its power over the western wilderness.

The trouble which finally destroyed Franklin was internal rather than external. Sevier's chief political rival was John Tipton, and when Tipton failed to win the ascendancy in Franklin he proceeded to obtain recognition and authority from North Carolina. Then followed a comic opera war between the followers of Sevier and those of Tipton, Tipton of course receiving some aid from North Carolina, which outlawed Sevier in 1786. Sevier was finally captured by the Tipton forces in 1788. He was rescued by his friends before he was arraigned for trial, but the affair resulted in the collapse of Franklin, North Carolina resuming control. Sevier was pardoned immediately, and participated in the North Carolina convention of 1788, which considered the adoption of the federal constitution. During the next year North Carolina ceded its western lands to Congress by a decisive vote, although by this time it had sold most of them.

STATEHOOD FOR KENTUCKY AND TENNESSEE

The achievement of statehood for Kentucky was not long delayed. The county organization of the far distant Kentucky soon proved unsuccessful and a movement developed for statehood, with some talk of complete independence. Here as elsewhere a good many people opposed statehood as being more expensive. During the years 1784 through 1790 there were nine Kentucky conventions to discuss the desirability of statehood, while Virginia passed four enabling acts. Ultimately agreement was reached, and Kentucky was admitted to statehood by Congress in 1792 — the first of the trans-Appalachian states.

Tennessee did not attain statehood so promptly. With the North Carolina land cession, Congress in 1790 created a territorial government to parallel that of the Northwest. The governor was William Blount, prince of land speculators, who filled the offices under his control with friends, relatives and business associates, giving special preference to men formerly connected with the state of Franklin. The speculators remained firmly in control until the arrival of statehood in 1796, at which time Sevier became governor and Blount went to the United States Senate.

Before leaving the Old Southwest it may be interesting to enquire into the later lives of the chief actors in the early drama. Sevier, Robertson, and Henderson settled permanently in the Tennessee-Kentucky region and played important parts in the development of the country. Sevier was active and influential in politics for many years. George Rogers Clark performed notable exploits north of the Ohio, which will be recounted in the next chapter. Daniel Boone, true to his pioneer instinct, continued to move. In the period during and immediately after the Revolution he took up much land in Kentucky and western Virginia, but because of faulty surveys and recording it was all later lost. After the Revolution he had a varied life as hunter, trapper, guide, and store and tavern keeper. By the latter 1790s Boone felt that Kentucky was too crowded, and proclaimed that he wanted more " elbow-room." So in 1799 he moved to present Missouri — about forty-five miles west of St. Louis. Here for many years he was an object of interest and admiration to all travelers who visited that part of the country. He lived with his sons and succeeded in saving enough money to pay off his old Kentucky debts. More hunting trips were made, carrying him as far as the Yellowstone River in 1814, when he was eighty years of age. His strength was not as great as it had been in the old days, but his eyes and ears were keen and his mind active. He even contemplated again moving farther west as population began to crowd him, but his last move had been made, and on September 26, 1820, he died at the age of eighty-six, having outlived most of his own generation.

READINGS

LAND SPECULATION: C. W. Alvord, *The Mississippi Valley in British Politics* (2 vols., 1917), vol. 1, ch. 3, vol. 2, ch. 5; K. P. Bailey, *The Ohio Company of Virginia* (1939)—detailed; E. Dick, *The Dixie Frontier* (1948), ch. 6; W. S. Lester, *The Transylvania Colony* (1935)—only fair; G. E. Lewis, *The Indiana Company* (1941); S. Livermore, *Early American Land Companies* (1939), ch. 4; A. M. Sakolski, *The Great American Land Bubble* (1932), chs. 1–4—interesting; A. T. Volwiler, *George Croghan* (1926)—scholarly.

NORTHERN MIGRATION: L. D. Baldwin, *Pittsburgh* (1937)—

good; T. Boyd, *Simon Girty* (1928); S. J. and E. H. Buck, *The Planting of Civilization in Western Pennsylvania* (1939), chs. 7–21; P. D. Evans, *The Holland Land Company* (1926)—scholarly; J. W. Harpster (ed.), *Pen Pictures of Early Western Pennsylvania* (1938); S. E. Slick, *William Trent and the West* (1947)—monograph on Pittsburgh region; J. E. Wright and D. S. Corbett, *Pioneer Life in Western Pennsylvania* (1940)—interesting.

SOUTHERN MIGRATION: T. P. Abernethy, *From Frontier to Plantation in Tennessee* (1932), chs. 1–12; C. H. Ambler, *West Virginia* (1933), ch. 7; J. Bakeless, *Daniel Boone* (1939); J. D. Barnhart, *Valley of Democracy* (1953), chs. 3–8; T. D. Clark, *A History of Kentucky* (1937), chs. 5–7—reads well; R. S. Cotterill, *The Southern Indians* (1954), chs. 2, 3; E. Dick, *The Dixie Frontier* (1948), chs. 1–5—reads easily; C. S. Driver, *John Sevier* (1932)—good but pedantic; C. Eaton, *A History of the Old South* (1949), ch. 5; A. Henderson, *The Conquest of the Old Southwest* (1920), chs. 8–20—Chronicles of America; J. A. James, *The Life of George Rogers Clark* (1928), chs. 1–5; R. L. Kincaid, *The Wilderness Road* (1947), chs. 5–7; W. H. Masterson, *William Blount* (1954), chs. 4–9; W. A. Pusey, *The Wilderness Road* (1921); C. L. Skinner, *Pioneers of the Old Southwest* (1921), chs. 5–11—Chronicles of America; S. E. White, *Daniel Boone* (1922)—simple and popular; S. Williams, *History of the Lost State of Franklin* (1924)—detailed.

CHAPTER 3

CONQUERING
THE OLD NORTHWEST

THE trickle of the first white settlers into the region south of the Ohio River was paralleled by a white invasion of the territory north of that stream. Even before the Revolution some small settlements had appeared here and there in the Old Northwest (this term being used to designate the region between the Great Lakes and the Ohio River and between the Appalachian Mountains and the Mississippi River). These early settlements were composed almost entirely of French traders and trappers, but they also frequently included small French military garrisons in the years before 1763. Among the more important of such towns were Kaskaskia on the Kaskaskia; Cahokia on the Mississippi; Vincennes on the Wabash in the present Indiana; Michilimackinac (present Mackinac) at the junction of Lake Huron and Lake Michigan; Detroit, and the future Pittsburgh. At the end of the Seven Years' War all of these places became at least nominally British, and the French inhabitants accepted the new rule with seeming equanimity. Their essentially French character made reasonable their addition to the Province of Quebec by the Quebec Act of 1774.

REVOLUTION IN THE NORTHWEST

The outbreak of the Revolution found none of the English colonists in the Old Northwest, except in the settlements in the vicinity of Pittsburgh. The nearest hostile English forces were the troops which occupied strategic points along the Lakes. If the war were to be fought in the West it would have to be over long distances. Actually the available English troops were few, and campaigns through hundreds of miles of wilderness to attack a few unimportant western settlements seemed profitless. On the other hand it was desirable to harass the western fringe of the colonies to necessitate the withdrawal of colonial troops from the more important operations in the East, or at least to prevent the westerners from having time or energy to join the eastern forces.

An effective weapon for the attack on the western settlements lay ready to use. The Indians already resented white encroachments, and needed little urging to harry the border settlements. Lieutenant Governor Hamilton, who was in command at Detroit, held numerous councils in which he encouraged the Indians to consider their grievances and to attack all settlers within reach. Probably he made reasonable efforts to persuade the Indians to conduct their operations as humanely as possible, but it was quite unlikely that the red man would change his method of fighting to suit the squeamishness of a British officer. From the standpoint of the British the colonists were rebels who were encroaching upon territory from which they had been legally excluded.

The American defense against Indian raids, as aided and encouraged by the British, was anything but well-organized. The states most subject to attack, particularly Pennsylvania, Virginia, North Carolina, and Georgia, made some provision for their own defense, but were usually glad to let the attacked settlers or the central government take the main burden. The settlers were few and poor, so that providing men and materials for extensive operations proved an almost insurmountable task. The Continental Congress was more than busy in the East and could be persuaded to furnish troops and supplies only when the danger was extremely pressing. By a law of 1775 three Indian departments were created, each with commissioners to try to quiet the Indians; these men held conferences, made treaties and gave presents, but the Indians were anything but peaceful.

The year 1777 was the bloodiest and gloomiest of the war in the West. Hostile Indians, and particularly the Shawnee and other Ohio tribes, drove back or killed settlers, and even attacked such fortified towns as Boonesborough. The situation was so obviously serious that Congress sent Brigadier General Edward Hand to strengthen Fort Pitt, lest this key position fall to the British and Indians. During the following year Washington sent some of his badly needed troops under General Lachlan McIntosh from Valley Forge, which indicates something of the vital urgency of the danger. Both Hand and McIntosh led expeditions against the Indians, but both failed because of the lack of men and supplies; their only accomplishment was to irritate the Indians still further.

GEORGE ROGERS CLARK

Out of this desperate situation came one of the outstanding exploits of the war — the expedition of George Rogers Clark against the Illinois country. Clark was the son of a Virginia planter and was trained as a surveyor. Moving west in 1772 he did exploring, fought the Indians, and helped to organize the militia defense of the Kentucky settlements at the outbreak of the Revolution. His trip to Virginia for powder still remains a noteworthy exploit.

In contrast to the majority of westerners, who thought only in terms of protecting themselves from Indian attacks, George Rogers Clark was bold and active-minded. As early as 1775, during his trip to Virginia, he conceived the idea that the only effective way to protect the new settlements from the Indians was to undertake offensive operations. He realized that real security could be obtained only by impressing the Indians convincingly of white superiority, and that in all probability the English posts, and particularly the one at Detroit, must be captured if peace were to come to the frontier. While conditions were at their worst in Kentucky (1777) and even Boonesborough itself was attacked twice, Clark had sufficient foresight to send two courageous spies to investigate the situation farther north. Their reports indicated that the northern posts were practically unprotected.

Obviously the West itself could not furnish the men, supplies, and munitions necessary for an extensive expedition into the northwest country, and so, late in 1777, Clark made the long trip back to Virginia to try to obtain assistance. Immediately upon his arrival he called upon Governor Patrick Henry and outlined his ambitious plans for the conquest of the Northwest. Governor Henry was timid, as well he might be, in view of the situation in the East; on the other hand such a conquest, if successful, would be of advantage in the prosecution of the war in the East, would greatly enhance Virginia's prestige, and would reinforce her claims to western land. Henry consulted with some of his close friends, including Thomas Jefferson, and after some hesitancy they decided to give Clark as much support as was possible at the moment.

Clark was given two sets of orders. The first contained the ostensible reason for his activities, by authorizing him to raise seven companies (350 men) for the defense of Kentucky, and to purchase arms, ammunition, and supplies on the credit of the state of Virginia. To pay the troops and keep them loyal he had £1200 in depreciated colonial currency and glowing promises of future gifts of land in the West. The second set of orders, which was to remain secret, empowered Clark to undertake offensive operations and to capture " Kaskasky."

Armed with these instructions Clark made his way to Pittsburgh, which was a logical gathering place for any expedition planning to descend the Ohio River. Here and at Wheeling he gathered such adventurers and wanderers as presented themselves, and obtained as large a quantity of supplies as he could. Actually he found it impossible to enlist the total 350 men, and when he started down the Ohio only 175 answered his commands. He even experienced difficulty in attracting this small number, for the Pennsylvania authorities could not wholly approve an expedition gathered in Pennsylvania to protect Kentucky, by a man with orders from Virginia. The men were a heterogeneous group; they dressed as they pleased, carried a motley array of guns, and were unwilling to obey any command which they did not think reasonable. Some were frankly homeseekers and were accompanied by their families so that they could take up desirable land upon the first favorable opportunity.

The first part of Clark's plan was to descend the Ohio as far as the mouth of the Kentucky and there disembark and drill his men. The topography of the land led him to change his mind and to camp instead at the falls of the Ohio. Here some of the homeseekers built houses and began farming, thus founding the first white settlement at the present Louisville. Here also Clark divulged his larger plans to his followers. At first there was much grumbling and dissent, but eventually objections were silenced and the expedition was ready to begin its real work.

On June 24, 1778, the little army shot the falls at Louisville and started to float down the Ohio River. Clark had hoped to capture Vincennes immediately, but with the small force under his command he now decided to concentrate his attention on the weaker Illinois towns; then if his plans went awry he could at least escape to the Spanish side of the Mississippi. Nine miles below the mouth of the Tennessee the party left its boats and started overland, partly because of the possibility of being discovered if it continued by water, and partly because of the slow and tedious work involved in going upstream. In the trip by land the party was led by a stray hunter who had been encountered accidentally, but his knowledge of the country was not accurate, and the men suffered during the march from lack of food and water.

Eventually Kaskaskia was reached. Sufficient speed and secrecy had been maintained so that the invasion was a complete surprise; Clark and his men met no resistance in entering the town. The French inhabitants were just as amenable to American rule as to British, and gladly changed their allegiance as soon as the new conquerors arrived. Even if resistance had been desired, it could hardly have been made effective. The British garrison had been removed the preceding year, and the total population of the whole region probably numbered under a thousand whites of both sexes and all ages. Cahokia and several other small communities were easily taken by a detachment of thirty men.

Clark's policy with the French settlers was to encourage their good will by giving them generous treatment, and at the same time to convince them of his military power. Old laws and customs were retained, and all disputed questions were settled quickly and justly. The idea of military strength was impressed by spreading the rumor that the force in Illinois was only a small part of a large army, which even then was camping at the falls of the Ohio. A friendly French priest was sent to Vincennes, where he succeeded in inducing the inhabitants to change their allegiance to the United States. In 1778 the entire occupied region was organized by Virginia as the County of Illinois, and the following year John Todd arrived as its civil governor.

While Clark was conquering the Illinois region, rumors were beginning to reach Hamilton at Detroit that all was not well. In a leisurely way he had been planning an attack upon Pittsburgh, and now he concluded he would first have to defeat Clark. His new plans were to retake Vincennes and then move on the Illinois settlements. After hurried preparations he left Detroit on October 7, 1778, with a force composed of thirty-six regulars, forty-five local volunteers, seventy-nine local militia and sixty Indians; his army was augmented on the way, mostly by Indians, so that by the time he arrived at Vincennes he had over five hundred men. His route was an old familiar Indian pathway—down the Detroit River, through a part of Lake Erie, up the Maumee, portage to the Wabash, and then down the Wabash to Vincennes.

When Hamilton reached Vincennes in the middle of December he found the town unprotected and easily taken. Again the French inhabitants conveniently changed their allegiance to their latest conqueror. From Vincennes, Hamilton planned to move against Clark when travel was again feasible in the spring, and so he settled down to winter quarters, erecting fortifications and drilling his men. It seemed both to him and to his staff that there was no danger of an attack from Clark at a time when cold weather and flooded rivers made the drainage basin of the Wabash a veritable swamp.

Clark was placed in an exceedingly awkward position by Hamilton's expedition. He was several hundred miles from home and could hope for no reinforcements. His men were on short-term enlistments which would soon expire. The Indians were not friendly and the French had but little interest in the success of their new master. If he stayed at Kaskaskia until spring it seemed evident that Hamilton, aided by the Indians, could defeat him and would then have no difficulty in conquering Kentucky at his leisure. Another than Clark might well have thought the obstacles insuperable, but here was a man whom difficulties did not daunt, and whose idea of fighting was to go, not halfway to meet the enemy, but all the way, and then to engage him upon his own ground. And so Clark again decided to move forward; the march on Vincennes was to begin at once.

Before the expedition left Kaskaskia a vessel, the *Willing*, was sent ahead to carry supplies and ammunition for use in the capture of Vincennes. The main body of 170 men was reenlisted and left Kaskaskia on February 5, 1779, for the march across the wilderness. The project was an exhibition of sheer, reckless courage, rare even on the frontier. In reality it was Clark himself who furnished the greater share of the perseverance and valor that kept the party moving. He spent most of his time in trying to keep the men in good spirits by joking, laughing, telling stories, aiding the footsore and encouraging everyone. At the same time he maintained a wary vigilance for unfriendly Indians, and used all of his woodcraft to keep on the right path. In spite of his many duties, he never failed to carry his share of the supplies and to do his part in the necessary manual labor.

Much of the country which Clark and his men traversed was flooded, and for days at a time everyone was soaking wet. For hours they would wade through swamps and creeks, with the water at times to their shoulders, so that the shorter drummer boy had to float on his drum. Food was scarce and many times a tightening of belts took the place of a meal. Fires were often impossible because of the wetness of the wood, and everyone had to sleep in his wet clothes. As they neared Vincennes conditions became worse. The country was practically one large lake, and both fires and shooting were impossible because of the danger of making their presence known. All this, too, in the depths of winter, when cold weather intensified all of the other discomforts.

To add the final touch of annoyance and trouble, the *Willing* was not waiting for Clark when he arrived at the Wabash on February 18. Little wonder that the men became discouraged after their two weeks of hardship, cold, and hunger, and that the expedition seemed doomed to failure within sight of its goal. But Clark's indomitable purpose carried him on. After a wait of two days without food, canoes were finally constructed to ferry the men across the stream. Then the forward movement was resumed. The water was often deep, there was no food, and the rear guard had to be given orders to shoot all deserters. The greatest trial of all was the passage of the Horse-Shoe Plain, then a shallow lake four miles wide. Canoes were used to rescue the men whose strength gave out, and to help the shorter men through the deepest places. Eventually a sigh of relief was possible when Vincennes was sighted.

The approach to Vincennes raised new problems. It seemed somewhat doubtful if a small, wet, hungry, poorly armed band of Americans could capture a fortified post garrisoned by upward of six hundred fighting men. Again Clark proved himself equal to the emergency. His first effort was to impress the French villagers and keep them neutral. A letter was sent to them offering peace and good treatment if they refrained from participating in the hostilities, but promising severe treatment otherwise. Then Clark marched and countermarched his men as fast as possible to give an impression of a large force. The result was that the French remained neutral.

The attack upon the fort started immediately, and was a complete surprise to Hamilton. Clark's ammunition was insufficient for a protracted siege, but as luck would have it Hamilton was so impressed by the supposed size of the attacking force that he immediately asked for a truce. Clark refused to grant a truce and insisted, with a heroic gesture, upon unconditional surrender. He did not finally receive quite his unconditional surrender, but the terms of the capitulation were sufficient to satisfy even the most ardent patriot. The Americans took complete possession of Vincennes on February 25, 1779. Hamilton and some of his officers and men were sent under guard to Virginia, imprisoned, and eventually paroled. The French volunteers in Hamilton's army were freed to return to Detroit, on the promise that they would not engage further in the war; Clark had neither food, clothes, shelter nor guards sufficient to keep them as prisoners.

The meteor of Clark's accomplishment continues to glow as one of the brightest lights not only in the history of the West but also in that of the United States as a whole. It was unfortunate that with this episode the career of Clark did not come to an end, and thus leave his reputation in undimmed glory.

With the capture of Vincennes, Clark was apparently in a secure position. The Northwest had been subdued and Detroit, the center of British influence, lay open to easy conquest. And yet the way was not as clear as it seemed. Clark's men had no stomach for further hardships, and as fast as their enlistments were completed, they went home. Supplies and ammunition were scarce, and certainly could not be replenished until spring. Clark had no option but to settle down at Vincennes with as good grace as he could muster, and wait until spring brought him new men and supplies. But when spring came the reinforcements failed to appear. Clark himself made a trip to Kaskaskia in a vain effort to improve his situation. By July some 350 men had gathered at Vincennes, but the lack of stores and provisions would have made an attack on Detroit foolhardy; most of the men were barefoot. Eventually all plans for offensive operations were given up for the year, and Clark moved his headquarters to the falls of the Ohio.

LAST YEARS OF REVOLUTION

With the opening of the year 1780 the British evolved plans of their own for the reconquest of the West, both north and south. General Campbell was to move from Pensacola with 1500 men, capture New Orleans, and then advance toward St. Louis. General Sinclair was to start from Michilimackinac, capture the Illinois towns of Kaskaskia and Cahokia, and then take St. Louis. Three smaller forces were to keep Clark engaged and to punish the Indians; the first was to advance from Detroit toward Vincennes, the second was to watch the plains between the Wabash and the Mississippi, and the third was to move down the Illinois River and chastise the Sauk and Fox Indians. All of these plans eventually failed. Campbell never felt he had a sufficient force to move north, and finally was forced to surrender Pensacola to the Spanish commander Galvez. The Illinois River expedition burned a few Indian towns and then returned home. The Detroit expedition heard rumors of a superior American force and so retreated, leaving Clark free to go westward and defeat Sinclair near St. Louis. In 1781 Spain undertook a retaliatory expedition against England, and succeeded in advancing as far as the present Niles, Michigan.

Following the defeat of Sinclair there again seemed to be an excellent opportunity for the conquest of Detroit, and so Clark hurried to Virginia to obtain support for his plans. He found little difficulty in getting encouragement, but unfortunately such aid was almost entirely verbal, and words would not pay troops or feed hungry men. Clark organized a new expedition at Pittsburgh, but when the commander of one division of the little force was defeated overwhelmingly by the Indians under Joseph Brant, the entire plan had to be abandoned.

Conditions became even worse in 1782 when an expedition under Col. William Crawford was butchered on the Sandusky plains by the Indians, aided by the British. Crawford ended his life at the stake. Emboldened by this success the Indians went so far as an unsuccessful attack upon Wheeling. The arrival of fresh troops from Kentucky proved of no advantage to the white settlers, since the new arrivals were defeated disastrously at Blue Licks. With these defeats the prospect of the frontier appeared exceedingly gloomy, but once more Clark saved the day. Receiving recruits from Kentucky he advanced northward, and late in 1782 defeated the Indians decisively at Chillicothe. In the next year the war officially came to an end, but it was some time before the English succeeded in persuading the Indians that actions which had been considered highly commendable in the past were both inappropriate and offensive after certain officials had uttered the magic word " peace."

TREATY OF PEACE

At the conclusion of active fighting the statesmen of the East had the task of confirming the conquests which Clark had made in the West. The commissioners were instructed to make peace only with the concurrence of our principal ally, France, but soon discovered that this procedure contained an almost fatal error. France was not interested primarily in the United States, but rather supported Spain, and Spain was opposed to American expansion. France and Spain agreed that the best plan was for the latter to take the Floridas, for the Indians to be guaranteed the country between the Appalachians and the Mississippi south of the Ohio under the joint protection of Spain and the United States, and for England to retain the country north of the Ohio, or better, to divide it with the United States.

When the American commissioners heard of these plans of France and Spain they cast their instructions to the winds and independently formulated a treaty with England. They were favored in this procedure by the attitude of England, which preferred American expansion to Spanish. The provisions of the Treaty of Paris as they related to the West were as favorable as the United States had any reason to expect. The entire region south of the Great Lakes went to the United States. The northwestern boundary was to run from Lake Superior to the Lake of the Woods and then directly west to the Mississippi (actually such a line was impossible to run, because a line directly west from the Lake of the Woods would not touch the Mississippi). From this point the boundary was to follow the Mississippi south to 31° north latitude and then along the 31st parallel and the present northern boundary of Florida to the Atlantic Coast. A secret agreement provided that if England retained West Florida its northern boundary would be the parallel of the mouth of the Yazoo River (32° 28'). These terms were eminently satisfactory to the United States except for the slowness with which Great Britain evacuated the Great Lakes posts which were within the limits of the United States.

But what happened to George Rogers Clark, the chief actor of the drama, and the one man to whom the conquest of the Northwest was due? His reward consisted chiefly in the gift of some 6000 acres of land in the wilderness of southern Indiana. In addition to the land he received a letter of thanks from the Governor of Virginia, and an ornamental sword. These munificent gifts of a grateful commonwealth had been won by Clark at the cost of the best years of his life, and the undermining of his health by the privations and hard work which he had experienced. Both he and his friends were weighted with debts which had been contracted during the Revolution, when they had dug into their own pockets to make up the gap between the appropriations of Virginia and the cost of carrying on the war.

When Virginia removed Clark from his command (1783), the sad spectacle of a hero without a job led Jefferson to make the suggestion that Congress commission the conqueror to explore the Far West. Congress failed to act, but a renewal of Indian warfare again called Clark into the field during the middle 1780s. After his return from fighting the red man, he was drawn into intrigues with the government of Spain, during which he received some funds from the Spanish commander at New Orleans (1787). A little later he was involved in an effort to free Louisiana from Spanish control, but the expedition never materialized. The remainder of his life was a losing struggle to cultivate his Indiana land, and he died in 1818, poor and discouraged.

READINGS

C. H. Ambler, *A History of West Virginia* (1933), ch. 7; L. D. Baldwin, *Pittsburgh* (1937), chs. 8, 9; J. D. Barnhart, *Henry Hamilton and George Rogers Clark* (1951)—includes Hamilton journal; N. M. Belting, *Kaskaskia Under the French Regime* (1948)—scholarly; T. Bodley, *George Rogers Clark* (1926); B. W. Bond, Jr., *The Foundations of Ohio* (1941), ch. 8; S. J. and E. H. Buck, *The Planting of Civilization in Western Pennsylvania* (1939), ch. 8; R. C. Downes, *Council Fires on the Upper Ohio* (1940), chs. 8–11—fine book; L. Esarey, *A History of Indiana from Its Exploration to 1850* (1915), chs. 11–18; W. Havighurst, *Land of Promise* (1946), ch. 7; J. A. James, *The Life of George Rogers Clark* (1928), *Oliver Pollock* (1937)—western merchant in Revolution; L. P. Kellogg, *The British Regime in Wisconsin and the Old Northwest* (1935), chs. 9–12; R. L. Kincaid, *The Wilderness Road* (1947), chs. 8–12—emphasizes Indian troubles; J. F. McDermott, *Old Cahokia* (1949)—detailed; W. H. Mohr, *Federal Indian Relations* (1933)—monograph; F. Palmer, *Clark of the Ohio* (1929); T. C. and M. J. Pease, *George Rogers Clark* (1929)—good; T. C. Pease, *The Story of Illinois* (1949), chs. 2, 3; M. M. Quaife (ed.), *The Capture of Old Vincennes* (1927); E. H. Roseboom and F. P. Weisenberger, *A History of Ohio* (1953), ch. 3—brief and factual.

CHAPTER 4

GOVERNMENTAL PROBLEMS

THE first settlers who came west of the Appalachians had a new world to build. They were confronted by a virgin wilderness in which the many essentials of white civilization did not exist. To fulfill their varied desires, which ranged from the simplest necessities of life to complicated cultural ambitions, the new inhabitants had to meet and conquer their strange environment.

CHARACTER OF WESTERN MIGRANTS

The methods used in solving western problems were conditioned by the character of the new inhabitants. Although many and diverse elements were represented in the western population, a few general statements can be made about them as a whole. The most obvious generalization is that most of the people moving west had for one reason or another not been successful in the East. Speaking broadly, a successful easterner would not leave the field of his achievement to move to an untamed wilderness. Consequently it follows that the vast majority of this new population was poor; men came because they had fortunes to make, and not because they had capital to invest or leisure to cultivate. The most important exception was the land speculator, but he usually either lost his money and became a typical westerner, or made more money and moved back east.

Lack of success in the East did not imply that the westerners necessarily lacked in ability. Frequently they belonged to a desirable, but unfavored, portion of the community from which they came. Younger members of large New England families sought more opportunity than their few relatively unfertile acres of New

41

England soil afforded. Poor whites from the South were driven to seek freer conditions of labor to avoid the competition of the slave-worked plantations. Slave owners sought replacements for their worked-out land. Independent farmers and artisans sought to improve their conditions. Immigrants from Europe drifted to the West, attracted by the lure of cheap land. Along with these desirable groups came a sprinkling of the less desirable — criminals seeking an escape from the law, or attempting to start life over again in new communities where their past deeds were unknown; the reckless and footloose, who would probably never become adequately adjusted to any human society.

The greatest single group was that of young unmarried farm boys, and the favorite age for migration was twenty-one. Presumably these young men had just completed their legal obligations to their parents and were now moving West to seek their fortunes. Frequently they returned East to obtain brides, for women were scarce in the West. When family groups migrated, the head of the family often made a preliminary trip to discover a suitable place to settle. At other times the family depended upon reports of friends and relatives who had moved West earlier. A family seldom migrated unless it had a fairly definite objective.

Naturally these various population elements went west by the most convenient routes, which meant that the migrants from particular eastern regions tended to congregate in groups in the West. This process was furthered by the tendency of all prospective frontiersmen to settle near former friends and neighbors. During the Revolutionary years the greatest mass of migration came from the South, passed through Cumberland Gap, and settled in Kentucky and Tennessee, or up the Potomac and then overland to the region of Pittsburgh. Eventually these streams of settlers overflowed into the region just north of the Ohio River — into what are now the southern parts of Ohio, Indiana and Illinois. Later they occupied Missouri and moved as far north as Iowa. Settlers from the Middle Atlantic states came west by way of Pittsburgh and mixed with the southern stream in the Ohio Valley. The New England migration of the eighteenth and early nineteenth centuries flowed for the most part into New York state with the fringes touching the Great Lakes; a few New Englanders, however, went into the Ohio Valley, usually traveling by way of Philadelphia, although sometimes proceeding west through southern New York state.

MAIN WESTERN PROBLEMS

Several of the most important of the problems facing these new settlers deserve particular mention, since efforts toward their solution ran throughout the entire history of the West. Of fundamental importance was the danger from the Indians. As said before, conditions were so bad in this respect during the 1770s and '80s that the settlers hardly dared leave their cabins unprotected, and few had sufficient temerity to travel at night. The outlook was particularly discouraging because of the slight hope for any quick alleviation. Neither the central government nor the settlers themselves had the manpower or the resources to prosecute successful Indian wars. The only hopeful indication was that a few leaders such as Washington saw the importance of the subject, and maintained a continuing interest in the progress of the West.

The second important problem of the West was the method of disposal of the land. Each settler wanted land which was both good and cheap, but he was prevented from fulfilling his desires by the chaotic conditions which existed during and immediately after the Revolution. At the end of the war the United States was confirmed in the control of the country extending as far west as the Mississippi, but it was hampered in the exercise of this control by the conflicting claims of its various component states. When these claims eventually were released in favor of the federal government, Congress had to find some adequate plan for the disposition of western lands. Here again the Indian problem was of significance, for western lands were not actually vacant, but rather occupied by numerous tribes of natives. Should the claims of the Indians to the land be respected, and if so, to what extent?

A third big problem confronting the West was that of money and credit, for the West needed as much of both as it was possible to obtain. When settlers went West they were poor, and found difficulty in meeting even their necessary expenses. The cost of moving had to be defrayed, and life supported until the first crop was harvested. Land had to be bought, as well as tools and seeds. Furthermore each new community had to do a variety of building — roads, bridges, schools, jails, and churches. Large amounts of credit were highly desirable. For many years the West was to be influenced by the fact that it was a debtor community.

The problem of transportation also troubled the new communities of the United States. The very foundations of their future prosperity rested upon the development of methods for transporting their goods to market cheaply and quickly, and for bringing news and goods from the East and from Europe. Each transportational novelty that became popular in the East found a host of ready adherents in the West. It was in this field that the lack of capital in the West was most felt, and various plans and devices were employed in an effort to obviate the lack of ready money.

Finally, the West was exceedingly interested in the development of good and effective government. Life and property had to be made secure; the Indians must be defeated; wills, deeds, and marriages must be recorded; roads and bridges must be built. The first efforts to solve the governmental problem were local and spontaneous in their origin, but sporadic local efforts proved unsatisfactory at the best. It was the problem of government that was first settled in a way which gave permanent satisfaction.

In addition to these five large problems there were innumerable others of a less pressing and vital importance. Religion, education, literature, art, medicine, law, and all the other perquisites of civilization had to be supplied. All of them must be considered if a true picture of the development of the West is to be presented. Those of land and government, however, deserve first treatment, for it was in regard to them that the first important actions were taken.

LAND OWNERSHIP

The importance of the ownership and disposal of western land in the period immediately after the Revolution cannot be overemphasized. The United States was an agricultural nation, and land was the fundamental necessity of life. In the West, with its few industries and its little shipping, land was the most important single economic element.

The land which today composes the United States had been granted originally to proprietors or companies who intended to exploit or colonize the New World. Because of the inadequacy of the existing geographical knowledge, the boundaries specified in the charters sometimes overlapped, and their terms often left a very real doubt as to the exact territory specified, with the result that colonial disputes over dividing lines were not uncommon. Some of the charters provided for grants beyond the mountains. As settlement progressed the original grantee would sell or give away such land as was needed to provide for the increase of population. The limits of such sales or donations were sometimes so ill-defined that they were impossible to mark, and frequently two or more grants overlapped. Then came the Proclamation of 1763, which forced the various colonies and proprietors to allow their far-western claims to lapse for the time being.

With the outbreak of the Revolution each colony with claims to western territory proceeded to revive its hopes and aspirations. Virginia proved the most active and fortunate, for it was under her auspices that George Rogers Clark conquered the Northwest. While Virginia organized Kentucky and the region north of the Ohio into counties, North Carolina did the same for the Tennessee country, so that all of the settled West had at least nominal government. The Georgia claim had not as yet been peopled. While this situation had some advantages for the states with western counties, it was not without its drawbacks. Other states also had western claims, and what was to become of them if Virginia and North Carolina were able to monopolize almost the entire West? Furthermore, the West itself was not fully satisfied, for it wanted cheap land and a government that would spend money freely to fight the Indians and to make public improvements; Virginia and North Carolina not only had no money to spend, but were very desirous of increasing their revenues.

Just at the time when the central government needed unusual power to deal with western problems, it was at the nadir of its effectiveness. The Continental Congress, from its first meeting in 1774, was a purely voluntary and noncoercive body, with little power and less desire to arouse local enmities by interfering with the West. The new Articles of Confederation finally went into effect with the ratification of Maryland on March 1, 1781, after having been before the states since 1777, but here again was an incredibly weak central authority; no executive, no effective courts, and no power to enforce legislation, made the Articles a frail support on which to lean. But in spite of the serious handicaps which surrounded Congress under the Articles of Confederation, it succeeded in putting into force some legislation which was exceedingly important in relation to the West.

STATE CESSIONS

Even before the Articles of Confederation were adopted by Maryland it was proposed by some states (those not having land claims) that all unsold western land be turned over to the central government as a common possession. The states with land claims could see quite obvious objections to such a proposal, but on the other hand they could also see good reasons for making the cessions. Conflicting state claims made problematical the amount of land which any one state would be able to hold. The Indians were in the main hostile, and their subjugation would be a long and arduous task. All kinds of public improvements would have to be constructed with eastern money, while the poor westerners would not be able to pay any considerable taxes for many years. Altogether, it seemed to many persons that the disadvantages of holding western territory far outweighed the possible future benefits which might accrue from land sales.

In view of these various factors the states began to look upon the Congressional proposal with favor, and actually began to cede their western claims to Congress. New York had the honor of being the first (1780) — possibly in part because her claim as heir of the Iroquois pretensions was scarcely tenable. Other states followed, the last being Georgia in 1802. Some of them, such as Virginia and North Carolina, had already sold a considerable share of the lands they were theoretically ceding to Congress. Others made reservations. The unsold land of Kentucky and Tennessee never came under Congressional control. The " Connecticut Reserve," including the present city of Cleveland, Ohio, was retained for the benefit of certain sufferers of the Revolution. Virginia withheld large amounts of land, of which the greater share was to go to her Revolutionary soldiers. The Georgia cession actually cost the United States more than was received from the lands remaining unsold at the time of the transfer; this outcome was due in large part to the Yazoo frauds.

LAND DEBATES

As a result of these cessions Congress was endowed with an immense public domain, and a continually increasing influx of population meant that immediate provision must be made for the survey, sale, and government of the regions which had proved attractive to settlers. A considerable number of these settlers had paid no attention to legal ownership, merely occupying and beginning to cultivate whatever land seemed to them good. What should be done with such " squatters "? Furthermore, soldiers of the Revolutionary army had been promised land as part payment for their services in the war, and the Newburgh petition of

1783 demonstrated that at least a portion of them had a real desire for the land. What, if anything, should be done for them? Here were two classes that were insistent upon virtually free land — but free land did not sound attractive to a government that was desirous of collecting every possible cent of revenue. Furthermore, both East and West were agreed that some sort of action would have to be undertaken immediately to protect the white man from red depredations. And finally, it was evident to such men as Washington that, if the United States did not act immediately and effectively, there was a real possibility that the West might either try to settle its own affairs as an independent state or appeal to some foreign power such as Spain for protection.

The debate in Congress on the disposition of the public lands was long and acrimonious. New England practice, in which each township was sold as a unit and then subdivided by its purchasers, was compared with the southern procedure, in which each man picked his land, placed his own boundaries, had his title recorded at the county seat, and then paid a lawyer to fight the cases which arose over disputed boundaries and ownership. The battle between indiscriminate and exact location was won by New England. Furthermore, there were debates as to whether the new land should be plotted in large or small townships, and whether large or small tracts should be offered for sale. In both these cases compromises were eventually effected. The progress of the discussion is best illustrated by the reports made to Congress in 1784 and 1785.

ORDINANCE OF 1785

Out of the welter of discussion eventually emerged the Ordinance of 1785, applying to the region north of the Ohio and designed primarily to obtain revenue from the public domain. Townships six miles square were to be surveyed prior to sale; each township was to be subdivided into thirty-six sections, each section thus being one mile square and containing 640 acres. These amounts varied slightly in practice, since the earth is round. The land was to be sold in the eastern states at auction, with a minimum price of one dollar an acre plus the cost of survey. Half of the land was to be sold in townships and the remainder was to be sold in sections. Reservations were made for the Revolutionary soldiers and for schools.

Sales of land under the new ordinance were disappointingly

6	5	4	3	2	1
7	8	9	10	11	12
18	17	16	15	14	13
19	20	21	22	23	24
30	29	28	27	26	25
31	32	33	34	35	36

HALF SECTION
320 ACRES

QUARTER
SECTION
160 ACRES

HALF QUARTER
SECTION
80 ACRES

QUARTER
QUARTER
SECTION
40 ACRES

System of Land Surveys

small to a government badly in need of immediate funds. Seven ranges of townships adjacent to the western boundary of Pennsylvania were surveyed in the years 1785–87 and put upon the market. Auctions were held in the city of New York, but only a few speculators attended and little land was sold. Most of the settlers merely squatted and hoped that Congress would some time take pity on their plight; certainly they had no money to go East and buy land at auction.

ORDINANCE OF 1784

Efforts to solve the problem of the survey and sale of the public domain were paralleled by discussions of the form of government which would be given to the West; in fact, the first governmental legislation came a year earlier than the land ordinance of 1785. The Ordinance of 1784 was based upon a report made by Jefferson to Congress in the same year; kind critics have said it was a temporary aberration on the part of the usually brilliant Jefferson. The report suggested limited local self-government for the West until its population was sufficiently large to make necessary the creation of states. To produce conveniently sized areas for statehood, the land west of the mountains and north of the Ohio was to be divided in a nice checkerboard fashion on every other degree of latitude, with a transverse line through the center of the territory. The result produced would have been ten approximately equal divisions, which were to be given the mellifluous names of Sylvania, Washington, Michigania, Cherronesus, Saratoga, Illinois, Polypotamia, Pelisipia, Metropotamia and Assenisippia. When any one of these regions had a population as large as the smallest of the United States it was to be admitted to the Union under whatever government it desired. When the report was finally put into law the boundaries were changed, Jefferson's names abandoned, and provision made that each region should have a delegate to Congress as soon as it had attained a population of 20,000.

The ordinances of 1784 and 1785 were not final solutions of the land and government problems, but they were important steps in that direction. Most observers agreed that these acts were in themselves not satisfactory. Land was not being sold and consequently no revenue was being produced. There was still no real provision for government before statehood. In consequence, Congress continued to debate the whole matter, and further action was only a question of time.

OHIO COMPANY

While Congress was trying to make up its mind, a movement started which was destined to have an important influence both upon Congress and upon the settlement of the West. As has been mentioned, the soldiers in the Revolutionary army had long been interested in obtaining western land as part of their reward for services in the war. The Newburgh petition of 1783 had this end in view, and in 1786 two generals, Israel Putnam and Benjamin Tupper, called a meeting of all interested parties at the " Bunch of Grapes " tavern in Boston. At this meeting was formed the Ohio Company, with a nominal capital of $1,000,000. Each member was to subscribe $1000 in depreciated Continental currency, which was easy to obtain, and $10 in cash, which was more difficult. The $10 subscriptions were to be used for immediate expenses, while it was hoped that Congress would accept the paper money in payment for western lands. General Samuel H. Parsons was delegated to present the proposition to Congress.

When Parsons arrived to talk with Congress he found no Congress in session — a quorum failed to appear from May 12 to July 5, 1787. He finally succeeded in presenting his petition, but it seemed exceedingly unlikely that any action would be taken concerning it, since the members of Congress were anything but optimistic about its chances. In fact Congress was practically only " marking time," waiting to see what was to happen in the Constitutional Convention, which began its meetings on May 25.

The gloomy outlook in Congress caused the Ohio Company to

take further thought, and finally to send a new representative to Congress — the Reverend Manasseh Cutler. Cutler had been a chaplain with the Revolutionary army and was a man of wide interests and broad culture. He immediately mounted his horse and rode to New York to see what might be done. His first efforts seemed so fruitless that he took a vacation and rode down to Philadelphia to attend some of the meetings of the Constitutional Convention. When he returned to New York he found his prospects more promising, and so embarked upon a strenuous program of calling on members of Congress, attending clambakes and receptions, and of cultivating particularly the friendship of the president of Congress, Arthur St. Clair.

The petition of the Ohio Company for land was but one of the matters pressing upon Congress for attention. The necessity of affording a better government for the West was a paramount problem, and it was but natural that Cutler, in lobbying for his own pet measure, should become interested in the governmental legislation and have a hand in both affairs. Another modifying factor was the speculative interest of many members of Congress and their friends in western lands. In fact, one of these men, Colonel William Duer, was so influential that Cutler felt it necessary to come to an understanding with him. The bargain they finally made was that Cutler promised to buy extra land for Duer and his associates in return for their support of the proposed Ohio Company purchase. But the Congressional committee which was considering Cutler's proposal remained hesitant. Thereupon Cutler grew impatient and threatened to buy his land from the individual states if Congress did not act. According to his own statement his threat " appeared to have the effect I wished "; the committee was " mortified," and eventually the grant was made.

When the grant was finally made, it included 6,500,000 acres of Ohio land — 1,500,000 acres for the Ohio Company and the remainder for Duer and his associates. The price to the Ohio Company was one dollar an acre, with one third off for bad lands, to be paid in Continental currency, which was then worth twelve and a half cents on the dollar. The actual price was therefore about eight cents an acre, which certainly was not an excessive price for good Ohio land, even when that state was a wilderness. According to the terms of the contract $500,000 was to be paid immediately and the remainder when the surveys were completed.

The grant to the Ohio Company immediately stirred that organization to activity. The down payment was made, and plans were evolved for the settlement of at least a part of the tract. In 1788 a group of New Englanders made the trip across New York and northern Pennsylvania, and then floated down the Ohio River to the mouth of the Muskingum, where they founded the town of Marietta. Being good New Englanders they produced a good New England village, including the usual Congregational church. When the Ohio Company eventually found itself unable to pay the remainder of the purchase price, Congress remitted it and cut the grant in half, so that the company finally received 750,000 acres.

SCIOTO COMPANY

Meantime the Duer group (usually known as the Scioto Company, although not organized formally) went ahead with plans to settle its land. Joel Barlow, the well-known author of the *Columbiad,* was sent to France to sell American farms. While in France he became associated with an Englishman by the name of William Playfair, who took the initiative in organizing a French company to do the actual selling. The wild land of the Scioto Company was advertised as very fertile, well populated, and suited particularly to artisans and mechanics of all kinds; no mention was made of the lack of a final title by the company. " Consumer resistance " was broken and 3,000,000 acres were sold. In 1790 some 600 of the purchasers started for America. For the most part they were members of the upper middle class, and included professional men, artisans, wood carvers, watch and clock makers, tailors, wig makers, and dancing masters. There was something pathetically humorous in the idea of wig makers and dancing masters migrating to the untamed wilderness of Ohio.

Duer and his friends were both pleased and embarrassed by the success of Barlow and Playfair. They were particularly concerned over their ability to make the necessary payments on their grant, for the cost of the 5,000,000 acres was a huge sum, even though the price was only two-thirds of a dollar an acre and payments could be made in six installments. When they tried to obtain the proceeds of the French company it was found to be insolvent due to the manipulations of Playfair. The result was the bankruptcy of the Scioto Company, and by the time the French settlers landed in Virginia their prospects were exceedingly gloomy. Eventually the migrants were escorted to the West and there, instead of finding populous towns and plenty of work, they discovered a wilderness containing a few partly completed log cabins. Some drifted away to other parts of the country, others stayed to form the town of Gallipolis. Actually they were on Ohio Company land where most of them remained in spite of a Congressional donation of land in the present Scioto County.

In addition to the Ohio Company and the Duer group many other individuals and companies applied to Congress for the purchase of large areas of land in the West. The only other sale was made to John Cleves Symmes, a member of Congress from New Jersey. Symmes received (1788) a grant of 1,000,000 acres east of the Little Miami. The terms were similar to those made to the Ohio Company: he was to pay $82,198 down and the remainder in seven installments. He made the down payment, but defaulted on the remainder, and the grant was eventually reduced to 300,000 acres along the Ohio River.

NORTHWEST ORDINANCE

While these various tracts of land were being granted the matter of government was finally settled. The act which provided for the government of the new West was probably the most remarkable piece of legislation passed by Congress under the Articles of Confederation, particularly when one considers that the old government was giving its last feeble gasps of life before the new Constitution was completed and put into effect. True it is that the act was mixed with the lobbying efforts of Cutler, Duer and others, that Cutler himself had a hand in the final outcome, and that Arthur St. Clair aided it in part because he had been promised the governorship of the new territory; and yet the Ordinance of 1787 was a remarkable bit of constructive legislation, of which the principles were to remain in effect during the whole process of frontier advance from the Appalachians to the Pacific. Any act which was used successfully for a century and a half under varying conditions is worthy of respect.

The Ordinance of 1787 applied only to the Old Northwest. This territory was to be divided into three, four, or five states. If three, the dividing lines should run as follows — one along the Wabash River to the meridian of Vincennes and then following that meridian due north to the international boundary; the other was the meridian of the mouth of the Great Miami. These are approximately the present boundaries on the east and west of Indiana.

If four or five states were to be created, then an additional line should be drawn directly east and west through the tip of Lake Michigan. The latter line was later modified.

Even more important than the division of territory were the provisions for government, which remedied the defects of the Ordinance of 1784 by an effective administration before statehood. Three stages of government were provided. The first, which was to go into effect immediately, gave control to a governor, a secretary and three judges, all elected by Congress, which maintained control. When the population of the territory had increased to include 5000 free adult males, the second type of government was to go into effect; all the old officers and provisions remained, but an elective legislature was provided to give the electorate its first taste of self-government. Finally, when the total population reached 60,000 free inhabitants, a constitutional convention could be held and the prospective state apply for admission to the Union. In addition to these provisions there was also a bill of rights similar to that of the United States Constitution, and a prohibition of slavery, excepting those slaves already in the territory.

Immediately following the passage of the Ordinance of 1787 Arthur St. Clair was appointed the first governor of the Northwest Territory. After a leisurely trip he finally arrived in Marietta on July 9, 1788. He had but little to govern, either in terms of land or population, and as a man of ambition he was anxious to increase both, which meant that he was particularly desirous of pushing back the Indians who were occupying the larger part of his new domain.

The fact that the Ordinance of 1787 applied only to the Old Northwest is sometimes forgotten. A similar act of 1790 made provision for the territory south of the Ohio. In later years the principles of the Ordinance of 1787 were reenacted many times to provide for all new regions west to the Pacific, with only the exceptions of Texas and California.

FURTHER DEBATES ON LAND

If anyone believed that the idea of making large grants such as that to the Ohio Company would replace the necessity for smaller sales to individuals he was soon disillusioned by the difficulties encountered before the large grants were adjusted. For the most part, existing Congressional legislation had no effect whatsoever; settlers continued to go where they pleased without consideration of the law. Certainly it seemed an imposition to ask a poor land seeker to make the long trip east to have a chance to bid at auction for the land he had already improved. If the prospective settler bought before he moved west, he found himself in equally bad circumstances; either he must buy his land unseen or he must make an expensive and time-consuming trip to the West before he bought. The only logical solution was to establish local land offices reasonably near the land to be sold.

The question of price also disturbed Congress. Everyone agreed that the land should produce a revenue to the central government, but there unanimity ceased. What sort of price would produce a maximum return? Too expensive land would mean that the poorer settlers could not afford to buy, and would just squat, whereupon the government would be faced with the unpleasant necessity either of ejecting large numbers of settlers from their homes or giving them the land. Closely allied with this problem was that of deciding the minimum size of a tract which would be sold to one person. Too large a minimum would mean that only the speculator could buy, while a very small amount would raise the cost of administration to a prohibitive figure. These and other phases of the land situation were debated by Congress continuously after 1789.

Alexander Hamilton contributed to the discussion in 1790 by a report to Congress in which he suggested a policy designed to increase the stability of the nation. He recommended that preference in land sales be given to the large companies, and that the small settler be pacified by making it possible for him to buy tracts of not over 100 acres. The price should be thirty cents an acre and credit should be given for three-quarters of the purchase price. Branch land offices would supply local needs. Influenced to some extent by this report, Congress eventually passed the act of 1796, which constituted one more step toward the solution of the land problem. Its terms were unimportant in view of the more effective act which succeeded it four years later.

ACT OF 1800

The most significant land legislation of this period came in 1800, when Harrison's Frontier Bill became a law. William Henry Harrison was the first Congressional delegate of the Territory of Ohio, and his measure represented the western desires of the time — modified to some extent, of course, by the necessities of practical politics. Most of the provisions were not novel, having long been discussed and having been expressed in considerable part in the act of 1796. Local land offices were established at Cincinnati, Chillicothe, Marietta and Steubenville; each office was to be manned by a Register (for drawing up the deeds) and a Receiver (to control the finances). East of the Muskingum the land was to be sold entirely in tracts of a section apiece (640 acres); west of that stream half was to be sold in sections and half in half-sections. The auction system was retained, with a minimum price of two dollars an acre, the purchaser also paying the cost of survey. Any land remaining unsold after the auction was open to private entry at the minimum price. Only about one-twentieth of the purchase price was due at the time of the sale, the remainder of the first quarter being due in forty days, and the other three-quarters in three annual payments, with the last payment at the end of four years. Interest was charged on the deferred payments, with a discount given for earlier settlement.

The act of 1800 fulfilled in general the desires of the West. The size of the individual purchase had been decreased, but even 320 acres of uncleared land proved a large amount, and was reduced in 1804 to 160 acres and in 1817 to 80 acres. The price was still high from the viewpoint of the westerner, but this trouble was alleviated by the credit system; the westerner might now make the first payment on twice the amount of land which he could formerly (before 1796) have bought at a dollar an acre; true he was in debt, but few worried about that for it was considered only a question of a few years until most everyone would be rich.

With the passage of the land act of 1800 two of the important western problems had been settled for the time being. No other important land legislation was passed for another twenty years. A scheme of government had been devised which was to last throughout the entire period of the continental expansion of the United States. In view of these accomplishments it becomes possible to consider some of the other problems and conditions of life which surrounded the people of the West in the period immediately after the Revolution.

READINGS

T. P. Abernethy, *Western Lands and the American Revolution* (1937); C. W. Alvord, *The Illinois Country* (1920), ch. 18— scholarly; J. A. Barrett, *Evolution of the Ordinance of 1787*

(1891); T. T. Belote, *The Scioto Speculation* (1907)—monograph; B. W. Bond, Jr., *The Civilization of the Old Northwest* (1934), ch. 10, *The Quit Rent System in the American Colonies* (1919)—comprehensive; J. S. Davis, *Essays in the Earlier History of American Corporations* (2 vols., 1917), ch. 2—Scioto speculation; W. Havighurst, *Land of Promise* (1946), chs. 10–12; B. H. Hibbard, *A History of the Public Land Policies* (1924), chs. 1–5—fairly good; S. H. Holbrook, *The Yankee Exodus* (1950), chs. 2, 3—scrappy; A. B. Hulbert, *Ohio in the Time of the Confederation* (1918), (ed.), *The Records of the Original Proceedings of the Ohio Company* (1917), Introduction; R. M. Robbins, *Our Landed Heritage* (1942), chs. 1, 2—best history of public domain; E. H. Roseboom and F. P. Weisenburger, *A History of Ohio* (1953), chs. 4, 5; A. M. Sakolski, *The Great American Land Bubble* (1932)—speculation; P. J. Treat, *The National Land System* (1910), chs. 1–4—good on origins; F. E. Wilson, *Arthur St. Clair* (1944), chs. 1–3—very sympathetic.

CHAPTER 5

REMOVING
THE INDIAN MENACE

EARLY settlers in the West were surrounded by numerous dangers, by no means the least was the Indian. While the Indian was in many ways an interesting and admirable person, he made a very unpleasant neighbor for the white frontiersman. From time to time, and without due formality, he went to war; then the forest became alive with lurking savages, and no settlement was safe. Peace and prosperity for the settler was impossible without the pacification of the Indian. Settlement could not proceed tranquilly until the Indians were subdued.

IMPORTANCE OF THE INDIAN

The fear of attack was only a part of the westerner's problem. The Indians were in prior possession of the lands which the frontiersmen desired to occupy, and had a claim to their ownership which the central government was willing to accept, at least in theory. On this subject the westerner disagreed with the federal government. Few westerners took Indian land ownership seriously, for to most the Indians were savages whom God, for some inscrutable reason, had allowed to hinder the progress of his chosen white people. After the whites had overcome the evil (the Indians) they could enter upon the joy of possessing their rightful heritage. Killing Indians was like killing snakes — entirely desirable except from the standpoint of the victim.

The Indians were in an exceedingly anomalous position in relation to the government of the United States. On the one hand they were considered by the national government as composing independent nations, each with partial sovereignty; they owned

57

the land which they occupied, and any kind of agreement either for land cessions or for other purposes had to be in the form of a treaty made by the executive power and ratified by the Senate. On the other hand it was perfectly evident that no matter what polite fiction was devised concerning Indian rights, the Indian tribes were actually not free and independent states. They lived within the territorial limits of the United States and were not recognized by foreign powers.

Both the United States and the Indians suffered because of this attempt to maintain the theory of Indian independence. Indian lands were considered legally as foreign territory; white settlers were prohibited, and strict laws were passed to govern the relations between the two races. Actually these acts were never effective, for the settlers continued to move west without the least respect for Indian boundaries. Then the United States was placed in its perpetual quandary as to how to treat the frontier advance. Of course the land belonged technically to the Indians and the whites had no rights which need necessarily be respected, but a white government was not inclined to act against its own people, particularly when they had votes and the reds did not. Furthermore, with the source of power several hundred miles away, it seldom seemed practicable to dispossess thousands of white settlers when they exhibited an inclination to resist.

INDIAN TREATIES

The method usually followed in settling a conflict between Indian rights and white desires was to buy the land in dispute and then open it formally to white settlement. The Indians were summoned to meet at some central spot, where a large council was held. Governmental agents would talk with the Indian chiefs, and by a mixture of cajolery, threats, food, clothing, and liquor could usually arrange a treaty providing for the cession of the land in question. Ordinarily the compensation for such cession was in blankets, cloth, weapons, jewelry, annuities, and often some white aid to settled agriculture for the Indians. After the Indian chiefs and the United States representatives had signed the treaty it was sent to the Senate for approval. In many instances the Senate modified the terms, necessitating an effort, usually quite futile, to have the modifications signed by the original participants.

As soon as the treaty was made and ratified it was considered by the United States to be binding permanently upon all members of the tribes whose chiefs had signed it, and also upon their descendants. Flagrant violations frequently resulted in the sending of a punitive military expedition to visit justice upon the violators; no clear line of demarcation could be drawn, of course, between the individual violators and the tribes of which they were members. As for the land itself, it was formally surveyed and opened for settlement; usually the original settlers, who had come while the land still technically belonged to the Indians, were able to have their possessions confirmed.

In spite of certain inconsistencies, this policy of the federal government was reasonably logical if one could accept the fundamental theories on which it was based and could overlook certain bad features of its administration. In point of fact, however, the whole procedure rested upon a legal fiction. The Indians were not in reality independent in the white sense of the term, and they never really understood the white attitude toward land ownership. To the Indians there was no such thing as permanent individual ownership and sale of land. In a vague way they recognized an ownership by use, but even here their concepts were not clear-cut. They never understood that the land which they sold was to be closed to them forever. Land was like air or water — plentiful enough for the use of everyone — and it was a perpetual surprise to the Indian when objections were raised to his returning to land on which he had formerly hunted.

The Indians also never saw eye to eye with the whites concerning treaties. Both the Indians and whites held that any treaty had to be ratified — by the Senate and by the tribe respectively. Both sides, however, overlooked this ratification process in respect to their cosigners. The whites in particular felt that a treaty was in force as soon as any Indians signed it. Much trouble was caused by the attempted enforcement of treaties which had been signed only by a handful of Indians who had been bribed or coerced, and who could in no sense bind their tribes. Furthermore, certain treaty provisions were never understood by the Indian signatories, so observance would have been impossible.

When the Indians violated a treaty, possibly because of lack of understanding, a failure in ratification, or complete unawareness of its existence, further differences between red and white ideology became important. The violation was usually committed by one or more small groups acting independently. The tribe as a whole might have no knowledge of these violations, and feel no responsibility, but the United States professed to see no difference between the part and the whole. Viewed practically, it was difficult to discover and punish the real offenders, and so the resulting punitive expedition waged war on that portion of the tribe within reach, and sometimes on any group of Indians within the district in which the trouble had occurred.

These differences in attitude between white and red made conflict inevitable, particularly as long as white settlers continued to view the Indian lands with covetous eyes. The resulting clashes must be blamed as much on unavoidable differences of viewpoint as on bad faith on either side. Some of the disastrous results of this conflict might have been avoided if the United States had come to realize at an earlier date that the Indian tribes could not be treated as equal and independent nations.

WEST AT END OF REVOLUTION

The end of the Revolution found the frontier in turmoil. The fortunes of war had varied, but never had there been a decisive and large scale defeat of the Indians. For the Indians war still continued, and they harried outlying settlements, killing individuals, capturing families, driving off stock, stealing crops, and destroying improvements. Arguments that the war was over because a few far distant whites had uttered the magic word " peace " carried little conviction. From the Indian standpoint, white intruders were still arriving and the new ones were no less objectionable than their predecessors.

White settlers were on the march, both north and south, and their increasing number made conflict with the reds unavoidable. Indians loved their homes and would not move voluntarily. In the south, the expansion was from Georgia and the infant state of Franklin. In the north the occupation of Ohio had begun with streams of settlement converging from Kentucky and western Pennsylvania. A sprinkling of towns such as Marietta had appeared on the northern bank of the Ohio River.

Also to the north and to the south a foreign power complicated the situation. In the south Spain was anxious to keep the Indian trade and to provide a buffer against further United States expansion. To accomplish these ends it was friendly toward Franklin, which it even talked of attaching to Spain. It was likewise cordial toward the Indians. In the north England continued to hold such western posts as Detroit and Mackinac, and to cultivate friendly Indian relations — with the object, of course, of retaining the fur trade. A gesture was made toward restraining the Indians from active war, for American good will was desired, but an Indian confederation was encouraged, and British statements at least implied that assistance would be forthcoming for the Indians in any future trouble with the United States.

Northwest and Southwest were also similar in the existence in each area of an Indian confederation. The southern combination was inspired by Alexander McGillivray and the northern one by the equally able Joseph Brant. In each case the federation was hostile to any further land cessions to the whites and agreed not to consider such cessions as valid.

INDIAN TREATIES AFTER THE WAR

The federal government under the Articles of Confederation was somewhat more optimistic about the future of Indian relations than the facts warranted. Flushed with victory, Congress held (1783) that the Indians, as unsuccessful British allies, had lost the war and hence had forfeited all claim to their land — a proposition which proved impossible to maintain in fact. During the same year Congress ordered all white intruders off the Indian lands and sent commissioners to obtain treaties of peace and friendship with the various tribes. A little later (1786) it provided for the administration of Indian affairs through two departments, which divided their duties at the Ohio River; both were subject to the Secretary of War.

When the Congressional commissioners went west to talk to the Indians they found their job extremely difficult. Most Indians had little desire to talk and even less to sign treaties — and particularly treaties for land cessions. Ultimately the southern Indians were brought into line — Cherokee (1785), Chickasaw and Choctaw (1786) and Creek (1790). Of these tribes, the Chickasaw and Choctaw were generally friendly to the whites. The Cherokee and Creek were generally hostile, in spite of the treaties, and in spite of various military operations, notably by Sevier, but also by the Georgia militia.

In the north the Congressional commissioners made a parallel series of treaties, but with even poorer results, if that were possible. The Iroquois at Fort Stanwix (1784) promised once more to give up their western claims. Most of the northwestern tribes agreed in two treaties within the next two years to accept American sovereignty and to cede their claims to most of Ohio. Viewed realistically, however, these treaties were not really very helpful. Comparatively few groups were represented and most of the Indians did not consider the agreements binding.

The commissioners tried to show their good faith by ordering Colonel Josiah Harmar in 1785 to eject all unauthorized white settlers who were in the Indian country. Harmar made a few feeble gestures in this direction, and constructed Fort Harmar at the mouth of the Muskingum, but then decided — quite wisely — that his force was too small to accomplish the task with which it was charged.

All of these treaties made a brave show on the statute books, but produced remarkably little change in western conditions. Indian raids continued, to the danger and distress of the West. At this juncture the whole problem was transferred to the hands of the new government established under the Constitution. Some sort of action was inevitable, especially since President Washington had long been greatly concerned with the West and had watched developments in that section with a keen and active interest.

Arthur St. Clair, as governor of the Northwest Territory, tried his hand at Indian affairs by concluding a treaty with all the available Indians at Fort Harmar in January 1789. Again the Indians bound themselves to keep earlier treaties of peace, but once again they showed very little enthusiasm for keeping their agreements. The consequence was that Brigadier General Harmar (his rank had been raised by this time) was sent on a raiding expedition against the hostile tribes. In spite of some minor successes, Harmar's expedition was a failure; it resulted rather in making the Indians more hostile than in pacifying them.

HARMAR

The failure of Harmar made more drastic measures necessary, and in the summer of 1790 Congress empowered President Washington to call out the militia of Kentucky, Virginia and western Pennsylvania for the defense of the frontier. In a short time the troops began to pour into Pittsburgh. General Harmar was placed in command, and as he was at this time at Fort Washington (Cincinnati) the new troops were allowed to straggle down the Ohio River on their own initiative and at their own convenience.

The army which finally gathered at Fort Washington was composed of 1453 men, of whom 320 were federal troops with a background of military experience gathered in the Revolution. The remainder were militia, mostly from Pennsylvania and Kentucky, and were far from satisfactory as a body of fighting men. They ranged in age from the very young to the very old. Many were physically incompetent and few had even an elementary idea of how to care for and use a gun. Their supplies were poor, the clothing which was issued was inadequate and shoddy, and the food was very bad. These conditions occasioned much grumbling. The men had the usual militia resentment against military control; disciplining a western company of militia was only slightly easier than enforcing orders on the Ohio River. In addition, the militia and the regulars were perpetually jealous of each other. Each looked upon the other with contempt, and came to the assistance of its rival only in case of dire mutual necessity.

Late in September, after the most desultory training, this ill-assorted army left Fort Washington to fight the Indians. Very soon the militia threatened mutiny; some of the volunteers actually started to go home, so that it was necessary to use force to recall them to their duty. A little later, after the army had covered some 170 miles, a small group of Indians was encountered accidentally. Both parties were surprised and alarmed, but the militiamen were more quick-witted than the Indians and started to run first. Again they had to be brought back ignominiously.

The general route of Harmar's slow and badly organized march was up the Little Miami and then north in the region of the present Ohio-Indiana boundary. Supplies were inadequate and the men were discontented, but luckily no considerable body of Indians appeared along the line of march. Finally the army reached one of the more important Indian towns, which was situated at the present site of Fort Wayne; the Indians fled, and Harmar's men had the satisfaction of destroying the Indian lodges and crops.

This " brilliant " victory was followed by other engagements which were less satisfactory. On September 19 a white detachment was surprised and overwhelmed. Two days later a general engagement was fought. Harmar's army was disorganized and retreated hurriedly; two hundred whites were killed and thirty-five wounded, the proportion between the two figures showing the thoroughness of the Indian operations. The only reason that more men were not killed was that the Indians were so occupied with taking scalps and loading themselves with plunder that they had no time to continue fighting. Eventually Harmar's army was restored to partial order, but it was thoroughly disheartened. On November 4, the survivors arrived at Fort Washington.

Harmar's operations were hardly effective in subduing the Indians. A court of inquiry examined into the affair, but finally exonerated the general. He had probably shown considerable personal bravery and had done the best of which he was capable with very poor materials, but these factors were of very little importance to a West looking for peace with the Indians. The net result was that a white expedition had been defeated disastrously, and that the Indians continued their depredations with increased self-assurance. Two other small expeditions were sent early in 1791, one of them led by James Wilkinson. They succeeded in doing some damage, but not enough to frighten the red man.

ST. CLAIR

In this extremity President Washington ordered Governor St. Clair to take personal command, cautioning him of the many mistakes that had been made in the past and impressing upon him the necessity for a successful campaign. St. Clair was a high-minded gentleman of the Federalist school, with noble ideals and great personal courage. At this time, however, he was becoming elderly and choleric; his strength was waning, his fat was increasing, and he was troubled periodically with the gout. He overrated his own military ability. In spite of these impediments he developed a good plan of campaign, which had as its principal object the construction of a line of forts from the Ohio River to Lake Erie.

St. Clair's men, like those of Harmar, were poor material with which to fight an Indian war. They were gathered for the most part from the cities of the East, often being drawn from the poorhouses and prisons. Most of them were six months' militia, receiving $2.10 a month, lacking military experience, and thriving on dissipation and disorder. This nondescript array came west by way of Pittsburgh, being allowed to follow its own pleasure in descending the Ohio to Fort Washington. Theoretically St. Clair had some 3000 men, but actually his total number of effectives was never larger than 2000. All the bad conditions which had bothered Harmar also harassed St. Clair.

St. Clair's first operation was the dispatch of an advance guard which built Fort Hamilton on the Great Miami about twenty-five miles from Cincinnati. The main army started its advance early in October 1791, but not without much grumbling at the necessity of leaving the pleasures of garrison life at Cincinnati. In practice the wilderness was made endurable by continued gambling and drinking, as well as by the continued presence of many women followers. On October 12 Fort Jefferson was built six miles south of the present Greenville, Ohio, and here the army rested twelve days before advancing farther north. November 3 saw the expedition encamped on a plateau of the Wabash a hundred miles north of Cincinnati and on the present Ohio-Indiana line.

At daybreak of the 4th the soldiers were startled from their slumbers by Indian war whoops and a shower of arrows coming from the surrounding forest. When the whites — partially clothed — rushed from their tents they had to fire at an unseen foe. The resulting engagement included many feats of personal bravery, but no effectively organized resistance. St. Clair was so weak that he had to be lifted to his horse, but once there he displayed great valor. Three horses were shot from under him, eight bullets went through his clothes and one clipped his hair. His best efforts, however, failed to produce any semblance of order among his troops. The Indians lurked in the forest, shot down the easily visible whites, and now and then rushed forth to take a scalp. The troops were unaccustomed to Indian fighting, and probably never saw their foes. Soon they began to retreat and shortly their walk turned into a run. As in the case of Harmar, the Indians were so busy collecting booty that they did not pursue their defeated adversaries.

When St. Clair's army had recovered enough to count its losses it found that 630 had been killed and 283 wounded — in other words that approximately half of the total force had been put out of action. Many of the bodies were left in the field of battle, and these were mutilated by the Indians; a later investigation showed a considerable number of females among the dead. The remnants of the so-called army gradually straggled back to Cincinnati, thoroughly beaten and demoralized. When the news of the defeat reached Washington, it is related that he had one of his few fits of extreme anger. The conduct of the expedition was investigated by Congress, but St. Clair was eventually exonerated. His resignation from the army was accepted in April 1792.

WAYNE

Immediately upon the defeat of St. Clair, Washington began to search for a man who would not repeat previous disastrous campaigns. After much cogitation he gave his approval to a former

Revolutionary hero, Anthony Wayne, even though " Mad Anthony's " daring exploits during the Revolution raised some question as to his prospective caution in fighting the Indians. A new army was gathered at Pittsburgh, and again it was composed of the kind of men who had " fought " under Harmar and St. Clair. But at this point all similarity with preceding expeditions ended. Wayne joined his command at Pittsburgh and immediately started to drill his 2500 infantry, cavalry and artillery.

Wayne desired to win his war in a hurry and return to the more pleasant life in the East. The Secretary of War, however, backed by the President, caused him to change his plan. Accordingly, he moved twenty miles down the river in the fall of 1792 and spent the winter at Legionville doing more drilling. By this time the West was becoming impatient with a " mad " general who spent his time in the barracks while his enemies were laying waste the settlements he was supposed to protect. But Washington insisted that no offensive action be undertaken until after the Indian councils of 1793. In April of that year Wayne moved his camp to near Cincinnati, where he proceeded to devote the summer and early fall to still more drilling. Discipline was strict and no detail of training was overlooked, the men even being taught how to yell. Undoubtedly this was the best prepared and drilled army that had ever existed in the West. " Mad Anthony " was in a fair way to lose his hard-won nickname — although by no means entirely through his own desire.

While Wayne drilled his men, American commissioners underwent the ignominy of following the Indians to Detroit to try to make peace. The commissioners were authorized to make real concessions, even to the extent of restoring all Indian lands except the Ohio Company and Symmes grants, or to make large additional payments. But the Indians proved arrogant and untractable and refused any solution short of recovering all their land north and west of the Ohio, and the commissioners were forced to return home with nothing but humiliation.

Immediately upon the failure of negotiations, Wayne was given the signal to advance. During the fall he moved north slowly, acclimating his men to actual campaigning. At the present Greenville he built Fort Greenville, an imposing stockade, did more drilling, sent out spies and started road construction. An advance guard was dispatched late in the year to construct Fort Recovery on the scene of St. Clair's defeat.

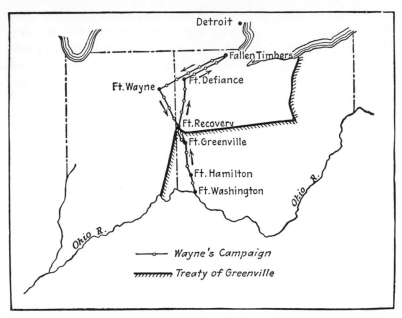

The Indians gathered some 2000 warriors in the spring of 1794 to oppose the Wayne advance. They made the mistake of attacking Fort Recovery instead of confining themselves to cutting off isolated parties and interfering with supply trains. Discouraged by the failure of their attack on the fort and by the lack of expected British aid, many of them returned home, so that only 1300 remained when Wayne started to move.

Wayne's advance, beginning late in July, was slow and impressive. Due attention was given to communications and to possible surprises. Fort Adams was built on the St. Mary's River and Fort Defiance at the junction of the Maumee and Auglaize. The main body of Indians was encountered August 20 at a place called Fallen Timbers because of the presence of trees overturned by a heavy storm. Amazingly enough the Indians were willing to fight one of their rare pitched battles. Wayne repulsed the attack but won no clear-cut victory: the Indians lost only some fifty braves and were by no means demoralized. The decisive nature of the battle lay in the Indian realization that they were to receive no active English aid; the silence of the guns at nearby Fort Miamis (British) was more significant than the actual battle.

After Fallen Timbers, Wayne returned to Fort Defiance, from

which base he destroyed the nearby Miami towns and built Fort Wayne. The winter of 1794–95 was spent at Greenville. Wayne's object had been attained. The Indians realized the futility of further immediate resistance, and for the first time in many years the frontier was freed of the menace of Indian attack. Both in the North and in the South the Indians were cowed and peaceful.

Wayne finished his work in the West by putting the results in treaty form. Starting early in 1795 he called the Indian chiefs to a large conference at Fort Greenville. By June there had arrived 1130 Delaware, Potawatami, Wyandot, Shawnee, Miami, Chippewa, Ottawa, Wea and Piankeshaw, Kickapoo and Kaskaskia. Fifty days were occupied by feasts, speeches, and ceremonies before any action was taken. The resulting Treaty of Greenville settled the status of the Indians of the Old Northwest temporarily — not because it was the first and only treaty of its kind, but because it was the first one to be based on a thorough intimidation of the Indians. By its terms a definite line was drawn between red and white territory. Roughly speaking the whites received the southeastern two-thirds of the present state of Ohio and the southeastern corner of present Indiana, while the rest of the Northwest was left to the Indians. In return for these land cessions the Indians were to receive immediately goods to the value of $20,000 and about half that amount annually thereafter. As soon as the treaty was signed Wayne returned to the East where he was greeted as a hero and given numerous ovations.

JAY TREATY

While Wayne was engaged in his victorious campaign in the West, there was in progress another mission of a far different nature, in which the West was also vitally interested. Negotiations concerning the outstanding differences between England and the United States had been in progress for some time, and in June 1794 John Jay was sent on a special mission to England to carry on direct negotiations. The final treaty (Nov. 19, 1794) was a victory for British diplomacy, and intensely unpopular in the United States, where it was accepted by the Senate with the narrowest of possible votes. In so far as it directly affected the West it provided for the surrender of the northwest posts which England had not evacuated. This surrender actually took place in June 1796, and it was only fitting that Anthony Wayne should be the man to accept the most important of them — Detroit.

With the surrender of the northwest posts and the submission of the Indians, the trans-Appalachian region was more available for settlement than it had ever been in the past. The Indians were not again to be ready for any widespread hostilities until the period of the War of 1812. With American possession of the Great Lakes posts the possibility of English encouragement to the Indians was decreased, and more freedom was possible for American traders and trappers. Although the Indian cessions in the Treaty of Greenville did not open any large quantity of unclaimed land for new settlement, the whites, as in the past, showed little respect for Indian land ownership.

The result of these developments was an ever-increasing flow of migration to the West. Whereas most of the early settlers had come from the South by way of Cumberland Gap, now they began to come in larger numbers from the central and northern states. The inevitable cycle of Indian relations was soon completed, and almost before the ink of the Greenville treaty was dry, new settlers were again pushing into Indian country. And again the government followed these pioneers, forcing the Indians back still farther. Half a dozen new cessions in the ten years after Greenville served to emphasize the ephemeral nature of Indian treaty lines and promises.

READINGS

B. W. Bond, Jr., *The Civilization of the Old Northwest* (1934), ch. 9, *The Foundations of Ohio* (1941), chs. 9, 11; T. Boyd, *Mad Anthony Wayne* (1929), pp. 234–249, chs. 14–17—good, *Simon Girty* (1928), chs. 9–12; J. P. Brown, *Old Frontiers* (1938), chs. 15–27; J. W. Caughey, *McGillivray of the Creeks* (1938)—reprints many documents; R. S. Cotterill, *The Southern Indians* (1954), chs. 4, 5; R. C. Downes, *Council Fires on the Upper Ohio* (1940), chs. 12, 13, *Frontier Ohio, 1788–1803* (1935), ch. 1; L. Esarey, *A History of Indiana* (1915), chs. 19–21; G. D. Harmon, *Sixty Years of Indian Affairs* (1941), ch. 4; W. Havighurst, *Land of Promise* (1946), ch. 8; J. B. Jacobs, *The Beginning of the United States Army, 1783–1812* (1947), chs. 1–7; L. P. Kellogg, *The British Regime in Wisconsin and the Old Northwest* (1935), chs. 13, 14; W. H. Mohr, *Federal Indian Relations, 1774–1788* (1933), chs. 4, 5—good monograph; M. B. Pound, *Benjamin Hawkins—Indian Agent* (1951)— southern Indians, mostly 1780s; E. H. Roseboom and F. P. Weisenburger, *A History of Ohio*

(1953), ch. 5—factual; H. E. Wildes, *Anthony Wayne* (1941), chs. 15-20—detailed; F. E. Wilson, *Arthur St. Clair* (1944), chs. 4, 5—laudatory.

CHAPTER 6

ADVANCING SETTLEMENT

THE end of the Revolution brought the first really large flow of migration across the Appalachians — a flood that was to increase with the years. The movement naturally was not a steady increase, for it tended to slow with eastern wars and depressions and with western Indian troubles. The Old Northwest, for example, did not compete for settlers on even terms with the Old Southwest until after Greenville. Also the movement did not go to all parts of the West equally. Certain regions were more attractive at certain times, not only because of the quality of their land, but because of the opening of new means of transportation.

Among the more evident developments of this post-Revolutionary period was an increased arrival west of the mountains of citizens of the middle and northern states. New York, New Jersey, and Pennsylvania people became numerous, as did the Yankees who now were spreading through western New York into the Great Lakes region and the Ohio Valley.

The vast majority of these self-elected westerners were native-born, and represented a part of the natural increase of population. Throughout the late eighteenth century and most of the nineteenth the United States doubled in population each generation, and without much relation to the flow of immigration. Some of these extra people moved to eastern cities, which grew throughout the period. Others migrated to farms or towns of the West. Either move represented search for economic opportunity. As for the immigrants, they also settled in the cities and in the West, but with reverse emphasis; more went to the cities than to the West — the settlement of such a town as Gallipolis was the exceptional case.

71

The eastern states viewed the departure of their sons and daughters with mingled pride and alarm. The populating of the wilder sections of the country was in some ways fine and patriotic: national power and prestige would be enhanced, trade with the East would increase, and possibly some of the migrants would retain sufficient love for their home communities to do business with them. On the other hand the departure of many young and vigorous citizens decreased the strength of the eastern states. Now these young people were also needed at home, particularly those who would normally do much of the unskilled labor on the farm, and in the store and mill. As industrial enterprises came into existence their operators found labor comparatively scarce and expensive, which meant increased difficulty in the competition with English manufacturing.

Westward-bound settlers were of all ages and both sexes, but, as already stated, the largest single element consisted of young men who had just attained their majority and were traveling alone or in small groups. Such a man might be sufficiently lucky to have enough funds to buy a farm immediately — after no more than a brief exploratory trip to find the most favorable location. More likely he possessed only a few dollars and planned to do farm work, storekeeping, boating, trapping, surveying, schoolteaching, or similar work until he acquired needed capital. Although he might squat on unsurveyed land he still needed capital to purchase supplies, and obtain animals, implements and seed. Before setting up as an independent farmer he might well return to the East to marry his boyhood sweetheart. A wife for a frontier farmer represented not only a person to love and to cherish, but also a needed companion and coworker on the farm.

PROCESS OF MIGRATION

When an entire family moved, the process was somewhat more complicated. A family was not as foot-loose as an unmarried man and wanted at least a general idea of where it was going. Possibly friends or relatives had moved earlier and had found a desirable region, or else the father or an older son would make a preliminary tour. In any case a man seldom took his wife and children west of the mountains without some feeling of assurance that he could provide for them, and there must have been many evenings of earnest conversation before the decision was made to leave old friends and surroundings for the newness of the West.

The migrating family sold its eastern possessions before it departed — partly because few articles could be packed into the single farm wagon, and partly because funds would be required to start farming and to tide over the first year until crops could be harvested and marketed. Frequently father enlarged his own small funds by borrowing from neighbors and friends, for he realized that even with the greatest frugality moving was costly. Every westerner advised a good supply of cash, but the eastern family seldom fulfilled the specifications; indeed, if the family had been well-to-do it would have stayed in the East.

Only the bare necessities of life could be given space in the one farm wagon that was the sole means of transportation. Of first importance were implements for erecting a home and for farming — particularly an axe, an auger, an adze, a hammer. Guns and ammunition were necessary. Food included primarily such staples as flour, bacon, sugar, salt, yeast, and vinegar. A spinning wheel was vital, and seeds for the first planting might be included. Other desirable articles were almost innumerable, and might include clothes and cloth, needles, thread, pots and pans, dishes and cutlery. Possibly some of the precious space was absorbed by a clock, bureau, bedstead, chair, or other specially prized family possession.

The westward-bound wagon was usually protected from sun and rain by canvas stretched tightly over curved strips of wood. Sometimes it was drawn by horses, but more frequently by the even more useful and hardy oxen. Mother and the younger children might ride in the wagon, while father plodded beside the team and the larger children followed in the rear. A cow or two or an extra horse might be included in the caravan, and it was not unknown to have the children chase chickens along the road to their new home in the West. The speed was that of men and animals walking. At night the family camped by the side of the trail and fried its bacon and cooked its biscuits by the heat of an open fire. Rain slowed the progress and made life miserable for the migrants.

AREAS OF SETTLEMENT

People moving west at the turn of the century, as in every period, moved as directly west as possible. Belts of settlement were being created, in which the culture of a particular section of the East was reproduced time after time under new conditions. Early settlement had been largely from the South. Now the bulk of the Virginia and Carolina migration was going to Kentucky and Tennes-

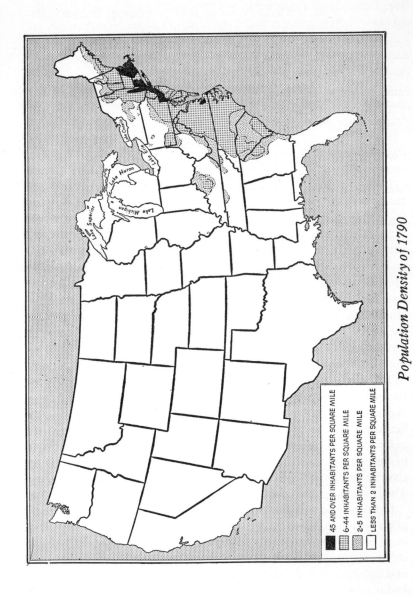

Population Density of 1790

Legend:
- ■ 45 AND OVER INHABITANTS PER SQUARE MILE
- ▦ 6-44 INHABITANTS PER SQUARE MILE
- ▨ 2-5 INHABITANTS PER SQUARE MILE
- □ LESS THAN 2 INHABITANTS PER SQUARE MILE

see, Pennsylvania migration to Ohio, and New England migration to central New York and the region of the Great Lakes.

The most popular mecca for the earliest trans-Appalachian settlers was Kentucky. Its population of 74,000 in 1790 tripled within the next ten years and almost doubled again in the succeeding decade. While early settlers came largely over the mountains through the Cumberland Gap, later arrivals came more and more by way of Pittsburgh or Wheeling and then down the Ohio River. Louisville was the most important of the Kentucky River towns; its chief rival was Maysville, which lay across the river from the terminus of Zane's Trace, which originated at Wheeling.

Lexington was the great interior metropolis of Kentucky, even though it could claim less than 2000 inhabitants in 1800. It dominated the blue grass country, overshadowing such rivals as Frankfort, Paris, May's Lick. Lexington was the trading center for nearby farmers and could boast such varied industries as ropewalks, tanneries, potteries and powder mills. It was proud of its literary and cultural achievements, being a publishing center of note and the home of the earliest western college — Transylvania. Quite naturally it was a political center and became the capital for the first six months of statehood. Little wonder that an energetic and ambitious young lawyer such as Henry Clay decided that Lexington was the proper place to settle during the 1790s.

The more southerly Tennessee was about half the size of Kentucky in population, although in the generation after 1800 the gap decreased. The earliest settlements were naturally near the Cumberland Gap, in the eastern part of the state; the road through the gap was improved for wagon traffic during the 1790s. Eastern Tennessee, a region of mountains and valleys, was particularly attractive to small white farmers practicing a diversified agriculture. The center of population came to be Knoxville, founded in 1789.

Central Tennessee was in reality a continuation of the bluegrass region of Kentucky; it permitted cotton culture and slavery on a profitable basis, even though there were comparatively few slaves in the early days. Nashville was the metropolis of the area, and experienced a boom after the opening of a wagon road in 1795. Industries, lawyers, doctors, ministers, churches, and comfortable homes soon appeared, and slavery increased. Cumberland College was organized in 1806. West of the Nashville area, in western Tennessee, there was little settlement before 1810.

South of Tennessee, restless Georgians were pushing into the central and north central sections of the present state, with a roving and avaricious eye cast as far west as the Mississippi — for Georgia had claimed the land to the Mississippi. The state had been exceedingly reluctant to grant this immense empire and possible source of wealth to the federal government, even though powerful Indian groups made immediate settlement impossible. Georgia's policy shortly after the Revolution had been to grant western land as a reward to people who had served the state and to prospective settlers ; in fact it developed a sort of early homestead policy. Unfortunately these early grants usually did not produce settlement. The grantees tended to sell their claims to speculators, and in some cases one person amassed a million or more acres. In addition, warrants were issued for several times the amount of land existing in several counties, and these warrants were then resold to unsuspecting buyers in Philadelphia and elsewhere. All of which meant much future trouble.

The Georgian land situation was further hopelessly involved by several large sales (Yazoo grants). Ostensibly to help the precarious Georgian finances seven companies in 1789 and 1795 were sold land estimated at somewhere between 50,000,000 and 70,000,000 acres. Bribery and fraud were rampant in getting the grants, prices were ridiculously low even for wild western land, and some of the payments were in worthless Georgian currency. After the second set of grants the legislature experienced a change of heart and tried to repeal them, whereupon the companies carried the fight to the courts. Ultimately Georgia found relief from her embarrassment by turning her claims over to the United States in 1802. The federal government gained only obligations, except that the deal opened the way for the governmental organization of the western area.

Along the Gulf Coast and up the Mississippi as far as Natchez had come colonial settlers after the region was acquired by England at the end of the Seven Years' War. Many of these people obtained grants from the English government. The growth of population was slight, and up to 1810 these small communities continued to cling to the coast and the lower river. Spain reconquered the whole area during the Revolution, and then argued with the United States as to the proper boundary. When Spain withdrew her troops from the disputed area, the United States set up Mississippi Territory (1798) and as governor sent Winthrop Sargent, who had been secretary of the Northwest Territory. In 1804 Mississippi was enlarged to include the Georgia land cessions, while other changes, to be recounted later, came with the acquisition of Louisiana.

North of the Ohio River settlement came very slowly until the Wayne campaign quieted the Indian menace. Present Ohio had a negligible population in 1790 and only 45,000 in 1800, but by 1810 the number had jumped to an impressive 231,000 — almost as many people as in Tennessee. Early settlements clung closely to the banks of the Ohio, but after 1800 they began to fill the general area of the cessions made at Greenville. A surplus of settlers drifted farther down the Ohio into southern Indiana and Illinois, but prior to 1810 few men were sufficiently courageous to venture far from the river. The one exception was the increased occupation of the Vincennes area along the Wabash.

The earliest migrants to the Old Northwest were predominantly southern in origin, and this southern flow continued into the nineteenth century, coming either by way of the Potomac or through Kentucky. By this later period, however, other population elements were attaining more prominence. The New England settlement at Marietta, the New Jersey settlement at Cincinnati, and the foreign settlement at Gallipolis were symptomatic of the change.

The most important Ohio metropolis was Cincinnati, even though it could boast but 500 residents in 1800. Cincinnati had been founded in 1789 on the Symmes purchase and had early begun to outdistance its nearest competitors. The growth was due in part to its position on the Ohio opposite the mouth of the Licking, and also to the favor of Governor St. Clair, who moved his original capital from Marietta to Cincinnati in 1790. Cincinnati was a product of land speculation, as were many other towns such as Dayton (1795) and Chillicothe (1796).

Settlers bound for the Ohio Valley tended increasingly to come by way of Pittsburgh. The population of this thriving potential city was little over 1500 in 1800, but the next few years saw Pittsburgh grow rapidly and outdistance such early competitors as Steubenville, Wheeling, and Marietta. Early Pittsburgh was primarily a commercial rather than a manufacturing center. Its most important early industries were milling and shipbuilding, with ships constructed for ocean as well as for river business. The coal and iron businesses were growing, so that within a few years Pittsburgh was to be known as " the Birmingham of America."

Another and more northern stream of migration had begun to

flow into the region of the Great Lakes by 1800. Settlement had been expanding through central New York state, with the Holland Land Company planning the town of New Amsterdam (Buffalo) in 1799. This young village was to become the northern entry to the West, and thus similar to Pittsburgh, but for the time being the growth was small and the town was burned during the War of 1812. Real expansion came after the war, and particularly after the opening of the Erie Canal.

West of Buffalo a string of hamlets was coming into existence along the southern shore of Lake Erie. Most important was Cleaveland, in the Connecticut Reserve; it was founded in 1796 by Moses Cleaveland and a group of settlers from Connecticut. At first it had to provide its own government, but in 1800 the administration was assumed by the Northwest Territory. Beyond Lake Erie was Detroit, a small trading settlement.

CONDITIONS OF TRAVEL

Roads from East to West were much the same as in an earlier period, although improved enough to permit wagons on all the main thoroughfares. Wagon roads were likewise being opened in the West during the 1790s and later to connect the principal towns, as Lexington and Nashville. Smaller inland towns had to be content with blazed trails, or at most paths that were passable only for pack animals.

Road construction meant cutting the trees, but leaving the stumps, and clearing away most of the brush. Grades were not improved and no roadbed was constructed. A few places might be given some special attention; a swampy sector, for example, might receive a few logs over which the wagons could jolt to the comparative safety of higher land. Such roads were bad at any time of the year, but were particularly atrocious during wet weather. Streams were ordinarily forded, except that a few of the larger ones had private ferries operated at the caprice of their owners, who charged all that the traffic would bear.

Bad roads meant that whenever possible the migrant moved by water, and water transportation meant that the heaviest movement of population was down the Ohio River, with the current furnishing the motive power. The obvious point of embarkation was one of the most easterly towns, which increasingly meant Pittsburgh. Here a westward moving family acquired a rough and box-like flatboat. This boat served two functions. First and most obviously it was a means of transportation, carrying the entire possessions of the family. Second, it was an important source of planed lumber and nails for a future home. Both articles were scarce, and consequently the flatboat was carefully disassembled so that wood and nails could be used again.

CHOOSING A NEW HOME

Upon arriving in the West, the migrant found nothing more important than his choice of land. Several attributes were important, and not the least was fertility — a surprisingly difficult characteristic to recognize. One sure test seemed to be whether the land in its native state produced vegetation; this criterion gives part of the explanation of why frontiersmen preferred the densely wooded lands near the rivers and why the ring of the woodsman's axe was the most characteristic sound of a new settlement. Houses, barns, and fences were inevitably of wood. The new settler did not, however, find himself attracted by the overflow land of the river bottoms. The other sure test for a new settler was to find land that looked similar to that which he had found good in his old home, and here he made many mistakes. The New Englander who looked for oak clearings or the Pennsylvanian who sought reddish soil was starting his western life under a severe handicap.

Practically as important to the settler as good land was the availability of water — both for drinking and for transportation. A spring or small brook sufficed for drinking, but a navigable stream was necessary for transportation and could also be used for drinking; true it might be dirty, but the dirt would settle and no one worried about bacteria since no one had heard of them. Here again the tendency was for settlers to build their houses near the larger streams.

Finally, the migrant preferred to be reasonably near a settlement — not only for protection from the Indians, nor to be able to buy and sell easily, but largely to provide human companionship and assistance. The transplanted easterner was no hermit and his family had no desire to be lost in the bosom of the wilderness. The average settler was a farmer looking for greater opportunity and did not propose to forego eastern advantages any longer than necessary. If he had sufficient funds he bought land that had been cleared and improved; if not, he sought to reproduce his old surroundings as quickly as possible. The frontiersman who made the original clearings at the very tip of civilization frequently sold out and moved to a newer frontier, which meant that a large share of arrivals took land that had been at least partially cleared and transformed it into productive farms.

ACQUIRING LAND

The land selected by the settler might be acquired in any one of several ways. Quite frequently he bought it from the original frontiersman or from a speculator, and the importance of the speculator should not be overlooked. Western speculation in land was as prevalent as the later speculation in mining stock by miners. The speculator was obiquitous, including not only the most outstanding men such as Clark, Boone, Sevier and Blount, but thousands of less known persons down to the poorest frontiersman who hoped that his land would inflate in value with the increase of settlement. Eastern speculators were also numerous. The companies obtaining Yazoo grants, the Ohio Company, Symmes, and the rest were merely the outstanding illustrations of eastern land speculation. While eastern speculators might buy their land in the West, the large companies of the early years were more likely to operate from the East. Some bought directly from the United States or from states with western claims. Others collected land warrants issued by the United States for Revolutionary veterans, or by such states as Connecticut, Virginia, North Carolina, and Georgia. Apparently a large proportion of the land donated to veterans eventually got into the hands of the speculators. The veteran seemed to be more interested in immediate cash than in a prospective farm.

Speculators were interested in good agricultural land, but even more in water power, mill sites, and town sites, for here lay the best chances of large profits. An impressive proportion of western towns was the work of speculators. Marietta, Cincinnati, Chillicothe, Dayton, Boonesborough, and Nashville were but a few of the hundreds that received their original impetus from speculators. And for every such successful settlement there were a dozen that remained entirely in their originators' minds or that eventuated only in a few log cabins. Probably the majority of speculators lost money, with only enough successes to keep the will-of-the-wisp of big profits glowing brightly to attract other adventuresome souls.

The alternative to buying from an original settler or from a speculator was to purchase from the government. Legally the settler could not occupy land until it had been surveyed and sold at auction, but thousands of settlers occupied land without the formality of purchase. They hoped that the government would later confirm their occupancy or that they could buy it at the minimum price when the auction arrived — and this feat was frequently accomplished with the assistance of neighbors who were similarly situated.

Once a man had picked his land — and sometimes bought it — he started the arduous labor of making it into a real farm. Ordinarily he arrived in the spring to give himself the maximum possible time to prepare for the winter. For a settler arriving around 1800 the process of starting a farm was similar regardless of whether he lived in the North or in the South. If in the South he might have a slave or two without thereby changing the picture radically. The movement of large slave coffles, with the establishment of big western plantations, was not common until after the War of 1812.

BUILDING A HOUSE

The first requirement for a family was shelter. Temporarily an open three-sided camp might be constructed from poles and thatched; the front was higher than the back, and the fire was built before the open front of the structure. The labor of erecting such a camp might be avoided if some near neighbor offered his hospitality.

Before a family could consider itself settled it needed a permanent home. Father and the older sons immediately got out their axes and started to chop down the trees on the site of their future home and garden. These trees were to be transformed into a house, a barn, and rail fences, for the wooden rail fence was practically universal. In the meantime the smaller children collected brush and grubbed out small trees and bushes. Ultimately the whole mass of trash was burned in large bonfires.

The actual construction of the house was a community undertaking, since seldom had a family sufficient grown sons to perform the necessary back-breaking work. On the day of the house-raising, neighbors gathered from miles around. The logs were rolled to the site of the cabin, notched or dovetailed at each end and lifted into place; alternately they were placed on one pair of opposite sides and then on the other pair. Meantime the women had been cooking a feast, which was probably followed by a dance in the new home. A little later the family might aspire to a cabin of squared logs, which excluded more of the weather and permitted better interior and exterior finishes.

The construction of a roof represented a considerable problem as long as nails remained a luxury. The frame of rafters was held in place by wooden pins driven into auger holes. Over the rafters might be placed bark or rude shingles, but more frequently the roof was of clapboard construction, with the boards held in place by saplings fastened with wooden pegs.

After the frame of the house was completed an opening was cut, and in the opening was placed a wooden door swung on leather or wooden hinges. Security could be attained by a heavy wooden bar fitting into brackets on the inside. A simple iron lock or a swinging wooden bar could be opened from outside by means of a leather thong passed through an auger hole in the door; the latch string hanging outside was an indication of hospitality.

Another opening was cut for the fireplace, which was constructed of stone or of logs or sticks covered with clay, depending on the region; the chimney was built ordinarily of logs, and but rarely of stone. The earliest cabins had no windows, but by 1800 most of them had at least small openings to admit light and air; sometimes the openings were barred to exclude wild animals. Window glass was a rare luxury, but oiled paper furnished a more or less satisfactory substitute. The floor of the log cabin was ordinarily hard packed earth, but the more particular and industrious frontiersman used puncheons — that is, logs which had been split in the middle, and of which the more or less flat surfaces were placed uppermost. The finishing touch for the cabin was the filling of the chinks between the logs with moss or dirt or clay.

The usual log cabin was neither beautiful nor commodious, and certainly could boast but little comfort. It had the one artistic value of being appropriate to its surroundings. Its materials and method of construction made unlikely any great size, and in fact the usual cabin was no larger than a moderate sized modern living room — say fifteen to eighteen feet long and twelve to fourteen feet wide. A partition might create two rooms, but generally there was no such division. A windowless loft could be used as a store room and as sleeping quarters for the children. Now and then two such cabins were built side by side with a common roof. In the South the two-room and even the two-story log cabin soon appeared; the kitchen might be in an ell, and other rooms were added as the family grew.

CLEARING THE LAND

The building of the cabin entailed clearing a portion of the land, but in many cases little more than enough for a garden and chicken yard. Further efforts were necessary before a crop could be planted. The really radical method was to cut down all trees and use oxen to pull the stumps, thus producing completely open fields, but in actual practice this procedure was seldom used, since it meant years of labor before reasonably sized fields could be obtained. Most common was the cutting of girdles around the trees, thus killing them, while postponing their removal to a later date. Corn which must be tilled poorly because of the multiplicity of roots and which received only the sparse sunlight filtering between deadened trees could hardly be luxuriant, but some corn was better than none.

The process of conquering a wilderness was slow and laborious. Even though the family left the East in the spring as soon as the roads dried and grass was available for the stock, so much time was consumed that first year in the long trip west, in selecting land, in building a cabin, and in clearing the land that nothing more than a small garden could be grown. In fact, with girdled trees, the crops of the first few years might all be very small. This interval between migration and marketable crops emphasized the need for a cash reserve. Even though father shot game and everyone went on starvation rations, money was still necessary to permit survival, and the traditional hospitality of the West was of little advantage since nearly everyone in a particular region was in similar circumstances. Well over a year must elapse before the family could again be self-supporting.

READINGS

C. W. Alvord, *The Illinois Country* (1920), ch. 19; F. C. Bald, *Detroit's First American Decade, 1796 to 1805* (1948); L. D. Baldwin, *Pittsburgh* (1937), ch. 11; E. J. Benton, *Cultural History of an American City* (2 vols., 1943–44)—brief on Cleveland; R. W. Bingham, *The Cradle of the Queen City* (1931); B. W. Bond, Jr., *The Civilization of the Old Northwest* (1934), chs. 1, 2, *The Foundations of Ohio* (1941), ch. 12; S. J. and E. H. Buck, *The Planting of Civilization in Western Pennsylvania* (1939), ch. 10; E. M. Coulter, *A Short History of Georgia* (1933), ch. 15 —very good; F. G. Davenport, *Ante-Bellum Kentucky* (1943), chs. 1, 2; E. Dick, *The Dixie Frontier* (1948), chs. 1–6—readable; R. C. Downes, *Frontier Ohio* (1935), ch. 2; D. Drake, *Pioneer Life in Kentucky* (1948)—good reminiscences; H. Hatcher, *The Western Reserve* (1949), chs. 1–9—reads well; W. Havighurst, *Land of Promise* (1946), ch. 14; S. H. Holbrook, *The Yankee Exodus* (1950), chs. 2, 3; L. K. Mathews, *The Expansion of New England* (1909), chs, 6, 7; M. M. Quaife and G. Glazer, *Michigan* (1948), chs. 11, 12—dull; E. H. Roseboom and F. P. Weisenburger, *A History of Ohio* (1953), ch. 4; H. R. Shurtleff, *The Log Cabin Myth* (1939)—origin of the log cabin; L. D. Stilwell, *Migration from Vermont* (1937), ch. 1—excellent monograph; H. Toulmin, *The Western Country in 1793* (1948)—contemporary, informative on Kentucky; W. T. Utter, *The Frontier State, 1803–1825* (1942), ch. 5—Ohio; J. E. Wright and D. S. Corbett, *Pioneer Life in Western Pennsylvania* (1940).

CHAPTER 7

LIFE
IN THE WEST

THE newly established western families were confronted with the problem of building a civilization with simple materials and tools. Most migrants were in no sense revolters from traditional ways of life, who desired a new, different and simpler environment. They sought only economic opportunity, and were anxious to reproduce the well-known trappings of eastern society as soon as possible. Crude houses and furniture were considered to be only makeshifts until better could be acquired.

HOUSE FURNISHINGS

While the new civilization was in the making the settler lived in the simplest of home surroundings. The crude, homemade furniture was confined largely to a rough plank or puncheon table and a few three-legged stools which stood most solidly on the rough floor. The absence of closets was compensated in part by pegs in the wall, with possibly a few shelves. Beds were built against the walls, preferably in the corners; the walls furnished the main supports, but needed the supplement of forked stakes driven into the ground. In lieu of springs was a lattice work of leather thongs, rope, or slats. Mattresses were filled with straw until enough feathers were collected to produce the favored feather beds, which were most comfortable if resting on straw ticks. Covers consisted of bear and buffalo robes or a second feather bed. All reports indicate that in the average cabin these articles were filthy and full of vermin. If cleanliness is next to Godliness these people deserved the fears for their religion that the East lavished on them.

Privacy in a frontier cabin was practically impossible to attain, since the entire family dressed, undressed, and carried on a major portion of its activities in the one room. Here occurred everything from spinning and making bread to childbirth. Some saving of modesty was possible because cold weather deterred one from removing all his clothes at night, while the all-over bath was ordinarily reserved for warm weather and the neighboring stream. Favored western stories dealt with the embarrassment that resulted when a group of travelers of both sexes spent the night with a large family in a log cabin.

Of the varied activities that made the cabin a busy workshop none was more important or more frequent than the preparation of food. Cooking was done at the fireplace, and consequently most of the food was either boiled or fried. A crane or iron hook held the pot for boiling, and the three-legged frying pan or spider was either held over the coals or allowed to rest on them. Some of the more elaborate fireplaces included ovens, but this was unusual. Roasting could be done on a spit. Frequently the baking was done in a skillet with a tight cover or in a Dutch oven, a large cast iron pot with a tight lid, which was pushed into the coals and then covered with them. Sometimes the article to be baked was wrapped in cabbage leaves and pushed directly into the coals. The fireplace, in addition to its use in cooking, furnished the only heat for the cabin in winter and light at night. Tallow candles were made by the women, but it was more economical of labor to use the light of the fire whenever possible.

Cooking and eating utensils were of the simplest. The family brought with it from the East a few skillets, pots, and pans, as well as pewter dishes, plates, and spoons. Additional utensils were homemade, and the men spent many a long winter evening in carving wooden bowls, trenchers and noggins (cups). Gourds could be used as cups and other containers.

FOOD AND CLOTHES

The food was limited largely to the products which the family raised. Wild game was available in the early days, and a deer or some wild ducks or turkeys were welcome additions to the family menu; bears were plentiful, but their meat was coarse and greasy. A staple article of diet was corn, which was used in every conceivable form, including johnnycake, pone, and mush. Mush and milk was a favorite supper; the big meal of the day was at noon. Equally universal was pork. Hog and hominy was better known than ham and eggs, for eggs were scarce. The pigs were allowed to run wild in the forest and were shot like wild animals. The meat had to be dried, smoked, or salted for summer use, since there was no ice available. The resulting demand for salt encouraged the development of western salt manufactories at the important saline springs.

Cane sugar was always scarce on the frontier, and the white variety was used even less than the brown; frequently its place was taken by maple sugar, honey, or molasses. Milk was also rare, and whenever possible, as on mush, it was replaced by such liquids as gravy or bear's oil. Tea and coffee were luxuries which had some substitutes. On the other hand there were plenty of vegetables — corn, beans, potatoes, peas, squash, pumpkins. Also there were within a few years adequate supplies of peaches, melons, apples, cherries, plums, and grapes. Taken all in all, the frontiersman had a plentiful variety of good food — at least in the summer. In the winter his diet was less satisfactory, for then he depended on such staples as corn meal and salt pork. The preserving of fruits and vegetables was an unknown art except by pickling or by drying, which produced a leathery, tasteless substance that may have been nourishing but was certainly not appetizing.

One of the commonest articles of western diet was corn whiskey, which was drunk by everyone upon any or no pretext. A hospitable home kept a jug of whiskey and a gourd near the door to refresh visitors. A considerable share of western corn was made into whiskey because the decreased bulk and increased value were advantageous in transporting it to market. Distilleries were an early and important feature of western life. Tobacco was almost as widely used as whiskey, and was raised and consumed in the West at an early date. Chewing became almost as universal as eating, and very few travelers could refrain from commenting upon the common art of chewing and the lack of delicacy in disposing of the surplus juice.

Frequently shoes or moccasins were made at home by the father with tools brought with him from the East. The tanning of the leather was a difficult operation for the individual family and in consequence the tanning industry, as carried on by professionals, soon began in the West. To save shoes the family went barefoot whenever possible.

Clothes were nearly all homemade. Flax, hemp, and wool were all produced on the farm and carried through the various processes which included combing, carding, spinning, dyeing, weaving, cutting, and sewing the garments. The resulting cloth (usually linsey-woolsey) was heavy and strong, but colors were limited and the finish was not professional, so that garments were more praiseworthy for wearing qualities than for beauty. The frontiersman tended to copy his costume from the Indians, even to the extent of leather hunting shirt, leggings, moccasins, and breechcloth, although he might have a cloth shirt and pantaloons. Women were adequately but not elegantly clothed in loose plain dresses something like modern smocks; one or more better dresses for church going or other occasions followed eastern styles. A prosperous westerner might become " swanky " and buy broadcloth to be made into a suit by a tailor; such a suit was worn only on special occasions and would last for years.

The activities of the interior of the cabin, including the preparation of the food and the making of the clothes, were the particular domain of the woman. Her tremendous range of activities included making soap and candles, caring for the small children, and acting as family physician. Lest she have any spare moments she usually tended a garden and a flock of chickens, while it was not unknown for her to work in the fields. The West could echo with heartfelt fervor the old jingle which insists that " a woman's work is never done." Men worked hard, but women worked if anything harder, and the operation of a farm was almost impossible without the presence of a woman.

FARMING

The main business of farming was the province of the man, and he would have been justified if he had frequently felt discouraged. Not only was he confronted with the prodigious task of clearing and breaking the virgin land, but even after the farm was cleared he suffered from poor tools and methods. Foremost among his tools was a plow, which might be nothing more than a forked stick, and which at the best was a straight wooden implement, sometimes tipped with iron, which necessitated at least two yoke of oxen; its operation was a man-killing job. A harrow was a wooden triangle fitted with wooden or iron teeth to be dragged through the ground.

All grain was planted by hand. Cutting was done with a scythe, and the greatest farm improvement of the period was the introduction of the cradle scythe in the late eighteenth century. The grain was separated from the chaff either by driving horses over it or by using a hand flail composed of two sticks connected by a leather thong. This required considerable dexterity if the wielder were to avoid cracking his own skull. Then the grain was tossed in the air, and, if no timely breeze were available to blow away the chaff, a sheet could be flapped by two men.

Simple tools used on fields filled with dead trees could not be expected to produce a large crop, and in fact the first corn crop was seldom as much as fifteen bushels an acre. As time passed and the fields were better cultivated the corn crops on the more fertile Ohio and Kentucky land averaged forty to fifty bushels an acre, with some going as high as seventy-five. Even at best, however, work was hard and yields were low. Tools remained poor and no proper rotation of crops was followed; in fact the same crop was grown year after year on the same field. Chemical fertilizers were unknown and manure was generally unavailable because the animals were allowed to roam freely.

The dominant western crop was corn, which was planted in check-rows about three feet apart. Seven or eight kernels were planted at each intersection, and all but two or three were weeded out when they started to grow, at which time there was one additional plowing. Ultimately the corn was picked, shucked, and shelled by hand. For home use it was either ground in a hand mill or treated with homemade lye to produce the ubiquitous hominy. If marketed it never brought over 25 cents a bushel. Sometimes it was shipped as kernels, but more frequently it was ground into meal, packed into small barrels, and loaded on flatboats for shipment to New Orleans.

While corn was the dominant western crop, it exercised no complete monopoly. Such grains as wheat, oats, barley, rye, and buckwheat were grown in considerable amounts. Wheat was the usual cash crop of the Northwest. Tobacco was widely cultivated, particularly in Kentucky; much of it was used in the West, while shortly after 1800 several thousand hogsheads were floated down the river each year. Hemp was exported both raw and as rope; every western town of importance had one or more ropewalks. Flax was grown primarily for home use, but a marketable excess was sold mainly as rough cloth. A considerable variety of poor fruit was produced, with peaches most popular — probably because westerners were told that peach trees became productive within two years. A large share of the peach crop was transformed into brandy, which sold commonly at a dollar a gallon. Vegetables were produced for home use, while a few were sold to the residents of the towns.

Western livestock was never impressive in comparison with eastern stock. Oxen, horses, beef cattle, pigs, and sheep were necessary for home use, but their quality was poor and tended to deteriorate. Many times they were branded and allowed to forage for themselves, which indicated both why their quality was poor and why fences were necessary for the cultivated fields. The pig was supreme from the standpoint of numbers, furnishing the meat staple of the West; a surplus was marketed as ham and salt pork. Cows were fewer, although in the more developed areas there were sufficient numbers so that butter could be sent to New Orleans. Cattle and hogs were driven over the mountains from the Ohio Valley to be fattened in Pennsylvania for the eastern market. The raising of blooded horses was becoming a recognized Kentucky industry, but semiwild horses remained so common that their skins were exported.

MERCHANDISING

The western agricultural surplus was ordinarily bartered for articles that the West wanted, and little money changed hands. The family with extra cloth or corn or pigs took them to the nearest store and traded with the merchant for salt, spices, iron implements, window glass, cloth, or whatever else the family wanted. Even in the early days the western stores had a surprising array of commodities, ranging from coffee to flutes and from nails to Havana cigars. This variety increased rapidly with time.

The business of the frontier merchant was by no means simple and uncomplicated. Ordinarily he had but little capital, and consequently did most of his business on credit. The articles which he sold came from some eastern city, usually Philadelphia but possibly Baltimore, Richmond, or elsewhere. These goods were purchased on credit, which meant that the merchants of Philadelphia financed a large part of western business. They were hauled over the mountains by wagon and bartered for western products. The western goods were then loaded on a flatboat and floated down the river to New Orleans, where they were frequently resold to the West Indies and sometimes to other parts of the world. Often this sale was again barter, as for sugar or molasses, which was then sailed to the eastern seaboard, thus completing the circle.

This circular trade meant that the great majority of the transportation for the western business within the United States was from East to West. Manufactured articles moved in this direction, while but few of the western bulky products could stand the high freight charges for the eastward trip, particularly since most of them were produced also in the East. Consequently most of the wagons returned empty. Furs and whiskey were prominent among the few articles that were shipped east. Obviously both East and West were anxious for improved transportation, which was expected to reduce prices and to increase the traffic both ways.

Exports from the trans-Appalachian West moved toward the west and south, since that was the direction in which the rivers flowed. Not until after the War of 1812 was there a cheap way to reverse the trip: before this time the keel boat was too expensive for widespread use, while overland traffic was almost impossible. The usual method for hauling goods was by flatboat, which could move only with the stream. For example, a flatboat would be built on the Ohio, loaded possibly with 300 barrels of corn meal, and placed in the charge of a supervisor and four boatmen. After about a month the boat would reach New Orleans, where the meal was sold and the boat broken up and sold. The men then returned overland.

MONEY

The lack of currency was always a serious deterent to western business. The little existing money came largely from new migrants, from New Orleans sales and from the army as it bought supplies and paid its members — which was one reason why every western community was delighted to have an army post. Even these small amounts of currency tended to be drained back to the East, with the result that the average westerner seldom saw even a few dollars in cash during the course of a year. The prevalence of barter was a partial solution of the difficulties, but barter was not always satisfactory; paying the schoolteacher in corn or the Yankee peddler in pork was at best cumbersome.

The necessity for a greater circulating medium encouraged the use of anything which came to hand. Various foreign coins, and particularly Spanish, were in common use. Westerners also circulated a great variety of eastern banknotes, of which many had a very dubious validity. Likewise they began to circulate currency of their own, as issued by such organizations as the Kentucky Insurance Company (1802) and the Miami Exporting Company (1803).

Such currency was none too well backed and produced tremendous profits at the expense of westerners, but its existence showed clearly the pressing western need for more circulating medium, and this problem was to remain in existence for many years in spite of numerous efforts at solution.

MANUFACTURING

As the West continued to develop, many of the functions which at first were performed by individual families were taken over by commercial enterprises. Among the earlier industries were mills for grinding corn, salt manufactories, distilleries, flour mills, tanneries, ropewalks, boat yards, sawmills, textile mills, glass factories, paper mills, shoe factories and tobacco processing concerns. The desirability and even necessity of professional production in these fields was quite evident, even though most of the new shops were small, representing little more than the master and a handful of apprentices and workmen. In time some of these enterprises grew in size, while specific industries developed importance in favored places — as iron at Pittsburgh and pork packing at Cincinnati. Consolidations, with price fixing tendencies, began to appear by the 1820s in such fields as salt, iron, cotton, glass, and transportation. Water furnished the early power, but the steam engine began to appear before the nineteenth century was very old.

Obtaining the necessary supply of labor was always a difficult problem for the western manufacturer. Most men moving to the West were farmers, and even the fair number of migrating " artisans " tended to be more interested in becoming independent farmers than in working for wages. Eastern artisans were frequently not highly specialized and often had some background of farming experience. At times workmen were bribed to come from the East, and to some extent women and children supplied the need for labor, although even apprentices were hard to find. The result was that wages, both money and " real," were high, while early nineteenth century strikes had more than normal success in comparison with eastern and European strikes of the same period.

In addition to the employees of manufacturing enterprises, the towns contained a host of independent professional and business men. As the communities grew there appeared the usual collection of doctors, lawyers, ministers, and teachers, with the lawyers and ministers outnumbering their other professional colleagues. Shopkeepers and clerks furnished a perceptible part of the population. Blacksmiths, shoemakers, tinkers, seamstresses, and tailors soon appeared to perform functions which were difficult for the untrained man. Some of them were itinerant, taking the job to the customer — a desirable procedure with a sparse population unconnected by good roads.

GOVERNMENT

One occupation that was not generally recognized as a full-time job was that of the politician. Politics was considered an avocation, even a sport, for many men. Any average adult male was assumed to be competent to fill any public office within the gift of his fellow citizens, and in the early communities the politician might also be a farmer or lawyer, land speculator, trader, or miller. Quite naturally the West accepted the most democratic egalitarianism then in existence, for westerners were in fact more nearly equal than any other society in the world. Little wonder that in the 1790s they accepted Jefferson's agricultural democracy and that later they became enthusiastic for Jackson. Only very gradually, and after the government became much more complex, did the West begin to think of politics as a full-time and moderately specialized occupation.

The earliest of the western governments were frequently extra-legal if not outright illegal, since they were self-constituted organizations within the limits of existing state or nation. Their occasion was the failure of eastern governments to bring law and order as fast as settlement expanded. Watauga, Nashville, Cleveland, and the state of Franklin come quickly to mind, but there were hundreds of other cases. Even in the Northwest Territory counties were formed slowly, and many communities established their own organizations before the properly constituted authorities began to function.

The need for governmental organization was particularly evident in the newer and wilder sections of the country, which gave ocular proof that the West attracted the lawless and dissolute as well as the sober and industrious. Without direct law enforcement the strong and well-armed man could dominate his region, and there were never lacking bullies to take advantage of more timorous men. Personal violence, ranging from fist fights and gouging matches to punctilious duels, were common in the West for a long time.

BANDITRY

Best known evidence of western lawlessness were the bandits who preyed along the routes of travel; such gentry were to remain highly visible until the disappearance of the frontier. The criminal class was in part transplanted from the scenes of other illegal activities in the East — and sometimes just ahead of vengeance. In part, however, it arose from western conditions, for certain men found outlawry more interesting than cutting trees or plowing virgin soil, and but little more dangerous. Some were intrigued by the excitement and adventure, but others merely sought a way of living which did not require continuous hard work. A few of those operating in the early nineteenth century acquired sufficient notoriety that their deeds have continued to live, albeit in a somewhat legendary form.

Colonel Fluger, commonly known as " Colonel Plug," kept a tavern just above Cairo, Ill. His chief stock in trade was his wife " Pluggy," who gave of her charms freely to keep boatmen and traders occupied while her husband was robbing them. Now and then the crew of a plundered boat returned for vengeance, and in at least one case the Colonel needed his wife's best ministrations to ensure his recovery from the effects of such a visit. Later he covered up each theft by boring a hole in the boat and allowing it to sink. While engaged in one such robbery the hawser broke before the Colonel had disembarked, but after he had bored the hole; that was the end of " Colonel Plug."

Another noted outlaw was James Girty of Pennsylvania, a nephew of the notorious Simon Girty reviled as a renegade by the frontiersmen of the latter eighteenth century. Girty boasted that no man could whip him, and as far as the records go, his boast was justified. One of his paramours insisted that, instead of having ribs like those of more ordinary human beings, his chest was one solid bone.

Various groups of bandits had their headquarters at one time or another at Cave-in-Rock, a large limestone cavern on the Illinois bank of the Ohio River. Here it was that early in the 1800s a certain Wilson and his family conducted a tavern and collected a group of robbers who prayed on the travelers by land and water. The gang eventually was dispersed and driven out of the neighborhood by indignant settlers. Wilson was killed by a henchman for the reward which had been placed on his head.

Connected with the Wilsons were Big and Little Harpe, whose proper names were respectively Micajah and Wiley. When Wilson and his followers were driven from Cave-in-Rock the Harpes wandered through Kentucky into North Carolina and then back West again. At this time the entourage included Big Harpe with two women and Little Harpe with one woman and a child. The child disturbed the quiet meditations of Big Harpe so he brained it. The downfall of the Harpes, as told later by the western writer James Hall, is worth recounting. One night the two men posed as ministers (an interesting commentary on conditions on the frontier) and accepted the hospitality of a certain Moses Stigall in Kentucky. Another man, by the name of Love, also spent the night with the Stigalls. In the morning Stigall left early on a business trip, whereupon the Harpes killed his wife and child and the innocent bystander Love. A posse, including Stigall, pursued the two murderers. Eventually they caught Big Harpe and shot and killed him. According to Hall's story, Stigall then in a spirit of revenge and to warn other evil-doers cut off Big Harpe's head and nailed it to a tree, thus giving that vicinity the name of Harpe's Head, Kentucky.

The most notorious of western bandits of the early nineteenth century was John A. Murrell, " The Great Land Pirate," who operated during the '20s and '30s. Murrell was both picturesque and able. In person he was tall, muscular, handsome, and an excellent leader of men — in fact he was everything that the outlaw leader of fiction should be. He traveled continuously and widely, being a real cosmopolitan. His early crimes were simple holdups or horse thefts, but later he favored stealing Negroes, whom he ordinarily sold and recovered several times before he finally killed them to destroy any possible incriminating evidence. His greatest achievement was the formation of a Mystic Clan which he organized on his many trips along the Ohio and Mississippi. The Mystic Clan was a secret criminal organization specializing in Negro stealing. It had secret grips, code, passwords and all the other regular fraternal symbols. At its height it contained possibly 1500 members, of which a small inner group was cognizant of all the more important plans and the rank and file did specified jobs, for each of which they were paid. It also had the superluxury of a legal staff; lawyers were retained at strategic points to be ready to defend any member accused of any crime.

Murrell's early successes led him to expand his plans until he formulated the idea of a general slave rebellion in the South which would result in a Negro empire of which he would be emperor. To further these plans he traveled widely, even joining the Catholic Church and visiting Mexico. Unfortunately Murrell was but human and liked admiration and praise, with the result that he talked too much to a spy. As a result he was captured, brought before the court on the charge of stealing Negroes, convicted, and incarcerated. While in prison he contracted the " prison sickness " and died at the age of forty-three.

The suppression of outlawry was desirable, but other reasons for the establishment of government were more important, even if more prosaic — the recording of wills, commercial contracts and land sales, the improvement of roads, the building of jails, the judicial settlement of disputes. These and other matters of every-day life were not in themselves thrilling, but together they consti-tuted an important difference between a wilderness and a settled community.

NEW STATES

The earliest governmental interests of the West centered largely in actions of the eastern states, but later attention was turned to legislation of Congress. The provisions of the Northwest Ordinance and of its counterpart in the Southwest had to be tried in practice. The performance of a governor with practically dictatorial powers, the change to partial self-rule, and the ultimate transformation to a state of the Union were all matters of intense interest to the westerner.

Actually it was not a western, but a New England state, that became the fourteenth member of the Union. Northern New Eng-land remained a frontier approximately as long as Ohio. The Ver-mont district had long been in dispute between New Hampshire and New York, with both making land grants in this intervening area. Upon the outbreak of the Revolution Ethan Allen and his Green Mountain Boys engineered an independence movement which harsh critics have held was concerned primarily with land speculation. At any rate independence was achieved in 1777 and maintained throughout the war, including negotiations with Con-gress and intrigues with England. Ultimately Vermont adopted the new federal Constitution and was admitted to the Union by Congress in 1791. This admission at least recalls the existence of a frontier which stretched from Maine through central New York, and which was the New England equivalent of Kentucky and Tennessee.

Following Vermont in the procession of new states came Kentucky and Tennessee, as described earlier. Neither was a typical " public land state " any more than Vermont had been, because in each case the available unoccupied land had been practically exhausted before Congress took control. Kentucky never came under direct Congressional regulation before its admission as the fifteenth state in 1792, but Tennessee had experienced the territorial form of government before it was admitted as the sixteenth state in 1796.

OHIO

The experiences of Ohio in its progress toward admission to the Union were more significant than those of its predecessors, since Ohio represented more nearly the usual process of development that was to take place in the great majority of the coming states to the west. Governor Arthur St. Clair arrived in 1788 at Marietta, which was the only settled community in present Ohio. The remainder of the officials appointed by Congress under the terms of the Ordinance of 1787 were three judges, and a secretary of the territory, one Winthrop Sargent. St. Clair created one county immediately and others as settlement progressed. A code of laws was promulgated, courts were established, and efforts made to increase the land open to whites by purchases from the Indians.

The affairs of the Northwest Territory never proceeded smoothly. Governor St. Clair was an intelligent man with high ideals of public service, but his aristocratic federalism conflicted sharply with the Jeffersonian republicanism of the majority of the territory. Furthermore, St. Clair was absent much of the time — in the East, treating with the Indians, or prosecuting an Indian war. During his absences the secretary acted in his place, and Sargent was even more objectionable than St. Clair; ultimately he was advanced to the governorship of the newly created territory of Mississippi in 1798.

The second stage of government became possible for the Northwest Territory when a census in 1798 showed the requisite 5000 adult white males. Governor St. Clair immediately called for the election of a legislative lower house of twenty-two, which met the following year. This body nominated ten men, of whom five were selected by the President to form an upper house. St. Clair and his legislature never saw eye to eye. Frequently he acted on his own initiative, to the loudly expressed rage of the representatives. In turn he found much of their legislation displeasing and so vetoed it. He obtained the nomination of his son for territorial representative in Congress, but William Henry Harrison was elected. Ultimately St. Clair's irritation overcame his discretion and he publicly criticized both Congress and the President, whereupon the President removed him.

The growth of the population of the Northwest Territory led many people to think of statehood, but for this purpose some reduction in boundaries was necessary. After many suggestions and much discussion Indiana was finally sheared away in 1800, with the dividing line the present Indiana-Ohio boundary, except that it was continued north to the international border. The section which is now a part of Michigan was later removed, but the boundary was sufficiently uncertain to cause a near war. The new Territory of Indiana included at first all the remainder of the Old Northwest, and to this lordly domain was added, for a short time in 1804–05, the vast bulk of the Louisiana Purchase, exclusive of Louisiana. Gradually this mass was reduced by eliminating the region west of the Mississippi (1805), Michigan (1805) and Illinois (1809), thus producing the present boundaries of Indiana.

As for the future Ohio a strong movement for statehood received added impetus from the disputes between the legislature and St. Clair. Congress was quite willing, and on April 30, 1802, passed an enabling act to permit the region to construct a constitution and apply for admission; this enabling act was the first of a long series passed for later areas farther west. Under its terms Ohio formed a constitution, and early in 1803 was admitted by Congress to the Union as the seventeenth state. Not surprisingly the new Ohio constitution gave the governor no power of veto.

Ohio furnished the prototype for other states which were later to be carved from the public domain. It participated successively in the three stages of government outlined by the Ordinance of 1787. The Territorial legislature had the seemingly inevitable quarrels with the governor. Surplus lands were removed to make new territories. A state constitution was formed under the authority of an enabling act and the state admitted to the Union; at this point a few states varied by not waiting for the enabling act. This general process soon became so standardized that only exceptions from it seem worthy of notice.

READINGS

T. P. Abernethy, *From Frontier to Plantation* (1932), ch. 9—Tennessee; C. H. Ambler, *A History of West Virginia* (1933), chs. 8, 9; J. D. Barnhart, *Valley of Democracy* (1953), chs. 9, 10 —Ohio statehood; B. W. Bond, Jr., *The Civilization of the Old Northwest* (1934), chs. 8, 11, 13, *The Foundations of Ohio* (1941), chs. 13, 14; S. J. and E. H. Buck, *The Planting of Civilization in Western Pennsylvania* (1939), chs. 11–14, 18–20; T. D. Clark, *A History of Kentucky* (1937), chs. 5, 6; R. M. Coates, *The Outlaw Years* (1930)—banditry; F. G. Davenport, *Ante-Bellum Kentucky* (1943), ch. 8; E. Dick, *The Dixie Frontier* (1948), chs. 6–10, 23; R. C. Downes, *Frontier Ohio* (1935), chs. 3–8; D. Drake, *Pioneer Life in Kentucky* (1948)—reminiscences; L. C. Hunter, *Studies in the Economic History of the Ohio Valley* (1934); R. Phares, *Reverend Devil* (1941)—banditry; H. Sinclair, *The Port of New Orleans* (1942), ch. 8—easy reading; H. Toulmin, *The Western Country in 1793* (1948), pp. 60–136—Kentucky; C. W. Towne and E. N. Wentworth, *Pigs* (1950), chs. 9, 10; W. T. Utter, *The Frontier State* (1942), chs. 6, 8, 10—Ohio; E. N. Wentworth, *America's Sheep Trails* (1948), ch. 5; F. E. Wilson, *Arthur St. Clair* (1944), chs. 6–9; J. E. Wright and D. S. Corbett, *Pioneer Life in Western Pennsylvania* (1940).

CHAPTER 8

REPRODUCING A CULTURE

WESTERNERS in the years near 1800 did not devote their entire time and energy to earning a living and to providing a government. Periodic relaxation was necessary for even the most ambitious and hard-working, while the majority of people had conscious strivings for the more intellectual and emotional interests of literature and religion. In such cultural strivings the westerners were distinctly children of the East. The idea of a characteristic western civilization developed slowly and painfully, and in the early years practically no one had any such idea. The main object was to reproduce eastern ways of life — and before long a westerner could be made " fighting mad " by the insinuation that he was deficient in any of the traits that distinguished the East. The only difference to which he would not object was that of superiority. Buildings must be as impressive, canals as long, the women as charming, penitentiaries as depressing, horses as fast, and parties as magnificent as in the East.

In the development of such interests as sports, the arts, education, and religion the West was under certain definite and obvious disadvantages. Population was sparse and generally deficient in money and leisure, which made the development of the arts extremely difficult, even in the towns. Furthermore, few westerners were thoroughly familiar with the more important intellectual productions of the East and of Europe of their time. Migrants were not drawn from the leisured and cultured classes, but from the less prosperous farmers and artisans. While they were endowed with perfectly adequate native intelligence, they lacked the background, time, and funds which might have provided an excellent education and wide reading. In fact many of them were illiterate, and their children were no less handicapped.

LITERATURE

While westerners were generally deficient in book education, there were many exceptions. European visitors never ceased to marvel when they arrived at the roughest of new log cabins to find a modest collection of books, newspapers, and magazines which had been read understandingly by their frontiersman owner, who talked long and informatively of national and international politics. Thousands of families had at least the minimum of the *Bible, Pilgrim's Progress,* and the poems of Milton. Their speech and writing showed the influence of these literary masterpieces.

Best circulated of western literary productions were the almanacs and newspapers. The almanac by no means confined itself to the calendar and the weather, but printed all kinds of advice and information, from the proper season for planting various crops to medical hints and moral precepts. The first to receive wide circulation was the *Kentucky Almanac,* which started publication in 1794.

Newspapers appeared quite early in most western towns, but their mortality was frightful; subscription lists were small, and many of the subscribers forgot to pay. The first paper west of the mountains (except in New York) was the *Pittsburgh Gazette* (1786), which was soon followed by *The Kentucke Gazette* (1787) at Lexington. First in the Old Northwest was the *Centinel of the North-Western Territory* (1793) at Cincinnati. Early newspapers were predominantly of four pages. Their contents were almost entirely national and European news. The lack of local news may be credited in part to the feeling of the editor that everyone in a small western town knew all the gossip anyway, but more to the ease with which a paper could be filled with items clipped from the eastern and European press. Nearly every paper was issued weekly, with the daily paper unknown. More frequent issues were impossible because of the lack of good communication to obtain news, the paucity of subscriptions, and the shortage of advertising.

Western books and magazines were scarce, but not unknown. The first book printed west of the mountains was the third volume of *Modern Chivalry,* which saw the light of day at Pittsburgh in 1793. The author was a prominent resident of Pittsburgh, Hugh Henry Brackenridge. The story was a long and rambling account of the troubles of an illiterate Irish servant, Teague O'Regan, who perpetually was being rescued from distressing and precarious situations by his master, Captain Farrago. *Modern Chivalry* is no masterpiece of fiction, but it does contain interesting comments on western life of that time. Much more widely sold and read was that eminently practical book *The Navigator,* written by Zadock Cramer, the first edition of which appeared in 1801. The most important early publishing center west of Pittsburgh was Lexington, Ky.

Other western literary productions included most numerously a variety of highly ephemeral religious and political pamphlets. The first magazine to be published in the West was *The Medley, or Monthly Miscellany,* begun at Lexington in 1803. Probably the earliest poem to be both written and published in the West was *The Kentucky Miscellany,* written by Thomas Johnson sometime before 1800; Johnson disliked Kentucky heartily and made his views known with more force than beauty.

Lack of funds and interest meant that libraries were few and small. Many families had a handful of books, but a collection of as many as a hundred was very rare. Booksellers made precarious livings in the larger towns. Here and there a subscription library was established, as at Lexington in 1795, Belpre in 1796, and Cincinnati in 1802; the famous " Coonskin Library " of Athens County, Ohio, was opened in 1804.

EDUCATION

Lack of writing and printing could be traced in large part to a meagerness of education. Few people were competent to write effectively, while even more important, few could read with sufficient ease to make that occupation a pleasure to themselves. And unfortunately the situation showed little prospect of improvement. Most farmers of the early nineteenth century were not enthusiastic about education, and felt especially skeptical of anything more than an irreducible minimum. Education seemed a luxury at a time when every penny loomed large. While southerners were even less enamored of education than northerners, both agreed that schools operated at the public expense meant an unjustified increase in taxes. To their minds it seemed obvious that those parents who desired the luxury of education for their children should pay for it themselves. The orator's panegyrics about an educated population received only lip approval from the masses of farmers.

All schools were private, and the teacher was paid by the parents of his students. Since the parents had little or no ready cash the teacher frequently received his compensation in the form of pigs, vegetables, and corn. Ordinarily he was " boarded around," staying for a short time at the home of each of his students. Such a life did not attract capable and interested teachers, particularly since it was commonly assumed that anyone who could read and and write was thoroughly competent to teach. The teaching profession had no important standing in the community and therefore attracted many of the misfits — men without steady occupation, who found schoolteaching the path of least resistance. It also attracted a somewhat more desirable group of young New England men who used it as a means of becoming acquainted with the country and saving a little money before they started their chosen work.

Education was usually limited to the three Rs. It was given only to children, and then only at times when they could not be employed usefully on the farm, which meant a few weeks or months in the winter for the older children and a little additional summer work for the younger children. Many children never attended school. The " little red schoolhouse " was as yet an institution of the future, for the best that the West could afford in 1800 was a small log schoolhouse of a single room. The children were ungraded and studied their lessons aloud simultaneously, after which they recited them from memory. Texts were scarce and father's books were considered good enough for little John ; the diversity of population might sometimes mean that no two books in the school were alike. Paper was scarce and consequently little used; its substitute was a slate, on which marks were made with a piece of soapstone. The summit of education was the knowledge of the elementary rules of reading, writing, spelling, and ciphering.

Secondary and higher education in the West were almost nonexistent prior to 1800. Here and there were a few seminaries (sometimes called colleges) for either boys or girls. For the girls they offered polite " finishing " courses in such departments as fancy needlework, deportment and painting. For the boys they offered the classical subjects which were necessary for entrance to an eastern college. The only institution of higher education in the West prior to 1800 was Transylvania University at Lexington. Its requirements were not high, and it was having a hard struggle to continue its existence; eventually it was to become important. Between 1800 and 1810 a few other feeble institutions raised their heads, as Jefferson College and Washington College in Pennsylvania (later united), Ohio University (Athens) and Vincennes University in the Old Northwest, and Cumberland College in Tennessee.

SOCIAL GATHERINGS

Lack of education and of the more formal types of culture which are connected with it, did not mean that life was all work and no play. The westerner had many moments of relaxation. Frontier life frequently was lonely, with each rural family fairly isolated and economically self-sufficient, but actually there were few people who really desired continual solitude. In addition, a number of occupations could not be performed by the family by itself. The result was that the West grasped eagerly at every occasion for a necessary gathering, and even created some that were not absolutely essential. Work was combined with play so that the work was lost to view in the general fun and merrymaking. Such occasions as a logrolling, house-raising, cornhusking, maple sugar gathering, a wedding, a funeral, harvesting, quilting, fulling, sewing, and weaving attracted the entire neighborhood. More self-consciously, the singing school and the spelling bee brought similar gatherings.

The announcement of a community enterprise meant the presence of everyone within traveling distance. The men spent the day in raising the house, husking the corn, or doing whatever work had been planned, while the women prepared an immense feast — and neither sex was mute during these activities. Then everyone ate and drank all he could, told jokes (often crude), recounted gossip, and debated politics and religion. In the evening the older folk continued their conversation while the young people danced to the playing of a fiddle. Square dancing was the rule, with some stentorian-voiced male calling off the figures. While dancing was quite general in the back country it had opponents; some of the more religious felt it to be immoral, and in this attitude they were backed by most of the churches.

Western parties tended to be boisterous, earthy, and even crude. These were vigorous and hard-working people who had not as yet arrived at the Victorian period. Kissing games were frequent; for example, the cornhusker who found a red ear could kiss the girl of his choice, and the kiss was seldom a perfunctory peck. Lovemaking was frequently coarse, vigor being the common substitute for finesse when youthful couples strolled off into the moonlit woods. A wedding was the occasion for riotous fun and pointed jokes; frequently the happy couple was put to bed in the loft while the party continued downstairs — and not without lewd remarks. When to the natural relief from backbreaking toil was added the consumption of too much whiskey the result might approach a riot. Westerners lived close to the basic facts of nature, and were not oppressed by the prudishness of a later generation.

DRAMA

One amusement that was largely absent from the West was the drama. A few theaters were constructed before 1810, as at Pittsburgh and Cincinnati, but there were no regular professional companies of actors. Amateurs presented a few plays — at Lexington even before 1800 — but the performances were bad. Many people throughout the country felt that the theater was basically immoral, while an even greater number held that professional actors, and certainly actresses, lived lives of sin. The general feeling that the theater had a contaminating effect on women influenced the amateur actors to use men in all female parts. The results may have been highly moral, but they had no other virtue to recommend them.

ATHLETIC CONTESTS

The West was always interested in athletic contests, which it commonly combined with gambling. Horse racing was highly popular, with race tracks in operation at various towns, both North and South, before 1800. Shooting matches, foot races, and wrestling all had their devotees, each with a stake on the outcome. The stake was usually more than the bettor could afford, which of course made the event the more exciting. Each contest was accompanied by copious drinking, and sometimes the drinking occurred without the contest. Shooting was possibly the most utilitarian of these sports, and each westerner was proud of his prowess with a rifle. While the shooting was actually not remarkably good from a modern standpoint, it was next to miraculous when consideration is given the heavy gun, the poor powder, and the small and often irregular shot.

Athletic contests were frequently highly objectionable from the point of view of a later, more squeamish generation. Rough and tumble fist fights had no Marquis of Queensbury rules. The contestants kicked, butted, bit, and gouged, and the loss of an eye, an ear, or a finger was not uncommon. Even making allowances for the tall stories that the West liked to impose upon credulous easterners, the fact still remained that the West was rough and uncouth, and that its fun was boisterous.

RELIGION

Among the various cultural developments in the West none was more important than the establishment and growth of organized religions. The best informed guess is that in 1800 less than half of western families were affiliated with any church. This small proportion depended partly on obstacles other than irreligion. Money to build and repair churches and to pay ministers was hard to obtain. In fact, ministers were in themselves difficult to acquire, since all divinity schools were in the East, and a graduate needed considerable fervor and missionary zeal to forego a comfortable living in the East in favor of the hardships of the frontier.

A special western difficulty existed in the multiplicity of sects which made the establishment and support of any single church more difficult. In the East these various sects tended to separate geographically, but in the West a dozen or more might be represented in somewhat equal proportions within a single small community — not only larger churches such as the Methodist, Presbyterian, Congregational, Roman Catholic, Episcopal, and Lutheran, but also such small groups as the Moravian, Dunkard, United Brethren in Christ, Anabaptists, Quakers, and Shakers. No one group might have sufficient strength to build a church and support a minister, while the idea of a community church would have been viewed generally with horror.

The religious lag of the West brought great distress of mind to thousands of people, both East and West. In the East, men feared that irreligion would grow in the West, infect the East, and thus destroy one of the foundations of the Republic. To avert this potential tragedy, proselyting groups were formed. Home missionary societies mushroomed during the 1790s, including notably the Missionary Society of Connecticut (1798), the Massachusetts Missionary Society (1799), and the Boston Female Society for Missionary Purposes (1800). Various Female Cent Institutions collected a cent a week from each member. These societies sent a considerable number of men on missionary tours of the West. In addition, tract societies provided religious pamphlets and books without charge, while Bible societies distributed the " word of God." Each regular denomination devoted part of its funds for work in the West.

Thousands of westerners were likewise concerned with the dangers of irreligion, for they had been reared in religious eastern homes and wanted their children to have the benefit of church teaching. They realized that, although worship could be an individual or family matter, for most people group worship was important.

Religion for the westerners had not only the usual moral and emotional values, but also a special importance in relation to frontier conditions. It helped to give a meaning to the hard western life. The hazards of a wilderness occupied by hostile Indians became more supportable if one felt that God watched over each of his creatures. Incidentally a strong Christian could feel that, since the Indian was an unbeliever, his destruction was a victory of right over the powers of darkness.

Organized religion also offered the westerners social and emotional outlets which were highly important. On Sunday the whole family walked or rode to church to spend the entire day. Sunday school was followed by a morning service, then dinner, and finally afternoon service. While sermons were long and the seats hard, the singing of hymns gave a joyous occupation to the lungs; hymns were " lined out " two lines at a time, since many people could not read. The noon dinner brought a chance for the latest news of crops, politics, and new babies. Furthermore, religious emotionalism gave a welcome release from the hard and prosaic task of making a living. Few westerners thought of the frontier as having in itself any emotionally stimulating experiences.

A church with real hopes for success in the West should have been optimistic in its faith, with stress on the importance of the individual. It should have provided social and emotional content. It should have had an organization adapted to the widely scattered western population. Further, it needed a clergy which could speak the language of the crude and hard-working West. The refined and sophisticated product of the eastern theological seminary was no doubt eminently satisfactory to an educated and intelligent audience, but its appeal to a relatively uneducated and uncultured West was slight.

METHODISTS

One church well-fitted for western needs was the Methodist as reorganized after the Revolution to give the American branch relative independence. Most effective work was done by Francis Asbury, called Bishop Asbury even though the title was not justified officially ; he was the best known American leader of the Methodist

Church. In spite of a feeble body and much sickness Bishop Asbury traveled widely, preaching, talking, and praying. Under his guidance Methodism became an important part of the religious life of the United States. Methodism crossed the mountains in the early 1780s and spread rapidly. The Western Conference, organized in 1800, included some 2500 members in Kentucky and Tennessee, while an additional 350 members belonged to three circuits north of the Ohio. Even before 1800 Methodist preachers had pushed into Missouri. By 1811 western Methodists numbered 30,000 (of whom 1500 were Negroes) and were at least as numerous as any other sect.

The Methodist doctrines of free will, free grace, and individual responsibility evoked an enthusiastic response from the hopefully individualistic westerner. Furthermore, the organization which was developed to care for the more sparsely settled sections of the country was admirably adapted to the conditions of the West. A minister, instead of devoting his entire time to the care of one church, might " ride circuit," thus distributing his attention over a considerable region. During his absence from any one community the work was continued by specially designated lay members, who were called " exhorters," or " local preachers." These laymen both preached and conducted religious services. Methodist ministers often appealed to their congregations with more effectiveness than did the leaders of other sects, because the Methodist Church was willing to use forceful men regardless of their education. Such men talked in the strong and vivid language of the frontier, and although they might be confused by the subtleties of theological disputation or be entirely ignorant of Greek and Latin, they could paint the terrors of Hell in compelling terms, and could call upon the sinner to repent with a vigor, earnestness, and pathos that put their more learned brethren to shame.

The most important and picturesque element of the Methodist system was the circuit rider himself. He ordinarily rode a horse, and his circuit required continuous traveling for four or five weeks. He preached daily at noon in any convenient gathering place such as a cabin or clearing. His salary in 1784 was sixty-four dollars a year, out of which he paid his own traveling expenses, but in 1800 he was given eighty dollars and traveling expenses for himself, plus an allowance for his family. This munificent salary often took the form of agricultural products, and it was frequently supplemented by entertainment and gifts from parishioners. The circuit rider usually wore a straight-breasted waistcoat, a high collar, and a plain necktie. Suspenders were a luxury. His hair was allowed to grow to his shoulders, according to the usual western custom of the time; barbers were rare, and with long hair it was possible for each man — or his wife — to do the necessary trimming.

The Methodist circuit rider threw his influence in the direction of civilization and culture in spite of his own crudities and frequent lack of education. Often he carried books in his saddlebags, and these he loaned to the people with whom he stayed. On many occasions he was the only visitor whom a family would entertain for months at a time, and to them he would bring the news of the outside world — tales of wondrous cities, new styles in dress and social intercourse, marvelous mechanical improvements, and neighborhood gossip. His advent was awaited eagerly, for he was more informative than the newspaper.

BAPTISTS

The chief frontier rivals of the Methodists were the Baptists, who were distinguished by believing in immersion and in close communion. Great freedom was allowed the individual churches, which varied widely in their practices. Instead of a regular circuit system the Baptists licensed local preachers and encouraged very small congregations. Like the Methodists they were more interested in fervor than education for the ministry, and favored rapid evangelization by emotional pleas. Also like the Methodists they established their first trans-Appalachian churches in the 1780s and then expanded rapidly, until by 1800 they had crossed the Mississippi.

The Baptists were the unwilling parents of the Disciples of Christ, commonly known as the " Christians " or " Campbellites." The originator of this new sect was Thomas Campbell, who migrated from Scotland to western Pennsylvania in 1807, but the important leader was the founder's son Alexander. The Disciples favored a " purer," more primitive Christianity to combine the true believers of all churches. After flirting with the Presbyterians they joined the Baptists (1813) and grew within that church. Ultimately, in the late 1820s they withdrew from the Baptist Church to produce, rather ironically, a new sect. Their belief in poverty and self-sacrifice did not prevent them from carrying along all the church property which they could.

PRESBYTERIANS AND CONGREGATIONALISTS

Third in size among western Protestants sects was the Presbyterian, which was handicapped by the more gloomy doctrines of Calvin, the lack of an effective frontier organization, the insistence on an educated clergy, and a reluctance to accept revival methods. On these issues occurred two southwestern schisms in the years immediately after 1800. The " New Lights " raised doubts about the doctrines of election and predestination, but soon died out. The Cumberland Presbyterian Church (1810) seceded largely on the educated ministry dispute, holding that piety was more important than book learning and that high educational qualifications meant a deplorable lack of ministers in the West. The parent church tried to fill western needs by promoting western colleges, but this procedure was too slow for many impatient westerners.

Closely allied with the Presbyterians were the Congregationalists. These two churches were in such community of feeling that in 1801 they adopted a plan of union by which they collaborated in founding new churches and then allowed these churches to decide for themselves whether their services, church rules, and ministers would be Presbyterian or Congregational. The general result of this cooperation was the development of Presbyterian rather than Congregational churches. Congregationalism became most important when an increased flood of New Englanders carried it to Michigan, Wisconsin, Iowa, Minnesota, and other regions of the Far West.

ROMAN CATHOLICS

The Roman Catholics did the earliest missionary work in the region west of the Appalachians. Jesuit priests had labored long among the Indians and with the French and Spanish settlers, but this early work was of practically no importance to the American West of 1800. Catholicism expanded from east to west in the period after the Revolution in the same way as did other faiths. The Diocese of Bardstown (Kentucky) was erected in 1808 and Joseph Flaget arrived to take charge of it in 1811. By 1815 there were probably 10,000 Catholics among the white settlers west of the mountains. Later migration was to increase Catholic membership to the great distress of many Protestant Americans who had considerable question as to whether Catholicism was not worse than paganism.

CAMP MEETINGS

The frontier community had a definite need for vital religious experiences that could not be satisfied by the occasional preachings of a peripatetic Methodist minister. Frequent emotional outpourings were necessary to alleviate the deadly seriousness of daily life. All believers must at times be assembled to obtain consciousness of common purpose and strivings. The frontier needed some religious expression which would weld isolated families in a sense of emotional unity. The institution which ultimately met this need was the camp meeting. In its original form as an emotional expression of religious strivings, the camp meeting was not distinctively western, but in its increased use and in the typical form which it later assumed it was a western contribution to the religious life of the nation.

As early as 1796 James McGready, a Presbyterian minister who had been inspired by the success of eastern revivals, arrived in Kentucky to help advance the work of God in the West. Personally McGready was unprepossessing and had a coarse, tremulous voice; but his lack of beauty combined with the peculiar timbre of his tones gave a curious and unearthly effect which was extremely impressive. Utilizing his powers to the full, he held a series of emotional meetings in which Hell was pictured frequently and vividly, and in which occurred much weeping and ecstasy. The unusual effectiveness of these meetings aroused widespread interest among westerners desiring the advance of religion.

Among the people to be attracted to hear McGready were the McGee brothers — William, who was a Presbyterian, and John, who was a Methodist. The McGees heard McGready in 1799 and were so much impressed that they began to hold similar meetings throughout the West. Of William it is related that " he would sometimes exhort after the sermon, standing on the floor, or sitting, or lying in the dust, his eyes streaming, and his heart so full that he could only ejaculate, ' Jesus! Jesus! ' "

Emotional religious meetings had an immediate and profound appeal to the West. The numbers which attended them soon became too large to be accommodated by the small country churches. Tents and cabins were found necessary, tents probably being used first in 1800. The length of the meetings increased, until it became common to hold them through an entire week end, from Friday until Tuesday. The largest of such meetings, and the one which may be said to have marked the height of the " Great Revival," took place at Cane Ridge, Kentucky, in August 1801; the number of participants was variously estimated as between ten and twenty thousand. While the " Great Revival " ended by 1805 the camp meeting continued to be used frequently and successfully.

Whole families traveled twenty, thirty, and even a hundred miles to attend a camp meeting. They brought with them tents, food, cooking utensils, clothes, and even furniture to make their stay enjoyable. Upon their arrival they raised their tents or constructed rude cabins on the edge of the cleared space which was to be used for the large meetings. Living quarters were furnished in semipermanent fashion. Cooking was done over open fires.

The main meetings were held in the large clearing in the center of the campground. A high platform at one end served as a pulpit for the ministers, eight, ten, or even more serving in relays. Most of the participating clergy were Methodists, with a sprinkling of Baptists and Presbyterians. The seats for the congregation were usually the halves of split logs arranged in parallel rows. Between the congregation and the platform was a litter of loose straw, destined to support the knees of repentant sinners. Meetings were held in the morning, afternoon, and evening, with pine torches affording the illumination after dark. Simultaneously with the large meeting there were usually a number of smaller meetings in tents along the sides of the cleared space.

The camp meeting stressed primarily the mystical and emotional appeal of religion. Songs by the congregation and prayers by the ministers served only as prefaces and interludes to the main business of exhorting. Such appeals included lengthy descriptions of the horrors of Hell, laid somewhat less stress on the glories of Heaven, and contained many admonitions for sinners to repent. At frequent intervals they were punctuated by shouted " amens " and " yes, Lords " and " glories " from members of the congregation and other clergy.

Bombarded by soul-harrowing discourses, some of the " sinners " came forward to repent of their sins, and the ministers " labored " with them individually. Flaming calls for repentance caused even the purest woman or young girl to feel a conviction of deadly sin which must be acknowledged and repented. Adolescent girls seemed to be particularly affected by threats of Hell and damnation. The response of a few people was contagious, and soon the whole meeting was raised to a pitch of hysterical enthusiasm. Since the ministers had experienced many such meetings they knew the proper psychological appeals to produce the maximum of religious exaltation. The conditions for emotional releases were most favorable at night, when the wild flare of the torches contrasting with the blackness of the surrounding forest and the talk of unearthly and eerie subjects made the meetings particularly impressive. Of almost equal effectiveness were the small submeetings in the tents, where the hot, stuffy, unwholesome air, the blaze of lights, and the exhortations for repentance were a combination difficult to resist.

The intensity of the emotional strain produced by the camp meeting was shown by the convulsive and involuntary actions of those people most affected. They leaped, ran, jumped, laughed, sang, sobbed, shouted, and swooned, for the better the meeting the larger was the number of the " slain." Some beat the ground in agony, while others barked like dogs, or emitted the " holy laugh." Many twitched in every joint with the " jerks," which were reputed to be so contagious that even scoffing onlookers were similarly affected. Trances and visions, in which conversations were held with Christ or the apostles or the dear departed, were not unusual. The more powerful the reaction of the individual, the more the Lord had worked, and the more the sanctification of the person affected.

The emotional displays of the camp meeting were expected, and plans were laid carefully to create them, but other results of the gatherings were achieved less consciously. The camp meeting was designed primarily for religious devotion, but it incidentally was an occasion for meeting friends and neighbors, and for discussing subjects of common interest. Families came in part to see other families, and in the intervals between meetings and while the food was being prepared over the open fires, gossip was exchanged and old friendships renewed. The small children played together during the day, and it was not unknown for their elders to miss meetings to discuss the crops or the latest candidate for the legislature.

The social intercourse of the camp meeting was in itself good, but at times it was accompanied by less desirable manifestations. People not interested in the religious exercises would come for the excitement and human companionship, and their presence would detract from the sincerity of the worship. Other hangers-on would also be attracted by the size of the meeting. The presence of large numbers of people necessitated an extensive supply of foodstuffs, thus leading to the establishment of a number of small stores on the edge of the grounds. Among other merchandise, these stores frequently handled whiskey, which attracted a rowdy element from the near-by towns. Frequently there was friction between the religious and nonreligious elements, sometimes ending in a free-for-all fight. The westerner, even when religious, was not docile, and did not consider seriously the admonition to "turn the other cheek."

The camp meeting encountered another difficulty in the tendency of some of the young people to confuse human and divine love and to obey too literally the injunction to "love thy neighbor as thyself." Some meetings found it necessary to post guards at night to prevent young couples from wandering into the surrounding woods. In the emotional orgy of the meetings women at times threw themselves upon the ground in suggestive attitudes, tore open their clothes, and hugged and kissed everyone they met. This overemphasis on sex was undoubtedly linked closely with the emotionalism of the whole camp meeting. Observers commonly noted that adolescent boys and girls were most subject to religious exaltation, and it is not hard to believe that at times sex was not sublimated, but took direct and earthly means for expression.

In spite of minor difficulties, the camp meeting was useful to the West both as a social meeting place and as an occasion for the emphasis of religious idealism. It provided a socially accepted vehicle for the expression of emotions which frequently were given no outlet in life on the frontier. Friendships were made or renewed, common problems were discussed, courtships begun or continued, information and experiences exchanged, and the inhabitants of the region given a feeling of unity and religious fellowship which helped to make more bearable future months of isolation. Many of the people were influenced to live more socially desirable lives, although of course there was the inevitable backslider who was "saved" at each successive meeting. In consequence, the camp meeting must not be considered as a picturesque but unimportant western eccentricity; rather it was an institution which added necessary elements to western life.

READINGS

T. P. Abernethy, *From Frontier to Plantation* (1932), ch. 13; C. H. Ambler, *A History of West Virginia* (1933), ch. 13; H. Asbury, *A Methodist Saint* (1927), chs. 8, 9—Asbury; W. C. Barclay, *Early American Methodism* (2 vols., 1949)—long and informative; B. W. Bond, Jr., *The Civilization of the Old Northwest* (1934), chs. 14, 15; S. J. and E. H. Buck, *The Planting of Civilization in Western Pennsylvania* (1939), chs. 15–17; T. D. Clark, *The Rampaging Frontier* (1939)—humor; C. C. Cleveland, *The Great Revival in the West* (1916); F. G. Davenport, *Ante-Bellum Kentucky* (1943), chs. 3–7, 9, 10; E. Dick, *The Dixie Frontier* (1948), chs. 12–20, 26–31; W. E. Garrison, *Religion Follows the Frontier* (1931), chs. 1–8; W. E. Garrison and A. T. De Groot, *The Disciples of Christ* (1948), chs. 1–14; C. B. Goodykoontz, *Home Missions on the American Frontier* (1934), chs. 4, 5; H. H. Grant, *Peter Cartwright* (1931), chs. 1–4; D. R. Guthrie, *John McMillan* (1952)—Presbyterian; F. L. McVey, *The Gates Open Slowly* (1949), chs. 1–3—schools in Kentucky; T. Maynard, *The Story of American Catholicism* (1941), ch. 14; J. M. Miller, *The Genesis of Western Culture* (1938)—upper Ohio valley; J. Neal, *By Their Fruits* (1947)—Shakers in Kentucky; E. K. Nottingham, *Methodism and the Frontier* (1941)—Indiana; W. B. Posey, *The Development of Methodism in the Old Southwest* (1933), *The Presbyterian Church in the Old Southwest* (1952); J. H. Schauinger, *Cathedrals in the Wilderness* (1952)— early Catholic Church in Kentucky; W. W. Sweet, *Religion on the American Frontier* vol. 4 *The Methodists* (1946), *Religion and Development of American Culture* (1952), chs. 4, 5, *Revivalism in America* (1944), ch. 6, *The Rise of Methodism in the West* (1920), chs. 1–4, *The Story of Religions in America* (1930), chs. 14, 15; W. T. Utter, *The Frontier State* (1942), chs. 12–14.

CHAPTER 9

THE WEST
ACQUIRES PATRIOTISM

WESTERNERS of the late eighteenth century had not as yet acquired the patriotism which within a few years led Stephen Decatur to vow allegiance to " my country, right or wrong." Westerners were interested primarily in their personal fortunes, and considerably less in the fortunes and glory of the young federal government. Government was meant to serve the interests of individuals, and not to be a supreme end in itself. If an independent trans-Appalachian state or connection with the Spanish empire seemed more advantageous, then there were plenty of westerners who would favor such a move, and this fact was commonly recognized both East and West.

The West was dominated by the Ohio-Mississippi river system in its economic life. Connections between East and West were tenuous, with travel slow and expensive. The great and easy artery of travel was the river, on which one could float in comfort to New Orleans. In consequence the control of the Mississippi, and particularly of its mouth, was vital to the West, and at times overshadowed the cultural and governmental connections with the Atlantic seaboard. This sentiment of separatism naturally led to a plethora of plots and intrigues. Its disappearance was one of the important developments in the history of the West.

The situation of the West during the Revolution provided no opportunity for gratitude to the East, and the end of the war brought little improvement. The Indians remained hostile, while England retained the northwestern posts that dominated the Indian trade. The result was that a very large share of the magnificent domain that had been transferred to the new government in the peace treaty was actually not available for settlers. Even if freed from Indians this land was still claimed by the individual states; only New York had completed its cession, and the important claims were those of Virginia, North Carolina and Georgia. Unceded state land claims meant that as yet there was no national land system and no national provision for government. State provisions for land sales and government were late in coming and unsatisfactory. Though the national government obtained power, Congress under the Articles of Confederation was nearly impotent. While these problems were in time solved, their existence even for a short period irritated the impatient West.

IMPORTANCE OF SPAIN

More important to the West, the end of the Revolution placed Spain in control of the complete range of territory to the south and west — East Florida, which was present Florida extending as far west as St. Marks on the Gulf; West Florida, roughly from St. Marks to Baton Rouge on the Mississippi, but with the northern boundary in dispute; Louisiana, including the present state of that name, but also a vast domain north of that state and of present Texas from the Mississippi to the Rockies. Of greatest immediate interest to the United States was the Gulf Coast, since here were the outlets of many important rivers, particularly the Mississippi.

Not only did Spain control the highly strategic mouth of the Mississippi, but she showed some evidence of an increasingly vigorous colonial policy during the 1780s and gave absolutely no indication of any enthusiasm for United States interests. In 1784 she closed the Mississippi to all but Spanish traffic as one step toward weakening the American West. Negotiations with the southwestern Indians brought some success with the Creek, who were hostile toward the United States. The establishment of new frontier posts brought Spanish garrisons to the Yazoo River (1791) and Chickasaw Bluffs (near present Memphis) in 1795. Farther north was St. Louis, which further encircled western settlements. These developments, and particularly the closing of the Mississippi, seemed highly vital to all westerners.

Spanish show of vigor tended to obscure for the moment the essential weakness of the Spanish position. The truth was that the Floridas and Louisiana represented only the extreme outposts of a large empire, and that while Spain desired to place a dam in front of Anglo-American advance, she had neither men nor money to do an effective job. West Florida and Louisiana were under a single governor, who was also an army officer; these areas contained almost all of the white population, with four-fifths of all whites in the towns from Mobile to New Orleans. Under the command of the governor of Louisiana in 1786 were less than 1400 effective men, of whom almost half were stationed at New Orleans and St. Louis; New Orleans was the only southern post that was fortified at this time. Farther east at St. Augustine was stationed the governor of East Florida, but his command included exceedingly few white settlers. Both governors were handicapped by a scarcity of money, while reinforcements had to be brought from Cuba or Mexico, either of which was too remote for prompt action.

SPANISH POLICY

The most obvious Spanish policy designed to hold Spain's possessions against American aggression was to strengthen her military position as much as possible, close the river to handicap American westward expansion, and exclude American settlers. The most obvious drawback to this policy was that the closing of the river hurt New Orleans as much as or more than it did the American West. Louisiana shipped principally tobacco, indigo, furs, and lumber, and in all of these found a limited market or strong competition from more favored regions. The closing of the river consequently produced a strong local movement to readmit American products. The result was an order of 1788 allowing the sale of American goods for export on the payment of a 15 per cent tax, which was later reduced.

The other principal difficulties with a strong Spanish policy were that Americans in considerable number had already trickled into the Gulf region and that the American settlers of Kentucky and Tennessee vastly outnumbered the Spanish residents to the south. Any strict policy might well inspire a revolt which existing forces would have difficulty in suppressing. It might also lead to an attack from the north which could not be withstood.

In view of these and other complexities Spanish policy fluctuated. A good share of the time American settlers were encouraged to come to Louisiana — provided they would swear loyalty to the Spanish King and embrace the Catholic faith. The hope was that in time they would become good Spanish subjects and strengthen the empire. This policy was actually a bad mistake, just as it was later in Texas. American settlers always preferred connections with the home folk to loyalty to a rather remote Spanish government.

Spanish policy, no matter how wisely or foolishly conceived, was badly damaged in its administration. Spanish officials were notoriously corrupt, and the bribe was a recognized institution. The closing of the Mississippi never really stopped trade because enforcement officers frequently winked at violations — for a consideration. The only effect was to restrict trade because of the increased costs necessitated by bribery.

WESTERN INTRIGUES

The American West was deeply concerned over Spanish policy, and particularly over the closing of the river, which seemed to many to portend economic disaster. Fervent western demands for immediate and drastic action brought little response because American governments, both state and national, were either uninterested or impotent, and consequently there arose a considerable sentiment for independence and even for union with Spain. Spain liked the idea of an independent western state, which would lessen the American danger, and was willing to help in the formation of such a state and to treat it well. The formation of an independent Franklin demonstrated that western talk was not all rant and bombast.

Independence for the West concerned only the Southwest region in the 1780s, because this area contained practically all of the western population of the time. In Tennessee intrigues were promoted primarily by Dr. James White, but involved other important leaders such as Sevier, Blount and Robertson. White proposed (1786) to the Spanish ambassador, Don Diego de Gardoqui, that the West declare its independence and that the new state be taken under the protection of Spain. Gardoqui was at first interested, but a little later his enthusiasm cooled and he suggested that westerners who preferred Spanish rule could easily move to Spanish territory. Incidentally, Blount's involvement in this affair represented only a second choice, since he preferred Congressional action, which ultimately made him governor of the Southwest Territory. Sevier, as head of the state of Franklin, treated with Spain, and in 1788 intrigued with Spain to obtain the revival of Franklin.

WILKINSON

The Kentucky agitation centered in the vigorous and egotistical James Wilkinson. Wilkinson was the son of a Maryland planter, and when little more than a boy had volunteered for the Revolutionary army. His war career was typical of his virtues and defects — he was involved in numerous and sometimes questionable intrigues, criticized his superiors severely, talked and wrote indiscreetly, quarreled and fought a duel, but still impressed the authorities enough to obtain several good jobs. At the youthful age of twenty (1777) he became a brevet brigadier general, and shortly later was made clothier-general. Wilkinson was certainly energetic and probably moderately able, but trouble seemed to gather around him. His morals, both personal and official, were not above reproach and he had the unfortunate failing of talking too much at the wrong time to the wrong people.

After the Revolution Wilkinson lived for a time in Pennsylvania, where he sat in the legislature. Finding economic success elusive he moved to Kentucky in 1783 as the representative of Philadelphia merchants. In Kentucky he was immediately outstanding, for as a youthful and vigorous retired general, suave and persuasive, he seemed to be a coming man. He built a large house in Lexington, speculated in land, as did his neighbors, and did some trading. He was active in the Kentucky statehood movement, participating in several of the conventions, and was one of a group which favored complete independence rather than statehood; in this attitude he had plenty of good company.

As a Kentucky merchant Wilkinson was intensely interested in the closing of the Mississippi in 1784. In spite of the closing he loaded two flatboats with tobacco and started downstream, interrupting his journey only long enough to persuade the Spanish commander at St. Louis that he carried important information of a proposed expedition headed by George Rogers Clark and aimed at Natchez. Arriving at New Orleans he talked long and earnestly with the governor, Esteban R. Miró, warning him of a potential attack from Kentucky. Expressing his usual urge toward literary composition, he then addressed a memorial to the Spanish government, advising that it should either foment a western revolt and take the new republic under its wing, or encourage Kentucky settlers to come to Louisiana; with either plan, Wilkinson was to become chief Spanish agent in the West. These conversations and compositions were so persuasive that Wilkinson was given a loan of $7000 in 1789 and a pension of $2000 a year a little later. Whether Wilkinson believed his own tales is doubtful, and particularly later when they became more complex and contradictory. Probably he was interested only in personal advantage in trade and in pensions, both of which he obtained from the somewhat credulous Spanish governors. Toward the end of his associations with Spanish officialdom no other explanation seems plausible than that he was milking them of everything possible, with no idea of ever completing his side of the bargain.

When Wilkinson returned to Kentucky he worked hard to maintain the confusion from which he might profit. In local politics he was vigorous for independence and for an alliance with England if Spain would not open the Mississippi. To Miró he wrote that he was working for independence and union with Spain, and that the Mississippi should be kept closed. To England he addressed a memorial in which he suggested he be made the English agent for the West to work for independence and an attack on New Orleans if the Spanish did not open the river; to his disappointment the English were not as credulous as the Spanish and refused his offer.

Western conditions meantime were clarifying, and the change was reasonably apparent by 1790. All the states but Georgia had ceded their western claims to Congress, which had provided for the survey and sale of the public land. The Northwest and Southwest Territories had both been established and statehood for Kentucky was obviously coming soon. The new government under the Constitution was distinctly stronger than its predecessor. In consequence Spanish intrigue seemed somewhat less promising as a full-time occupation, and Wilkinson, in debt as usual, went back to the army; he was in command at Cincinnati when St. Clair's defeated army returned. Rumors that he was in the pay of Spain reached President Washington, but did not stop the issuing of a commission. Wilkinson fought acceptably in the Indian wars of the 1790s, while at the same time he continued to receive his Spanish pension and to ask for more.

GENÊT

A new western complication arose with the arrival in the United States of Citizen Edmund Charles Genêt (1793) as representative of a France in which the Girondists were in power. The Genêt mission as regards the West was to acquire Florida and Louisiana, where supposedly the oppressed inhabitants were panting for an opportunity to accept the ideals of the French Revolution. The general plan was to recruit a frontier American army, pay it with money which the United States still owed France, and float down the Mississippi. Genêt depended on American enthusiasm for France and the Revolution, and in truth there was a considerable amount of such sentiment in the South and West.

Genêt's representative in the West was André Michaux, who discovered what he considered the perfect man to lead a western expedition in George Rogers Clark. Clark was resentful at what he held to be the ungrateful treatment that he had received for his services in the war, and his feelings were so intense that he had smashed the ceremonial sword given to him by Virginia. Since the war he had been engaged in land speculations and in Spanish intrigues, neither one of which had proven very lucrative. Now he was commissioned commander in chief of the proposed western expedition and began to raise men and supplies. Wilkinson capitalized on the furore by warning Spain of the expedition; in return, money was sent to him, but unfortunately it was appropriated by bandits en route.

The promising Genêt plans collapsed when President Washington proved unexpectedly hostile. The President felt that the United States would do well to avoid being entangled in a European war, and that an armed expedition raised within the United States to act against a supposedly friendly power could have no other effect. Consequently he requested the Governor of Kentucky to stop Clark, and asked France for the recall of Genêt.

While the Genêt plot was hatching in Kentucky, Wayne was preparing to crush the Indian power in the Northwest. Wilkinson was second in command and participated in the battle of Fallen Timbers, for which action he was given official praise by Wayne. Wilkinson, however, could never be happy as second in command, and privately expressed his contempt for Wayne by labeling him "a liar, a drunkard, a Fool, . . . a Coward, a Hypocrite, and the contempt of every man of sense and virtue."

ENGLISH AND SPANISH TREATIES

The Wayne campaign was one of the indications that the national government was increasingly solicitous of western interests and desires. Western impatience with the continuation of English control in the Northwest and of Spanish control of the Mississippi was extremely apparent to President Washington and other eastern statesmen, who had long feared the possibility of western revolt. In consequence a sincere effort was made in the 1790s, not only to quiet the Indians, but also to negotiate treaties that would remove at least the major western grievances. First came the Jay Treaty with England (1794) which brought the transfer of the western posts the next year. After Wayne's death in December, 1796, Wilkinson became head of the western army; his receipts from Spain were then some $30,000, and the end was not yet.

The English treaty opened the way for an agreement with Spain, since Spain was no longer allied with England and consequently feared a joint English-American occupation of her North American possessions. This agreement took the form of the Treaty of San Lorenzo as negotiated by Thomas Pinckney in 1795. Spain agreed to accept the American contention of a northern boundary at 31° and to withdraw her troops to below that line. Even more important she agreed to the free navigation of the Mississippi and to a three-year right of deposit at New Orleans — the privilege of landing and storing goods for reshipment without paying duties. This right of deposit was to be continued after the three years, but not necessarily at New Orleans.

The signing of the Pinckney Treaty did not bring vital changes overnight. The right of free navigation was not exercised until December 1796, while the right of deposit and the completion of the transfer of western posts did not come until 1798. Governor Carondolet of New Orleans retained hope that the West might be detached from the Union and hence delayed in carrying out the concessions of the treaty while he dispatched bribe money to the north. The changing times became very evident when Wilkinson jailed the Spanish agent, Thomas Power.

While Carondolet procrastinated an American commissioner, Andrew Ellicott, arrived at Natchez to accept the land north of 31° and to survey boundaries. Quickly growing impatient at the failure of the Spaniards to withdraw, he gathered a small force of his own, persuaded some United States troops to come, and engineered a " revolution " by the American settlers. After the revolution the Spanish commandant still remained in nominal control, but the actual power was wielded by a committee of citizens from June 1797. When the Spanish posts were finally handed over to the United States Wilkinson was on hand to give all possible courtesies to the departing Spaniards.

FILIBUSTERING

The Natchez revolt was but one small indication of American interest in Spanish territory and of American willingness to use direct and drastic action if other means of acquisition failed. One of the more magnificent American plans was that of William Blount (1796), who probably had the idea of wresting Louisiana and the Floridas from Spain, presenting them to England, and receiving land grants in return; the premature disclosure of the plot led to Blount's expulsion from the Senate in 1797. During this same general period Philip Nolan, a Wilkinson protégé, was adventuring into Texas. William A. Bowles led several Florida filibustering expeditions, of which the most impressive was that of 1799–1801, which captured a trading post and fort, and fought a regular battle with a Spanish force. Ultimately Bowles died in Morro Castle.

These filibustering expeditions were based on a variety of motives. Uppermost, perhaps, was the idea of personal gain in plunder or trade or land. But along with this commercial spirit ordinarily went considerable patriotism, which was at least advanced as a justification. The authors took credit for the intention to free oppressed peoples or to add new territory to the United States. Whatever the real motivation such expeditions constituted one of the important steps by which the United States was to acquire new bits of territory during the coming half century.

FRENCH PLANS

The United States was not the only nation with an interest in Spanish territory, and actually it was France who first succeeded in detaching a piece of it. The French interest in Louisiana had existed throughout the 1790s, but had become particularly strong after 1795. Revolutionary France felt that it had a world mission, and that in particular the people of this former bit of the French colonial empire would welcome eagerly the French deliverer from a foreign oppressor. Prospective French control, however, was even more objectionable to the American West than Spanish ownership, since France would make a stronger and more aggressive neighbor. Western plots to join Spain or England or to conquer Louisiana were hence based in part on the desire to forestall French plans.

Easterners as well as westerners worried over the possibility of

French expansion. In the closing years of the century Alexander Hamilton backed an amazing plan to encourage war between Spain and France, and then in alliance with England to conquer the Floridas, Louisiana, and possibly untold other parts of the Spanish empire. Hamilton himself was to be in supreme military command. He sounded out many people, including Wilkinson, but ultimately nothing came of the plans. All such intrigues were meat and drink to Wilkinson, who could use them to frighten Spanish governors and thereby extract more Spanish money. In cold fact the plots were fairly chimerical, partly because the West in general was hostile to England and partly because Spanish concessions by 1800 had removed many of the causes for western action.

While Americans talked and plotted France was negotiating to obtain Louisiana. Spanish diplomats were superficially coy and reluctant, and frequently changed their minds, but they had no real objection to selling Louisiana any time after 1795 if the price were right. They saw the immense wilderness of Louisiana, inhabited by only some 50,000 people, as nothing but a drain on the Spanish treasury. The French-Spanish dickering eventually produced the mutually satisfactory Treaty of San Ildefonso in 1800, by which France received Louisiana. This treaty was secret, and for the time being the actual transfer of Louisiana was not made.

Napoleon had his hands freed for a prospective American colonial adventure in March 1802 when he signed the Peace of Amiens with England. Immediately he pushed for a quicker Spanish transfer, and signed a new treaty. The general French plan was for a populous North American colony which would trade primarily with the French West Indies sugar islands and with the homeland. As a basis for operations Charles V. E. Leclerc was sent to Santo Domingo with 20,000 troops; he arrived on the island early in the summer of 1802.

The year 1802 was a troublous time for the United States, and particularly for the West. Rumors were circulated of the transfer of Louisiana to France, and these rumors became more convincing as news came of the expedition of Leclerc. And then on October 18 the Intendant of Louisiana stopped the right of deposit at New Orleans. Even though the closing was actually brief and did not prevent American navigation of the Mississippi, the West went wild and talked freely of war. Quite commonly it added two and two and concluded that the end of the right of deposit had been inspired by Napoleon — which was actually not the case.

LOUISIANA PURCHASE

President Jefferson found himself in a difficult and embarrassing situation. He had long felt that the advance of American settlement would in time take care of the Spanish difficulties, but now this long-range optimism was less easy, and he did not underrate the willingness of the West to take its own action, nor did he minimize its separatist tendencies. Although Jefferson was a great lover of France and his French minister, Robert R. Livingston, was an even greater Francophile, conversations with Talleyrand brought only denials that Louisiana had been acquired. Meantime the Federalists were making political capital of the situation by urging immediate and forceful action, and Jefferson was always sensitive to political factors. Finally, and possibly most disturbing, Jefferson had grave constitutional doubts as to the right of the federal government to acquire new territory.

Jefferson at first tried to calm the West, while at the same time he put indirect pressure on France by suggesting that her American adventure might push the United States into an alliance with England. Simultaneously Livingston was making efforts to buy New Orleans, together with possible additional territory, but making no visible progress. As American sentiment increased in violence, Jefferson became more and more convinced of the urgency of the situation and finally decided upon a special French mission. His choice of an emissary was James Monroe, who was popular in the West; a $2,000,000 fund was made available for the use of Monroe. When Monroe sailed he had instructions to buy the Floridas and the Isle of Orleans (New Orleans) for not over $10,000,000, and permission to promise favored treatment to French vessels and trade, and even to guarantee French possession of the remainder of Louisiana. Alternate instructions envisaged the purchase of less territory even to the acquisition of a single town on the Mississippi for deposit. Finally, if Napoleon should sell nothing, Monroe and Livingston were authorized to cross the channel and make an English alliance.

Before Monroe appeared in France Napoleon had changed his mind about his proposed American empire. Difficulties in Santo Domingo possibly played a part in the change. The heroic resistance of the natives under Toussaint L'Ouverture had been backed effectively by the ravages of the yellow fever to produce thousands of French graves. But Napoleon was a soldier and expected to lose men in making a conquest, so late in 1802 he gathered a new expedition to occupy New Orleans; this armada failed to sail because of the cold winter. By the spring of 1803 a prospective renewal of the English war was the decisive factor in pushing the colonial project into obscurity. Napoleon exclaimed pettishly: " Damn sugar, damn coffee, damn colonies." To obtain funds for the English war he decided to sell Louisiana — and of course it would not be too difficult to conquer Louisiana if he changed his mind again.

While Monroe was still traveling toward Paris Talleyrand offered to sell Livingston all of Louisiana. Livingston exercised great self-restraint and reluctantly postponed a decision until Monroe appeared. The two men dickered but briefly before they closed the deal. The final treaty (1803) transferred all of Louisiana to the United States for about $15,000,000, of which approximately a quarter was used to settle United States claims on France. The boundaries of the acquisition were stated but vaguely, thus opening the way for many future disputes. The United States had taken advantage of European troubles to aid itself. Jefferson's scruples over the constitutionality of adding territory seemed easily overcome — apparently he was untroubled by the fact that the seller had promised not to dispose of the country and therefore the title might be considered defective.

The change of masters occurred late in 1803 at New Orleans, then a dilapidated city of some 8000. On November 30 Louisiana was transferred formally from Spain to France, and on December 20 from France to the United States. The American commissioners who accepted the cession were William C. C. Claiborne, the prospective governor, and James Wilkinson, head of the western army and the future governor of upper Louisiana Territory. Wilkinson must have felt considerable sorrow at the disappearance of his paymaster from New Orleans, but for the moment that sorrow was abated by a Spanish payment of $12,000, in return for which he penned lengthy " Reflections," of which he sent a modified version to Jefferson.

Permanent government provision for the new region was made early in 1804. All the portion outside the present Louisiana was made into Louisiana District, with Wilkinson as governor but with the judicial administration attached for the time being to Indiana Territory. In 1805 this area became Louisiana Territory and in 1812 Missouri Territory. The present Louisiana was constituted

Orleans Territory, but its eastern boundary fluctuated several times within the next eight years. Governor Claiborne was received by the French and Spanish with considerable skepticism and had serious administrative difficulties in his first years. In 1805 Orleans was given a goverment like that of the neighboring Mississippi Territory, and with the passage of years the administration came to operate with considerable smoothness. American occupation brought an immediate increase of population, so that in 1812 Louisiana could be admitted to the Union.

BURR

The acquisition of Louisiana should have put an end to western separatist movements and to the intrigues with Spain. Such, however, was not the case, for it was after the purchase of Louisiana that there occurred the most spectacular scheme of all, that associated with the name of a former United States Vice President — Aaron Burr.

Aaron Burr was an attractive personality — brilliant, restless and ambitious — with an ability to make money easily and an even greater ability to spend it rapidly. Trained as a lawyer, he fought in the Revolution and then entered politics, becoming successively Attorney-General of New York, member of the state legislature, United States Senator, and Vice President of the United States (1801–05). With the last of these positions the path of political opportunity seemed closed. Jefferson, head of the Republican party, had never forgiven Burr for failing to eliminate himself as a candidate for the Presidency when the election of 1800 was thrown into the House; while outwardly friendly, he continually frustrated Burr's desires. Furthermore, Burr had shot and killed his bitter enemy Hamilton in a duel on the fields of Weehawken, July 11, 1804. While Hamilton was at least as guilty in the quarrel as Burr, and while both men had had experience in such affairs of honor, a great popular outcry arose against the slayer of Hamilton.

Burr's troubles caused him to look forward to the end of his term as Vice President with uncertainty. Elective office either in New York or the nation seemed highly unlikely, and Jefferson refused to appoint him to any post commensurate with his attainments. On the other hand he was still active and vigorous, being as yet under fifty. In this unhappy situation his thoughts turned more and more to the West, where his duel with Hamilton would not injure his prestige, and where a fertile and ingenious mind would find plenty of stimulation in the traditional intrigues and plottings. Before making any decision Burr talked to a number of westerners, among whom was Wilkinson; in fact the two men corresponded for years in code, which was not unusual in a day when the carriers of dispatches frequently read their contents.

The plans which Burr eventually evolved still remain doubtful in content — probably in part because he changed his story with each auditor and partly because the people who later repeated his conversations wanted to justify themselves. Burr tried to raise money by approaching both the English and Spanish ministers. To the former he proposed an independent western state, with Burr to furnish the western army and England to provide $500,000 and a fleet at the mouth of the Mississippi. To the latter he outlined a fantastic plan which included western freedom and the capture of both New Orleans and Washington. Burr's plausibility receives strong testimony in the fact that he convinced both men of the desirability of giving him money; unfortunately he was too far distant to influence their respective bosses, and the funds did not materialize.

Soon after Burr completed his duties as Vice President in 1805 he and his beloved daughter Theodosia made a tour of the West. Burr was received everywhere with enthusiasm and acclaim, while his daughter was taken to the West's heart. Inevitably Burr talked to hundreds of men, including Jackson and Clay, but what he said to them is uncertain, since as usual he probably varied his story to appeal to the particular listener. Four days were spent at Fort Massac in earnest conversation with Wilkinson, but again the subjects discussed remain uncertain.

Burr returned to the West in August 1806, at which time he began to collect men and supplies for a rendezvous late in the year on an island in the Ohio River. These activities inspired the wildest of rumors and the revival of old plots and intrigues. Accusations of treason were made and twice Burr was arrested; each time he convinced the grand jury that he planned nothing more than colonization. Jefferson heard these rumors of treason, but took no immediate action. Ultimately a disappointingly small party of thirty men embarked on nine boats and started the long trip down the river. By this time Jefferson had apparently become alarmed, for he issued a warrant for Burr's arrest, which followed the expedition down the river.

The actions of Wilkinson during 1806 are as difficult to explain as those of Burr. Wilkinson had been in perpetual trouble as governor at St. Louis, and so in June 1806 had been ordered to move to the vicinity of New Orleans. These orders he obeyed with the greatest of leisure, moving first by way of Natchez to Natchitoches, where a slight border trouble gave some pretext for deviation from a direct route. At Natchitoches he inquired among his men concerning a possible expedition against Mexico, but could evince no enthusiasm. By September he had returned to Natchez, leaving his army to make its own way to New Orleans.

At Natchez Wilkinson apparently finally made up his mind as to his proper actions. Rather belatedly he sent a note to Jefferson warning him of the Burr expedition, of which the destination was given as Vera Cruz. Incidentally he also warned Spain and Mexico, even dispatching a man on an unsuccessful mission to Mexico City to collect payment for this information. After warning Jefferson he rushed to New Orleans, where to the surprise of everyone he declared martial law and worked frenziedly to prepare the city against an attack. Apparently he had decided to become the " Savior of the West."

Meantime Burr had been floating leisurely down the river, unaware of the warrant for his arrest and the preparations of Wilkinson. Ultimately he heard of the warrant, became panic-stricken and tried to escape overland in disguise. He was captured by Edmund Gaines on February 19, 1807, and taken to Richmond to stand trial before Chief Justice Marshall for a misdemeanor and for treason. He was adjudged not guilty, but the political factors of the trial made the verdict not completely satisfactory. Burr's public career was ended, even though he lived until 1837. As for Wilkinson, he gave very inconclusive testimony in the Burr trial, since he had also to vindicate himself. His own conduct was so obviously suspicious that he was investigated by Congressional and military committees. His explanations of various peculiar actions and letters were rather thin, but conclusive evidence was lacking and he was exonerated in each case. Before his retirement he participated in the War of 1812, but with no credit to himself.

Before leaving Burr, it is only fair to give him the opportunity to say a few words in his own behalf. During his last years he described his early plans and ambitions by declaring: " I am not a libertine · I am not a murderer; I am not a traitor. I never broke a promise to a woman in my life. I did not intend to kill Hamilton and did not shoot first. I never got within ten thousand leagues of a wish to break up the United States by a separatist or a secession movement, although I did hope to establish an empire in Mexico and to become its emperor."

The Burr episode marked at least a temporary end of western plans for independence; not until settlement crossed the Rockies were any such ideas again advanced seriously. By the early nineteenth century there no longer was any question that the Mississippi Valley would remain a part of the United States. In fact the West was in the process of becoming even more blatantly patriotic than the East, with desires of expanding the Union to bring its blessings to neighboring peoples. This highly nationalistic and expansionist sentiment was soon to be given vivid expression by Henry Clay and the other War Hawks.

READINGS

T. P. Abernethy, *The Burr Conspiracy* (1954)—very good, *From Frontier to Plantation* (1932), ch. 6; H. Alexander, *Aaron Burr* (1937)—adverse; E. S. Brown, *The Constitutional History of the Louisiana Purchase* (1920)—accurate; C. M. Burson, *The Stewardship of Don Esteban Miro* (1942); J. W. Caughey, *Bernardo de Galvez in Louisiana* (1934)—fine; W. Havighurst, *Land of Promise* (1946), ch. 13; T. R. Hay and M. R. Werner, *The Admirable Trumpeter* (1941)—Wilkinson; C. N. Howard, *The British Development of West Florida* (1947)—monograph; J. R. Jacobs, *The Beginning of the United States Army* (1947), chs. 8–10, 12, *Tarnished Warrior* (1938)—Wilkinson; J. A. James, *The Life of George Rogers Clark* (1928), chs. 17, 18; L. Kinnaird (ed.), *Spain in the Mississippi Valley, 1765–1794* (7 vols., 1949); E. W. Lyon, *Louisiana in French Diplomacy* (1934)—monograph; W. H. Masterson, *William Blount* (1954), chs. 10, 11; N. Schachner, *Aaron Burr* (1937)—defense; R. O. Shreve, *The Finished Scoundrel* (1933), chs. 4–17; J. W. Silver, *Edmund Pendleton Gaines* (1949), ch. 2—dull; S. H. Wandell and M. Minnigerode, *Aaron Burr* (2 vols., 1925), vol. 2, parts 6–8; A. P. Whitaker, *The Mississippi Question* (1934), *The Spanish American Frontier* (1927)—fine monographs; J. Wilkinson, *James Wilkinson* (1935)—defense.

CHAPTER 10

BEYOND
THE MISSISSIPPI

THE territory which the United States acquired by the purchase of Louisiana was sufficiently vast and vague to stagger the imagination of most men. Only small parts of it had ever been visited by white men, and rumors as to its characteristics were wild and undependable. Even its exact boundaries were unknown. For the time being it was something of a white elephant to the young and struggling republic.

EXPLORATION OF LOUISIANA

The Louisiana country, like any unexplored region, attracted considerable attention merely because it was unknown. Even in earlier years various adventurous souls had looked at it speculatively. Jefferson had been interested scientifically many years before he had any thought of buying the territory. In 1786, while minister to France, he talked with the migratory John Ledyard in Paris, and the two men planned that Ledyard would cross Siberia to Kamchatka, then sail across the Pacific and finally make the overland journey through the Louisiana territory. Ledyard was a happy choice for such an expedition, being an inveterate wanderer of considerable ability, and happy only when seeing new places and people. He started across Russia in 1786, traveling mostly by foot, but he was eventually stopped and turned back by Russian officials, whereupon he went to Africa, where he died in 1788.

Other plans to explore the Far West soon followed those of Ledyard. Captain John Armstrong made the attempt in 1790, but was turned back by the Indians. André Michaux, the French botanist, started west in 1793, but was embroiled in the Genêt intrigue and did not travel beyond the Mississippi. Michaux was backed by America's most important scientific body, the American Philosophical Society, which supported him because of Jefferson's recommendation. Other persons also considered the long overland trip to the Pacific, but none of these projected expeditions was completed within the territorial limits of the present United States prior to 1800.

LEWIS AND CLARK

These various plans, and especially those sponsored by Jefferson, made it almost certain that when Louisiana became United States territory (at the same time that Jefferson was President) further plans for the exploration of the territory would be inaugurated. Actually Jefferson had requested and received permission from Congress even before the purchase of Louisiana to organize an expedition for the exploration of the region west of the Mississippi (January 1803). For its leadership he chose Captain Meriwether Lewis (born 1774) and William Clark (born 1770). Lewis had been Jefferson's private secretary and Clark was a brother of the famous George Rogers Clark. These men were personal friends, and both were acquainted with the ways of the wilderness. Lewis started west shortly after his appointment, arriving at Pittsburgh in the summer of 1803. Both here and farther down the Ohio he gathered men and supplies. The party spent the winter of 1803–04 in Illinois, nearly opposite the mouth of the Missouri.

The real start of the expedition occurred on May 13, 1804, at which time the ascent of the Missouri River was begun. The party was composed of some 30 men, of whom about half were drawn from the army and the other half enlisted for the duration of the trip. Each man was expected to keep notes of all he observed, and oilskin wrappers were provided to protect the notes from the elements. The general aims of the expedition, as stated in its instructions, were primarily scientific. The men were to explore the land, rivers, and mountains from the Mississippi to the coast, to take observations of all animal and vegetable life and all mineral resources, to observe the manners and customs of all the natives, and to promote friendly relations with the Indian tribes of the region. These aims were anything but modest for a small body of white men entering the thousands of square miles of unknown country which extended westward from the Mississippi.

Progress up the Missouri was necessarily slow. A fifty-five foot keelboat carried most of the supplies and equipment; it was outfitted with a large square sail, but most of the time the wind was not favorable and the vessel had to be dragged upstream at the end of a rope. Progress was further delayed by the necessity of conferring with the Indians, informing them of their new masters, and trying to obtain their good will by means of presents. By the end of October the party had progressed as far as the Mandan villages, which were near the site of the present Bismarck, North Dakota. The winter of 1804–05 was spent among the Mandans, who were friendly to the whites. After building a stockade and several log cabins the men rested and collected provisions; they also added to their party an interpreter, who was a necessity for the trip farther west. Even with the interpreter, who was an Indian woman, there was great difficulty in communicating with some of the tribes which were encountered. Sometimes it was necessary to translate a speech half a dozen times before the principals could understand each other. Such a procedure, particularly when carried out badly by natives of insufficient linguistic knowledge, was not conducive to an accurate understanding.

With the coming of spring the expedition resumed its journey up the river in pirogues and canoes; the keelboat was sent back to St. Louis. It left the Mandan villages on April 7, and on the 26th of the same month arrived at the mouth of the Yellowstone, where some difficulty was experienced in determining which was the main stream. After spending a month portaging the Great Falls, it eventually arrived (July 25) at the three forks, which were given the names Jefferson, Madison, and Gallatin. Any one of the three branches offered almost equal possibilities for the continuance of the journey, and consequently considerable time was spent in exploring all three. Finally the most westerly, the Jefferson, was chosen and it and then the Beaverhead was followed to about the present Dillon, Montana. Then the party abandoned the river and prepared to make the next stage of the trip by land.

Lewis and Clark were in an unenviable position when they left their canoes and started forward on foot. Already they were nearly two thousand miles from civilization, having crossed an untracked wilderness and braved the perils of starvation, accident, and disease. They had traversed countless miles of wilderness in which an unwise gesture would have meant annihilation by the Indians. All these difficulties remained to be met again on the return trip,

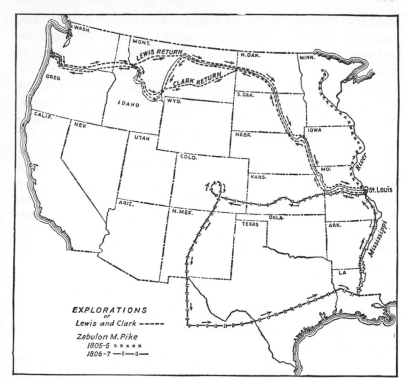

EXPLORATIONS
OF
Lewis and Clark - - - - -
Zebulon M.Pike
1805-6 × × × × ×
1806-7 —‖—‖—

but the hardest part of the journey still lay ahead of them if they were to reach the Pacific. The unknown Rocky Mountains had to be crossed in the face of approaching winter; supplies were running low, native guidance was poor, and the hostile Blackfeet occupied the country which they were approaching. The decision to push farther west in the face of these obstacles required the highest courage and resolution.

The pedestrian part of the trip was begun in August under the leadership of unwilling guides who had to be guarded to prevent their desertion. Snow fell by September 3, making the mountain passes exceedingly dangerous. On September 7 the party was near the present Idaho line at Grantdale, Montana, and from there it followed the Lo Lo Creek and Lo Lo Pass (Nez Percé Pass) through the mountains. Frequently the men floundered in the snow; most of the time they were wet and cold, and provisions were so scanty that hunger was the ordinary condition. Eventually they passed the mountains and struck a branch of the Clearwater, where they built five canoes. The remainder of the westward trail followed the Clearwater, the Snake, and the Columbia, including a portage at The Dalles on the Columbia. The main objective of the expedition was attained when the Pacific Ocean was sighted on November 7, 1805.

Reaching the Pacific Ocean was a notable accomplishment, but from the standpoint of Lewis and Clark, a good half of the work remained to be done. The homeward trip still bristled with obstacles, and additional exploration was much to be desired. For the time being, the men constructed winter quarters at the mouth of the Columbia and made preparations for the return trip. The eastward journey began on March 23, 1806, the party retracing the path which had been followed westward through the mountains. Difficulties in obtaining food increased with the depletion of trading goods, and Lewis and Clark posed as doctors to secure the needed supplies. After the mountains had been crossed, the group was divided, half going north with Lewis and then descending the Marais River while the other half under Clark followed the Yellowstone. The two parties were reunited at the mouth of the Yellowstone on August 12, and from this point the trip down the river was comparatively easy. The Mandan villages were passed on August 14, and on September 23, 1806, the party was back in St. Louis.

The significance of the Lewis and Clark expedition lay in the fact that it was the first trip by white men overland through the present continental United States to the Pacific Ocean. The magnitude of the feat was in no wise lessened by the even more marvelous trip of Alexander Mackenzie, who had reached the ocean through Canadian territory a full decade before — on July 22, 1793. It marked the beginning of accurate knowledge concerning the Far West, for the journals kept by the men were gradually published in the East. Unfortunately some of the diaries were lost, but those which remained gave the only reliable facts which hitherto had been collected about the Far Northwest.

The expedition was also notable for the remarkably effective way in which it had been handled. Thirty white men had been taken without a serious mishap through 6000 miles of wilderness inhabited by potentially hostile Indians. For this service, Lewis was rewarded with the governorship of Louisiana Territory, which post he held until a bullet cut short his life in 1809. Clark entered the fur trade, and was governor of Missouri until it became a state. He then became Superintendent of Indian Affairs at St. Louis, holding this position until his death in 1838.

OTHER EXPLORERS

The expedition of Lewis and Clark was but the first of a long series of governmental efforts to obtain complete and accurate information concerning the country west of the Mississippi. Even before Lewis and Clark were well started, Congress authorized (1804) the exploration of a number of the rivers in the Great Plains region — the Panis (Platte), the Paduca (Kansas), the Morsigona (Des Moines), and the St. Peters (Minnesota). Separate parties were picked for surveying each of these rivers but, while all of them did some work, the total results were disappointing. William Hunter and George Dunbar, both well-known scientists, led a small party up the Ouachita of Louisana in the winter of 1804–05; while they covered this river satisfactorily they did not reach the Red River, in which Jefferson was particularly interested. A short time later (1806) Thomas Freeman ascended the Red River for some 600 miles before he was turned back by a superior Spanish force.

PIKE

Of the minor expeditions the most important were the two under the command of Zebulon Montgomery Pike. Pike was a young army officer and did his exploring under the orders of James Wilkinson, who was in command in the West. By orders dated July 30, 1805, he was instructed to ascend and find the source of the Mississippi, survey Indian conditions, and locate possible military routes. On his way north he stopped at the present St. Paul, Minnesota, where he bought a considerable area of land just south of the falls of the Mississippi as a site for a military post. Resuming his journey, he was much troubled by the difficulties of travel, for by this time it was mid-winter. At Sandy Lake (January 8, 1806) he found a post of the Northwest Company, a Canadian venture. Here Pike made a noble and futile gesture by ordering the company to pay duty on all goods brought across the international boundary, and to refrain from selling liquor to the Indians. Considering the smallness of Pike's force, its distance from effective support, and the actual nonexistence of an ascertainable boundary, such orders must have sounded ludicrous to Canadian ears.

Pike continued from Sandy Lake to Leech Lake, where he arrived on February 1, 1806. Here he ended his advance to the north, since he mistakenly considered Leech Lake to be the source of the

Mississippi. His return trip to St. Louis was slow and uneventful. The results of this first expedition of Pike were disappointingly meager. He had found what he thought to be the source of the Mississippi; he had bought land which was later to furnish the site of an important army post; he had made a futile gesture toward the Northwest Company; and he had added a little information to the slowly growing body of knowledge about the West.

Immediately upon his return (1806) he received new orders to explore the headwaters of the Arkansas and Red rivers. Leaving St. Louis on July 15 with twenty-two men he ascended the Missouri and Osage rivers and then crossed overland to the Arkansas River which he followed through what is now southern Kansas. His plan was to ascend the Arkansas, cross to the Red, and descend the latter stream to its junction with the Mississippi. The farther west he moved, the nearer he came to Spanish territory, and although the exact boundary line was as yet undetermined, the Spanish government became alarmed. A force of 600 Spanish dragoons under Lieutenant Don Facundo Malgares was therefore dispatched to keep Pike and his party out of Spanish territory. Pike heard rumors of this hostile Spanish expedition and so stopped and built fortifications on the site of Pueblo, Colorado. Incidentally he took the time to start the ascent of the peak which now bears his name. As it happened his fears of the Spanish force proved groundless, for Malgares never found him.

In December Pike took a small part of his force and started south, ostensibly to find the source of the Red River. The weather was bitterly cold, he had but the vaguest idea of where he was going, and the men had to fight a grim struggle with snow and hunger. Eventually they came to a river, which Pike said later he thought was the Red, and built a stockade. The building of the stockade was a very wise precaution in view of the fact that the river on which it was constructed was actually the Rio Grande and the party was probably within Spanish territory. Unfortunately the rude fort did not prove a sufficient protection and when a hundred Spanish troops appeared on the scene, Pike was forced to give himself up as a prisoner.

After the capture of Pike, there remained the perplexing question of what should be done with him. If his party were considered hostile the penalty might be severe, but if the presumed invasion of Spanish territory were actually an accident, then the invaders should be treated more leniently. The Spanish captain felt incapable of deciding the case and so took Pike first to Santa Fe and then south through El Paso to Chihuahua. Meantime Pike was making copious notes on the country through which he passed, hiding them carefully so that they would not be confiscated. At Chihuahua it was decided to return Pike to the United States, and so he was escorted by way of San Antonio to Natchitoches and there handed over to the United States troops (July 1, 1807). During this return trip he again took voluminous notes. The net result was that Pike, although not carrying out his orders to explore the Red River, brought home a great amount of information to be added to American knowledge of the Southwest, and which resulted in the stimulation of interest in the Texas region.

All these governmental expeditions, as well as a considerable number of private ventures, helped to push back the frontier of knowledge concerning the Far West. The principal geographical features became known, although vast quantities of detailed information still remained to be gathered. The wild animal and plant life of the western plains was revealed. The main tribes of Indians were differentiated and their characteristics enumerated. Of especial importance to the later explorer and trapper were the location and traits of the Indian tribes of the western plains, and although their greatest significance did not come until some years later, the general tribal habits of life merit at least a brief description.*

PLAINS INDIANS

The plains Indians were among the most powerful groups on the continent, and their general characteristics were somewhat similar because of the uniformity of the country over which they roamed. As a whole they were less agricultural than the tribes farther east. Part of the explanation for this lay in the lower stage of development of Indian civilization, but the greater part was accounted for by the nature of the country. The open, treeless, semiarid plains of the Far West offered less encouragement to agriculture than did the better watered country farther east. In addition the western plains were ideally suited to the support of what seemed to be an inexhaustible supply of food — the buffalo. It was upon this noble animal that the Indians depended for the greater share of their necessities of life. Its meat, which was preserved by smoking and drying, was the Indians' principal food. Its skin, after being tanned

* For the general location of the principal tribes see the map on p. 13.

with its brains, made clothing, shoes, tents, and blankets; its bones furnished such implements as knives and hoes, and even at times bows; its tendons were used for thread and for bow strings. Even its entrails furnished a part of the Indian domestic economy, for the intestines were used in making sausages and the bladder for a water bag.

The buffalo moved across the plains in huge herds, so the Indians too were nomadic. The usual Indian domicile was the temporary wigwam or tepee — constructed of a framework of slanting, crossed poles covered with joined buffalo skins. Permanent wooden houses were rare. Traveling was done with the aid of a travois, which was an arrangement of poles, with one end lashed to the horse and the other dragging on the ground; on these poles were lashed the wigwam, clothing, sleeping robes, and cooking and eating utensils, with frequently a child or two perched on top. Horses were a necessity, being used much more than farther east. These horses were small and shaggy, and had their origin in the Spanish territory to the south. Every Indian was a good horseman, since children were taught to ride almost as soon as to walk. The greatest use of the horse, outside of traveling and fighting, was in hunting buffalo. In the usual buffalo hunt, horsemen rode into the herd and shot their quarry from close range. A miscalculation probably meant death under the hoofs of the frightened animals. Because arrows were scarce and hard to make they were recovered at the end of a hunt, and it was considered very unfortunate if an arrow only wounded a buffalo, for then the arrow was lost. Buffalo hunts sometimes took the form of driving the animals into a corral, where they could be dispatched at the hunter's leisure. At other times the buffalos were driven over a cliff and thus slaughtered by the hundred.

Many of the activities of the western Indians were similar to those of their eastern brethren. Chiefs obtained their offices from popular choice, and had but vague powers. Scalps taken in war proved that the brave had come sufficiently close to the enemy to touch him. Horse stealing conferred on the thief honor only second to touching the enemy. Prisoners were rarely tortured; usually they were either enslaved or adopted into the tribe. The division of labor was practically the same as in the East. The men hunted, fished, and fought, while the women did the rest of the work. The position of a woman was comparatively good. She had rights that her husband must respect, and often participated in ceremonial dances and tribal councils. Children belonged to the clan of the mother.

Marriage customs were fairly uniform all over the western plains, even though they varied in detail. Women married young and were ordinarily acquired by some form of purchase. Polygamy was accepted universally, but was practiced only by a few of the wealthier men. Divorce occurred in most cases only on the wish of the husband, but here and there either party could take the initiative. Infidelity by the wife was frequently punished by the amputation of the end of her nose by her husband; infidelity by the husband was punished by the relatives of the wife. Women were ordinarily considered unclean during their menstrual periods, at which time they frequently lived by themselves in small temporary shelters. Childbirth seemed to be accomplished with ease, and was not allowed to interfere with the regular activities of the mother. No assistance was given except in the case of the first-born child. Immediately after the birth the woman washed herself and the new baby in the nearest stream, even if the weather were so cold that she must first chop a hole in the ice.

Medical care was furnished by medicine men in almost the same way as in the East. The main effort was to drive out the wicked spirits by elaborate ceremonies, although simple herbs and sucking were also used. Infectious diseases were beyond the power of the Indian doctor, and white men's diseases such as smallpox and syphilis brought frightful mortality. Surgery was so primitive that when an arm or leg was broken it was almost never set properly, and there was no assurance that the limb could be used in the future.

Burials were made in every conceivable form — on a platform, in the trees, on the ground and covered with stones, and in the ground. Surviving friends and relatives had a period of mourning in which they lamented with loud and doleful howls. Female members of the household (particularly the widow) would often cut their hair, gash their arms and legs, and even cut off fingers to show their grief.

Utensils and weapons varied so widely among the western Indians that generalization becomes impossible. Vessels might be simple wooden, horn, or bone receptacles, but they might also be glazed clay with elaborate designs. Material for clothes, blankets, and tents ranged from poorly tanned buffalo hides to well-woven cloth and waterproof blankets. Bows, arrows, lances, clubs, shields, and knives varied from tribe to tribe, depending largely on the kind of material which was available in the particular region.

Each tribe had elaborate dances and ceremonials, of which many were long and complex. They were designed to ward off evil spirits and propitiate good ones, so that the corn would grow well, rain would fall, buffalo would be plentiful, the young men brave, war successful, disease and accident absent, and all other good things which the Indian desired would come true. Frequently a dance was mimicry of the thing desired, as in the case of a pantomime buffalo hunt. The dancing took the form of short, jerky steps, together with a vertical movement of the body. Most of the dances were only for men, but a few were especially for the women, and some were for both sexes. In almost every case there was an accompaniment of song and instrumental music. The most common musical instrument was the drum. The drummer and the singer made no effort to agree in their rhythms, each doing a solo; the result was weird and unearthly to the visitor accustomed to the musical traditions of the whites. In addition to all sizes and shapes of drums, a varied assortment of rattles and simple whistles were in common use. More rare was the flute, which was a variation of the whistle, and was made only by a few tribes. The flute was used only for love songs, and even then but rarely, so that few whites ever heard it in its original Indian use.

The western Indians loved funny stories and practical jokes. They had strong family affection and were reasonably loquacious. They reveled in games of all kinds. A child had a sled and a hoop, bow and arrow, dolls, and other similar delights; the boys favored war games and the girls liked to play house. Adults had many sports including several ball games, kissing games, guessing contests, and various dice games — the dice being possibly marked plum pits or bones. Both men and women participated, and betting was universal.

Each Indian tribe had its legends of spirits, mythological heroes, and animals who spoke understandably, as well as fabulous tales of the origin of particular kinds of animals, parts of the country, and the human race. Many good and bad spirits were thought to inhabit the world, and usually there was a supreme good spirit and a happy hunting ground. Great dependence was placed on dreams and visions. Most tribes had their mythological " culture heroes," about whom long tales were told. Other stories explained the making of the world, the appearance of people, the creation of the buffalo, and similar great mysteries. Ordinarily such tales were told only at night, and then by a commonly accepted story-teller, who made an elaborate ceremony of the narration.

In spite of their general similarities, the plains Indians were by no means a homogeneous people. Racial stocks varied, and customs, equipment, mythology, and personal characteristics were dissimilar. Some tribes were traditionally friendly with each other, while others were ordinarily hostile. Each group occupied a fairly definite portion of the plains, although periodic migrations served to change the whole picture from time to time. It would be erroneous to consider all of the tribes as but a part of one large group with uniform characteristics.

INDIVIDUAL TRIBES

Probably the most highly civilized, friendly, and peaceful group in the West was the Mandan. Lewis and Clark spent the winter of 1804–05 with them, and later travelers almost inevitably visited at least a few days with these hospitable people. The Mandan were a branch of the Sioux and probably at one time were a numerous group, but by the early nineteenth century they had been reduced to two comparatively small villages. They fought but little, and were more agricultural than their neighbors. Personal cleanliness was carried to a high point, baths in the Missouri River being a daily occurrence for most. In addition they utilized a primitive type of steam bath — a tight hut in which water was thrown upon hot stones. After the bather had remained in the hut as long as possible, he plunged into the river for a final dip.

A Mandan house was large and permanent, being forty to sixty feet in diameter. Four large center poles supported the roof. The walls were constructed of logs, and were built vertically at the bottom, tapering toward the top. The entire structure was covered with mud and was sufficiently strong to support the weight of the entire family on pleasant days. The ground inside the house was dug down for about two feet and then trampled hard. The fire was in the center and the smoke escaped through a hole in the roof. Such a house was sufficiently large to be the home of between twenty and forty persons.

Family life was highly developed among the Mandan. Polygamy was commonly accepted, but was too expensive except for a few of the chiefs. Female chastity was valued highly. A girl ordinarily became a bride somewhere between the ages of eleven and fourteen, being sold by her father to the successful suitor. Young children, especially boys, were trained carefully to be brave and self-reliant. Every summer the boys participated in a sham battle, which gave them a realistic sample of future war.

The most important celebration of the Mandan was a long symbolic ceremony in the spring. It honored the falling of the water in the river after the spring floods, celebrated the appearance of new vegetation, and initiated the young men into the full membership of the tribe. Songs and ceremonies occupied four days, with the height of the festivity coming on the fourth day. At this time all the young men to be initiated were gathered in a central lodge. Each in turn had portions of the skin of the chest or back, upper arm, lower arm, upper leg, and lower leg lifted, incisions made, and splints introduced. Then the youth was hoisted by ropes attached to the splints of the chest or back until his feet left the ground; weights were hung to all the splints, and he was revolved until he fainted. Meanwhile everyone in the building shouted to sustain the group morale and to drown the young man's groans. After the initiate fainted he was lowered and allowed to recover consciousness. Then he was taken to one side of the room and the little finger of his left hand chopped off. Finally he was escorted outside and run or dragged until the weights at the ends of the splints tore the wood through the flesh and freed him.

The Mandan initiation ceremony was unusually cruel, but it furnished unmistakable proof of the endurance and stoicism of the initiate, and indelibly impressed upon him the importance of full membership in the tribe. It also illuminated the paradoxical nature of the Indians, for these gruesome rites were practiced by a tribe which was one of the most peaceful, friendly, and good-natured in the West. Ultimately the Mandan were almost annihilated by a yellow fever epidemic in the latter 1830s.

On all sides of the Mandan, but particularly to the west, lay the powerful Sioux. They occupied the entire country from the Minnesota region to the sources of the Missouri, and numbered about 50,000 persons. In general they were typical of the majority of the plains Indians. They lived in buffalo skin tepees, were nomadic, and excelled as horsemen, hunters, and fighters. They had an initiation ceremony which was like that of the Mandan, but not so severe.

The proudest of the plains Indians were the Crow, who lived near the headwaters of the Yellowstone in present southern Montana. The Crow despised the whites as inferiors and were continually at war with the neighboring tribes. By common report their women were noted for their lack of moral standards. The Crow were exceeded in their warlike propensities by the Blackfeet, who lived to the northwest in the present Idaho and eastern Montana. The Blackfeet were more consistently hostile to the whites than any other plains tribe, and they were known as both ferocious and cruel. They lived entirely by hunting, practicing no agriculture. Like many other Indians, they removed all the hair from their bodies.

In the Rocky Mountain region and along the Pacific Coast were innumerable tribal groups. For the most part these tribes by the early nineteenth century were small, poverty-stricken, filthy and degraded. They lived chiefly on fish and roots, with now and then such delicacies as grasshopper pie. Their principal accomplishment was the weaving of baskets, of which some were so well constructed as to hold water. One of the northern tribes flattened the heads of its children by strapping a board on the top of the new baby's skull; this group, however, was not the one known as the Flathead. The best of the Far Western tribes, and one which furnished a notable exception to the general characteristics of the inhabitants of the region was the Nez Percé. These Indians lived on the lower Snake River and its tributaries, and were an extremely able and dignified group of people.

In the Central Plains region lived several very powerful tribes. The Cheyenne and the Arapaho (in permanent alliance) occupied the region of the headwaters of the Platte, and were typical plains Indians. The Cheyenne have received in the writings of George Bird Grinnell the best description given any Indian tribe. East of the Cheyenne, in present western Nebraska, were the Pawnee — another typical plains group. The Pawnee have received unusual attention because of one of their ceremonies which included a human sacrifice, and which was practiced as late as 1838. In the spring, a young girl, a virgin, was shot, and her flesh and blood used in an elaborate and symbolic ceremonial to fertilize the fields of corn. South of the Pawnee lived the Osage, a small tribe roaming over the region which is now western Kansas and eastern Colorado; its hereditary chieftainship was one of its few unusual characteristics. West of the Cheyenne were the Shoshoni of the Salt Lake district, who were commonly known as " Root Diggers " or " Snakes " (the name coming from the Snake River). They were poor, miserable, and dirty, living mostly on roots since game was scarce and the land was not easily cultivated. Usually they were peaceful.

Two of the most feared tribes of the plains, the Apache and Comanche, lived to the south in the present Arizona, New Mexico, and western Texas. Both were wild, uncivilized, cruel, fierce, and warlike. Prisoners were enslaved, and sometimes tortured; women prisoners were almost always raped. Both tribes were migratory, not practicing agriculture and having no permanent villages.

Two minor groups in the South were notable for their high civilizations. The Pueblo Indians, living for the most part in present New Mexico, were the remnants of a highly organized and prosperous tribe; their stone houses, excellent implements, and irrigated fields all indicated a former state of opulence. West of them, on the lower Colorado, were the Navaho. Although the Navaho lacked permanent homes, they raised various grains and fruits, herded cattle, sheep, mules, horses, and asses, and made excellent blankets and coarse woolen goods.

It was with these various plains Indians that Lewis and Clark, Pike, and their later successors came in contact. At times they were peaceful and encouraged the process of western exploration and settlement; at other times they were hostile and necessitated the use of thousands of soldiers for their subjugation. In any case, their mere existence was one of the most important potential dangers which the western explorer and settler had to face. Many years were to pass before they were finally reduced to a powerless state of dependence.

READINGS

EXPLORATION: J. Bakeless, *The Eyes of Discovery* (1950), ch. 20—Lewis and Clark—*Lewis and Clark* (1947)—very good; J. B. Brebner, *The Explorers of North America, 1492–1806* (1933), ch. 24; C. H. Carey, *A General History of Oregon* (2 vols., 1935–36), ch. 10—dull on Lewis and Clark; W. E. Connelley, *History of Kansas* (5 vols., 1928), vol. 1, chs. 4, 6—factual; B. De Voto, *The Course of Empire* (1952), chs. 10–12—Lewis and Clark— (ed.), *The Journals of Lewis and Clark* (1953); G. W. Fuller, *The Inland Empire* (3 vols., 1928), vol. 1, chs. 6, 7; L. R. Hafen (ed.), *Colorado and Its People* (4 vols., 1948), vol. 1, ch. 5; B. Harris, *John Colter* (1952)—accompanied Lewis and Clark; W. E. Hollon, *The Lost Pathfinder Zebulon Montgomery Pike* (1949)—very good; E. Hueston, *Star of the West* (1935)—journalistic on Lewis and Clark; J. Mirsky, *The Westward Crossings* (1946)—semi-popular; J. Monaghan, *The Overland Trail* (1947), ch. 2—Lewis and Clark; A. P. Nasatir, *Before Lewis and Clark* (1952)—upper Missouri River; B. Nelson, *Land of the Dacotahs* (1946), ch. 5—Lewis and Clark; G. L. Nute, *Caesars of the Wilderness* (1943)—early French explorers; R. G. Thwaites, *Brief History of Rocky Mountain Exploration* (1904); M. S. Wade, *Mackenzie of Canada* (1927)—good.

INDIANS: E. D. Branch, *The Hunting of the Buffalo* (1929); J. W. Caughey, *California* (1940), ch. 2, *History of the Pacific Coast* (1933), chs. 2, 3—well written; C. Coan, *A History of New Mexico* (3 vols., 1925), vol. 1, chs. 2–9—detailed; F. Densmore, *The American Indians and Their Music* (1926); E. Fergusson, *New Mexico* (1951), ch. 8; G. W. Fuller, *The Inland Empire* (3 vols., 1928), vol. 1, chs. 4, 5; G. B. Grinnell, *By Cheyenne Campfires* (1926)—stories—*The Cheyenne Indians* (2 vols., 1923), *The Fighting Cheyennes* (1915); F. B. Linderman, *American* (1930), *Red Mother* (1932); F. C. Lockwood, *The Apache Indians* (1938)—good; R. H. Lowie, *The Crow Indians* (1935)—good; B. E. Mahan, *Old Fort Crawford* (1926), chs. 1–3; B. Nelson, *Land of the Dacotahs* (1946), ch. 2—Sioux; R. H. Ogle, *Federal Control of the Western Apaches, 1848–1886* (1940), ch. 1 —reads fairly well; R. N. Richardson, *The Comanche Barrier* (1933), pp. 15–53; R. Santee, *Apache Land* (1947)—random and episodical; J. W. Schultz and J. L. Donaldson, *The Sun God's Children* (1930)—Blackfeet; H. H. Sibley, *Iron Face* (1950)— reminiscences of Sioux warrior; L. Standing Bear, *My People the Sioux* (1928); R. M. Underhill, *Red Man's America* (1953), chs. 8–13; E. Wallace and E. A. Hoebel, *The Comanches* (1952) —sociological approach; G. D. Wagner and W. A. Allen, *Blankets and Moccasins* (1933); R. K. Wyllys, *Arizona* (1950), ch. 1— thin and factual.

CHAPTER 11

THE
FUR TRADE

A WILDERNESS drew traders and trappers as well as explorers, since wild country was valuable chiefly for its furs, and trail breaking paid the largest dividends. Lewis and Clark met trappers on the Great Plains and Pike found them near the source of the Mississippi. The Daniel Boone type of frontiersman was the one who ordinarily first surveyed the country and whose reports led to the coming of agricultural settlers. The trapper was thus important both because of the magnitude of the business which he represented and because of his position in the vanguard of white settlement.

The first large-scale American business upon any new frontier had always been the collection of furs, whether by catching the animals or by trading with the Indians. Fine furs such as beaver, otter, mink, and fox were especially desired, but coarse furs such as buffalo, bear, and deer could be used for lap robes and heavy coats. Buffalo tongues, buffalo and bear tallow, and a few other commodities could be marketed.

SPANISH AND FRENCH

The Spanish, who were the first arrivals in the New World, evinced but little interest in the fur business in the early days. They dreamed of precious metals and stones, and trading for furs seemed a less profitable and more prosaic business. From time to time individual trappers and trapping companies were licensed, but for many years they remained relatively unimportant. Not until Spanish power in North America had nearly vanished did the trappers and traders of Spanish extraction attain any considerable importance.

It was the French who were responsible for the development of the American fur business as a large-scale enterprise. They worked up the St. Lawrence and through the Great Lakes to the Mississippi basin, with trading centers as far afield as Kaskaskia, Cahokia, and Vincennes. The French adapted themselves quickly and well to both trapping and trading. They isolated themselves for years in the wilderness, apparently happy, and on the most friendly terms with the Indians, often marrying Indian girls and raising half-breed progeny. Even after French political power had disappeared in North America the French trader and trapper continued to set the tone for the fur business of the West all the way to the Pacific Coast.

ENGLISH

With the elimination of France from North America, England fell heir to the control of the fur traffic of the new country. The business was transacted largely by English and Scotch merchants who used Montreal as their main American trading center and London as their chief distributing point. London set the fur prices of the western world. In spite of English control, the mass of the men engaged in the fur trade in America was not Anglo-Saxon, but French, and the French influence remained dominant in the wilderness.

The most important of the English fur trading companies was the Hudson's Bay Company, chartered in 1670 with absolute power over the vast and vague region of the Northwest which was tributary to Hudson's Bay. The " Great Company " made an enviable record of fair treatment of the Indian, insisting upon the principles of one price, no rum, and no violence. In spite of minor lapses in the application of these precepts in the face of special conditions, the dealings of the Hudson's Bay Company were on the whole commendable.

Chief among the other and less important English companies interested in the fur trade was the Northwest Company. A group of Scottish Montreal traders headed by Benjamin and Joseph Frobisher and Simon McTavish originated the company in 1779 in a tentative agreement which was made permanent in the winter of 1783–84. Its general field of operations was from the Mandan country to the Pacific and from the Hudson's Bay territory to Louisiana. At the height of its power it employed some 2000 men. It not only had trading posts like those of the Hudson's Bay

Company, but also equipped expeditions to trade with the Indians in the more important Indian villages.

The proximity of the regions worked by the Northwest Company and the Hudson's Bay Company threw the two into a conflict which began almost with the organization of the younger concern. Geographical concepts were vague, so that there was a real doubt as to the proper limits of the jurisdiction of each company. Competition between them sometimes included such devious and objectionable practices as the excessive use of whiskey in trading, stealing of furs, and the inciting of the Indians. In 1811 a settlement sponsored by Lord Selkirk at the present Winnipeg was encouraged by the Hudson's Bay Company as a buffer between the rival organizations; the object was attained, but at the expense of the settlers. Eventually (1821) the Northwest Company was absorbed by its older competitor and good trading methods were restored.

The most productive fur center in the West until a generation and more after the Revolution was the Great Lakes region. Here were the English and Scottish traders, whose operations were pushed north, south, and west so rapidly that Alexander Mackenzie actually succeeded in reaching the Pacific Coast as early as 1793. Here also were the Spanish and French, operating from Vincennes, Kaskaskia, Cahokia, and St. Louis, and also pushing up the valley of the Missouri. Finally, here were the American traders who had come from over the mountains with the hope of participating in the rich fur business farther west. With the advent of the Americans, the greatest competition for western furs was between the English and American traders. This rivalry was largely responsible for the refusal of England to surrender her Great Lakes posts at the end of the Revolution, and also explained in part the campaigns around Detroit in the War of 1812.

FEDERAL REGULATION

One of the early problems faced by the federal government under the Constitution was the regulation of the western fur trade. Unrestricted private competition clearly produced demoralizing effects, as had been apparent for many years. The immediate solution was the first of a long series of laws which provided for the licensing of private traders and the exclusion of all other persons from the Indian country. A trader was to be licensed only if he could show a good moral character and give a bond that he would not sell liquor to the Indians. These provisions looked fine on paper, but were never enforced effectively. Licenses were easy to obtain and unlicensed persons were not ejected, while liquor sales and other unfortunate practices were widespread. No good method was ever developed to prevent the Indians from being cheated unmercifully by private white traders.

Another possible improvement of the fur trading situation came in 1795 when the federal government itself entered the business by establishing trading "factories" in the Indian country. The hope was that a non-profit-making organization providing first-rate goods at moderate prices would improve Indian-white relations. Originally the use of liquor and of credit were outlawed, but while the first objective was at least approached, the second proved impossible. Private traders were still permitted, but with the expectation that their number would decrease, and that they would merely supplement the government system.

The small government establishment was less effective than those of the large private companies. Government prices forced those of the private operators somewhat lower, but in the process the government was faced with steady losses. Among the troubles were the poorer locations of government posts, the inability of the "factors" to travel widely among the Indians, the less specialized and less efficient employees, many poor purchases of trading goods, poor furs and their mishandling, and the excessive credit to poor risks, including white soldiers of neighboring garrisons.

The outstanding opponent of the government factory system was the American Fur Company, which even went to the extent of trying to arouse Indian hostility against the United States government. In the economic field it undercut the government on staples and advanced the prices on other articles. In the political field it lobbied vigorously. Among the politicians opposed to the government in business Lewis Cass and Thomas Hart Benton were outstanding. Cass was governor of Michigan Territory, which had much fur business and consequently many traders. Benton's home state was Missouri, which contained the most important western center of the fur business. Political agitation led to the abandonment of the government venture in 1822, at which time there were nine government factories and 126 licensed traders. The license system was continued, as were the violations.

The Americans, entering the fur trade rather late, found the most lucrative business monopolized by the English and Scottish companies. The long overland trip across the Appalachians was a serious handicap, especially when it competed with the easier St. Lawrence route. Marketing and distributing facilities were underdeveloped until after 1800.

ASTOR

The most important single figure in the development of the fur business of the United States was John Jacob Astor, whose antecedents and early life gave no indication of his later activity. Astor was born in Germany in 1763, and at the age of sixteen left home to join his brother, who was in the musical instrument business in London. During the winter of 1783–84 he realized a long desired ambition by migrating to the United States. Having no capital but seven flutes he found work in New York, first as a baker's helper and then as an assistant to a fur merchant. After learning the fur business he set up shop for himself, combining the trading in furs with the sale of musical instruments. Eventually he confined his business to trading activities. At first he gathered most of his own furs in central New York state and bought the rest from Canada, but gradually he developed an efficient collecting organization and was able to confine most of his attention to merchandising. About 1800 he expanded his operations to the Great Lakes region.

Along with his growing fur business Astor combined trading with China, which was an excellent fur market, and by the beginning of the century had his own ships engaged in the trade with the Far East. Astor's energy and strength were apparently inexhaustible. Everything which he touched seemed to turn to gold, and by the early 1800s he was one of the richest and most powerful men in the United States.

Then came the purchase of Louisiana, and Astor's mind was fired with the possibilities of the fur business in this new and unworked territory. Why should he not expand his operations and monopolize the new region for himself? A vision appeared of a huge company with posts on the Great Lakes, and then along the Missouri and Columbia rivers to the ocean. He even saw the furs being taken to China to exchange for teas, silks, and spices, which would be returned to the United States to complete the circle of transactions. Included in the traffic would be the supplying of the Russian posts which stretched along the Pacific Coast of North America. Truly it was an ambitious dream, including a territory as large as an empire and embracing the entire world in its operations.

Astor's first move in his new plans was to consolidate his existing position and obtain new capital by organizing the American Fur Company (1808) to control the region of the Great Lakes. Two years later he chartered the Pacific Fur Company, which was to be used in furthering his plans in the Far West. In practice, it was difficult to distinguish the operations of these two companies. Astor controlled them both, and used the funds, supplies, and men interchangeably.

ASTORIA

The realization of Astor's dream of a series of forts along the Missouri and Columbia rivers was entrusted to the Pacific Fur Company. Partners were added to control operations in the field, and were given a total of approximately half of the stock. Astor himself advanced the necessary funds ($400,000) and agreed to assume any loss which might be incurred within the first five years. Traders and voyageurs (boatmen) were hired from the Northwest Company.

The first fort of the projected chain to be founded was the western one at the mouth of the Columbia. Two parties were to participate in its construction, the first to go west by sea and the second by land. The former started in 1810 on the trip around the Horn in the vessel *Tonquin,* commanded by Captain Jonathan Thorn, an able navigator, but a stern and forbidding disciplinarian, arbitrary in his actions and requiring strict obedience to his orders. Under ordinary naval conditions Thorn may have been a successful seaman, but he did not appeal to the extremely individualistic fur traders, who had ideas and wills of their own. The result was a series of misunderstandings and disputes, mostly personal, that marred the trip.

The *Tonquin* arrived at the mouth of the Columbia early in 1811 but had much difficulty in entering the river, finally losing a small boat with all on board before the entrance was effected. Upon entering the Columbia Thorn discovered that the overland party had not as yet arrived. Some time was spent in sailing up and down the river to pick a good place for a trading post, but finally the men disembarked and built a small fort which they named Astoria in honor of the principal partner, John Jacob Astor. The *Tonquin* and her crew left Astoria on June 1, 1811, to trade with the Indians along the coast. A surprise attack by the Indians resulted in the killing of most of the crew. The survivors blew up the ship. Four of the men escaped in a small boat but eventually were killed.

Meantime the overland group under the leadership of Wilson Price Hunt had left New York in July 1810. Hunt first went to Montreal to engage voyageurs for the long trip, but difficulties were thrown in his way by the older companies, and after having taken all the men he could obtain he still had to hire others on his way west. His route from Montreal was by way of Lake Huron and Lake Michigan, overland to the Mississippi, and then down that stream until he arrived at St. Louis in September. After ascending the Missouri to near the present site of St. Joseph a permanent winter camp was established and Hunt returned to St. Louis to obtain additional supplies and an interpreter.

It was the middle of April 1811 before Hunt and his latest recruits joined the main group and the whole party started up the Missouri. They planned to ascend the river to the mouth of the Yellowstone, or as far as it was navigable, and then cut overland to a branch of the Columbia. Part way up the Missouri they heard rumors of the hostility of the Blackfeet and therefore changed their plans. Leaving the Missouri in present South Dakota, Hunt led his party on foot through the Black Hills and ultimately across the Rockies to the headwaters of the Snake, which was descended by canoe until the river became impassable. The one large group was found to be unwieldy so it was divided into four parties, each of which was to seek its own route to the Pacific. Each of the parties experienced terrible hardships and privations in their wanderings, and several deaths were recorded; the last of the survivors reached Astoria on February 15, 1812.

The arrival of the overland party, together with the coming of additional supplies by the ship *Beaver,* gave new spirit and vigor to the settlement at Astoria. The fort was strengthened, cabins were built, fish were caught and dried, trading was done with the Indians on the coast, and detachments were sent to deal with the tribes in the interior. Then came rumors of war between the United States and England, and the Astorians decided (1813) that they were so completely isolated and England's control of the sea so secure that it would only be a question of time until they were captured, and in consequence they might as well abandon the fort.

Before Astor's men could depart, a force of Northwest Company traders arrived. To both groups the arrival seemed opportune.

Many of the Astorians were Canadian, and were easily persuaded to sell their post in the fall of 1813, particularly when they heard rumors of an approaching English warship. Some of them joined the Northwest Company. The Astorians were pleased to sell their property instead of having it captured by a British man-of-war, while the Northwest Company was glad to buy out a competitor at a moderate price. Within a month of the sale the British warship *Raccoon* arrived and " captured " Astoria. The commander was exceedingly disgruntled when he saw the insignificance of the small wilderness fort which he had crossed half the world to conquer.

The loss of Astoria ended Astor's plans in the Far Northwest, and he dissolved the Pacific Fur Company. The failure of the enterprise was not due to any fault in the central idea which lay back of it, and only in a small degree to the accident of the outbreak of the war. The decisive factors in the collapse were the lack of adequate communication with the East, the failure to construct the series of forts originally planned to link East and West, and the mismanagement of the two parties which took the field.

AMERICAN FUR COMPANY

After his failure in Oregon, Astor concentrated his attention on the regions farther east. His influence on the Great Lakes country was strengthened until it became a monopoly, while his control in the upper Mississippi Valley was almost as great. The trading policies of the company were anything but commendable. Zachary Taylor, commanding infantry in the upper Mississippi Valley in the 1820s, insisted that : " Take the American Fur Company in the aggregate, and they are the greatest scoundrels the world ever knew."

Agents of the American Fur Company entered the Missouri Valley in 1822, when the headquarters of the western department was established at St. Louis. Gradually the employees of the company worked farther and farther up the valley, consolidating with or crushing competitors until the American Fur Company reigned supreme. In 1829 it established Fort Union at the mouth of the Yellowstone. Its boat the *Yellowstone,* which ascended to Fort Union in 1832 and later to Fort Benton, was responsible for the opening of steamboat business on the upper Missouri. While Astor retired from the company in 1834, when its business was at a peak, the American Fur Company remained dominant in the Missouri Valley for another decade.

The establishment of the western headquarters of the American Fur Company at St. Louis was one of the many illustrations of the increasing importance of that city as a center for the trans-Mississippi fur business. St. Louis, with its strategic position on the Mississippi just below the mouth of the Missouri, was the natural outfitting point for traders and trappers and the logical place for the marketing of the furs they bought back. Here a considerable number of companies doing business in the Far West had their headquarters.

MISSOURI FUR COMPANY

The earliest important company with its main headquarters in St. Louis was the St. Louis Missouri Fur Company, commonly known as the Missouri Fur Company. This firm was started by prominent St. Louis men in the winter of 1808–09, and included many of the best trappers, traders, and hunters in the West. Its first trading expedition, leaving St. Louis in 1809, was an imposing body: 150 men with their necessary supplies, materials for the establishment of four or five permanent posts, and outfits for equipping several smaller subparties. It ascended the Missouri River and built its first post on the Bighorn River. Then it continued farther west, constructing a second fort at the three forks of the Missouri; here it was attacked by the Blackfeet who killed some 25 whites and caused the abandonment of the fort. Farther west, a third post was established on the Snake River.

This first expedition of the Missouri Fur Company seemed pursued by an evil fate, for it met one misfortune after another. The attack by the Blackfeet was followed by other Indian encounters, physical obstacles proved unexpectedly difficult to overcome, some of the furs were accidentally burned, and all of the forts eventually had to be abandoned. In spite of these troubles, however, the expedition showed a small profit. The Missouri Fur Company, like other similar groups of the period, was reorganized frequently. Most of the fur companies changed their names and personnel so rapidly that it is almost impossible to follow consecutively the history of any one group. The Missouri Fur Company ended its precarious existence in the early 1820s.

ROCKY MOUNTAIN FUR COMPANY

The Missouri Fur Company was succeeded by the Rocky Mountain Fur Company. The succession was not in any sense formal, but the same men who composed the earlier group were also active in the later. The principal leaders of the new company were William H. Ashley, who had been born in Virginia, and Andrew Henry, who came originally from Pennsylvania. Henry controlled operations in the field, while Ashley spent most of his time in St. Louis arranging the financial affairs of the company, purchasing supplies, hiring men, and disposing of the furs.

The first expedition of the Rocky Mountain Fur Company left St. Louis in 1822 and was gone two years. It too included some of the most famous trappers of the West. Among them was Jedediah Strong Smith, who later was responsible for the exploration of a large share of the hitherto unknown Southwest. There also was James Bridger, soon to become one of the best known of the plainsmen. Not least was Hugh Glass, whose exploits have been immortalized in the poetry of John G. Neihardt. Glass was at one time left for dead after an encounter with a grizzly bear, and crawled some two hundred miles without a gun, food, or adequate clothes to reach the nearest white habitation. Because of these many famous trappers, the first expedition of the Rocky Mountain Fur Company was notable in the history of the fur trade.

The later history of the Rocky Mountain Fur Company is difficult to follow. Like similar organizations, the company frequently changed its name. At times it either lapsed completely or used no name at all. The title which is commonly given it is more a convenience than an exact designation. The company's field of operations was the upper Missouri Valley and the mountainous region beyond. A great part of its business was done in what is now the southern part of the state of Idaho.

HUDSON'S BAY COMPANY

The chief competitor of the Rocky Mountain Fur Company in the Far Northwest was the Hudson's Bay Company, which had continued to push southwest after its absorption of the Northwest Company. Its chief agent in the Oregon country was John McLoughlin, who had established himself at Fort Vancouver in 1825, and who became sufficiently powerful in the twenty years of his residence to deserve the title of " the King of Old Oregon." McLoughlin's power was absolute and he wielded it with choleric vigor. At the same time he was wise, generous, and hospitable, so that his monarchy was of the benevolent variety. Every traveler and trader who visited the region stopped at Fort Vancouver, where

he was invariably well treated. There was but one exception —
Hall J. Kelley — to this rule, and then the circumstances were
unusual.

McLoughlin as representative of the Hudson's Bay Company
was engaged in a three-cornered fight with the American Fur
Company and the Rocky Mountain Fur Company for the control
of the Oregon region, but in spite of the bitterness with which
this contest was waged, McLoughlin's business dealings were
always fair and honorable. He treated the Indians generously and
his own trappers justly. The profits of the fur trade of the region
were only moderate, and one reason for continuing the post was
the desire of the Hudson's Bay Company to have an outpost to
halt the advance of American trappers. Because of this situation
McLoughlin was encouraged in his preferred policy of trying to
make the post self-sufficient. He fenced his fields, conducted a
varied agriculture, raised stock, and built comfortable homes.
When the first real agricultural settlers came to Oregon, McLoughlin was their friend, adviser, and helper — services for which he
was later ill repaid. His control of Oregon was one of the brightest
spots in the history of the fur trading West.

NATURE OF FUR TRADE

The activities of the fur trading companies were conditioned by
the fact that the business was essentially European — in spite of
the obvious consideration that the furs originated on the North
American continent. Most of the furs were obtained in trade with
the Indians, and for this purpose European-made articles were
given in exchange. The furs themselves found their largest market
in Europe, and European demand set the price in America. Even
the direct participants in the trading were usually European —
French and Spanish, rather than American. The French language
was in more common use than the English, and many of the terms
of the business were French in origin.

The fur trade was also characterized by the large amount of
credit that was involved in most transactions, and by the considerable element of hazard which produced either large profits or
large losses. A period of approximately four years elapsed from
the time that the manufactured goods were shipped from Europe
until the furs were returned and sold, and almost every operation
occurring in the interim was based on credit. The sale of goods,
transactions of the middleman, trading with the trappers and In-

dians, transportation, preparation, and sale of the furs were all normally credit operations. This emphasis on credit, added to difficulties and dangers inherent in the business, produced a highly speculative industry. An annual profit of 50 per cent was not unusual; frequently the figure was much higher. On the other hand the operations of any single year might result in a total loss, often including the sacrifice of human lives.

PERSONNEL OF FUR TRADE

The personnel of the fur trade of the West was both interesting and distinctive. The most important individual was the " bourgeois," who was head of the permanent trading post and frequently a partner in the business — for employee ownership of stock is not a new device. The position required considerable administrative ability, for it was the " bourgeois " who performed such functions as hiring hunters and trappers, supervising the trading, ordering the necessary goods and supplies, and setting the prices. Next in rank was the " partisan " who commanded field operations and held a rendezvous if there were no permanent post in the region. The first lieutenant of the " bourgeois " was the clerk, who was second in authority at the permanent post, taking complete command when his superior was absent; sometimes he held stock in the company.

In addition to the managerial force there was an army of men who performed the heavy manual labor. First of all there were two main types of white trappers — those who were hired by the year and those who had no direct connection with any particular company. The man hired by the year was paid a wage of about $400, for which he would give his entire catch to the company, while the " free trapper " disposed of his furs annually for whatever they would bring. Of lower social rank than the members of either of these groups was the camp keeper, who received approximately $200 a year. His duties were all performed in camp, where he tended the stock, and cleaned and dressed the furs. Another large group was that of the " voyageur " — usually a French creole from Canada or Louisiana — who did the arduous work of handling the boats. At the larger posts were artisans such as blacksmiths and carpenters. Unskilled labor went by the name of " mangeurs de lard " (" pork eaters ") and came principally from Canada. Last but not least in importance were the Indians who gathered the majority of the furs and traded them annually.

The most interesting and picturesque of these groups was the white trapping fraternity, which included such well-known men as Kit Carson, Jim Bridger, Jedediah Smith, Ewing Young, Bill Williams, and William Wolfskill. The white trappers were gaunt, brown, gloomy, taciturn men, with a dry native humor. Physical courage was a prime essential for their existence, and human life was considered of little value. They were the direct heirs of the Boone tradition, and knew the forest as intimately as the city dweller knew his front yard. They lived in the wilds, going to a trading post but once a year to exchange the season's catch for the necessities of life and for the ornaments which were so dear to their hearts. Most of them were improvident, and were usually in debt to the trader — although it should be added that the trader's high prices, faulty measurements, and inaccurate bookkeeping contributed to this situation. The trapper spent his earnings immediately, and then bought on credit as long as the trader would trust him. By winter he was penniless and found it necessary to go back to work.

The trapper's costume was a curious mixture of Indian and white habiliments. Ordinarily he wore a light blue cotton shirt, and over it a knee-length leather hunting shirt. Sometimes he wore breeches, but just as frequently he wore a breechcloth and allowed his thighs and hips to remain bare. Indian leggings and moccasins protected the feet and ankles, while a handkerchief turban warded off insects and added a touch of color. Decorations were at a premium and included colored porcupine quills, feathers and beads to fasten to his clothes, and feathers to thrust into his hair. His ammunition bag was attached to a belt which hung over his left shoulder in such a fashion that the bag came close to his right hand. In his girdle was a knife, a hatchet, tobacco, sugar, and salt. A buffalo robe served for bed and cover, while a saddle made a high but hard pillow. Most of the trappers were excellent horsemen and very proud of their horses and equipment; the saddle and harness were painted, or embroidered, or decorated with feathers, beads, or silver. In the winter the trapper frequently lived in a rude hut, with an Indian wife to keep him amused and do his hard work. His language was a medley of bad English, French, and Spanish. Rather curiously he had no interest in minerals except for decorative purposes; deposits of gold and silver were common knowledge, but no self-respecting trapper ever seriously considered descending to the ignoble work of mining.

TRADING POSTS

The permanent posts of the fur trade were notable landmarks in the wilderness of the West. Ordinarily they were rectangular or square, with sides between 100 and 400 feet in length. The walls were built of pickets twelve to eighteen feet high and four to eight feet thick, except in the South, where adobe walls were more common. Frequently a wooden path was bracketed some four feet from the top for defense. At diagonal corners there were two blockhouses, each fifteen to eighteen feet square, two stories high, and surmounted by a roof. The blockhouse jutted out from the walls so that it could command a clear view of the sides of the fort. The ground floor was designed for the use of cannon, while the upper story had peepholes for rifles. The strength of the blockhouse was attested by the fact that none was ever attacked successfully by the Indians. Somewhere in the picket wall of the fort was a heavy wooden door, well-buttressed, and usually with a small wicket to permit a view of the person desiring admittance without opening the main gate.

The buildings inside the stockade included barracks for the men, a storehouse, shops, the trader's house, and the clerk's house. Often there was a garden just outside the wall, and sometimes it too was barricaded. All livestock was ordinarily kept outside of the walls, but in case of danger it was brought inside. Life at the fort was slow and monotonous, but exciting moments came with the arrival of a caravan of goods from the East, a skirmish with the Indians, a hunting trip, or the departure of a trading expedition. In addition to the larger and more important posts were a number of smaller and less powerful stations scattered here and there throughout the West.

The alternative of the permanent trading post was the rendezvous, of which the first was held by Ashley in 1822 and the last by the American Fur Company in 1839. Its greatest use was in the region which is now southern Idaho and western Wyoming. The rendezvous was a specified gathering place for trading and had its principal advantage in obviating the necessity for a permanent post with a large personnal. A locality was chosen which had a good supply of grass and water, and to it would come the trappers, the Indians, and the traders from the East with their goods. The caravan left St. Louis early in the spring and arrived at the meeting place in late June or early July. Here it would stay and trade for the year's catch until either the furs or the goods were exhausted. Articles in special demand by both the Indians and the trappers were blankets, cloth, trinkets, beads, mirrors, jewelry, salt, sugar, tobacco, guns, ammunition, knives, and large quantities of liquor. Athletic contests, gambling, and drinking would occupy all of the day and most of the night, and everyone was merry. Eventually the items to be traded would be exhausted and the caravan would start its return trip in time to arrive in the East before winter.

Trading at all the posts was in goods and very little actual cash changed hands; the unit of value was the beaver skin. Manufactured products were overvalued and furs undervalued (from the standpoint of the trader), and whiskey was plentiful, with the result that the trapper was ordinarily in debt and the Indian impoverished. This situation was on the whole favorable to the trader, for then he was assured that the trappers would be forced to make a good catch the next year; in addition, if the trapper were in debt he would be more likely to do business again with the same trader.

The fur trade reached the peak of its importance in the United States during the 1830s. In the next decade it declined in relative significance even though not in value. The cream of the American fur supply had been skimmed, and advancing settlement was driving the trapper to newer fields.

READINGS

J. C. Alter, *James Bridger* (1925)—good; C. H. Carey, *A General History of Oregon* (2 vols., 1935–36), chs. 11–14; H. M. Chittenden, *The American Fur Trade of the Far West* (3 vols., 1935)—reprint of classic account; R. G. Cleland, *This Reckless Breed of Men* (1950)—very good on trappers; L. H. Creer, *Founding of an Empire* (1947), chs. 2–4—Utah; G. C. Davidson, *The Northwest Company* (1918); L. J. Davidson and F. Blake (eds.), *Rocky Mountain Tales* (1947), ch. 1—Bridger stories; B. De Voto, *Across the Wide Missouri* (1947)—mostly fur trade —*The Year of Decision, 1846* (1943), ch. 2—mountain men; E. Dick, *Vanguards of the Frontier* (1941), ch. 1; A. H. Favour, *Old Bill Williams* (1936)—very good; H. Fergusson, *Rio Grande* (1933), ch. 7—mountain men; G. W. Fuller, *The Inland Empire of the Pacific Northwest* (3 vols., 1928), chs. 8–10; B. C. Grant (ed.), *Kit Carson's Own Story of His Life* (1926), part 1; L. R. Hafen (ed.), *Colorado and Its People* (4 vols., 1948), vol. 1, ch. 6;

L. R. Hafer and F. M. Young, *Fort Laramie* (1938), part 1;
G. D. Harmon, *Sixty Years of Indian Affairs* (1941), chs. 9, 10—
detailed; H. Hatcher, *The Great Lakes* (1944), ch. 22; H. A.
Innis, *The Fur Trade of Canada* (1930), chs. 3, 4—scholarly;
L. P. Kellogg, *The British Regime in Wisconsin and the North-west* (1935), chs. 4–17; D. Lavender, *Bent's Fort* (1954), chs. 2–4, 8, 9; C. Lindsay, *The Big Horn Basin* (1932), ch. 2—limited
in scope; J. Monaghan, *The Overland Trail* (1947), chs. 3–5;
R. G. Montgomery, *The White-Headed Eagle* (1934), chs. 1–12—
McLaughlin; D. L. Morgan, *The Great Salt Lake* (1947), chs. 4–7—good; B. Nelson, *Land of the Dacotahs* (1946), chs. 4, 5—
reads easily; G. L. Nute, *The Voyageur* (1931)—excellent;
H. O'Connor, *The Astors* (1941), chs. 1–3; O. B. Peake, *A History of the United States Indian Factory System* (1954); R. E.
Pinkerton, *Hudson's Bay Company* (1931), chs. 14–36; K. W.
Porter, *John Jacob Astor* (2 vols., 1931)—scholarly; M. M.
Quaife, *Lake Michigan* (1944), ch. 16; E. E. Rich (ed.), *Letters of John McLaughlin* (1941), (ed.), *Peter Skene Ogden's Snake Country Journals* (1950); G. Simpson, *Fur Trade and Empire* (1931)—Simpson journal; C. L. Skinner, *Beaver, Kings and Cabins* (1933); A. D. H. Smith, *John Jacob Astor* (1929), books 3–5—good; K. A. Spaulding (ed.), *On the Oregon Trail* (1953)—
Stuart journal; W. E. Stevens, *The Northwest Fur Trade, 1763–1800* (1928)—fine monograph; M. S. Sullivan, *Jedediah Smith* (1936), *The Travels of Jedediah Smith* (1934); C. A. Vandiveer, *The Fur Trade* (1929), chs. 16–28; S. Vestal, *The Missouri* (1945), ch. 2, *Jim Bridger* (1946), *Kit Carson* (1928), *Mountain Men* (1937); F. Waters, *The Colorado* (1946), part 2, ch. 3;
O. O. Winther, *The Great Northwest* (1947), chs. 3–6, *The Old Oregon Country* (1950), chs. 1–8; R. K. Wyllys, *Arizona* (1950),
ch. 4—factual.

CHAPTER 12

WAR
IN THE NORTHWEST

THE center of the fur trade in the opening years of the nineteenth century was the area tributary to the Great Lakes, and consequently it was here that the Indian problem became most acute as English and Americans struggled for control. In general the Indians favored the English traders — partly because Canadian settlements did not encroach on the land of the western Indians in any important fashion. Their attitude toward the United States tended to be hostile. Wayne's campaign had overawed them temporarily, but the Indians, angered by white encroachments and with a fading memory of white military power, were willing again to try to drive off the invaders by force.

INDIAN GRIEVANCES

The Indian had many rankling and irritating grievances to arouse his hatred of the whites. The contact of the two civilizations always meant the eventual supremacy of the white, and the eventual decay and destruction of the red. The Indian of the Old Northwest realized that the period of his total elimination was not far distant if he did not fight back, for with the beginning of the nineteenth century thousands of white settlers poured into Ohio and Indiana, driving off the game and taking possession of the land. The federal government continued to give lip service to the fiction of Indian independence and land ownership, but the Indian was more impressed by the rapidity with which the whites obtained any area they coveted. No opposition short of war seemed to have the least chance of damming back the white flood.

The Indian was also increasingly resentful of the way in which he suffered from the worst traits of white society. He was cheated

164

at the trading posts. He was plied with whiskey until his powers
of reasoning were gone. He traded a year's catch of furs for a few
trinkets and a little bad whiskey. He soon gave the trinkets to his
wife and drank the whiskey, with the result that his season's work
was gone and all that remained was a dark brown taste and im-
paired health. The white man's diseases then completed the havoc.
Gambling and stealing were traits common to both races, but
now they became for the Indian mean and degrading instead of
remaining a part of the life of every self-respecting adult. The
traits of the warrior were turned into those of the sneak thief. The
white had taught him new and more expensive ways of eating and
of dressing; with his money gone for bad liquor, he was often
reduced to slinking about the white settlements and resorting to
petty pilfering, which injured his self-respect and was punishable
if he were caught. The crimes committed by the Indians were
always punished if the culprits were detected, but the opposite was
by no means always the case. Furthermore, the Indian women
were comparatively easy prey for the aggressive frontiersmen.
The result was the introduction and spread of venereal disease,
which further sapped the strength of the Amerinds. No wonder,
with these and other causes for resentment, the Indians were becoming increasingly hostile toward the whites.

The Indian who best exemplified the growing rancor toward
white civilization was Tecumseh, one of the ablest leaders the
Shawnee ever produced. Tecumseh was born about 1768 and consequently was a young brave at the time of the campaigns of
Harmar, St. Clair and Wayne. As he grew older and watched the
advance of the whites and the progressive deterioration of the reds,
he felt an ever-increasing surge of anger against this seemingly
inexorable process. He became certain in his own mind that the
land belonged to the Indian tribes forever, no matter by what
show of legality it might be taken from them, and that they should
cling to their traditional ways of life. In this belief and in his later
plans he was joined by his brother the Prophet, who claimed to
have magical powers. Both men gradually came to the realization
that the only possible way of opposing the white advance successfully was to obtain the cooperation of all the Indians and to have
them act as a unit. With this plan in mind they traveled widely,
particularly in the first decade of the nineteenth century, talking
with Indians both north and south in an effort to form an alliance
against white aggression. Beginning in 1808 their headquarters

were at the confluence of Tippecanoe Creek and the Wabash; here was built Prophet's Town, with its extensive agricultural fields and large herds, and with no whiskey.

WILLIAM HENRY HARRISON

The white man who best represented the point of view diametrically opposed to that of Tecumseh was William Henry Harrison. Harrison was a frontiersman only by adoption, having been born in Virginia on February 9, 1773, of a family which had lived in that part of the country for over a century. He was given a good education in the expectation that he would enter the medical profession. But military life attracted him more and in 1791 he joined the army, receiving a fairly good rank because of political influence in governmental circles. His command was ordered west, arriving at Fort Washington just as the remnants of St. Clair's defeated army were returning. Harrison subsequently took part in Wilkinson's campaigns against the Indians and then distinguished himself at Fallen Timbers with Wayne. Returning to Fort Washington in 1796 he was given command of the fort with the rank of captain. Two years later he resigned because of lack of action.

Harrison spent much of his life in seeking remunerative positions by the use of political influence. In 1798 he wangled the job of secretary of Northwest Territory, but proved more interested in farming and distilling than in keeping records. The following year he took advantage of a factional fight in the Ohio Legislative Council and was elected as delegate to the United States House of Representatives. His victory by the close vote of eleven to ten probably was due to the fact that his opponent was the son of the then unpopular Governor St. Clair. In Congress Harrison was active in supporting a revision of the land laws and the division of the Northwest Territory to permit the statehood of Ohio, playing an active role in the construction and passage of the land act of 1800 and in the formation of the Territory of Indiana. Then once more he pulled all the political strings within his grasp to obtain the appointment of governor of Indiana.

When Harrison arrived at his new post early in 1801 he found himself with but few people to govern in spite of his nominal control of a considerable area. The total white population of the present states of Indiana, Illinois, Michigan, and Wisconsin was then only a little more than 5000; the most populous town, Vincennes, had 700 inhabitants. Consequently the new governor had plenty of spare time in which to try a little farming, dabble in land speculation, and take an interest in the schemes of Burr. He was personally ambitious, which meant that as governor of Indiana he desired to enlarge his constituency by buying Indian land for the benefit of white settlers. On the other hand his immediate aim was to continue in office, and since he felt that Jefferson favored a policy of benevolent noninterference in Indian affairs he was content for the time being to sit idle and do nothing.

Harrison was soon freed to follow his own desires by a plain intimation from President Jefferson that new land acquisitions would not be looked upon with disfavor. Immediately (1802–03) he entered negotiations with the Indians and another million acres was added to the land available for white settlement. Other treaties followed, and the resulting Indian resentment was attributed by the governor to British influence, which since the surrender of Detroit centered at Malden (Amherstburgh) across the river. Harrison had some sympathy for the Indians as they suffered from " unprovoked wrongs," but he was convinced that the only possible way to deal satisfactorily with them was to destroy them. He had visions of himself as a second Wayne, and read all the old military masters. He mapped out wonderful prospective campaigns, and felt that all he needed was an opportunity to exhibit his abilities as a strategist.

His attention was not called to Tecumseh until 1806, but during the succeeding years the men came into closer and closer contact. In the same year (1808) that Tecumseh took up his residence in Prophet's Town he had an interview with Harrison, in which he promised peace if the United States did not make further treaties including land cessions with individual Indian tribes; if such cessions were made, Tecumseh threatened an English alliance and war. A similar interview was held the following year, but by this time events were occurring which made peace impossible. The Territory of Illinois was created, leaving Indiana with its present boundaries. Harrison received permission from the Secretary of War to buy more Indian land, and a purchase of 2,500,000 acres made in the fall of 1809 increased the number and wrath of the hostile Indians. Rumors of war became current on the frontier.

TIPPECANOE

The new land purchase led Tecumseh in his conversations with Harrison in 1810 to insist more strongly that Indian land was held in common and could not be alienated by a few individuals. Harrison might well have commenced war at this time if the government had not been busy in West Florida, but he waited until August 1811, at which time he felt that his opportunity had come. Tecumseh, after an interview in which he had asked that no immediate action be taken, departed on a tour of the South to talk with the southern Indians. As soon as he had gone, Harrison gathered 1000 men (mostly volunteers) and, with a well-planned campaign already formulated, prepared to annihilate his unsuspecting enemies.

When Harrison left Vincennes on September 26, 1811, his objective was to crush the Shawnee power by destroying Prophet's Town. Moving directly up the Wabash, he paused only long enough to build Fort Harrison on the present site of Terre Haute, and on the night of November 6 was encamped on Tippecanoe Creek. Although he stated that he did not intend to attack Prophet's Town, the Indians feared treachery and under the leadership of the Prophet attacked the white camp early in the morning of the 7th. In spite of the surprise, Harrison maintained his position. The white casualties were 185, while the losses of the Indians were unknown. Both sides claimed victory, but popularly Harrison received the credit. He became a military hero largely because he had the foresight to dispatch messengers to the East immediately after the battle with news of an overwhelming defeat of the Indians. In later years there was much controversy as to whether or not Harrison had actually won. He had avoided rout and repulsed the Indians, but on the other hand he had found it necessary to retreat almost immediately, stopping only long enough to destroy Prophet's Town. He was back in Vincennes on November 18.

The battle of Tippecanoe had far-reaching effects, even though they were somewhat different from those that Harrison had anticipated. Prophet's Town did not disappear, for the Indians immediately rebuilt it. Indian troubles did not stop, for new depredations occurred at once. From a larger point of view, however, the Indians suffered greatly. Tecumseh lost some of his prestige, and plans for a general Indian alliance never again came so near to success as they had in the years just prior to 1811. The United States encountered no further resistance in expanding its land purchases to Lake Michigan after the War of 1812. For Harrison's personal benefit the encounter inspired the battle cry of " Tippecanoe and Tyler too " which was an important factor in his successful Presidential campaign of 1840.

WESTERN WAR SENTIMENT

Scarcely had Harrison returned from his Indian campaign when the outbreak of the War of 1812 took the center of the stage. The causes of the war, according to the diplomats, involved primarily the freedom of the seas, but more realistically the war was based on western problems as expressed by western men. The West had long blamed its Indian troubles on English incitation, and looked hopefully toward breaking English power and succeeding to the control of the fur trade. The perfect solution, in western eyes, was to annex Canada — a project not new to Americans. Almost as good a case could be made for a war with Spain and the annexation of Florida, but two wars at one time were somewhat excessive, and if a choice had to be made the preference went to war with the traditional enemy England.

War sentiment was brought to the boiling point in Congress by Henry Clay and his " War Hawks," mostly from the West and South. Loudly and vaingloriously they shouted in the session of 1811 for a larger army and navy for " defense," and for the armed protection of American " rights " on the sea and elsewhere. Quite frankly they advocated the annexation of Canada and Florida, for were not these territories necessary for our defense, and a " natural " part of the United States? The War Hawks were certain that they would be better utilized by the superior American brand of civilization. Clay thundered that the Kentucky militia alone could conquer Canada.

The western war spirit just prior to 1812 showed vividly that the West was no longer thinking in terms of independence and foreign alliance. It had become belligerently and jingoistically patriotic, sensitive to national insults and eager to expand United States influence in the world. The intrigues of the previous decade were ancient history. Now the West was growing rapidly in population and exercising an ever-increasing influence in the halls of Congress, which meant that it could attain its aims through the machinery of the federal government. The westward movement of population meant the eastward movement of separatist plans — first to New England and then later to the South.

HULL OPERATIONS

The West obtained its war, and looked forward eagerly to the immediate conquest of Canada. The first campaign in the Northwest was undertaken by William Hull, then governor of the comparatively new Territory of Michigan, which had been created in 1805. Hull did not feel competent to undertake a military expedition, opposed his own appointment as leader, and finally accepted only under protest. His orders were to reinforce Detroit and then to invade Canada; in these operations he was to be supported by an offensive movement at Niagara by General Henry Dearborn. From the very beginning Hull's plans went wrong. His boat containing supplies and orders for Detroit, which he sent ahead of his main advance, was captured by the British under Brock at Malden. On July 5, 1812, Hull and his army of 1600 men arrived at Detroit. A week later he crossed the Detroit River and entered Canada, issuing a proclamation promising real freedom to the British inhabitants of the region; he delayed, however, in his attack on Malden.

William Hull has been criticized severely for his failure to attack Malden, when his effectives outnumbered the British three to one. It must be remembered, however, that he realized his own incompetence as leader of the expedition. He was entirely lacking in military ability; by nature he was timid and fearful, leaning toward persuasion rather than force. He was opposed by Isaac Brock, a comparatively young man with a background of active military life, and the traditions of a British family of soldiers. In addition, Hull was hampered by the necessity of using part of his men to keep open his communications to the rear, and was never given the cooperation he expected. The Niagara offensive and the more easterly invasion of Canada failed to materialize, while Lake Erie remained in English hands. In the West, Mackinac was lost, and the troops from Fort Dearborn (present Chicago) were annihilated in an unsuccessful effort to join Hull. All these factors led Hull to decide that he was too weak to advance farther, and so he recrossed the river and returned to Detroit. In fact, he wanted to evacuate Detroit and retire to the Maumee, but his officers, led by Lewis Cass, objected effectively to any such retreat.

Hull's timidity encouraged Brock to cross the river and lay siege to Detroit. On August 15 he demanded the surrender of the city, and the next day, much to his surprise, Hull acceded to the ultimatum. News of this ignominious capitulation soon reached the East, where it was received with amazement and chagrin. A considerable body of American troops which had been expected to capture Canada had been taken prisoner by an inferior body of

British, and without even attempting to defend themselves. Hull was immediately court-martialed and sentenced to be shot, although his sentence was later remitted. His punishment, however, did not advance the American cause. The hostile Indians were lined up solidly with the British, and for the time being the frontier of defense had to be withdrawn to the line of the Wabash and Maumee. General James Winchester was sent with a relief army to recover some of Hull's losses.

HARRISON'S CAMPAIGNS

While these events were occurring in the north, William Henry Harrison was forced to remain in a position not at all to his liking. He had expected that upon the outbreak of the war he would be made a major general and given charge of offensive operations, for had he not shown his military acumen by his successful campaign against the Indians? But no such appointment was made, and so Harrison deserted his Indiana job and went to Cincinnati to use his political influence to obtain a high army command. He was successful in raising a body of Kentucky militia and in persuading his friend the Governor of Kentucky to commission him major general of the Kentucky militia. The appointment was curious in view of the fact that Harrison was not an inhabitant of the state.

Harrison's first offensive operation was to move on Cincinnati. There he found Brigadier General Winchester with a mixed army of militia and regulars, and with indefinite orders to reinforce Hull. Harrison thereupon browbeat Winchester and took control of the whole army. Then came the news of Hull's defeat and definite orders from Washington for Winchester to lead the relief army. Harrison was in an exceedingly embarrassing position, and found it necessary to say — possibly with his fingers crossed — that he would restore Winchester's army immediately. Then he interpreted his " immediately " to mean after the capture of Terre Haute, which had been taken by the Indians. Just at this time he was given some measure of justification by the news that he had finally been appointed a brigadier general of the United States army, largely through the influence of his friend Henry Clay.

Harrison advanced upon Fort Wayne with his borrowed army, entering it on September 12, 1812. The victory was actually barren, since the Indians had already departed. Winchester now demanded the return of his army, and even Harrison could no longer find a reason for refusal, since he was the junior officer. To add to his disgruntlement, he received orders from the War Department to support Winchester with his Kentucky militia; such action would make him distinctly a subordinate, with little power of his own. While Harrison had no choice but to obey, he kept control of his militia and decided in his own mind to act independently and capture Detroit. Meanwhile the influence of Henry Clay had been at work in Washington, with the result that President Madison came to appreciate the merits of Harrison, and gave him complete charge of the armies of the West. It is not recorded what Winchester thought when these new orders reached him, but he had a good army training and obeyed the commands of his superiors.

As soon as Harrison took command he decided to divide his 10,000 men into three armies and advance toward Detroit at once. Both decisions were probably bad; the army should have been kept united and given more training before it undertook offensive operations. As it was the roads were either nonexistent or nearly impassable, supplies were poor and inadequate, the leaders were jealous, and the army showed its disaffection in desertions and threats of mutiny. Harrison became less sure of the desirability of an advance, and corresponded voluminously with the Secretary of War on the subject. While the troops under the immediate command of Harrison were thus loitering in October and November, the column under Winchester continued to advance — upon the assumption that it was being supported by the rest of the army. On the Raisin River, January 22, 1813, Winchester was attacked by a small force under Henry Proctor, who had succeeded Brock in the command of the British troops, and was defeated completely, in part because of his own bad strategy and in part because of a lack of expected support by Harrison. If Proctor had continued to advance he probably would have defeated the rest of the army under Harrison, but his force was small and so he hurried back to defend Malden.

Winchester's defeat caused Harrison to abandon his plans temporarily, and to retreat to the Portage River, where he established winter quarters. His explanation for the withdrawal was that the support of the West for his campaign had been lukewarm and ineffective. While in winter quarters, the enlistments of many of the six months' militia expired, and most of them went home. Consequently Harrison found it necessary to postpone his advance still longer while he spent the summer of 1813 in raising new troops in Ohio and Kentucky. It was at this time that he learned that his rank had been raised to that of major general. Luckily his leaderless force was not attacked during his absence.

Activities on the northern frontier were resumed in the late summer. Both Proctor and Harrison advanced, and a number of indecisive skirmishes were fought. Then came the news of Oliver H. Perry's victory on Lake Erie on September 10, 1813, and Harrison was encouraged to move more rapidly. In the latter part of September he embarked for Malden. When he arrived there on September 27, he found the town deserted. Greatly outnumbered Proctor had felt that discretion dictated a retreat rather than a battle. Harrison, after some hesitation, decided to follow his retreating enemy. By means of forced marches he overtook Proctor at the Thames River on October 5, 1813. The superior number of the Americans left no doubt of the outcome, and the British were defeated decisively. The Indian allies deserted the British cause, although Tecumseh remained to end his life fittingly on the field of battle.

After the battle of the Thames, Harrison was again a hero, and could return to enjoy the fruits of his victory. Coming back by way of Detroit and the southern shore of Lake Erie, he eventually reached the East, where the " hero of the Thames " was given a proper reception — parades, banquets, speeches, toasts, and eulogies. American victories had been sufficiently infrequent that even the least of them was the occasion for enthusiasm which approached adoration of the victor.

Harrison returned to Cincinnati in January 1814, and there found that interest in the war had given way to a state of boredom. Therefore he resigned his army position. The war, although technically still in progress, was at an end as far as the Northwest was concerned. The easy victories which had been expected at the opening of hostilities had failed to materialize. Hoped-for glory had been reduced to one small victory and a number of defeats. The net result had been the loss of several posts in the Far Northwest. Since the war was not advantageous and the conquest of Canada now was recognized as impossible, there was no point in continuing hostilities.

EFFECTS OF THE WAR

The results of the War of 1812 for the Northwest were of mixed value. Several ignominious defeats had injured patriotic confidence.

The expected conquest of Canada had not materialized. Men had been killed, property destroyed, and farms had their production reduced because of the absence of manpower. On the other hand, the power of the Indians had been broken. Tecumseh had been killed, and the possibility of a general Indian confederation had vanished. No further Indian outbreak was to occur until the Black Hawk War, a minor episode 20 years later. The subjection of the Indians also meant new purchases of land in the succeeding years. Some of these cessions were engineered by Harrison, as was only fitting. In all, he bought some 33,000,000 acres.

The war was also responsible for the first real beginnings of settlement in Michigan, which from 1818 to 1834 included not only its present territory but also the region westward to the Mississippi. Returned soldiers advertised the opportunities in the vicinity of Detroit when they told their friends of their war experiences and observations. People from farther south moved northward in increasing numbers, although it was another decade before large-scale emigration came to Michigan.

The development of Michigan was closely asociated with the life and work of Lewis Cass. Cass had commanded an Ohio regiment in Hull's army in the early stages of the war. He opposed Hull's strategy and advocated the defense of Detroit, but his efforts were unavailing. In the general capitulation he was taken prisoner, but was later paroled. His parole was removed in January 1813, at which time he gathered a new army and joined Harrison, whom he followed through the succeeding campaigns. When Harrison occupied Detroit, Cass was placed in command of the fort and the town.

Cass was appointed governor of Michigan on October 29, 1813, and immediately set to work to rehabilitate his territory, which had seen such rough usage up to that time. For twenty years he was active in developing and advertising Michigan. He traveled widely, both on exploring trips and on missions to deal with the Indians, covering the territory as far west as the Mississippi. He also was instrumental in influencing Henry Schoolcraft to do exploring. In recognition of his abilities and services, he was appointed Secretary of War by Andrew Jackson in 1831.

The end of the War of 1812 marked the beginning of a definite stage in the development of the Old Northwest. The early hunters, trappers, and explorers had long been giving way to the advancing agricultural frontiersmen, but now, with the removal of the last

Indian barrier, the way was opened for a still more rapid increase of white settlement. Frontier conditions were soon to be replaced by the peaceful development of a more stable society.

READINGS

C. W. Alvord, *The Illinois Country* (1920), ch. 20; F. C. Bald, *Detroit's First American Decade* (1948)—1796–1805; H. P. Beers, *Western Military Frontier, 1815–1846* (1935), pp. 1–53; F. Cleaves, *Old Tippecanoe* (1939), chs. 1–17—Harrison; L. Esarey, *A History of Indiana* (1915), chs. 34–36; D. B. Goebel, *William Henry Harrison* (1926); J. A. Green, *William Henry Harrison* (1941), chs. 1–8; W. Havighurst, *Land Of Promise* (1946), ch. 9; L. P. Kellogg, *The British Regime in Wisconsin and the Old Northwest* (1935), chs. 17–20; B. Mayo, *Henry Clay* (1937), chs. 11–13; J. M. Oskison, *Tecumseh and His Times* (1938)—good; A. Pirtle, *The Battle of Tippecanoe* (1900); J. W. Pratt, *The Expansionists of 1812* (1925), chs. 1, 4; M. M. Quaife, *Lake Michigan* (1944), chs. 11, 12; J. W. Silver, *Edmund Pendleton Gaines* (1949), ch. 3—detailed monograph; G. G. Van Deusen, *The Life of Henry Clay* (1937), chs. 5, 6; W. Wood, *The War with the United States* (1915)—Canadian view; F. Woodford, *Lewis Cass* (1950), chs. 3–8.

CHAPTER 13

THE SOUTHWEST AND JACKSON

A ROUGH similarity existed between the Northwest and the Southwest before and during the War of 1812. Both regions were most heavily populated near the Ohio River, and became less densely settled as one moved away from the river banks. The Algonkin tribes harassed the northern frontier, while the Five Civilized Nations were only slightly less hostile in the South. The frontiersmen coveted English Canada in the North and the Spanish Floridas in the South. But here the similarity ceased. American leadership and its results in the South were entirely different from those in the North.

The history and situation of the Floridas were unlike those of Canada. The portion of the Floridas east of the Perdido River had been Spanish, and the portion west of that river French until the end of the Seven Years' War (1763) when they were given to England in return for the restoration of Cuba. Under English rule immigration was encouraged by liberal land grants and new settlements appeared. During the Revolution these settlements provided bases for expeditions into Georgia and havens for Tory refugees. At this time their northern boundary was the parallel of the mouth of the Yazoo River (32° 28′).

The end of the Revolution saw England in the role of the vanquished, and the Floridas were ceded to Spain. Spain would have preferred to keep the old English Yazoo line west of the Chattahoochee, but the treaty of peace drew the line along the 31st parallel to the Chattahoochee, down the Chattahoochee to its junction with the Flint, directly to the head of the St. Marys, and down the St. Marys to the coast. This line is the present northern boundary of Florida, but extended to the Mississippi. A secret agreement made at the same time with the United States provided that if England retained West Florida its boundary should be 32° 28′, but this contingency did not arise.

After the Revolution the Spanish holdings of Florida and Louisiana were continual sources of irritation and trouble, including as they did the control of the mouth of the Mississippi and other important rivers such as the Tombigbee, Alabama, and Apalachicola. For the immediate present the navigation of the Mississippi overshadowed all other considerations, taking preference both in private plots and in governmental negotiations. The results, as described earlier, were the Pinckney Treaty of 1795 and the subsequent purchase of Louisiana.

EFFORTS TO ACQUIRE FLORIDA

The acquisition of Louisiana soon proved an altogether too meager morsel for the appetite of American expansionists, and agitation for the taking of the Floridas — and of course Canada — continued. The Americans who had settled on the Gulf Coast and the lower Mississippi preferred the United States to the Spanish government. The outlets of the principal southern rivers began to look more important as the Georgia and Tennessee settlements pushed toward the Southwest. The weak Spanish administration was a perpetual invitation to fugitive slaves, hostile Indians, and outlaws of all kinds.

American desire for the Floridas went a good deal further than hopeless dreaming. Pinckney made an effort to buy them in 1797 but failed. This failure, together with increased western irritation, brought frequent rumors of war in 1803–06 and thus furnished part of the background for the Burr plans. After 1806 the talk of war decreased. Negotiations for the purchase of the Floridas were reopened, but Spain proved adamant. Thereupon Jefferson turned to France, for having bought one property from a country with dubious title he saw no reason why he might not do business again that way. His idea was sound, but Napoleon asked more money than Congress was willing to appropriate (1806).

Failure to buy the Floridas led people to consider other methods by which the region might be acquired. Most convenient and satisfactory was the supposition that at least West Florida might have been included in the Louisiana purchase. Truly, no one had thought of this possibility when the purchase was made, but when Napo-

leon's delightfully vague boundaries were reconsidered it seemed
only reasonable to make them cover as much ground as possible.
As early as 1803 Robert Livingston came to the conclusion that
his earlier ideas of the boundaries of Louisiana were wrong and
that the United States had bought also part of West Florida. In
the same year Congress agreed with this pleasant theory and provided for the establishment of customhouses as far east as the
Mobile River. Naturally Spain protested, and since the United
States did not want war at this particular time, the objectionable
act was held in abeyance.

ACQUISITION OF WEST FLORIDA

While the United States was making efforts to buy the Floridas,
American citizens were filtering into the coveted region, and soon
there were rumors that these settlers planned to revolt from
Spain and either set up their independent government or ask annexation to the United States. That these rumors were not merely
idle gossip was demonstrated by a convention of American settlers
meeting in West Florida in 1810. While the meeting confined its
action to petitioning the existing authorities for better treatment,
a considerable number of its members emphatically favored a declaration of freedom. Immediately after the convention, the liberty
party took matters in its own hands. Philemon Thomas and 104
men seized Baton Rouge, captured the Spanish military commander, declared West Florida independent, formed a constitution,
elected a president, and applied to the United States for annexation.

Here was the plum which the United States had so long desired,
now ripe for the plucking. President Madison furbished up his
claims to the territory and issued a proclamation declaring the
region as far east as the Perdido River was a part of the United
States. He received the necessary support from Congress in the act
of January 15, 1811. The western army was dispatched to the south
and seized all of West Florida except Mobile, which was held by
a fairly strong Spanish garrison. Upon the admission of Louisiana
to the Union in 1812 it was given the portion of West Florida west
of the Pearl River, while the remainder was added to the Territory of Mississippi. This incident of the acquisition of West Florida was interesting in part because of its immediate effects, but
more because it served as a startling parallel to later expansions
of the United States.

The acquistion of West Florida left East Florida as the center of interest. President Madison decided that the pattern of events of the earlier acquisition might well be repeated, and sent to the scene of prospective expansion the elderly, stocky, redhaired, and aggressive George Mathews, brigadier-general of Georgia militia and a former governor of Georgia. He was instructed that he could accept any territory offered by local authorities or threatened by a foreign power, and he interpreted these instructions as giving him a free hand to take East Florida.

General Mathews established himself on the St. Marys River, where he collected "Florida patriots," largely from Georgia; many of them had never been in Florida. The invasion of the "homeland" was begun in March 1812, supported by an American naval squadron, which cooperated reluctantly, and by a regular army group, which required a change of commanders before it would act. Amelia Island and Fernandina were taken, and siege was laid to St. Augustine. Freedom was declared for East Florida, a constitution was adopted, and a flag was designed with a blue soldier presenting a fixed bayonet on a white background. John H. McIntosh became Director of the Territory of East Florida, with the obvious implication of early annexation to the United States.

Unfortunately for the plans of Mathews, the administration then had a change of heart due to pressing war difficulties farther north. Mathews was dismissed on the pretext that he had exceeded his instructions—a repudiation which practically killed the old man. American troops were removed upon the promise of the Spanish governor to grant amnesty to all rebels, and the "revolution" contracted to a few guerrilla groups that looted the countryside. The West Florida technique had failed in East Florida, and hence other measures became necessary.

ANDREW JACKSON

In the Southwest the War of 1812 was notable principally because of the activities and rise to power of one man—Andrew Jackson. Jackson was Scotch-Irish by descent, and his parents had moved west before the Revolution (1763) to the Catawba region, where Andrew was born in 1765. His father died before Andrew's birth and his mother when he was fourteen, so that for most of his life he was forced to depend on his own resources. He spent his youth and early manhood among rough and uneducated people, so that it is not remarkable that he swore fluently, drank, chewed, dueled, gave way to violent fits of temper, and never commanded good English. In contrast to these less desirable traits he had the frontier virtues of straightforwardness, trustworthiness, truthfulness, self-sufficiency, and loyalty to his friends.

Andrew Jackson began his mature life with the study of law in North Carolina, and in the latter 1780s moved to the Tennessee frontier, where he developed a successful legal business and participated in local politics. He was a member of the state supreme court, and held the rank of major general of militia after 1802. When the war with England began he immediately raised an army of volunteers and offered his services to the government. His offer was accepted, and early in 1813 he received orders to move south and help capture Florida. His best route lay down the Mississippi, so he marched his troops to Natchez, preliminary to following the river to New Orleans. He was willing to promise with easy confidence the capture of Mobile, St. Augustine, Pensacola, or any other place that was desired. While at Natchez he quarreled with Wilkinson over the question of who was superior in rank, and then he quarreled with Thomas H. Benton because Benton thought Wilkinson was right. At a later time Jackson engaged in a tavern brawl with the Bentons (the future Missouri Senator and his brother) and received a serious arm wound.

Jackson's orders to move south were part of a general plan which included three armies and was probably designed to conquer all of the Floridas. The ostensible purpose was to prevent a Spanish invasion, Spain then being controlled by England. Whatever the general plans may have been they were not put into operation, since the Senate would authorize no more than the occupation of Mobile. General Wilkinson obtained the honor of investing that city on April 13, 1813, thus rounding out the American control of West Florida.

By the time Jackson arrived in Natchez the government had changed its mind about the advisability of a Florida expedition, and so ordered him to disband his troops. This order displeased Jackson intensely. Not only did it destroy his hopes of a successful military expedition, but also it implied that the volunteers would have to make their way as best they could over several hundred miles of wilderness, since no provision was made for returning the men to their homes. For a person of Jackson's temperament there was only one thing to do — and that one thing did not include obeying orders. Disregarding his instructions, he marched his men home, placing himself liable for the necessary expenses. It was a brave and humane action — bad military etiquette, good politics. Eventually he was paid for his expenses.

CREEK WAR

The return of Jackson to Tennessee coincided with a new outbreak by the Indians of the Southwest. The Civilized Nations had long resented white aggression, and now were heartened by the defeat of Hull in the North. More immediately important, however, were internal conflicts, particularly between those who favored adopting white methods of life and those who preferred traditional Indian customs, and even the peace tour of Tecumseh could not allay the dispute. As part of this intratribal struggle there came on August 30, 1813, an attack by Creek primitives upon the half-breeds at Fort Mims, which lay at the junction of the Alabama and the Tombigbee. In the ensuing battle the attackers were carried away by their martial enthusiasm, and ended by killing all the people of Fort Mims, white as well as Indian.

Almost before the last of the scalps had been torn from the heads of the slaughtered whites at Fort Mims, plans had been made for punitive expeditions into the territory of the hostile Indians. As a matter of fact these plans had largely been prepared before, and needed only the finishing touches before they were put into effect. Three armies were to take the field — one from Georgia under John Floyd, a second from Louisiana under W. C. C. Claiborne, and a third from Tennessee under Jackson. In practice the three divisions failed to cooperate according to plans, the generals quarreled over precedence, supplies were poor and insufficient, and the troops were disaffected. The Jackson column was by far the most important of the three.

The orders for Jackson to take the field against the Indians arrived when Jackson was confined to his bed as the result of his shooting fray with the Bentons. In spite of his illness he assumed command of his army at once, and conducted the early part of the campaign when he could scarcely sit on his horse and should have been in bed. His plans called for a movement down the Coosa and Alabama rivers, with the establishment of permanent forts along the route. As he progressed he found himself opposed by the

Indians in continual skirmishing, with here and there a more important engagement.

Jackson's major difficulty was not with the Indians but with his own men. Most of them were new recruits, not anxious to fight the Indians at any time, but particularly opposed to fighting on empty stomachs. From time to time portions of them started to desert. Then Jackson had to use one part of the army to keep the remainder from going home, and subsequently to use the second group to keep the first in camp. To preserve discipline he punished infractions of all rules severely, which was an almost unknown procedure with frontier militia. On one point, however, the men succeeded in having their own way. In the middle of the campaign the enlistments of a majority of them expired and they decided to go home. Jackson blustered and raged, but still the men went home. Left with only a 1000 men, of whom most were enlisted for terms which would soon be over, he found it necessary to return to civilization to gather more troops.

By March 1814 Jackson again had 5000 troops at Fort Strother. Resuming his movement to the south he won decisive victories at Horseshoe Bend (March 27) and at the junction of the Coosa and the Tallapoosa ; on the latter battlefield he erected Fort Jackson, where in August he dictated a treaty by which the Creek ceded 22,000,000 acres of land, permitted military posts and roads, and agreed to keep the peace in the future. In the meantime his militia had been dismissed (April 21, 1814) and marched home. The southwestern Indians had been crushed.

Jackson was rewarded for his successful Indian campaign with the major generalship in the regular army left vacant by the resignation of Harrison. He made his headquarters in Mobile to be ready for either a recurrence of Indian trouble or an attack by the British. Having some leisure he entered into an acrimonious dispute with the governor of Florida over the return of fugitive Indians, and also built a fort west of Pensacola — clearly within Spanish territory. Finally, becoming impatient at the slowness with which the war was being fought, he asked permission of the War Department to take Pensacola, justifying his proposed action by the presence of English troops, whose capture he felt would be a " defense " of Spain. The War Department denied his request, whereupon Jackson captured Pensacola in November 1814. Desk generals could not keep Jackson from doing what he thought desirable.

BATTLE OF NEW ORLEANS

By this time it had become fairly certain that the British contemplated a southern invasion which would begin at New Orleans, and so as soon as Jackson had completed his occupation of Pensacola he hurried west to the hitherto defenseless New Orleans. Arriving on December 2, 1814, he displayed his usual energy in completing the defenses, collecting supplies, and in recruiting and training soldiers. Unified action was obtained by placing the city under martial law. As Jackson's preparations were nearing completion the British arrived, making a careful landing below the city. They were led by General Edward M. Pakenham, an able soldier who had seen service under Wellington.

After preliminary skirmishing the final attack on New Orleans was launched on January 8, 1815, and resulted in a complete victory for Jackson. The British advance was halted, Pakenham was killed, and soon the red-coated troops took boat and sailed away. It was a glorious victory for Jackson, who was thereupon toasted throughout the United States as the " hero of New Orleans." A picture of him riding a hypothetical white charger came to be a commonplace in the barrooms of the country. The glory of the feat was in nowise dimmed by the fact that it occurred two weeks after the signing of the Treaty of Ghent. Carping critics have insisted that Jackson's troops were superior in number and equipment and had their choice of a position to defend, while Pakenham's men were confused by the terrain. Even admitting these conditions, the credit which Jackson received for his effective handling of the defense of New Orleans was deserved.

After the victory of New Orleans Jackson continued to rule despotically. Military discipline was enforced vigorously and the very unusual punishment of death was given for desertion. New Orleans remained under martial law, and Jackson's word was supreme. Such a situation was endurable in time of imminent danger, but now that peace had returned the people of New Orleans became restive. Collisions between civil and military authority were increasingly frequent and acrimonious. Jackson involved himself in disputes with many people, including United States Judge D. A. Hall, Governor Claiborne, and the state legislature of Louisiana. The situation did not improve until the spring of 1815, when the army was restored to a peacetime basis. At this time Jacob Brown was placed in command north of the Ohio, Jackson

in the Southwest, and Edmund Gaines on the Florida border.
Jackson felt himself sufficiently relieved of military duties to
travel in the East, where he was acclaimed as the outstanding hero
of the late war.

FLORIDA TROUBLES

While Jackson was receiving a deserved ovation from his admir-
ing countrymen, the Florida situation remained as troublesome as
ever. Although active operations in that region had been curtailed
for the duration of the war, the United States had by no means
lost its interest in annexation. Now new sources of irritation made
the acquisition of Florida still more desirable. The Indians who had
been defeated farther north found an asylum in the Florida swamps,
from which they emerged to harass the border settlements. Escaped
Negro slaves also went to Florida, where they could not be re-
captured. Both groups remained actively hostile, partly because
of the activities of English traders who operated south of the
borders of the United States.

The center of the Florida trouble was the so-called " Negro
Fort " on the Apalachicola River. Here the escaped Negroes ral-
lied and showed disdain of their pursuers by desultory firing on
the Americans on the other side of the river. This situation was
no more pleasing to the Spanish governor of Florida than it was
to the Americans, so he gave permission for the capture and destruction of the fort. After a brief attack it was demolished by
hot shot on July 27, 1816.

Negotiations for the purchase of Florida were resumed by President Monroe after the War of 1812. In the latter part of 1817 he
felt sufficiently doubtful of the possibilities of peaceful purchase
to send troops to the border to invade the territory if the occasion
demanded. Gaines was ordered early in December to capture Amelia
Island, which was a well-known rendezvous of smugglers, and
Jackson was put in charge of border operations. When Gaines
arrived at Amelia Island he found a body of American filibusters
in control, and in consequence his occupation was bloodless.

When Jackson took control of the border late in 1817 he had a
not unreasonable feeling that the administration might be pleased
if he conquered the desired territory. Before acting upon his own
authority he took the precaution of writing to Monroe, asking
for at least tacit permission. Under normal conditions he would
have written to the Secretary of War, but in this case he disliked

the Secretary, even to the extent of forbidding his subordinates to obey any orders coming directly from the Department of War. This action was called treason by General Winfield Scott, whom Jackson then immediately challenged to a duel, which Scott refused on religious and patriotic grounds. Jackson's letter to Monroe was never read by the President, since he was sick at the time. His friend John Rhea, however, wrote to Jackson intimating that the President approved of the General's plans — or at least this was the tenor of the letter according to Jackson's later statements. Unfortunately Jackson had burned the original document before he quoted it to others.

With these hypothetical instructions Jackson raised troops in Tennessee and marched to a position near the site of the old " Negro Fort," arriving in March 1818. Then, pursuing some fleeing Negroes, he crossed the border into Florida. Later he supported this action on the grounds that hostile Indians were given encouragement from Florida, and that the Englishmen in the region were a continual source of trouble to the United States. In this advance into Florida he pushed the Indians ahead of him, killing a few of them as well as executing two Englishmen who happened to be in his path. The latter act caused the United States some diplomatic trouble. Eventually Jackson captured St. Marks, at the same time ordering Gaines to take St. Augustine. On his way home he made a final gesture by recapturing Pensacola, which had been returned to Spain.

Jackson's operations in Florida threw the government at Washington into turmoil. Spain was angry, and asked for the punishment of Jackson and the return of the captured territory. The negotiations for the purchase of Florida, which had been progressing fairly well, came to an end. Long Cabinet meetings debated whether or not Jackson should be upheld; Adams backed the General while Calhoun was his chief opponent. Congress was restive, and Henry Clay brought in a motion censuring Jackson for his precipitous action. Apparently Jackson himself was amazed and resentful of all this hubbub. In respect to the Cabinet he was entirely in error for he credited Calhoun with his defense and for many years hated Adams because of his supposed opposition. Jackson also missed the political significance of the move of Clay, and considered it as a personal affront.

Eventually the Cabinet adopted a compromise position. Pensacola and St. Marks were returned to Spain as requested, but Adams intimated plainly that the presence of Florida as a constant source of irritation was bound to produce just such invasions unless Spain sold the territory to the United States. The soundness of this attitude was demonstrated later in Spain's sale of Florida, but for the immediate present it only served to infuriate the irascible Jackson, who was certain in his own mind that he had obeyed orders. The compromise also displeased the people of the United States, who admired the spectacular exploits of the impetuous General. Monroe attempted to placate Jackson by a friendly letter, and the general public by an open communication to the *National Intelligencer*.

PURCHASE OF FLORIDA

The results of Adams' diplomacy came in the purchase of Florida in 1819 — the treaty not being ratified, however, until two years later. In addition to transferring title to Florida, the treaty also finally settled definitely the northern limits of Spanish claims in the Southwest. Starting at the mouth of the Sabine it followed that river to its intersection with the 32° of north latitude, then due north to the Red River, up the Red to 100° west longitude, north to the Arkansas River, along the Arkansas to its source, north to the 42° of latitude, and thence along that parallel to the Pacific. In view of later developments, it is interesting that not even Jackson desired to acquire Texas at this time.

After the acquisition of Florida Jackson was finally and completely vindicated by being appointed governor of the new Territory. As in previous similar situations, he at once proceeded to involve himself in quarrels with many of the people with whom he had dealings ; this time his chief opponent was the former Spanish governor. Jackson's temper was further ruffled by the scarcity of offices which he could bestow upon his relatives and friends. By October he had come to the conclusion that his health was not adequate for the governorship of Florida, and therefore resigned. Two years later he was offered a mission to Mexico, but refused because he thought that the mission was not needed.

The series of events in the Southwest which terminated with the acquisition of the Floridas had many and varied results. The United States had acquired a considerable body of new territory, rounding out its possessions east of the Mississippi, and leading many people to think that the end of expansion had been reached ; the Indians had been defeated and were to remain harmless for another generation; a new figure from the West — Andrew Jackson — had risen to prominence and assumed an important role on the national stage, while two of his principal rivals, Henry Clay and William Henry Harrison, also western, were brought into prominence by the war. Possibly most significant was the method which had been used for expansion — a method which was to appear again and again with but minor variations.

READINGS

K. T. Abbey, *Florida* (1941), chs. 6–8; J. S. Bassett, *The Life of Andrew Jackson* (2 vols., 1911), vol. 1, chs. 6–16; C. M. Brevard, *A History of Florida* (2 vols., 1925), vol. 1, chs. 1–5; P. C. Brooks, *Diplomacy and the Borderlands* (1939); F. E. Chadwick, *The Relations of the United States and Spain* (1909), chs. 4–7; R. S. Cotterill, *The Southern Indians* (1954), chs. 6–9; E. M. Coulter, *A Short History of Georgia* (1933), ch. 16; I. J. Cox, *The West Florida Controversy, 1798–1813* (1918)—definitive; H. B. Fuller, *The Purchase of Florida* (1906), chs. 1–11— old but still useful; C. N. Howard, *The British Development of West Florida* (1947)—heavily political; M. James, *Andrew Jackson the Border Captain* (1933), chs. 9–20; C. Johnson, *British West Florida, 1763–1783* (1943); G. W. Johnson, *Andrew Jackson* (1929), chs. 13–21; D. Karsner, *Andrew Jackson* (1929), chs. 13–21; S. W. Martin, *Florida During Territorial Days* (1944), ch. 1; R. W. Patrick, *Florida Fiasco* (1954)—Mathews and East Florida; J. W. Pratt, *The Expansionists of 1812* (1925), chs. 2, 5, 6; J. W. Silver, *Edmund Pendleton Gaines* (1949), ch. 4—detailed.

CHAPTER 14

THE GREAT MIGRATION

THE end of the War of 1812 was marked in the West by a vastly increased influx from the East. As with all population movements this resulted from conditions in both the old and new homes, for people were both propelled and drawn. The causes for the movement and the location of the migrants are the basic essentials of the western story.

PROSPERITY AND MIGRATION

From the standpoint of the East the decade of 1805–15 was generally a period of depression. The Napoleonic Wars created havoc for New England shipping and nearly ruined southern markets. The North began to turn to manufacturing, but the shift was as yet too small to be of widespread importance. Business was in the doldrums and times were hard.

Depression in the East might theoretically have meant an increase in the movement to the West by those brave souls who were willing to undertake a risk to obtain more economic opportunity, but actually no such expanded movement occurred. The costs of moving and of settling could not be dismissed with a shrug of the shoulders, and where was a man to obtain the necessary capital in hard times? The truth was that people could not afford to move in bad times, and consequently migration slowed, although of course it never came to a complete halt.

The attractive power of the West also declined in bad times, for the West felt the pressure of adversity as well as the East. Western agricultural prices fell, work was scarce and wages low. Serious handicaps were faced by the migrant who planned to leave the East without funds and to earn a stake in the West. Westerners wrote to their eastern friends advising them to defer their movement until times were better. Any potential migrant found the West much more attractive in good times than in bad.

Several types of evidence support the generalization that most westward movement occurred during periods of prosperity. Census material would seem to be the most obvious, but actually the federal figures are not very helpful, since a decennial count has no particular correlation with the business cycle. Here and there a state has useful figures, and particularly where a western territory counted its people several times in prospect of statehood. The dates of the admissions of the various states are in themselves helpful when ranged alongside of the business cycle. Accounts of western residents give clues to the times in which migration was heaviest, as do the toll receipts of certain roads and canals. Land sales can be tabulated, although with reservation that by no means all sales meant settlement or all settlement meant sales. But no matter what method is used the same conclusion appears — that the great flow of migration came in prosperous times.

While the depressed decade of 1805–15 discouraged migration, at the same time it contained seeds which germinated a little later into a large-scale push of population. Various striking events were giving the West effective advertising. The purchase of Louisiana, the Lewis and Clark expedition, the Burr episode, the travels of Pike, the boundary disputes, the Florida disturbances, the Indian wars, and the War of 1812 all helped to increase the general knowl-edge of the West and to encourage an interest in its possibilities. Then, too, the West was becoming more attractive and accessible. The Indian menace was practically eliminated with the operations of Harrison and Jackson. The National Road was under construction and the first steamboats were appearing on western waters. More land was available with the new land purchases and surveys. Land was becoming cheaper because of the land bonuses given to the soldiers in the War of 1812. These were given in the form of script, which most of the soldiers sold instead of exchanging for land. The throwing of considerable amounts of land warrants on the market made available large quantities of good land at comparatively low prices.

The factors at work in the period prior to the close of the War of 1812 produced an increased movement to the West which came to a peak in the years 1818–19 and ended with the panic of 1819. So great was the movement of population that it came to be known as the Great Migration. Over a million acres of land were sold in 1814, this total being greater than the sales in any one previous year, and the amount continued to increase until sales of approximately three and a half million acres were recorded for each of the years 1818 and 1819. After 1819 the figures decreased.

ACQUIRING LAND

The land settled during the Great Migration was theoretically occupied under the provisions of the land act of 1800, which provided for local land offices, the auction system, and then private sales at two dollars an acre, with possible credit for the greater part of the purchase price. Surveys of the new land were made as rapidly as possible and local land offices were opened as fast as they were needed; by 1820 there were thirty-four western land offices, of which fourteen were in Ohio. The auction system did not prove profitable, since the average selling price remained very near the legal minimum.

In actual practice the settlers paid but little attention to government surveys and sales. All surveys were necessarily made slowly and systematically, and included all the land, no matter whether it were good or bad. Settlement, on the other hand, skipped the seemingly poorer sections and took only the best land along the rivers. The result was that some of the settlement was always ahead of the surveys, and a large per cent of the new inhabitants were forced to take up unsurveyed land to which they had no legal right and trust to luck that they would be able to buy it at a later time. Their number was increased continually by those persons who lacked funds and sought consciously to elude the governmental land system.

The subdivision of the government which handled land sales prior to the War of 1812 was a bureau in the Department of the Treasury, but a more effective control of the public domain was made possible on April 25, 1812, with the creation of the General Land Office. The new bureau remained, however, a part of the Treasury Department until it was transferred to the Department of the Interior after that department was organized in 1849.

REGIONS OF SETTLEMENT

The greatest flow of settlers during the Great Migration followed the central route through either Pittsburgh or Wheeling and then down the Ohio River. The state of Ohio received more popu-

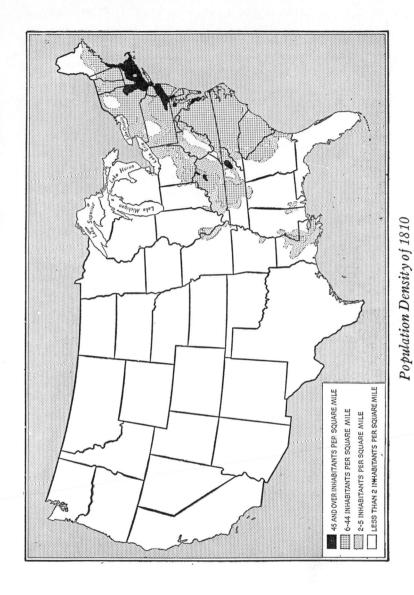

Population Density of 1810

Legend:
- 45 AND OVER INHABITANTS PER SQUARE MILE
- 6-44 INHABITANTS PER SQUARE MILE
- 2-5 INHABITANTS PER SQUARE MILE
- LESS THAN 2 INHABITANTS PER SQUARE MILE

lation than any other region, so that by 1820 its nearly 600,000 made it the most populous state west of the mountains. Farther to the west new families occupied southern Indiana and Illinois, followed the Mississippi both north and south, and pushed up the Wabash and Missouri. To the north a string of settlements blossomed along the entire southern shore of Lake Erie and as far west as Detroit, but again the density of population was small. Migrants clung closely to navigable waters and wooded land, and hence did not touch central and northern Indiana and Illinois or the great bulk of the present Michigan and Wisconsin. In 1820 the entire Michigan Territory (which included the present Wisconsin) contained less than 9000 persons.

To the south additional migration flowed into Kentucky and Tennessee, so that by 1820 the former was almost as large as Ohio, while the latter had well over 400,000 residents. In general the land extending north and south through the central section of the two states attracted most people. The real beginning of Memphis came in 1819, but any important growth waited until later. Still farther south the largest concentration of population was in Louisiana, where 150,000 people produced the fourth largest of the western states. Mississippi was settled almost exclusively in the south. Alabama had a sprinkling of farms covering most of the western half of the state, but with the greatest concentration in the region of the great bend of the Alabama River. West of the Mississippi, and in addition to the Louisiana and Missouri settlements, were a few residents in Arkansas Territory — particularly along the Mississippi and Arkansas rivers.

Even though the great majority of the West of 1820 was but sparsely settled the new states and territories west of the mountains could still boast a total of some two and a quarter million people, which gave it almost a quarter of the total population of the United States. Here lies the reason for the ever increasing power of the West in the federal government. In the House its votes might be decisive, while in the Senate its proportionate strength was even greater. Consequently the West had better than an even chance of obtaining any legislation which it really desired wholeheartedly. The great limitation was that the West was not itself always united. Clay and Jackson were both westerners, but not necessarily in accord for that reason. The more highly developed states such as Ohio and Kentucky by no means always agreed with the smaller and younger communities.

METHOD OF SETTLEMENT

The process of hewing homes from the wilderness during the Great Migration was very similar to that of twenty years before. There was the same long and tedious trip to the West, the same effort to pick out good land near eastern friends, the same clearing of a plot of land, the same community house-building, and the same girdling of trees and planting. Amusements were still furnished by dances, house-raisings, singing schools, weddings, camp meetings, and husking bees. Life had changed but little since the first pioneers had followed Daniel Boone into the wilderness.

The crops of the newly settled lands in the Ohio Valley were, as before, chiefly corn, wheat, rye, oats, tobacco, hemp, and flax. Prices were comparatively high, but it was difficult to get the goods to market. Labor was scarce and expensive, and difficult tasks were done by community effort. Clothing, as in an earlier period, was made at home of wool and flax produced on the farm, the common cloth being linsey-woolsey. The component materials continued to be raised, carded, spun, woven, and sewed at home. Even shoes were still made by the frontiersman, although the tanning of leather was coming more and more to be a commercial process. Both clothing and shoes were saved as much as possible, particularly in the summer.

Centralized industry continued to develop slowly. Pittsburgh still grew and prospered with its manufacture of iron, glass, and rope, and its building of boats. Farther west Cincinnati was attaining commercial importance, particularly with the development of pork packing; the farmers were gradually learning that it was more advantageous to drive their hogs to a central slaughtering and packing plant than to do the work themselves. St. Louis was coming into prominence as a center of the fur business and as a distributing point for the Far West. New Orleans, with the increase of the steamboat traffic, continued to maintain her commercial dominance. Other smaller but bustling centers contained particularly water-driven lumber mills, grist mills, distilleries, and tanneries.

HEALTH

One of the most unsatisfactory conditions of frontier life was the lack of adequate medical facilities. During the first quarter of the nineteenth century there were very few properly trained doctors west of the mountains. Competent physicians preferred to remain in the East rather than to embrace the poorly paid and hardworking life which was inevitable farther west. Western medical practice included riding many miles over atrocious roads, day and night, in good weather and bad, to serve a widely scattered and poor population. Good hospitals did not exist, and medical schools and publications were rare.

The West was not an exceedingly healthful region in spite of the outdoor life and hard work of its inhabitants. Accidents were common as long as hunting, felling trees, and fighting Indians were regular pursuits. Fever and ague were omnipresent in the lowlands of the Ohio. Scarlet fever was frequent and at times epidemic. Yellow fever was prevalent in the New Orleans region during the summers, killing its hundreds and thousands. A typhoid epidemic caused great fatalities all over the West in 1816–17. Cholera had periodic epidemics, the worst being in 1832 at the time of the Black Hawk War. In addition to these outstanding diseases, the westerner suffered from many of the other ills to which the flesh is heir.

The earliest form of medical treatment on the frontier was given by any individual who possessed even the simplest knowledge of drugs and surgery. Every educated man was supposed to be competent to treat disease, and each family had its own supply of simple herbs such as calomel, jalap, and cinchona bark (containing quinine). The seventh son of a seventh son was presumed to have unusual healing powers; early morning dew was supposed to be excellent for the complexion. As for surgery, it vied in gruesomeness with torture by the Indians. For example, the incidents of an amputation without anesthetics (for ether and chloroform were not used until the 1840s) and performed with a butcher knife, a meat saw, and a hot iron are best left to oblivion.

The ministrations of the early pioneer doctor were little better than those of kind friends, for such a practitioner ordinarily had but little formal education, and learned his trade from his predecessors and by experience. His equipment, which he carried in his saddlebags, consisted of a few simple drugs, roots, herbs, calomel, a lancet, cupping glasses, and possibly a few other crude surgical instruments and a supply of leeches. He compounded all of his own medicines, for there were few drugstores; particularly bitter doses were concealed in a piece of apple or dough. The western physician had two principal cures for all diseases — calomel or jalap, and bleeding. Calomel (sometimes jalap) was prescribed for every known disease, and calomel was often given in such large doses that it caused intense salivation and loosening of teeth and gums. Bloodletting was almost equally universal, being ordinarily accomplished by either cupping or the use of leeches. The leeches were put in a tumbler and then the open end of the tumbler placed on the skin. Cupping consisted of opening a vein and applying a glass from which the air had been expelled by the burning of alcohol. Such bloodletting was done in reckless amounts and was considered especially efficacious for any illness which included a fever.

Early medical methods produced results which were marvelous, not in the large number of fatalities, but in the comparative size of the group which remained alive. Fresh air was taboo; in a case of fever or inflammation the patient was placed between feather beds and the doors and windows tightly closed. Cautery was performed with a white hot iron. Wounds were encouraged to discharge pus by being kept irritated with threads or a pea. Hemorrhages were treated by bloodletting.

Western doctors were bad and western health poor, but these assertions lose some of their force in view of the fact that American health in general was poor and few American doctors well-trained. Western epidemics were national and world epidemics, while peculiar western remedies were also general American remedies. Furthermore, the West had some of the nation's more progressive doctors. Dr. William Goforth introduced vaccination to the West at the early date of 1801. Dr. Sappington of Missouri popularized the use of quinine, particularly for malaria, in the 1830s with " Dr. John Sappington's Anti-Fever Pills." Dr. Crawford Long, a small-town Georgia doctor, probably made the first medical use of ether as an anesthetic in 1842 — for the removal of a neck tumor.

Curiously enough the West was responsible for first performing several notable medical operations. Dr. Francis Prevost of Louisiana claimed the use of the rare Caesarean section in four cases prior to 1832, with three of them successful. The best authenticated of the early Caesarean operations was performed by Dr. John L. Richmond in 1827 in rural Ohio. Dr. Richmond, who was also a Baptist minister, was called to the rude shack of a Negro woman late one night, and there he performed the operation by the light of candles and with only his pocket case of tools; the child died, but the woman returned to work in twenty-four days. Most amazing of all was the ovariotomy performed by Dr. Ephraim McDowell of Danville, Kentucky, in 1809. Without special training or equipment, and of course without anesthetics, Dr. McDowell was the first man in the world to remove an ovarian tumor successfully; this operation marked the real beginning of abdominal surgery.

After about 1820 medical science west of the mountains gradually improved. Here and there promising young men attended the medical schools in the East, while more and better doctors moved west as the population grew sufficiently large to support them. Medical schools were established in the West. The earliest of these schools was the medical department of Transylvania, which attained an excellent reputation by the 1830s. Other schools such as the Ohio Medical College (1819) and the Worthington Medical College (1832) helped to raise the tone of medical practice. Magazines such as the *Ohio Medical Repository* (1826), which later became the *Western Journal of the Medical and Physical Sciences* under the editorship of Daniel Drake, provided mediums for disseminating the latest scientific advances.

THE NEWER SOUTHWEST

During the period of the Great Migration the Southwest began to receive the distinctive migration which in time made this region very different from that north of the Ohio. The change was due largely to two important developments. The first was the invention of the cotton gin by Eli Whitney in 1793 and its subsequent rapid introduction after 1800, which made practicable the large cotton plantation operated by slave labor. The second was the opening of large quantities of virgin soil in the Southwest by Jackson's successful operation against the Creek. As a result of these two factors there was a gradual western push by the cotton planters and their slaves. The movement first became noticeable about 1810, and after that time grew very rapidly.

The new southern migration did not change radically the old pioneer process; rather it brought it to a different conclusion. The first stages of settlement, both North and South, remained approximately equivalent, with the appearance of the trapper and hunter, followed by the agricultural pioneer who cleared the land and planted the first crop of grain. Sometimes the frontiersman had one or two slaves, but such was ordinarily not the case. After the land had been cleared and planted, the process of further development diverged widely in North and South. In the South, the first settler either bought more slaves and started the cultivation of cotton or else sold his holdings to a large eastern planter and mover farther west. No matter what procedure was followed, the result was large plantations with slave labor, a one-crop system, and no efforts to prevent soil exhaustion. The prosperous farming communities and small towns of the North did not appear. Eventually the soil was depleted and the planter moved again, leaving behind him exhausted and deserted land. The wise planter did not remain in one place until the exhaustion of the soil made his farming unprofitable.

By the end of the War of 1812 the southern roads to the West were so crowded with planters and gangs of Negroes that there was a scarcity of provisions. The Negroes, sometimes shackled, traveled on foot while the planters rode. Most went overland, although a few moved to the lower Mississippi Valley either by ocean or by way of the Ohio and Mississippi rivers. The roads, as elsewhere, were very bad, often being little more than bridle paths. The most important one in the Far South was the Federal Road, authorized by Congress in 1806, which ran from Athens, Georgia, by way of the Tombigbee settlement to New Orleans; in the east it connected Athens with Greenville, Charlotte, Salisbury, Fredericksburg, Washington, and Baltimore. A few slaves appeared in Kentucky and Missouri, and more in Tennessee, but the main influx was in the lower South.

The majority of the planters who moved West came from the piedmont region of the East rather than from the coastal plain, and carried to their new homes the customs with which they had been familiar. They soon constructed large ramshackle " mansions " in which they dispensed typical southern hospitality. They raised but two important crops — cotton and corn — and cotton predominated, in part because its price was unusually high in the period immediately after the War of 1812. The first plowing came in February, and the cotton was planted in March. Later the plants required thinning and frequent cultivation. Picking occurred late in August and on into the winter. After picking, the cotton was ginned, although a certain amount of impurities had to be removed by hand, and then pressed into 350-pound bales. There was no fertilization of the soil and no rotation of crops, so that the land was soon exhausted. Often the plantation depended on the outside for even its necessary food and clothing.

The labor of the southern plantation was performed by Negro slaves, who were worked in large gangs under continuous supervision. Each slave was given clothing twice a year, in the spring and fall. His total cost per year to his master was about twenty to twenty-five dollars, exclusive of food. With full-time work he was supposed to be able to cultivate from five to six acres of cotton or corn, with the result that for each slave there was about a thousand pounds of ginned cotton. In some cases the individual slave would be given a limited area of land and allowed to cultivate it at his own discretion. All the planter's profits were in any case put back into the business to purchase new land and slaves, so that he seldom had any reserve capital and was frequently in debt. When a dwindling yield threatened disaster in any one area, he might move his whole laboring force and equipment farther west.

The most obvious characteristics of the southern system of agriculture were the increasing importance of cotton and the rapid exhaustion of the soil. In the decade 1811–21 only one-third by value of the crops raised west of Georgia was cotton, but by 1831 the proportion had grown to one-half and by 1834 to two-thirds ($75,000,000). From the standpoint of soil depletion, older communities such as Virginia had shown evidences of exhaustion as early as colonial times, and districts farther west soon exhibited the same tendency, so that a decrease of population and wealth in the older communities was by no means unusual.

Another characteristic of the southern system was a continued and increasing demand for slaves. Instead of dying, as southern colonial leaders had expected, the institution of slavery grew progressively stronger. While the demand for additional western labor was filled in part by the increase of illegal slave trading, more important was the selling of Negroes from the worn-out farms of the East to the new lands of the West. Eastern slave owners were confronted with exhausted lands and an oversupply of Negroes to be fed and clothed, while the West was willing to pay high prices for the same undesired eastern slaves. The result was the development of a recognized and lucrative profession of buying Negroes in the East, shipping them to the West, and selling them to western plantation owners. The traffic was so profitable that in some cases slave owners were accused of breeding their slaves like cattle to profit by their sale.

To the Negro, being sold to the West was the acme of misfortune, and many of the more humane owners refused to sell their slaves for the western trade. The West meant hard work, poor food, inadequate clothes, and an excessive amount of sickness. The swampy cotton plantations of Mississippi or sugar plantations of Louisiana were especially dangerous, and slaves died by the hundred. The general attitude of the Negro toward being moved to the wilderness is fairly well expressed by the popular old song " Darling Nellie Gray ":

One night I went to see her, but, " She's gone ! " the neighbors say,
The white man bound her with his chain ;
They have taken her to Georgia for to wear her life away,
As she toils in the cotton and the cane.

Free Negroes were not numerous in the West except at New Orleans, where they included many artisans and small shop owners. Generally they were well-behaved, although a slave revolt in 1811 had made the whites extremely fearful. Curiously enough they supported slavery and themselves had slaves. City life produced some unusual factors for the Negro. Many mulatto girls became the mistresses of white men, while likely looking mulatto female slaves found a good market among the " sporting class." The result was a lack of women to marry Negro men.

NEW STATES AND TERRITORIES

Advancing settlement brought agitation for statehood, since most westerners desired greater self-government than existed under territorial organization. Each region followed the steps outlined in the Northwest Ordinance — Congressional control, limited self-government, and finally statehood. In each case a Congressional enabling act and a constitutional convention preceded admission to the Union. The state constitutions showed the definitely democratic tendencies of the times, with limitations on executive power, removal of religious and property qualifications for voting, and the election of judges by the legislature. These trends were not original with the West, but had their fullest expression in that region.

North of the Ohio the western fruits of the Great Migration in terms of new states were Indiana and Illinois. Indiana Territory had come into existence in 1800, and with the arrival of settlers its size was reduced by the creation of Michigan (1805) and Illinois (1809) Territories. The second stage of territorial government came in 1805, and ten years later an Indiana census showed sufficient people for statehood — 60,000. The Indiana desire for statehood was satisfied by Congress in 1816. A strict adherence to the boundaries stated in the Northwest Ordinance would have meant that Indiana only touched Lake Michigan at a single point, but the extension of the northern boundary of the state for ten miles at the expense of Michigan produced the lake frontage that now includes the city of Gary. Indianapolis, founded in 1819, became the state capital in 1825 for no better reason than that it was approximately the geographical center of the state.

Illinois' first governor was Ninian Edwards, who remained in office until statehood. The second stage of territorial government was achieved in 1812, and a growing movement for statehood attained fruition in 1818, even though the population was then considerably less than the 60,000 that was supposedly required. Like Indiana the new state was given a lake frontage — this time by extending the northern boundary some sixty miles; in consequence many loyal Wisconsinites have long felt resentful that Chicago is in Illinois rather than in Wisconsin. North of Indiana and Illinois the country to the international boundary had been realloted several times, depending largely on southern conditions. From 1818, upon the admission of Illinois, until Wisconsin became a territory present Michigan and Wisconsin were included as the Territory of Michigan.

South of the Ohio River the first new state of the nineteenth century was Louisiana, which had been populated largely before the Americans took control and hence should not be considered as a result of the Great Migration. Its admission in 1812 was opposed bitterly by New England Federalists, who foresaw dire results if the entire Louisiana Purchase, with its semi-wild people, were to be carved into states and admitted to the Union. The eastern boundary of the new state was extended to the Pearl River, thus including a part of West Florida, which had but recently been annexed by the United States.

Mississippi Territory had come into existence in 1798 to provide for the region between 31° and the mouth of the Yazoo, which had just been evacuated reluctantly by Spain. The addition of the Georgia land cession of 1802 expanded the new territory to the present size of Mississippi and Alabama, except for the Gulf Coast, which was not added until 1812. After Jackson crushed Indian resistance settlement flowed in increasing amounts — particularly to the rich black land of the Mississippi, the Gulf Coast, and the valleys of the Alabama and Tombigbee. Expanding population brought a division of the territory in 1817, the year in which

Mississippi became a state. Two years later Alabama followed it into the Union; by 1820 the population of Alabama was about 128,000, which was well over half again as large as that of Mississippi.

The last two states to be produced by the Great Migration were Maine and Missouri, admitted respectively in 1820 and 1821. Maine had been a part of Massachusetts, but in 1820 was separated in accordance with the wishes of both parties. Missouri could boast a more checkered career; in fact it had been something of an administrative problem, since for many years the St. Louis settlement had been the only important area of population west of the Mississippi. The entire Louisiana purchase exclusive of the prospective state of Louisiana had been successively Louisiana District (1804) attached to Indiana Territory, Louisiana Territory (1805), and Missouri Territory (1812). In 1819, two years before Missouri became a state, Arkansas Territory was created to include not only present Arkansas but also the land west to the existing international boundary.

The only important white settlements west of the Mississippi were in what is now Missouri, which had benefited from its proximity to the junction of the Mississippi and the Missouri. Early settlements had hugged the Mississippi, with Ste. Genevieve the earliest — a little past the middle of the eighteenth century — and St. Louis a little later. Even before 1800 the advance fringe of settlement, led by Daniel Boone, had advanced up the Missouri. Upon the acquisition of Louisiana, present Missouri had a population of possibly 10,000; it then grew rapidly, particularly in the period of the Great Migration. By 1820 its population was well over 60,000 and clamoring for statehood.

The application of Missouri for statehood called attention to the fact that with the admission of Alabama in 1819 the slave and free states each numbered eleven. This equality of sectional interests seemed important to the politicians of the time, for it insured the South half of the votes of the Senate in a day when its influence in the House was declining. Consequently Congress, after a heated debate, accepted (1820) the admission of Missouri and Maine as compensating states, but with the proviso that no later state formed from the Louisiana Purchase and north of the principal southern boundary of Missouri (36° 30′) should have slavery. The " Missouri Compromise " led to the immediate admission of Maine, but Missouri was delayed until the following year (1821).

The delay was caused by the action of Missouri which adopted an extremely stringent pro-slavery constitution to demonstrate its independence, and thus made a new compromise necessary. Missouri was the twenty-fourth state to enter the Union. Of the twenty-four states nine were west of the Appalachians.

LAND LAW OF 1820

One of the most important consequences of the Great Migration, from the standpoint of the West, was its effect on the land legislation of the United States. Glaring faults in the public land system, which otherwise might have gone unnoticed, were brought to light by the desire of thousands of new citizens for homes and farms. Outstanding were the difficulties produced by the credit feature of the act of 1800. Western farmers were always too optimistic, and insisted upon buying all the land on which they could make the first payments, with the result that they were frequently unable to meet succeeding installments. Theoretically they should then have been dispossessed and their first payments forfeited. Actually it was difficult to evict thousands of farmers when they became obstinate and bitter, and such a procedure was politically questionable when votes were needed by the party in power. Not only the delinquent farmers, but all of the West was opposed to dispossession and forfeiture, for each westerner realized that at some future time he might have the same sort of trouble.

The credit situation became worse and the number of defaulters increased when hard times swept the country. Such a period came during the Napoleonic wars, the Indian troubles in the West, and the War of 1812, when a depression was general and the existence of a farmer militia prevented many westerners from tilling their land. To add to these difficulties, the existence of a disorganized currency in the West made it hard to tell the well-to-do from the paupers, for wealth did not depend on the amount of money as much as upon the institution which issued it.

The immediate result of western difficulties was a flood of petitions asking for Congressional assistance. Congress responded by the passage of a long series of relief bills which aided particular persons and localities by postponing or remitting payments, or by alloting reduced amounts of land to correspond with the amount of money already paid. In spite of this relief, $21,000,000 was still overdue and unpaid in 1820, and with the panic of 1819 the future looked dark.

The failure of Congress to modify the land act of 1800 at an earlier time than it did was due in part to a very real division of opinion as to what should be done. The East continued to feel that western land was a trust fund for the nation, and should be made to produce the largest possible amount of revenue. Furthermore, many easterners favored a high price for the land to discourage western migration so that the new manufacturing establishments of the East would not suffer from a lack of labor. The West, on the other hand, was strongly of the opinion that the land should belong to the people who worked it and gave it value. It was further argued that a reduced price would encourage settlement and thus add to the wealth and strength of the United States.

Out of this sea of conflicting purposes eventually emerged the land act of 1820. The credit system was abolished with general consent. The smallest unit to be sold was eighty acres. The auction system was to be retained, and was to be followed, as before, with private entry at the minimum price, but now the price was reduced to the compromise figure of $1.25 an acre. Defaulters under former legislation were to be aided by being given outright an amount of land corresponding to the money which they had already paid.

The act of 1820 was a distinct improvement upon former legislation concerning the public domain. The credit idea was never revived. The smaller minimum unit was found desirable and retained. On the other hand, the auction system continued to prove less and less satisfactory. The settler wanted the right to settle on the land before it was surveyed and then to be assured that the speculator could not bid it away from him at an auction. The most pressing demand of the West continued to be, as ever, low-priced land. These western desires came to be mixed with sectional conflicts in the twenty years after the passage of the act of 1820 and were a continual source of trouble in Congress.

The Great Migration was significant in carrying settlers to, and even beyond the Mississippi, although large areas remained unsettled farther east, both in the North and South. Half a dozen new states had been added to the Union, until the older West was no longer the frontier of settlement. Ohio, Kentucky, and Tennessee were soon to consider themselves old and well-settled regions, and to resemble seaboard communities more than the regions on the newer frontier. The conquest of the continent had been well begun.

READINGS

T. P. Abernethy, *The Formative Period in Alabama, 1815–1828* (1922); E. H. Ackernecht, *Malaria in the Upper Mississippi Valley* (1945); C. W. Alvord, *The Illinois Country* (1920), ch. 21; J. D. Barnhart, *Valley of Democracy* (1953), chs. 11–13— Indiana and Illinois statehood; S. J. Buck, *Illinois in 1818* (1918), chs. 2–11; R. C. Buley, *The Old Northwest* (2 vols., 1950), vol. 1, chs. 1–5, vol. 2, ch. 9—detailed; L. Esarey, *History of Indiana* (1915), chs. 29–33; B. H. Hibbard, *Public Land Policies* (1924), chs. 5–7; S. H. Holbrook, *The Yankee Exodus* (1950), ch. 6— episodical; A. L. Kohlmeier, *The Old Northwest* (1938), ch. 1; J. F. McDermott (ed.), *The Early Histories of St. Louis* (1952) —extracts; J. B. Martin, *Indiana* (1947), chs. 2, 3—thin; T. C. Pease, *The Story of Illinois* (1949), chs. 5, 6; M. E. Pickard and R. C. Buley, *The Medical Pioneer* (1945); R. M. Robbins, *Our Landed Heritage* (1942), ch. 2; F. C. Shoemaker, *Missouri and Missourians* (5 vols., 1943), vol. 1, chs. 5–16; L. D. Stilwell, *Migration from Vermont* (1937); W. T. Utter, *The Frontier State* (1942), ch. 12—Illinois; E. M. Violette, *A History of Missouri* (1918), chs. 5, 6—text; E. N. Wentworth, *America's Sheep Trails* (1948), ch. 5—detailed; S. C. Williams, *The Beginnings of West Tennessee* (1930), chs. 10–37; C. G. Woodson, *The Negro in Our History* (1922), ch. 7.

CHAPTER 15

TRANSPORTATION BY ROAD

THE West of the early nineteenth century had no more pressing and perplexing problem than that of providing adequate transportation. Rivers were extremely useful, but even they had certain definite and inescapable drawbacks. Most obvious was the sad fact that a river ran in only one direction while traffic desired a two-way route. Migrants could use a flatboat to Illinois and corn meal could be floated to New Orleans, but the reverse trip was always arduous and expensive. Rivers also frequently became low in the fall and froze in the winter. Furthermore rivers did not pass every one's front door, but left many communities without transportation; this situation became worse as an increasing flow of settlers were forced to make their homes farther and farther in the interior. Possibly the greatest trouble of all was that rivers did not flow over mountains, and hence generally made no connections between East and West.

The various defects in water transportation meant that road travel was always an integral and important part of the American system of transportation. From the trapper who plodded along a blazed trail through the wilderness to the streamlined automobile that rolls over a concrete highway, a large and important part of American travel has always been performed over land and by road.

Road building was an exceedingly primitive art before 1790. Prior to that date there were no paved roads in the United States, and but few were improved in any way; to say merely that they were bad is to be generous. The ordinary road was an imperfectly cleared path which exhibited two deep ruts in dry weather and seas of mud in wet; the streams were crossed at fords, with here and there a ferry. Regular coach lines did not become common until after the Revolution.

Road making was revolutionized by the discoveries of McAdam and Telford in England about 1790. These two men were respon-sible for the crushed rock, drained highway. The first application in the United States of the knowledge of better road building was made on a turnpike traversing the sixty-two miles between Phila-delphia and Lancaster. This road was built by a private company, and for many years after its opening in 1794 was one of the finest in the United States, attracting travelers from many miles to ride on its comparatively smooth surface. Both this and later similar roads were " Macadamized," but at that time the process did not include the use of any " tar " binder. Various sizes of crushed rock were placed on the roadbed and packed down by the traffic; the result was a fairly level surface as long as sufficient repairs pre-vented the formation of ruts.

WESTERN ROADS

The early roads of the West performed the difficult feat of being worse than those in the East. Originally they had been In-dian trails following the uplands wherever possible. With the com-ing of the whites the paths were blazed (notches made in the trees along their borders) and gradually became broader from the in-creased travel and the larger packs carried. Eventually pack horses and mules could be used on them, but wagons and coaches were impossible before 1800 except on specially favored routes such as Braddock's Road and Forbes Road. Not only were most of the trails too narrow for large conveyances but their roughness made horseback riding more comfortable than traveling in a springless wagon or coach.

In the period from 1800 to the close of the War of 1812 western roads improved with exasperating slowness. A few were broadened by cutting down more trees; the worst mud holes were made pass-able by logs laid side by side, and here and there ferries were estab-lished. In general, however, there was very little real road build-ing, and most highways remained only broadened trails, difficult for the passage of wagons and impossible for coaches.

The roads became worse as the traveler went farther west. While the rocks of the mountains never were conducive to smooth trans-portation, the bottomless mud pits of the plains were even less desirable. Rumor said that such mud holes could swallow horse and rider at one gulp. The paths were but partially cleared, and the traveler had to weave his way back and forth among the stumps of felled trees. A few crude and erratic ferries seemed as gifts of a beneficent Providence to the harassed wayfarer.

Western vehicular traffic seldom moved in anything as impressive as a coach in the years around 1800. Passengers ordinarily rode in a farm wagon with seats placed crosswise, and sometimes covered by canvas top and curtains. Freight was carried in a Pennsylvania or Conestoga wagon. The Conestoga was distinctive in being tipped upward at each end, reputedly to avoid losing freight on the hills. A sixteen-foot box was covered by a twenty-four foot canvas top, and the whole rig hauled ordinarily by six horses. The blue underbody, red upper, and white top produced a vivid and patriotic display on the roads. The poorer roads would hold nothing more than a wooden cart with two wide wooden wheels, while even more usual was the horseback rider, with his entire baggage contained in a pair of saddlebags.

The building of good roads was an almost insuperable problem in view of the immense distances and lack of funds. The federal government was willing to strain its resources for little more than military roads in the territories and mail subsidies — for even on the main western routes mail was usually carried at a loss. The states legislated concerning some of the main highways, but their somewhat grandiose plans produced but meager results because their funds were utterly inadequate. Private businessmen now and then opened a toll road, and in a few cases were subsidized by the federal government. Counties and townships performed most of the road building in practice, but instead of collecting taxes for this purpose, they ordinarily permitted a citizen to work out his taxes on the roads; the results seem to indicate that most men working for the government at that time seized the opportunity for a good rest.

In spite of the many difficulties in the generation after 1790, the West succeeded in opening a number of main roads that usually, but not always, permitted wagon travel. Among the best known was Zane's Trace from Wheeling to Limestone (later Maysville) Kentucky. Its construction, which was aided by a Congressional land grant in 1796, consisted in felling the larger trees — but not removing the stumps — and clearing away the brush. Zane's Trace connected with another to Lexington and that in turn with still another to Nashville, from which place one could follow the famous

Natchez Trace to Natchez. This route, followed in the other direction, was used extensively by men returning home after having taken their flatboats to New Orleans. Among other main highways was the one directly over the mountains to Nashville, and the one through Georgia to New Orleans, both of which have been mentioned earlier in other connections.

The badness of western roads was advantageous at least to the city of New Orleans, which blossomed vigorously after the purchase of Louisiana made certain the freedom of the river. But the pleasure and profit of New Orleans merchants did not seem the most desirable goal for the rest of the United States. Westerners gnashed their teeth when they viewed eastern markets with their higher prices — markets which could not be exploited because the cost of transportation increased the prices of western products to impossible levels. Then too, shipments to Europe could be made more cheaply from the eastern seaboard than from New Orleans provided the charge to the seaboard were only smaller.

The West was interested in purchases as well as in sales. As it grew in size and wealth it increasingly desired the luxuries of civilization, and these luxuries were almost prohibitive with the expense of poor transportation. For example, freight rates from Philadelphia to Pittsburgh about 1800 were ordinarily $5 a hundred pounds and the stage fare some $20; the cost of a piano delivered in rural Indiana would have staggered the purse of any but a John Jacob Astor.

ROADS BETWEEN EAST AND WEST

The East was also distressed about the lack of adequate transportation to and in the West. Shippers and manufacturers regretted bitterly their impotence in reaching the expanding western market, and viewed the western traffic floating down the river to New Orleans with anything but joy. Consequently the East joined the West in clamoring more and more loudly for improved transportation between the sections. The main objective of the agitation was an improved road and, as is usual in such cases, Congress was implored to provide for its construction.

Congress was perfectly willing to aid the project as long as it did not mean an immediate expenditure of cash. In the Ohio Enabling Act of 1802 (as modified in 1803) provision was made that five per cent of the proceeds of land sales in Ohio should go for roads; three-fifths of the total amount should be used for roads within the state and the other two-fifths should be spent for roads from elsewhere to the borders of the state. Similar provisions were made for other states admitted later to the Union, and as the land was sold a fund gradually accumulated in the treasury of the United States. The three-per-cent fund soon permitted Ohio to build a number of roads, particularly between Lake Erie and the Ohio River, although other states with less land sales were not so lucky. The two-per-cent fund soon permitted the forming of plans for the building of a road to connect the East and the West.

NATIONAL ROAD

As soon as this proposed road had passed from the stage of speculation to that of a near possibility, the problem of selecting its route became important. Each town which felt it had a chance of being placed on the main line of east-west travel did its best to attract the road. The eastern terminus finally was set at Baltimore, although actual construction started at Cumberland. For the western terminus Pittsburgh, Wheeling, and Steubenville were all strong contenders, but the prize finally went to Wheeling. Because of the influence of Albert Gallatin of Uniontown, the road was planned to run through the Pennsylvania towns of Washington and Uniontown. The route made necessary by these decisions was first embodied in a Congressional report in December 1805. In general it was that of Braddock's Road, but with its western terminus at Wheeling instead of Pittsburgh. It passed through the states of Maryland, Pennsylvania, and Virginia, and these states immediately gave their consent to the construction.

Provision for the definite location of the road was made by act of Congress on March 29, 1806. The general route was stated, but the formulation of detailed plans was left to a commission to be appointed by the President. While this commission completed definite plans within the next few years, so that it was possible to let the first contracts in 1811, actual construction was delayed by the War of 1812 and did not commence until 1815. By 1818 the United States mails were running between Washington and Wheeling over the new road. The eastern part was cheaper to construct than the western, and the total cost was $1,700,000 or an average of $13,000 a mile, which was probably too much. The desirability of the route which the road followed is easily apparent to the modern user of the National Road, for the present highway follows its predecessor very closely.

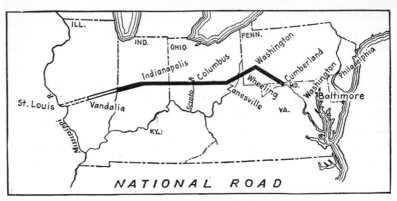

Cumberland to Wheeling opened by 1818. Ohio portion opened by 1837. Indiana section graded and bridged by the national government, but opened privately in 1850. Illinois portion never built by the national government, but graded and bridged to Vandalia.

The right of way of the National Road (often called the Cumberland Road) was thirty feet wide in the mountains and sixty-six feet elsewhere. Bridges were of solid masonry and built so strongly that many are still in use. The roadbed was raised in the center and ditches were dug on each side in order to drain off the water. The roadbed was composed of stones, of which those comprising the lower stratum were broken to pass through a seven-inch ring and those of the upper stratum through a three-inch ring. The stones were broken with a round hammer weighing about a pound, although larger stones required a larger hammer. The laborer who broke the smaller stones sat on a rock pile to do his work, and received an average wage of about a dollar a day. The stones were packed into the roadbed by the traffic. A layer of stones was dumped into place, traffic was permitted to pass over it, then another layer of stones was added, and the process continued until the stones were packed to the requisite depth.

Even though the National Road was a great improvement upon its predecessors, it too had serious deficiencies. A gravel road made of loosely packed stones was fairly smooth when it was built, but soon deteriorated. A steady flow of traffic produced bad ruts, while melting snows and heavy rains made deep gullies and from time to time washed out portions of the mountain construction. The eastern part of the road had been worn out before the western part was opened, and continual repairs were a necessity if the road were to be kept in good condition.

Congress had apparently considered only the original construction of the road and had not thought of the necessity of repairs. But this attitude became difficult to maintain almost before the highway was completed, and the rapid deterioration of the road produced a continually increasing popular pressure for further outlays for upkeep. The obvious method to provide for repairs was to erect toll gates and to use the toll money for replacements, and a bill for that purpose passed Congress. To the dismay of friends and users of the road, Monroe vetoed the bill. The President had come to the conclusion, after long and complicated Constitutional reasoning, that Congress had the power to build and repair the road, but not to charge toll. Congress refused to make appropriations out of general governmental funds, and so for a decade the road became poorer and poorer while its friends wrangled over the Constitutional aspects of toll collections by the federal government. The Gordian knot was finally cut when Congress provided for the repair of the road from current funds, after which it was to be given to the states in which it lay. These cessions occurred in the years 1831–34, and after this time the states erected tollhouses and used the collections for repairs.

TRAVEL ON THE NATIONAL ROAD

The National Road was crowded with traffic immediately upon its opening, for it afforded by far the best existing highway between East and West. Immigrants and their families, travelers, salesmen, farmers with their produce, freighters, stages, pedestrians, and cattle being driven to market filled the way between Cumberland and Wheeling. In the West, Wheeling grew in size and importance, while in the East Baltimore looked forward to a long period of commercial development.

Large freighting and coaching companies came into existence to care for this important and increasing traffic. Effective transportation of both goods and passengers required considerable amounts of equipment. In the passenger field the largest and most important of the stage lines was operated by the National Road Stage Company; its chief competitor was the Good Intent Line. Stages ran both day and night, and their arrival was the chief event of each town through which they passed.

A stage was ordinarily drawn by four horses, which were changed about every twelve miles to keep them in good condition and to permit rapid traveling. The stage itself had three seats, of which the front one faced the rear and the middle one had a strap for its back. Each seat held three passengers, and another place, beside the driver, was much coveted in fair weather. The driver was on top in front, and the baggage was placed in a " boot " in the rear. Leather straps were the only springs, and leather curtains were but partially successful barriers against rain and cold. A coach ride over the Alleghenies, with the coach rattling and jolting over the ruts and around the corners, with magnificent vistas in the distance and frightful chasms in the immediate foreground, was an experience not easily forgotten.

The aristocrat of the road was the stage driver, whose importance was comparable to that of the captain of a boat at sea. Every small boy along the road knew the drivers by name, and received an imperishable halo of glory in the eyes of his friends if one of the drivers condescended to recognize him. The importance of the driver did not depend on his salary, which was ordinarily twelve dollars a month and keep, but on his courage and skill. He drove rapidly and well, averaging ten miles an hour, which was an excellent rate of speed on the sharp grades and abrupt turns of a mountain road. Driving was a dangerous occupation even under the most favorable conditions, but on a dark night, or in a heavy rain, or when the roads were icy it was so hazardous that only the most competent or the most foolhardy man would undertake it.

Stage fares were collected by the hotel landlords, who acted as agents for the various companies. The landlord gave a bill of lading to the driver, and this list told the next landlord the names of the passengers and the distances for which they had paid. The fare varied somewhat from year to year, the average being a little over six cents a mile. The price of the trip from Baltimore to Wheeling was usually a little less than twenty dollars.

The average distance covered by each stage per day tended to increase, varying of course with the time of the year and the condition of the highway. During the 1830s the trip from Washington to Wheeling could be made in thirty hours, although the usual time with stops at night was two and a half days. By then the construction of the road had been continued farther west, reaching Columbus, Ohio, in 1833 and being graded, but not hard surfaced, into Illinois. By 1837 the trip from Washington to Columbus could be made in forty-five and a half hours, to Indianapolis in sixty-five and a half hours, and to St. Louis in ninety-four hours. The usual times to these places were respectively three days, sixteen hours; six days, twenty hours; ten days, four hours.

Freight, like passengers, was handled mostly by large companies. Farmers with their teams and wagons offered competition during the slack farming seasons, but the greater part of the business the year round was carried by the large companies. The usual wagon was of the Conestoga variety, which gave an attractive touch of color to the business. Wheels were continually made wider as the traffic developed, for it was found that the broader tire was more satisfactory on the gravel road. Brakes were poor, and therefore on heavy grades saplings were sometimes fastened around the rear wheels, or heavy logs tied to the back of the wagon. The average load was about 6,000 pounds, although there is a record of as much as 13,280 pounds (10,375 net) being carried in one wagon in 1835. The wages of the wagoner were paid by the trip and not by the day. The freight rate between Cumberland and Wheeling varied from $1.25 to $2.25 per hundred pounds. The average daily trip was about fifteen miles. Unlike the stages, the wagons stopped every night, and the same horses were used throughout the trip.

Taverns lined the whole route of the National Road at frequent intervals, even in the mountains. Food was plentiful but plain, and whiskey was sold everywhere. The bar was the most important room of the inn, usually being in the front and serving also as an office for the landlord. Drivers of wagons were not given rooms in these hotels, but had to sleep either on the barroom floor or outside. Here and there along the road were so-called " wagon houses," which were rude shacks for the use of the teamsters; the teamster was obliged to furnish his own bedding and food, and do his own cooking.

HAZARDS OF ROAD TRAVEL

The National Road was by no means a fair example of western roads during the '20s and '30s. With all of its roughness, its ruts, its dangers, and its lack of repair, it was immeasurably superior to the roads elsewhere in the West. Most of them were like their predecessors of a decade or two earlier; a so-called " road " was often no more than a single track through the woods, and at the best an unimproved double track which was almost impassable in the early spring. A traveler between Nashville and Memphis in 1831 penned a description which might have been repeated with variations throughout the West: " Frightful roads. Precipitous descent. No regular highway. The road is only an opening cut in the forest. The stumps of the trees are not completely cut away, so that they form so many impediments over which we jolt."

Of the various results arising from the prevalence of bad roads the most serious was the high rates for hauling freight. The usual charge in Illinois about 1820 was 50¢ per hundred pounds for twenty miles, which was so forbidding that the farmer lost money if he had his corn hauled even twenty miles. In consequence there might be a near-famine in one region while a neighboring area had an unmarketable surplus. Or, stated in another way, prices varied tremendously from place to place. In 1825 wheat brought 25¢ a bushel in Illinois and $2 on the eastern seaboard, while the comparable range in corn was between 10¢ and $1.75. Obviously, agricultural and industrial specialization could not proceed rapidly until better transportation permitted a wider exchange of products.

Western coach travel was an experience to be undertaken only by the hardiest traveler or under extreme necessity. Most main roads had one or more coach lines, although sometimes there was no regular schedule, and cases are on record in which a traveler waited days and even weeks for a coach. With a well-organized line, travel might continue day and night, but more usually stops were made at night. The usual day's travel was between twenty and fifty miles, but under exceptional circumstances as much as a hundred miles might be covered, at a rate of some six or seven cents a mile, exclusive of board and lodging. For a long trip the coach departed as early as 3 or 4 A.M. and kept going until 10 P.M. or later, with stops only for meals. Three or four such days were excessive punishment for even the strongest traveler and he would then be glad to stop a week or more to regain his vigor.

A stage coach could not put into practice the axiom that a straight line is the shortest distance between two points, for most roads meandered leisurely back and forth on no recognizable principle. Stumps had to be avoided, and the failure to do so was responsible for the phrases " up against a stump " and " stumped," which described an ordinary experience in the West. In dry weather the coach bumped unmercifully over the rutty road, enveloped in clouds of dust from the horses' feet. In rain, the leather curtains of the coach afforded but little protection and the passengers were usually thoroughly soaked. The coach continued to plow through the water, with here and there a detour through fields to avoid the worst mud holes. When the coach stuck in the mud, which was not unusual, the male passengers would alight, cut limbs of handy trees, and pry and push the vehicle until it reached a drier spot.

Accidents were so frequent as to be commonplaces of western travel. With the roughness of the roads the coaches rocked dizzily from one side to the other, and the passengers were forced to sway in the opposite direction to keep the vehicle upright. Sometimes, in spite of all efforts, the coach lost its balance and fell over on its side. In such an emergency the passengers nonchalantly crawled out of the wreckage, bound up their wounds, righted the coach, and proceeded on their way. The breaking of an axle or a wheel was more serious, even though the driver carried implements to take care of just such emergencies. If the men could not make temporary repairs, the driver set out on foot for the nearest settlement, while the passengers invited themselves to stay for the night at the most convenient log cabin. Such accidents were taken with philosophic calm and good humor. More irritating in the long run was the continual bumping of the passenger's head against the roof as the coach lurched and swayed along the uneven road; many a traveler ended his day's journey nursing a sore head and a splitting headache.

Western coaches forded the smaller streams. Frequently the more timid souls would first alight, thus giving the occasion for appealing scenes of gallantry in which the men would carry the younger and better-looking of the opposite sex through the water. Floods meant that days might be spent waiting for the waters to subside; sometimes the coach moved too soon and was washed down the stream. In high water a wagon might replace the coach. Ferries were operated on the largest streams, but it was ordinarily necessary to visit the home of the ferryman to obtain his services. The coach would be carried on the first trip of the ferry, and the passengers on the second.

Roads were almost never repaired or improved. The worst holes were sometimes filled with logs, not to make traveling more comfortable but to prevent the coach from being stuck. A few experiments were made with plank roads, but their cost was too great to make them generally practicable. Due appreciation was felt for the wonders of a macadam surface such as on the Albany-Troy road opened in 1829, but the only road of this type in the West except the National Road was the one out of Lexington.

TAVERNS

The arrival of a stage at any town or tavern was always the occasion for an impressive flourish. The horses were raced for the last few rods and the horn tooted; then the brakes were set with a grinding roar, the driver leaned back on his reins, and the horses slid to a stop in a cloud of dust. Since most stages ran only in the day, the night stops meant late to bed and early to rise. When there were no taverns, as sometimes happened, the travelers stayed in private homes. Westerners were very hospitable, and it was rare for any family to refuse accommodations, even though a large family in a small log cabin scarcely had room for a coach-load of strangers.

Western taverns were fairly numerous, although they were not as profuse as in the East. They varied in nature from commodious frame buildings to small log cabins where the traveler slept in the same room with the landlord's family. The keeper of the inn always acted as host; he met his guests at the door, showed them to their rooms, and presided at meals, where he led the conversa-tion. The largest chamber of the inn was the bar, which served as the gathering place for the men. Its decorations might be such articles as a wooden clock, a map of the United States, a map of the state, a framed copy of the Declaration of Independence, a looking glass with brush and comb attached, and a few engravings or wood prints.

The rooms of the western inn were frequently large and airy, but these were almost their only desirable qualities. Washing facilities consisted of a shallow tin pan, a pitcher, and a bucket; at times even these were absent and the traveler was expected to use the pump and a tin basin outside. Any kind of personal service was nonexistent; the traveler used the cold water which was in his pitcher when he arrived, or went without washing. Bedding was ordinarily both scanty and filthy. The western landlord econo-mized on linen and blankets by putting two travelers into each bed, regardless of whether or not they had ever seen each other before. Sometimes, when there were several beds in a room, they were filled with little regard for age or sex; possibly two men would be given one of the beds, two women the next, and a married couple the third. Naturally this kind of arrangement was by no means universal. In the smaller inn the first floor was sometimes given to the ladies for their sleeping quarters, while the loft was occupied by the men. The ordinary price for accommodations in the West was a dollar a day for board and lodging.

Tobacco and liquor were both common in the West. Tobacco was used by almost every man — but not for smoking. There was a cud in each masculine cheek, and, if the chroniclers have told the truth, spitting was done with a fine disregard for consequences; the floors, the coaches, the boats, and the great open spaces all provided convenient receptacles for surplus tobacco juice. Drinking was equally universal among the men. The better hotels had long wine lists, but the smaller establishments concentrated on the cheaper and more potent whiskey, which was even put on the tables at meal time in place of water.

Meals were served at the taverns at regular hours and were eaten by everyone together. The usual routine was breakfast at 7:30, dinner at 2 and supper at 7. Immense quantities of food were consumed rapidly and silently. Everything was put on the table at once in large dishes, and the guests helped themselves, except that a servant girl passed the tea and coffee. Table appointments were usually scarce; tablecloths were common, but napkins were rare; the only silver ordinarily used was spoons; the knives and two-pronged forks were of steel and had horn handles. Eating with a knife and without major tragedy was a fine art.

Western food varied with the type of tavern, the size of the community, the region of the country, and the time of the year. In the North the traveler might expect such viands as venison steak, bread, butter, honey, tea, coffee, beefsteak, eggs, apple sauce, corn bread, fat pork, chicken, and potatoes. In the South the common bill of fare included such items as beef, turkey, venison, chicken, sweet potatoes, corn cake, ham, and bacon. Everywhere was a strong emphasis on meat, which was served in great variety, even at breakfast. Pork was ubiquitous. Whenever feasible the preparation of the food consisted in frying in grease, and the effects of this method were particularly objectionable in the case of meat, which often swam in grease. Coffee was poor, and when sugar was served it usually was brown. The one dish that was typically American was corn on the cob. Characteristic of western hotel meals was a lack of green vegetables. They were scarce in the summer and almost never seen in the winter. New Orleans was one of the few places where the traveler might be served such vegetables as radishes, peas, asparagus, lettuce, and spinach.

In spite of all the difficulties the United States was a nation of travelers. Horses and all kinds of wagons and carriages filled the roads, for the nation was restless and feeling its young strength. Discomforts were accepted with resignation — particularly since more comfortable travel was unknown. Such acceptance did not mean, however, that people were satisfied. They wanted an ever increasing amount of transportation, even though poor, and even more they desired greater speed and cheapness. These goals were particularly important to the westerner with his farm products and long distances. In time, after much experimentation, he was to approach within reasonable distance of his goal.

READINGS

T. P. Abernethy, *The Formative Period in Alabama* (1922), ch. 8; R. C. Buley, *The Old Northwest* (2 vols., 1950), vol. 1, ch. 7; S. Dunbar, *A History of Travel in America* (4 vols., 1915), vol. 1, chs. 2–13, vol. 2, chs. 32, 33, vol. 3, ch. 34; L. Esarey, *A History of Indiana* (1915), ch. 11; W. E. Gephart, *Transportation and Industrial Development in the Middle West* (1909), chs. 3, 8; A. F. Harlow, *Old Post Bags* (1928), ch. 17; A. B. Hulbert, *The Paths of Inland Commerce* (1920), chs. 2–4; P. D. Jordan, *The National Road* (1948); H. and E. Quick, *Mississippi Steamboatin'* (1926), ch. 2; N. F. Schneider, *Y Bridge City* (1950)—Zanesville and Zane's Trace; G. R. Taylor, *The Transportation Revolution* (1951)—more than the West; W. T. Utter, *The Frontier State* (1942), ch. 8.

CHAPTER 16

THE COMING
OF THE STEAMBOAT

THE development of roads was important to the advancement of the West, but until the coming of the railroad, transportation by land was always secondary to that by water. The water traffic on the Ohio and the Mississippi and their subsidiaries loomed as the most significant phase of western transportation until well beyond the middle of the nineteenth century. The center of western economic interest was New Orleans. Down the river went the heavy and less perishable commodities such as flour, salt, rum, potatoes, brandy, pork, bacon, linen, and cordage. Up the river came articles such as molasses, sugar, coffee, and tea, with large value in small bulk. This river traffic helped give the tone and tempo of western life.

EARLY WATER TRAFFIC

Before 1790 almost all western travel by water was by canoe, and long after that date the canoe was a common sight. The ordinary canoe in use between the Appalachians and the Mississippi was a " dug-out " hollowed from the trunk of a tree; the bark canoe was practically unknown. The " dug-out " had an average length of about twenty feet, and could be constructed by four men in four days. A few were larger, sometimes being as long as thirty feet, with a beam of three and a half feet, and carrying a square sail. The majority were divided into four compartments which were formed by allowing portions of the tree trunk to remain as partitions. The front and rear divisions were used respectively for paddling and steering, while the two center divisions contained the cargo. When the canoe was used for commercial purposes it was ordinarily handled by Indians or by French from

Canada or Louisiana. The native French creole boatmen were a picturesque group — hard-working, but happy and carefree; their songs rang out joyously in the silence of the river and the lonely forests along its banks.

Several modified forms of the canoe were in common use, and these variations were somewhat loosely given the name of pirogue. One of the most ordinary forms of the pirogue was a canoe with a square stern, in which case the name was used to distinguish it from pointed end boats. Another form was that of two canoes lashed together and floored over, and frequently using a sail for motive power.

The most used boat of the whites, and one which grew rapidly in popularity after 1790, was the flatboat. This craft was given its name, quite obviously, because of its flat bottom. It might vary greatly in size, with common varieties anywhere from twenty to a hundred feet in length and eight to fifteen feet in width; the depth was usually little over three feet, but might be much more. The crudest of the boats was little more than a good-sized raft; if used by migrants it might have a barn for the livestock and a small cabin for the family. A boat used for a comparatively short commercial trip might be partially roofed, but the New Orleans boats were completely covered and somewhat more sturdy.

Each flatboat was equipped with four oars, but these were not used to furnish motive power, for the current of the river was utilized to do most of the hard work. On both sides were thirty-foot oars to row the boat to shore for a landing and to take it from shore into the current; their position and appearance sometimes caused the boat to be called a " Kentucky broadhorn." In the stern was another oar some forty or fifty feet in length, which was used for steering. In the front was a small " gouger " which aided the steering through unusually rapid water. Since the flatboat depended upon the current of the river for its speed, it was an exceedingly slow-moving craft, except for such exciting moments as when it shot the falls of the Ohio at Louisville. Ordinarily it was tied to the bank every evening, for sand bars and other river obstructions made night travel dangerous. The favorite aid to navigation was Z. Cramer, *The Navigator*.

The passengers on a flatboat had their living quarters aboard. Bunks took the place of beds, and the food was prepared in a rude fireplace. Migrants took aboard all their possessions, even their livestock, and it was one of the humorous sights of the river to see cows riding peacefully on the deck of a flatboat. Such a migrating family demolished its boat at the end of the trip and used the boards and nails for the construction of a home on land. When a cargo was carried to New Orleans the boat was ordinarily broken up and sold at that point. The men returned by land over the Natchez Trace.

The principal up-river craft was the long narrow keelboat, which usually measured about fifty feet in length and seven to ten feet in width. Being destined for longer use than the flatboat it was better constructed, with pointed ends and a regular keel — which gave the boat its name. Its draught was only from twenty to sixty inches because of the shallowness of the rivers on which it operated. In spite of this small draught, it could carry between twenty and forty tons of freight. A roof protected the cargo from rain and sun.

The keelboat made use of every possible method of propulsion. Three to six oars on each side gave facilities for rowing. A square sail of some hundred square feet was rigged to a thirty-foot mast and was helpful in the event of a favorable wind. A " cordelle " (rope) was stretched from the top of the mast to the shore, with an auxiliary line to the bow to keep the boat from yawing, and was used to tow the boat through troublous waters. This form of progress was both slow and arduous, with twenty to thirty men scrambling over the rocks and through the water to drag the boat upstream; at times it was even necessary to employ a block and tackle. Because of its difficulties, towing was used only when all other means of locomotion failed. Whenever the water was sufficiently shallow the boat was propelled by poles, and for this purpose a fifteen-inch platform was built on each side of the deck. Half of the crew took their places on each side. Each man thrust his pole into the bed of the river and put his shoulder against the socket at the other end. Then they all walked from fore to aft, and as each man arrived at the stern he took out his pole, walked to the bow, and repeated the trip.

The only advantage of the keelboat was that it was the one boat in common use which could transport a fairly heavy cargo upstream. Such trips were long, arduous, and expensive, and required large crews. They were practical only for the shipment of valuable goods which would not spoil in transit; the expense of a long trip was larger than would permit the profitable carriage of cheap, bulky freight. Since the majority of western products were of the latter variety, the number of keelboats engaged in traffic on western waters was never very large, even though such craft handled the bulk of up-river traffic.

In addition to the main varieties of western boats, there were a number of craft whose names appear less frequently. The arks and Kentucky broadhorns were varieties of the flatboat; ordinarily the various terms were used interchangeably. The barge was a large edition of the keelboat. At times transportation took the form of the simplest kind of log raft, with a cabin and fireplace, and oars to make the craft manageable. The model boat of the river was the galley, with dimensions of approximately forty-five by twelve feet. It was propelled exclusively by oars and carried only passengers and mail.

West of the Mississippi two other types of boats were in common use. The Mackinaw boat was shaped like a rowboat, but was often as large as fifty by twelve feet, and was constructed of inch-and-a-half plank. It was peculiar in being five feet deep at the ends, while only three and a half at the center. The cargo was carried in a watertight compartment in the center. Four oarsmen rowed in the front, while the steersman sat on an elevated perch in the rear. Another conveyance which was peculiar to the rivers of the Far West was the bullboat, which had the general appearance of an inverted rimless hat. Its usual dimensions were thirty by twelve by twenty feet, and it was constructed of a willow frame covered with buffalo hides, the seams being caulked with a mixture of tallow and ashes. Its virtues were that it could be constructed quickly, was light, and could carry up to 6000 pounds. At night it could be turned upside down and used as a shelter. It was navigated by two men with poles and consequently did not move very fast.

River traffic grew rapidly as white immigration to the West increased. In 1810 an observer counted 197 flats and 14 keelboats passing the falls of the Ohio within two months. Six years later a traveler from Natchez to Louisville met 2000 flats within twenty-five days. A recent scholar estimates an average of 3000 flatboats a year on the Ohio River between 1810 and 1820. By the end of the War of 1812 the river was covered with slow-moving, crude crafts floating with the current.

RIVER MEN

The increase of river traffic meant the growth of a " floating population " to furnish the labor on the flatboats and keelboats, and work on the waterfronts. Such " half horse, half alligator " men were rough and tough. Only the less educated, stronger, and more restless element of the population could live the hard life of the river, with its attendant dangers, hard work, poor food, and small pay. Naturally such men tended to concentrate in the river cities such as Cincinnati, Louisville, Natchez, and New Orleans. The most noted of the smaller Ohio River towns was Shawneetown, Illinois, which afforded a southern entrance to Illinois, and was reputed to be the wildest, most lawless town in the West.

The one river man to live through the years in story was the exaggeratedly typical, semi-legendary Mike Fink, whose proud boast was that " I kin outrun, outhop, outjump, throw down, knock down, drag out, and lick any man in the country. I'm a Salt River roarer. I love the wimmen and I'm chock-full of fight." Fink's usual methods and point of view are well illustrated by the story of how he killed a deer. One day he was out hunting and saw a deer, but as he had only one bullet he crawled closer to make sure of his quarry. Just as he was ready to fire he observed an Indian stalking the same prey. Being afraid that if he used his one bullet on the deer he would be killed by the Indian, he waited until the Indian had shot the deer and then shot the Indian, thus making certain of both his life and his venison.

Fink was noted for his fine marksmanship, and it was this reputation which finally led to his demise. According to a story which has many versions, Mike and a pal were in love with the same girl. They had a pleasant little custom of taking turns shooting a tin cup filled with whiskey off each others head, thus deluging whoever was the target with the liquor. On one occasion when Mike and his pal were performing this stunt, Mike had first shot; in spite of his well-known ability with a gun the bullet went several inches too low and pierced his friend's skull. Mike got the girl, but a friend of the dead man " got " Mike.

The river man had two striking traits which were immediately evident to the casual spectator. The first was his varied and picturesque vocabulary. Many of the river man's phrases explained both themselves and the object invoking their use — " quicker nor a alligator can chaw a puppy "; " dumb as a dead nigger in a mud-hole "; " harder nor climbin' a peeled saplin' heels upward "; " travel like a nigger in a thunder-storm "; " hell's a-snortin'."

The second was his tendency in spare moments to sing songs, frequently of local derivation. As with other analogous groups engaged in distinctive and appealing occupations, indigenous verse sprang spontaneously and anonymously from common experiences. Unfortunately in the case of the Ohio River boatmen this verse has never been collected in any systematic way, and most of it has disappeared. Two fragments will give some idea of its nature:

> " And it's oh! she was so neat a maid,
> That her stockings and her shoes
> She toted in her lily white hands,
> For to keep them from the dews."

> " Here's to those that has old clothes,
> And never a wife to mend 'em.
> A plague to those that has halfjoes,
> And hasn't a heart to spend 'em! "

EARLY STEAMBOATS

Early western river traffic was handicapped not so much by its slowness, although that difficulty was obvious and important, as by its inability to move upstream without the expenditure of tremendous amounts of capital and labor. In this respect the West was no different from the rest of the world, for although steam had been applied to other industrial processes by the late eighteenth century its use in transportation did not come until much later. Experiments to utilize steam in the movements of vehicles on both land and water were a prolific source of interest for the ingenious minds of the age.

The eventual emergence of the steamboat was not due to the work of any one man, and consequently credit for it cannot be given exclusively to one person. Robert Fulton has usually received more than his fair share of recognition because of his spectacular demonstration of the commercial possibilities of the steamboat in his trip on the Hudson with the *Clermont* in 1807. His name has further impressed itself historically because he and his backer Robert R. Livingston obtained a legal monopoly of the steamship transportation in the states of New York and Louisiana. If this power could have been maintained it would have given them control of a large portion of the shipping of the United States. The successful effort to break the monopoly, culminating in the case of *Gibbons v. Ogden,* made Constitutional history.

One of the earliest efforts of the Livingston-Fulton monopoly was to introduce and develop the steamboat in the West. Western commerce was large and the control of Louisiana was strategic.

In May 1809 Nicholas Roosevelt was sent West to sound out steamboat possibilities. For Roosevelt the trip was a honeymoon as well as a business venture and so he built a flatboat at Pittsburgh, fitted it with luxurious appointments, and floated leisurely down the river. At each town he discussed his plans with the leading citizens. He spent three weeks at Louisville, for here were the dreaded falls, and the old-timers were naturally skeptical of the proposed new machine; by stretching their imaginations they could conceive of a steam engine helping a boat down the river, but as for moving up against the current — well, it wasn't likely. The end of Roosevelt's journey was New Orleans, from which point he returned to the East by ocean, arriving at New York in January 1810.

Roosevelt's report to the monopoly was apparently favorable, for in 1811 the steamboat *New Orleans* was built at Pittsburgh. The *New Orleans* had the dimensions of a hundred thirty-eight by twenty-six and a half feet, burned wood, and cost $38,000. Whether it was a side or stern-wheeler is still argued. It was launched in March 1811 and started down the river in October. On the second day it arrived at Cincinnati, where the people admired it but were not convinced that it could move upstream. The following day it arrived at Louisville, where a big reception and dinner were given in honor of the occasion. Some of the leading citizens were taken on a short ride to demonstrate the boat's possibilities; for the first time the skeptical were convinced that progress could be made against the current and they were duly impressed, even though the maximum upstream speed was only about three miles an hour. After waiting for high water the boat shot the rapids at Louisville and continued downstream, arriving at the city for which it was named on January 10, 1812. Its life was short, for while engaged in regular trips between New Orleans and Natchez it struck a snag and sank on July 14, 1814. Despite the briefness of its career, the *New Orleans* had demonstrated the possibilities of steamboat traffic on western waters.

THE WESTERN STEAMBOAT

The technical development of the steamboat and the increase of the traffic which it carried were very rapid both in the East and in the West. Competition was introduced when the Livingston-Fulton monopoly was beaten after a long court struggle. Steamboat machinery was improved so that greater speeds could be maintained. Keels gave way to the flat bottoms which were so necessary for western rivers. More decks were added and the decorations were elaborated. By the 1820s the river boat had reached the general form which it was to maintain during succeeding decades. It penetrated practically every navigable western river and also the Great Lakes, where the first American boat was the *Walk-in-the-Water* (1818).

Every steamboat carried its freight, machinery, and fuel at water level. The engines burned wood, which produced multitudes of sparks and necessitated frequent refueling. The woodcutter's home, on the bank of the river, near the source of supply, soon became a recognized western institution. The wood was carried aboard in part by the deck passengers, who traveled at lower rates and usually slept on the rear of the first deck. The second deck was the domain of the cabin passenger, and had sleeping quarters, a dining room, a men's room and bar, and a ladies' parlor. The ladies' parlor was always in the rear — not because the ladies were considered unimportant but because the not infrequent explosions of the boilers in the front of the boat made the stern the safest position aboard. The top, or " hurricane," deck was occupied by the pilothouse and the officers' quarters, commonly known as " the Texas " in later years.

The cost of steamship travel varied with the amount of competition, but tended to decrease with the passing years. In 1819 a cabin passage from New Orleans to Natchez was $30, to the mouth of the Ohio $95, and to Louisville $125; the return trip from Louisville to New Orleans, being with the current, cost only $75. A deck passage was of course much cheaper, since such passengers furnished their own food and bedding, slept on the deck and helped carry the wood. By 1832 the traveler could make the trip from New Orleans to St. Louis for $25 and return for $20; the deck passage either way was $5. Freight also was cheaper, with a common rate of 62½¢ a hundred pounds from New Orleans to St. Louis in the '30s.

Along with decreased fares came increased speeds. In 1817 the *Enterprise* made a record run of twenty-five days, two hours, and four minutes from New Orleans to Louisville. By 1825 the *Tecumseh* was holding the record for this trip with eight days and four hours, while in 1853 the *A. L. Shotwell* covered the same distance in four days, nine hours, and thirty minutes. Every boat was proud of its speed and cherished any record which it made. Each new record soon became common gossip up and down the river.

The effort to make new speed records was one of the many factors producing frequent accidents on western waters. Part of the trouble, however, was due to nature and not to man. The Ohio and Mississippi were dangerous rivers even with the most careful navigation. Snags and sawyers were omnipresent and difficult to avoid; a snag could, and often would, rip the wooden hull so that the boat would sink in a few minutes. Effective snag removal did not begin until the late '20s. In the summer and fall both rivers were low, and with the changing channel caused by shifting sandbars it was easy to go aground. In the spring the floods, carrying large quantities of debris, occasioned other forms of trouble which were just as damaging.

Serious accidents were also frequently caused by mechanical failures. Western steamboats used dangerous high pressure boilers to get more power with less weight. The metal of the boilers was poor and sometimes burst under high pressure of steam or lack of water. At times when the captain wanted a high speed a Negro would sit on the safety valve to keep an abnormally high pressure of steam — the result was that the pressure always went up, and sometimes the Negro and most of the passengers went with it. Then too the wooden boats were highly combustible and the large quantity of sparks produced by the wood used for fuel often set fire to the boat. This danger was increased when greater speed was obtained by the additional use of such substances as pitch, oil, turpentine, and lard, which produced a hotter fire and more steam, but also evoked a greater shower of sparks.

Another prolific cause of accidents was racing, carried on for the most part by the sporting southern element. Each captain considered his own boat the best on the river, and when rival claimants met they frequently tested the merits of their respective crafts. Some of these races were accidental encounters, but some were planned long in advance, with each captain placing a wager on his own boat. The races were particularly spectacular at night, with the lights of the two steamers showing against the blackness of the surrounding darkness, and the open furnace doors bringing into strong relief the muscular bodies of the firemen, stripped to the waist, as they rushed wood to the all-devouring fires. The engine roared, the paddles churned, whistles shrieked, and the passengers gathered at the rail to lay odds on the outcome. Masses of sparks shot out of the funnels and the heavy black smoke would indicate the addition of lard or turpentine. Not infrequently the boat would catch fire or the boilers would burst from the increased pressure, and the spectacle would end in a tragedy.

The most noted race of them all came after the Civil War (1870), when the *Robert E. Lee* and the *Natchez* sped up the river from New Orleans to St. Louis. The *Lee* was stripped for action and had made special preparations for refueling, with the result that it won the race even though the *Natchez* was probably the faster boat under ordinary conditions. Mile after mile they raced neck to neck, their progress being followed all over the country by telegraphic dispatches. They arrived at St. Louis within a few minutes of each other, having covered the 1278 miles in three days, eight hours, and fourteen minutes, or an average of fourteen and a sixth miles per hour, including stops.

The possibilities for disaster were illustrated in a few of the more notable accidents of the time. The *Brandywine,* while participating in a race thirty miles above Memphis on April 9, 1832, caught fire and 100 persons were lost. The *Ben Sherrod* was racing the *Prairie* on May 8, 1837, when it caught fire and shortly later its boilers, together with some gunpowder and liquor in the cargo, exploded; the *Prairie* failed to stop to rescue the survivors, and some 200 people lost their lives. The *Moselle* was just leaving Cincinnati on April 25, 1838, to race down the river against time when all four of its boilers burst simultaneously, throwing debris and bodies a quarter of a mile; the result was eighty-one known dead and fifty-one missing.

The height of the steamboat business came during the 1850s, at which time the Mississippi and Ohio were the most important streams, although the Missouri and other tributaries carried some part of the business. This was the period of huge, many decked boats embellished with gingerbread scrollwork and bright paint. Rich carpets covered the floors and elaborate glass chandeliers multiplied the brilliance of the many lights, while luxurious furniture rivaled that of the best hotels in the land. Excellent food was prepared by a corps of cooks and served by a host of well-trained black waiters. Elaborate bars and long wine lists were provided for the convivial guests. Orchestras and brass bands added the romance of gay music to the scene. After the Civil War the splendor of the steamship waned as the traffic on which it was based was rapidly diverted to the expanding railroads and taken directly to the East.

The development of the steamboat during and after the 1820s

made it the home of many activities which in an earlier time had been confined entirely to dry land. Photographers bought their own boats and worked the river towns, antedating in thought if not in words the injunction that there is " always a picture just ahead." Patent medicine vendors followed the same procedure in presenting their sales talks and vaudeville, and selling their nostrums. Gamblers, saloonkeepers, and prostitutes took to the river, both running their own boats and exploiting the opportunities available on regular commercial craft. " Show boats," with dulcet strains of the calliope and the seductive glare of multitudinous bright lights, brought to many of the river towns their only touch of the drama. In spite of the inadequacy of the small theater on the boat and the poorness of the players, the show boat filled a very real need in the emotional life of the West. Even preachers sometimes navigated their own boats and brought salvation to the river population, who certainly needed it if anyone ever did. Add to these the immigrant, the migratory worker, the river man, and all the other people who found water transportation desirable, and the diversity and size of the river traffic can be partially understood.

BOAT CREWS

The navigation of the river boats was in the hands of a group of comparatively well-trained and experienced men. Of these, the most skilled was the pilot, who has been so well described by Mark Twain that it seems almost sacrilegious to venture a new portrait. In importance the pilot was scarcely inferior to the captain, and his salary was sometimes as much as $1000 a month. He was in absolute command of the movements of the boat except that the captain could give orders as to the time to start and stop. The knowledge of the Mississippi pilot can only be estimated justly when it is remembered that he had to know intimately 1500 miles of the most changeable river in the world. The channel varied continually with the shifting of sand bars, and even the shifting of banks and cutoffs. The whole appearance of the river was different at night from in the day, and at high water from at low water. There were no lights or buoys as at present, and consequently the pilot had no guide except his own sight and memory.

The captain of the boat, frequently a part owner, was absolute master of the ship except that he could not give orders to the pilot concerning navigation; he acted as host to the passengers, much as did the proprietor of an inn on land. Of slightly less importance was the engineer, who was absolute ruler of the machinery, giving obedience only to the tinkling orders of the directing bell. A mate and a clerk had their chief duties in accepting and reckoning the charges on freight. A semi-official personage on most boats was the barkeeper, who usually made good profits by operating his bar as a concession. In early days most of the drinks that he served were simple, with straight whiskey in most favor and the mint julep ranking second in popular estimation; later times saw more elaborate concoctions.

The passenger lists of most boats contained the names of a number of professional gamblers, who generally found it advantageous to operate in small groups. These professional gentlemen were usually quiet, well-dressed, courteous, and soft spoken. Their favorite game was poker, although they would participate in any diversion which included the exchange of the currency of the country. Their most important rule for success was " always let the sucker think that he is going to beat you." The chief gathering place of the Mississippi gamblers was Natchez, since here had been the beginning of the overland road to Nashville. Natchez was one continuous line of saloons, billiard parlors, gambling halls, and houses of prostitution until the 1830s, when the more peaceful citizens became sufficiently outraged to use forceful measures to eject the disorderly element. When Natchez proved inhospitable many of the gamblers made their headquarters at Vicksburg, but in time they were forced to leave this later haven and go elsewhere.

One of the most picturesque groups on the river boats were the roustabouts who did the common labor of cleaning the boat, carrying wood, stoking the furnace, and loading and unloading cargo. A few of these workers were old river men who had drifted to the steamboat when the slower-moving vessels were driven off the rivers. In addition there were a considerable number of Irish immigrants who were employed during the '30s and later. By far the largest group, however, and the one which eventually monopolized this sort of work, was the Negro. Happy and carefree, the Negro gave much of the tone to the life on the river. As with the Ohio River boatmen they developed a folklore, poetry, and songcraft distinctively their own. Some of these songs drew from incidents of life elsewhere, but many of them gave pictures of river life which were excellent as descriptive writing. Consider, for example, the picture of the life of a Negro deckhand on a Mississippi steamboat as given in the words of the following song:

" Oh, roll, Nancy gal, roll, gal,
I'll meet you by and by ;
We gwine to roll de cotton
Way up ten tiers high.

" A dancin' up de river,
A dancin' down again,
With rousters all a-hustlin',
Jes' look at ' Tobin's train ';
Her wheels is beatin' ' Juba,'
While b'ilers sing de tune,
De whistle calls de figgers,
De chimbleys scrape de moon.

" Oh, all aroun' de capstan
Jes' clear de deck awhile,
An' wake de Mississippi
In good ol'-fashioned style.
De jackstaff is a-hummin',
De guys is clangin' loud,
De furnace is roarin',
De mate's done lef' de crowd.

" Oh, Cotton-hook Jim, come pat yo' time,
Oh, Sandbar Joe, come shake yo' heel,
Oh, Yallerback Bill, come shout yo' rhyme,
Ontwell we make her tremble to the keel !
Oh, shuffle an' cut an' walk aroun',
De ' coon in de holler,' an' de ' corn in de groun','
An' ' possum fat ' an' ' taters ' and ' Betsy Brown,'
Twell even de capstan j'ines de reel.

" Backstep, front step, set 'em down ag'in,
Sachez to de left and swing to de right ;
Polish up de planks like de debil beatin' sin,
Fo' you gwine ter roll cotton tonight ;
Rattle up de middle, clatter down de side,
Jolly as a clam at de floodin' o' de tide,
Happy as a groom a-huggin' o' de bride,
Twell de fus' signal landin' is in sight.

" You hear dat whistle shoutin',
You hear dat little bell;
Oh, swing aroun' de derrick,
We's gwine ter work a spell;
And dar's de mate a-comin',
De captain's up on deck,
Oh, hurry up, you rousters,
You'll cotch it in de neck!

" Dong! From de landin' backin,'
Oh, look out for dat stage!
De safety valve is hissin',
De greaser's at de gauge;
Oh, shovel up de furnace
Twell de smoke put out de stars,
We's gwine along de river
Like we's bound to beat de cars.

" Oh, roll, Nancy gal, roll, gal,
I'll meet you by and by;
We gwine to roll de cotton
Way up ten tiers high."

READINGS

C. H. Ambler, *A History of Transportation in the Ohio Valley* (1932), pp. 31–184; L. D. Baldwin, *The Keelboat Age on Western Waters* (1941)—excellent; W. Blair and F. J. Meine, *Mike Fink* (1933); B. W. Bond, Jr., *The Civilization of the Old Northwest* (1934), ch. 12; H. E. Chambers, *Mississippi Valley Beginnings* (1922), ch. 30; H. M. Chittenden, *A History of Early Steamboat Navigation on the Missouri River* (2 vols., 1903), vol. 1, chs. 9, 10—classic account; F. E. Dayton, *Steamboat Days* (1925), chs. 17, 20—detailed; E. Dick, *Vanguards of the Frontier* (1941), ch. 7; F. L. Dorsey, *Master of the Mississippi: Henry Shreve* (1941)—readable but none too accurate; S. Dunbar, *A History of Travel in America* (4 vols., 1915), vol. 1, chs. 14–17, vol. 2, chs. 19–21; G. L. Eskew, *The Pageant of the Packets* (1929); P. Graham, *Showboats* (1951), chs. 1–3—good; J. M. Hanson, *The Conquest of the Missouri* (1946); M. L. Hartsough, *From Canoe to Steel Barge* (1934), chs. 1–3; H. Hatcher, *The Great Lakes* (1944), ch. 20; A. B. Hulbert, *The Paths of Inland Com-*

merce (1920), chs. 5, 6, 11; L. C. Hunter, *Steamboats on the Western Rivers* (1949), chs. 1–13—definitive; W. J. Peterson, *Steamboating on the Upper Mississippi* (1937); M. M. Quaife, *Lake Michigan* (1944), chs. 13–15; H. and E. Quick, *Mississippi Steamboatin'* (1926)—somewhat fictionalized; O. A. Rothbert, *The Outlaws of Cave-in-Rock* (1924)—Ohio River; L. Saxon, *Father Mississippi* (1927), chs. 14–20; G. R. Taylor, *The Transportational Revolution, 1815–1866* (1951), ch. 4—excellent, includes more than the West; W. T. Utter, *The Frontier State* (1942), ch. 7; S. Vestal, *The Missouri* (1945), ch. 1, 2, 3.

CHAPTER 17

CANALS
MAKE THEIR BOW

THE burning fever of western desire for better transportation was by no means cured with the introduction of the steamboat and the improvement of roads; rather was the disease encouraged. Steamboats were fine, but even their most ardent protagonists had to admit that they were no great help to inland towns and to communities on very small streams. Traffic had to follow the river and could not always go where the buyer and seller might prefer. As for roads, even with their improvement the cost of transportation remained high, since one team could haul no more than a single loaded wagon, with possibly the addition of a trailer if the roads were very good.

WESTERN DESIRES

The westerner was convinced that good transportation was the shortcut to prosperity. He argued that with smaller carrying charges he could make more money on what he sold and likewise could buy more cheaply. Consequently he was sure in his own mind that cheaper transportation meant more wealth for the West. Unhappily this utopian ideal always remained just around the corner, no matter what improvements were made. Better transportation decreased shipping costs and hence the price of what the westerner bought — so far the ideal was achieved — but it also lowered the price of farm products and hence the westerner was somewhere near the place from which he had started. Corn and wheat fell at least as rapidly as plows and hardware, and the general trend of prices through most of the nineteenth century was down. In spite of this unfortunate development successive generations of westerners continued to hope for economic salvation through improved transportation, and each generation made some advance that looked hopeful at the time but that never quite justified the original optimism.

EASTERN PLANS

The East likewise favored improved transportation, and for obvious reasons. Not least among its desires was better connections with the West, but there was a striking lack of unanimity in naming the routes that should be improved, for each seaboard town from Maine to Florida had rosy visions of a golden future in which it would draw the bulk of western business and become great and opulent. While hundreds of towns had such dreams, the principal competitors were Boston, New York, Philadelphia, Baltimore, and Charleston. From 1818 to 1825 the advantage lay with Baltimore because it was the terminus of the National Road. True enough the National Road was by no means a perfect method of communication, but it was so much better than anything else in existence that every other city viewed it with a jealous eye.

Boston had the poorest outlook of any of the five cities. While its connections with the remainder of New England were comparatively good its links with the West were quite the reverse. In particular the Berkshires frowned menacingly across any route westward, and the greatest imagination and optimism were required to foresee the bulk of western freight and passengers traversing these mountains to Boston when they could embark on a steamboat at Albany for an easy and pleasant voyage to New York. As for New York, the Hudson River was splendid, but the long and painful road from the Hudson to Lake Erie was a headache. Even more distressing, the great bulk of western settlement before 1820 was along the Ohio River and to the south, so that presumably good communications to Lake Erie would be of comparatively little advantage.

Philadelphia was likewise in distress. The Pennsylvania (Forbes) road did not improve with age, and consequently even the traffic from Pittsburgh tended to swing south and over the National Road to Baltimore. Presumably Baltimore should have been happy over these developments, but in fact it was not. Baltimore merchants were painfully aware that western traffic was mainly going down the river to make New Orleans rival New York as the ranking port of the United States, and that conditions threatened to become worse as steamboats improved and the center of trans-Appalachian population continued to move westward. As for Charleston, the outlook was really dark, for its western connections were blocked by mountains and untamed Indians. Its only nearby rivers were short and hence not very useful. The best river of the region was the Savannah, but it lay far south of Charleston, and the trade which it carried was monopolized by the city at its mouth.

Each eastern city wanted improved connections with the West to draw business both from New Orleans and from its eastern competitors, and consequently each grasped eagerly at the transportational panacea of the '20s and '30s — the canal. Each community minimized local physical obstacles so that it could dream and plan itself the center of a national system of canals. Public-spirited citizens gave and solicited funds, governments helped, and even the loafer at the grog shop could speak learnedly of locks and water levels.

Canals seemed at the time to be the ultimate achievement in transportation. What could be superior to the easy movement of canalboats over the smooth paths of water which were to connect all the important centers of the country. The wilder enthusiasts even talked of canals to span the continent, linking the waters of the Atlantic and the Pacific. Their unreasonable enthusiasm continued unabated until it felt the damper of the panic of 1837; after that time transportational utopians turned their energies to a still newer panacea — railroads.

BOSTON

In Boston, canal enthusiasm produced but small results. One early piece of construction, the Middlesex Canal, connected Boston harbor with the navigable portions of the Merrimac and thus gave water connections as far as Concord, New Hampshire, which was hardly a move toward the conquest of western business. Boston boosters could do little but grind their teeth in bitter frustration until the newer railroad opened additional possibilities.

NEW YORK

The great project designed to fulfill the desires of New York City, as well as those of the entire state, was a canal from the Hudson River at Albany to some point on Lake Erie. The original form of the plan provided merely for improving the Mohawk River where rapids and falls obstructed the free passage of shipping.

Such action became a necessity as settlement advanced along the river, and by 1796 five locks around the Little Rapid permitted navigation as far as present Rome. The larger idea of a canal along the Mohawk was advocated as early as 1810, and two years later the legislature gave official sanction to the project; actual work was delayed by the outbreak of the war with Great Britain.

Agitation for the canal was renewed at the close of the War of 1812, and the project was enlarged by the advocacy of a connection between the Hudson River and Lake Erie. The legislature was again acquiescent, and this time work was started at Fort Stanwix (Rome) in 1817. The length of the proposed waterway caused many people to chuckle sardonically at the visionary plans. Here was a prospective canal to be dug through hundreds of miles of virgin wilderness, with no existing traffic along much of its route, and with but few people farther west who might use it to ship their products to the East. Building a canal under such circumstances seemed both unreasonable and fool-hardy. To add to the inescapable physical obstacles, fever and ague were very severe among the workmen, so that at times the digging almost came to a stop. Only the utilization of hundreds of recently arrived Irish immigrants made possible the continued progress of the work.

The Erie Canal was built rapidly in spite of physical obstacles, disease, and the scoffing of skeptics, and by October 1825 it was ready to open for traffic. The inauguration ceremonies consisted of a trip by Governor De Witt Clinton and his party along the entire line by boat from Buffalo to Albany, and then by steamship to New York. Each town they visited honored the occasion with an imposing celebration, including parades, bands, dinners, speeches, toasts, and fireworks. The final ceremony occurred in New York City on November 4, 1825, when, amid elaborate ceremonies, a keg of Lake Erie water was emptied into the Atlantic Ocean, thus symbolizing the wedding of those two bodies of water.

The Erie Canal was little more than a large ditch. Its width at the top was forty feet, at the bottom twenty-eight feet, and it was four feet deep. The locks were ninety by twelve feet and the largest boat which they would hold could carry only one hundred tons. The total cost was about $7,000,000. The smallness of the canal soon meant that its facilities were overtaxed by the amount of traffic which it carried, and so it was enlarged between the years 1835 and 1862. Numerous branches increased its usefulness. It retained considerable importance for many years, even with the completion of the competing New York Central Railroad; within recent years it has been succeeded by the Barge Canal, which is still significant.

The early importance of the Erie Canal far exceeded the hopes of even its most enthusiastic supporters. It was a significant factor in the development of central and western New York state, being directly responsible for such cities as Herkimer, Utica, Syracuse, and Lockport. Buffalo grew mightily, particularly with the harbor improvements which began in the 1820s. The canal had also a vital role in the development of regions farther west, contributing largely to the early growth of the Great Lakes country, including Michigan, Wisconsin, Minnesota, Iowa, northern Ohio, Indiana, and Illinois. It brought an immense amount of business to New York City, being one of the more important causes for the development of the commercial supremacy of that port. For a visionary scheme it had decidedly practical results.

PHILADELPHIA

Philadelphia, being the chief commercial rival of New York, viewed with apprehension and alarm the building of the Erie Canal. This fearfulness was increased by the obvious impossibility of constructing a similar project over the mountains farther south, although a few of the most optimistic souls were unwilling to admit that the hills of Pennsylvania were an insuperable obstacle to canals. Just at the time that the Erie Canal was being completed, Pennsylvania ordered a survey of the water routes across the state (1824–25). The plan which eventually emerged and was adopted included a marvelous combination of canals, inclined planes, and " new-fangled " railroads. For lack of a better name it was dubbed the " Pennsylvania system." Work was started in 1826 and the entire line opened for use in 1834 at a cost of $13,500,000, which was borne entirely by the state.

The " Pennsylvania system " was an excellent example of American energy and ingenuity, and one of the mechanical marvels of its age. Travelers came from far and near to see it and to ride over it. In general the route lay along the old Kittanning Path and was the one later followed by the Pennsylvania Railroad. The distance from Philadelphia to Columbia (on the Susquehanna River) was covered by one of the earliest railroads in the country; the grades at each end of the line were surmounted by the use of inclined planes on which cars were drawn over iron rails by ropes attached to sta-

tionary engines. In the early years the cars were pulled over
the railroad by horse power. From Columbia a canal followed the
Susquehanna and Juniata rivers to Hollidaysburg. This canal had
a total of eighteen dams, thirty-three aqueducts and one hundred
and one locks.

The most interesting and unusual feature of the system was on
the part which traversed the mountains from Hollidaysburg to
Johnstown (thirty-seven miles). Here was the greatest application
of inclined planes ever to be put into operation in the world. On
both sides of each mountain were inclined planes with grades of
between ten and a quarter and a hundred feet per mile. The cars
were hitched to the stationary engines with ropes, and then pulled
up one side of the hill and lowered down the other side. Horses
and stages were used in the intervening spaces; within a short
time the coaches were replaced by railroad cars, and still later
steam locomotives were introduced. At Johnstown the traveler
again boarded a canalboat, on which he remained until he arrived
at Pittsburgh. This western canal had a total of sixty-four locks,
ten dams, two tunnels, and sixteen aqueducts.

The " Pennsylvania system " was easily the most ingenious
transportational device developed up to that time in the United
States. Its 363 miles of line included almost every known type
of conveyance. Its chief drawbacks were its cost of building and
maintenance, and its necessarily high charges for the transportation of freight. The frequency of reshipment was reduced with the
invention of a sectional canalboat, each part of which could be
loaded on a railroad car for the trip across the inclined planes. But
even at the best the system was expensive, and it was later superseded by the Pennsylvania Railroad, chartered in 1846.

BALTIMORE

Just as Philadelphia had been stimulated, Baltimore was spurred
to new efforts for improved transportation by the opening of the
Erie Canal. The National Road, in spite of its drawbacks, had
seemed fairly adequate until New York's canal approached completion, at which time the Baltimore region found desirable the
chartering of the Chesapeake and Ohio Canal (in Virginia in 1824
and Maryland 1825) to connect the navigable waters of the Potomac and Ohio rivers. This project was the successor of several efforts to improve the navigation of the Potomac River. Because of
the nature of the land the canal was planned to begin above the

falls at Georgetown and then to follow the Potomac north and west; in consequence, Baltimore finally received only a branch. The beginning of work was considered of sufficient importance that the ceremonies were attended by President Adams, who threw the first shovel of dirt on July 4, 1828. In spite of this auspicious start, construction proceeded slowly. The canal did not reach Cumberland until 1850, and there the work stopped permanently. It was never a financial success, partly because of its incompleteness and partly because even the operating sections were opened after the period of maximum usefulness of canals had ended.

The Chesapeake and Ohio Canal very soon proved unsatisfactory to the citizens of Baltimore. For one thing the work progressed too slowly for the eager spirit of the southern metropolis. Furthermore, Baltimore was never content to be on the branch line of anything, even a canal. The result of the city's impatience was the development of a timely transportation innovation, the Baltimore and Ohio Railroad. Charles Carroll of Carrollton, the last living signer of the Declaration of Independence, threw the first shovelful of dirt on the very day that President Adams performed the same function for the canal. The railroad moved in its early years only a little more rapidly than the canal, but eventually it was completed and made a success.

CHARLESTON

Farther south, Charleston was also interested in the northern developments, and worried by their significance. For a while she toyed with the idea of canals, but even the most sanguine boosters could find little that could be done to attract Mississippi Valley business. She turned to railroads, chartering a road between Charleston and Hamburg, and starting work in 1827. By 1833 the road was completed to Hamburg, on the Savannah River and opposite present Augusta, Georgia. The 136 miles of its line was the longest single piece of track in the United States. The main object of the road was to divert the business of the Savannah River from Savannah to Charleston.

The result of eastern competition for western business was the emergence of New York with a clear advantage in the Erie Canal, which furnished the most adequate East-West transportation. Philadelphia had established reasonably good communications, although there was still much to be desired. Baltimore continued to depend upon the National Road until the completion of the

Baltimore and Ohio Railroad in the '50s. Boston and Charleston lagged distinctly, with the condition of Charleston much more serious. The situation of the '20s and '30s helps to explain the comparative importance of the chief cities of the present day.

WESTERN PLANS

The enthusiasm for canals which manifested itself in the East was no whit greater than that which the West displayed at the same time. If the East looked to canals for increased business, the West viewed them as the greatest possible attraction to lure a reluctant economic prosperity. Each individual westerner and each western community saw the canal as its one outstanding chance for financial salvation, and no cankering doubts clouded the clear face of hope. Each man was an inexhaustible fund of information concerning water levels, locks, aqueducts, dams, stump pullers, and the cost of labor; he could paint a most alluring picture of how one or more canals through his particular community would result in untold riches for everyone.

The main western projects, and each community had at least one pet idea, were for artificial waterways connecting the Great Lakes with the Ohio-Mississippi system. The small and unnavigable tributaries of the larger rivers would be used to furnish the water for the canals. In this way all-water routes would be opened from New York to New Orleans by way of the Hudson River, Erie Canal, Great Lakes, projected western canals, and principal western rivers. Western products could be carried more easily either to an eastern or a southern market. Naturally any such route would favor New York at the expense of her southern competitors, but this result seemed unavoidable as long as a water-level route was necessary and there were mountains to the south.

Enthusiasm for canals together with the formulation of a multitude of plans for their construction did not produce the actual waterways. The principal western handicap was lack of capital, for the West was poor. Individual subscriptions were solicited successfully, but their collection was anything but easy. States borrowed freely to further the desired projects, but even under the best conditions their credit was definitely limited. In consequence the West looked beseechingly to the national government for aid. Henry Clay furnished a fair example of western ambitions. When he linked his proposed help to " internal improvements " with a national bank and a protective tariff he was not only trying to produce a platform on which he might ride to the Presidency, but was expressing the sentiments of the older and more developed parts of the West.

The West was definitely unlucky in its early efforts to obtain federal aid for transportational improvements. Both Madison and Monroe objected on constitutional grounds to any assistance to projects of a local nature, and they were fairly strict in deciding between local and national projects. John Quincy Adams was more generous, and during the four years of his Presidency considerable aid was extended to roads and canals. Jackson, even though a westerner, reverted to earlier practice and vetoed a number of measures which he considered to be local. Best known was his veto (1830) of an act for the aid of a road from Maysville to Lexington. This veto was a brave political act since it disappointed constituents in the President's home country. On the other hand he was glad to sign bills for the aid of internal improvements when he felt that the projects were permissible to the federal government under the Constitution.

The western canal mania was also limited in effectiveness by the plenitude of proposed plans. Each community felt certain that if it were on the line of a canal it would become prosperous, but shuddered to think of the possible results if the canal were built elsewhere. In consequence any specific canal proposal tended to receive the opposition of all the population not directly benefited, which meant that in most cases the opposition was in a majority. The obvious solution was to charter and aid several plans at the same time, and thus enlist the support of a majority. With such logrolling the only limitation to authorized routes would be the necessity for obtaining water, and even that limitation was not very rigid since partisans of any plan had a habit of seeing water wherever they wanted it. The profusion of plans brought of course a diffusion of labor, so that the completion of any single project was delayed.

OHIO

The first western state to undertake actual canal construction was Ohio. This priority was but natural since Ohio was the most populous state west of the mountains. Between the eastern and western borders of Ohio were half a dozen feasible routes which might have been used to connect Lake Erie with the Ohio River. Even before 1820 there was some discussion of these possibilities, and in 1822 the legislature responded by authorizing a commission to survey and report upon the existing options. The commission worked for three years and finally approved four routes, advising early construction on one or more of them.

Acting immediately upon the report of the commissioners the state legislature early in 1825 authorized the construction of two canals across the state. The first started at Portsmouth and ran north along the Scioto, then cut east to the Muskingum and followed the Muskingum and Cuyahoga to Cleveland. The second followed the historic Maumee-Miami route from Cincinnati to Toledo, on Maumee Bay. Immediate construction on the second of these routes was authorized only between Cincinnati and Dayton. It was due to this project that Toledo received the importance which made Ohio willing to fight a war over the territory in which it lay. The authorization of these two projects was an instance of magnificent courage and optimism, not to mention rashness, on the part of the state of Ohio. The estimated cost of the work was $5,700,000, which was almost exactly one-tenth of the value of all the taxable property in the state, and actual costs are notoriously somewhat greater than preliminary estimates.

The work on the Scioto-Muskingum route, commonly given the name of the Ohio Canal, was begun on July 4, 1825. Governor Clinton of New York came west to help celebrate the occasion, and dug the first spadeful of dirt at Licking Summit, near Newark. Labor was scarce, but by November 2000 men were at work; German and Irish immigrants were imported to keep the labor supply from diminishing in amount or increasing in price. Preliminary estimates of cost were found to be too low and some of the contractors absconded. In spite of these setbacks work continued steadily, so that the whole 333-mile project from Cleveland to Portsmouth was completed in 1832. The dimensions of this waterway were approximately those of the Erie Canal. On the whole it was built both well and cheaply.

The other Ohio project, commonly known as the Miami Canal, was also begun in 1825. It was opened between Cincinnati and Dayton in 1829, but later work went much more slowly because the Ohio Canal was considered the more important and pressing undertaking. The Miami Canal was finally completed to Lake Erie and opened to traffic in 1845. In addition to these two state projects, there were other private canal ventures, some of which were aided by Ohio. None of them was very important.

INDIANA

Indiana, like Ohio, had canal schemes before 1820, but they did not assume vital importance until after the beginning of work by Ohio in 1825. All the difficulties which hampered Ohio operated in Indiana to an even greater extent because Indiana had fewer people and less wealth; the total taxes collected in Indiana in 1827 were $33,000. Congress gave some slight assistance through its land grant of 1827, but main dependence was placed on a $15,000,000 issue of state bonds. Of this imposing sum, about $2,000,000 was embezzled, another $4,000,000 was lost in worthless securities, while much of the remainder was frittered away.

The principal route upon which the Hoosiers looked with favor began at the navigable portion of the Wabash River and ran northeast until it entered Lake Erie near Toledo — another historic portage route. A small part of the line lay within the borders of Ohio, and the consent of the latter state for building was not obtained until 1829; Ohio later backed out of her agreement and had to be repersuaded. Work was started in 1832, but was bungled from the beginning. Money was spent haphazardly, management was too large and inefficient, and the Irish labor was engaged in continual riots between the partisans of North and South Ireland.

In spite of these various troubles, the Wabash and Erie Canal was finished in 1842 and opened the next year from Lafayette to Toledo, 215 miles. Work was then pushed farther south, so that by 1853 boats could go all the way to Evansville. Several other projects, particularly the " Cross Cut " venture, were complete failures, but for a time in the early '50s the main canal carried much traffic, while the Whitewater Canal in southeast Indiana was a fair success. Business then declined steadily, to come to an almost complete end with the opening of the Wabash Railroad in 1856. The floods of 1875 stopped all traffic and the canal was never repaired.

OTHER WESTERN CANALS

Illinois also had its pet project — the Illinois and Michigan Canal — designed to connect Lake Michigan and the navigable portion of the Illinois River. The idea was old, but not until the 1820s was the route surveyed and a tract of land donated by Congress. One of the results of the surveys was the plotting of the town of Chicago near Fort Dearborn in 1830. Actual construction of the canal was not begun until 1836; it was opened for use twelve years later.

These four canals in the states immediately north of the Ohio River were the most important projects completed in the West. Of the smaller canals, the most significant was the Louisville and Portland around the falls of the Ohio at Louisville; it proved exceedingly profitable after its opening in 1830. A modest original investment by the federal government grew to complete control by 1874. Other minor enterprises ranged from the portage canal at Portage, Wisconsin (built in the '40s), to a number of waterways in the vicinity of New Orleans. For every canal which was built there were a hundred plans for others, and every western state toyed with at least eight or ten projects which it considered important.

The majority of the canals completed during the two decades after 1820 were in the Northwest rather than in the Southwest. The sparser population and lesser wealth of the South had their influence, as well as the development of the plantation system which eliminated the urban centers so necessary for canal promotion. Furthermore, the rivers of the South were more adequate than those of the North, being frequently slow and deep, and allowing steamboat navigation practically to the front door of the plantation.

The real and unalterable limit of canal construction in both the North and the South was set by the lack of capital. The little Congressional assistance that was given did not greatly aid building. The one hindrance which the canal did not have to meet was a lack of imagination. It was during the '20s that the idea of an ocean to ocean canal through Nicaragua received its first real support. Visionary enthusiasts also talked of a trunk line canal from ocean to ocean through the territory of the United States. In its projected form, this waterway was to include the Hudson River, the Erie Canal, Lake Erie, then a canal around the tip of Lake Michigan to the Illinois River, the Illinois, Mississippi, Missouri, another canal to the Columbia River, and then the Columbia to the coast. Just how it was to cover a few small stretches such as the Rocky Mountains was left mostly to the imagination of the listener.

CANAL TRAFFIC

As canals became an ordinary part of the system of communication in the United States. canalboat traffic settled into a regular routine. Its outstanding characteristic to the modern observer was its slowness of movement, for the usual speed was between two and four miles an hour. This leisurely traffic was satisfactory for the transportation of heavy nonperishable freight to a fairly stable market, but was not so desirable under other conditions. Passengers were reasonably comfortable, at least in comparison with their accommodations on a stage coach. Certainly the traveler who was interested in the country through which he passed had plenty of time to observe the scenery.

Most canalboats were painted in bright colors and, excluding those which handled only freight, could be classified as either line boats or packets. The line boat ordinarily carried only local traffic, and did not afford sleeping facilities; the usual charge was one cent a mile without food and two cents with food. The packet was larger and finer in every way. It furnished both food and beds, and made faster time due to its continuous travel day and night, so that it could cover some hundred miles a day. The cost of transportation, including food, was about five cents a mile, which was less than the rate charged by the stages.

Boats carrying passengers were arranged somewhat alike. In the front was a tiny cabin, with five or six bunks for the crew. Next came a small room to be used by the women for washing and dressing. Then there was a women's cabin, where the lady traveler could retire from the prying eyes of the male passengers and where all the women slept at night. In the center of the boat was a large general apartment, which might be as long as forty-five feet. In the day it was used as a general assembly room in which the passengers could entertain themselves or doze, and in which small parcels were kept (the larger baggage was kept on deck). Here meals were served on planks supported by wooden trestles. At night the cabin was used as the sleeping quarters for the men. Bunks were suspended on iron brackets, of which the ends on one side were pushed into the wall and on the other hung by ropes from the ceiling. Such shelves were six by three and one-half feet, and were arranged in tiers three high, so that there was little room between them. When all the bunks were filled the surplus men slept on the tables or the floor. Small straw mattresses and filthy blankets completed the rest of the equipment; these bedclothes were piled in a corner of the room during the day, and were seldom washed. Behind the large room was a bar and then the kitchen; the cook was generally also the barkeeper, and worked both day and night.

The usual crew of the boat consisted of a captain, two steersmen, two drivers, and a cook; just which of these dignitaries had any duty in caring for the wants of the passengers is not clear. The drivers and steersmen alternated in six-hour shifts.

Most of the passengers spent the fine days on deck, talking, playing games, sewing, reading, painting. Some of them would from time to time get off the boat and obtain a little exercise by walking along the towpath and chatting with the driver. The principal hazard of deck travel was the bridges, which were encountered every mile in some sections and still more frequently in the towns; these bridges were so low that everyone had to duck to avoid being knocked into the water. On bad days it was necessary to go below to the cabin, which was close and stuffy under the best conditions and almost insupportable in warm weather. Ventilation was an unknown art, with the result that some travelers preferred the rain to the cabin. An additional drawback was that even the most fastidious individual could not avoid the company of his fellow passengers, some of whom were highly objectionable. Filth and vermin were by no means rare. Sometimes traveling ministers would seize this opportunity to hold religious meetings, at which they were certain of a considerable congregation no matter how long and tedious the service.

One of the current amusements of canalboat travel was to watch the manipulation of the vessel, which was usually drawn by one to three horses or mules. The towpath was on only one side of the canal and so when two boats met, one of them would let its towline slack for the other to pass over the top. When the towpath crossed the river, considerable agility was necessary on the part of the horse and the driver. The horse would first go under the bridge and then gallop over it to arrive on the other side before all the slack of the line was taken up by the drift of the boat. Now and then the horse was too slow and was pulled into the water. Mules found a bridge a poor place on which to exercise their ancient prerogative of becoming stubborn.

The canal was an exceedingly important factor in the development of the West, even though its period of dominance was but brief. It afforded cheap and safe, although slow, transportation, its only superior at that time being the steamboat, which did not compete. Even when state-built and -operated canals did not show a profit, they helped to advance the economic well-being of the communities which they served. Prices for farm products improved, while the cost of imported articles decreased. Many towns all over the country traced the beginnings of their commercial importance to the influence of the canal.

One of their greatest services was to bring population into new areas. Often their very construction produced a settlement of the workers along the line of the canal. When completed they attracted settlers because of the improved transportational facilities, and in consequence surrounding land increased in value. All of them carried hundreds and even thousands of settlers to the West, and the flow of migration was facilitated by the better connections between East and West.

The desire for canals represented the peak of a movement for better transportation which included all types of internal improvements. The emphasis was placed on canals because they were the latest and most desired form of transportation. Other projects such as building roads, removing obstacles from the rivers, marking river channels, and placing lighthouses and buoys on the lakes also received sympathy and support. While the canal was at the height of its popularity an even newer idea was being expressed in the first experimentation with the railroads. Eventually the railroad was to overshadow its predecessor.

As with similar enthusiasms, the canal mania was carried to excess. Plans were always greater than completed projects. More work was started than could be finished. Excessive loans were made to complete waterways which could never be financially successful. Many canals were built far in advance of any possible usefulness. This over-expansion inevitably helped to produce a financial panic — that of 1837.

READINGS

C. H. Ambler, *A History of Transportation in the Ohio Valley* (1932), ch. 6; E. L. Bogart, *Internal Improvements and State Debts in Ohio* (1924), chs. 1, 2; R. C. Buley, *The Old Northwest* (2 vols., 1950), vol. 2, ch. 12; S. Dunbar, *A History of Travel in America* (4 vols., 1915), chs. 35–38; L. Esarey, *A History of Indiana* (1915), ch. 16; W. F. Gephart, *Transportation and Industrial Development* (1909), ch. 7; H. Harlan, *The Western Reserve* (1949), ch. 10—Ohio Canal; A. F. Harlow, *Old Towpaths* (1926)—reads easily; H. Hatcher, *The Great Lakes* (1944), ch. 21; L. T. Hemans, *Life and Times of Stevens Thomson Mason* (1920), pp. 276–282, ch. 19; A. B. Hulbert, *Paths of*

Inland Commerce (1920), chs. 3, 8, 9; G. L. Nute, *Lake Superior* (1944), ch. 10—Sault canal; J. N. Primm, *Economic Policy* (1954), chs. 5, 6—Missouri; B. L. Pierce, *A History of Chicago* (2 vols., 1937–40), vol. 1, chs. 4, 5; J. W. Putnam, *The Illinois and Michigan Canal* (1918); G. R. Taylor, *The Transportational Revolution, 1815–1866* (1951), ch. 3—all the United States; N. E. Whitford, *History of the Canal System of the State of New York* (2 vols., 1906).

CHAPTER 18

A
DELUGE OF PEOPLE

THE flood of settlers which had ebbed after the panic of 1819 again rose to magnificent proportions during the prosperous period of the late '20s and early '30s. In the one year of 1835 over 12,000,000 acres of the public domain were sold — an amount twice as large as the sales of any previous year, while the next year sales jumped to 20,000,000 acres. And once again history was repeated as the new flood dried up upon the arrival of another financial crisis — this time the panic of 1837.

The trans-Appalachian West grew rapidly, not only in absolute numbers, but in comparison to the remainder of the United States. The West's 2.2 millions of 1820 became 3.7 millions by 1830 and 6.4 millions by 1840, which represented a rate of growth almost twice as large as that for the United States as a whole. Westerners had comprised something less than a quarter of American population in 1820, but twenty years later they could boast of over a third. A list of the ten most populous states included Ohio, Kentucky, and Tennessee in all three census periods, and in 1840 they were joined by Indiana. Clearly the importance of the West was increasing, and particularly economically and politically.

In spite of the rapid growth in western population, there was no great increase in the number of organized states and territories. The only significant changes after the organization of Florida Territory in 1822 and before 1840 were the creation of the new states of Arkansas and Michigan and of the new territories of Wisconsin and Iowa. However, in 1840 the states west of the mountains numbered eleven, two less than half of the twenty-six states in the Union, and consequently the West was not to be discounted in national politics whenever it could agree on any proposal.

250

The western migration of the '20s and '30s was composed predominately of American-born farmers in spite of the very much increased foreign immigration of the period. The Irish immigrant tended to stay in the East, where he did unskilled labor, but a considerable number obtained jobs on western roads and canals, and many of these ultimately settled in the regions where they had worked for wages. An increasing flow of Germans went to the Ohio Valley and as far west as Missouri and Wisconsin, where they were joined by early Scandinavian migrants. And yet in spite of such population elements the American West remained largely native born.

OHIO VALLEY

The center of western population continued to remain in the Ohio Valley, which contained a good half of all westerners. Kentucky grew only moderately, but the states north of the river boomed. Ohio almost tripled between 1820 and 1840, while Indiana increased more than fourfold, and Illinois over eight times; in fact Illinois tripled within the single decade of 1830–40. This population showed signs of filling these states completely as it pushed into central and northern Indiana and Illinois.

Part of the population increase of the Ohio Valley did not represent an expansion of the agricultural frontier, but rather an increase in the size of the cities, since the valley contained an important share of western metropolitan centers. Pittsburgh dominated the upper valley in spite of the pretensions of Wheeling; by the 1830s the title of " gateway to the West " had lost much of its pertinence because of the competition of the National Road farther south, and increasingly Pittsburgh was known as a manufacturing center. " This city of smoke and mud, and ugly pavement " was all bustle and dirt and confusion. Commercialism was rampant, with visitors claiming that Pittsburgh men worked every waking hour except for the few minutes necessary to snatch hasty meals. Shipbuilding was a major industry, and included the construction not only of a considerable proportion of western steamboats but also of ships destined for the ocean-carrying trade. Coal mining and iron smelting were responsible for the general pall of smoke which was the despair of housewives; reputedly Pittsburgh residents never saw white snow. The making of glass, rope, cotton cloth, hardware, paper, liquor, and books were among the numerous Pittsburgh industries.

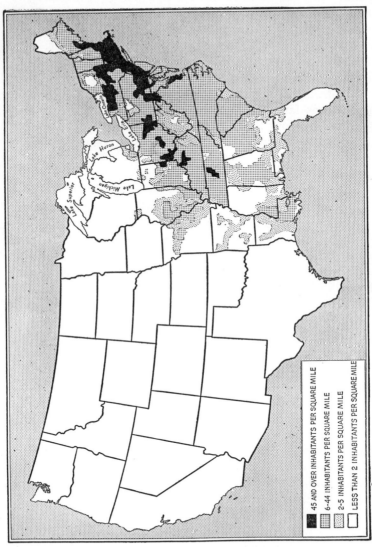

Population Density of 1830

45 AND OVER INHABITANTS PER SQUARE MILE

6-44 INHABITANTS PER SQUARE MILE

2-5 INHABITANTS PER SQUARE MILE

LESS THAN 2 INHABITANTS PER SQUARE MILE

Farther down the valley the cities of Louisville and Cincinnati were outstanding, with Louisville distinctly the less important, especially after the completion of the canal which avoided the necessity of transshipping goods around the falls. Louisville had a varied assortment of young industries, but its greatest importance was as a distributing and shipping center for the Kentucky hinterland. Here it was that the state's agricultural products, and particularly tobacco, were brought for shipment on the hundreds of steamers that plied the Ohio. Here it was that the people from the back country did their shopping in the many stores of which the town was justly proud.

The commonly recognized " Queen of the West " was Cincinnati, seventh American city in 1830 and sixth in 1840, when its 46,000 people displaced Charleston in the national ranking. Cincinnati was one of the more attractive of western cities, with clean, paved streets bordered by trees, well-tended houses, and good stores. Most visible architecturally was " Trollope's folly," a bazaar constructed as a speculation by Mrs. Anthony Trollope, one of the least liked of foreign visitors; the building had suggestions of Greek, Roman, and Moorish influences. In Cincinnati commerce boomed, stores were well filled, and steamboats crowded the wharves.

The principal industry of Cincinnati was pork packing, which assumed such proportions that frequently the city was dubbed " Porkopolis." The squeal of pigs was the city's dominant sound — partially because Cincinnati, like other American towns, allowed pigs to roam the streets freely to act as scavengers. Cincinnati had the first packing house west of the mountains in 1818, and twenty years later some 182,000 hogs were packed in a single year. Pork packing was an example of the best division of labor of the period, and utilized " everything but the squeal." One man drove the pig into a small pen, another knocked it on the head and stuck its throat, two more hauled the carcass away, and then another two immersed it in scalding water. After another man had removed the bristles in about a minute and a half, stretchers were put between the legs, and still two other men disembowled, beheaded and halved the animal. All these operations were completed in about three and a half minutes, so that the pig was dismembered almost before the last grunt had died away. After cutting, the hog was allowed to cool and then was packed in brine for shipment.

But Cincinnati was not devoted entirely to business. It was

also a most important literary and cultural center. Books, maga-zines, and newpapers flowed in a steady stream from its presses, and included several daily newspapers. The city counted among its residents such outstanding western authors as Hall, Flint, and Gallagher, as well as several painters. All kinds of professional groups were large in number. Schools, hospitals, and libraries were comparatively many and good, while the city was the western center for such philanthropic organizations as the American Sunday School Union.

Cincinnati was also interesting during the '20s and '30s because it was the greatest center of the increasing German immigration, which was coming in large numbers to central and southern Ohio. Cincinnati had German newspapers, clubs, and singing societies; German was spoken commonly on the streets, and peasant costumes could be seen here and there.

The growth of the Ohio Valley meant that by the 1830s the older sections along the river could no longer be considered as a frontier, unless one talks of literary, educational, medical, or other frontiers. In most of the ordinary cultural traits it was more akin to the East than it was to the newer regions farther west, and con-sequently it leaves the frontier picture.

NORTHERN OHIO AND MICHIGAN

To the north, migration flowed in vast quantities along the Great Lakes, filling such cities as Erie, Cleveland, Sandusky, To-ledo, and Detroit; Cleveland, for example, had a population of 1000 in 1830 and 6000 in 1840. Continuing west, migrants pushed into Michigan, northern Indiana and Illinois, Wisconsin, and even as far as Iowa. The travel of westward-bound migrants became ex-tremely impressive as they filled the boats and crowded the roads. During the year 1833, 60,000 people left Buffalo by water for the West, the next year saw 80,000, and succeeding years brought still more. These figures obviously did not include the great number of settlers who went by land; the explanation of the omission is that no one felt it worth his while to count the wagon trains.

The city of Buffalo, as noted earlier, experienced a boom with the opening of the Erie Canal, the improvement of the Lake Erie harbor and the vastly increased migration; by 1840 it numbered 18,000. With this rapid expansion the town was filled with land speculators and hotels. The buildings that rose on every hand were ordinarily large and cheaply constructed edifices, even though they included a theater which was considered one of the finest in the West. The streets of the town were crowded with immigrants, land speculators, runaway slaves and their masters, Indians — frequently drunk — merchants, canal drivers, and other elements of the heterogeneous population. Buffalo presented a fine opportunity for the energetic and ambitious, but it was no place for a lady alone on the streets at night.

The great northern area of opportunity during the early 1830s was Michigan, which was particularly attractive to Yankeee migrants, who arrived in great numbers.

" Then there's old Varmount, well, what d'ye think of that!
To be sure, the gals are handsome, and the cattle very fat:
But who among the mountains 'mid cloud and snow would stay,
When he can buy a prairie in Michigania?
    Yea, yea, yea, to Michigania."

Detroit, the gateway of Michigan, remained a fairly small town with a population of about 9000 in 1840, but it had large ambitions. It bulged with immigrants and merchants and speculators so that accommodations for food and lodging were stretched to the breaking point. Streets were wide and unpaved, and sidewalks no more than a few random planks; in rainy weather a caller drove his carriage directly to the front door of the house where he desired to call so that he would not be completely mired. Detroit was a city of the future, and consequently was attractive only to the man who could keep his eye on the new churches, banks, stores, newspapers, and homes that were springing into existence and have visions of a golden future.

Many visitors saw only the drab existing conditions and not the hoped-for future: " O Detroit, what a barren and inhospitable City thou art! Thou shalt sit enthroned as the Queen of Muddy Streets, through which do saunter the gaunt lean cows, which after feeding upon what thy generous inhabitants cast from their kitchen doors are killed and quartered to be cooked — but to be eaten — aye there's the rub — that is frequently an impossibility. Gristle, skin & bone, pervade thy very marrow & boiled, baked, or fried one's teeth suffer in the attack."

Michigan settlers came largely from New York and New England and concentrated in the southern third of the state. All of the inland towns in this area had been established after the War of

1812 and now they grew magnificently. Farther north such frontier settlements as Grand Rapids and Saginaw were receiving their first growth in the '30s. Land speculators held the lots in these hopeful metropolises at outrageous prices. To the west, the new towns of St. Joseph and New Buffalo were rivals of Chicago, with speculators dreaming of a rosy future in which they would outdistance the Illinois upstart. The Michigan boom was sadly injured by the panic of 1837, then revived a little only to collapse completely when the depression finally hit the West in full force in 1839.

MICHIGAN STATEHOOD

The growth of Michigan naturally led its inhabitants to talk about statehood. While the census of 1830 had shown a population of only 32,000, a new census four years later showed three times that number — more than sufficient for statehood. Assuming that Congressional approval would be easy to obtain, a constitutional convention was called in 1835 and after arduous labor produced a document that was accepted by the voters. So assured did the inhabitants of Michigan feel of the quick coming of statehood that they proceeded to elect state officers and to put them to work.

The admission of Michigan did not come promptly, but was delayed by a boundary dispute with Ohio. The southern boundary of Michigan as stated in the Ordinance of 1787 was a line directly east from the tip of Lake Michigan. When Ohio had been admitted to the Union there had been some doubt as to where, if at all, such a line would strike Lake Erie, but the matter did not seem of vital importance. Merely as a precautionary measure, the constitution of Ohio contained the provision that in case the line did not hit the western end of Lake Erie it could, with the consent of Congress, be changed to strike the most northerly cape of Maumee Bay.

The actual survey of the Michigan-Ohio boundary showed that it did in fact miss the western end of Lake Erie. Even more important the Toledo region was growing rapidly, with the prospective completion of the Wabash Canal. In consequence Ohio claimed the alternate line of her constitution, and Michigan promptly refused, positively and belligerently, to consider herself bound by a provision of the Ohio constitution.

Westerners believed in immediate and forceful action to support what they felt to be their proper claims, and consequently both

Ohio and Michigan breathed defiance and rolled up their sleeves for a fight. Ohio raised troops and started them north toward the disputed area. Michigan likewise raised troops and sent them on what turned out to be a delightful junket, while the legislature voted funds for " defense." Ohio surreptitiously held court and Michigan patriots kidnapped some of the officials.

A potential civil war brought the intervention of President Jackson, although he was embarrassed by his desire to retain the friendship of both sides in the coming Presidential elections. In this dilemma he followed good political practice by asking a truce, during which a federal commission would investigate the conflicting claims. The upshot of the investigation was the proposal of a compromise which Michigan felt was dictated by the electoral votes of Ohio: Ohio was to receive the line she wanted, while in return Michigan was to receive the upper peninsula, which she did not want in the least. Presumably the only people who should have been dissatisfied were the few residents of the Wisconsin region, but their votes were insignificant, and anyway they should by this time have become accustomed to losing territory to neighboring states.

The proposed " compromise " was utterly unacceptable to Michigan and was rejected with considerable heat at a convention which met at Ann Arbor in September 1836. Incidentally, the extralegal state government was continuing to operate during these troubled times. After the delegates to the September convention returned to their homes a small unauthorized group of men anxious for statehood convened at Ann Arbor in December 1836 and voted to accept the compromise. When Congress received the vote of this latest gathering it must have breathed a great sigh of relief, for immediately it turned a blind eye on the credentials of the members of the group and hastily admitted Michigan to the Union on January 26, 1837.

NORTHERN INDIANA AND ILLINOIS

A portion of the settlers who moved west by way of the Great Lakes ended their trips on the plains of northern Indiana and Illinois where they coalesced with other streams of settlement from the south. The result was the appearance of thousands of new farms and the establishment of such cities as Galesburg, Springfield, and Chicago. The land rejected by early settlers as unfit for farming proved to be the most productive of the entire area.

These new settlements came into existence largely on the relatively treeless prairies and hence were faced by a whole new set of problems that were later to become familiar beyond the Mississippi. Solutions were not found at this time, but at least the problems were recognized and faced. The absence of trees eliminated the labor of girdling and chopping, but increased the difficulties of the first planting; at least four oxen were required to drag a plow through the tough prairie soil, which meant that the cost of the first plowing was something like two dollars an acre, or more than the usual cost of the land. The scarcity of trees was most important in the great difficulties which it produced in the building of houses and barns, the fencing of the land, and the providing of fuel. For the time being old techniques were continued but at a greatly increased cost because of the necessity of hauling wood long distances.

The wonder city of Illinois was Chicago, lying on Lake Michigan at the mouth of the Chicago River. Historically the region had been fortified because it was on a trade route which ascended the Chicago River, portaged to the Illinois, and finally won through to the Mississippi. At the opening of the year 1830 the future Chicago consisted of one stockade — abandoned, a handful of cabins, and large wastes of sand.

The Chicago boom started with the plotting of the city in 1830 by the canal commissioners, and almost immediately the land speculators seized reins and whip. Reports had it that by 1834 the town had some 2000 inhabitants, but that enough building lots had been surveyed to provide for a population of 300,000 without slums. Every male inhabitant bought and sold town lots, and transmitted eagerly the gossip of how someone had made a profit of twenty to thirty per cent within a few days or a hundred per cent or more within a few weeks. Every speculator could show amazing paper profits, and all the inns and stores were crowded with men just on the point of making their fortunes — until the pin prick of the panic of 1837.

Before the arrival of the panic Chicago had managed to collect some 6000 residents and to furnish itself with a proper variety of houses, stores, churches, taverns, banks, and newspapers, not to mention a considerable variety of industrial enterprises. Many people felt assured of the future greatness of Chicago — but their prophetic vision was slightly dimmed by the existence of as many others who felt equally certain of the future opulence of dozens of towns that never actually matured. Optimism was in the air. The older and more important western cities such as Cincinnati, St. Louis, and New Orleans saw as yet no reason for alarm.

WISCONSIN

North of Illinois the present Wisconsin was receiving its first important settlements. Two areas had the preference. The first was the typical farming frontier which occupied the southeastern part of the state and reached west from Milwaukee, with tentacles west beyond Waukesha and north to Appleton. As in the case of Michigan, a considerable share of the new residents came from New England and New York, but Wisconsin also received many foreign-born, particularly German, Swedish, Danish, and Norwegian. The Scandinavians were particularly notable, since they were very enthusiastic about the new country and wrote in that spirit to their friends back home. The result was an ever increasing flow of Scandinavians to the Northwest — at first to Wisconsin, and then to Minnesota and Dakota.

As with other frontiers, Wisconsin was a happy hunting ground for the land speculator. In most new regions he was the first pioneer, occupying good agricultural land, mill sites and town sites. These early claims were generally respected without the benefit of law, and claim jumping was viewed askance even if the new occupant really wanted to farm. The result was that later arrivals had to choose between paying for land already claimed, taking inferior land, or going to a wilder district.

The activities of the speculator were not considered bad as long as tremendous areas of the state were unoccupied. In fact, any sign of either farming or commercial activity was considered a hopeful portent for the future. " Our object is to better our conditions." Wisconsin wanted more people, and quantity was more important than quality. It was the earliest state (1852) to give official encouragement to immigration. Later Iowa, Minnesota, Dakota, and other territories and states organized similar advertising ventures to attract people to their communities. Pamphlets were published in various languages, and quite typically a New York agent tried to route the settlers to the region he represented. Unfortunately many of these migrants were badly swindled before they arrived at their new homes.

The metropolis of the infant Wisconsin was Milwaukee, which had its first speculative boom in the years 1835–37. Quite appropriately the first newspaper (1836) was titled the Milwaukee *Advertiser* and devoted its main efforts to attracting settlers. The Milwaukee of 1836 had less than 1000 inhabitants, but great expectations. Houses were being built feverishly, living quarters were at a premium, wages and other prices high, and speculation rife. In other words Milwaukee was a typical frontier town.

The second important area of settlement in Wisconsin was the lead district which straddled Illinois and Wisconsin, stretching roughly from Galena, Illinois, to Mineral Point, Wisconsin. The lead appeared near the surface and was comparatively pure, so that it could be extracted from pit mines and then smelted before being moved down the river to St. Louis and New Orleans. Desultory mining had been in existence for many years as far west as Dubuque, but the real development of the mines dated from the early '20s. By 1826 there were an estimated 1600 miners in the region, and during the following year there was a boom which was not again equaled until the discovery of gold in California.

The lure of lead drew prospective miners mainly from the West and South, but also attracted considerable numbers of Irish and French. Trial holes were dug all over the landscape, and rumors of new finds resulted in the overnight production of such mining camps as New Diggings, Hard Scrabble, Coon Branch, Fair Play, Platterville, Mineral Point, Dodgeville, and Blue Mounds. The miner did his own prospecting and then mined and smelted his own ore, usually living in a cave that he had dug in the side of a hill. Now and then one attained prosperity but as in most mining booms the majority existed largely on hope. These mines were the lure that brought farmers to the Rock River region and hence were responsible indirectly for the Black Hawk War, in which the white volunteers included a sizable proportion of miners.

The imminent admission of Michigan as a state led Congress to split off the western section as the Territory of Wisconsin in 1836. As then constituted Wisconsin included not only the present state but all the land farther west between the Mississippi and Missouri from Canada to the northern border of Missouri; this region west of the Mississippi had been attached to Michigan in the years 1834 to 1836. In 1838 Wisconsin was cut to its present limits except that it continued to retain the region northwest of Lake Superior. The infant territory created in 1836 could boast some 22,000 inhabitants, and its governor was Henry Dodge. The location of the territorial capital was a matter of bitter rivalry between Mineral Point and Milwaukee; a compromise was finally arranged which provided for a town in the wilderness of the Four Lakes region — Madison. Wisconsin attained statehood in 1848, and Minnesota became a territory in the following year.

IOWA

West of the Mississippi settlement began to flow into present Iowa before 1840. New towns such as Keokuk, Burlington, Davenport, and Dubuque grew along the river in the tract of land forced from the Indians at the end of the Black Hawk War. As time passed and new cessions were obtained, settlement spread west; Iowa City was founded in 1839. These settlements were far distant from the territorial government at Madison and hence the new Territory of Iowa was created in 1838 to take care of them; its inclusion of much country to the north and northwest was of little practical importance since there were almost no whites outside the present limits of Iowa.

KENTUCKY AND TENNESSEE

South of the Ohio River the slowing growth of Kentucky was almost as striking as the rapid expansion of the states to the north. Kentucky's diversified agriculture might have been expected to attract the same stream of settlers that appeared on the other side of the river, but several factors changed the outcome. The existence of Negro slavery deterred both northerners and immigrants from abroad. Its comparative density of population and absence of public land produced a preference for the open spaces farther south. The very diversity of agriculture seemed unpromising to southerners interested in raising cotton. The consequence was that Kentucky grew slowly. While in 1820 she was a close second to Ohio for the lead in western population, by 1840 Ohio had obtained twice as many residents as Kentucky, and Indiana had almost come abreast of her southern neighbor.

The situation of Tennessee was quite different from that of Kentucky in that the fertile western part of the state remained open for settlement after 1820. Planters flooded into this section and produced a great boom in the most important town, Memphis. Memphis was the nearest important river town south of St. Louis, and did a flourishing business as a shipping and distributing center. Farmers, traders, and migrating Indians crossed the river at this point. Cotton and other agricultural products were heaped on the docks waiting to be moved by river steamer. Planters, Indians, trappers, gamblers, and prostitutes rubbed elbows in the streets in typical western fashion.

LOWER SOUTH

Still farther to the south the new Territory of Florida was making but little advance in population, with the settled areas confined entirely to the northern parts of the territory. Neither the orange nor the tourist business had as yet been conceived as the foundation of permanent prosperity. Most of Florida was characterized mainly by its marshy land, its scrubby trees, and its imposing wastes of sand — unless one were more impressed by the hostile and dangerous Indians, for the Seminole troubles did not end until after 1840. In spite of inadequate population Florida desired statehood, and consequently formulated a constitution and applied for admission in 1838. The plea was not accepted.

The great bulk of southern migration moved into western Georgia, Alabama, Mississippi, and Louisiana. The older of these states, Georgia and Louisiana, almost doubled in the years from 1820 to 1840, while the newer ones, Alabama and Mississippi, increased by five times. The new settlement of the lower South was composed predominantly of planters moving their slaves to cultivate cotton, although eastern Louisiana had a very considerable sugar industry. A few of the migrants moved by water, either around the tip of Florida and into the Gulf or by way of the Ohio and Mississippi, but most of them departed from Virginia or the Carolinas and moved overland through Georgia. Any night would exhibit the twinkle of lights as the slaves prepared their evening meals over their campfires. Eastern planters who moved to the West frequently bought out the holdings of the earlier frontiersmen who had cleared the land, and these pioneers continued farther west.

The southern frontier was even more boisterous and lawless than the northern — if common rumors of the time are credible. Indian troubles tended to attract the dissolute and the vicious, since the Indians were just being forced to move west, thus affording a splendid opportunity for the none too scrupulous to seize Indian land and improvements. Furthermore the towns were comparatively small, isolated, and badly policed, which made them splendid refuges for the lawless. As usual land speculators were as much in evidence as farther north.

Cotton culture in a region with navigable rivers that permitted shipping directly from the front door of the plantation, discouraged development of the hundreds of bustling communities that were so much in evidence north of the Ohio. The main shipping centers were largely on the coast. For the eastern portions of the Deep South Augusta and Savannah were the important outlets, and with the existing methods of transportation Augusta could compete with Savannah on almost even terms. Farther to the west most of Alabama and a portion of Mississippi were tributary to the city of Mobile; the growing business of the rural regions was beginning to crowd the unpaved streets and wooden sidewalks of the Alabama metropolis. While Mobile still contained a fair number of French- and Spanish-speaking residents, the dominant class was now Anglo-American.

Western Mississippi, Louisiana, and in fact the whole area bordering on the Mississippi looked to that stream for its transportation. Such cities as Vicksburg, Natchez, and Baton Rouge drew the business of their back-countries, even though they tended to be overshadowed by New Orleans. Natchez was the best — but not most favorably — known of these towns.

New Orleans was unquestionably the dominant western city of the '20s and '30s. Its location was such that it could control the business from the two-thirds of the continent drained by the Mississippi and its tributaries, and few people questioned the proposition that New Orleans was destined to become and remain America's most important city. This accepted present and future importance attracted great numbers of people who wanted to get rich with the country, and the population of New Orleans reached the neighborhood of 100,000 by 1840.

Steamboats from the upper Mississippi and the Ohio lined the wharves, where they nudged ocean-going vessels from all over the world. As early as 1821 New Orleans exported some $16,000,000 of western products during the year, while in return silks, French wines and brandies, British cutlery, rum, coffee, and other exotic products jammed the warehouses. Before the Civil War, annual exports had passed the hundred million mark in spite of the bad river channel about which people talked but did nothing. New York could well look to its laurels.

The most obvious drawbacks of New Orleans were its swampiness and its high morbidity. The two were of course connected, and not only because of the reputed necessity of weighting coffins to keep them underground. New Orleans suffered from all the usual western ills, and in addition was a notable center for yellow fever. The mosquito was considered a great nuisance, but was not connected in the popular mind with the disease. Every inhabitant who could find time and money went north during the sickly season.

New Orleans continued to remain quite foreign in appearance — somewhat Spanish, but more French. French architecture was in evidence, French was spoken commonly on the streets, a French theater operated successfully, and a magnificent Catholic cathedral served the Spanish-French populace. Across Canal Street was the American section of the town, slightly cleaner and more bustling, with its own theater and hotels and stores. None of the streets of the city was paved; ultimately paving stone had to be brought from the North as ship ballast. Most of the houses were constructed of wood, but some of them were covered with stucco.

New Orleans was famous for its gaiety, which visitors often called wickedness. Sailors gambled and brawled in the saloons, poolrooms, and gambling halls of the waterfront. Pickpockets jostled each other on the streets. In 1836, with a city of some 60,000, there were 543 licensed saloons, cabarets, and taverns, plus an unknown number of others. Brothels were numerous. The more leisured inhabitants — and slavery permitted freedom for many — engaged in a round of balls, dinners, and masquerades. The Mardi Gras was new. The gaslights of the theaters shone brightly, and the St. Charles Hotel, opened in 1837, was considered the most imposing building west of the mountains.

Part of the city's reputation for sin can be traced to its use of Sunday as the main day for shopping, visiting, theater attendance, and party giving. For northerners who arrived on business, and particularly for conscience-ridden New Englanders, this procedure was a desecration of the Sabbath and inevitably indicated natural depravity.

The creole ladies of New Orleans were noted for their beauty, but some doubt was expressed as to their virtue — a doubt which was probably not justified. Their dark, voluptuous charms and their soft, languorous drawls were enchanting to all save the most captious critics, who professed to detect a deplorable lack of animation. When feminine charms were combined with the peaceful and romantic beauty of a moonlit river they erased even the unpleasantly monotonous music of the clouds of mosquitoes.

In addition to the creoles New Orleans had many mulattoes, of whom the girls seemed quite attractive to the white men. A whole section of the city was devoted to the small attractive houses inhabited by white men and mulatto (usually quadroon) girls. The couples were prevented from marriage by both law and social custom. If the white man married, the quadroon received the house and furniture; reputedly the girl seldom contracted a new alliance, and not infrequently committed suicide. As for the white ladies, they met this delicate situation by ignoring it.

MISSOURI AND ARKANSAS

West of the Mississippi the great population center north of Louisiana was the state of Missouri, including the important city of St. Louis. The number of residents increased sixfold between 1820 and 1840, as settlers from both north and south of the Ohio River spread themselves over the greater part of the state, and as foreign immigrants began to arrive. In particular German migrants came in considerable numbers, which was probably a mistake, since they were frequently unhappy in a region that was aggressively pro-slavery. Older towns such as Carondelet and St. Charles, Ste. Genevieve and Cape Girardeau, retained considerable numbers of French Catholics, but the newer towns were entirely Anglo-American, and even the older towns were overrun by English-speaking people until they began to lose their former ways of life.

The city of St. Louis dominated the Missouri area and much of the trans-Mississippi West, even though its population in 1840 was little over 16,000. Old and well-established as cities of the newer West went, it looked down with disdain on such young upstarts as Memphis, Milwaukee, and Chicago. Any St. Louis resident was completely confident that the location of his home town near the confluence of the Mississippi and Missouri gave it the command of the business of each of these streams. Its control of the fur trade was held a harbinger of a similar dominance in any other business that might be developed west of the Mississippi. Like other boom towns of the period its wharves were jammed with steamboats, its stores crowded with purchasers, and its streets filled with the heterogeneous population of the West.

The business section of St. Louis inevitably lined the river, and this part of the town was badly drained, filthy, and overwhelmed by millions of flies. Some sections of the city showed evidences of French settlement, including an imposing Cathedral, a Catholic college, and the Convent of the Sacred Heart. Other parts of the city were entirely American, with broader streets and many new buildings among which was one of the finest theaters west of the Appalachians.

Lying between Missouri and Louisiana was the Territory of Arkansas, which had been but sparsely populated upon its creation in 1819. In early territorial days Arkansas extended as far west as the international boundary, but by 1828 it had been reduced to its present limits. The settlement of Arkansas continued but slowly, in part because of the considerable areas occupied by swamps and mountains. As more easterly states were occupied the overflow entered Arkansas, settling primarily along the Arkansas, White, Black, and Red rivers — a pleasant color scheme. Development was hastened by the construction (1821–33) of a military road between Memphis and Little Rock and by the removal in the early '30s of the obstructions to navigation in the Arkansas River by that well-known steamboat man Henry M. Shreve, whose work on the Mississippi was even more important.

New Arkansans were not large in numbers but were vigorous in self-expression. A demand for statehood brought a convention at Little Rock in 1836; a constitution was formulated and an appeal for admission addressed to Congress. Statehood came immediately, with Arkansas offsetting the northern state of Michigan. The population of Arkansas in 1840 was slightly under 100,000, but was spread so thinly that very few areas could boast as many inhabitants as six per square mile.

With the admission of Arkansas and Michigan and the formation of the territories of Wisconsin and Iowa the eastern half of the United States had almost assumed its present form politically. East of the Mississippi only Florida and Wisconsin remained eligible for statehood. For the first tier of trans-Mississippi states, Iowa remained to be admitted, while Minnesota was still a matter for the future; otherwise settlement had reached the longitude of the great bend of the Missouri.

READINGS

T. P. Abernethy, *The Formative Period in Alabama* (1922), chs. 6–14, *From Frontier to Plantation* (1932), chs. 15, 16, 18; H. R. Austin, *The Milwaukee Story* (1946), chs. 3–8—episodical; E. J. Benton, *Cultural Story of an American City*, part 2 (1944); T. C. Blegen, *Norwegian Migration to America, 1825–1860* (1931); R. C. Buley, *The Old Northwest* (2 vols., 1950), vol. 2, chs. 10, 11; Mrs. R. Burlend, *A True Picture of Emigration*

(1936)—firsthand on Illinois; E. E. Calkins, *They Broke the Prairie* (1937)—Galesburg, Illinois; F. Copeland, *Kendall of the Picayune* (1943), ch. 3—New Orleans; F. G. Davenport, *Ante-Bellum Kentucky* (1943), chs. 1, 2; E. Dick, *Vanguards of the Frontier* (1941), ch. 6; J. Drury, *Midwest Heritage* (1948)—pictures of Old Northwest; W. F. English, *The Pioneer-Lawyer and Jurist in Missouri* (1947); L. Esarey, *A History of Indiana* (1915), chs. 10–13; J. G. Fletcher, *Arkansas* (1947), chs. 4–7—popular in tone; P. W. Gates, *Frontier Landlords and Prairie Tenants* (1945)—scholarly on Illinois; H. H. Grant, *Peter Cartwright* (1931), chs. 5–12; L. T. Hemans, *Life and Times of Stevens Thomson Mason* (1920), chs. 3–13—Michigan; H. C. Hockett, *Western Influence on Political Parties to 1825* (1917); S. H. Holbrook, *The Yankee Exodus* (1950), chs. 7, 9—scrappy; B. Knollenberg, *Pioneer Sketches of the Upper Whitewater Valley* (1945)—Indiana; S. W. Martin, *Florida During Territorial Days* (1944), chs. 2–9; L. K. Mathews, *The Expansion of New England* (1919), pp. 220–236; W. Nowlin, *The Bark Covered House* (1937)—contemporary; L. Pelzer, *Augustus Caesar Dodge* (1908), chs. 2–8—Wisconsin; B. L. Pierce, *A History of Chicago* (2 vols., 1937–40), vol. 1, ch. 3; J. Plumbe, *Sketches of Iowa* (1948)—contemporary; V. P. Pooley, *The Settlement of Illinois from 1830 to 1850* (1908); M. M. Quaife, *Lake Michigan* (1944), ch. 18; M. M. Quaife and G. Glazer, *Michigan* (1948), chs. 13–15 —text; C. C. Qualey, *Norwegian Settlement in the United States, 1825–1860* (1938), chs. 1, 2; W. F. Raney, *Wisconsin* (1940), chs. 4–7; E. H. Roseboom and F. P. Weisenburger, *A History of Ohio* (1953), ch. 8; E. D. Ross, *Iowa Agriculture* (1951), chs. 2, 3; J. Schafer, *The Wisconsin Lead Region* (1932); H. Sinclair, *The Port of New Orleans* (1942), chs. 11–13; H. J. Smith, *Chicago's Great Century* (1933), chs. 1–3—journalistic; B. Still, *Milwaukee* (1948), chs. 1–3—scholarly; C. W. Towne and E. N. Wentworth, *Pigs* (1950), chs. 9, 10, 14–16; S. C. Williams, *The Beginnings of West Tennessee* (1930), chs. 16–41.

CHAPTER 19

THE
MONEY PROBLEM

THE western prosperity of the early '30s, with its orgy of speculative investments in transportational innovations, its rise of land and commodity values, its flood of immigration, and its high hopes for the future, came to an end with the panic of 1837. The resulting collapse of the economic life of the nation damaged the West more than had any other similar preceding event, and focused the attention of the country upon the financial condition of the West as well as upon that of the nation at large.

The West had been handicapped throughout its entire history by a lack of ready money and of credit. The West of a century ago, like the West of today, was predominately a debtor community. The migrant to the new lands of the frontier was not a rich man, and he needed capital even for his original settlement. A horse and wagon had to be bought, provisions acquired, land purchased, a house built, and the family supported until the first crop was harvested. The usual frontiersman raised these necessary funds largely through the East. Possibly he had saved some money or had property that he could sell, or relatives or friends might advance him the needed capital; or on the other hand, of course, he might work for some years in the West and acquire land before he returned East to claim a bride or to join his family. In any case the obtaining of credit was largely a personal matter, carried on outside of commercial banking institutions.

CREDIT BY MERCHANTS

After the migrant to the West arrived at his new home further financial requirements were satisfied in part by credit from local

268

merchants. Surplus corn, tobacco, furs, honey, or pork could be traded for tools or cloth, and frequently the merchant was willing to wait for payment. The consequence was that western merchandising was a complicated and hazardous occupation. From time to time the merchant would find the necessity of traveling to New Orleans both to sell and buy. He also might travel to the East Coast for manufactured articles. Hardware was more likely to come from Pittsburgh. The result was a considerable stock of goods from coarse cotton cloth to gauze veils, and from sets of Shakespeare to Bateman's Drops. The freight charges were high — possibly a third of the final cost of the article. Payment by the merchant was difficult, and he delighted in the cash of a nearby army post. Currency might well be lost in transit, while bills of exchange on the East were hard to obtain. These difficulties of the western storekeeper measure his services to the struggling communities of the West. He was an important source of credit, which in turn was advanced in part by eastern firms.

But there were many desires which could not be satisfied by the merchants. Each settler was hopeful of the future and wanted more funds to buy additional land, acquire new machinery, construct new buildings, and buy seeds and stock. He could hardly borrow from friends and neighbors, since one man was nearly as poor as another. Even westerners of the most prosperous group were almost hopeless when they looked enviously to such commercial enterprises as factories, packing plants, canals, and railroads — not to mention such community necessities as churches, courthouses, and jails. For these purposes new sources of credit must be found.

EARLY BANKS

The first tramontane settlers came West at the time of the Revolution, when organized commercial banking was as yet unknown in the United States. The only lending of money was done by men who had a surplus of ready cash and were willing to lend it to trusted individuals. The first refinement of this simple operation came when people realized that paper credit was not always redeemed immediately. An order to pay the bearer a specified amount of money might pass from hand to hand for many years without being redeemed, thus serving in itself as currency. This practice afforded the basis for much of the later banking activities of the world. It meant that a person or company might issue paper promises to pay definite sums of money to the holders of the notes and

feel confident that no large share of them would be presented for
payment at any one time, thus avoiding the necessity of maintaining a cash reserve equal to the face value of the notes. Furthermore these paper tokens might be loaned the same as money.

Discovery of the first simple principles governing paper credit
led to the establishment of several kinds of banks in the United
States in the period immediately following the Revolution. The
first United States Bank (1791–1811) acted as financial agent for
the federal government as well as doing a private business of its
own. Local banks were incorporated by the states, each such bank
having its own peculiar charter provisions, since general and uniform banking laws were still a thing of the future. Lastly, since
there was no prohibitory legislation, private persons and groups
of persons engaged in banking at their own discretion; sometimes
such private enterprises were sufficiently small that the entire
bank could be moved from place to place in a trunk. Members of
both of the last two groups frequently carried on other businesses
at the same time. The rapid growth of banking in the United States
is evident from the fact that the three banks in existence in 1789
had increased to twenty-six by 1800; in 1811, which was the year
that the charter of the United States Bank lapsed, there were
eighty-eight such institutions.

WESTERN BANKS

The attitude of the West toward banks and banking was dictated
by the desire for more credit. As far as a westerner was concerned,
the one important service of a bank was to issue large quantities
of paper money and to loan it to anyone who wanted it. The idea
of requiring adequate security for a loan was approved, but only
in theory; everyone was optimistic about the future, feeling that
wealth was just around the corner and that repayment of any
loan, no matter what its size, would be painless. In this frame of
mind the westerner naturally objected to the repayment of a loan
at any specified time. If wealth lay just ahead, then it was cruel
as well as unbusinesslike for the bank to remove the steed on which
its patron was galloping down the broad path to prosperity. The
function of the bank was to increase the money in circulation, and
not to recall any of it. Finally, the West carried its well-known
democratic concepts into bank management. Just as any average
man should be able to fill any post in the government, so should
he be able to operate a bank satisfactorily.

On the basis of these simple precepts the West began to acquire banks of its own during the first decade of the nineteenth century. The Lexington (Kentucky) Insurance Company (1802) did a banking business. The Miami Exporting Company (Cincinnati, 1803) was organized to finance New Orleans trade, but soon confined its business to commercial banking. The bank of Michigan and the bank of Kentucky started operations in 1806. The very famous Nashville bank opened its doors in 1807 and continued operations until the panic of 1819. Other small banks appeared throughout the West. Most of these organizations were short-lived, but they all succeeded in issuing large quantities of paper money before their respective demises.

The checks on the transactions of the early western banks were few and comparatively ineffectual. Some reliance could be placed on the honesty and good business sense of their promoters, but this control was somewhat vitiated by the proprietors' lack of banking training and experience. A more effective and immediate check was exercised by the United States Bank, which felt some responsibility for banking conditions all over the country. The United States Bank followed the policy of collecting the paper money of banks which were rumored to be unstable, and then presenting a considerable amount of such paper for immediate payment in cash; either the bank then gave convincing proof of its stability or it was forced to admit its insolvency and close its doors. Even the potential threat of such action was sufficient to make many of the smaller banks follow a comparatively conservative policy.

The only real limitation upon irresponsible operations by the smaller banks disappeared when the first United States Bank was not rechartered in 1811. The small banks then saw their opportunity and multiplied like rabbits, and even after the Second National Bank of 1816. By 1820 there were in the United States 307 banks, of which the West had its fair share. In the one year 1818 Kentucky authorized forty banks with a total capitalization of $8,000,000, and other states were not much less generous. The country was deluged with a flood of paper money, whereupon the West gave loud cheers and asked for more. The answer of the small banks was that if all the large banks were eliminated still more paper money could be issued. This statement was undoubtedly quite accurate, even though students of the subject both then and later deplored the removal of the last check upon conservative banking.

Failure to recharter the first United States Bank was followed immediately by the outbreak of the War of 1812, and banking conditions became increasingly confused. The last vestige of control over the smaller banks disappeared with the suspension of specie payment all over the country. The result was that the field of banking was left wide open to all comers, and so hundreds of men decided that the easiest way to amass riches quickly was to print their own money. As long as public confidence remained, any sort of paper currency could be circulated, at least for a short time.

As might have been expected, many of the new banks were badly managed by their amateur owners. Usually a company was organized on the basis of a small cash subscription; then paper money supplied the deficit of gold, or capital was raised by loans on the company's nice fresh new stock. Actual currency of the realm was a rarity, kept mostly for the purpose of display. Paper money was backed by little or no specie reserve. Most of the bank's loans appeared as " frozen assets," that is, long term loans which could not be called in case of sudden need. Short term or call loans were of little use in the West, where the farmers needed money for at least a year at a time, and consequently the average bank had little option but to tie up its money in permanent form. Even worse, many of the loans were based on the scantiest of security, for frequently the banks accepted the farmer's own optimistic statement of the value of his land. Such security was fairly satisfactory in prosperous times, but became practically worthless in times of economic depression and low prices. In such a period the bank might call the loan, but then it received the hostility of the borrower and his friends and was left with large amounts of unsalable cheap land on its hands; its only choice was to allow the loan to continue indefinitely, with every prospect that it would never be repaid and the excellent chance that the bank would be bankrupt in the meantime.

The evils inherent in western banking practices were supplemented by a considerable amount of fraud. The " saddlebag bank " was notorious. A man would ride his horse into a small town, and his saddlebags would be crammed with beautiful crisp new bank notes. He would then set up an office and loan his paper money to all the neighboring farmers on easy terms and with but little security. After collecting all the promissory notes that were available he disposed of them to the store owner or innkeeper at a discount for ready cash and decamped with the proceeds. The storekeeper was thus left with the job of placating the irate farmers when they discovered that their nice new bank notes were practically worthless.

Another common type of fraud was counterfeiting. All bank notes were poorly printed and easily copied, thus offering great temptations to the dexterous man who possessed a printing press, was desirous for easy wealth, and was not burdened with an excessive amount of moral scruples. The number of notes which were counterfeited became so great that anyone handling large sums of money required a " counterfeit detector," which was a thick book describing the most common frauds. The situation was so bad that all bank notes were looked upon with suspicion. Usually they were accepted at par only in the community in which they were issued; at other places they were discounted, with the size of the discount depending upon the reputation of the issuing bank and its distance from the place of presentation. Many notes would not be accepted at any value if taken far from home.

SECOND UNITED STATES BANK

Conditions were sufficiently bad that well-informed people did not question the need of the ameliorating influence of a federal bank, and so the Second United States Bank was chartered in 1816 for a period of twenty years. The new bank sought to establish specie payments, in which effort it was finally successful, and like its predecessor kept an eye on the smaller banks throughout the country. It also engaged in a vigorous policy of expansion, establishing eleven branches within a few years, and issuing much paper currency of its own.

The West was by no means enthusiastic over this new federal fiscal agency. The pressure of the United States Bank immediately caused some of the more feeble western institutions to close their doors, and the westerners who held the notes of these defunct organizations could be pardoned for not viewing with pleasure the increase of sound banking. Furthermore, all the influence of the central bank was toward decreasing the issues of paper made by the smaller and less stable institutions, with the result that the West found its credit contracted and its currency less. When the westerner considered that all of the West was in debt and needed money, and that no one had any doubts as to eventual prosperity, it seemed to him both sad and unreasonable that the whole credit structure should be contracted.

The obvious villain of the scene from the standpoint of the West was the United States Bank, which was the prime mover in the much deplored contraction of credit. Consequently the West did all that it could to curtail the power of the Bank. Between 1816 and 1819 the states of Ohio, Kentucky, Tennessee, Maryland, North Carolina, and Georgia made efforts to tax the branch banks out of existence. Unfortunately for the success of their attempts the Supreme Court was not imbued with the western spirit and judged the tax legislation to be unconstitutional in the cases of *McCulloch v. Maryland* and *Osborn v. the United States Bank.*

Then came the crash of the panic of 1819, and the West saw the United States Bank as the chief cause of this tragedy. Actually the debacle had resulted chiefly from the bad banking and extravagance of an earlier period, but the West was not willing to look for complicated explanations; it wanted an immediate scapegoat. It preferred a simple and logical train of thought — everything had been fine before the chartering of the Second National Bank — now conditions were chaotic — ergo, the Bank had done the damage. The debtor part of the West was very bitter on the subject. Kentucky tried to relieve the situation by passing a series of stay laws to prevent the collection of debts by the banks, but after a bitter political struggle which affected even the courts the more conservative element won, and the laws were declared unconstitutional by the state courts.

When the worst effects of the panic of 1819 disappeared and prosperity returned during the '20s the West lost some of its resentment against the National Bank, but there remained an undercurrent of hostility and distrust. Certainly the Bank never attained any considerable popularity in the West. Many individuals such as Andrew Jackson continued to harbor a grudge which was to produce bitter fruit some fifteen years later.

SPECULATION

The new period of prosperity reached its highest point with the migrations of the middle '30s. New communities came into existence, property values increased, trade expanded, and the West looked toward the future with renewed hope. Along with the general expansion went an increase in the number of banks; by 1834 there were 506 banks operating in the United States under state charters, and three years later this number had reached 788. The amount of paper money per capita in circulation, which had decreased from $6.96 to $6.69 between 1820 and 1830, now rose to

$9.86 in 1835 and $13.87 in 1837. With the expanding currency went an increase of prices, which pleased the westerner because the enhanced value of the products which he had to sell more than offset the increased cost of his purchases. Furthermore, high prices were a boon to all debtors with goods to sell; each $100 borrowed in 1825, for example, had a greatly decreased real value when it was returned ten years later, due to the general rise of prices in the meantime.

As prosperity continued to grow, the energy and enthusiasm of the West knew no bounds. Everyone was confident of the future and bought all the land he could. Immense speculations took place in farms, town sites, city lots, and water sites. New homes, barns, stores, theaters, schools, prisons, and wharves were constructed. The greater part of this expansion was of course based on credit, and again the credit took the form of long-time loans which could not easily be liquidated. But no one was worried. Times were good and would be better. A small investment today would return a fortune tomorrow. No speculation was too wild or hazardous to be inviting.

Individuals transmitted their enthusiasms to their respective states, and each state launched an immense program of public improvement. Canals were dug, rivers dredged, railroads constructed, harbors marked, roads built, and educational facilities expanded; in every way preparation was made for a glorious future. The South was a trifle less involved than the North, because of a lack of credit rather than a lack of desire. Nearly all public works throughout the country were constructed on the basis of borrowed capital, with each state issuing its bonds to be sold at a discount in the East or in Europe. The total figure of American state loans by 1839 was at least $170,000,000. The West again illustrated its confidence in the future by bonding itself far beyond its prospective capacity to pay.

JACKSON AND THE BANK

The only important brake on western banking optimism was the pressure of the United States Bank as it held country bank notes and forced their issuing institutions at least to approach solvency. The older and more developed portions of the West, as represented by Henry Clay, approved this concession to sound banking, but the majority of the younger West felt otherwise. A decrease in central control would permit a greater expansion of credit, with more paper money for everyone, and the West felt that such a development would be desirable and would benefit all poor people. Before the general feeling of the West could become effective, however, it needed crystallization and a popular leader.

The man who finally dramatized western hostility and made the Bank appear as the ogre which gobbled up nice little children, was Andrew Jackson. Jackson remembered vividly the panic of 1819, and as President of the United States was in a position to put his prejudices into practical effect. His opposition to the Second Bank was an unreasoning emotion, based on few immediate and specific grievances. Probably it was increased by the failure of the bank to make appointments satisfactory to the President; the charge that the Bank was using its power to oppose Jackson politically was not justified until the fight was in full swing.

Jackson lost no time in letting his hostility to the Bank be known. Four years before the expiration of the Bank's charter the President made it evident that he was implacably opposed to renewal. The result was that the issue became political, with Clay and the Whigs supporting the Bank and Jackson and the Democrats opposing it. A recharter bill was passed by Congress in 1832 and immediately vetoed by Jackson in a vigorous message, whereupon the rechartering of the Bank became one of the most hotly contested points in the election of the same year. Jackson won the election and took his victory as a vindication of his policy in respect to the Bank. In 1833 he followed his victory by removing the government deposits which were in the national bank, even though it took two changes of Secretary of the Treasury to do it, and placing them in " pet banks " in various parts of the country. The removal of deposits curtailed the power and usefulness of the Bank, which finally was reduced to insignificance when its charter expired in 1836 and was not renewed. Jackson had " slain the octopus " and the people of the United States were " free."

STATE BANKING

The opposition of Jackson and the West to the Second United States Bank did not mean that they were necessarily opposed to all large banks or even to government banking. Their hatred was centered in one institution which had been performing functions which they did not like. There was considerable feeling that a legitimate function of government was the development of a proper credit system, and several western states had themselves engaged in banking ventures before, during, and after the '30s. The results were by no means always bad, but even if they had all been unfortunate they would still have demonstrated that the West was not opposed to governmental banking.

Of the western states which established their own banks, Indiana was unlucky in her first venture, which came in the year of the panic of 1819 and had a short life. A new state bank was chartered in 1834 and was quite successful, weathering the depression which started in '37 to attain the banking leadership of the state. A third bank was established later. Illinois also planned three banks, but with very sad results. The first was chartered in 1819 and not even organized. The second was incorporated in 1821, and was so badly run that it succeeded in losing half a million of state funds before its charter expired a decade later. The third was chartered in 1835 and its childhood growth was stunted by the panic of 1837 which brought insolvency; it expired in a long death agony during the '40s. Missouri chartered a bank in the depression year of 1837 and gave it a monopoly position; the bank weathered its early difficulties successfully and was sound and prosperous during the '40s and '50s.

The southern states tended to subsidize private banking rather than to establish state banks. Louisiana, Mississippi, Florida, and Arkansas all furnished such aid during the '20s and '30s. The usual plan was for the state to subscribe to the capital stock of one or more private banks, although sometimes it made further guarantees of other bank securities. The state subscriptions were made from the receipts of the sales of state bonds, which were sold mainly in the East or in Europe.

State banks in the West were on the whole successful, particularly when compared with the many contemporary private enterprises that were notoriously badly managed and frequently insolvent. This success was particularly noteworthy in view of the bad surrounding conditions, which included outstandingly strong political pressure to make state banks more lenient in their lending policies and thus to speculate in the future of the country. The use of state credit to furnish capital for private banks was not nearly so fortunate, since such banks seemed to spend more time in trying to cheat the state than in doing regular banking business; the inescapable results were poor banks and enormous state debts. In general this period of state banks and state aid, and of specially chartered private corporations, came to an end during the '40s and '50s, when general state laws provided for uniform bank incorporation and at least a minimum of regulation.

Even though state-operated banks were reasonably conservative, their number was few and their influence small. Other banks were less careful, especially when the restraining influence of the Second United States Bank decreased as deposits were removed in 1833 and the charter lapsed in 1836. Less control and the impetus of the demands created by a period of rampaging prosperity brought new banks into existence daily, and each one issued large quantities of paper currency. Everyone had plenty of money — more than he ever had before. Prices continued to rise to the benefit of the debtor and anyone who had anything to sell. Internal improvements were constructed on a magnificent scale, giving plenty of employment and putting much money into circulation. By 1839 the West had spent on such improvements possibly $50,000,000, of which the greater part had been borrowed from the East and from Europe.

FEDERAL FINANCES

The federal government was affected by this wave of prosperity by receiving more revenue than it had ever before collected. Land sales reached a staggering total, producing the greatest return ever. The compromise tariff of 1833 had resulted in unusually large receipts. For one time in its history the government had more money than it well knew how to spend.

The flow of money into the treasury of the United States was so large in the early '30s that Congress became embarrassed. Legislative ingenuity concerning the spending of government income failed to keep pace with the flow of gold into the treasury, with the result that the legislators began to be worried about the situation. Some suggested that the surplus be used for internal improvements, others talked of lowering the price of land or the tariff, while still others proposed giving the unused funds to the states. Each legislator had his pet scheme for disposing of the extraordinary receipts.

The result of Congressional cogitations was the passage of a Distribution Bill in 1836. The act provided that the Secretary of the Treasury should take the balance which he had on hand (excluding a reserve of $5,000,000) and divide it among the states according to population. Payments were to be made in four quarterly installments. In theory these payments to the states were loans, and were technically called " deposits," but in practice no one expected that the federal government would ever ask for their repayment. They have in fact never been returned.

With the passage of the Distribution Bill the Secretary of the Treasury immediately notified the " pet banks " to turn over the governmental funds they had on deposit to make the payments to the states. Then the trouble began. Most of these banks had loaned all of their available cash to patrons and when they tried to recall the loans a cry of distress went up all over the country. Many debtors were forced into bankruptcy and the whole credit structure of the country showed signs of strain. The banks managed to meet the first and second payments in January and April 1837, but by that time they were in serious difficulties and on May 10 they stopped specie payments. This precautionary measure enabled them to meet the third installment on July 1, but the fourth was never paid.

The financial difficulties of 1837 were increased by an earlier maneuver on the part of Jackson. Like other westerners, Jackson resented large land purchases by eastern speculators. These speculators used mostly paper money borrowed from the " pet banks " and based on land receipts. For some time Jackson had tried unsuccessfully to persuade Congress to prohibit this practice. Ultimately, on July 11, 1836, he issued his famous " specie circular," which was an executive decree requiring that all payment for public lands be in gold and silver coin, with certain possible exceptions for actual settlers. This order produced an immediate rush upon the banks by land purchasers for specie. As this money was paid to the government it was shipped east to the treasury, thus depleting the specie of the West and disorganizing the currency of the country. Land purchases fell tremendously in amount, since borrowed paper could no longer be used. The more serious results of this procedure became evident with the added stress of the attempts to carry out the terms of the Distribution Bill.

PANIC OF 1837

The financial difficulties of the country came to a climax with the suspension of specie payment in May 1837. The currency and credit situation which had long been bad needed only a slight touch to topple over the unsteady pyramid which had been constructed, and now that touch had come. Suspension by the banks caused the earlier optimism about the country's future to suffer a temporary eclipse, and people became suspicious, economical, and conservative. Few bank notes remained at par, and many of them were refused under any circumstances. The banks became cautious, called their loans as they came due, and refused to make new ones. The resulting contraction of credit was a severe blow to all debtor classes of the country. Western farmers were particularly hard-pressed; many of them could not pay their debts and in consequence lost the products of years of labor by foreclosure. Moreover, the westerners were also adversely affected by a contraction of credit by the business houses with which they dealt. Merchants tried to settle outstanding accounts, and refused to open new ones. This was a bitter blow to the western farmer, who so long had been accustomed to live largely on credit.

The results of the depression of 1837 were not only visible in the affairs of the banker, merchant, and farmer, but also in the business of government; the receipts of both federal and state governments decreased as land sales fell to a minimum and the prices of all taxable property went down. With the exception of immediately necessary work, construction of public improvements came to an end; partially completed canals and roads were deserted, and machinery was allowed to rust beside the abandoned work. Many of the states had issued large amounts of bonds based on future hopes, with the result that they were hopelessly in debt. Often they had but little to show for their large expenditures, and found it difficult even to raise the money for the payment of the interest on the bonds. Taxes were hard to collect since most people were in debt and property values had gone down. Some of the states avoided their financial troubles by exercising their sovereignty in stopping payments of their bonds.

One of the most easily visible results of the panic of 1837 was the widespread unemployment which existed, particularly in the East, during the late '30s and early '40s. The closing of factories and the cessation of work on public improvements forced large numbers of men to join the ranks of the unemployed. Their number was further swelled by the addition of the clerical employees of businesses which had found retrenchment necessary, by unemployed farm labor, and by former farm owners who had lost their farms. The contrast with the prosperity of the early '30s was startling, and the future looked black.

Rather surprisingly the panic of 1837 was not at first very severe in the West, and after the early necessary readjustments there came a period of improvement, in which it seemed as though the West would weather the storm. This return of optimism proved premature, for a second collapse, coming in 1839, pushed the West into the depths of financial confusion. Prosperity did not return until well into the '40s.

The panic of 1837 was but one of a long series of similar cataclysms which have swept over the United States at fairly evenly spaced periods. Among them, the panics of 1819, 1837, 1857, 1873, and 1893 were the more important in the nineteenth century. In each case the panic was preceded by a crescendo of prosperity, enthusiasm, and optimism which found expression in public and private construction, rising land values, improvements in transportation, full employment, and large profits. Ultimately the prosperity bubble was pricked, and frequently the prick came from abroad, since most periods of depression were world-wide. Then came a period of gradual recovery, leading to another boom and another panic. Even at the present time, with much increased social control, apparently no good device has been perfected to prevent men from being alternately optimistic and pessimistic. Cyclical swings of business and even major depressions seem to be still with us.

READINGS

T. P. Abernethy, *The Formative Period in Alabama* (1922), ch. 10; L. E. Atherton, *The Pioneer Merchant in Mid-America* (1939), *The Southern Country Store* (1950); J. S. Bassett, *The Life of Andrew Jackson* (2 vols., 1911), vol. 2, chs. 27–29; R. C. Buley, *The Old Northwest* (2 vols., 1950), vol. 1, ch. 8; J. R. Cable, *The Bank of the State of Missouri* (1923), chs. 1–12; R. C. H. Catterall, *The Second Bank of the United States* (1903) —the classic account; E. Channing, *History of the United States* (6 vols., 1927–30), vol. 5, ch. 14; G. W. Dowrie, *The Development of Banking in Illinois, 1817–1863* (1913), chs. 1–4; L. Esarey, *State Banking in Indiana, 1814–1873* (1912), chs. 1–4; S. J. Folmsbee, *Sectionalism and Internal Improvements in Tennessee, 1796–1845* (1939)—very detailed; A. B. Hepburn, *A History of the Currency in the United States* (1915), chs. 8, 9; M. James, *Andrew Jackson* (1937), chs. 11, 13, 15–17; R. C. McGrane, *Foreign Bondholders and American State Debts* (1935), chs. 1–12, *The Panic of 1837* (1924); F. D. Merritt, *The Early History of Banking in Iowa* (1900), chs. 1–4; T. C. Pease, *The Frontier State* (1918), ch. 16; B. L. Pierce, *A History of Chicago* (2 vols.,

1937–40), vol. 1, ch. 6; J. N. Primm, *Economic Policy* (1954), ch. 12—Missouri; E. M. Violette, *A History of Missouri* (1918), ch. 7—text; M. S. Wildman, *Money Inflation in the United States* (1905), part 2, chs. 2, 3; S. C. Williams, *The Beginnings of West Tennessee* (1930), ch. 29.

CHAPTER 20

CULTURAL ADVANCE

THE West of the '20s and '30s included both frontier communities struggling to conquer a wilderness and older towns which considered themselves rising cultural centers. Population ranged from criminal fugitives to the leisured few who read the latest European periodicals and tried their hands at poetry. Cities of the Ohio Valley boasted daily newspapers, theaters presenting the outstanding stars of the American stage, and authors of more than local repute, while newer settlements in Michigan, Wisconsin, and Arkansas consisted of hard-working farmers who thought themselves lucky when they were able to keep their families from starvation.

Even allowing for well-educated and informed westerners the general cultural level of the West was low. Large numbers of people were illiterate and hence unread, with no other thought than to make their fortunes by any means at their command. Speech was crude and actions direct. Jokes were coarse and amusements rough. The pistol-carrying, swearing, tobacco-spitting westerner cared little for the polite usages of eastern society. Many easterners and a few westerners feared that this reversion to the primitive would in time contaminate the entire nation.

RELIGION

In no realm of culture were western deficiencies more deplored than in religion, for the West was notably less religious than the East — that is, in the obvious sense of belonging to and attending church, and of following such religious customs as the observance of the Sabbath. To religiously minded easterners, and particularly to New Englanders, the West was on the road to perdition and might well carry the East with it. For example one minister reported that the people of Green Bay in 1836 " seemed to be agreed in only one thing and that was to blaspheme God and indulge in all kinds of wickedness." Irreligion inevitably implied to the godly improper speech and action, immorality, the degradation of the family, the failure of democratic institutions, and the collapse of patriotism. No descendant of the Puritan tradition could view these dire possibilities without serious concern.

Many Protestants also felt that the lack of any religion was no worse, and possibly less bad, than the acceptance of Catholicism, which was distinctly on the ascendant in the Mississippi Valley. New clergy were coming. New schools and churches were being opened. European missionary societies of the '20s and '30s were pouring money into the American West. Irish and German Catholics were developing communities in the eastern cities and in the Great Valley. The more easily alarmed Protestants saw deep-laid plots to undermine the United States and every Protestant experienced forebodings, which were soon to be translated into political action.

While Protestants were alarmed at the growth of Catholicism supported by European money, the Catholics actually faced serious difficulties. Most of the older Americans were Protestant, which meant that the flood of new Catholic arrivals could have little hope for support from within the United States. A typical priest would write that his little church " can scarcely accommodate all who come to worship," and that he found difficulty in raising funds for a larger church with its expensive equipment. Moreover, while the Protestant minister might hold a lay job, such as farming, the Catholic priest had no such alternative.

MISSIONARY WORK

Part of the western irreligion which seemed so alarming to the East was more apparent than real. While the West may have attracted the irreligious and encouraged a lack of attention to the church, its sparse population, poverty, and diversity of sects were probably more important in giving the appearance of irreligion. A westerner who was breaking his back to attain wealth parted reluctantly with the dollars necessary to build a church and maintain a minister. The obvious solution was home missionary work supported by pious easterners, although notable accomplishments also came from such groups as the American Education Society (1815), American Bible Society (1816), Sunday School Union (1825), and

American Tract Society (1826). These societies exhibited in their names the growing nationalism of the American people.

Most important of the home missionary groups was the American Home Missionary Society (1826), in which Congregationalists and Presbyterians cooperated. In addition there were a Presbyterian Board of Missions, an American Baptist Home Mission Society (1832), which replaced an earlier and ineffective organization, a Methodist Missionary and Bible Society (1819), an Episcopal Domestic and Foreign Missionary Society (1821), and others. Least important of the societies formed by the major denominations was the Methodist, since the entire church was organized on a missionary basis. These organizations combined and directed the earlier state and local societies, which now became affiliated, although in some cases they continued to do independent work of their own.

New methods appeared with the new societies. The older plan of sending missionaries on western tours became rare, and the main effort was to provide settled pastors for regularly organized churches. The American Home Missionary Society, for example, encouraged appeals by western churches, and to such a church it would grant ordinarily $100 a year, which was presumed to be a quarter of the salary of a minister. In time the church was expected to take care of the entire salary. Other societies acted similarly. In addition each society had agents to travel among affiliated groups encouraging mission interest and collecting funds, and to visit the aided churches to give advice and assistance. By 1835 the American Home Missionary Society was raising some $100,000 a year, with which it was paying over 700 representatives. Hundreds of churches were thus brought into existence or their continuance made possible.

The home mission movement was not without its opponents. A certain number of westerners resented being considered a mission field. A section of the western clergy was also dissatisfied, and this feeling was strongest among the Baptists, where it produced a rather bitter internal war during the 1820s. Argumentatively the western ministers held that the doctrine of predestination made a mission movement silly if not impious, but mission sympathizers contended that the real objection arose from the fears of badly educated western ministers that they would be overshadowed by the better trained easterners.

The work of the missionary societies made possible the more

rapid organization of new churches, which followed the frontier closely. In the '30s, for example, men were sent to Iowa, Texas, and Oregon. Possibly best known were the " Illinois Band," the " Iowa Band," and the later " Kansas Band," all Andover mission projects; individuals such as Asa Turner, J. M. Peck, Philander Chase, and E. P. Lovejoy did notable work.

The missionary movement was always connected closely with educational activities. A lack of qualified western ministers depended in large part on the absence of the proper educational institutions, and consequently many churches and missionaries worked for better western education. A high proportion of western schools and colleges was established under church auspices. In addition, funds were raised in the East for western schools or to educate ministers for the West. Several churches had funds for the education of poor boys for the ministry. Best known was the Education Society, formed in 1815 by the Congregationalists and Presbyterians as the American Society for Educating Pious Youth for the Gospel Ministry. A Ladies' Society for the Promotion of Education in the West (Congregational) took form in 1846 largely through the inspiration of Catherine Beecher. It was designed to help western education, but also aided energetic unmarried girls to migrate to the West.

ELEMENTARY EDUCATION

The advance of western education proved slow and painful. In the elementary field the private school remained the rule, with parents paying for their own children — say a dollar or two per year for each child; the usual session was thirteen weeks, with six eight-hour school days each week. The presiding genius of the ordinary ungraded one-room school was a male teacher, usually without proper training, and teaching only the most elementary subjects for short terms. The number of such schools continued to increase with the growth of population, but their standards were not perceptibly raised except in the large urban centers. They remained handicapped by the lack of textbooks and were forced to use the same old miscellaneous collection of books year after year. Most popular were such texts as Noah Webster's spelling book, Jedidiah Morse's geography, and Lindley Murray's grammar, all of which originated prior to 1800. The famous McGuffey readers were first published at Cincinnati in the late '30s and in the course of time became the most popular texts of their kind. Most of the generation after the Civil War, and many children as late as the end of the century, had been raised on McGuffey.

The proportion of children who attended school even for a short time in any year was low. It was estimated that in 1840 only one-eleventh of the western population was in school, while in the East the proportion was one-sixth. In 1829 there were reported to be 2114 children of school age in Bullitt County, Kentucky, of whom 160 were being educated; in the same year it was said that sixty families in the county contained no member who could either read or write. The lack of educational facilities was in general greater south of the Ohio than north of that stream, although it was deplorable in both cases. The state of Ohio, being most populous, had the best educational record of any state in the region.

Interest in the development of an adequate educational system grew rapidly in the West during the '20s, with particular emphasis on the desire to furnish free public education to all those who might wish it. By 1830 a few cities such as Cincinnati, Louisville, Lexington, and Detroit had made their first efforts to provide free public schools, although of course even in these places such schools were by no means adequate to take care of the entire population. Within the next decade their number increased greatly, and the states of Ohio, Illinois, and Michigan had at least the beginnings of state systems of education. By 1837 Cincinnati boasted that its public school system of ten schools cared for 3300 of its 5500 children between the ages of six and sixteen. The salary list of $14,000 a year provided for forty-three teachers of both sexes; male principals received $500 and their assistants $300, while female " mistresses " received $250 and their assistants $200. The average cost per child per year was eight dollars, which was then considered very liberal, even though today it would seem a mere pittance.

The slowly developing support for western elementary education for everyone received additional impetus from the growth of a class of professionally minded teachers, whose existence was observable by the '30s. These men and women considered teaching a profession comparable to that of law or medicine, and not a temporary stopgap to be used until more profitable work could be found. These forward-looking teachers organized a society in 1831, the Western Literary Institute and College of Professional Teachers, published the proceedings of the society, and founded an educational periodical — the *Common School Advocate*. Educational problems were discussed, new methods were given publicity, and the desirability of increased educational facilities urged. At no time during the period, however, were western teachers trained specially for their profession; the first normal school of the United States was opened in Massachusetts in 1839.

SECONDARY AND COLLEGE EDUCATION

Next in rank to the elementary schools were the academies or grammar schools, of which there were possibly 400 west of the mountains by 1840. All of them were private, for even in the most advanced educational centers the idea of the public secondary school had not taken root. The high school movement was born in the East during the '20s and '30s, but did not reach the West until later. The duty of the secondary school continued to be the training of boys for college and the " finishing " of the girls. A few of them took some interest in the training of teachers; none was co-educational. The work that they gave was much less advanced than that of the modern high school. Entering students were frequently as young as ten or twelve and never had more than a common school education in the elementary subjects. While the academies taught a comparatively large proportion of the classics, their graduates had little more than the equivalent of two years' work in a modern high school or preparatory school.

The peak of the educational system was the college or university, and here Transylvania University at Lexington, Kentucky, reigned as the most influential school of collegiate rank in the West. Transylvania was founded as a seminary in 1783, and while it nominally became a college before 1800, it was really little more than an academy until the administration of Horace Holley (beginning in 1818). In spite of increasing competition of rival schools Transylvania rapidly became the outstanding college of the West, and its faculty included the best known men in their respective fields. By the '30s the medical department had become so strong as somewhat to overshadow the rest of the university.

Other colleges came into existence to challenge the leadership of Transylvania in the generation after 1815. The Presbyterians in particular did outstanding work in providing higher education for the West; in fact they controlled Transylvania until 1823, when they withdrew to found Centre. Presbyterian-founded colleges included the University of Pittsburgh, Indiana College (later the University), Muskingum, Wabash, Knox, and Ripon. In conjunction with the Congregationalists the Presbyterians were responsible for such institutions as Western Reserve, Beloit, and Illinois College. Other denominations did their part. The Baptists founded Shurtleff; the Episcopalians, Kenyon; the Catholics, St. Louis University; the Methodists, Augusta, Allegheny, McKendree, Lawrence, and Indiana Asbury (later De Pauw); the Methodists also took over Transylvania in 1841. State universities such as Missouri and Michigan were opened. Of considerable importance in the period was Miami University (Oxford, Ohio) which was opened in 1824 under the presidency of R. H. Bishop, a former member of the Transylvania faculty. William Holmes McGuffey, the textbook writer, was at one time on the Miami faculty.

Western colleges were generally small and poor, with one or two buildings for both classrooms and dormitories, two or three professors, and a handful of students. A considerable number of the students actually did preparatory work instead of pursuing studies of collegiate rank. The instruction was generally poor, although a few good men drifted West from the better eastern institutions, notably Yale and Princeton. The rank of professor carried little social prestige and its possessors were mostly recruited from the ministry; most men preferred farming or some other " useful " occupation.

In addition to the regular colleges there were a number of western professional schools by 1840. Half a dozen medical schools were in existence, of which the largest were the medical department of Transylvania, Louisville Medical College, and the Medical College of Ohio at Cincinnati. Three law schools presented the principles of Blackstone and Coke, and again Transylvania had the largest enrollment. Ten theological schools prepared candidates for the ministry. Seven of them were Presbyterian, two Baptist, and one Episcopalian. The largest was Lane Seminary (Presbyterian) at Cincinnati, of which Lyman Beecher became president in 1832. A secession from Lane because of the slavery issue led to the establishment of a new school at Oberlin, near Cleveland, which soon became practically as large as its unwilling mother. Oberlin was particularly notable as being the first college to admit both men and women as candidates for degrees.

BOOKS AND LIBRARIES

Educational progress in the West was continually hampered by the lack of cheap and easily available books. The publishing business of the West was of slow growth because of the difficulty and expense of obtaining the necessary materials, and because the sparseness of western population made the sales of any publication comparatively light. Prior to 1820 the publishing center of the West was Lexington, but most western books were printed in the East and transported across the mountains. After 1820 Cincinnati became the dominant literary center.

A lack of books meant a lack of libraries, public or private. Here and there were libraries for the use of subscribers, but none of them was open to the general public. Among the oldest of these semi-public libraries was the one at Lexington, which was opened before 1800, and contained approximately 4000 volumes by the 1830s. Similar organizations at Cincinnati, Louisville, and other western cities could not boast of as large stores of books; anything over 1000 volumes was considered a noteworthy collection. Most of the colleges also had libraries of their own, but they were small, composed mostly of texts, and used but little; the largest of them in 1840 was that of Lane Theological Seminary, which contained 10,000 volumes, and was the largest single library in the West.

OTHER TYPES OF EDUCATION

A less formal educational feature of the West during the '20s and later was the lyceum, of which at least one existed in each of the larger towns. The lyceum comprised a group of persons interested in the discussion of what they considered important problems, and had as its principal activity the presentation of a series of lectures during the winter. The subjects for discussion might vary from the desirability of the abolition of capital punishment to the occupation of the Oregon country. A subject of much interest during the '20s, '30s and '40s was phrenology, particularly because of its advocacy by Charles Caldwell, a member of the medical faculty of Transylvania University. Through his teachings, Henry Ward Beecher and others were converted to this new medical science.

First rate work in the sciences was by no means unknown in the Ohio Valley of the '20s and '30s. William McClure and R. D. Owen were doing able work in geology. In fact McClure has been known as the father of American geology. Thomas Say, American-born, has been best known in entomology. John James Audubon, of dubious parentage, was in business in Kentucky for some years; his epochal *Birds of America* was published in 1826, and in time brought him fame and fortune. Most unique was C. S. Rafinesque, who taught at Transylvania, and who did creditable work in practically every science, not to mention sorties into the arts and social sciences. Some quarter century before Darwin, he wrote (1833): " There is a tendency to deviations and mutations through plants and animals by gradual steps at remote irregular periods. This is a part of the great universal law of perpetual mobility in everything."

Both politics and religion interested the West, and were discussed at length in the lyceum, in other public speeches, and in impromptu social gatherings. Political opinions were frequently expressed with great vigor and intense partisanship, for western politicians such as Andrew Jackson, Henry Clay, William Henry Harrison, and " Davy " Crockett had their strong followers and bitter opponents. Similarly, a discussion of religion would always draw an interested crowd. Of particular interest were the debates held by Alexander Campbell, the founder of the " Christian " Church. His debate with Robert Owen at Cincinnati in 1829 drew capacity houses in spite of its lengthy theoretic arguments. Robert Owen was visiting the United States at this time to further his utopian experiment at New Harmony, Indiana, and was anxious to meet all comers on the proposition that all religions were bad and contrary to human nature. The Owen-Campbell debate continued hour after hour and day after day, even though the men orated at cross-purposes; the audience was solemnly attentive up to the last minute, which was a tribute to the West's interest in religion. More exciting were the Lyman Beecher diatribes against the advance of Popery. The West also came to listen to the feministic radicalism of " Fanny " Wright, who was then involved in an experimental community at Nashoba, Tennessee, to raise the standards of the Negroes. Westerners disapproved of Miss Wright's radical beliefs and her lack of the current feminine virtues, but it paid her respectful attention.

The lyceum and the lecture found an important rival in the musuem, which was an exceedingly popular place of amusement. Each larger town had a museum where the visitor, upon paying a small fee, could see Indian relics, old coins, collections of animals and plants, mummies, curious monsters, clothes and utensils from the Far East, and wax figures of the great rulers, statesmen, soldiers, and criminals of the world. Particularly notable was Dorfeuille's museum in Cincinnati, where on the top floor was a " pandaemonium " of Hell, in which there were dwarfs that grew into giants, imps of ebony with eyes of flame, large reptiles devouring youth and beauty, cakes of fire, and mountains of ice; the surrounding railing was even connected with one of the new electrical machines, and gave a shock to anyone who leaned on it. Most visitors satisfied their own consciences that this exhibit was educational and taught an excellent moral lesson.

The museum was closely allied to various types of traveling exhibitions. Minstrel shows were coming into favor, although but few of them toured the West. Traveling menageries attracted many of the curious, particularly when they were supplemented by the gyrations of acrobats. Automatons, of which the automatic chess player was best known, were viewed with interest. Balloon ascensions were high in popular favor. The greatest of American showmen, Phineas T. Barnum, was beginning his career by tours through the West. All of these forms of amusement, however, were periodic in their nature, and were enjoyed by comparatively few citizens.

MUSIC AND OTHER FINE ARTS

The music of this new and growing West of the early nineteenth century was usually primitive. The piano was rare, and the most common instruments were the flute and the fiddle, with the greater popularity going to the latter. The fiddle (it did not attain the aristocratic name of violin in the West until later) was essential for all dances; the musician frequently made his own instrument and almost always taught himself to play it. The beauty of his music may be imagined. Any attempt to cultivate good instrumental music was rare. There is a record that as early as 1807 a group of young men from Pittsburgh organized an Apollonian Society and gave acceptable renditions of compositions by Haydn, Pleyel, Bach, Mozart, and Handel, but such efforts were exceedingly few in the first half of the nineteenth century.

Vocal music was used largely as a means of amusement for social gatherings. Few people could read music and consequently the song books were printed with only the names of the tunes or with " patent notes," which showed their pitch by their shape. Singing classes were popular, particularly with young men and women desiring recreation ; any person with even the vaguest possible knowledge of music would act as teacher, give the pitch, and sing the tune, after which the others would repeat the song. Singing in the churches was by the congregation, unaccompanied. An organ would have been considered sacrilegious, even had there been sufficient funds to pay for its installation.

If western music was in its infancy, the other fine arts were new-born babes. A few westerners with artistic leanings, such as S. N. Clevenger and Hiram Powers, did a little sculpturing, but they were self-taught and their work was crude. It was Hiram Powers who made the figures for the representation of Hell in Dorfeuille's museum at Cincinnati, and this work proved so arresting that a patron of the arts subsidized Powers to study in Europe. Eventually he produced some work which was fairly good. His best known figure, the *Slave Girl,* probably attracted more attention for its nudity than for its artistry.

Architecturally the best building was the despised log cabin, which adapted western materials to western needs, and was much better than two Wisconsin innovations of the '40s — an octagon house of fifty-seven rooms, and one of the earliest concrete buildings of the United States. Homes and public buildings with pretensions toward style copied eastern forms, and the East was in the throes of a Greek temple craze. Most distinctive and challenging of western buildings was Mrs. Trollope's bazaar at Cincinnati. According to an eyewitness it was " Græco-Moresco-Gothic-Chinese." Luckily it was early covered with whitewash.

Painting obtained a slightly better reception in the West than architecture or sculpture. A few foreign artists, such as Lesueur and Bodmer, visited or moved to the West, painted western scenes and taught some appreciation of pictorial art. George Catlin came from the East and did hundreds of Indian portraits. Now and then a foreign artist would come to a western city and try to give lessons in his art, but while the West always entertained him hospitably, it could not waste its time in viewing or acquiring this effeminate talent. The most that the average westerner would concede for painting was that talented daughters of well-to-do families might make worse use of their time than to paint pictures on velvet.

A few westerners were willing to brave the lack of popular appreciation and teach themselves the rudiments of painting, after which they could try to exist on the dollar a head that farmers were willing to pay for their wives' pictures. Some evidence of an increasing interest in art came with the founding of an Academy of Fine Arts in the frontier town of Chicago in the late '30s. Such proofs of a growing artistic appreciation, however, were but faint clouds in the sunny sky of western materialism. Even in the East the prospective painter could not obtain proper instruction or materials, while in the West the business of making a living was so important that it left no time for the non-essentials. The few picture galleries in existence were nearly all in the museums, and constituted sorry collections of paintings.

The West furnished a fair market for portraits, provided they were not too expensive, since the camera was not available in the West. Landscapes could now and then find purchasers. If sufficiently large they found a wondering audience. Quite popular was the panorama, which at its most impressive might be a picture of the entire Mississippi, painted on three-quarters of a mile of canvas so that it might be rolled past the popeyed patron. There was no western demand for still life, and portraits of nudes were banned by all polite society as fit only for a barroom.

Most important of the western painters of the period was the Missouri artist George Caleb Bingham. Largely self-taught, he succeeded in making his living by painting portraits at some fifty dollars a head, including portraits of Clay for a political banner. In time he raised sufficient money to go East and to Europe. His descriptive paintings concerning local elections, pioneers, and river life are excellent both as paintings and as historical evidence. Very possibly he was correct in his not very modest claim: " I am the greatest among the disciples of the brush, which my native land has yet produced."

DRAMA

The type of art which obtained the most secure foothold in the early West was the drama. Amateur theatricals were presented in Lexington before 1800, and appeared very early as a part of the amusements of such towns as Pittsburgh, Cincinnati, Detroit, and St. Louis; military garrisons in the West spent spare moments in producing their own plays. Boys usually took the women's parts, and the result was considerably worse than that of the modern all-male college production. Theaters did not exist in the early days, and so any vacant room was equipped with a rough stage and crude seats. Candles gave the necessary light, one or two small rooms furnished dressing facilities for the whole cast, and the scenery was entirely homemade. Plays produced under these circumstances were designed primarily for the amusement of the families, friends, and acquaintances of the amateur actors.

The first professional company to show in the West was recruited in Montreal and Quebec, and opened in Lexington, Kentucky, in 1810 with the tragedy " Jane Shore." It was followed by other companies, of which the most notable were those headed by Samuel Drake and N. M. Ludlow. The life of the traveling player was extremely arduous and uncertain, for western towns were small and far apart, and the patronage of their theaters variable. Frequently the town fathers would consider the drama an immoral influence and try to close the theaters by heavy taxation. Audiences were composed largely of men, with a sprinkling of prostitutes, and the rowdy element was not averse to hurling overripe vegetables or breaking the furniture if either the play or the acting was not pleasing. These audience protests were often justified.

The theaters of the West remained few and poor before 1820. A traveling company might play one night in a regular theater, the next in a billiard hall, then in a brewery, a vacant store, or the hall above the courthouse. At times it was even forced to play in clearings in the woods. The trip between stops was often long and always over bad roads. The poverty of receipts caused many companies to disband, often leaving their members stranded penniless in the wilderness. The chance of a western actor rising in his profession and becoming a star in the East was remote.

But the western theater began to make progress in the late '20s and the '30s, due in large part to the efforts of the rival producers James Caldwell and Sol Smith. Caldwell centered his activities at New Orleans, but also worked more northern towns such as Natchez, Nashville, and St. Louis. Sol Smith spent most of his time in the Kentucky region, but also made trips north into Ohio and south into Georgia, Alabama, and Mississippi, and had a theater in St. Louis. He was probably the best known and most popular comedian in the West.

The best theatrical town in the '20s and '30s was New Orleans, where there was both an American and a French theater. Even grand opera was produced: " The Barber of Seville," " The Marriage of Figaro," " Cinderella " (the English version of Rossini's opera), and others. Cincinnati was next to New Orleans in dramatic importance, particularly after the opening of Caldwell's new theater in 1832. This structure held between 1300 and 1500 people and cost $40,000. It was decorated elaborately and was lighted with lamps instead of candles. The magnificence of the Cincinnati theater was exceeded in 1837 with the building of a new St. Louis theater which, even though it was not completed because of the financial panic, was the most impressive that had ever been attempted in the West. Its stage was fifty-five feet wide and seventy-three feet deep, and the auditorium could hold 1400. The seats and floor could be removed to permit the presentation of the equestrian performances which were so popular at that time.

Each theatrical company which played in the West had an almost unlimited repertory, since no one play received sufficient support to permit its production on many occasions. To avoid daily jumps the company had to be exceedingly versatile. A certain amount of variety was also achieved for the audiences by the system of starring then in vogue. Outstanding actors and actresses toured the country in a limited number of plays, appearing with one company after another. In this way the West was able to see such famous performers as Junius Brutus Booth, Edwin Forrest, Charles Kean, James H. Hackett, Jane Placide, Ellen Tree, Fanny Elssler, " Jim Crow " Rice, and the Ravel family. Ellen Tree was a sure favorite, always drawing large houses. Edwin Forrest was well liked in his Shakespearean roles. Fanny Elssler the dancer was one of the most attractive artists, but asked such a large salary that it was always a question whether even full houses would produce a profit for the manager of the theater.

The usual dramatic performance consisted of a three- or four-act play followed by a one-act farce, and with singing and dancing specialties between the acts to keep the audience from becoming restless. Acrobats, such as the Ravel family, drew good houses. Equestrian companies were all the rage for a time during the '30s, but soon passed from popular favor. A fake dancing match arranged by Barnum in New Orleans about 1840 drew large crowds. Infant prodigies such as Master Burke were favorably received, and several of them toured the country.

Of the plays ordinarily presented to western audiences, the productions of Shakespeare easily led in the number of performances, particularly " Richard Third," " Othello," and " Hamlet." The majority of the plays were English in origin. Most popular were the works of Thomas Morton — " Town and Country," " Speed the Plow," " A Roland for an Oliver," and others. Efforts by such American actors as Edwin Forrest to encourage American playwrights had only limited success, although his *Metamora* by J. A. Stone was very popular. During the '30s a few costly spectacles were staged, including a battle of the war with Tripoli, the eruption of Mt. Vesuvius, a wild horse in " Mazeppa," dogs, camels, monkeys, a Hercules, pugilists, and fireworks. These expensive treats were enjoyed by their audiences but were not popular with the poor western producers.

HISTORY

Not only in the drama, but also in more scholarly writing, the West had not as yet realized its distinctive raw materials and the proper technique for their development. Medical and legal treatises were few. Historical writing was in its infancy, in spite of the efforts of John Filson and H. Marshall to record the narrative of Kentucky. Even Indian material was poorly presented, with the possible exception of the work of Henry Schoolcraft. On the other hand the West was beginning to evince an interest in its own history, as is shown by the founding of the Vincennes Historical and Antiquarian Society (1808), the Antiquarian and Historical Society of Illinois (1827), the Historical Society of Michigan (1828), the Historical Society of Indiana (1830), the Historical and Philosophical Society of Ohio (1831), the Kentucky Historical Society (1838), and similar organizations.

NEWSPAPERS AND MAGAZINES

The most common reading material of the West was the newspaper, and a newspaper press was one of the first nonessentials to be brought to a new community. Before 1800 newspaper subscription lists were small, advertising was very limited, paper, ink and type were expensive, deliveries were uncertain, and news hard to obtain, so that all the papers were weekly and depended largely upon public printing for their support. After 1800 they entered a period of rapid growth which was particularly evident during the '20s and '30s. In 1790 there had been but one newspaper to each 75,000 people, but by 1840 the proportion had grown to one to 12,000. The daily paper (six days a week) had become well established in the larger cities such as Cincinnati. With all of this growth, however, newspaper printing remained a hazardous business and the mortality rate among publishing companies was high.

In addition to the newspaper there was the monthly magazine (or other periodical). The majority of these were literary or religious in nature, although a few scientific journals made their appearance. For the most part they depended upon exchange material. Timothy Flint tried to encourage the writing of original western material for his *Western Magazine and Review* (1827–30) but was not successful. William Davis Gallagher did a little better in *The Western Literary Journal and Monthly Review* (1836). Best of all in this respect was the *Western Monthly Magazine* (1833–36) edited by James Hall. This publication printed a considerable amount of western material, written for the most part by Hall himself.

LITERATURE

The western poet who probably did the best writing during the period was W. D. Gallagher, and his work was extremely dry and conventional; even fresh western themes were ruined by the treatment he gave them. Of considerable popularity in the West was Richard Emmons whose great work *The Fredoniad: or, Independence Preserved. An Epick Poem on the Late War of 1812* was published in 1827. Emmons' work received warm praise and a moderate financial return from the West, but to the modern reviewer it is no better than Barlow's terrible *Columbiad*.

The two outstanding western authors of the '20s and '30s were Timothy Flint and James Hall. Flint was born in Massachusetts, attended Harvard, and then entered the ministry. He was continually sick and so undertook missionary work in the West in 1815 partly to improve his health. For twenty-five years, in spite of ill health, he lived an exceedingly active life, traveling widely in the West, in the East, and in Europe. He died at Natchez in 1840. Among his many literary labors were the editorship of the *Western Magazine and Review,* the editing of the Far Western travels of James Ohio Pattie, and a life of Boone. Other writings included autobiography, description, and several novels. Practically all of Flint's work was based on frontier themes, but unfortunately he had a romantic imagination and an instinct for melodrama, so that his writings cannot be trusted to depict western life fairly.

Much more important than Timothy Flint was Judge James Hall, the foremost western writer of his day. Hall was born in Philadelphia in 1793, where he had just begun the study of law when the War of 1812 broke out. He joined the army, participated in the Niagara campaign, and fought against the Barbary pirates. Finally in 1820 he returned to Philadelphia to complete his law course. Instead of remaining in the East, however, he moved to that famous town Shawneetown, Illinois, and became prosecuting attorney for twelve counties. His title of Judge was not honorary, for he held the office of circuit judge for twelve years. In his spare moments he found time to edit at least two newspapers — the *Illinois Gazette* of Shawneetown, and the *Illinois Intelligencer* of Vandalia.

One of Hall's greatest contributions to the literary development of the West was his editing of the *Illinois Monthly Magazine* at Vandalia in 1830–32. This magazine was the first literary journal in Illinois and emphasized western material, of which Hall himself had to write the greater share. It was responsible for preserving many western figures such as Mike Fink. In 1833 Hall moved his periodical to Cincinnati, renaming it the *Western Monthly Magazine*. He still insisted on filling it with original western contributions to increase the literary self-consciousness of the West. It was he who discovered Harriet Beecher (Stowe).

Hall did not confine his literary efforts to editorial work. Novels, short stories, descriptive works, and texts flowed continuously from his tireless pen. *The Harpe's Head, Legends of the West, The Soldier's Bride, Tales of the Border, The Western Reader, Letters from the West, Notes on the Western States, Sketches of . . . the West, Statistics of the West, The West,* were but a part of his prodigious production in the twenty years from 1828 to 1848. His graphic accounts of western life and customs were only rivaled by Albert Pike's *Prose Sketches and Poems Written in the Western Country* (1834), A. B. Longstreet's *Georgia Scenes* (1835), Mrs. C. M. Kirkland's *A New Home — Who'll Follow* (1839), and J. G. Baldwin's *The Flush Times of Alabama and Mississippi* (1853). The best Indian stories were from the pen of William J. Snelling. Hall was undoubtedly the greatest single advertiser and popularizer of the West, and did more than any other one man in developing a real western literature.

EASTERN LITERATURE IN THE WEST

The necessity which such men as Hall and Flint felt for developing an indigenous western literature indicated that ordinarily the West consumed the literature of the East and of Europe. British productions were widely reprinted and read, in good part because there were no copyright restrictions to prevent them from being pirated. Apparently the West wanted romance, for it bestowed its favor on the sickly sentiment of Felicia Hemans and Hannah More, both of whom were well known in both East and West. Byron also had a large and devoted following; it has been estimated that the sales of his poetry in the United States were around

200,000 volumes, of which a fair share went to the West. Works like *Beppo* and *Don Juan* were published west of the Alleghenies within a year of their publication in England (1818 and 1819). Best and most favorably known of all, however, was Sir Walter Scott; his new works were republished in the West as fast as they appeared and were devoured eagerly. Most western writers such as Hall, Flint, and Gallagher were influenced by Scott.

Eastern authors also had their readers in the West, although western taste in this respect was generally bad. Holmes, Whittier, and Longfellow were creating reputations, but Hawthorne, Emerson, and Poe were almost unknown. Irving had some following but Cooper was viewed with distrust, most people feeling that his stories would have been better if he had known more of the West. Bryant was known but little and liked less.

EASTERNERS USE WESTERN THEMES

Eastern literary lights by no means overlooked the fact that the West was a splendid source of material for not only works of travel and description, but also for short stories and novels. The situations which particularly appealed to them were tales of travel and of Indian life and wars. In regard to the first of these possibilities such books as Paulding's *Westward Ho!* (drawn largely from Flint), and R. H. Dana, *Two Years before the Mast* — a delightful book — were outstanding.

The dean of American letters, Washington Irving, was attracted toward western material partly because of the interests of his friend, John Jacob Astor. He wrote historically and descriptively rather than romantically. His *Astoria, Captain Bonneville,* and *Tour of the Prairies* were all published during the '30s and dealt with the trans-Mississippi West. The description of the Astoria enterprise is the best of them. The other two are interesting chiefly for their style and for their descriptions of the western plains. All three are readable, but none is among the best of Irving's work.

Of much more general appeal to eastern writers than travel and exploration was Indian life and warfare. The entire American public seemed bitten by the desire to see and read about Indians. George Catlin could draw large crowds wherever he exhibited his collection of Indian portraits and curiosities. T. L. McKinney's *The Indian Tribes of North America,* largely pictorial, was reputed to have yielded a profit of $100,000 to its publishers. Innumerable plays utilized the Indian as either hero or villain. Best known was the prize play *Metamora* by John Augustus Stone, with Edwin Forrest monopolizing the part of Metamora from the opening of the play in December 1829. Dramatic realism flew out the wings as Forrest ranted, orated and gesticulated, but thousands of Americans hung on the words of Metamora, as this fearless lover of nature pursued his tragic life until he finally perished with his wife and child.

As for the novelists of the period, few before 1850 failed to do at least one Indian story. Starting with Philip Freneau and Charles Brockden Brown each author found occasion either to praise or to condemn his red-skinned brother. A few of these efforts, such as Longfellow's poem *Hiawatha* still retain currency, but most have disappeared. Among the best was James Kirke Paulding's *Koningsmarke, the Long Finne* (1823), written in light vein but giving a credible picture of the Indian as a human being.

Among the best liked works of their own day were the novels of James Montgomery Bird and William Gilmore Simms. Bird's great work was *Nick of the Woods, or the Jibbenainsosay* (1837), a dark tale of violence and bloodshed in Kentucky immediately after the Revolution. The Indians were the villains and the Jibbenainsosay was an avenging white who slaughtered the reds right and left. Simms did a more plausible job, and particularly in his novel *The Yemassee* (1835). The scene is laid in the Carolinas of the early eighteenth century and the book abounds in fights and hairbreadth escapes, and yet the Indian is given a sympathetic treatment as a sociable being with loves and hates, virtues and vices, who is in the sad but inevitable process of being overwhelmed by a civilization of greater power than his own.

The writer whose Indian stories have had the greatest power of survival is James Fenimore Cooper. The five volumes of his *Leather-stocking Tales,* dealing with the lives and contacts of the Indians and the frontiersmen, appeared between 1823 and 1841. Cooper had lived in central New York state as a boy and felt himself to be an authority on the frontier even though he actually had known no Indians except the degenerate remnants of once powerful tribes, and had never revisited the scenes which he was to describe. Quite typically Cooper was dogmatic and intolerant in his conclusions. This trait in time destroyed his contemporary popularity, since he quarreled with nearly everyone in sight and became very critical of American institutions — a frame of mind that did not endear him to the American public.

Cooper's tales are not bad pictures of the frontier, in spite of certain errors of fact. They are primarily masculine and juvenile in content and appeal; Cooper's women were always wooden and unconvincing, and his love affairs mawkish. The Indians tend to be types rather than individuals. Either they are everything that is good and noble and true or they comprise all of man's less admirable traits. Possibly these very literary and psychological defects are the basic causes for the popularity of the volumes, both then and later. Nearly every small boy since the middle of the nineteenth century has marveled at the feats of the frontiersmen, shuddered at the dangerous situations, felt relieved at the miraculous escapes of his heroes, applauded the good Indians, and felt angry at the bad.

Taken all in all, the early nineteenth century made considerable use of frontier themes. And yet much remained to be done. The emphasis on travel and Indian troubles left large masses of material unexplored. The western thriller had not as yet appeared; its reputed originator E. C. Z. Judson published his first book in 1845 but it did not deal with the West. Even more important there was as yet no fiction which the modern critic would label as realistic. Much work remained for the American novelist before he had exploited western themes properly.

READINGS

F. W. Allsopp, *Albert Pike* (1928); R. C. Buley, *The Old Northwest* (2 vols., 1950), vol. 1, ch. 6, vol. 2, chs. 13–15; J. F. Cady, *Missionary Baptist Church in Indiana* (1942); W. G. B. Carson, *Managers in Distress: The St. Louis Stage, 1840–1844* (1949); D. Crockett, *Autobiography* (1923); F. G. Davenport, *Ante-Bellum Kentucky* (1943), chs. 3–5, 7–10—straightforward; E. Dick, *The Dixie Frontier* (1948); D. A. Dondore, *The Prairie and the Making of Middle America* (1926)—detailed on Mississippi Valley in literature; J. T. Flanagan, *James Hall* (1941); C. B. Goodykoontz, *Home Missions on the American Frontier* (1939), chs. 6, 7, 12; L. Hazard, *The Frontier in American Literature* (1927)—scholarly; H. C. Hubbart, *The Older Middle West, 1840–1880* (1936), chs. 2, 3; A. Keiser, *The Indian in American Literature* (1933)—many quotations; J. E. Kirkpatrick, *Timothy Flint* (1911); F. L. McVey, *The Gates Open Slowly* (1949)—education in Kentucky; S. W. Martin, *Florida During Territorial Days* (1944), ch. 9; T. Maynard, *The Story of American Catholi-*

cism (1941), ch. 16; R. Newcomb, *Architecture of the Old North-west Territory* (1950)—many pictures; E. K. Nottingham, *Methodism and the Frontier* (1941)—Indiana; B. L. Pierce, *A History of Chicago* (2 vols., 1937–40), vol. 1, chs. 7–9; W. B. Posey, *The Development of Methodism in the Old Southwest* (1933); E. H. Roseboom and F. P. Weisenburger, *A History of Ohio* (1953), ch. 9—text treatment; R. L. Rusk, *The Literature of the Middle Western Frontier* (2 vols., 1925)—carries to 1840; G. Spencer, *The Chicago Public Library* (1943), chs. 1, 2; W. W. Sweet, *Methodism in American History* (1933), ch. 11, *The Presbyterians, 1783–1840* (1936), chs. 2, 3, *Religion on the American Frontier* (1931), ch. 2, *The Story of Religions in America* (1930), ch. 16; J. D. Wade, *Augustus Baldwin Longstreet* (1924); F. P. Weisenburger, *The Passing of the Frontier, 1825–1850* (1941), chs. 1–7—Ohio; S. C. Williams, *The Beginnings of West Tennessee* (1930), chs. 26, 31; *see also* writings of authors mentioned in the chapter.

CHAPTER 21

THE PERMANENT INDIAN FRONTIER

THE expansion of western population presaged the elimination of the Indian tribes east of the Mississippi. If settlement continued to grow, and there was every reason to believe that it would, the available agricultural land in the eastern half of the United States would soon be occupied. What then would become of the Indian? In the past his domain had merely been contracted. Now the time seemed near when the remainder of his lands would be viewed covetously by the oncoming whites.

A NEW INDIAN HOME

Luckily for the whites the solution of the problem of the Indian appeared obvious and easy. West of the Mississippi lay millions of acres of wild land which everyone felt sure would never be desired for white settlement. Remote from the eastern seaboard, they were viewed not only as extremely dry, but as practically sterile. Until after the Civil War the great majority of American citizens were satisfied that the plains of the Far West comprised the " Great American Desert," and it was so marked in school geographies. Such a region was impossible to cultivate, and would support nothing but tough prairie grass, buffaloes, and Indians. In fact, many people thought that even a good deal of the land east of the Mississippi was comparatively sterile.

Well-informed people, including travelers to the western plains, helped to foster this idea of a western desert. Lewis and Clark described a considerable share of the region as " desert and barren." Pike likened the Southwest to the African deserts. Stephen H. Long in 1820 found this portion of the West " wholly unfit for cultivation." Even farther east, an observer found (1817) that southeastern Wisconsin was " laboring under permanent defects of coldness of soil and want of moisture." As late as 1847 Horace Greeley was certain that northern Illinois had " the great, formidable, permanent " drawback of " deficiency of water." With trained observers reporting barren and arid lands it was little wonder that the average citizen believed in the Great American Desert. This belief did not decrease perceptibly until the forties and was not extinguished until the sixties or later.

In view of the apparent unavailability of the Far West for white settlement it seemed reasonable to send the Indians to that part of the country. The first treaty to accomplish this object was signed in 1818, and others soon followed. There was no conscious policy involved in the removal of these early tribes; no place for them existed east of the Mississippi and so they were moved west. Within a few years, however, the statesmen in charge of Indian relations began to realize that their first desultory efforts to remove racial frictions might be expanded into a permanent and desirable policy. If the Indians could all be moved west of any possible white settlement, racial frictions would be at an end and the Indian problem would be solved.

The new Indian policy was definitely proposed by Secretary of War Calhoun in January 1823, when he presented to Congress a report which included a detailed statement of the number of the Indians within the boundaries of the United States, and which recommended that they all be moved west of the Mississippi. This policy was adopted by Monroe and continued by his successors. It included persuading the eastern Indians to move west and the western tribes to provide room for the migrants; neither process was easy. Along with the removals went an effort to control and police the Indian country, and to keep out white trespassers.

The new western homes for the Indians were expected to be permanent. Congress authorized (1830) the President to make the necessary treaties and " solemnly to assure the tribe . . . that the United States will forever secure and guarantee to them, and their heirs or successors, the country so exchanged with them." Nearly every treaty had such a provision; one of 1838, for example, gave the Cherokee " *a permanent* home, and which shall, under the most solemn guarantee of the United States, be, and remain, theirs forever." The "forever " of the United States government actually meant less than a generation in most cases.

NORTHERN INDIANS

The removal of the northern Indians was relatively easy, since no strong and warlike tribes remained to oppose the will of the United States. A long series of treaties provided for the removal and for the limitation of western boundaries to provide the necessary room. A St. Louis treaty of 1825 with the Kansa and Osage was particularly remarkable, and together with other agreements provided space between the Platte and the present Oklahoma for the Kickapoo, Delaware, Shawnee, Kaskaskia, Peoria, Miami, and others.

Farther north the Indians were a trifle more vigorous, but still comparatively peaceful and inoffensive. The Ioway, Sauk, Fox, Sioux, and Chippewa were persuaded in 1825 to agree to boundary limitations. The negotiations at Prairie du Chien were among the more notable of western gatherings, with the white negotiators including such men as William Clark, Lewis Cass, Henry Schoolcraft, and Lawrence Taliafero. White advances soon made necessary further agreements, and particularly a new Prairie du Chien treaty five years later.

BLACK HAWK WAR

The one outbreak that resulted from northern removals was the Black Hawk War, which has been better advertised than its importance warranted. The disturbing nations were the allied tribes of the Sauk and Fox, and from a legal standpoint their resistance to white advance was entirely unjustified. By a treaty made with Harrison in 1804 and reaffirmed several times later, they had sold all of their land on the east side of the Mississippi between the mouths of the Illinois and Wisconsin, retaining only the right to use this land until it should be demanded by the white settlers. For two decades no whites encroached upon their principal town near Rock Island at the mouth of the Rock River, but finally in the '20s the first settlers came. Their number continued to increase yearly so that by 1830–31 they were sufficiently numerous to be menacing. Relying on the old Indian treaty they paid no attention or respect to their red neighbors, but plowed up Indian villages and graveyards to plant their fields of corn.

The Indians were surprisingly mild and docile in view of white encroachment, particularly since the squatters had no more legal right than the Indians. Keokuk, the principal chief, counseled moving west of the Mississippi. Black Hawk, now sixty years of age, wanted to resist, and to remain in the country in which he had spent his whole life. During a visit to Malden, Black Hawk was advised by the British that he could not be forced to leave, and when he returned home he ordered the white settlers away. The whites immediately petitioned Governor John Reynolds of Illinois for assistance, and in response to this plea the governor declared Illinois " invaded " and called for volunteers. Almost immediately General E. P. Gaines of the United States army moved to the scene of the trouble with 600 volunteers and ten companies of regulars. As soon as Gaines arrived (1831) the Indians deserted their villages and fled across the Mississippi. A new treaty was signed confirming the old agreement of 1804.

Unfortunately for the Indians they crossed the Mississippi too late in the year to grow crops of corn before winter, and in consequence they were soon near starvation. In this extremity some of them stole back across the river and pilfered a portion of the corn that they had planted in the spring. Immediately there was another loud outcry from the settlers, who had visions of being murdered and scalped in their beds.

Conditions among the Indians went from bad to worse, whereupon Black Hawk concocted a wild plan for mitigating the suffering of his people. The main part of his project was to cross the river in the spring, join the friendly Winnebago, and jointly raise a crop of corn. Probably he also had a vague idea of obtaining British aid for the regaining of his old village. Certainly he had a childish faith that he would not be harmed if he did not enter his old village.

To carry out these vague plans Black Hawk and 400 warriors with their families crossed the Mississippi in April 1832 and started up the Rock River toward the Winnebago country. Colonel Henry Atkinson immediately sent orders for him to return, but he refused to do so. The frontier was once more in an uproar. Volunteers were gathered in Illinois amid scenes of wild excitement, with the men enlisting for adventure and fun. General Winfield Scott started from the East with some thousand regulars, including the West Point cadet corps; these troops never saw action because of a cholera epidemic which held them at Fort Dearborn (Chicago).

The enlistment of these hundreds of white soldiers worried Black Hawk, who had expected no such reception. Then too his greeting by the Winnebago was not warm, and no encouragement came from the British. In consequence he dispatched a small party with a flag of truce to arrange for a surrender. When the white volunteers saw the Indians they paid no attention to the white flag, but started firing at once; some of the Indians were killed, the others were captured, and the whites made a wild scramble to take part in the complete destruction of Black Hawk's band. Black Hawk was naturally amazed at this reception of his flag of truce and decided that if he could not surrender he would at least die fighting, so with forty warriors he awaited the oncoming rush of the whites. When the whites came within range, the Indians rushed from the woods uttering their death cries of defiance, and as soon as the Indians charged the white troops turned and ran. Again the Indians were astonished at this new turn of events — so much so that when they did start to pursue the fleeing troops, the whites were out of range.

After the white troops had returned to safety they told awe-inspiring stories of doing battle with 1500 to 2000 bloodthirsty and ferocious savages under the Machiavelian military genius of Black Hawk. More troops were raised until their total number was about 4000. As for Black Hawk, he was elated by his easy and unexpected victory. The whites were after all not invulnerable, and so the Sauk and Fox warriors attacked the frontier at various unprotected spots, keeping the outlying settlers in a continual shiver of apprehension.

One Indian victory did not make a war, and Black Hawk soon found it necessary to retreat before the superior white force. Up the Rock River he went, but his flight was hampered by the presence of women, children, the aged, and the sick, and provisions became scarcer each day. Finally the Indians were reduced to horseflesh and whatever barks and roots they could find along the line of march. As the situation became worse, Black Hawk's one thought was to return to the main part of the tribe, and so he crossed over to the Wisconsin River and descended it toward the Mississippi. Most of the women and children were put on rafts to float down the Wisconsin, while the warriors went on foot, always remaining sufficiently far in the rear to cover the retreat of their dependents.

The pursuing army floundered and grumbled through the woods. Fighting Indians was an exciting occupation, but pursuing them through hundreds of miles of wilderness was anything but a holiday excursion. For a long time the troops moved rather blindly, depending largely on a general impression of the direction the Indians were going, but in the Four Lakes region of Wisconsin the whites finally discovered the trail and there was a small engagement with the Indians who were acting as a rear guard for the crossing of the river. As luck would have it a portion of the whites blundered upon a party of women and children floating down the river on rafts. For a time the troops had great sport shooting at these nice open targets, until the entire party was either shot, drowned, or captured.

Eventually Black Hawk and the remnants of his party reached the Mississippi. Here he again tried to surrender, this time to the steamboat *Warrior,* which happened to be passing. Again the whites failed to respect a flag of truce and fired on the Indians. About this time the white troops also reached the Mississippi and partly by accident discovered a band of 300 men, women, and children. The ensuing slaughter continued for three hours until all but fifty women and children had been killed. Black Hawk was captured, and the remainder of his force taken back to Iowa; only 150 of the original thousand Indians survived the expedition.

General Scott finally arrived and took command of the situation on August 7, 1832. Under his auspices a new treaty was signed, in which the Indians agreed to remain west of the Mississippi and in which they ceded a fifty mile strip along the west bank of that river as expiation for their sins. Black Hawk was taken east and exhibited as an object of curiosity to throngs of thrill-hungry easterners, who were exceedingly disappointed because he did not look more fierce and savage. He was released in June 1833 and went back to Iowa. His own comment on the episode was terse — " Rock River was a beautiful country. I loved my towns, my cornfields, and the home of my people. I fought for it. It is now yours. Keep it as we did."

SOUTHERN REMOVALS

The removal of the southern Indians was a much more difficult proposition since the Five Civilized Tribes, numbering possibly 60,000 and occupying some 18,000,000 acres of land, resisted strenuously. The United States had promised Georgia at the time of her land cession in 1802 to quiet the Indian land titles of the region in the near future, but with Indian objections had found the promise difficult to fulfill. Now in the late '20s and '30s, with the desire for a permanent frontier added to an influx of settlers and gold miners, drastic action became necessary. The resulting Indian re-movals constitute one of the least savory incidents in a long his-tory of none too happy racial contacts; the details of the story were repeated with monotonous and depressing regularity for each of the five tribes.

The Choctaw up to this time had been consistently friendly to-ward the United States in spite of a number of provocations, in-cluding several fraudulently obtained land cessions. They had a fairly high civilization during the 1820s and in fact presented a laudable example to the whites by outlawing whiskey. Efforts by the whites during the '20s to buy more land failed, even when various chiefs were bribed. Mississippi thereupon became impa-tient and attached the Indian lands adjacent to white counties (1829–30), making the Indians citizens of the state.

Spurred by the action of Mississippi the United States obtained a treaty of cession in 1830, but the circumstances were so unsavory that even President Jackson agreed that the document was fraud-ulent. The Senate rejected it, but more because of the cost than because of the fraud. A new council in 1830 found the Choctaw still steadfast in refusing to sell their eastern land — even in the face of threatened military action. After this council had officially disbanded the white commissioners bribed the remaining Indians to sign the desired treaty, and this treaty was ratified by the Senate and proclaimed by the President.

In spite of Choctaw resentment a considerable share of the tribe migrated in the years 1831–33; others remained, so that a fair number still lived in Mississippi at the end of the century. The whites did not wait for Indian departures, but seized land, cattle, homes, and other property at once. Most Indians started their mi-gration with no more possessions than the clothes on their backs. They were cheated unmercifully by merchants and ship captains, and encountered blizzards, near-starvation, cholera and other dis-eases. In the West they found completely unimproved land, with no provision for their arrival, and were harassed by thieving settlers, dishonest traders, and wild plains Indians. To their im-mense credit was their construction of a fairly prosperous civiliza-tion, which included churches, schools, newspapers, and a tribal government under the constitutions of 1834 and 1838. Quite under-standable was their law which provided death for any chief who agreed to a further land cession.

Chickasaw removal followed much the same pattern as Choctaw, including early unsuccessful efforts to purchase land, the extension of Mississippi laws in 1830, and white appropriation of Indian land and improvements. Cession treaties of 1830 and 1832 were never put into force because of the difficulty of obtaining western lands, but the treaty of 1834 gave the basis for the real migration which started in 1837. By this time the eastern Indians had become almost completely demoralized by white encroachments, whiskey salesmen, and the cholera. Arriving in the West they were greeted by a smallpox epidemic and a drought, while being outnumbered by the Choctaw, with whom they were supposed to live in peace and amity. Subsequent Chickasaw history is no subject for the sensitive investigator.

The Cherokee had also been advancing rapidly in civilization during the 1820s. They had become a settled agricultural people, adopting white ways of life and even a constitution (1827) based on that of the United States. Red policemen produced at least as good order as in neighboring white communities and taxes were collected equally as poorly. Most remarkable was the work of the Indian genius Sequoyah, who had developed an alphabet of eighty-two symbols which made possible a written language. The *Cherokee Phoenix,* printed in both English and Cherokee, began publication in 1828.

An agricultural civilization produced Indian stability, and removal treaties could be obtained only by fraud. Even then the Indians refused to move. In consequence Georgia became increasingly impatient, and especially after the gold discoveries of 1828. In that year she annexed the Indian lands and then provided for their distribution among white Georgians by lottery. As usual miners and settlers did not wait for the law, which was scheduled to go into operation on June 1, 1830, but began immediately to seize Indian land and property. President Jackson approved the Georgia action and removed federal troops. The Indians provided heavy penalties for anyone signing a treaty of cession, and appealed unsuccessfully to the federal government.

Even the Supreme Court of the United States became involved in the Cherokee troubles, and found difficulties of its own when it tried to define the status of the Indians. It finally labeled the Cherokee a " domestic, dependent " nation, which meant whatever the Court wanted it to mean, and refused to allow the tribe to appear as a litigant. In each of the three cases appealed to the Court the state of Georgia refused to appear, and in each case Georgia carried out the provisions of her own laws regardless of the Court's decision. In the best known of the cases, which concerned two missionaries imprisoned by Georgia, the Supreme Court held the Georgia law unconstitutional. Georgia refused to recognize the decision, but avoided some unpleasantness by freeing the missionaries by executive clemency. The federal administration supported the actions of Georgia rather than the decisions of the Court. President Jackson is reported to have remarked about the decision on the missionary case — " John Marshall has made his decision — now let him enforce it! " Even if the words are apocryphal, the sentiment is accurate.

The Cherokee resisted white pressure, and defiantly refused to leave their homes. Treaties of 1834 and 1835, signed by a few Indians who had been bribed, were rejected by the tribe. A new treaty of 1835 was signed by some twenty men, none of whom was a chief, and then repudiated by the overwhelming majority of the tribe. The United States apparently then despaired of doing any better, so ratified this document and declared it to be in force.

The mere assumption that a fraudulent treaty was binding did not move Indians west, and consequently General Winfield Scott was sent in 1838 with 7000 regulars to do the job. Detachments were ordered to round up the Indians, and all too frequently as a party of white soldiers surprised and surrounded an Indian family, white adventurers stood ready to grab the property that was about to be abandoned. This particular summer was unbearably hot and consequently the removals were in part postponed until fall. Winter removals proved even more unhappy, and more than a quarter of the 16,000 migrants died en route, while the remainder ended their trip in poverty, squalor, and sickness.

Creek removals parallel those of the Cherokee. The Creek had been the most civilized tribe upon the advent of the whites, with a settled agriculture and a reasonably stable government. Land cessions had been forced by Jackson at the end of his southern campaign, but no later ones were signed except through bribery, and the signers were frequently put to death. President Adams was conscientious and disapproved of the fraud while he was in power, whereupon he was denounced vitriolically by Georgia authorities. Georgia then seized the bit between her teeth and appropriated Creek territory. Whites overran the Indian country, seizing land and property and debauching the natives. In the process, however, Georgia got rid of the Creek.

All of the eastern Creek finally accepted a removal treaty in 1832, and started to move west the next year. Traders and contractors took advantage of them, and the militia fired on them — presumably by mistake. Some 1500 of the Indians were so angered that they went on the warpath, harrying outlying western settlements. Immediately 11,000 troops were sent under General T. S. Jesup to put down the insurrection. While most of the Creek were corraled and sent west, quite a number evaded the soldiers; during the '50s an additional 4000 were removed — part of them in irons. As a result of their troubles the Creek declined almost fifty per cent in numbers within a generation.

SEMINOLE WAR

A few of the Creek who disliked the idea of moving West escaped to Florida, where they joined their racial brothers the Seminole. These Seminole had always been exasperating, not only because they occupied desired land, but because they raided outlying settlements, killing and plundering, and offered an asylum for escaped Negro slaves. After the American acquisition of Florida a treaty was drawn in 1823 by which the Seminole agreed to withdraw to the poorer lands, but this treaty was not always observed, and the Floridians desired ardently the removal of the Indian population.

A Seminole removal treaty was signed in 1832, although probably the majority of the tribe opposed it. In accordance with its terms a band of prospective migrants gathered at Tampa in the winter of 1832–33. While there they heard of an Indian raid and consequently dispersed for fear of white retribution. Then followed ten years of sporadic warfare between the United States army and a handful of half-starved and poverty-stricken natives. In behalf of the army it should be added that the Indians could find their way through the almost impenetrable swamps, emerging only for short raids, and pursuit was extremely difficult. The best known Indian leader was Osceola, who finally died in captivity. A succession of white generals included E. P. Gaines, T. S. Jesup, Zachary Taylor, G. C. Macomb, and W. J. Worth. Even though they utilized treachery their results were not impressive.

The last real battle of the Seminole War occurred in 1842, at which time Taylor estimated that less than 3000 Indians had been removed at a cost to the federal government of $20,000,000 and the lives of 1500 soldiers. These figures did not include the serious damages suffered by the Floridians. When hostilities finally ended some 500 Seminole had not been removed; today their descendants still remain in Florida, although they no longer merit the hostility of the whites.

WESTERN CONDITIONS

The removal of the Five Civilized Tribes was not a feat in which Americans can take much pride, but at least it opened the remainder of the South to cotton culture. As for the Indians, they ended their mournful hegira in present Oklahoma, where they were anything but happy. The plains Indians — particularly the Osage, but also the Kiowa, Comanche, and others — objected strenuously to their new neighbors, and the Civilized Tribes fought back to the best of their ability. The federal government forced cession treaties on the western Indians to provide room for the eastern arrivals, established new forts to preserve the peace, and sent expeditions to overawe the plains tribes. Several Indian councils were held, notably those of 1842 and 1843, to create amity between the old and new inhabitants of the present Oklahoma. While these were a real contribution to the settlement of grievances and the creation of friendships, they by no means eliminated all frictions.

Not least of the difficulties confronting the migrant Indian was that of leaving an agricultural way of life to enter a plains country without houses or barns or stock, and where the plow had not as yet broken the tough prairie sod. For the time being they were entirely dependent on the bounty of the government as it trickled through the sticky fingers of private contractors. The Indians seldom received what the government theoretically had provided, and the government was none too generous in any case. Then too illegal traders entered the Indian country and found the natives altogether too willing to trade anything which they possessed for a few hours of forgetfulness. Furthermore, and quite unexpectedly, white settlers found the country attractive and became a perpetual source of friction.

Rumors of fraud and mismanagement in the West reached the War Department, which sent Major Ethan Allen Hitchcock (1840) to investigate. The Major filled nine fat notebooks with circumstantial stories of bribers, falsified accounts, short weights, spoiled meat, and similar unfortunate transactions. His report was duly filed, but the Department took no action — some said because too many prominent men would have been involved. When Congress became insistent in its demand for this information, the War Department discovered very conveniently that the report had been mislaid.

With the removal of both northern and southern tribes, excepting only a few harmless and isolated groups, the Indian problem east of the Mississippi had finally been solved. The resulting Indian frontier was not a vague general region but a definite line that could be drawn on the maps of the 1830s. Starting from a point on the northern part of Lake Michigan it struck across Wisconsin to the Mississippi, with a little dip for the Menominee. It followed the Mississippi to the northern boundary of Missouri in 1830, but moved a little west in Iowa during the decade because of the Sauk and Fox cessions. Then it followed the northern line of Missouri and the western boundaries of Missouri and Arkansas to the Red River. West of this frontier lived some 350,000 Indians in 1840, of these, some 100,000 or their ancestors had originally lived east of the Mississippi.

The permanence which this frontier was expected to assume was demonstrated by the provisions made for marking and guarding it. A road from the mouth of the St. Peters to the Red was ordered surveyed by Congress in 1836, and while the surveys were not made some of the road was actually constructed and a long line of forts instituted to guard the frontier. An Indian commission suggested the creation of a neutral no-man's land between the Indians and whites, to be controlled by rangers. General Gaines, who commanded in the West, proposed in 1838 the creation of permanent stone forts that would at least outlive the century, but before his recommendations received favorable attention the frontier line had again advanced — and this time the lack of sufficient undesired land to which the Indians might be pushed necessitated a new and different " solution."

The administration of Indian affairs was strengthened during the early '30s. General supervision was given to the office of Commissioner of Indian Affairs, the Commissioner being responsible to the Secretary of War. The entire country was divided into three superintendencies, and under each superintendent were numerous agents and subagents who dealt directly with the Indians, settling disputes, allotting rations, and presumably avoiding the necessity of using the army to keep peace. The agency was not a new insti-

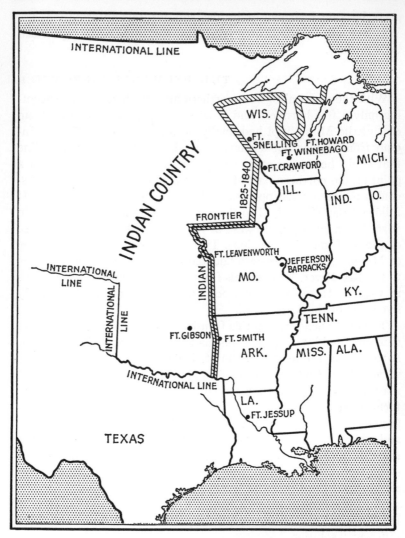

Permanent Indian Frontier

tution, but the functions of the agent were stated more specifically and more carefully.

Among the functions of the Indian agent was the licensing of traders who could enter the Indian country. A new Indian Inter-course Act of 1834 made more stringent the licensing provisions for traders and the exclusion of whiskey. Presumably all unauthor-ized persons were expected to stay east of the permanent frontier.

Some hope existed that in time the Indians could be persuaded to adopt the ways of white civilization, although a number of critics insisted that settled agriculture was unlikely until the Indians were given individual rather than tribal ownership of their lands. The annuities provided by the federal government had long included agricultural and other implements, sometimes at the request of the tribes themselves. Furthermore the government had for many years aided missionaries in the establishment of schools and churches, and this policy became more regular and extensive as the years passed. The expenditure of the government in 1825 was some $200,000, which went to thirty-eight schools. Many of the mission establishments had been moved west along with the Indians, and they were particularly concentrated in the Southwest. The Congregationalists and Presbyterians, acting mainly through the American Board of Commissioners for Foreign Missions, were most active, but other denominations also participated.

WESTERN ARMY

The main work of controlling the Indians remained basically in the hands of the army. Starting in 1837 the entire region west of the Mississippi was constituted the western department and placed under the control of Gaines, so that administration of the entire frontier was unified. The American army of this period grew from some 6000 men in 1830 to 11,000 by 1841. Even though a majority of the men were stationed on the frontier, they did not constitute a large legion for 1500 miles of border. Many of them were down-and-outers or immigrants trying to learn English. Their arms were rather nondescript and sometimes they had no uniforms. Supplies were often lacking — as overshoes and mittens. Altogether the army was seldom very alarming.

Beside the army of the western department, a special western force was created in the '30s to meet the peculiar problems of the frontier. A corps of rangers was raised under the authority of a law of 1832, but lacked both uniforms and discipline, so that the next year it was replaced by a regiment of 600 mounted dragoons. These men were never impressive in appearance, but they did good work in the wilderness; they comprised a good quarter of the western army. The Colonel of the regiment was Henry Dodge, the Lieutenant-Colonel Stephen Watts Kearny, and one of the second Lieutenants was Jefferson Davis.

The western army spent a large share of its time in the various forts. Most important in 1830 were Forts Howard (Green Bay), Winnebago (Portage), Snelling (St. Paul), Crawford (Prairie du Chien), Armstrong (Rock Island), Leavenworth (Leavenworth), Gibson (on the Arkansas River in present northeastern Oklahoma), Jesup (Natchitoches), and Jefferson Barracks at St. Louis. During the decade a number of changes were made, including the establishment of several new posts among the Civilized Tribes of the Southwest. The busiest of the western forts was Fort Gibson, which ordinarily contained the largest complement of men.

A western fort, ordinarily built by the soldiers, resembled a fur trading fort in appearance. Usually constructed of pickets, but sometimes of stone, with few exceptions it had the typical two-story towers at diagonal corners. Inside the walls were the barracks for the men, homes for the officers, kitchen, dining hall, offices, school, storehouse, magazine, guardhouse, and hospital. Ordinarily a small civilian community sprawled near by, while a fur trading post was not uncommon. The frontier fort was impregnable to attack from the outside, even though badly manned and equipped. The wide spacing of the forts, however, made reinforcements difficult in the event of an Indian outbreak.

Life in the fort was outstandingly monotonous, and particularly so in the winter when the little community might be completely isolated for months at a time. Routine filled most of the day from reveille at daybreak to the reading of orders and taps at night. In addition to the regular drilling, cleaning, and guard duty the soldiers spent most of their time in farming and construction work, for soldier labor erected most of the buildings and grew and collected hay for the horses, vegetables, and other crops. During the summer the soldiers' diet might be palatable because of vegetables from the post garden, but during the rest of the year the staples were bread and soup, neither very good. Special delicacies in food and drink and wearing apparel might be purchased from the authorized post sutler, but prices were high and pay low.

The chief diversion for the army was gambling — cards, horse races, checkers, and even the weather. Whiskey was a possible means of relieving the tedium, but the War Department became moral in 1832 and stopped whiskey rations, while the soldier's pay did not permit him to get drunk many times a month. A post library had some possibilities, but the books were few and badly chosen. For the officers and their wives there was the usual round of dinners, teas, dances, and calls, but many of the officers were graduates of West Point and curtailed their own enjoyment by a rigid insistence on the dignities of rank. As we have seen, amateur theatricals were common, but women were excluded from the boards; men donned their wives' clothes and squeaked the female parts with more ardor than artistry. A school generally catered to the children of the post, and the sutler devoted part of his income to such worthy projects as the school, hospital, library, and care of widows and orphans.

The few army amusements alleviated but slightly the dreariness of life, which was made even less bearable by the frequency of sickness — not usually fatal, however, because the men were young and resilient. The inevitable results were many infractions of the rules, mutinies, and desertions. From an army of 6000 in 1830 there were some 1250 desertions. The situation was not improved by the severe punishments visited on men for such minor offenses as having a missing button and imbibing too much whiskey. An iron yoke, stocks, solitary confinement on bread and water, hard labor, stoppage of pay, or extra guard duty, possibly carrying a log or bag of shot, were common. Whipping was still in vogue, being done by the drummers taking turns. The man was stripped to the waist, tied to the flag pole, and whipped with a knotted instrument of nine leather throngs.

The monotony of the life at a western fort made any alternative seem attractive, and even Indian outbreaks were viewed with some enthusiasm. Periodically a detachment was sent into the wilderness to remind the aborigines that the United States was not a pacific nation and had the power to enforce its desires. Such an expedition tried to remove causes of friction and to obtain promises of good behavior. Its commander had to be a man of both energy and discretion — an explorer, strategist, and diplomat. The limited number of his troops and the wildness of the country counseled extreme care, and even with great diligence he might lose much of his command through Indian attacks, accident, starvation, and disease. His negotiations with the Indians were difficult, since they required both moderation and firmness, while his small force hardly permitted aggressive domineering. Among the western expeditions of this type, those of Colonel Henry Dodge and his dragoons during the mid-1830s were notable. Dodge covered a large share of the country from the Arkansas to the Red, and west as far as the Rockies.

Other special army details were also necessary. Sometimes a detachment was used to enforce the decision of an Indian agent, as for example to bring to the agency a native accused of theft or murder; such a mission had dangerous possibilities, since lack of tact might drive an entire tribe into open hostilities. From time to time officers and men were sent on exploring expeditions, some of which are described in the next chapter. Sometimes detachments were used to guard the overland traffic. The Santa Fe trade was thus protected in the years 1829, 1834, and 1843. This work was comparatively dull, since it meant long hours of slow travel in the dust kicked up by the traders' mules. Even such a trip, however, had advantages over the dull routine of the fort.

The idea of a permanent frontier was delightful in theory but somewhat disappointing in fact. The Indian problem was not solved, but merely moved across the Mississippi, where all of the old difficulties soon reappeared. The Indians never succeeded in living in permanent peace either with the whites or with each other. Indian agents found themselves without adequate power to control their charges, and even the support of the army was sometimes insufficient.

The worst trouble with the frontier was that it failed to divide. Traders and trappers, both licensed and illegal, flowed across the border and the Indian agents were powerless to stop them. Explorers and traders occupied the plains country in increasing numbers. Even worse, the " desert " proved far from as forbidding as had been expected. Before the outbreak of the Civil War settlers had begun to seep into the Indian country all the way from Minnesota to Texas. The frontier which had looked so permanent and useful in the 1830s had definitely outlived its usefulness by the 1850s, and treaty obligations proved no real barrier to the advance of the American nation.

READINGS

GENERAL: E. Bandel, *Frontier Life in the Army, 1854–1861* (1932); H. P. Beers, *Western Military Frontier, 1816–1846* (1935), pp. 94–149; J. P. Brown, *Old Frontiers* (1938), chs. 30–35; E. Dick, *Vanguards of the Frontier* (1941), chs. 3–5; B. Dyer, *Zachary Taylor* (1946), chs. 5, 6—good on Black Hawk and Seminole wars; H. Hamilton, *Zachary Taylor* (1941), chs. 8–10; A. R. Johnson, *et. al.*, *Marching with the Army of the West, 1846–1848* (1936); S. B. McKinley and S. Bent, *Old Rough and Ready* (1946), chs. 7, 8—Taylor; W. C. Macleod, *The American Indian*

Frontier (1928), chs. 29–31—permanent frontier; J. C. Malin, *Indian Policy and Westward Expansion* (1921)—permanent frontier; L. Pelzer, *Marches of the Dragoons in the Mississippi Valley* (1917)—scholarly; F. P. Prucha, *Broadax and Bayonet* (1953)—army in upper Mississippi valley; F. W. Seymour, *The Story of the Red Man* (1929), chs. 7–9—readable; J. W. Silver, *Edmund Pendleton Gaines* (1949), chs. 7, 8—Black Hawk and Seminole wars; E. B. Wesley, *Guarding the Frontier* (1935).

NORTHERN INDIANS AND BLACK HAWK WAR: T. C. Blegen and P. D. Jordan, *With Various Voices* (1949)—contemporary on Fort Snelling; C. Cole, *I Am A Man* (1938)—Black Hawk, *Iowa Through the Years* (1940), chs. 11–19; W. W. Folwell, *A History of Minnesota* (4 vols., 1921–30), vol. 1, chs. 6, 7; M. L. Hansen, *Old Fort Snelling* (1918); G. D. Lyman, *John Marsh* (1930), chs. 8–24—includes Black Hawk War; B. E. Mahan, *Old Fort Crawford* (1926), chs. 7–16; T. C. Pease, *The Frontier State* (1918), ch. 8—Illinois.

SOUTHERN INDIANS: K. T. Abbey, *Florida* (1941), ch. 10; A. Bass, *Cherokee Messenger* (1936)—good; C. M. Brevard, *A History of Florida* (2 vols., 1925), vol. 1, chs. 10–14; R. S. Cotterill, *The Southern Indians* (1954), chs. 10–13; E. M. Coulter, *A Short History of Georgia* (1933), ch. 17; E. E. Dale and G. Litton, *Cherokee Cavalier* (1939), chs. 1, 2—letters; E. E. Dale and M. L. Wardell, *History of Oklahoma* (1948), chs. 4–8; A. Debo, *The Rise and Fall of the Choctaw Republic* (1934), chs. 2, 3, *The Road to Disappearance* (1941), chs. 3, 4—both books very good; G. Foreman, *Advancing the Frontier, 1830–1860* (1930), *The Five Civilized Tribes* (1934), *A History of Oklahoma* (1942), chs. 2–5, *Indian Removal* (1932), *Indians & Pioneers* (1930), *The Last Trek of the Indians* (1946), *Sequoyah* (1938)—scholarly; R. H. Gabriel, *Elias Boudinot* (1941); E. C. McReynolds, *Oklahoma* (1954), chs. 5–8; S. W. Martin, *Florida During Territorial Days* (1944), ch. 10; M. L. Starkey, *The Cherokee Nation* (1946)—excellent; M. L. Wardell, *A Political History of the Cherokee Nation* (1938), chs. 1–6.

CHAPTER 22

FAR WESTERN EXPLORATION

THE establishment of a permanent Indian frontier was conceivable only because of the vague and inaccurate ideas about the great trans-Mississippi West which were commonly accepted. This immense area became more attractive to the whites as an increasing flow of traders and explorers brought back reports of its desirable features. Even before 1840 a few hopeful whites saw agricultural possibilities in country as remote as the Pacific Coast.

In the early years following its purchase the exact boundaries of Louisiana were not known. The northern limit depended on an understanding with England, and the matter was discussed only halfheartedly for a number of years, since it seemed of little importance. For a time there was talk of following the watershed of the Missouri, but ultimately it was decided that it would be simpler to draw a straight line along the 49th parallel from the Lake of the Woods to the Rocky Mountains. The boundary west of the Rockies was not specified in this treaty of 1818, partly because no one knew just how much territory was included in the Louisiana country, and partly because both England and the United States had claims based on exploration and settlement and could not agree on an acceptable compromise. Provision was made that the Oregon country be left open to joint occupation for a period of ten years. In 1827 this provision was continued indefinitely until one of the parties should give notice of the termination of the treaty.

The boundary between the Louisiana territory and Mexico was settled in the year after the agreement with England, and in the same treaty that gave Florida to the United States. The line as

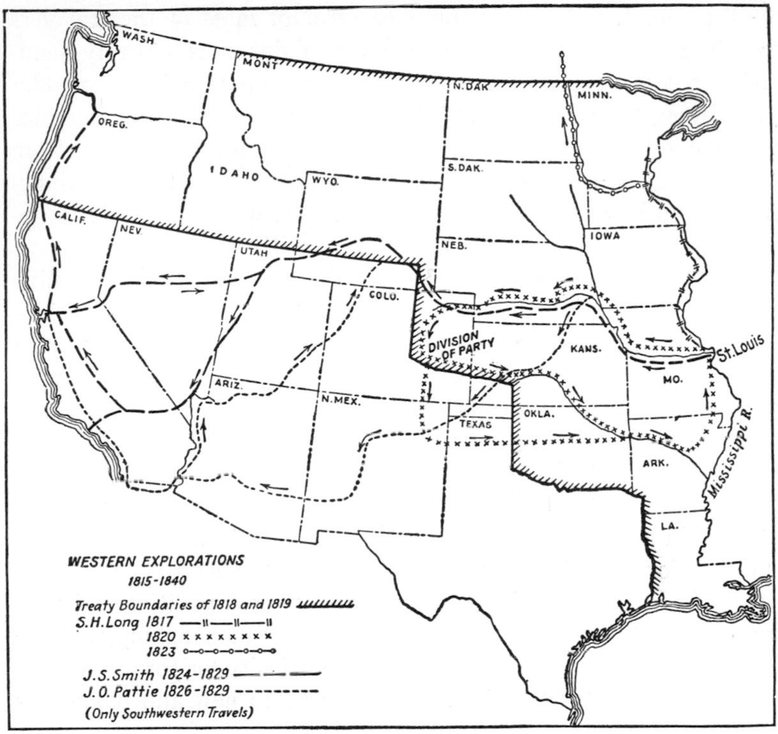
WASH.
MONT.
N.DAK.
MINN.
OREG.
IDAHO
S.DAK.
WYO.
CALIF.
NEV.
UTAH
NEB.
IOWA
COLO.
DIVISION OF PARTY
KANS.
St.Louis
MO.
ARIZ.
N.MEX.
OKLA.
TEXAS
ARK.
Mississippi R.
LA.
WESTERN EXPLORATIONS
1815-1840
Treaty Boundaries of 1818 and 1819
S.H. Long 1817
1820
1823
J.S. Smith 1824-1829
J.O. Pattie 1826-1829
(Only Southwestern Travels)

it was then drawn excluded the present American Southwest from Louisiana to the coast. Probably the Texas region could have been included in Louisiana if the United States had been sufficiently insistent.

The defining of western boundaries was a necessary undertaking, but it was much less interesting to the general public than efforts to obtain accurate information about the soil, climate, physical features, flora and fauna, and native inhabitants of the Far West. This interest, coupled at times with the hope of monetary gain, lured a continuous procession of explorers across the continent, so that by the late '30s the outstanding physical features of the Far West were reasonably well known to everyone who had the desire and energy to learn of them.

The observations made by these explorers were remarkably keen and accurate, considering the difficulties of traversing an unknown wilderness and the lack of precise scientific instruments by most parties; in fact many of the observations were made without aid of any instruments and represented only the experienced guesses of the explorer. The most obvious error of most of the travelers was the assumption that the western plains were entirely semi-arid or desert places which could never support a white popula-tion living by agriculture. This mistake was easy to make, since an explorer judged the character of the soil almost entirely from the nature of the vegetation which it supported. The trans-Missis-sippi country had but few trees, so that it was reasonable to de-duce that the soil was comparatively sterile.

The expeditions going to the Far West were of every possible variety, but for purposes of convenience they can be divided into three general groups. The first was the government party, moving under direct instructions, but frequently commanded by a man who was interested in western exploration; it was ordinarily guided by a westerner who had a firsthand knowledge of at least a portion of the country to be traversed. The second type, that of the fur trader, was motivated largely by the hope of personal gain, al-though in part the wanderings of the fur trader were dictated by a desire for adventure in unknown parts of the country. The third group included the miscellaneous remaining expeditions of men going west to make their fortunes from salmon fishing, for the pure love of adventure, from scientific curiosity, or for any one of the several reasons that lead men to perform new and dangerous exploits.

STEPHEN H. LONG

The long list of government explorers to the Far West was begun with Lewis and Clark and Pike. Most noteworthy in the period after the War of 1812 was the name of Stephen H. Long. Long's first trip was made in 1817, when he ascended the Mississippi and built Fort St. Anthony at the junction of the Mississippi and St. Peter's (Minnesota) rivers. The expedition had little importance except that the fort which it established later became Fort Snelling and was on the site of the city of St. Paul.

The next year Major Long was given command of the most pre-tentious expedition to be sent to the Far West since the days of Lewis and Clark. Its aims were both military and scientific, in-cluding a demonstration of power meant to impress the Indians and the exploration of the region of the Missouri River. The mili-tary section was under the immediate command of Colonel Henry Atkinson, and started its forward movement in 1818; by Septem-ber 1819 it was at Council Bluffs, where it spent the winter. In spite of extensive plans the troops never advanced much beyond this point.

The scientific portion of the expedition, under the direct command of Long, included a botanist, a zoologist, a geologist, an assistant naturalist, a painter and sketcher (for there were no cameras), and a topographical engineer, besides the laborers necessary for moving the equipment and supplies. It was transported in the *Western Engineer,* a specially constructed seventy-five-foot vessel which was one of the first steamboats to navigate the Missouri. The boat had its machinery hidden, and its bow was built to represent a serpent's head, so that when the fires were burning the smoke issued from the snake's nostrils. The vessel was more effective in frightening the Indians than it was in carrying men and supplies.

The scientific party made its way very slowly up the Missouri, taking observations as it went, and also spent the winter of 1819–20 at Council Bluffs. By this time Congress was becoming impatient; the party was moving slowly, the cost was great, and little was being accomplished. A Congressional investigation resulted in cutting off financial support and the expedition came to an end, which was unfortunate in view of its eminent personnel.

The failure of Long in 1819 did not prevent his being placed in charge of a new expedition (1820) which was designed to explore the Platte, the Arkansas, the Red, and other rivers of the region. This was the same general task that had been given earlier to Pike. Long left St. Louis in June of 1820 and made a leisurely trip up the Platte, arriving at the present site of Denver on July 5. He failed to locate the headwaters of the Platte, but he viewed the peak which now bears his name. Turning south he sent half of his party home by the Arkansas; with the remainder he made a half-hearted effort to find the source of the Red and then descended the Canadian. By October he was back in St. Louis, having accomplished little and having added almost nothing to the knowledge of the region which he had traversed. Like Pike, he classified the Southwest as a country which was uninhabitable for white settlers.

In spite of the meager results which Long had produced so far he was called upon to make another expedition in 1823. This time he was to explore the region between the Mississippi and the Missouri. Possibly because of his previous experiences he was to accomplish more important results than he had in his three former expeditions combined. His party included a zoologist, a mineralogist, a geologist, and a landscape painter, all of whom came from the East. The entire group left Philadelphia on April 25 and went west by way of Fort Wayne, Fort Dearborn, and Prairie du Chien, adding a few soldiers en route.

The real start of the expedition was from Fort Snelling. During almost all of the trip the force was divided, part going by boat with the luggage and the remainder exploring the shore; at night the parties came together to camp. The expedition moved down the Mississippi and then up the Minnesota, making careful observations along the way. The sources of the Minnesota and the Red River of the North were explored, and then the party started the descent of the Red River toward Pembina (present North Dakota). Near Pembina the international boundary was located and marked.

Major Long's orders instructed him to leave the Red River at the international boundary and follow the 49th parallel on his return trip to the East. Actually he found these orders impossible to follow because of the swampy nature of the ground and so he continued along the Red River into Canada as far as Lake Winnipeg. Then he crossed to Lake Superior and followed the Great Lakes as far as Rochester, N. Y. He arrived again in Philadelphia on October 26, 1823. The results of the expedition were satisfactory, including as they did a large amount of information about a hitherto comparatively unknown part of the country.

OTHER GOVERNMENT EXPLORERS

While Major Long was the most outstanding of the western military explorers of the period of 1815 to 1840, he was but one of a considerable number of such leaders. Leavenworth, Atkinson, Dodge, and other western commanders who dealt with the Indians found it necessary to range far afield and to collect both fact and rumor concerning the unknown parts of the country. One of the best known of their expeditions was the demonstration of Colonel Henry Leavenworth against the Missouri River Indians in 1823, which resulted more in geographical information than in effect on the Indians. Fort Leavenworth, named after the Colonel, was established in 1827. Colonel Henry Atkinson led an Indian peace commission up the Missouri River in 1825, and with his 476 men made a great display of military force and obtained treaties of peace from the Indians whom he visited. In this trip he traveled as far as a point 120 miles above the mouth of the Yellowstone, but established no permanent posts. In the '30s Colonel Henry Dodge led several Indian expeditions, of which the most important (1835) ascended the Platte and South Platte, coming back along the Arkansas and then cutting overland to St. Louis.

Probably the expeditions of Henry R. Schoolcraft, the Indian agent at Mackinac, should also be classified as military. The most important of his several trips was the one in 1832. With a party of thirty, including a geologist and a missionary, he skirted Lake Superior and ascended the St. Louis River. Portaging to the Mississippi basin he eventually arrived at Sandy Lake, an important trading center which had been visited by Pike a quarter of a century earlier. Continuing his trip he came to the farthest limits of previous exploration at Cass Lake, discovered and named by Lewis Cass. Here he reduced his party to those best able to continue the arduous trip upstream, and finally his troubles were rewarded by the discovery of Lake Itasca, that will-o'-the-wisp source of the Mississippi. Schoolcraft's discovery was important in itself, but it was eclipsed by the literary contributions of the author toward an understanding of the Far West. Schoolcraft had an immense knowledge of Indian ways and customs and a ready pen, so that in his writings he was able to expand greatly the knowledge of the East concerning the western country and its inhabitants.

The best known of all the military explorers was John C. Frémont, the "Pathfinder of the West." His first trip to the West was an exploration of the Minnesota River in 1838. At this time he was only twenty-five years old, bright, quick, clever, handsome, and impetuous. The party of which he was a member was commanded by the eminent French scientist J. N. Nicollet, who gave Frémont much of the information and training which were to make him successful on his later trips in the early '40s.

These and other minor military expeditions increased vastly the information which was available about the plains region of the Far West in the period before 1840. The main rivers such as the Missouri, Platte, Minnesota, Arkansas, and Red had been examined and described. The outstanding physical characteristics of the plains had been recounted. Obviously this information still contained large gaps which would require many years to fill, but the main essentials had been stated. Also of significance was the fact that practically no knowledge had been obtained about the region west of the Rockies, unless vague rumors were to be given credence. No military expedition followed Lewis and Clark across the mountains until after 1840, partly because the United States held no exclusive possessions on the coast.

FUR TRADERS

Almost as important as the army men, and often ahead of them both geographically and chronologically, were the fur traders. The fur trade constantly opened new regions, in part because of the normal expansion of the business and in part because of the push of settlement and the exhaustion of eastern fields. This necessity for expansion was by no means always unpleasant, for many of the trappers found happiness and satisfaction in the exploration of new parts of the country. Frequently the traders went much farther than business necessitated, and often they lost both time and money in their operations. The lure of unexplored wilderness always called such men, whether they were a Marco Polo, a John Ledyard, an Amundsen, or an Alexander Mackenzie.

The most active and able of the trapper-explorers was Alexander Mackenzie, a Scotsman operating in Canada. Fifteen years before the purchase of Louisiana and the exploration of Lewis and Clark, Mackenzie descended the river that now bears his name far enough to see the whales and the ice sheet of the Arctic Ocean at North Latitude 69° 14' (1789). Four years later he was embarked on the adventure of reaching the Pacific Ocean overland. Ascending the Peace River, he then crossed the mountains, descending the Fraser, and finally painted his name on a rock on the coast on July 22, 1793. This feat was undoubtedly one of the most remarkable in the annals of the West. Mackenzie's small party was much of the time without food, wet, surrounded by wild beasts, and facing unknown natives. The trip was a monument to Mackenzie's endurance, to his mastery over men, and to his driving personality.

Other Canadian traders followed Mackenzie into the wilderness. David Thompson operated between Lake Winnipeg and the Mandan villages after 1795. He crossed the Rocky Mountains to the Columbia River in 1805, just failing to meet Lewis and Clark. Between 1807 and 1809 he traveled widely in the Oregon country. Donald McKenzie explored the Columbia and ascended the Snake River into present Idaho in the years beginning in 1818. Alexander Ross traversed much of present northern Idaho in 1824. Peter Skene Ogden was also in the Idaho region during the '20s and later claimed to have discovered the Great Salt Lake in the winter of 1824–25; recent investigations, however, have raised some doubts as to whether this body of water was seen by a white man before 1828–29.

Traders of the Canadian companies moving southwestward were met by American traders moving to the northwest. Representatives of such companies as the Missouri Fur Company, Rocky Mountain Fur Company, and American Fur Company were pushing north and west from St. Louis during the early nineteenth century, the Pacific Fur Company even going the entire distance to the coast to establish Astoria. The American groups were particularly strong in the valley and near the headwaters of the Missouri, and in the southern Idaho region, where many a rendezvous was held in the '20s and '30s. Their greatest single discovery was the mountain route since known as South Pass, which was probably first used by the party of Robert Stuart returning from Astoria in 1812. This pass is in present southern Wyoming and is by far the best crossing of the mountains, since it has only a very gradual grade all of the way. After its discovery and popularization nearly all travelers to the Far West used it, and but few people traversed the more arduous passes near the headwaters of the Missouri.

The one great region that the trappers had failed to explore by the middle '20s was the Far Southwest beyond the mountains. This portion of the country was of course outside the boundaries of the United States, but international boundaries never hampered the traders. More important to the trapper, it was an arid region of mountains and deserts, difficult to traverse and lacking a large supply of fur-bearing animals. Incidentally it was far from any available rivers: the Colorado was impassable, the Rio Grande flowed through an inhabited part of Mexico, and the navigable rivers emptying in the United States came nowhere near the region. There seemed every reason why trappers would have no interest in this part of the country.

JEDEDIAH STRONG SMITH

In spite of the obvious drawbacks of the Southwest, several trappers became interested in it during the '20s — more because of the excitement of prospective exploration than because of the opportunities for profitable trapping. The most important was Jedediah Strong Smith, who was responsible for the first exact information about the Far Southwest. In many ways Smith was an unusual man. He came from a New England family at a time when most traders were southern or western in origin, and he was deeply and sincerely religious. He drifted west in search of opportunity, going by way of New York state, Erie, Pennsylvania, and Ashtabula, Ohio. While in Ohio, he was attracted to St. Louis by the lucrative possibilities of the fur trade, and in 1822 he became a member of the first expedition of the Rocky Mountain Fur Company.

Smith accompanied William H. Ashley on the annual caravan of the Rocky Mountain Fur Company in 1826, but when Ashley stopped in present southern Idaho, Smith continued west. Following in general the later route of the San Pedro, Los Angeles, and Salt Lake Railroad, he eventually entered California, where he stayed through the winter. Early in 1827 he returned by the present Union Pacific route, leaving most of his party in California to await his return. He attended the rendezvous of 1827 where he joined two other men in buying out Ashley's business, and then persuaded his partners to commence trapping operations in the Southwest.

Upon the completion of his business at the rendezvous Smith rejoined his party in California and started north along the coast. The trip proved unexpectedly difficult and dangerous, and a surprise attack by the Indians brought disaster. The only men to escape with their lives were Smith and two others, and the furs which they had worked a year to collect were gone. After many trials and a vast amount of wandering Smith finally reached Fort Vancouver, where he was well received and kindly treated by Mc-Loughlin. In fact McLoughlin went much further than the laws of hospitality required, and recovered and paid for Smith's furs; in return he received Smith's promise not to compete in the Oregon country. After Smith had rested he set out on his return trip by way of the Missouri. At St. Louis he decided to give up trapping and enter the Santa Fe business; it was in this trade that he met his death at the hands of the Comanche in 1831.

Smith's travels and adventures in the West were worthy of the pen of a Homer. Traveling thousands of miles through an unknown wilderness, penetrating forests full of wild animals, crossing raging torrents, paddling his canoe into unknown dangers, plodding across weary miles of sand, crossing snow-capped mountains, and surrounded continually by hostile savages, his activities in the decade that he spent west of the Mississippi verge on the miraculous. His own statement of motives is illuminating; " I of course expected to find Beaver, which with us hunters is a primary object, but I was also led on by the love of novelty common to all, which is much increased by the pursuit of its gratification."

THE PATTIES

Two other trappers naturally are classed with Smith in the exploration of the Southwest during the '20s. Sylvester and James Ohio Pattie, respectively father and son, roamed over the present states of New Mexico, Arizona, and California during the years 1824–30 mining copper, hauling supplies, trapping, hunting, and fighting Indians (by whom James was nearly killed on several occasions). In 1827 they gathered a small party and started down the Colorado River toward the ocean. Eventually they were forced to leave their boats and go overland, but the country was inhospitable and they nearly died of privation. Food gave out and they ate their horses. Water gave out and their mouths became so parched they could only speak with the greatest difficulty. Sylvester, being the oldest, collapsed first and begged to be left behind so that the rest of the party might be saved, but his son refused and they staggered on their way, partially supporting the old man.

When the travel-stained and miserable Pattie company finally arrived at San Diego they received anything but a friendly greeting from the Spanish governor. The whole party was thrown into prison and fed on spoiled food. The prison regimen was unbearable for men who had been accustomed to vigorous outdoor life and who had just passed through a period of terrible hardship, and the elder Pattie soon sickened and died. Shortly after his death a smallpox epidemic broke out on the coast and James Ohio, who was a jack of all trades, offered to vaccinate everyone if he and his party were set free. His offer was accepted, and to fulfill his share of the bargain he vaccinated thousands of whites and Indians up and down the coast. For this service he was given his freedom, and eventually made his way back through Mexico to the United States, where he arrived penniless and in bad health. His travels, as edited by Timothy Flint, make a fascinating story of adventure and suffering.

PRIVATE EXPLORERS

The western explorations made by governmental parties and by fur traders were but a few of the many trips to the region west of the Mississippi. Other travelers included private adventurers, observers, missionaries, sick men looking for health, and scientists in search of specimens. These men were responsible for the large increase in the eastern knowledge of the West, for they often kept and later published journals of their travels. Brief résumés of the travels of a few of these private adventurers will give an idea of the kind of work which they accomplished.

John Bradbury was an English scientist, primarily interested in botany; he traveled up the Missouri River in 1809–11 to make scientific observations, and his published account of this trip was both interesting and illuminating. Colonel John Shaw started in 1809 to go from Missouri along the 37th parallel to the coast, and although he was turned back by Indians before he attained his objective, he succeeded in reaching the mountains. The two years after his return (1809–11) Shaw spent in exploring considerable portions of Missouri and Arkansas. H. M. Brackenridge, an amateur botanist, published a good account of a trip which he made up the Missouri River in 1811.

The best known of the many botanists who explored the Far West was Thomas Nuttall, who made numerous trips to the Northwest after 1810. Nuttall was the true scientist of fiction, and many stories were told of his care of specimens. After a hard day's work, when the entire company was wet, hungry, and completely tired, Nuttall would spend hours over the campfire classifying and labeling with painstaking care the specimens which he had collected during the day. At one time the party was caught in a sudden and terrific storm on the Missouri and was only saved from destruction by Nuttall's presence of mind in grabbing a shrub on the bank and thus keeping the boat from being blown out into the river; Nuttall's account of the incident consisted mostly in a classification of the shrub.

A few of the other western travelers can only be mentioned. Henry R. Schoolcraft explored for pleasure as well as for business and in 1818–19 made an extensive tour through the Ozark region of Missouri and Arkansas. One of the many titled visitors, Maximilian, Prince of Wied, made a considerable trip up the Missouri in 1833–34; his account of his observations was interesting, but even more valuable were the paintings made by the very excellent artist who accompanied the Prince. Another painter, George Catlin, made several tours through the West in the '30s and drew hundreds of pictures, mostly of the Indians. An entirely different type of man was Father Pierre de Smet, a Jesuit priest who did very effective missionary work during the '30s, particularly in the Idaho-Wyoming region. J. N. Nicollet, another scientist who has already been mentioned, made extensive surveys of the Mississippi and Missouri valleys between 1836 and 1840.

Another private adventurer, who has been given more than his just meed of publicity because of the writings of Washington Irving, was Captain B. L. E. Bonneville. Bonneville had received a leave of absence from 1831 to 1833 to engage in a trading venture of his own. He outfitted at Independence and then journeyed over the Platte River route, trading as far west as present Idaho. As a commercial venture the trip was a failure, and as a scientific enterprise it was unimportant, since the ground which Bonneville covered had been known for two decades, and he had neither the knowledge nor training for accurate scientific observations.

NATHANIEL J. WYETH

The most spectacular of all the private trading expeditions were those of Nathaniel J. Wyeth, a solid and substantial New England ice merchant. Wyeth's interest in the West was mainly the result of the enthusiasm of Hall J. Kelley, a New England schoolmaster who was greatly impressed with the future of the Oregon country and who had plans for settling a group of colonists on the Columbia River. Wyeth liked Kelley's proposals for an expedition to the Far West and so gathered a group of his friends and neighbors to par- ticipate in them. Every Saturday night these prospective western- ers met at Wyeth's house and made grandiose plans for their trip across the continent and for the operations they expected to carry on when they arrived at the coast. In general they projected a trad- ing expedition, but just what or where they would trade was left delightfully vague. Of course they expected to barter with the na- tives, but why not also treat with the white inhabitants of Cali- fornia, the Hudson's Bay Company, the Russian traders? Some talked also of the possibilities of salmon fishing on the Columbia.

Wyeth's group eventually became tired of waiting for Kelley's larger plans to materialize, and decided to go on ahead. The total membership of the Wyeth group was twenty-one, mostly farmers and artisans. Each man wore a sort of uniform, of which the main elements were a coarse woolen jacket and pantaloons, a striped woolen shirt, and rawhide boots. Their equipment included food, clothing, axes, beads, and trinkets. For the trip across the plains they provided themselves with three amphibious monsters, part wagon and part boat. These transportational novelties were care- fully fitted and caulked canoes with removable wheels, so that they could be used on both land and water. They were early given the name " Nat-wye-thium " in honor of the leader of the expedition.

The party decided that before it started its travels it needed some real wilderness experience to acclimate itself to western life. The result was ten days spent on an island in Boston harbor. The party proved a real " ten days' wonder " to the people of Boston, who came in large numbers to view this curious looking group of Far Western explorers.

The actual start for the West came in March 1832, when the party left Boston by water for Baltimore. At Baltimore the members of the group rode on the newly opened track of the Baltimore and Ohio Railroad to the end of the line. The remainder of the journey over the mountains proved long and arduous, largely because of the necessity of dragging the wagon-boats over the hills. At one place the innkeeper refused to give them rooms, alleging a fear of Yankee shrewdness; possibly the curious appearance of the party with its remarkable method of transportation played some part in his decision. Upon reaching the Ohio River the party continued its trip to St. Louis by boat. Here the wagon-boats were sold, since every westerner advised Wyeth and his followers that such vehicles could not be pulled through the forest, over rough ground and through mountain passes, or paddled over the rapid streams of the West.

The expedition crossed the western plains by way of the Platte River, being guided by an old fur trader. Some of the members became discouraged from time to time, deserted their companions, and went home. Eventually the more persistent reached the southern part of present Idaho, but by that time everyone was thoroughly disheartened. All of them would have started back except that the return trip was more difficult than continuing west and then taking ship to Massachusetts. In consequence Wyeth and eleven others persisted, and eventually arrived at Fort Vancouver on the Columbia River, where the group was completely disbanded. Wyeth was back in Boston before the end of the year, defeated but not discouraged.

Wyeth certainly possessed one great virtue, persistency, for he immediately laid plans for a second trip, which occurred in 1834. This time he was able to benefit by his former western experiences, and while the expedition was a financial failure it did not end as disastrously as the first. Wyeth trapped, and fished for salmon, but without profit. More important, he built Fort Hall on the Snake River in present southeastern Idaho, and this fort was an important outfitting point for many years. Eventually he gave up his western dreams and returned to Boston, where he re-entered the ice business and died a fairly wealthy man.

The principal result of these and many other expeditions was that by the end of the '30s the Far West had become fairly well known. It was still generally considered uninhabitable, but it was no longer an unexplored wilderness. As the reports of governmental exploring expeditions were printed, the journals of private travelers published, and the tales of the trips of the fur traders passed from mouth to mouth, the average easterner came to have a fairly adequate concept of the main physical features of the Far West. In addition, these many expeditions helped produce a considerable body of guides who were later able to lead other parties to the newer parts of the country with but a fraction of the difficulties of their predecessors. The Far West was becoming known.

TRAFFIC ACROSS THE PLAINS

The main distributing center for business to and from the Far West was St. Louis, which was strategic for commerce in the Missouri Valley, on the South Pass route, and to Santa Fe. For the usual traveler, however, the actual outfitting and jumping-off point was farther west, nearer the great bend of the Missouri. The town of Franklin, opposite present Boonville, was the busiest of such centers until 1828, when the river exercised its unpleasant habit of changing its course, and washed the town into oblivion. Its successors were most notably Independence and Westport (present Kansas City), but other towns also participated in the business.

Traffic across the plains started in the spring as soon as the grass was adequate for feeding livestock and the ground sufficiently firm to support wagons. To be ready for the earliest possible move, traders, trappers, soldiers, interpreters, hunters, guides, boatmen, and missionaries crowded the Missouri River towns for several weeks in the early spring. By the late '30s and '40s the congestion was increased by the addition of settlers migrating to the Pacific Coast. A chaos of tents, livestock, wagons, and equipment made the towns bedlam.

Parties traveling across the plains varied in equipment and personnel depending upon their numbers and aims. Traders bound for a mountain rendezvous or for Santa Fe carried an irreducible minimum of clothes and food, since they conserved all possible space for trading goods. A few staples such as flour, bacon, coffee, sugar, and salt were used to supplement a diet that depended mainly on game shot along the route. The army expedition carried more food, although it hoped to vary its meals with game; if engaged in an elaborate survey, both the personnel and the equipment were exceedingly varied. Settlers carried the greatest amount of personal possessions, since they needed household furnishings similar to those of their predecessors in the Ohio Valley. Their covered wagons were filled with everything that the owners felt could be hauled across the continent, and the frequency of errors in judgment was attested by the large amounts of discarded equipment that soon lined the road.

Motive power was a matter of some differences of opinion. Horses were fastest, but also most easily exhausted; they were most useful in the fur trade. Mules were more sturdy and not quite as fast; they were preferred in the Santa Fe trade where speed was desirable but where long arid stretches made horses a risky gamble. Oxen were slow but hardy; they were the pick of most settlers and freighters. The difficulties of travel necessitated more than one team per wagon. Ordinarily the Santa Fe traders used eight mules and settlers four or six oxen, with other animals for emergencies.

Travelers usually moved in groups to be able to cope with the natural and human dangers that might be encountered. A fur caravan might have fifty to a hundred men, with three to four times that many horses and mules, while other parties might range from five wagons to a hundred or more, the larger group becoming more prevalent as settlers increased in number. The smaller party could move faster and was less troubled by internal dissension, but the larger group was safer.

The usual practice was for individuals and families to leave the Missouri River as they felt the urge in the early spring and then to stop at Council Grove in present eastern Kansas to organize parties for the rest of the trip, whether to Santa Fe, California, or Oregon. Semimilitary organizations were created, and the various jobs such as cooking, gathering wood, feeding the stock, and standing guard were allocated.

The average day of plains travel was anything but exciting — a plodding, dusty trip broken only by lunch and by short rest periods in the middle of the morning and the middle of the afternoon. A camp site depended on grass and water, and if possible the caravan stopped early enough to complete all necessary chores before dark. The wagons were arranged in a circle and a guard set, but the horses were brought into the circle only in time of Indian danger. The usual day's trip was possibly fifteen miles, but ranged widely from the two or three miles made by settlers confronted with adverse conditions to the thirty or forty miles by professionals. Sundays were often used for rest and repairs.

The prevailing impression of plains travel was the slow pacing of countless miles in the scorching heat of the sun, enveloped in clouds of dust and irritated by inadequate water. Fear of hostile Indians was much less pressing than worry over the necessary minimum of water, grass, and game. A severe storm might flood the camp and stampede the animals. Sickness was common, particularly the internal upsets caused by an improper and monotonous diet. Accidents might result from an undesired contest with a bear, a snake, a mule, or a horse, by a misstep on a mountain, or by a bursting gun. The necessary human repairs which then came were as rough as wagon repairs. A snake bite brought incision and searing with a hot iron, with the sufferer first fortified by whiskey taken internally; some men confined the treatment to the whiskey. An amputation might be performed with a butcher knife and a meat saw, but gangrene ordinarily carried off the sufferer.

Not the least of the dangers of plains travel was the Indian menace. Indians normally were friendly and hospitable, but there were important exceptions. Young men attained dignity and older men reputation by joining war parties to steal horses and collect scalps, neither of which feats received the approval of the whites. In addition the Indian was sensitive to personal slights and believed in personal retribution for any damage to himself or his family. When seeking revenge he was not always careful to harm the same white who had harmed him.

The whites were not without sin in the relations of the two races. White traders cheated the natives, white hunters drove off their game, and the white government took their land. Like the Indians, the whites were not discriminating as to whom they punished for any trouble. An Indian raid frequently brought retribution to someone, but very possibly not to the person or group connected with the original disturbance; all Indians looked very much alike to white eyes. In fact most westerners were still convinced that the only desirable Indian was one who had ceased to breathe, and many were willing to help along the good work. Not infrequently a white took a shot or two at a stray Indian just for the sake of the target practice.

Indian attacks were made but seldom on large white parties. Most Indians were armed with bows and arrows and were not anxious to face white rifles. Small white parties, however, might have their possessions stolen or even at times be attacked. The resulting engagement might be bitter and bloody, with each side employing every stratagem which generations of frontier warfare had developed. Mutilation of the dead was common for both Indians and whites, for plains warfare followed no strict military code.

Indian troubles tended to increase as the years passed. The first explorers and trappers found the various tribes generally peaceful, but as racial contacts increased so did friction. In part the conflicts were caused by the less desirable and more headstrong of each race, but in part they were the inevitable outcome of an aggressive culture moving into control of a region occupied by a proud and warlike people. The possibility of a completely peaceful removal of the Indian control of North America was difficult to imagine.

READINGS

J. C. Alter, *James Bridger* (1925), chs. 4–27; J. C. Bell, *Opening a Highway to the Pacific, 1838–1846* (1921), ch. 3; R. G. Cleland, *A History of California* (1922), chs. 5–7; W. E. Connelley, *History of Kansas* (5 vols., 1928), ch. 7—Long; L. H. Creer, *Founding of an Empire* (1947), chs. 2–7—Utah; H. C. Dale, *The Ashley-Smith Explorations* (1918); G. C. Davidson, *The Northwest Company* (1918), chs. 2, 3, 5; E. Dick, *Vanguards of the Frontier* (1941), ch. 8; G. W. Fuller, *The Inland Empire* (3 vols., 1928), vol. 1, chs. 8–10; W. J. Ghent, *The Road to Oregon* (1929), ch. 1; E. W. Gilbert, *The Exploration of Western America* (1933), chs. 10–12; L. R. and A. W. Hafen, *Old Spanish Trail* (1954); W. E. Hollon, *The Lost Pathfinder* (1949)—Pike; J. F. McDermott (ed.), *Up the Missouri with Audubon* (1951); L. McFarling, *Exploring the Northern Plains* (1955), chs. 8–13— original accounts; J. Monaghan, *The Overland Trail* (1947), ch. 6—Wyeth; D. L. Morgan, *The Great Salt Lake* (1947), chs. 4–8, *Jedediah Smith and the Opening of the West* (1953)—very good; A. Nevins, *Fremont* (1939) chs. 7–9; H. R. Schoolcraft, *Narrative Journal* (1953); C. A. Vandiveer, *The Fur-Trade and Early Western Exploration* (1929), chs. 12–17; S. Vestal, *The Missouri* (1945), ch. 4; *see also* fur traders in Chapter 11.

CHAPTER 23

MEXICO ATTRACTS

ANGLO–AMERICAN advances toward the west met the resistance not only of a wilderness to be conquered and red men to be brushed aside, but also of another European frontier — that of Spain. Along the southern fringe of the United States lay the " Spanish borderlands," where the clash of civilizations became a three-way affair.

The Spanish occupation had begun in the Caribbean as the result of an error plus an accident. The error was Columbus' geographical knowledge, and the accident was the place of his landing. The result was that Spain occupied first the West Indies and Mexico, and then used Mexico as the base for expansion to the north. Within a half century much of the Caribbean area had been overrun, while venturesome Spaniards had explored the northern continent as far as its Kansas heart. By 1540 Spanish expeditions had touched the present states of California, Arizona, New Mexico, Texas, Louisiana, Arkansas, Oklahoma, and possibly Missouri. Names like those of Cabeza de Vaca and Hernando De Soto should rank at least as high as those of Lewis and Clark.

Most imposing of the early expeditions was that of Francisco Coronado, 1540–42. Coronado's main power lay in some two hundred horsemen, many of them titled Spanish adventurers elaborately caparisoned in burnished suits of armor, and bearing swords and lances. In addition, however, there were seventy foot soldiers and hundreds of servants and friendly Indians, together with artillery, livestock, and provisions. A portion of this impressive array finally advanced as far as present Kansas. Even though Coronado failed to find the precious metals that were the main object of his search, and though his expedition returned bedraggled, discouraged, and disappointed, he pushed existing geographical knowledge more than one step further. The magnitude of his achievement can be measured only with the realization that it came within fifty years of the time Columbus first sighted the new continent, and over half a century before the English tried to establish a permanent settlement at Jamestown.

EARLY SPANISH SETTLEMENT

Spanish failure to find gold, silver, and precious stones in the northern country reduced but did not end interest — for were there not other desirable articles to be obtained? And was there not reason for trying to meet and check the French empire, and later the English and Russian? And, above all, were there not pagan souls to be saved? Other expeditions, both lay and cleric, plodded through the weary, sandy miles to the north. The church and the state, cross and sword, went side by side, while soldier and settler often combined in a single person. Small Spanish settlements began to appear from the easternmost outpost at St. Augustine (1565) to the far reaches of the Pacific West.

The most easily attainable and most desirable region west of the Mississippi and north of the present Mexico was the valley of the Rio Grande in present New Mexico. Here in 1598 under Juan de Oñate came settlers to establish the first permanent white settlement west of the Mississippi. San Juan, north of the present Santa Fe, was founded nine years before Jamestown. A little later (1609) the village of Santa Fe was established to become the capital and metropolis of the area.

Succeeding years brought an increasing flow of friars, soldiers, and settlers to the northern wilderness, even though their maximum number was not sufficient to make any tremendous breaks in the wilderness. The Rio Grande settlements grew most rapidly, particularly as the colonists intermarried with the natives and produced numerous offspring. Vassals of the Spanish king struggled as far as East Texas to counteract the French advance from Louisiana, and Spanish Nacogdoches offset French Natchitoches. Hopeful priests, cattlemen, soldiers, and miners trickled into the present southern Arizona. The army and priesthood joined forces to advance up the Pacific Coast as far as the Golden Gate to forestall the Russians.

The occupation of the California coast from San Diego (1769) to San Francisco (1776) was the last important expansion of Spanish power in the American West. Thereafter Spain was to be on the defensive — a defensive that was soon to become a final stand to maintain existence. Spain's ultimate failure was based on the fact that there were too few Spaniards west of the Mississippi to hold the country against aggressive outsiders. By the late eighteenth century there were probably not over 15,000 people of white blood in the American Southwest, while two-thirds of these were located in the Rio Grande Valley of New Mexico. Many of these were at least half Indian, and the likelihood of their uniting in effective resistance to the Anglo-Americans was small.

The Spanish empire was theoretically the private property of the king, but in practice it was controlled by two Spanish bodies — the Council of the Indies, with legislative and administrative duties, and the House of Trade, which enforced colonial trade restrictions. In America the top official was the viceroy, of which there were several, and then the descending hierarchy went through the governor to the alcalde and cabildo in the individual town. On paper the organization was fine, but in practice it tended to creak at the joints since complete control from the top had many obvious difficulties in a period of slow communication. Furthermore the Spanish bureaucracy had a notable reputation for inefficiency and graft — a meaningful reputation in view of the number of competitors for the honor.

Control of the sparsely settled wilderness depended largely on the army, as it was stationed in presidios (garrisons) throughout the Southwest. The paucity of soldiers attested both a lack of funds and a touching faith in Spanish arms. Best known were the garrisons at San Antonio (1718), El Paso (1683), Santa Fe (1609, replacing San Juan), Tucson (1776, replacing Tubac, 1752), San Diego (1769), and San Francisco (1776).

Spanish garrisons were widely scattered and infinitesimal in size. Twenty or thirty soldiers were considered a good sized force, while some posts had no more than five to ten. Twenty soldiers could hardly overawe Indian tribes numbering thousands, and the natives were at times ill-disposed. In fact outbreaks and depredations were almost continuous throughout the whole area. Worst of them was the Pueblo Revolt of 1680, which brought death to a sixth of the white population in New Mexico and harried the rest to El Paso, but at many other times and places life was precarious for the Spanish " conqueror."

Even more visible than the military in the new communities were the Franciscan and Jesuit priests who in many cases, as at El

Paso, arrived first. Not infrequently High Mass, a Te Deum, and a salvo of cannon fire were the opening ceremonies. Church and state were indivisible, with the state preserving order to permit the saving of souls, and the church civilizing and Christianizing to produce good, loyal subjects of His Catholic Majesty.

The work of the church centered around the approximately sixty-five missions, at which were congregated Indian converts or potential converts. Here the good friars worked and taught and prayed to save the pagans from eternal punishment, and the results were impressive when stated in the number of those baptized. As early as 1630 the New Mexico missions claimed 60,000 converts. Unhappily this total came not entirely from the attractiveness of the Gospel and its preachers, but also from the lure of Spanish goods and the power of Spanish arms. From time to time the Indians discarded their allegiance to the Prince of Peace to engage in theft, arson, and murder; when Spanish military power lapsed most Indians reverted to their original ways of life.

The head of a mission was by no means interested exclusively in matters spiritual. He was the head of an economic and social unit of considerable size and variety. Large herds of cattle and horses, flocks of sheep and goats, great fields of grain, considerable numbers of artisans, and hundreds of Indian workers presented problems to challenge the keenest business intellect. Missions produced their own food, much of their clothes and tools. They traded, and functioned as inns, hospitals, and schools. In particular the missions of California waxed fat and prosperous with broad acres of wheat and fruit, and with horses, sheep, mules, and cattle to be counted by the thousand. Nor did they overlook vineyards and wine making, while distilleries were far from rare. Successful large-scale business must be credited to these factory-farm-church establishments.

Alongside each mission was an Indian town or pueblo, for the fathers felt that their best work could be accomplished if the Indians were concentrated. In New Mexico these towns already existed as a part of native culture, but elsewhere they had to be produced by a mixture of cajolery and force.

White settlers were sometimes grouped in towns, but frequently lived as isolated ranchers. These whites were encouraged from time to time by the Spanish administration; now and then the settlement was forced, as when soldiers were required to bring their families and remain in the north. The usual town grew near a presidio or mission or both and was highly dependent on them. In many cases the whites intermarried with the natives. Outside the towns were numerous cattle ranches. Land seemed inexhaustible and was donated in immense tracts, while cattle were almost equally as cheap. The lack of an easily available market meant that the average rancher lived in a crude log or adobe cabin, constructed with an eye to defense, and existed very close to the margin of starvation even though by custom he dispensed an openhanded hospitality.

The golden age of the Spanish Southwest was approximately the years 1790 to 1810. Missions and towns were beyond their first crude youth and worried mainly about hostile Indians; many of the missions were highly prosperous. Spanish administration had been routinized, and was not too severe. France had been eliminated from North America. The Russian menace had proved less terrifying than its advance notices. The bulk of United States population was still far distant, while the acquisition of Louisiana would seem to have channelized American energies away from the Spanish possessions. The few American visitors and settlers seemed no more than the casual sparks from a locomotive headed in a different direction.

INCREASING DISORDER

But the peacefully static conditions of the years around 1800 were not to last. A series of revolts starting in 1810 brought increasing domestic disorder which did not end with Mexico's successful revolution of 1821. Garrisons were reduced and even the few remaining troops were paid but irregularly. Instead of a concrete wall against internal and external troubles they became a barrier of tissue paper.

Wavering internal control was matched by shaky external domination. Even early in the nineteenth century pirates in the region of the Gulf of Mexico were bold and vigorous. Their principal rendezvous was Barataria, which was within fifty miles of New Orleans; in fact there is reason to believe that the New Orleans merchants encouraged piracy as a means of getting cheap supplies. The audacity of these pirates was illustrated by plans to seize and loot Pensacola, and to invade Florida and sell it to the United States. Outstanding among the pirates were the Lafitte brothers (the name has been spelled variously) and particularly Jean, six feet two, dark, handsome, unsmiling.

The Barataria retreat was made untenable by United States forces in 1814 and many of the pirates were thrown into the New Orleans calaboose. As luck would have it their services were needed in the defense of New Orleans and in time they were pardoned by Madison. After the war they found little happiness in legal trade and soon reverted to piracy. Jean Lafitte took over Galveston Island in 1817 and there he made piracy a well-organized and efficiently managed business. In consequence, Americans who came overland generally figured that the wise procedure was to make their peace with Lafitte.

AMERICAN FILIBUSTERS

Anglo-Americans in the regions near the Texas frontier looked southwest at the lax Mexican control and saw numerous attractive possibilities. In Texas were immense herds of cattle and horses, as well as millions of acres of fertile land within easy distance of Gulf ports. To the west lay trapping opportunities, soon to be exploited by the Patties and others of their stamp. In Texas, but particularly along the Rio Grande, were dozens of isolated settlements panting for American products, especially since the various revolutions had interrupted their slender communications to the south. And if trade went to Texas and New Mexico, why not to California and even to present Mexico itself? In addition, California offered a supply of hides and of sea otters and other furs, together with an opportunity for the outfitting of American ships. Energetic and optimistic Americans viewed each of these opportunities enthusiastically.

The earliest Anglo-American infiltration of Spanish territory was characterized mainly by individual traders and by raiding expeditions led by filibusters. Even before 1800 various American traders had seeped into Texas — generally for trade with the Indians but at times to do business with the whites — and it was not long before they were making the trip overland to Santa Fe. Their fortune was universally bad — quite consistently their goods were confiscated and they were jailed.

More spectacular than the traders were the filibusters as they advanced in ever increasing waves to seek fame and fortune. Leading the procession came Philip Nolan, horse trader, friend of Jefferson, and protégé of Wilkinson. Leaving Natchez in October 1800 with a small party he trapped wild horses as far west as the Brazos. Discovered and attacked by Spanish soldiers he was killed and his men imprisoned. Spanish power was declining, but not so greatly as to be unable to cope with a handful of adventurers.

Other Americans seemed not intimidated by Nolan's sad fate, and the name of James Wilkinson recurred with almost monotonous regularity. Wilkinson was involved in the Burr plans, which looked toward the Southwest. He boasted of his relations with Nolan. He sent out Pike, who traversed a large part of New Mexico and Texas. He encouraged dissidents. His son was a member of the Gutiérrez-Magee expedition and his nephew James Long led still another party.

The Gutiérrez-Magee expedition of 130 men invaded Texas in 1812 in the name of Mexican patriotism. Bernardo Gutiérrez de Lara had barely failed to obtain official American support for the revolution in which he was engaged. His partner, Augustus Magee, resigned his colonelcy in the American army to participate in the venture, thus bringing to mind similar incidents in East Florida at about the same time. Moving into Texas by way of Nacogdoches the leaders called on all Mexican patriots to embrace the revolutionary cause. The growing army surged ahead, defeated an opposing force, and invested San Antonio, although by this time Magee had died. Internal dissension and a loyal army brought the collapse of the movement, with neither side showing mercy in the fighting. Reports claimed that ninety-three Americans escaped from a force that at its maximum included 700 Americans plus three times that many Mexicans and Indians.

Nothing daunted by this disaster James Long, formerly a surgeon in the United States army, planned a new invasion in 1819. Recruiting some fifty volunteers at Natchez he advanced on Nacogdoches, captured the town, and declared Texas free. He tried to obtain the assistance of the noted pirate Jean Lafitte, but Lafitte clung to piracy as safer and more lucrative than filibustering. Long maintained a precarious independence for two years, and then upon his defeat suffered the usual penalties — he was shot and his men imprisoned.

American filibustering in Texas received no governmental encouragement, with the possible exception of the somewhat devious efforts of Wilkinson. In fact, Washington showed a most notable lack of interest in Texas. The boundaries drawn in the treaty of 1819 specifically excluded Texas, even though plausible claims might have been advanced for at least part of this area. The Long expedition was largely a protest against this action. And yet, for anyone east of the Appalachians, including the king of Spain, the American colonization and subsequent acquisition of Texas seemed such a remote possibility as hardly to be worth consideration.

SANTA FE TRADE

Conditions west of the Sabine changed markedly in 1820, when a Spanish revolution resulted in the permission of foreign settlements in the Empire. Hardly had this news reached America before a successful Mexican revolution produced a new nation and abrogated the old colonial restrictions. The way was opened for American trade and settlement, depending only upon the policy of the Mexican government, which was never strong, and even less so in the remoter places of the north.

The most important trade to develop was that with Santa Fe, which meant, of course, with the New Mexican settlements of the area, not to mention extensions of the trade into California and Mexico. The start of the business is ordinarily credited to William Becknell and his successful venture of 1821. During the first few years only a scattering of traders ventured the trip, but their successes ultimately brought large yearly caravans, which continued until railroad connections appeared over half a century later.

The articles taken to Santa Fe were only those which had fairly large value in small bulk, for the long and expensive trip across the plains prohibited the carrying of large cheap goods. Usually such merchandise included woolens, cottons, silks, velvets, shawls, looking glasses, and hardware. These goods were carried in Pittsburgh or Conestoga wagons, each drawn by eight to twelve mules or oxen and holding three to seven thousand pounds. On the trip back to the United States the usual articles returned were mules, horses, beaver skins, and bullion.

The Santa Fe business prospered in spite of numerous obstacles. In the path of the trader lay treeless and waterless plains, as well as one real desert; streams had to be forded; the Indians, particularly the Comanche, were dangerous. The customs restrictions at Santa Fe were always annoying, the tax which was levied being at times as high as sixty per cent of the total value of the imports. A flat rate of $500 per wagon was made effective in 1839, with the result that the traders used larger wagons for the trip. Bribery of the customs officials was an ordinary part of the business, with the usual arrangements giving a third of the tax to the government, a third to the official, and the remainder to the trader. Even with these various handicaps the trade prospered, an average trip returning a profit of between ten and forty per cent.

The total value of the trade was not as much as might have been expected. The average per year between 1822 and 1843 was $130,000 with the largest single year (1843) having a total of $450,000. The trade was stopped by Santa Anna in the years 1843-44, but was then revived, and the caravan of 1846 was valued at $1,752,250. The trade continued important through the Civil War.

Each year the caravan from the United States moved west as early as the ground was passable in the spring and each fall it returned before the coming of snow; travel was at the rate of about fifteen to eighteen miles a day. Most of the goods to be carried west passed through St. Louis, but the usual outfitting point for the traders was some town farther up the Missouri River. Each man going west carried for food approximately fifty pounds of flour, fifty pounds of bacon, ten pounds of coffee, twenty pounds of sugar, and some salt. These supplies, sometimes supplemented by a little game, were supposed to be adequate for the trip to Santa Fe.

The start from Independence or any outfitting town was a helter-skelter affair, each driver leaving whenever he was ready. The Indians of the region were not hostile and the plains were not dangerous, so precautions were unnecessary. The real dangers lay farther west, and so a rendezvous was held at Council Grove (in present Kansas) to provide protection for the rest of the journey. Here would gather all the men making the trip, and they would rest, fix their wagons, and fatten their stock. The company was then organized for mutual protection and assistance; officers were elected to assume command of the entire caravan, provide for both day and night guards, select the men to do the cooking, and take complete control in case of trouble. After the organization of the group it moved out of Council Grove in a body, and the actual trip had begun.

The trail from Council Grove went directly west to the great bend of the Arkansas River, which was reached at a distance of 270 miles from Independence. Then it followed the river to its crossing at the 392-mile mark. At this point there were two optional routes for the remainder of the distance. Most caravans cut overland from the Arkansas across the Cimarron desert to the Cimarron River (a branch of the Arkansas) and then up the Cimarron and finally cross country to Santa Fe. The optional route continued to ascend the Arkansas River as far as Bent's Fort, which was located near the present La Junta, Colorado. Here it turned directly south to Santa Fe. The second route was less hazardous, but longer, and in consequence most of the traders went by way of the Cimarron. At Santa Fe the traders sold their merchandise on the streets until they had disposed of their stock in trade or until winter began to approach. Then the caravan started the return trip, arriving in Independence before the first fall of snow if possible.

The trade to Santa Fe was one of the straws which showed the direction of the wind and forecast the eventual disintegration of the permanent Indian frontier. The government, however, was willing neither to admit the danger to its Indian policy nor to try to stop the trade. It was drawn into the anomalous position of continuing to support the permanent frontier and at the same time to give direct aid and encouragement to the Santa Fe traders. By the terms of the act of 1825 the road to Santa Fe within the limits of the United States was marked, although unfortunately the markings were placed on the little used route by way of Bent's Fort. Fort Leavenworth was established in 1827 for the principal purpose of restraining the Indians for the benefit of the Santa Fe trade. Military escorts were provided in the years 1829, 1834, and 1843, and protected the traders as far as the United States boundary; this assistance was not given every year since the value of the trade hardly paid for the cost of the escort, and a large share of the most dangerous part of the route was in Mexican territory.

The importance of the Santa Fe trade was actually much greater than its volume would seem to indicate, in part because its romance and adventure appealed strongly to a nation which had received its concepts of the West from Cooper and Irving. Fighting Indians and forest fires, shooting buffalo and other game, fording rivers, crossing deserts, attending Spanish fandangos, and eating chile con carne all seemed to be exciting occupations. Also there was a romantic appeal to the dusky Mexican beauty with her high combs, her long black cigaret, and her alluring eyes. Dirt and vermin were invisible over a space of a thousand miles.

The Santa Fe trade demonstrated the ease with which the United States might conquer the Southwest. The illusion of Mexican military power could not be maintained in the face of the observations of the traders. Furthermore the Santa Fe traders helped in some measure to dispel the illusion of a Great American Desert. The whole effect of the trade was to begin the disintegration of the permanent Indian frontier and to turn American attention toward the Mexican territory of the Southwest.

AMERICAN SETTLERS IN TEXAS

If the beginnings of the Santa Fe trade demonstrated Mexican weakness, the beginnings of American migration to Texas proved the point beyond contradiction. In the van was one Moses Austin, Connecticut Yankee by birth, who had pursued an elusive fortune to Pennsylvania, to Virginia, and to Missouri before he finally conceived of Mexican lands as a last resort. His application coincided with the new liberalized policy of the Spanish government and a grant was approved (1821) on condition that he bring 300 families.

Moses Austin died before he could utilize his new-found fortune, but his work was continued by his son Stephen F., who was forced to considerable effort before he succeeded in obtaining the reaffirmation of the grant by the new Mexican government. The land lay between the San Jacinto and Lavaca rivers on the Gulf side of the trail from Nacogdoches to San Antonio. In this region Austin had supreme power to distribute land, lay out towns, administer justice, and exercise the other necessary functions of government. At once he began to offer attractive terms to prospective American colonists and by the end of the decade had attracted some 5000 settlers.

At the same time that Stephen Austin was in the city of Mexico lobbying for the confirmation of his grant other Americans such as James Wilkinson and Haden Edwards were seeking grants of their own, and the Mexican Congress was considering some kind of general land legislation. The Congress finally delegated (1824) most power to the individual states, and so the next year the state of Coahuila and Texas acted very liberally by providing in general for *empresario* grants much like the one Austin had received. Each *empesario* was to receive a large tract of his own free if he brought a proper number of colonists, while each colonist was to receive one labor (177 acres) for agriculture and twenty-four labors (4251 acres) for grazing. The cost was small, and payment was spread over six years. Tariffs were removed on agricultural implements, and all taxes were to be remitted for six years and then halved for the next six years. The introduction of slaves was prohibited, except in the Austin colony, but this provision was soon modified.

The Mexican policy took concrete form in the next few years with large grants to such men as Green Dewitt and Haden Edwards, so that the entire area of Texas became a patchwork of claims. This policy was definitely dangerous to Mexican control of Texas in so far as it succeeded. While an increase of power and wealth, and consequently of taxes, might be expected, the comparable examples of East and West Florida might well have caused Mexico to be more cautious. The day was soon to come when it would rue the policy bitterly.

American farmers found Texas desirable. By 1827 their number was possibly 10,000, three years later it had doubled, and by 1835 it had reached 35,000. Most of them were from the southern states, and largely from Kentucky and Tennessee, but some came from as far as New England, while a few hailed from Germany and Ireland. Theoretically they were all loyal Catholic citizens of Mexico, but actually both their patriotism and Catholicism were scarcely skin deep. Catholic priests and Mexican soldiers were greeted with apathy. Some of the late arrivals married Mexican girls — an indication not of Pan-American unity but of the scarcity of women and of the larger grant available to a married man. Here and there settlers spoke openly of their desire for United States control, but most of them followed Austin's lead in preserving at least technical loyalty to the Mexican government.

The handwriting on the wall became more obvious with the Fredonian revolt of 1826–27. Haden Edwards had been awarded an *empresario* grant which included Nacogdoches and had immediately gotten into trouble with earlier settlers, largely Mexican, over their claims. On appeal to the government the older claims were upheld and the Edwards' grant cancelled — whereupon Edwards established a revolutionary government with the usual constitution and the equally usual appeals for United States assistance. The United States turned a deaf ear and the revolt was suppressed by a Mexican army aided by some of the Austin colonists.

The Fredonian trouble underlined a situation which was giving more and more concern to informed and intelligent Mexicans. Spanish and Anglo-Saxon cultures did not mix happily. Particularly in government and religion were there wide and deep differences. Each people looked on the other with suspicion and even hostility. Furthermore the American predominance in numbers was increasing year by year.

A prominent Mexican thus analyzed United States policy in

1830: " They begin by introducing themselves into the territory they covet, upon pretence of commercial negotiations or of the establishment of colonies. . . . These colonies grow, multiply, become the predominant part of the population; and as soon as a support is found in this manner, they begin to set up rights which it is impossible to sustain in a serious discussion. . . . These pioneers originate, little by little, movements which complicate the political state of the country in dispute, and then follow discontents and dissatisfaction, calculated to fatigue the patience of the legitimate owner, and diminish the usefulness of the administration and the exercise of authority. When things have come to this pass, which is precisely the present state of things in Texas, diplomatic intrigue begins."

Point was given to the final Mexican assertion of the preceding quotation by the fact that the United States had acquired an interest in Texas which had been absent in 1819. President Adams had only recently made a serious effort to buy Texas, and although he had to be content with a treaty which did no more than recognize the Sabine boundary, the Mexicans may be excused for fearing that action would be taken through United States-born citizens of Texas.

MORE SEVERE MEXICAN POLICY

Mexican fears produced a severely restricted policy in 1830, with the prohibition of further immigration from the United States. *Empresario* grants were to be cancelled as soon as legally possible. Foreign ships were admitted to Mexican coastal trade in the hope that inter-Mexican trade could be aided at the expense of the traffic with New Orleans. Texan military garrisons were reinforced in 1830 and 1831. Finally, an effort was made in 1832 to encourage immigration from non-American countries.

The Mexican reforms came too late to be effective, even assuming a conscientious administration. A handful of poorly paid and inadequately equipped Mexican soldiers could not guard a thousand miles of land and water frontier against United States settlers. Trade continued to go to New Orleans in spite of a tariff and shipping preference. Immigrants from other countries did not arrive. The only tangible accomplishment was to irritate the colonists so that even formerly loyal supporters of Mexico began to grumble at their many restrictions. And this result was produced without even really excluding United States colonists. Enforcement of the

law was exceedingly lax, and exceptions were immediately made
of colonists headed for the Austin and Dewitt colonies; in 1833
the prohibition was repealed completely.

Texan troubles increased during the early '30s. Internally, more
settlers appeared, with a direct increase of belligerent demands for
their " rights." Externally, President Jackson made a new offer for
Texas, and expanded his desires to California. Jackson's representative was the swashbuckling and vainglorious Anthony Butler,
who suggested wholesale bribery as the road to success; Jackson's
ideas of morality were outraged and he recalled Butler.

Just at the time that Butler's mission was becoming obviously
hopeless (1832) another friend of Jackson appeared on the scene —
Sam Houston; the coincidence in time may of course have been
an accident. Houston had been born in Virginia, but had grown up
in Tennessee and served with Jackson in the War of 1812. He then
entered law practice and politics, with his public offices including
a major-generalship in the militia and membership in Congress. At
the age of thirty-four (1827) he was elected governor of Tennessee
and two years later he married. Unquestionably he seemed headed
for a long and distinguished political career.

Within three months of Houston's marriage he threw up his
job as governor, deserted his wife, and fled to the Indian country,
where he soon took a native spouse. Houston himself never explained his actions, and hence most guesses have involved his relations with his wife. During the succeeding three years he was
twice in Washington, being entertained by Jackson at the White
House. When he crossed the border into Texas he was a marked
man, not only because of his past career and his friendship with
the President, but also because of his appearance and personality.
Well over six feet tall, built in proportion, handsome, with a deep,
rich voice and an attractive manner, he was an outstanding man.
At once he became the leader of the Texan groups favoring independence and there can be little question that thereby he was following Jackson's desires, which may or may not have been put
into words.

During the very year of Houston's arrival there occurred a small
Texan revolution, although there is no connection between the two
events. The abortive revolt was the result of an unpopular administration of customs restrictions. Luckily the revolt coincided with
a successful revolution by Santa Anna in Mexico. Santa Anna immediately sent an army to Texas, but along with the army went

Austin and promises of reforms if the revolutionists accepted the new Mexican administration. The Texan rebels were more impressed by the promises than by the army, laid down their arms, threw their hats in the air, and gave three cheers for the " liberal " Santa Anna.

Santa Anna's liberalism resulted in the repeal of the prohibition of United States immigrants, but there his reforms stopped, and the Texans wanted self-rule. Discontent increased when Santa Anna (1834) dropped even the pretense of liberalism, dismissed his Congress, and gathered all power into his own hands. As Texan mutterings increased, the new dictator decided that military chastisement would be salutary for Texas and at the same time increase his own prestige.

TEXAS REVOLUTION

Events moved rapidly to a crisis. General Martin Perfecto de Cos entered Texas in September 1835. A month later a Texas convention created a provisional government headed by a known advocate of independence and gave Sam Houston command of the army — but did not declare independence. Cos was defeated and driven out. Santa Anna then took command personally; he crossed the Rio Grande on Feb. 12, 1836, and on March 2 Texas proclaimed her independence.

When Santa Anna crossed the Rio Grande he had an army of some 6000 and visions of military fame. In numbers he was clearly superior to any possible opposing force, and he tended to overlook poor equipment and morale. He planned a campaign that would ferret out and destroy all rebel forces. No quarter was to be given and no prisoners were to be taken. Texas was to be given a taste of Mexican authority which would not soon be forgotten.

The situation of the Texans was precarious. Although hardy and self-reliant as individuals they were variously armed and equipped and without formal discipline. Their numbers were possibly 1000, but even these were divided into several small groups. Sam Houston was theoretically in supreme command, but in practice his orders could be no more than suggestions or requests.

Santa Anna took full advantage of Texan division. A force of about a hundred at San Patricio was annihilated — survivors of the battle being executed. A force of 182 men under W. B. Travis was trapped at San Antonio, which Houston had ordered abandoned; the heroic defense of the Alamo ended only with the death of the last defender. Four hundred men under J. W. Fannin at Goliad were surrounded. They surrendered on agreement that they would then be permitted to go home; actually they were marched out in three small groups and massacred on the order of Santa Anna. Apologists insisted that rebels risked death by revolting, but most people were horrified.

These slaughters had at least the effect of unifying the Texan command by killing all rivals to Houston. In addition, Santa Anna, flushed with victory, became increasingly less cautious. Most important, Texans were inspired to desperate resistance, for they clearly had no option between victory and death. The battle cries of " Remember the Alamo!" and " Remember Goliad! " were heard increasingly as Houston and his 350 men started retreating eastward, gathering recruits as they went.

Mexican victories and the Houston retreat brought into prominence the question of whether the United States would intervene. Throughout the Union public meetings demanded federal action, and meantime sent supplies, munitions, and men to aid the rebels. President Jackson undoubtedly prayed for Texan victory; certainly he followed the campaign closely and sent Gaines to the border with an American army. Possibly he hoped that Gaines would follow his own precedent as set in Florida. Possibly positive action would have come if Houston had been defeated. In fact, however, neither of these things happened. The United States government remained strictly neutral — except that it winked at the aid given by American citizens to the rebels.

Houston's retreat was at first an inescapable necessity, but later it seemed to become a habit. An enlarged and more disciplined army still brought only retreat. Even when Santa Anna's self-confidence and lack of military ability led him to divide his troops Houston refused to do battle — in spite of the fact that the Texans outnumbered the Mexicans. In consequence many of the Texans went home, others became bitter and sullen, and Santa Anna overran the capital of the new republic.

Ultimately Houston and Santa Anna confronted each other on the San Jacinto River near Galveston Bay. The Texans were the more numerous, but Houston delayed until Santa Anna was reinforced. Then, against the advice of some of his staff, Houston attacked on April 21, 1836. Judged by results, his campaign had been masterly, for he achieved a total victory. Apparently the Mexicans were taken by surprise because Mexican military traditions did not allow the possibility of an attack by an outnumbered army on a superior position. Houston's report of the engagement claimed more Mexican casualties than Santa Anna had troops, but there was no doubt that the Texans had won an overwhelming victory at little cost. Santa Anna was himself captured and demonstrated his plausibility by persuading his captors to release him upon his promise to use his influence toward the acceptance of Texan independence. This promise he later repudiated — after all, it had been extorted by force.

TEXAN INDEPENDENCE

With Houston's victory at San Jacinto, Texan refugees who had crowded the roads to the east began to return. The constitution which had been drawn at the time of the declaration of independence, was placed before the people and ratified. The temporary president was superseded by a regularly elected incumbent—naturally the hero of the hour, Sam Houston. A minister was sent to the United States and a proposal for annexation was adopted by an almost unanimous popular vote. The course of events that Texas anticipated was perfectly obvious to the world.

But annexation plans struck an unexpected snag in the person of President Jackson. Long desirous of acquiring Texas, he now not only proved cool toward the idea of annexation but also very lukewarm even about recognition. Possibly he feared trouble with Mexico and England, but more likely he was influenced by political considerations. At any rate he passed the buck to Congress, which replied in kind by authorizing him to recognize Texas whenever he thought desirable. Among Jackson's last official acts were the receiving of the Texan minister and the sending of a chargé d'affaires to Texas. After his retirement from the Presidency he became an ardent annexationist, while Van Buren continued his official policy of caution.

The issue of the annexation of Texas became mixed with the slavery question. Two pamphlets of the abolitionist Benjamin Lundy spread the idea that Texas was a den of the blackest iniquity, and that its settlement and revolution constituted a deep-laid plot by slaveholders to add more slave territory to the United States. With the issue thus confused a decade of Congressional debate was necessary before Texas could be admitted by even the narrowest of votes.

Balked in her desire for annexation Texas withdrew the proposal and tried to make independence succeed. In this effort she had not only the usual difficulties that face any postrevolutionary country, but also a small population (some 55,000 in 1840) and a lack of variety in resources and occupations. Her one obvious advantage was the ability of her leaders. During her independence she had four presidents, including the provisional one; Houston had two terms and would undoubtedly have continued in office continuously from 1836 had it not been for the constitutional provision prohibiting a president to succeed himself.

One of the earliest of Texan problems was to obtain world recognition of its independence, with the aims of trading and of borrowing money more easily. Recognition by the United States was soon followed by that of England and France. As for Mexico, the best offer Santa Anna ever made was home-rule if Texas returned to her Mexican allegiance.

Relations with Mexico were far from peaceful. Immediately after San Jacinto Houston had trouble persuading his army that it should not rush down into Mexico to find more Mexicans to thrash. In fact the army was itself a problem, being unruly and demanding. Shortly after independence, groups of Texans crossed the border to foment a revolution in Mexico — an effort that failed. Texas itself in 1841 undertook to conquer Santa Fe — for Texas claimed land to the Rio Grande — but the expedition was mismanaged and its members ended in Mexican jails. Mexico retaliated the next year with an effort to reconquer Texas, and succeeding years saw further raids both ways. Incidentally, Texas also had a very small navy which did as it pleased, refusing to obey orders it did not like.

The Indians presented still another problem as they raided across the borders. Treaties were made with some of the tribes, while some groups were forcibly expelled. Much trouble came from the Comanche, who refused to be cowed by several armed expeditions. Ultimately Texas developed a policy similar to that of the United States. Military garrisons occupied forts in the less populated areas. All Indian trade was put under governmental supervision (1843) and sales of liquor and firearms prohibited.

Undoubtedly the greatest internal problem was raising money, which would have been difficult even in the best times and was well-nigh impossible as the panic of 1837 tightened its grip. Taxes were levied on property but no one had money to pay them. Tariffs were enacted but remained unproductive as long as trade languished. Efforts to float loans in the United States and Europe were lamentable failures. Bonds were issued but could find few purchasers, even with interest at ten per cent. Paper money was issued, but so small was the confidence in Texan finance that its purchasing power soon fell to about a tenth of its face value.

The most valuable possession of Texas was its land, and consequently Texas early devised a land system — a system that was continued even after the state entered the Union. Outright sales were disappointingly meager, but gifts could be made to worthy projects. Her revolutionary soldiers were paid partly in land. Transportation was subsidized. An impressive school system was given a start with regal land subsidies. Immigrants were encouraged by liberal gifts, and the *empresario* system was revived. The result was the influx of many settlers, not only from the United States but also from the various German states, England, France, and elsewhere; the population of 1846 has been estimated as 100,000.

The decade of independence was not a satisfactory period for Texas. Only a few citizens, such as the second president M. B. Lamar, had ever wanted a separate existence. Most of them continued to think of the United States as their country. Annexation to the United States was the expected goal, and to some extent everyone marked time until that happy end was consummated.

READINGS

EXPLORATION AND FAR SOUTHWEST: M. Bishop, *The Odyssey of Cabeza de Vaca* (1933); H. E. Bolton, *Anza's California Expedition* (5 vols., 1930), *Coronado* (1949), (ed.), *Pageant in the Wilderness* (1950), *Rim of Christendom* (1936)—Kino—*The Spanish Borderlands* (1921); J. W. Caughey, *History of the Pacific Coast* (1933), chs. 4–10, *California* (1940), chs. 3–10; C. Coan, *A History of New Mexico* (3 vols., 1925), vol. 1, chs. 10–16; A. G. Day, *Coronado's Quest* (1940); B. De Voto, *The Course of Empire* (1952); J. M. Espinosa, *Crusaders of the Rio Grande* (1942)—De Varga; E. Fergusson, *New Mexico* (1951), chs. 10–15; H. Fergusson, *Rio Grande* (1933), chs. 1–6; C. Hallenbeck, *Alvar Nunez Cabeza de Vaca* (1940); G. P. Hammond, *Coronado's Seven Cities* (1940), (ed.), *Narrative of the Coronado Expedition* (1940); G. P. Hammond and A. Rey, *Don Juan De Oñate* (2 vols., 1953); T. M. Marshall, *A History of the Western Boundary of the Louisiana Purchase* (1914); P. W. Powell,

Soldiers, Indians, and Silver (1952)—Spanish advance 1550–1600;
H. I. Priestley, *The Coming of the White Man* (1929)—largely
before 1800, Tristán de Luna (1936); R. N. Richardson and C. C.
Rister, *The Greater Southwest* (1934), chs. 2–4; R. K. Wyllys,
Pioneer Padre (1935)—Kino.

SANTA FE TRAIL: G. D. Bradley, *The Story of the Santa Fe*
(1920), ch. 1; W. E. Connelley, *History of Kansas* (5 vols., 1928),
ch. 9—factual; S. M. Drumm (ed.), *Down the Santa Fe Trail*
(1926); R. L. Duffus, *The Santa Fe Trail* (1930); H. Fergusson,
Rio Grande (1933), ch. 8; M. G. Fulton (ed.), *Diary and Letters
of Josiah Gregg* (1941); J. Gregg, *Commerce of the Prairies*
(1954)—reprint of contemporary account; K. L. Gregg (ed.), *The
Road to Santa Fe* (1952)—surveys of route 1825–27; D. Lavender, *Bent's Fort* (1954), chs. 5–7; S. Vestal, *The Old Santa Fe
Trail* (1939).

TEXAS: E. C. Barker, *The Austin Papers* (3 vols., 1924–28),
The Life of Stephen F. Austin (1925), *Mexico and Texas, 1821–35*
(1928)—lectures—*Readings in Texas History* (1929); W. C.
Binkley, *The Texas Revolution* (1952)—fine scholarship; W. H.
Callcott, *Santa Anna* (1936); C. E. Casteñada (transl.), *The
Mexican Side of the Texas Revolution* (1928); F. Copeland,
Kendall of the Picayune (1943), chs. 5–12; D. Day and H. H.
Ullom (eds.), *The Autobiography of Sam Houston* (1954), chs.
1–16; R. M. Denhardt, *The Horse of the Americas* (1948), chs.
1–8, 9, 12; L. Friend, *Sam Houston* (1954), pp. 3–114; H. Gam-
brell, *Anson Jones* (1948); W. R. Hogan, *The Texas Republic*
(1946)—informative; P. Horgan, *Great River* (2 vols., 1954), vol.
1, book 2, vol. 2, book 3; M. James, *The Raven* (1929)—Houston;
O. Morton, *Terán and Texas* (1948)—good monograph; R. Phares,
Cavalier in the Wilderness (1952)—early trader; R. N. Richardson, *Texas* (1943), chs. 1–7—good; G. L. Rives, *The United States
and Mexico, 1821–1848* (2 vols., 1913), vol. 1, chs. 1–19; L. Saxon,
Lafitte the Pirate (1930); J. W. Schmitz, *Texan Statecraft, 1836–
1845* (1941); R. W. Steen, *The Texas Story* (1948), chs. 1–13—
scholarly; N. W. Stephenson, *Texas and the Mexican War* (1921),
chs. 1–7—Chronicles of America; H. G. Warren, *The Sword Was
Their Passport* (1943)—Texas filibustering; O. P. White, *Texas*
(1945), chs. 2–13; A. W. Williams and E. C. Barker, *The Writings of Sam Houston* (7 vols., 1938–42).

CHAPTER 24

DESTINY BECKONS

DRAMATIC developments in Texas did not monopolize the attention of all Americans who were looking for the reputedly greener fields of the distance. An increasing number were casting their eyes to the Pacific Coast and even farther. The aspirations and interests of a youthful America seemed limitless.

CLAIMS TO THE PACIFIC COAST

Historically the Pacific Coast of North America had been but one of the minor stakes in the game of world imperialism. Spanish, English, and French explorers had touched various points in their wide-flung efforts to understand and conquer the entire world. By the late eighteenth century these competitors had been reduced to Spain and England, and in spite of the thousands of miles of wilderness the two nations collided on Vancouver Island at Nootka Sound (1790). The result was that Spain was forced (1794) to relinquish her attempted monopoly north of her farthest settlement at San Francisco Bay.

The English-Spanish dominance lost ground as these nations became involved with the events flowing from the French Revolution and as other nations began to afford competition. Even before 1800 both Russia and the United States were giving evidence of making a real bid for the trade of the Pacific Coast.

Russia had been expanding from west to east. In 1725 the Danish-born Vitus Bering jumped the ocean on the first of his trips to North America. Bering was followed by Russian traders, who made their headquarters in Alaska, and near the end of the century the Russian-American Fur Company was organized to monopolize the business of the new world. Edging continually southward it established its southernmost post at Fort Ross (1812) not far north of San Francisco Bay. This advance furnished a good talking point for the Spanish occupation of California and helped to inspire the Monroe Doctrine. These results were utterly out of proportion to the very small menace existing in Russian trade expansion.

The last, but ultimately the most important nation to make its appearance on the Pacific Coast, was the United States. American interest manifested itself first with profit-seeking Boston merchants who projected a three-cornered trade whereby Yankee cutlery, textiles, and trinkets would be taken to the Pacific Coast to be traded for furs, which had an excellent market in China. In China the ships could be loaded with such products as tea, spices, and silks for the American trade. While Americans were not the first to undertake this business they soon dominated it.

The first Boston ships destined for the Northwest trade were sent out by an association of Boston merchants in 1787. One of them, commanded by Captain Robert Gray, was the first American ship to circumnavigate the globe, and was received with tremendous acclaim when it returned to Boston in 1790. Gray immediately reoutfitted and departed for the West, where he entered the Columbia River (1792) slightly ahead of the English Captain George Vancouver, thus providing an important element of the later American claim to Oregon, even though a Spaniard had actually entered the river some years earlier.

Within a few years American ships dotted the coastal waters from Alaska to Mexico. Theoretically such vessels were excluded from any Spanish port, but in practice shipmasters could almost always discover a complaisant official who was willing to become nearsighted — for a consideration. American ships were more warmly welcomed after Mexican revolutionary movements almost ended Spanish trade between Mexico and California.

The main trading interest of the early years centered in the seal and otter, which were available all along the coast. In return the Boston merchant provided manufactured goods and knickknacks which were highly attractive to the isolated coastal communities. As a concomitant part of the trade the ship captains seized the opportunity to scrape the hulls of their vessels and to reoutfit with meat, grain, vegetables, and water.

The character of American trade changed about 1820 with the virtual extinction of the seal and otter. Other furs remained in the

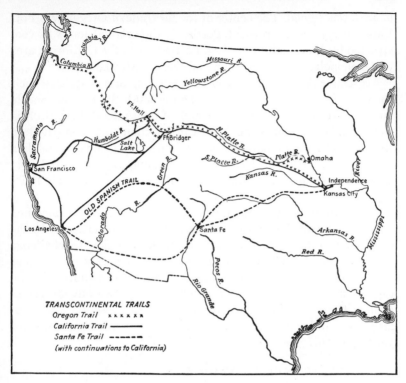

TRANSCONTINENTAL TRAILS
Oregon Trail ×××××××
California Trail ————
Santa Fe Trail ------
(with continuations to California)

northern country, but in California the visitors were increasingly whalers and hide and tallow ships. For the whalers California was second only to Hawaii as a favored place for refitting and provisioning. The hide and tallow business was the real descendant of the fur business of California. During the '20s and '30s its principal center was San Diego. The business was legal under Mexican law if the proper port duties were paid, but admittedly many ships evaded these taxes at least in part. The hides came from the large California herds and went into shoes manufactured in New England. The classic account of this business as it existed during the '30s is Richard Henry Dana's *Two Years Before the Mast*.

Following close on the heels of the explorers and traders by sea came the explorers, traders and trappers by land. Down from the Northwest swept the trading companies, with Alexander Mackenzie in the van. Then came the Americans, with Lewis and Clark in the lead. The failure of Astoria put a temporary end to the American invasion of Oregon; in fact there was no American in the Columbia River region when the joint occupation agreement of 1818 was signed. The center of the fur trade of Oregon was Fort Vancouver, opposite present Portland; the original fort was constructed by McLoughlin in 1825. Farther south the California area was monopolized first by Spain and then by Mexico.

Aggressive American trappers did not long accept quietly their exclusion from the Pacific Coast. To the south the Patties, Smith, and others crossed the Sierras in spite of their uncertain California welcome. To the north the American fur companies competed on the fringes of the domain of the Hudson's Bay Company, while a scattering of such men as Smith, Young, and Wyeth visited Fort Vancouver, even if they did not fight the monopoly actively in its own field.

The United States government was not entirely unconcerned with the westward expansion of the interests of its citizens. In the early years official Washington was in no position to challenge Spanish control of California, but the Oregon country was another matter. Here was the only practical Pacific Coast outlet for an expanding nation — an outlet which not only had advantages in trade with the Far East, but also contained rich resources, particularly furs and agricultural land; timber and minerals were not yet important.

DIPLOMATIC NEGOTIATIONS

The first official act of the United States was negative — an agreement with England (1818) whereby the Canadian boundary was continued west only as far as the mountains, with the Oregon country to remain open for joint occupation. Here England made a mistake. Depending on her existing monopoly of the fur trade and the absence of Americans in the region she underestimated the rapidity of American expansion. During the next year the Spanish treaty put a northern limit to Spanish claims at 42°, the present northern line of California, and the United States was enabled to argue that she fell heir to all Spanish claims farther north. Then came the Monroe Doctrine aimed partly at Russia, followed by an agreement with that country (1824) which limited Russian expansion from the north to 54° 40'. By these treaties the debatable western country was limited to the area between 42° and 54° 40' west of the Rockies.

Congressional interest in Oregon first reached print in 1820 and after that year there was a succession of bills to aid settlement, usually by improving and guarding the route to Oregon. Senators

Linn and Benton were especially active; both came from Missouri, which had the greatest immediate interest in Oregon. None of these suggested measures became law, partly because of a lack of interest, partly because of the cost, partly because of doubts as to the value of the country, and partly because of the distance. Many people felt that Pacific Coast settlement would inevitably mean an independent nation because of remoteness. Benton agreed to the likelihood of separatism but found an independent state undesirable.

While Congressional interest produced no positive action it did encourage the State Department to try to obtain a part of the Oregon country outright when the agreement of 1818 neared its ten-year expiration date. The United States suggested a continuation of the 49° line to the coast. England refused, and ultimately the old joint occupation agreement was continued indefinitely, with a provision for its abrogation by either party on twelve months' notice.

Diplomatic and Congressional maneuverings were but the reflection and not the substance of American interest in the Pacific Coast. The important fact for the future was that more and more individual Americans were envisaging opportunities in the Far West and seeking to embrace them. The first of these optimists had been an insignificant scattering of traders, trappers, and more or less casual travelers, but time brought more permanent settlers engaged in commercial, agricultural, or religious occupations. As their number increased United States policy reflected the change.

Until late in the 1840s American interest was much greater in Oregon than in California — a preference based partly on facts and partly on accident. California was under Spanish rule whereas Oregon was open to Americans — a factor that should not be weighed too heavily in view of the contemporary Texas situation. Oregon had more fur-bearing animals than California, more fish in the rivers, more well-watered agricultural land, and was closer to the Orient. The overland road to Oregon was possibly a trifle easier than that to California. Most important, however, was a factor which was at least partly accidental — successful advertising, including an unusual approach through religious interest.

HALL J. KELLEY

The first great ballyhoo artist of Oregon was the Boston schoolmaster Hall J. Kelley. Kelley was a neurotic, and many thought him completely insane. All his life he had poor eyesight, and eventually became almost blind; this physical handicap may largely explain why he was highly nervous, extremely sensitive, and diffident, and so excitable that at times he lost the power of speech. He was also deeply religious, almost completely lacking in humor, and increasingly obsessed by an oppressive sense of persecution. He released part of his nervous tension by writing textbooks from which he profited moderately, only to lose his savings in unfortunate investments.

Kelley's interest in Oregon originated with his reading an account of the Lewis and Clark expedition. The more he read the more excited he became, until the failure of Astoria seemed to him a world-shaking tragedy. By the 1820s Oregon had become a mania, and he spoke and wrote voluminously on his great love: Oregon was supreme for climate, soil, fishing, fur traffic, missions, trading, or what have you — " no portion of the globe presents a more fruitful soil, or a milder climate, or equal facilities for carrying into effect the great purposes of a free and enlightened nation." Kelley's work included elaborate plans for a great colony, and on this subject he memorialized Congress for aid. Disciples appeared so slowly, however, that ultimately, as already described, Kelley's most important convert Nathaniel Wyeth became impatient and started ahead with his own small group.

Kelley finally and regretfully abandoned his plans for a large settlement, and late in 1832 started west by way of New Orleans, Vera Cruz, and San Diego with a small party. Whether through bad management or bad luck he finally arrived at Monterey penniless and alone. There he joined Ewing Young and several others in a plan to drive a herd of cattle to Fort Vancouver. En route most of the cattle were lost and Kelley contracted malaria. His reception at the fort (1834) was marred by McLoughlin's belief that he was a cattle thief, so that while he was properly housed, fed, and doctored he was not entertained regally and felt himself to be persecuted. Eventually he returned to Boston by sea to spend the rest of his life in writing justifications which were frequently incoherent and sometimes completely incredible — " The colonization of Oregon was both conceived and achieved by me."

The Kelley effort at colonization was a complete fiasco, but the Kelley writings did much to stimulate a rapidly growing American interest in Oregon. Books and articles about Oregon flowed from the press in increasing numbers. Lyceum lectures on Oregon were popular. Even by the early '30s there was considerable sentiment that the acquisition and occupation of Oregon was only a matter of time.

OREGON MISSIONS

A new and forceful impetus in favor of Oregon came in 1831, when a little party of two Blackfeet and two Nez Percé appeared in St. Louis to see the white man's civilization and possibly to inquire into the religion of the " black robes." Even a small interest in the white man's religion was little short of startling, since the Indians had been anything but receptive. The story of " the wise men from the West " appeared first in the Methodist *Christian Advocate* for Mar. 1, 1833 and was then given wide circulation in the religious press. Money was solicited and missionaries enlisted for the new and promising venture. Rather curiously the first fruits of a request for Catholic missionaries in the interior was a Methodist mission primarily for the whites of the Willamette Valley.

The desirability of Oregon missions was not new at this time. Earlier reports on the country had stressed their need and during the '20s such appeals were numerous. Acting on these suggestions, and especially on the recommendations of Hawaiian missionaries, the American Board of Commissioners for Foreign Missions (Presbyterian, Congregational, Dutch Reformed) had sent the Reverend Jonathan S. Green to make a survey of the coast in 1829. The Reverend Mr. Green did not actually land in present Oregon, but he saw enough to deplore the moral conditions of the coast and to recommend work among the Indians. The American Board felt, however, that it had more profitable uses for its limited funds.

Vague hopes for a nebulous future mission were crystallized into action by the Indian pilgrims. First in the field were the Methodists, with a small party headed by Jason Lee and his nephew Daniel. Crossing the plains with the Wyeth party in 1834, Jason wrote home : " I rejoice that I am counted worthy to bear the news of salvation to these poor red men of the west, and I would not abandon the enterprise and return home for all the honors of Cesar, Alexander, and Boneparte united, and all the temporal pleasures of the civilized world in addition."

Upon his arrival at Fort Vancouver Jason Lee lost some of his enthusiasm as McLoughlin advised him that work among the Blackfeet was not hopeful and that he had much better stay near the coast. The Methodist mission was finally established in the

Willamette Valley near present Salem. In spite of the handicaps of the wilderness, of a lack of workers, and of sickness the missionaries constructed necessary buildings, planted crops, and began a school. Early realizing the ineffectiveness of work with Indian adults, attention was confined largely to the children and to the French-Canadians, formerly employees of the Hudson's Bay Company, who lived in the region.

Jason Lee felt his greatest handicap to be the lack of an adequate number of helpers and wrote fervent pleas for assistance. Finally he went East himself (1838) to get aid. The fruits of his efforts were several small groups and finally a large party in 1840, at which time several branch establishments were created. The later arrivals included teachers, farmers, and artisans as well as missionaries, but even with this help the results were not impressive.

The American Board was not far outdistanced, even though suffering from a lack of both funds and qualified missionaries. The elderly and ailing Reverend Samuel Parker was sufficiently enthusiastic for the " conversion of the world " but the Board doubted his qualifications and appointed him only reluctantly. Arriving at St. Louis too late in 1834 to join the annual overland caravan, the Reverend Mr. Parker waited until the next year when he was joined by another seeker after health, Dr. Marcus Whitman. When the two men got as far as Green River they decided they needed more help; Parker continued to Fort Vancouver and then home by ship while Whitman retraced his steps.

The trip west in 1836 was something of a bridal tour for Dr. Whitman, who apparently had more in his mind when he returned than the need for more missionaries. Also in the party were Mr. and Mrs. H. H. Spalding and a mechanic. Spalding was an Oberlin man, conscientious, pious, and hard-working, but lacking in humor and inclined to be critical of others; his wife was not in the best of health. The party took the first wagon to go as far west as Fort Boise, but the nature of the country prevented the ladies from riding in it most of the time.

After consultation with McLoughlin the Whitman party established its station at Waiilatpu, near present Walla Walla. As reinforcements arrived new stations were soon started at Lapwai (near present Lewiston) and Tshimakain (near present Spokane). Unfortunately the missionaries could not themselves live in peace and amity, with much of the blame going to Spalding's jealous and critical nature. The new stations were designed in part to separate the belligerent ministry. Then too the Indians proved disappointingly unreceptive to the Gospel or any other phase of white " civilization." Conversions were notably lacking, and braves could not be persuaded to stick to one wife and to give up hunting in favor of agriculture, which to them was " squaw's work."

The Board was discouraged by the bickering of the missionaries and by the lack of conversions; on several occasions it was on the point of abandoning one or more missions. Dr. Whitman's ride east in the winter of 1842–43, by which fable has it he persuaded Tyler and Webster to " save " Oregon, actually did persuade the Board to save the mission. The central mission was finally destroyed by the Indians in 1847 during an uprising in which a quarter of the mission population was killed; the others were abandoned a little later.

Shortly after the establishment of the Whitman mission the Catholics started their own efforts in 1838. They worked with both the Indians and the whites; McLoughlin himself was a Catholic. Best known of the Catholic workers was the Jesuit Pierre Jean De Smet, who came to the mountains in 1840. His field work was not particularly important, but his many popular writings and his raising of money were exceedingly significant. In December 1843 the Columbia mission was made a vicariate apostolic.

The work of the Oregon missionaries may have been of slight importance in the evangelization of the world, but it was highly effective in helping to advertise Oregon. Even the family which confined its reading to the *Christian Advocate,* the publications of the American Tract Society, or the annual reports of the American Board could hardly avoid knowing about, and being interested in, Oregon.

JOHN C. FRÉMONT

Last and greatest of the popularizers of Oregon was John C. Frémont. While he traveled widely in the West his title of " the pathfinder " was hardly merited; his importance was really as the pilot bird of American expansion. His great contribution was the vivid and exciting accounts of his travels that appeared over his name — actually they were written by his wife Jessie, daughter of Senator Benton of Missouri. These books not only stimulated men to desire to go to the Far West, which at the time meant Oregon, but also described the best route and the proper equipment.

Frémont's first expedition left St. Louis in June 1842 guided by that famous trapper and hunter Kit Carson, then thirty-three years old. Carson had been born in Kentucky, but as a boy had been brought by his family to Missouri, where he was apprenticed at the age of fifteen to a saddle maker. He soon ran away to join the Santa Fe traders, and later traveled widely over the West, going even to California. He probably knew more about the western country than any other one man. Under his guidance the Frémont expedition went west over the well-known South Pass route and as far as Wind River. The discoveries made by the party were few, but when Frémont returned to Washington he wrote (or rather his wife wrote) a compelling and attractive description of his adventures and of the country which he had traversed.

Frémont undertook his second expedition (1843) with an unusually large and well-equipped body of men. His equipment was in fact so military in its nature that his superior ordered him back to Washington to explain the cannon. The letter ordering Frémont to return was received and opened by his wife Jessie, who did not redirect it immediately, but wrote to her husband to leave for the West as soon as possible. He did. Near the headwaters of the Arkansas the Frémont party was joined by Kit Carson, and an attempt was made to find a pass through the mountains directly to the west. The failure of this effort forced the group to go north and use the South Pass route. Farther west Frémont examined the Salt Lake district, and it was his later written description which was largely responsible for the Mormon settlement in that region. From Salt Lake he swung north as far as the Whitman mission and Fort Vancouver, and then returned to the South, making a marvelous crossing of the Sierras near the present Virginia City in February. Continuing south through California he eventually returned by approximately the same route that Jedediah Smith had used earlier in going to California. After many adventures and narrow escapes from destruction he was back in St. Louis in 1844.

Frémont found himself a hero when he returned to Washington. Congress had printed 100,000 copies of the report of his first expedition, while additional copies were being sold by private publishing houses. The report of the new expedition was soon written, and proved more popular than its predecessor. The whole nation wanted to read the exciting adventures of Frémont and his party, and some of the readers were sufficiently impressed to pack their belongings and start overland for Oregon. Frémont's clear and accurate description of the route to be followed caused his reports to be used as handbooks for the guidance of immigrants going west.

FARMING MIGRATION TO OREGON

All of the varied interest in Oregon increased the attractiveness of that region for the pioneers considering a movement to the West. The result was that population began to move to Oregon, at first slowly, and then more rapidly. The first of these settlers went in 1839 under the leadership of T. J. Farnham, and thereafter at least a few people went each year. The first considerable group made the trip in 1842, at which time eighteen wagons and over a hundred persons were piloted by Elijah White, formerly a missionary and now a sub-Indian agent for Oregon. The next year a group of a thousand settlers was accompanied by Whitman. The annual migration of 1844 was somewhat smaller, but in the next year nearly 3000 migrants left Westport and other Missouri River towns, and in 1847 the number was between 4000 and 5000.

Immigrants to Oregon followed the well-known Platte River or South Pass route. The starting point was Westport, Independence, or some similar town, and here the migrants provided themselves with wagons, mules, or oxen, and provisions for a trip of about four or five months. If the party left Independence it followed the Santa Fe trail for a short distance and then struck north, with the routes from the other towns entering at various places along the line of march. The trail ran a little west of north, and after it reached the Platte River it followed that stream, eventually reaching Fort Laramie, a distance of 667 miles from Independence. Here a stop was made to rest both the human beings and the livestock, repair the wagons, and buy any necessary extra provisions. Leaving Fort Laramie the trail continued to follow the Platte to the mouth of the Sweetwater and then the Sweetwater. At 947 miles South Pass was reached — a beautiful pass, of which the even grade opposed no obstacle to the passage of wagon traffic. After leaving South Pass the trail followed branches of the Green River and then the Green River to Fort Bridger (1070 miles). Here it struck northward to Fort Hall (1283 miles) and then followed the Snake to the Columbia (1835 miles) and the Columbia to the ocean.

The South Pass route, as just described, was by far the best means of crossing the plains and the Rocky Mountains, and after the latter '20s practically everyone who went to the Far West followed this path. The whole trip to Oregon comprised something over 2000 miles, of which the worst part, in respect to the country traversed, was the Idaho region. Here the rocky country, the hills, the forests, and the lack of good water and grass in certain sections made the trip exceedingly unpleasant and at times dangerous. Farther east, in the plains region, physical obstacles were comparatively less important. Bad river crossings offered certain dangers, and in the course of time vegetation became scarce because of the passage of large numbers of caravans. The traveler also had to plan for a possible lack of food, sickness of his stock, accidents to persons or wagons, and similar misfortunes. The threat of hostile Indians was met by group migration, similar to that of the Santa Fe trade. Each night the wagons were placed in a circle with the tongue of one under the body of the next, to form an embrasure. Sometimes a rope was tied around the wagons and the stock driven inside the enclosure. A guard was posted both day and night to report any sign of hostile Indians. Actually the bloodshed in conflicts with the Indians was remarkably little.

The new settlers of Oregon found themselves in a position that was both isolated and somewhat embarrassing. They were under the joint control of two governments, neither of which had acted to produce even the semblance of law and order. Since the settlers were American in origin they turned to the United States as early as 1838 and asked for recognition and some kind of provision for government. Congress was now embarrassed in its turn, for it was hard to say just what kind of government should be given to a region that was under joint control. The easiest thing to do was nothing, which Congress proceeded to do. In the meantime McLoughlin and the Methodist missionaries furnished a certain amount of order and legal procedure. Eventually the settlers became tired of waiting for Congressional action and followed good frontier precedent by organizing a government of their own (1843).

The increase of the population of Oregon brought a rapid development of sentiment throughout the United States for aggressive action in respect to the Northwest. In 1836–37 Lieutenant W. A. Slacum toured the Pacific Coast for Jackson's information, and in 1838 Lieutenant Charles Wilkes started an extensive survey that ultimately lasted almost five years. These trips indicated quite clearly an increasing official interest in the entire coastal area.

When Ashburton arrived in the United States in 1842 to try to settle the outstanding differences between England and the United States he discussed, among other things, Oregon. Webster was at first willing to accept the boundary of the Columbia River but, when Wilkes returned with the report that while sand bars blocked the mouth of the Columbia there was a good harbor farther north at Puget Sound, he shifted his demands to the line of 49°. Since Ashburton would not accept this boundary the final treaty did not mention Oregon.

EARLY CALIFORNIA

The predominant interest of Americans in Oregon did not mean forgetting California, for California presented varied attractions, including its climate. Even in the early days it was considered a resort for invalids. As one trapper-booster proclaimed: " There never was but one man in California who had the ague. He was from Missouri and carried the disease in his system. It was such a curiosity to see a man shake with the chills that the people of Monterey went eighteen miles in the country to watch him."

The greatest advantages of California over Oregon derived from the fact that it was inhabited by whites. White men meant greater trade, more opportunities for outfitting ships, larger herds of cattle, more agriculture. Even doctors and other professional men found opportunities, while merchants might find settled communities in which to do business. The corresponding drawback was that whites also meant an existing government, which at times was definitely unfriendly. On several occasions American arrivals were jailed in one of the infrequent efforts to stop Anglo-Saxon incursions.

The people of California were themselves an attraction to Americans from the East, since their distinctive costumes and manners allowed them to be labeled " quaint " or " picturesque." The rancher was impressive in rich jacket, velvet or silk vest, velvet or satin breeches slashed at the knee — all decorated with quantities of gold and silver braid and embroidery; a broad red sash and a wide sombrero gave the finishing touches. Women's clothing in comparison was plain, but the lady when dressed in her best was loaded with jewelry, including conspicuous combs if she were married. Visiting New Englanders were shocked by the absence of sleeves and corsets, and completely horrified when the women smoked cigarets. These clothes and manners provided the starting point for juicy and shocking stories to be told to boon companions at home concerning the immorality of California women — stories which did nothing to deter other young men from going west to see these strange things for themselves.

Governmentally California was left largely to her own devices, particularly after Mexican independence, since home troubles were sufficient to occupy the complete attention of national politicians. Most of the time a Mexican appointee held office as governor, but when a local revolution brought a new incumbent he was ordinarily regularized by Mexico. On one occasion California proclaimed a short-lived and rather meaningless independence. In the years between 1822 and 1846 California was blessed by fourteen administrations.

Latin governments have long received the condescending smiles or sneers of Anglo-Saxons. The succession of parades, bombastic proclamations, revolutions instead of elections, and maneuvers instead of battles has seemed amusing, being blamed ordinarily on the Latin temperament and on governmental inexperience. The revolution may be considered, however, as only a more dangerous and therefore more exciting means of producing the results of an election. A succession of revolutions would have been extremely depleting in man power and wealth if fought to the bitter end, and hence the Californians quite intelligently made only a pretense of fighting, after which victory was conceded to the stronger side. The " Battle of Cahuenga Pass " in 1845, for example, brought only the killing of one horse and the wounding of a mule, but it was the decisive battle in a successful revolution.

From the standpoint of land ownership the period of Mexican control was important. Many new land grants were added to the few of Spanish days so that the entire state became a mass of claims. Furthermore, the missions were secularized and their land dispersed. This change had long been planned, but only feeble starts had been made before 1833. Decrees of that and the two succeeding years provided that the property of all twenty-one missions be taken from the hands of the friars, who retained only their religious functions. By the law half of the land went to the mission Indians individually and half went to state trustees. Presumably it could not be alienated, but actually it slipped rapidly into private ownership. Between secularization and land grants most of the state was claimed by individuals — a fact which produced great bitterness at a later time with United States acquisition and a flood of American settlers. Ultimately a United States law put the burden of proof on men who had acquired land before the American occupation — proof that was always difficult and sometimes impossible to obtain.

AMERICAN MIGRATION TO CALIFORNIA

California of the early nineteenth century had political turbulence but social and economic peace. The ranchers dispensed a crude but generous hospitality and the small villages slumbered in the sun. The most active groups were the visitors by ship or land — traders and trappers. Into this calm arrived the first permanent foreign settlers, with the first Americans appearing in 1816. The number of arrivals in any one year was small, probably never exceeding fifty before 1840. In fact the best estimate for California in 1840 gives 380 foreigners, of whom possibly fifty had come overland and the rest by sea. The influence of these strangers, however, was out of proportion to their numbers.

Several American groups in California may be distinguished. Sailors had deserted their ships, searching either for health or for economic opportunity. A scattering of trappers had settled permanently west of the mountains. These two groups were of little importance except as their numbers increased American influence. Some did trapping, either in the interior or along the coast, while others became cowboys (vaqueros) or even ranchers. More important was a handful of individuals who came to California to take advantage of specific opportunities. These men became agents for the hide and tallow trade, entered commercial business, or acquired ranches. They adopted Mexican citizenship, embraced the Catholic faith at least nominally, spoke Spanish, attended fandangos, and even took native wives. Within this small group there was soon vested a control of the majority of California business and the ownership of much California land.

Several Americans were preeminently outstanding. Most important was Thomas O. Larkin, who arrived in 1832 and soon became the leading merchant in Monterey; not only did he become wealthy, but he was first American consul in California, Polk's secret agent in promoting United States annexation, and in general a center of American influence. Isaac Graham found opportunity in a distillery near Monterey; he was always a troublemaker, and together with his band of American riflemen was decisive in the success of the California revolution of 1836. John Marsh was a Harvard graduate, intelligent and well-educated, but miserly and a misanthrope. He sought his fortune in ranching, but also was known as a doctor even though he had no formal medical training; his importance lay largely in his continuous urging of American immigration.

The greatest of the American influences was probably that of John A. Sutter, even though Sutter himself was not an American. He had been born in Baden and grew up in Switzerland. His ambition and ability were balanced by an over-active imagination, an openhanded generosity and a spirit of adventure, all of which brought to him a shot-gun marriage, five children, and a staggering mass of debts. When his varied obligations proved impossibly oppressive he made a hurried departure — just ahead of a warrant for his arrest.

Arriving in America in 1834 at the age of thirty-one, Sutter found himself drawn to a German community in Missouri. There he made many friends but even more debts, whereupon he decided to try his fortune in California. Traveling overland he constructed quite an eminent background and reputation for himself before he arrived at Fort Vancouver. Difficulties of transportation led him to Hawaii and Alaska before he finally reached California in 1839.

In California Sutter was taken at his own valuation. He acquired Mexican citizenship, large tracts of land, and borrowed capital. In the Sacramento Valley he created an impressive establishment which he called New Helvetia. An adobe fort, the necessary buildings, shops, fields, herds, orchards, and vineyards constituted a regal domain. Unskilled labor was done by the Indians under compulsion, but there were also many varied white artisans. Sutter himself lived on the best of food and drink, surrounded by his harem and his faithful retainers, dispensing hospitality in keeping with his self-admitted importance. Sutter even had his own coinage, his own artillery, his own soldiers — Indians in blue and green uniforms trimmed with red — and even the rank of captain in the Mexican army. Unfortunately his one military adventure was on the wrong side of the revolution of 1845, whereby he experienced hurt pride even if not material damage.

Sutter's main importance was in relation to the Americans he always favored. His fort was the first settlement reached by the usual overland traveler, and Sutter in California was just as hospitable as McLoughlin of Oregon. He was generous and helpful to the groups of migrants that started to arrive from over the mountains in 1841 and to Frémont upon several occasions. For these services he was badly paid. Later arrivals stole his property, while Frémont always looked upon him with suspicion and even dislike.

The real American invasion of California began in 1841 with the arrival of the first group of permanent settlers coming overland. First was the John Bidwell group of thirty-two, although other parties also came in the first year. Quite significantly the larger part of the original Bidwell party seceded to go to Oregon. These newcomers had no desire to adopt California ways of life; as their number increased the end of Mexican control of California came nearer and nearer. No additional migrants arrived in 1842, but each succeeding year saw more Americans top the Sierras. In 1845 some 250 arrived, drawn largely by the glowing reports of Frémont and of L. W. Hastings. The migration of 1846 included Sam Brannon and 200 Mormons arriving by ship and was the largest influx before the gold rush.

Migrants to California followed several routes, including the Santa Fe trail and the long swing around the Horn, but their usual path followed the Oregon trail as far as Fort Hall, where they swung southwest. Passing north of Salt Lake they followed the Humboldt River to its Sink. Early travelers then took the route of the Carson River, Walker Pass, and the Stanislaus, but starting in 1844 the favorite route went by the way of the Truckee River and the Truckee Pass.

The trip to California was long and arduous, largely because its worst section lay near the end. Even during the early years wagons could be taken as far as Fort Hall with comparative ease, but then came the arid stretches of present Nevada, where water and grass were infrequent, where equipment wore out, where supplies ran short, and where tempers became frayed. Finally appeared the intimidating masses of the Sierras, with no crossing like the famous South Pass over the main ranges of the Rockies. Progress was slow, difficult, and dangerous. A late start from the East, delays en route, or early winter in the mountains might bring snow which could easily be fatal. Most tragic was the fate of the Donner party, which was snowbound at Donner Lake in the winter of 1846 and was reduced to cannibalism before a fraction was finally rescued. Little wonder that the green vegetation of California looked like heaven to the foot-weary immigrant as he surmounted the last mountain range.

By 1846 California contained possibly 700 Americans, 100 British, 7000 Spanish and 10,000 Indians. While the Americans were still definitely a small minority they were sufficiently numerous to give pause for thought to any Mexican administrator who was familiar with the past history of American expansion.

READINGS

CALIFORNIA AND GENERAL: J. C. Bell, *Opening a Highway to the Pacific, 1838–1846* (1921); D. M. Brown (ed.), *China Trade Days in California* (1947); J. W. Caughey, *California* (1953), chs. 8–14, *History of the Pacific Coast* (1933), chs. 11–16; R. E. Chapman, *A History of California* (1921), chs. 30–35; R. G. Cleland, *The Cattle on a Thousand Hills* (1951), chs. 1, 2, *A History of California* (1922), chs. 1–10, *The Irvine Ranch* (1952), *Pathfinders* (1929)—travelers to California; J. Sutter, *Sutter of California* (1934); A. J. Davis, *Spanish Alta California* (1927); B. De Voto, *The Year of Decision, 1846* (1943), ch. 6—trails; G. P. Hammond (ed.), *The Larkin Papers* (4 vols., 1951–53); R. D. Hunt, *John Bidwell* (1942), chs. 1–6—California pioneer; R. D. Hunt and N. V. G. Sanchez, *A Short History of California* (1929), chs. 1–22; V. E. A. Janssens, *Life and Adventures in California* (1953)—contemporary; A. C. Laut, *The Conquest of Our Western Empire* (1927), chs. 1–5, *The Overland Trail* (1929); O. Lewis, *California Heritage* (1949), chs. 1–7—mostly pictures; G. D. Lyman, *John Marsh, Pioneer* (1930), chs. 28–38—California in 1830s; A. Nevins, *Fremont* (1939), chs. 10–13; A. Ogden, *The California Sea Otter Trade* (1941); W. W. Robinson, *Land in California* (1948); R. A. Rydell, *Cape Horn to the Pacific* (1952); J. A. B. Scherer, *Thirty-First State* (1942), part 1; G. R. Stewart Jr., *Ordeal by Hunger* (1936)—Donner party—(ed.), *The Opening of the California Trail* (1953)—Donner party reminiscences; R. L. Underhill, *From Cowhide to Golden Fleece* (1939)—Larkin; J. Van Nostrand and E. M. Coulter, *California Pictorial* (1948); J. P. Zollinger, *Sutter* (1939)—excellent.

OREGON: E. Allen, *Canvas Caravans* (1946)—trip to Oregon in 1852; B. B. Barker (ed.), *Letters of Dr. John McLaughlin, 1829–32* (1948); W. W. Bischoff, *The Jesuits in Old Oregon* (1945); C. J. Brosnan, *Jason Lee* (1932)—scholarly; C. H. Carey, *A General History of Oregon* (2 vols., 1935–36), vol. 1, chs. 5–19; B. De Voto, *Across the Wide Missouri* (1947), chs. 1, 2, 9, 10, *The Course of Empire* (1952), ch. 9—Grey, Vancouver; C. M. Drury, *Elkanah and Mary Walker* (1940), *Henry Harmon Spalding* (1936), *Marcus Whitman, M. D.* (1937)—detailed; G. W.

Fuller, *The Inland Empire* (3 vols., 1928), chs. 6–17; T. Gay, *Life and Letters of Mrs. Jason Lee* (1936); W. J. Ghent, *The Road to Oregon* (1929), chs. 1–7; D. Henderson, *The Hidden Coast* (1953), chs. 11, 12—Wilkes; F. V. Holman, *Dr. John McLaughlin* (1907); A. B. Hulbert (ed.), *The Call of the Columbia* (1934), *Where Rolls the Oregon* (1933), and D. P. (eds.), *Marcus Whitman, Crusader* (3 vols., 1936–41), *The Oregon Crusade* (1935); M. C. Jacobs, *Winning Oregon* (1938); W. I. Marshall, *Acquisition of Oregon* (2 vols., 1911)—exposes Whitman myth; F. Merk, *Albert Gallatin and the Oregon Problem* (1950)—scholarly; J. Monaghan, *The Overland Trail* (1947), chs. 7–10; R. G. Montgomery, *The White-Headed Eagle* (1934), chs. 13–20—interesting on McLaughlin; F. Parkman, *The Oregon Trail* (1943)—a reprint; F. W. Powell, *Hall Jackson Kelley* (1917), (ed.), *Hall J. Kelley on Oregon* (1932); J. Schafer, *A History of the Pacific Northwest* (1921), chs. 8–10; O. O. Winther, *The Great Northwest* (1947), chs. 2, 3, 7, 9, 10, *The Old Oregon Country* (1951), ch. 2—China trade.

CHAPTER 25

SPOILS
TO THE STRONG

NEW and attractive vistas were opening before delighted American eyes during the 1840s. While Americans had long been optimistic about their future and nothing loath to help make their dreams come true, there had hitherto seemed to be insuperable limits to the expansion of population. For many years the assurance of the existence of a " great American desert " in the plains area, the Spanish occupation of the Southwest, and English dominance in the Northwest had served to convince most people that the ultimate limit of American population was somewhere near the great bend of the Missouri River. Now the flow of settlers across the plains to the Pacific Coast together with the obvious weakness of Mexico gave new horizons to American hopes.

MANIFEST DESTINY

Population expansion and an active desire for more territory went hand in hand, but with some doubt as to which was leading the other. " Manifest destiny " became the current ideal, with the term itself coming into common use during the mid-1840s. More and more people felt that the United States must inevitably own and occupy the entire region from the Mississippi to the Coast, including not only existing parts of the nation, but also the entire area from Texas to the Pacific and north through Oregon. A vocal minority had even larger visions and talked of all of North America, including such neighboring islands as Cuba, while even Hawaii was not outside the orbit of American interest.

The American expansionist justified his desires in numerous ways, but deep in his heart he felt most strongly that the United States was the finest civilization as yet produced on the face of the globe, and that this nation was destined by the will of God to carry the blessings of democratic institutions to less enlightened peoples. In the words of that time, the United States " is destined to manifest to mankind the excellence of divine principles; to extend on earth the noblest temple ever dedicated to the Most High — the Sacred and the True." In fact " we should be recreant to our noble mission, if we refused acquiescence in the high purpose of a wise Providence." The idea of self-defense was seldom mentioned. Material advantages were stressed somewhat less than religious and moral arguments.

The idealistic claim of fulfilling a high mission as foreordained by the Deity was sometimes buttressed by specific claims to the desired territory. In the case of Oregon the joint occupation agreement was in itself an admission that the United States had plausible title to the drainage basin of the Columbia River. With Texas, American claims had been renounced in the treaty of 1819, but with Texan independence annexation was a distinct possibility, and with annexation the most extreme of the Texan claims could be sponsored. As for the Far Southwest, no plausible claims could be advanced.

The trend of American official opinion was made clear as attempts to buy Texas in the late '20s expanded within the next decade to efforts to acquire all of the Southwest, including California. That American public opinion was not as yet prepared for drastic action seemed apparent when both Jackson and Van Buren were cool toward Texan annexation. John Tyler had a more vigorous policy when he succeeded to the presidency upon the death of W. H. Harrison, but even as late as 1844 the Senate rejected decisively a treaty for the annexation of Texas.

The annexation issue became outstanding in the campaign of 1844. The Democrats nominated the expansionist James K. Polk, and the party platform called for the reannexation of Texas and the reoccupation of Oregon. Public opinion responded to this spur so obviously that Henry Clay, the Whig candidate, hedged on his original opposition to expansion until even his best friends had doubt as to where he stood. " Fifty-four forty or fight " became the most popular slogan of the campaign, although as events were finally to show, Polk did not take his battle cry too seriously.

The Polk victory, which included Democratic majorities in both houses of Congress, made certain that further American expansion was just around the corner. Tyler immediately pressed an earlier proposal that Texas be annexed by joint resolution, which would avoid the necessity of the two-thirds Senate majority required by a treaty. This time annexation won, even though only by a short head in the House and by an eyelash in the Senate. On December 29, 1845, the laws of the United States were finally extended formally over Texas, and in the following year Texas members were sitting in Congress.

The annexation of Texas was manifestly an unfriendly act toward Mexico, which had never recognized Texan independence. The immediate result was that the Mexican minister in Washington demanded his passport and left for home. War with Mexico in the near future seemed by no means unlikely, although for the immediate present neither side was willing to take up the sword.

OREGON

When Polk entered the White House he was confronted by the earlier completion of half of his expansion program and by a potential war with Mexico. He still desired to settle the Oregon dispute satisfactorily, but on the other hand he was not anxious to risk two wars at the same time. The English negotiations which had begun during the previous administration were continued. James Buchanan, the new Secretary of State, apparently did not feel himself bound by campaign oratory since he suggested the compromise boundary of 49°. The British representative refused; the greatest concession he had been authorized to accept was 49°, but with free ports to the south. The British negotiator then suggested arbitration, which Buchanan refused.

Polk put pressure on the British government in his annual message to Congress in December 1845. Stating vigorously the American claim as far as 54° 40', he asked Congress for power to give notice of the abrogation of the joint occupation agreement, which was promptly granted. By this time the British Foreign Office became convinced that the longer it delayed a settlement the worse it would be, because American settlers by the hundred were flowing into the disputed area. In fact the Hudson's Bay Company had already recognized the near end of its Columbia River business by moving its main station to Vancouver Island in 1845.

The new British proposal was the acceptance of the line of 49°, except that the entire Vancouver Island should remain British. This proposal was sent by Polk to the Senate without recommendation. The Senate passed a favorable resolution, whereupon a treaty embodying these terms was signed and ratified (1846). While these terms were not so favorable to the United States as some people had hoped, they actually represented an American victory. The American government had long desired the 49° boundary, and presumably the larger demands were principally for the purpose of bargaining.

The acquisition of Oregon did not produce immediately that stability of government which the people of the Northwest desired, for Congress was dilatory. Not until August 13, 1848, was Oregon made a territory, and its first governor, Joseph Lane of Indiana, did not arrive until 1849; the white population of Oregon then was approximately 9000.

The original Territory of Oregon included all the country west of the mountains between 42° and 49°. The first division occurred because of the desire of the handful of people north of the Columbia for a government of their own — in fact they even talked of statehood. The division was accepted by Congress in 1853, when the northern half of the territory was cut off and given the name of Washington; Isaac A. Stevens was the first governor. At the time of the admission of Oregon as a state in 1859 Washington was made to include all the country not within the present limits of Oregon. The present boundaries of Washington were established when Idaho was made a territory in 1863.

TEXAS AND MEXICAN WAR

While the fate of Oregon was still in the balance, Texan troubles went from bad to worse. Not only was the United States confronted by the inevitable hostility arising from the annexation of territory claimed by a neighboring state, but the exact limits of the annexation were in bitter dispute. Mexico had long insisted that the western boundary of Texas was the Nueces River, which had its outlet in Corpus Christi Bay. Texas insisted that its proper boundary was the Rio Grande, thus including a large section of New Mexico. Naturally the United States accepted the more favorable statement and sent General Zachary Taylor with an army to occupy the region in dispute. A border clash seemed only a matter of time.

Sending an army seemed to promise direct and drastic military action, but Polk at the same time made another effort to obtain his desires by bullion instead of bullets. John Slidell was sent as United States minister with authority to release Mexico from pay-

ing American claims which she had recognized if the boundary of
the Rio Grande were admitted. Furthermore Slidell could offer
$25,000,000, and possibly more, for the entire Southwest — that
is, approximately the region later ceded at the end of the Mexican
War. Finally, if this latter proposal were not acceptable, $5,000,000
could be offered for New Mexico. Unfortunately Slidell arrived in
Mexico at an exceedingly unpropitious moment, for a revolution
was in progress and neither side could risk the popular displeasure
that would result from land cessions. In consequence Slidell was
not even received; disgusted, he left Mexico in March 1846.

With the failure of the Slidell mission Polk was in a quandary
as to the proper course to pursue. Clearly he wanted to acquire the
Southwest, not only for itself but also to eliminate what seemed to
be a reasonable chance of England taking at least California in
payment of debts owed her by Mexico. However, there seemed no
way except by war, and Polk had no love for war. There was also
considerable doubt as to whether Congress would be willing to declare and support a war for the acquisition of further slave territory. Polk presented the disturbing problem to his cabinet and
lengthy discussions ensued. Ultimately (May 9) the entire cabinet
with the exception of George Bancroft agreed that the only solution was war. Polk was left to determine the ways and means for
starting such a war.

Even while the cabinet was holding its discussions Taylor had
moved his army as far as the Rio Grande and had seized ships
carrying supplies to the Mexicans on the other side of the river.
These actions were quite understandably labeled aggressive by
the Mexicans, and more important the Mexican government was
willing to risk an American war under the delusion that she had
a chance of victory in consideration of the division of American
opinion. A Mexican detachment crossed the Rio Grande in April
1846 with orders to harass the Americans. Almost immediately
there was a small clash of patrols, unimportant except that it gave
a good pretext for war.

The news of the engagement on the Rio Grande happened to
reach Washington on the very day that the cabinet had decided
on war, and even though Polk was a religious man and May 10
was a Sunday he devoted himself to a war message which was delivered to Congress the next day. The message recited the wrongs
suffered by the United States and the aggressions of Mexico, which
were capped by the invasion of the United States and the spilling

of American blood on American soil. " War exists . . . by the act of Mexico herself." Congress reacted properly and declared war. The rest of the country was aroused. The Mexican invader must be repelled. On to Mexico City!

Even after war had begun Polk made one final effort to achieve his goal by peaceful means. It so happened that at this time Santa Anna was out of power; through a representative he promised that if he were slipped past the American blockade he would favor American desires. Polk was undoubtedly somewhat credulous when he accepted this proposal, but he was not sufficiently naïve to withdraw the army. As might have been expected, the return of Santa Anna to Mexico merely added another Mexican general to be defeated.

CONQUEST OF CALIFORNIA

One of the first operations of the war was the dispatch of an overland expedition to capture Santa Fe and California; unquestionably the American negotiator at the end of the war would be in a stronger position if the United States were already in possession of the territory it desired. The command of the overland party was given to Stephen W. Kearny, then stationed at Fort Leavenworth. His rank was advanced from Colonel to Brigadier-General. Kearny immediately sent supply trains ahead, and then departed with some 1700 dragoons and sixteen cannon. On August 18 he entered Santa Fe without opposition, and soon he established a civil government under Charles Bent. Leaving the bulk of his army at Santa Fe under the command of Colonel A. W. Doniphan, he continued west with 300 men. Doniphan in turn was relieved upon the arrival of General Sterling Price and moved south to reinforce Taylor.

Kearny obviously was not impressed with the difficulty of conquering California or he would not have left the bulk of his army in Santa Fe. Not far from Santa Fe he met Kit Carson, who was riding to Washington with news that California had already fallen. Upon receiving this information Kearny sent back two-thirds of his men and continued with the remaining hundred. He arrived near San Diego in December 1846.

Following Kearny across the plains came the so-called Mormon Battalion, which had been enlisted from the ranks of the Mormons, who were just then starting their exodus across the plains. The march of the battalion across the continent was one of the more notable exploits of the war. Leaving the Missouri River on July 20 the Mormons limped into Santa Fe between October 9 and 12. There they acquired their second wind for continuing the march to San Diego, where they arrived late in January 1847 under the command of Philip St. George Cooke. This 1400-mile march was distinctly a remarkable bit of travel, even though the battalion had no influence on the course of the war.

The actual conquest of California had taken place before the arrival of the eastern groups, even Kearny. The story is remarkably difficult to relate in spite of a tremendous amount of research concerning its actors and actions. In particular, the relations of each man involved in the American conquest to the United States government, and the motives which influenced him at any particular time, remain matters of considerable speculation.

A preview of California's annexation came on October 19, 1842, when Commodore T. A. C. Jones seized the town of Monterey. Jones had orders to take this action if and when war began between the United States and Mexico. The day after the seizure he decided that his impression of war was an error, so he restored the town with apologies and sailed away. His actions made clear, however, the expectations of the American government and the feebleness of Mexican control of California.

The California pot began to simmer when Polk entered upon the Presidency in 1845. His confidential agent in California was T. O. Larkin, who had been United States consul since 1843. Larkin was given the rather equivocal suggestions that he should not plot against the existing California government, but that a revolution might be a very fortunate event. Larkin's reaction was to plot a revolution which was scheduled for 1847 or 1848. The revolutionists were to include not only recent American arrivals but also native Californians.

The second marionette operated by strings pulled in Washington was Commodore John D. Sloat, who was sent to the Pacific Coast with orders to seize Monterey in the event of war with Mexico. If he also had further and secret orders they remain unknown. The seizure orders were themselves standard in the navy, and designed not so much to help win the war as to forestall British action. Not long after Sloat left the East Commodore Robert F. Stockton was sent after him (October 1845) with sealed orders for Larkin.

A third actor in the coming drama was John C. Frémont, who

probably had hopes of becoming the star of the production. Through his contacts with his father-in-law Benton he had considerable information as to the interests and plans of the American government. Frémont was sent across the plains in the summer of 1845 ostensibly to explore the sources of the Arkansas, Rio Grande, and Colorado rivers, Great Salt Lake, and the Sierra and Cascade mountains. Later there was much dispute as to the exact meaning of the Frémont orders, and also question as to whether he had additional secret orders or at least suggestions. A decision is difficult because Frémont himself seems to have wavered between conflicting impulses and his later recollections were somewhat different from the statements he made at the time. But whatever his instructions there is no question as to the nature and accomplishments of his party.

Frémont's expedition had several curious characteristics, of which the first to become obvious was the unusual size and composition. Sixty-two members picked for their marksmanship and devoting their spare time to target practice were surely excessive for an avowedly peaceful exploration, even in a hostile wilderness. Then too they did no exploring on their way west, not even mapping the Oregon trail although this was one of their stated purposes. The fact was that the party headed straight for California by the most practicable route, dividing into two groups to cross the mountains. Frémont himself was at Sutter's Fort early in September and from this point he rode down to Monterey, where he had a long and confidential talk with Larkin. Presumably this conversation did not deal entirely with the beauties of California scenery, and certainly Frémont's stated instructions gave no authorization to enter a foreign country.

Instead of replenishing his supplies and leaving California, Frémont obtained permission to settle down for the winter. The only restriction on his stay was that he should not approach the coast. When spring arrived he still showed no signs of leaving — in fact he moved closer to Monterey and started to construct a fort. By this time Governor José de Castro had become justifiably suspicious of Frémont's intentions and ordered him to leave Mexican territory, whereupon Frémont refused, began to fortify his position, and in March 1846 one of his men raised the United States flag. In justice to Frémont it should be added that the flag was probably not raised as a result of his personal orders.

Just as an armed clash seemed probable Frémont apparently

changed his mind, for he started north. At first his progress was slow and defiant, with his well-equipped and rested force making only some six to eight miles a day, but after passing Sutter's Fort he moved more rapidly. Castro boasted of having driven out the Yankees. Just beyond the California border Frémont again seemed hesitant, for he slowed down and developed an intense interest in the painstaking exploration of a hitherto completely unattractive region. Almost it seemed as though he were waiting for something or somebody.

While Frémont was loitering in the north there appeared in California one Lieutenant A. H. Gillespie of the United States Marine Corps, traveling in the disguise of an invalid merchant and bearing new instructions for Larkin and Frémont. As published later these instructions were completely innocuous — certainly not worth the long trip to California; the curious aspect of the matter was that Gillespie had thought the messages so damaging that he had learned them by heart and destroyed them before traveling through Mexico.

When Gillespie arrived at Monterey he immediately sought out Larkin and the two men talked long and earnestly. Then he hurried after Frémont. As Frémont told the story almost a half century later he galloped back forty-five miles in a single day to meet Gillespie, for " then I knew the hour had come." The two men spent a long evening before the fire. What they said must remain a mystery, but the next day Frémont turned south.

The maneuverings of American officials coincided with a series of apparently unrelated events in California. The American settlers had grown progressively more hostile to Mexican rule and had started to talk revolution. Upon Frémont's return they carried on their plotting in his camp. Rather unexpectedly Frémont discouraged such talk; possibly his personal plans were different. Regardless of such discouragement, however, some thirty-five settlers, of whom the best known was William Ide, declared their independence (June 14, 1846) in an oratorical proclamation and raised the Bear Flag of revolt.

The first stages of the revolution were considered by native Californians as nothing but thievery by disaffected nomads, but the movement was taken more seriously after the occupation of Sonoma and the capture of several loyal Mexican citizens. Frémont talked to Ide and others of the revolutionists, but then decided to maintain something that he could at least call neutrality. He gave the rebels advice and guarded their prisoners — an unusual form of neutrality, even though he did no actual fighting.

The ultimate importance of the Bear Flag Revolt was negligible for by early July came the news of the war with Mexico. Immediately Sloat landed and took possession of Monterey; when Stockton finally appeared he took Sloat's place. Frémont enlisted most Americans, including the Bear Flaggers, in his " California battalion." Next Frémont and Stockton advanced jointly to the south and captured Los Angeles. The main American force then returned north leaving a small detachment under Gillespie to hold Los Angeles. California had thus been conquered easily and practically bloodlessly, and it was this news that was carried east by Kit Carson and influenced General Kearny to send most of his troops back to Santa Fe.

The only real fighting in California came after it supposedly had been conquered. Native Californians, finding the Gillespie rule of Los Angeles distasteful, revolted and drove him out of the city. Just at this time Kearny appeared on the horizon and was attacked by the Californians. While he reported the engagement as an American victory the facts seem otherwise, for his casualties were comparatively large and he did little more than prevent complete annihilation. Luckily Stockton and Frémont returned, and with the support of the Kearny forces were able to re-establish American control in southern California.

The noisiest of the California battles was waged at the end of the war between Frémont and Kearny as to whom should be in supreme command. Stockton had placed Frémont in control and then sailed away. Kearny bore orders from Washington giving himself the top command, and in any case he outranked Frémont. After a spirited exchange of insults Kearny started home, taking Frémont along virtually as a prisoner. Tried by court martial Frémont was found guilty of mutiny, disobedience, and unbecoming conduct. The President pardoned him, but Frémont was so angered by what he felt to be injustice after meritorious service to his country that he resigned his commission. Much of his later activity reflected no credit on his abilities as an explorer, a businessman, or a public servant, but his Presidential candidacy showed his continued popularity. His historical reputation suffered particularly from his speculations and from his unsatisfactory record in the Civil War. It would have been better if he had died before Kearny reached California.

TREATY OF GUADALUPE HIDALGO

The conquest of California was but a small part of the campaigns of the Mexican War. The first really important action was the southerly advance of Zachary Taylor. While Taylor was no military genius and has been much criticized both at the time and later, he did succeed in capturing Monterrey and in repulsing a larger army under Santa Anna. Actually this battle was only a very moderate success, since Santa Anna was himself not an excellent commander and his army was poorly trained and equipped, but Taylor became popular as the " hero of Buena Vista " and had the way opened to the Presidency.

Polk was by no means pleased with the Taylor movements, which he considered inconclusive, and put more trust in General Winfield Scott, who landed at Vera Cruz in 1847. During his advance toward the city of Mexico he defeated a new army under the command of Santa Anna. At the end of a completely victorious campaign he entered the city of Mexico on September 14, 1847. At this point he was in a position to dictate whatever terms of peace he desired.

Before the military operations were completely victorious Polk sent a representative to Mexico to try to conclude a peace. For this purpose he chose Nicholas P. Trist, chief clerk of the State Department, and a worse choice could hardly have been made, since Trist was a man of only mediocre ability, chronic indecision, great stubbornness, meticulous regard for the niceties of behavior, and great virtuosity with the pen. His instructions were to obtain Texas, New Mexico, Upper and Lower California, and the right-of-way across the isthmus of Tehuantepec. For these concessions he might offer $30,000,000 plus the cancellation of some $3,000,000 of American claims. The least he was to accept was the Rio Grande to El Paso and then due west to the coast; for this he could offer $15,000,000.

Trist's first trouble was with Scott, for the men disliked each other on sight and for a time refused even to speak, confining themselves to writing long letters of justification. Eventually the two became close friends and Scott permitted an armistice for negotiations. Santa Anna proved most amenable to such discussions, for he had hopes of getting the $30,000,000 to use on his army. Ultimately the armistice collapsed, Santa Anna fled the country, and Scott took the city of Mexico.

Polk was not pleased with the Trist negotiations, and particularly since American popular sentiment was beginning to insist that Mexico disgorge a greater part of her territory. Polk sympathized with these expanded aspirations and ordered Trist to come home. These orders were disregarded by Trist, who placed his individual judgment and morality ahead of his obedience to authority. Trist kindheartedly refused to injure Mexico more than necessary to encourage Mexican confusion. The treaty he signed early in 1848 was the minimum first orders — Texas, New Mexico, Arizona, California, and the region to the north for $15,000,000 plus claims up to $3,250,000.

When the Trist treaty arrived in Washington Polk was very angry, but at the same time embarrassed. His term was coming to an end and he had renounced a second candidacy. Opposition to the war raised some questions as to whether Congress would vote adequate funds for its continuance. In consequence he sent the treaty to the Senate, where it was ratified. The Treaty of Guadalupe Hidalgo marked the near end of American continental expansion. Later additions were the small Gadsden purchase of 1853 and the purchase of detached Alaska in 1867.

LATER FILIBUSTERING

The end of continental expansion can today be recognized, but at the time it was not immediately apparent. During the years after 1850 the preliminaries of expansion continued to occur as American settlers flowed across both the northern and southern boundaries and filibusters went to the south; the only difference from earlier years was that these expansions did not result in annexation. Most famous of the filibusters of the '50s was that " man of destiny " William Walker, slight, gray-eyed, dapper, cultured, and soft-spoken. With an " army " of thirty-three men he established in November 1853 the Republic of Lower California, with the necessary complement of president, flag, and constitution, and then " invaded " Mexico. The invasion failed, and Walker retreated to the United States where he was haled before a court for the violation of Mexican neutrality. The common story is that the jury took but eight minutes to bring a verdict of " not guilty."

Walker's next project showed more ingenuity and produced greater success. In 1855 he sailed to Nicaragua, landed, and seized control of the government, which he operated for two years. His ultimate defeat and execution can be traced not so much to Nicaraguan patriots as to the work of " Commodore " Vanderbilt, whom he had antagonized. Walker's untimely death was particularly sad in realization that he might well have been an American hero of the stature of Houston if only he had not lived so late that he did not fit into the ideology and desires of the United States.

Most fantastic of the expansionists were the Knights of the Golden Circle, organized at Lexington, Kentucky, in 1854. Their central theme was the development of a magnificent slave empire, which was to be a circle with Havana as the center and with a radius of some 1200 miles, which would include everything from southern North America through northern South America. The order had three degrees — Knights of the Iron Hand (military), Knights of the True Faith (financial), and Knights of the Columbian Star (governmental). It was credited with having helped inspire such men as Walker. Plans for a Mexican invasion in 1860 finally fizzled and the order was lost in the Civil War.

COMPROMISE OF 1850

As a result of the treaty of Guadalupe Hidalgo the United States was left in possession of an immense new domain for which some governmental provisions had to be made in view of the considerable white settlements. Texas was of course already a state, but her boundaries remained uncertain, while New Mexico and California were under military government, and the Mormon community of Utah existed under a government of its own devising. The problem of acceptable governments was made more acute by the slavery issue, and Congress debated acrimoniously. Before that debate ended President Polk's term of office had expired, President Taylor had died, and President Fillmore had assumed office.

The Congressional debate concerning the government for the new territories was highly significant for the future, but the men and women of the Southwest were hardly willing to sit passively and twiddle their fingers while Congressmen and Senators made oratorical reputations for themselves. The great interior basin, approximately present Utah and Nevada, was organized by the Mormons in 1849 as the state of Deseret, with the usual constitution and state officers (see Chapter 26). Population was inadequate for statehood, and there was considerable doubt as to whether Congress would be willing to tolerate polygamy, which shortly was to be linked with slavery as " twin evils."

The settlements of the upper Rio Grande had been organized

by Kearny as the Territory of New Mexico. Theoretically they
included the Arizona white population, but actually physical distance prevented any real control. A revolution early in 1847 was
suppressed by the military; in its progress Governor Charles Bent
was killed, which at least saved some future unpleasantness, since
Kearny had had no power to establish a territorial government.
During the Congressional debate after the war the people of New
Mexico petitioned for territorial government and ultimately (1850)
formulated a state constitution which was accepted by the voters
8371 to 39.

The New Mexico situation was further complicated by boundary
difficulties. The New Mexicans wanted an independent government of their own which would include the Arizona settlers —
somewhat to the distaste of the Arizonans. More important, Texas
had long claimed as far west as the Rio Grande — a claim that at
one time had been accepted by the United States government. To
reinforce her title Texas had organized the county of New Mexico
and sent county officials who were prevented by the army from
functioning. Incidentally there still remained the unsettled problem as to whether Texas itself should be divided into several states.

Californians were even more insistent upon a better local government than were their eastern neighbors. Americans had not
been enamored of Mexican rule, but they were almost equally
displeased with army control, and their number increased vastly
with the gold rush. In general the office of alcalde tended to continue under the new dispensation, but here and there communities
set up their own local governments. The desire for a more effective
and representative government became so strong that the military
governor finally called a convention to establish a state government, feeling that he could not prevent such a convention in any
case and that he might as well obtain the advantage of having
sponsored it.

The California convention met at Monterey in September 1849.
The place of meeting was in itself an indication of the fact that
it was more a creature of the old than of the new order. Three-
quarters of its members had arrived in California before the gold
rush, and included not only such men as Larkin and Sutter but
also a sprinkling of native Californians. The resulting constitution,
ratified overwhelmingly by the electorate, produced a frame of
government and also the present boundaries of the state. The first
governor was Peter H. Burnett. The first legislature met at San

Jose in December 1849, and among other actions selected John C. Frémont and W. M. Gwin as United States Senators. Here was a full-fledged and active, although extralegal government with which Congress was confronted.

The debate from which the Compromise of 1850 emerged was notable for the last important appearance of the three men who had done so much to dominate the American political scene of the past generation — Henry Clay, Daniel Webster, and John C. Calhoun. The final compromise was proposed by the aging Clay, supported by Webster and particularly in his famous Seventh of March speech, and opposed by Calhoun who as usual couched his arrogant demands in soft words. The original compromise was stated in a single bill but failed of passage because of the combination of opponents. Ultimately all of the separate measures were passed.

The Compromise of 1850 provided for the admission of California under the constitution which was already in operation, which meant as a free state. Texas was paid $10,000,000 to accept suitable boundaries, and of course remained a slave state. New Mexico, including present Arizona, became a Territory; statehood did not come for another sixty years. Utah also became a Territory, with statehood to be delayed some forty-five years, primarily on the polygamy issue (see Chapter 26). In addition, slave trade was prohibited in the District of Columbia and a more stringent fugitive slave law was enacted.

The Compromise of 1850 has long been recognized as a turning point in American history. In the East the old compromising spirit was ebbing rapidly with the passing of the conciliatory generation and the arrival of more drastically minded younger men. In the West the formation of new states and territories marked very clearly the breakdown of the old concept of a permanent Indian frontier; no longer could men hold that the limits of white settlement had been reached at the great bend of the Missouri. Equally important the total continental limits of the United States had been approximately attained. Only the small area of the Gadsden Purchase and the noncontiguous Alaska were later to be added. The old and aggressive spirit of the past, which had expanded the United States from Atlantic to Pacific, was to recede for over a generation, and was then to reappear only in terms of overseas interests. Much of continental United States remained to be populated, but only a little remained to be acquired.

READINGS

E. D. Adams, *British Interests and Activities in Texas* (1910);
G. W. Ames, Jr. (ed.), *A Doctor Comes to California* (1943)—
with Kearny; C. A. Barker (ed.), *Memoirs of Elisha Oscar
Crosby* (1945)—gold rush; A. B. Bender, *The March of Empire*
(1952)—army; A. H. Bill, *Rehearsal for Conflict* (1947)—Mexican War; J. W. Caughey, *California* (1953), chs. 15, 18, *History
of the Pacific Coast* (1933), chs. 15, 17, 21; R. G. Cleland, *A
History of California* (1922), chs. 10–16, 18; C. Coan, *A History
of New Mexico* (3 vols., 1925), vol. 1, chs. 19, 20; B. De Voto,
The Year of Decision, 1846 (1943); R. L. Duffus, *The Santa Fe
Trail* (1930), chs. 12–14; B. Dyer, *Zachary Taylor* (1946), chs.
8–11; W. H. Ellison, *A Self-Governing Dominion, 1849–1860*
(1950)—California; E. Fergusson, *New Mexico* (1951), ch. 18;
J. D. P. Fuller, *The Movement for the Acquisition of All Mexico*
(1936); P. N. Garber, *The Gadsden Treaty* (1923); G. R. Gibson,
Journal of a Soldier Under Kearny and Doniphan (1934); B. C.
Grant (ed.), *Kit Carson's Own Story* (1926), part 2; L. Greene,
The Filibuster (1937)—Walker; H. Hamilton, *Zachary Taylor*
(1941), chs. 11–18; R. D. Hunt and N. V. de G. Sanchez, *A Short
History of California* (1929), chs. 23, 24, 27, 28; M. C. Jacobs,
Winning Oregon (1938); M. M. J. Kelly, *Joseph Lane* (1942);
W. C. Kennerly, *Persimmon Hill* (1948)—with Doniphan; D.
Lavender, *Bent's Fort* (1954), chs. 10–17; S. B. McKinley and
S. Bent, *Old Rough and Ready* (1946), chs. 9–15—Taylor; A.
Nevins, *Fremont* (1939), chs. 15–21; R. N. Richardson and C. C.
Rister, *The Greater Southwest* (1935), chs. 6, 9; G. L. Rives, *The
United States and Mexico, 1821–1848* (2 vols., 1913), chs. 20–31;
J. A. B. Scherer, *Thirty-First State* (1942), parts 2, 3; J. H.
Smith, *The Annexation of Texas* (1911), *The War With Mexico*
(2 vols., 1919); N. W. Stephenson, *Texas and the Mexican War*
(1921), chs. 8–14; R. L. Underhill, *From Cowhides to Golden
Fleece* (1939)—Larkin; A. K. Weinberg, *Manifest Destiny*
(1935)—arguments; O. P. White, *Texas* (1945), chs. 14, 15;
R. K. Wyllys, *Arizona* (1950), ch. 5.

CHAPTER 26

THE MORMONS

EVEN as Taylor and Scott were driving south into Mexico a new type of migration was crossing the plains to the Far West as the Mormons began (1846) their magnificent trek to escape the unhappiness that had been their lot in the Mississippi Valley. This religious community became the first important white population element of the inter-mountain basin, and constituted an important part of the ever increasing evidence that the ideal of a permanent frontier was but temporary.

MORMON ORIGINS

The Mormons, or more properly the members of The Church of Jesus Christ of Latter-Day Saints, belonged to a recently developed Protestant Christian sect. Their prophet and originator was Joseph Smith, who had been born in 1805, the son of a poor Vermont farmer. Smith grew to maturity in central New York state, a region which was unusually concerned with religious experiences at that time. Even at an early age Joseph Smith saw visions and received revelations.

Mormonism was based not only upon the revelations to the prophet but also upon the sacred Book of Mormon, which was dug from the ground near Palmyra, New York, in 1827 by Smith, who was acting upon revelation. The Book of Mormon was engraved on golden plates, and its authenticity was attested by a " cloud of witnesses "; it could be read directly in English by the use of lenses which contained the magical stones Urim and Thummim. The book told how certain lost tribes of Israel had wandered to America, where ultimately the bad Lamanites (Indians) had destroyed the good Nephites about 400 A.D. The only remaining Nephites were the distinguished prophet Mormon and his son Moroni; Mormon wrote the bulk of the book describing the wanderings and fate of the Nephites, while his son completed the work. Smith's divinely revealed mission was to reconquer America, " the promised land," from the wicked Lamanites.

The authenticity of the Book of Mormon has often been questioned, and it has been labeled a farrago of nonsense stated in pseudo-Biblical language, with many near quotations from the Bible, Shakespeare, and Pope, and with particular attention devoted to the problems of the farmer of central New York. On the other hand thousands of intelligent and thoughtful people have accepted the book as genuinely inspired and a proper guide to the higher things of life.

After the publication of the Book of Mormon, Joseph Smith and his friends sold it from door to door. Purchasers were not easy to find in the comparative poverty of central New York, but many of the readers became believers and ultimately a formal church was established on April 6, 1830. The new Saints were disturbed by the skepticism of doubting neighbors and consequently some of them followed Smith in 1831 to establish a homogeneous group of their own at Kirtland, Ohio, near Cleveland. Here was developed a closely knit religious community, in which all property was vested in the church. A temple was built, houses constructed, farms put under cultivation, and stores and a bank opened.

Extensive missionary work was a characteristic of the Mormons from early days, and provided the basis for the later spectacular increase in numbers. Indian missions were obviously desirable in view of the purpose of the faith. In addition there were missions for white Americans, and before the end of the decade work was extended to Europe. Missionaries were sent in pairs as part of their religious duties and were highly successful, particularly in England. Thousands of European converts soon were streaming to the new world to expand the numbers of the Saints. England alone sent 4000 converts in the years between 1840 and 1846.

Most important of the early converts was Brigham Young, who saw the light in 1832. Young resembled Smith in having been born in Vermont and reared in New York. By trade he had been a joiner, house painter, and glazier. By nature he had a forceful and attractive personality, a ready tongue, and excellent judgment concerning men and affairs. His most important early work was as a missionary, and he had tremendous success in England. He was sufficiently prominent to be named a member of the Council of Twelve Apostles in 1835, but he never came into close contact with the prophet.

The Mormons were never happy in Kirtland. Gentile neighbors were suspicious and frequently outright hostile, accusing the Mormons of sacrilege and immorality; rumors of polygamy were passed from mouth to mouth in spite of indignant Mormon denials. Even more important the Mormons were rent by internal dissensions as various individuals claimed personal revelations to rival those of the prophet; each such individual tended to become the nucleus for a small group of malcontents. Then too the panic of 1837 brought serious distress. Smith's investments in land, industry, and banking began to show signs of strain; in fact the prophet agreed that his best abilities were not in the field of business.

The solution of the Kirtland difficulties was to move the community father west — actually an old plan, which had been in Smith's mind at least as early as his first western trip in 1831. The new " promised land " was Zion, Missouri, which was known to the gentiles by the name of Independence, and to this place the Mormons had been moving in larger numbers during the '30s than to Kirtland. Unfortunately the people of Missouri proved no more hospitable than those of Ohio. In 1833 the Saints were driven out of Independence, going to the Missouri counties to the north. Here it was that the prophet came when conditions in Kirtland became intolerable in 1838. But again the gentiles proved hostile, and mobs brought damage to Mormon life and property. The crisis came in 1839, and the governor of Missouri not only refused to act against the mob but said: " The Mormons must be treated as enemies and must be exterminated or driven from the State if necessary, for the public good."

NAUVOO AND JOSEPH SMITH

The new Mormon haven was the town of Commerce, renamed Nauvoo, which lay on the Illinois side of the Mississippi, about halfway between Fort Madison and Keokuk. An impressive city was planned, and by 1845 Nauvoo's 15,000 inhabitants made it the largest town in Illinois. As with each such settlement, one of the earliest activities was the beginning of construction of a temple. Necessary homes and public buildings were erected and farming begun. The people worked sufficiently hard to produce an almost immediate appearance of prosperity. Thrift, religious earnestness, and content were in evidence for even the most casual eye.

The Mormon community of the 1840s, both religious and lay, was dominated by the striking personality of Joseph Smith. While Smith considered himself a prophet he laid no claims to divinity or even to personal perfection. Naturally impressive, he was over six feet tall and could carry his 200 pounds easily and well. He was handsome in appearance and had a magnificent physique, which he delighted in exhibiting by wrestling with any and all visitors. A man of strong passions and lusty with life, he loved his friends and hated his enemies, worked hard, ate heartily, and sometimes drank to excess. His versatile mind embraced activities which ranged from the translation of Egyptian papyri to managing the combined grocery store and hotel named the Nauvoo House. His most magnificent gesture was to run for the Presidency (1844) on a platform of territorial expansion, abolition, a national bank, and penal reform; Mormon missionaries did his campaigning. With all these activities he never lost an almost childlike love of display, whether of his own mental powers and religious authority or of his impressive uniform, embellished with plentiful gold lace and brass buttons, which he wore as head of the Nauvoo Legion.

The Mormons always placed great stress on the importance of the individual, but also held that the individual could attain his maximum stature only by working with other individuals to develop the highest possible temporal and spiritual values. Spiritual values were of course the ultimate goal, and in this respect the Mormons differed from other Protestant faiths only in the extent of their application of religious teachings. The Mormons held that all property really belonged to the church and was permitted to individuals only on the tolerance of the church. The church was active in all phases of life, including economic endeavor, philanthropy, and even amusements. The individual went through elaborate rituals upon entering the church and on getting married, performed some kind of special mission for the church, and paid tithes through his life. Mormons could not lay aside their religion on weekdays and then parade it on Sundays.

While the church was extremely paternalistic it was also benevolent and democratic, at least in theory. Every male member of the church was also a member of one of the two priesthoods, and each higher officer was elective. No individual was neglected and no individual could go unclothed, unhoused, and unfed if he were willing to work. Child labor was opposed, but every adult was supposed to work. Women were especially well-treated, and were even allowed to vote in the early Salt Lake settlement. It was no accident that Utah became one of the first states to have woman suffrage.

The basic social institution for the Mormons was the family, not only to promote morality and care for children, but because the Mormons felt that marriage for the woman was a necessity for salvation. Herein lies an important reason for the institution of polygamy in a society which had a surplus of women. Here too lies the basis for the development of two kinds of marriage, of which one was for eternity only and did not include physical cohabitation on this earth. The family was the only proper place for sex expression, and large families were much to be desired. The man was head but not master of his family, for his wife was an individual and not a slave.

Most discussed of Mormon practices was that of polygamy, which was based on a revelation to the prophet, and hence looked to the future rather than to the past. While the practice was denied publicly until after the migration to Utah, the original revelation had come to Smith presumably in 1831. Not until Nauvoo did the prophet divulge his revelation to a few of the leaders, by whom it was received with considerable consternation and heart-burnings, since it violated deeply ingrained ideas of morality. Polygamy was but little practiced in Nauvoo except by Smith, who had a total of at least twenty-eight wives, and even this considerable family apparently did not entirely limit his affections.

Plural marriage among the Mormons has very properly been called " Puritan polygamy." A second marriage was undertaken only after much prayer and also after consultation with and acceptance by the first wife. Elaborate ceremonies emphasized the gravity of the occasion. Licentiousness and sensuality were frowned upon whether inside or outside of marriage, and adultery was punished severely. Marriage was a serious duty, both temporal and religious. By plural marriage the surplus women, many of them from England, were given the security of homes of their own, and an opportunity for salvation, while the number of children in the community was increased desirably. The husband was expected to treat his wives equally. Ordinarily the wives were good friends and enjoyed the companionship of living together in many cases.

Frequently a man married sisters. In fact the women gave little evidence of having any objection to polygamy.

Regardless of the possible justifications for polygamy, the gentiles near Nauvoo considered it as an evidence of moral turpitude, and held that it was a fitting concomitant of the sacrilege of calling " Jo " Smith a prophet. These Illinois farmers may have been just a little jealous of the pleasures they pictured in polygamy and certainly they were envious of the prosperity of the industrious Mormon community. In politics they also resented the Mormons, since the latter voted as a unit and were able to hold the balance of power within the state, with consequent favors for the city of Nauvoo. The enmity of the gentiles soon produced mob violence in the form of fires, thefts, malicious destruction, and personal attacks. Ultimately Joseph Smith and his brother Hyrum were placed in the Carthage jail, presumably for their protection; a mob stormed the jail and murdered both men (1844).

BRIGHAM YOUNG AND THE MOVE WEST

The murder of Joseph Smith inspired several rival claimants to compete for his power as head of the church. Most picturesque was James Jesse Strang, who later had himself crowned " King of Beaver Island " in northern Lake Michigan. Most able and ultimately successful was Brigham Young, who luckily returned from a missionary tour at the psychological moment. Young first obtained the confidence of most of the Mormons and then consolidated his power by excommunicating rival leaders. Several seceding bands, including one headed by Joseph Smith III, son of the prophet, claimed to be the real repositories of the true faith.

Brigham Young faced as serious problems as ever confronted any leader. The death of Smith had removed the central figure of the group and hence reduced its cohesion. Internal dissension continued to be troublesome even though the excommunication of rival leaders made it less effective. The hostility of the neighboring gentiles meant that again the entire community had to be moved if it were not to face dissolution. But where could the Mormons go? And could they find the depths of courage once more to abandon the fruits of years of work and start life again in poverty?

Young's answer to his problem was to start the evacuation of Nauvoo in February 1846, in the heart of the winter and with no definite objective in view. Led by a small party under Young, groups of Mormons crossed the ice of the Mississippi and struggled through the roadless mud of Iowa. These people were leaving a settled and prosperous community with little more than the clothes on their backs and the few possessions that could be packed in wagons. Their farms and homes were deserted to acquisitive Illinois farmers; furniture, crockery, and other personal possessions became the toys of future generations of Illinois children. Embarking toward the setting sun, they were hazarding their very lives for the attainment of an ideal — the right to live and work and worship God as they pleased.

The migration of 1846, like every Mormon undertaking, was organized thoroughly and effectively. Small groups went ahead to establish temporary camps, where cabins were frequently built and crops planted for the benefit of later arrivals. Then came the larger parties which included the old and young, the sick and the infirm, for by fall the gentiles had ejected the last of the Mormons from Nauvoo. Even with the best possible planning, provisions soon became scarce. Some of the young men worked for the Iowa farmers along their route, others sold the products of their hard work, while a brass band gave concerts both to help their own morale and to raise funds. But even at the best, conditions were desperately bad. Slogging through Iowa mud, pelted by spring rain, subsisting on a meager and monotonous diet, only the magnificent faith of these people kept them moving. Many a Mormon man or woman breathed his last on the Iowa prairie and many a Mormon baby was ushered into the world on a blanket placed under a wagon box.

The principal winter quarters for the cold weather of 1846–47 were near present Omaha, although other Mormon communities were scattered through the surrounding countryside. Here it was that the Mormon Battalion was recruited for the long march to San Diego. A forest of tents and crude cabins kept out at least part of the elements. Food was scarce and even the usual crude tools of frontier life were frequently lacking. The poor diet and exposure meant a dreadful mortality, and at times the living had difficulty in providing burials for the dead. Brigham Young and other leaders exhibited day by day the magnificent courage which alone insured the survival of the group.

WESTERN COLONIZATION

The Missouri River was but the first step in the march to a Zion which would be far distant from the troubles with hostile gentiles; there is no evidence, however, that the Mormons tried to get outside the boundaries of the United States. Early in 1847 Young received his first and only revelation — that the Saints should continue their march west. In April he took the road again, this time at the head of a party of 148, which included three women and two children; the bulk of the party was composed of young men of a variety of skills needed to establish a new community. Guided by Frémont's writings, Young followed the usual Platte River-South Pass route, except that he took the north rather than the more used south bank of the Platte. From Fort Bridger he cut directly to Great Salt Lake, where he announced, " This is the place." Immediately the party set to work to start houses and plant crops in preparation for later arrivals. As for Young, he again turned his face east to meet and direct later emigrants.

While Salt Lake Valley was described to the Saints in glowing terms, the actuality was exceedingly drab. The lake was beautiful but useless except for bathing parties. The land was treeless, and in fact had almost no vegetation except sagebrush. The ground was hard and baked by the sun. Everywhere was desolation and waste. Irrigation was necessary before the first crops could be planted with any hope of success. The first buildings had to be closely packed and arranged as a fort to provide against possible Indian attacks.

Other parties immediately followed the pioneers, although it was five years before the entire population of Nauvoo reached Salt Lake. Each party was well organized and experienced no more than the usual trials of wilderness travel. Part of the migrants were foreign converts, largely from England, who arrived by the thousand. Mormon agents planned their trips, met them on arrival — at New Orleans in the early years — and supervised their overland trip. Special rates were provided. A Perpetual Emigrating Fund, established in 1849, loaned money to the migrants who were poverty stricken; after reaching Utah they were supposed to pay back the advances plus interest from their earnings and thus furnish the funds for similar advances to later travelers. To reduce the cost of the trip across the plains the experiment was tried in 1856 of using two-wheeled handcarts instead of the usual ox-drawn wagons. Tragic results came to groups that started the trip so late that they were caught in winter weather before they completed their long walk, and consequently the use of handcarts was soon abandoned.

The Mormon settlement was not confined to Salt Lake City even in the early years. Hundreds of new " stakes " were established in the surrounding countryside, ultimately extending south beyond the Colorado River, north into Idaho, and both east and west. In 1850, for example, such towns as Lehi, Springfield, and Payson were founded. Settlers for each stake were picked by the church authority and went as a religious duty. Attention was given to such factors as general plans, leadership, a proper distribution of skills, and necessary supplies; little wonder that these new towns survived. As early as 1849 plans existed for lines of settlements to San Francisco and to Los Angeles. In connection with the latter objective a community was established at San Bernardino, California, but various difficulties led to the decision of the Church in 1857 to abandon it.

ECONOMIC DEVELOPMENTS

The first years in the Salt Lake Valley were a time of extreme hardship for everyone. As new arrivals appeared by the thousand food became so scarce that it had to be rationed. The building of houses was unusually difficult since all wood had to be hauled with tremendous labor from the neighboring mountains. Clothes, tools, furniture, and other equipment were of the scantiest, including only what was salvaged from Nauvoo and hauled by wagon over the plains. Even nature seemed adverse when the first crop failed because of the lateness of the planting. The crop of 1848 started well, but soon its destruction was threatened by the arrival of swarms of locusts; salvation came only with the providential appearance of large numbers of gulls.

The future prosperity of the Mormon community depended primarily upon irrigation, for agriculture was impossible without an adequate artificial supply of water. Irrigation canals were among the earliest ventures, being built and operated cooperatively under the supervision of the church; as early as 1865 they included over 1000 miles of ditches. Irrigation meant comparatively small farms, intensive cultivation, and closely packed communities. In Salt Lake City, for example, each resident was given a town lot and a farming lot; for an artisan the farming lot was quite small and near the city so that it could be used for garden crops. Everyone in the community was guaranteed the right to the necessities of life provided only that he was willing to work, and no one has ever accused the Mormons of lacking industry.

In agriculture, as throughout every phase of Mormon life, the activities of Brigham Young were omnipresent. He urged new migrants to bring all sorts of seeds, small trees, and shrubs. He sent parties to California to bring seeds and stock. He encouraged better agricultural processes by offering prizes for the largest crops of flax, hemp, wheat and other grains to be grown on a single half-acre. Some of the newer crops, such as cotton, silk, and sugar beets did not prove successful.

Young early appreciated also the necessity for developing as nearly a self-sufficient economy as possible, since connections with the remainder of the United States not only were difficult but awakened unpleasant memories. Iron mines were discovered and developed, thus providing the basis for the manufacture of nails and other hardware and for the construction of machines of various types. Among the industries to appear were tanneries, flour mills, lumber mills, potteries, a woolen mill, and a sugar mill. Many industries such as the manufacture of cloth remained primarily in the home. The medium of exchange was in part a domestic currency, which was backed by gold dust; a few gold coins were minted. A special effort was made to attract a proper variety of artisans, and Utah soon boasted men who could make boots and shoes, watches, caps and hats, paper, carriages; in addition there were stone masons, cabinetmakers, and other skilled workmen.

Mormon enterprises were frequently inspired and not infrequently owned outright by the church. The tendency toward community endeavor developed at some places into outright communism, although this trend proved to be transitory. Destined to live more permanently were the cooperative stores, which originated in 1869. The parent store (Z. C. M. I.) was the one at Salt Lake City. For the Mormons there was no distinct division between activities to be labeled religious and activities in which the church should have no part.

Transportation and communication were also important matters because even with the greatest possible efforts the Mormons could not in fact become completely self-sufficient or be entirely indifferent to the events of the rest of the world. The church early inspired a freighting company which made connections with the East, and later a mail route was established. When the transcontinental telegraph was strung in 1861 the Mormons were interested, and five years later completed their own connections. With the arrival of the Union Pacific Brigham Young obtained a contract for building part of the line in Utah, and this contract he sublet to other Mormon men. Salt Lake City was disappointed in not being on the main line of the Union Pacific, and consequently had to build its own branch, which was completed in 1870.

SOCIAL DEVELOPMENTS

The overwhelming importance of material progress overshadowed but never entirely eclipsed less vital social interests. Education was always a matter of concern to the Mormons, and schools were opened even in the first year in Utah. These, like all Mormon schools, were co-educational. The elementary schools long remained private, largely because Young was opposed to the use of taxes for the support of the schools. Higher schools were slow to open because only the most elementary education seemed vitally necessary for Mormon youth. In time academies were established and in addition theological training was given. A college had been founded at Nauvoo, and the University of Deseret functioned at Salt Lake City for a few years starting in 1850; this first effort failed, and the University was not reopened until 1867. Considered as a whole the Mormon educational efforts were not impressive, although of course allowance should be made for the immense difficulties which confronted Mormon educators in these early days.

The amusements favored by Young and the church were the theater, music, and dancing. As early as 1855 the church built a community center which was partly a theater. A quite magnificent show-house was opened by the church at Salt Lake City in 1862, being highly decorated with the products of the carpenter and painter. The actors included not only visiting companies and stars, but also local players, and Brigham Young could watch his own daughters perform on the boards. According to Young's beliefs the drama, music, and dancing were highly desirable. Dances were generally opened with prayer. Music was common both inside and outside the church, with numerous choirs, bands, and orchestras. The quality of the performances has received varying comments.

Other cultural interests of the Mormons were less impressive. One or more newspapers were always published, with preference going to the *Deseret News* from its origin in 1850. Magazines were scarce, books were even scarcer, and decent libraries were almost nonexistent. Poetry was encouraged but its quality was mediocre. Considerable interest was given to lectures that ranged in topic from science and farming to history and morals. Museums were reasonably numerous. Artists were rare. Literary, musical, and other societies had somewhat tenuous existences. Here, as in all phases of life, the attitude of the church was the decisive factor as to what activities would succeed and what would fail.

One of the early advantages of Utah to the Mormons was that they had a world completely of their own, untroubled by skeptical or hostile gentiles. The first important group of arrivals from the outside world came with the gold rush of 1849, but these argonauts proved helpful since they did not stop for long and had money and manufactured articles which they desired to trade for provisions — an exchange that was mutually profitable. But increasingly during the '50s and '60s, and particularly with the opening of the Union Pacific, further gentiles seeped into the Salt Lake area in search of wealth. Their reception was not cordial, since the Mormons were clannish and had good reason to be suspicious of outsiders. The establishment of cooperative stores was one method of curtailing the business that went to gentile traders.

This Mormon hostility to non-Mormons was illustrated most extremely in the " Mountain Meadows Massacre." In 1857, at the height of Mormon troubles with the federal government, a party of 140 Arkansas settlers passed through Salt Lake City on its way to California. At Mountain Meadows it was attacked by Indians, part of whom were Mormons disguised for the occasion. The emigrants prepared for defense by arranging their wagons in a corral and digging a protective trench. A group of Mormons then appeared and persuaded the beleaguered travelers to give up their arms and be escorted to safety. After the migrants were disarmed they were murdered in cold blood — all except seventeen children, who were too young to remember. This cruel act of butchery has been admitted by the Mormons, and the only argument concerns the extent of the participation, if any, of Brigham Young. The least possible complicity that can be claimed is that he had a knowledge after the act and made no effort to apprehend and punish the perpetrators.

GOVERNMENT

The situation of early Utah in respect to law and government would have been comparable to that of California or Oregon except that the Mormons were an unusually orderly and obedient people, and the church a strongly controlling force. Almost at once the church made and enforced civil as well as religious rules. Enforcement was easily possible since the church had the power of economic life and death, not to mention its purely religious sanctions.

As for distinctly civil government, the United States delayed in making any provision and hence the Mormons, like other westerners, set up a state government of their own. A convention meeting at Salt Lake City in 1849 wrote a constitution for the new state of Deseret, modeling the document along usual American lines. The infant state was not modest, but included within its borders all the land between the Rockies and the Sierras, and south of Oregon. The constitution was at once put into effect, and no one was surprised when Brigham Young was elected the first governor. A delegate was sent to Washington to request favorable action, but Congress decided in the Compromise of 1850 to make Deseret only a Territory, with the name of Utah. The area involved was reduced somewhat, but still included present Utah and Nevada, as well as parts of Colorado and Wyoming. Later legislation cut the territory still further until it attained its present boundaries.

Brigham Young was given the appointment as governor of the Territory of Utah, but the other federal officers were gentiles, which created immediate trouble. Some of the new appointees were definitely inferior and tactless men, but even the best possible officeholders could not have avoided all difficulties. The Mormons were sensitive, suspicious, proud, and dictatorial; under the best conditions they would hardly have taken the gentiles lovingly to their bosoms. The result was that the federal officers found great difficulty in performing their functions.

A crisis in federal relations came in 1857 when a territorial judge fled from Utah shouting that his life was in danger, and roaring diatribes against the Mormons, who he said were flouting federal authority with impunity. This incident occurred just as the practice of polygamy was receiving nation-wide knowledge and disapprobation. The church had publicly accepted polygamy as an authorized practice in 1852. Four years later the national Republican platform had linked polygamy with slavery as twin evils, and apparently more people deplored polygamy than objected to slavery. With considerable public sentiment to back him, Buchanan decided to send a non-Mormon governor backed by an army really to enforce federal authority. The new governor was Alfred Cumming of Georgia, and the army of 2500 was under the command of Colonel Albert S. Johnston, later to attain fame in the Civil War.

As the army moved across the plains the Mormons prepared

for defense, with Brigham Young breathing defiance against the United States, which he labeled somewhat inelegantly " a stink in our nostrils." Outlying settlements were abandoned and their inhabitants drawn back to the neighborhood of Salt Lake City. Salt Lake City itself was prepared for evacuation and for destruction if capture threatened. The Danites, a Mormon militia, harassed Johnston by capturing wagon trains, stampeding livestock and burning the grass. As Johnston approached Utah Young threatened to destroy Salt Lake City and to fight the invaders to the last man.

A federal mediator finally avoided the last desperate measures. Upon agreement with Young the new governor entered Salt Lake City without the troops and had his position recognized. Then the troops entered the city in the summer of 1858 without opposition, but camped outside the city and soon returned East. The Utah " rebels " were pardoned by the President. The entire episode had cost the federal government some $15,000,000 without any important results, since the general situation remained unchanged, with the same frictions as before.

The " Mormon problem " remained unsolved for a generation after the regrettable " Mormon War." No Congress could be found to accept an American state with polygamy as long as polygamy was frowned upon by the great bulk of American citizens. Public opinion was dominated by a flood of pornographic literature of the same general appeal as the *Police Gazette*. Wildly impossible tales which related how women were held in white slavery and how Brigham Young and other Mormon elders indulged in orgies at the Endowment House made the stories of the Arabian Nights seem like minutes of a chamber of commerce meeting. Numerous " confessions " of ex-wives appealed to the prurient and morbidly curious. Many good Christians professed to see Salt Lake City as little better than an immense house of prostitution, emitting an offensive stench which demanded purification.

The Mormons of course quite properly answered their accusers that polygamy was an ancient and well-recognized form of family organization, used extensively in Old Testament days, and that it was highly moral — decreasing rather than increasing the amount of prostitution. Such answers were completely ineffective because most Americans did not see them, but in any case they would not have been believed. Furthermore, polygamy was becoming increasingly less desirable for the Mormons themselves. The surplus of women was disappearing. The outside opposition was harder and harder to bear as communication and transportation improved, while the delay in obtaining statehood was undesirable.

Starting in the 1850s Congress passed a long series of laws designed to eliminate polygamy. The first laws were too weak to be effective and then the Civil War prevented any active effort at enforcement. With increasing experience Congress was finally able to meet the problem, not of outlawing polygamy, but of obtaining the enforcement of antipolygamy laws. As long as federal judges had to depend for their decisions upon Mormon juries, the possibilities of obtaining convictions for polygamy were nonexistent.

The first effective antipolygamy legislation was the Edmunds Act of 1882. Plural marriage was forbidden, and living with more than one wife at the same time was made punishable by fine and imprisonment. All children born before January 1, 1883, were to be considered legitimate and those born in plural marriage after that date were to be held illegitimate. The real teeth of the act came in the provisions that no person believing in polygamy could vote, hold office, or perform jury duty, and that a Presidential commission should be the final judge as to the beliefs of the voters, elected officials, and jurymen.

The Edmunds Act was enforced so vigorously that within five years 500 Mormons had been jailed under its terms. The church then saw the handwriting on the wall, and the president of the church officially banned polygamy by an order of September 25, 1890. Polygamy of course did not actually end overnight, if for no other reason than because conscientious citizens were unwilling to desert their wives, even though they were plural. Congress recognized the practical death of polygamy by passing an enabling act for the state in 1894. Two years later Utah was admitted to the Union.

READINGS

N. Anderson, *Desert Saints* (1942); H. Beardsley, *Joseph Smith* (1931); G. W. and H. P. Beattie, *Heritage of the Valley* (1951), chs. 16–29—San Bernardino; G. R. Bird, *Tenderfoot Days in Territorial Utah* (1918); H. Birney, *Zealots of Zion* (1931); F. M. Brodie, *No Man Knows My History* (1945)—Smith; F. J. Cannon and G. L. Knapp, *Brigham Young* (1913)—friendly; J. W. Caughey, *History of the Pacific Coast* (1933), ch. 20; L. H. Creer, *Founding of an Empire* (1947), chs. 8–13, *Utah and the Nation*

(1929); B. De Voto, *The Year of Decision 1846* (1943), ch. 3; E. Dick, *Vanguards of the Frontier* (1941), ch. 9; J. H. Evans, *Joseph Smith* (1933), *Charles Coulson Rich* (1936)—friendly; S. L. Bates, *The Life Story of Brigham Young* (1930); H. Hatcher, *The Western Reserve* (1949), ch. 12; M. R. Hunter, *Brigham Young the Colonizer* (1940); G. O. Larson, *Prelude to the Kingdom* (1947)—sympathetic; W. E. La Rue, *The Foundations of Mormonism* (1919); W. J. McNiff, *Heaven on Earth* (1940); J. Monaghan, *The Overland Trail* (1947), ch. 13; T. C. Pease, *The Frontier State* (1918), ch. 19—Nauvoo; M. M. Quaife, *The Kingdom of St. James* (1930)—Strang; R. N. Richardson and C. C. Rister, *The Greater Southwest* (1935), ch. 7; O. W. Riegel, *Crown of Glory* (1935)—Strang; B. H. Roberts, *The Mormon Battalion* (1919); F. C. Shoemaker, *Missouri and Missourians* (5 vols., 1943), vol. 1, ch. 21; S. Vestal, *The Missouri* (1945), ch. 8—Mormons in Missouri; M. R. Werner, *Brigham Young* (1925); K. Young, *Isn't One Wife Enough?* (1954)—by a Mormon; L. E. Young, *The Founding of Utah* (1923).

CHAPTER 27

FROM PREEMPTION TO HOMESTEAD

BY no means everyone seeking a new western home in the '40s and '50s was a religious refugee or a revolutionist or even a miner, in spite of the tendency of the spectacular occupation of Texas, Oregon, Utah, and California to overshadow the more ordinary advance of population. Most of the migrants were still the usual fortune-seeking Americans who pressed onward as they had done in preceding years, steadily adding one area after another to the settled portions of the country. Their volume increased rather than diminished during the period of the stirring events in the Southwest and on the Pacific Coast.

AGITATION FOR LAND LAW CHANGES

New settlers after 1840 had the advantage of a new land law that had resulted from dissatisfaction with the law of 1820. Westerners had long objected to the price of land and to the ability of the eastern speculator to use the auction to bid land away from original settlers. The objection of the West to the speculator of the East was in no sense an objection to speculation itself, for every westerner was himself a speculator. He preferred town sites, but in any case acquired as much land as possible, with the idea of later selling part or all of it at advanced prices. This kind of speculation he felt to be perfectly proper and even commendable, but the kind in which an easterner used only his money, with no thought of personal occupancy at any time, seemed positively wicked.

The West wrestled with the land situation both by appeals to Congress for new laws and by direct action. The direct action came through extralegal " claims associations," composed of farmers who

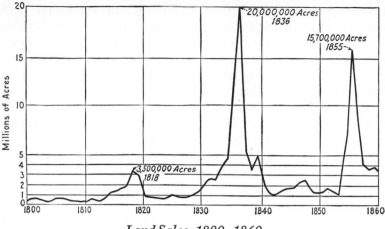

Land Sales, 1800–1860

had taken up land ahead of the auction and wanted to be certain of its purchase at the minimum price when it was finally offered for sale. With the usual American passion for organization each such group wrote a constitution, adopted bylaws and elected officers. The most active officer was the secretary, who recorded the claims of members.

When an auction was announced any interested association sent a bidder, usually the secretary, to act for all members. As each parcel was offered for sale the bidder consulted his little book of records; if the land were claimed by a member the agent bid the minimum of $1.25 an acre. Now and then some bumptious or uninformed outsider bid upon a member's land, which meant bad luck for the outsider. Some night he might receive a forcible invitation to be the guest of honor at a ducking, a whipping, or a tar-and-feather party. Competitive bidding was thereby discouraged. The association also settled conflicting claims between members, and failure to accept the award of a committee might bring the destruction of improvements or even the physical harm of the noncooperator. The land association was one of the many organizations in the history of the frontier that solved problems immediately and effectively in the absence of regularly constituted authority.

Westerners had no real desire to operate outside the law, and hence flooded Congress with a sea of petitions designed to obtain the kind of land law they preferred. Western agitation for land reform in the years after 1830 was more hopeful because of the political situation. Starting with Jackson, the Presidents were generally interested in western problems, while Jackson and Harrison were identified in the popular mind with the West. While western influence was not outstanding in the House it was quite imposing in the Senate, where the numerous new states constituted an important section of that body.

The power of the West in Congress was further enhanced by a sectional split between Northeast and Southeast, which enabled the West in some cases to wield the balance of power. Not that the West followed a consciously opportunistic policy, but rather that it represented a third section of the country which might attain its goal by combining with either of the other two, or which might receive favors in return for supporting measures in which either Northeast or Southeast was interested. On many issues the West was not itself unified, but when it had a generally accepted program it had a reasonable chance of victory.

Congressional action regarding the public domain was delayed partly by becoming mixed with those equally moot points the tariff and federal aid to internal improvements, and also by the many and varied laws that were proposed. From the welter of debate five proposals emerge with some clarity — cession, graduation, preemption, distribution, and increased prices. Most pleasing to the West was the idea of ceding all public lands to the states in which they lay. Benton, as an influential westerner, gave the proposition his rapturous support, but all of the East was generally opposed; Calhoun once favored the plan as a desperate effort to gain western support for legislation he considered really vital.

Next to outright cession, the West's favorite plan was graduation, which was the pet of Benton. The idea of graduation was to reduce year by year the price on unsold public land, thus giving some opportunity to the poorer land seeker and disposing of the less desirable parts of the public domain. The East was unsympathetic, since it saw a prospective decline in federal revenue and an increased drain of industrial labor to the West. More moderate was the proposal for preemption, by which the bona fide settler could buy land at the minimum price before auction. The West liked the idea but considered it as at best half a loaf, while the East was either noncommittal or tepidly enthusiastic. Preemption, like some of the other proposals, could of course be combined with other plans.

A fourth proposal, sponsored by Clay as part of his " American system," was to retain the existing situation but to divide the proceeds of land sales among the various states according to population. The idea was acceptable to the Northeast since that region had most population and hence would get most of the returns, while the whole plan included a high tariff. The Southeast envisaged the same results and hence was opposed. The West was moderately interested, for although land reform was excluded, the money would be helpful for internal improvements. Possibly the most appealing plan to the Northeast was to raise land prices or stop land sales; the latter proposal, as suggested by Senator S. A. Foot of Connecticut, produced the Webster-Hayne debate, which did nothing to clarify the land situation. Politically any such proposal was disastrous to the Northeast since it would push the West into the arms of the Southeast; hence it was not pressed.

While Congress was debating a permanent land policy, preemption went into effect gradually and unobtrusively. The federal government had long recognized the impossibility of ejecting thousands of squatters or of forcing them into actual competition in the purchase of their farms. Consequently Congress accepted the situation and in a series of laws starting in 1830 gave the right of preemption to particular regions within definite time limits. The passage of a general preemption law seemed increasingly only a matter of time.

Most advertised of the land proposals of the '30s was that of distribution, as favored by Clay. Sectional divisions gave way to political party pressure so that its passage in 1836 was by a party vote. Instead of a simple distribution of land proceeds, the measure provided for the deposit of the existing treasury surplus as a loan to the states according to population; the main purpose was to annihilate a large federal surplus, and of course no one ever expected the loans to be repaid. Distribution came to grief when the panic of 1837 ended the federal surplus, and Congress could start anew in the matter of land legislation.

PREEMPTION

The land issue was revived in Harrison's " log cabin and hard cider " campaign of 1840, in which the Whigs talked preemption in the West and distribution in the East. A measure combining these two propositions was finally forced through Congress in a bitter fight during which the divisions were almost entirely political. Necessary to insure its passage was an amendment which provided there should be no distribution if the tariff went over twenty per cent; this provision was deadly poison to distribution, for the tariff of 1842 proved to be well over twenty per cent.

The law of 1841 has been known commonly as the Preemption Act. Its distribution feature provided that 10 per cent of the land proceeds go to the states in which the land lay, while the remainder, minus administrative costs, be divided among the states according to the number of senators and representatives each had in Congress. In addition 500,000 acres were given to each of nine public land states. The preemption feature provided that a settler, upon evidence of having cultivated the land that he claimed, could buy a maximum of 160 acres at the minimum price without auction, except that no man could qualify for a preemption claim who thereby would own over 320 acres. There was no prohibition of a settler immediately selling his claim to another, but an amendment of 1843 prohibited the settler from making more than one preemption claim.

The adoption of preemption was a landmark in the history of the public domain, for it established the principle that an actual settler should be given special privileges and consideration. The only remaining important step for the small farmer was making the land free. Incidentally, Benton's idea of graduation was enacted into law in 1854, but apparently furnished no considerable help to the small and poor farmer.

The reception of preemption in the West was favorable but by no means enthusiastic, since westerners felt that Congress did not deserve any considerable praise for what they considered a long delayed act of simple justice. Agitation continued for cheaper, and preferably free, land and also for larger and larger grants to aid internal improvements. When the pressure became sufficiently great, Congress acted.

MIGRATION AND NEW STATES

While Congress continued to debate further modifications of the land laws, settlement moved steadily west. The migration of the '30s had produced the states of Arkansas and Michigan, and the territories of Wisconsin and Iowa. Declining after the panic of 1837 it again increased during the '40s. From 1840 through 1850 came the states of Texas and California, and the territories of New Mexico, Utah, and Oregon, as already mentioned, but also important developments farther east.

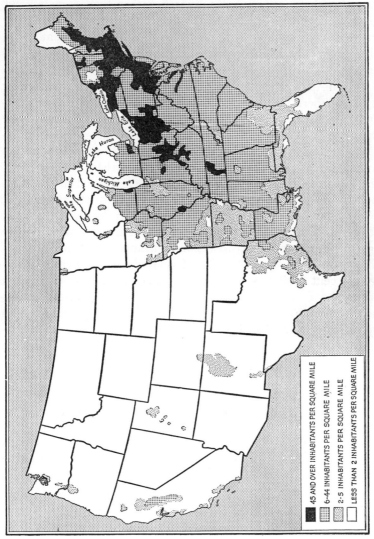

Population Density of 1850

45 AND OVER INHABITANTS PER SQUARE MILE

6-44 INHABITANTS PER SQUARE MILE

2-5 INHABITANTS PER SQUARE MILE

LESS THAN 2 INHABITANTS PER SQUARE MILE

One of the products of the migration of the 1840s was Florida, even though it represented a bypath rather than a main road. Neither citrus fruit nor sun had as yet been capitalized, and few Americans felt any enthusiasm over the Florida swamps, at a time when their only neighbors were hostile Seminole. Migration during the '20s and '30s had established many communities all the way from Apalachicola to Key West, but had concentrated largely in the northern part of the territory. A statehood movement produced a constitution in 1838 and the beginnings of a compromise capital at Tallahassee the next year, but Congress failed to exhibit the proper sympathy. Not until 1845 was Florida admitted to the Union, and then only to balance the northern state of Iowa. The Florida population of 1850 was 87,445, concentrated almost entirely in the north and north central sections of the state.

The main bulk of the movement to the West during the '40s and '50s went to or near the fringes of the frontier. In the South the movement was to Mississippi and Louisiana, but much more to Missouri, Arkansas, and Texas. Missouri increased over seventy-five per cent during each decade, while Arkansas and Texas each increased over a hundred per cent in each decade. During the '50s the expansion of southwestern population definitely lagged behind the increase in the Northwest, and this lag was accentuated during the '60s; presumably this situation was created largely by the effects of slavery and of the Civil War.

Part of the great migration to the Northwest in the two decades after 1840 was to the older states of Illinois and Michigan, but the bulk was to the newer regions of Iowa, Wisconsin, and Minnesota. As usual the peak of the migration came during prosperous times — in this case just previous to the panic of 1857. The new arrivals were remarkable for including an unusually large percentage of the foreign-born — notably the Germans, particularly in Wisconsin, but also Norwegians, Swedes, Danes, Dutch, and others. Preponderantly these people were components of the " old immigration " from northern and western Europe.

Iowa was the first of the new states of the upper Mississippi Valley after 1840. The first important white population had come after the Black Hawk War and had occupied the eastern fringe along the Mississippi, giving rise to the various river towns which later became important. Optimistic farmers immediately started to push farther west but with little predictable pattern of settlement since the comparatively open plains offered no obvious route

or place of settlement. These pioneers had the usual frontier disregard for technical Indian ownership, and especially since the Indians were impotent. Claims clubs made provision for land ownership whenever the government finally caught up with settlement.
The Indian cessions of 1837 and 1842 did no more than recognize
the existing white occupation. Early Iowa settlers grew considerable amounts of wheat, but the hog-corn economy so typical of
later Iowa was evident as early as 1840.

In government the Iowa region had been attached successively to
Michigan and Wisconsin, and then in 1838 had become a territory
in its own right. At that time it included most of present Minnesota and considerable parts of the Dakotas; the capital was at
Iowa City. Early statehood talk was somewhat muted because of
increased costs that were involved. A constitutional convention
finally met in 1844 and produced a constitution acceptable to the
people of Iowa. Congress, however, refused to accept the boundaries
that Iowa had drawn for itself, and in fact they had been drawn
with a somewhat lavish hand. A considerable wrangle over the
boundary issue finally ended in a compromise and Iowa was admitted to the Union on December 28, 1846; eleven years later
the capital was moved to Des Moines. Iowa's growth in population was magnificent; the 43,000 population of 1840 increased to
192,000 in 1850, and to 675,000 in 1860.

Wisconsin antedated Iowa in becoming a territory but was later
in attaining statehood. Early arrivals tended to congregate in the
mining districts of the south and the lake towns of the southeast,
but an ever increasing number pushed north and west into the
grain country, while a few hardy souls settled along the Mississippi
and on the shores of Lake Superior. Vast reaches of the northern
and western parts of the territory remained comparatively un-
populated for many years. The total growth of population was
spectacular, being from 30,000 in 1840 to over 300,000 in 1850,
while the next decade brought another increase of 150 per cent.

Wisconsin was apparently less anxious for statehood than some
other areas, for it took no positive action until Congress passed
an enabling act in 1846; among other factors, many Badgers were
irritated by the fact that Wisconsin as a territory had lost to
Illinois and Michigan two important areas that should have been
hers under the terms of the Ordinance of 1787. In time a constitutional convention was held and the results ratified by the people.
Wisconsin was admitted as a state on May 29, 1848. With the ad-

mission of Wisconsin, the Minnesota area was left without a government, but this defect was remedied the next year by the creation of the Territory of Minnesota.

By the time that the new states and territories of the '40s were joined by the products of the Compromise of 1850 the organized territory of the United States had assumed the appearance of a horseshoe. The eastern leg was formed by Minnesota, Iowa, Missouri, and Arkansas. The southern base comprised Texas and New Mexico. The western leg included California, Utah, and Oregon. White settlement, however, presented no such complete pattern. Between Texas and California the only important settled areas were those of the Rio Grande and Salt Lake valleys. The remainder of the trans-Mississippi West remained the hunting grounds of the Indians.

CHANGING INDIAN POLICY

The advancing white frontier together with the vast increase of the overland traffic inevitably made the Indians uneasy. The western Indians had already been compressed to make room for eastern tribes and now they saw white farmers pouring into the country west of the Mississippi, while hundreds of white travelers crossed the plains to Santa Fe, Salt Lake City, California, and Oregon. Little wonder that the Indians felt no thrill of gratitude for the " permanent " frontier which had presumably been arranged for their benefit. Apparently a frontier line was enforced by the whites only as a barrier to the Indians and did not interfere with the free flow of the whites to wherever their fancy dictated. Quite understandable was an increasing sullenness and resentment by the Indians, with more and more talk of making some final stand before they were completely annihilated.

From the white standpoint the permanent frontier was losing its desirability as the " great American desert " was proving to be far from a desert. Increasing plains travel produced the ambition to control the plains Indians more effectively, at least to the point of obtaining a safe right of way to the Far West. Even more important, white settlers were becoming interested in the country west of the great bend of the Missouri, while white miners were beginning their sporadic rushes which were in time to take them to all the hopeful parts of the West. Possibly the Indians could be pushed back still farther, with the ultimate hope of concentrating them in some completely undesirable parts of the country.

A change in the Indian policy of the federal government appeared during the early '50s, when commissioners were sent to make new treaties with the western tribes. In a few of the resulting agreements additional land was acquired, but the usual treaty provided only for the right of white travelers to cross the Indian country and for the United States to mark and construct roads. These treaties continued to be negotiated by the Indian Bureau, but from 1849 the Bureau was a part of the Department of the Interior rather than of the War Department.

Several of these treaties of the early '50s were of particular importance. The Sioux of Minnesota agreed in 1851 to make more land available to white settlers, and this treaty later furnished the background for the Sioux outbreak of the early '60s. The northern plains Indians, including the Cheyenne, Arapaho, Sioux, Assiniboin, Arikara, Crow, Gros Ventre, and Shoshone agreed in 1851 to permit the United States to build, fortify, and use a road or roads across the plains, and not to molest travelers. The southern plains Indians, and especially the Apache and Comanche, signed a similar agreement in 1853.

These treaties made clear once more that the primary concern of the federal government was the protection of the whites, and that in any conflict between the two races Indian hopes and rights would take second place. In justice to the Indians it should be added that during the succeeding years they observed their treaty obligations scrupulously. The conflicts which occurred were due invariably to the whites, and particularly to the frame of mind which held that every plains Indian was necessarily hostile.

KANSAS AND NEBRASKA

The most discussed and trouble-provoking of the white advances of the '50s was that going west of Missouri into present Kansas and Nebraska, particularly into Kansas. Here was the great bend of the Missouri which was long the springboard for travel to the Far West. Outfitting and distributing centers soon lined the river, and in time farmers began to occupy the country to the west. Theoretically all the land west of the Missouri was Indian property, with white entry forbidden by law, but actually the Indians were not sufficiently strong to make an effective barrier. Indian treaties of cession followed the advancing whites, notably the treaty of 1854, which ceded all land between 37° and 42° 40', or present Kansas and present southern Nebraska.

Due to the flimsiness of the Indian barrier, the main troubles of Kansas and Nebraska were between whites and other whites. Even before Kansas and Nebraska had enough settlers to frighten the coyotes they had entered national politics. As early as 1844 Stephen A. Douglas of Illinois was advocating the organization of Kansas and Nebraska, and for ten years he kept the issue before the country. His main interest was in obtaining a route for a transcontinental railroad, but he was not unmindful of the desirability of collecting the honey of national approval to satisfy the bee of Presidential aspirations that was buzzing in his head. His main obstacle in creating new territories was of course not the solemn governmental promise to the Indians of the permanent possession of their western lands but rather the fight between North and South over the slavery issue. The Douglas solution was the repeal of the Missouri Compromise, with the permission for each new territory to decide whether or not it would have slavery. This program he called " popular sovereignty." Ultimately in 1854 he got his plan enacted. Kansas, as then constituted, stretched west to touch Utah. Nebraska included roughly the immense area between the Missouri River and the Rockies, north of Kansas. A transcontinental railroad would pass only through organized territories and states.

Early Kansas arrivals consisted predominately of speculators looking for claims which might later be sold at a profit to actual settlers. They ordinarily employed military land warrants, or bought Indian land or railroad grants, since little opportunity existed for homesteading except west of 97° and in areas remote from the railroads. Early real settlers were largely the ordinary migrants engaged in their endless search for economic opportunity, but some of them did come directly from the East with subsidies, which included rifles, from the abolitionist Emigrant Aid Society. The opposing proslavery element came largely from the neighboring state of Missouri, and sometimes only to raid and vote instead of to settle. The abolition center was Lawrence and the proslavery center was Atchison. The main fight was in Kansas rather than in Nebraska because even the most ardent proslavery man could not imagine Nebraska as anything but free. Possibly somewhat harsh is the comment that sympathy with the Negro slave did not make the abolitionist charitable toward other nonwhite races, since Indian land was taken freely.

The political history of Kansas during the middle '50s was a depressing story of fraud and violence. Elections were frequently controlled by parties of armed men stationed at the polls, and in at least one case resulted in twice as many votes as there were qualified voters. Successive elections might produce almost unanimous votes on opposite sides, depending on which party dominated the polling places and did the voting. A steady stream of governors tried to achieve some semblance of order, but their success ranged from moderate to negligible. At one time two rival legislative groups were meeting simultaneously.

Most disturbing for the future was the increasing disorder and violence, with bands of armed men using the territory as a rendezvous, and the slavery issue as a pretext for depredations which redounded to their own personal and immediate advantage. For a time the conflict was so widespread that it was labeled the " Wakarusa War." On May 21, 1856 a Missouri mob sacked the town of Lawrence, and a reprisal in the form of a free-state march toward Topeka was so alarming that the governor asked for federal troops. Among the least creditable episodes was the Pottawatomie massacre in which John Brown and his four sons, on the plea that they were fighting for liberty, killed and mutilated seven men and stole their horses (1856).

Ultimately statehood became the vital issue, and in 1857 a proslavery constitution was adopted at Lecompton; the free-state men were suspicious of the governor and hence abstained from voting either for delegates to the convention or on the ratification of the constitution. This constitution was submitted by Buchanan to Congress (1858) and accepted by the Senate, but the House forced an amendment necessitating another popular vote. A Kansas election then rejected the document decisively by a vote of almost ten to one. A new constitution was written at Wyandotte, and Kansas was finally admitted as a free state in 1861. The population of Kansas by the census of the preceding year was 107,206.

The twin of Kansas did not occasion similar trouble, for even the most moral and conscientious New Englanders saw no reason to rush to " save " a territory that would obviously be saved without their active aid. A few settlements along the Missouri River plus even fewer along the Platte comprised almost the entire population of the '50s; the figure given by the census of 1860 was 28,841. Congressional leaders finally deemed a few extra votes desirable, so obtained the passage of an enabling act in 1864; the residents of Nebraska then promptly rejected this suggestion of increased responsibilities and expenses. A new proposal of state-hood was presented to the legislature in 1866; the legislature was unenthusiastic but passed the matter to the electorate, of whom only some 8000 voted, with a favorable majority of a scant hun-dred. A constitution was then formulated and accepted by Con-gress, only to meet the veto of President Johnson. Congress then showed its current respect for the judgment of the President by passing the bill over his veto in 1867. By 1870 the population of Nebraska had reached 122,993.

MINNESOTA

Although the Kansas-Nebraska bill and the subsequent struggle over Kansas occupied the center of the stage during the '50s, the growth of Minnesota was actually more important as far as the numbers involved. Early white settlement which centered at Fort Snelling, at the junction of the Mississippi and Minnesota, was exceedingly small, for as late as 1850 the federal census showed only 6000. As Wisconsin approached statehood, Congress specu-lated a little on the desirability of providing government for the handful of whites west of the Mississippi, but apparently any ac-tion was at least partially stymied by a difference of opinion as to how to spell the difficult name of Minnesota. At any rate Min-nesota was left without government when Wisconsin was admitted, and consequently a convention meeting at Stillwater memorialized Congress on the subject and sent H. H. Sibley as a representative to that body. The Congressional solution of what to do with a rep-resentative who had no territory was to accept and pay him as a delegate of the defunct Territory of Wisconsin. Minnesota became a territory in 1849, with boundaries that extended as far west as the Missouri River and with Alexander Ramsey as the first gov-ernor.

Almost all of Minnesota remained Indian country as late as 1850. The first big white accession came with the Sioux treaty of 1851, which was soon followed by other similar agreements, so that within the succeeding decade nine-tenths of Minnesota was opened for settlement. Frequently, in accordance with age-old frontier practice, the whites took up the land before the Indians sold it. Theoretically the Indians were paid for their cessions, but actually they seldom received any money. The " joker " in the usual treaty was a provision that before any money should be paid to an Indian all traders' claims against him should be satisfied. The Indians were perpetually in debt and the traders kept the accounts, so there can be little wonder that very little of the treaty money ever reached Indian hands.

The rush to Minnesota in the 1850s was spectacular even for the American frontier. An unending procession of wagons poured into the territory, with land occupied much faster than it could be surveyed, and with towns planned hopefully at every promising location. St. Paul was the expanding metropolis, with the usual preponderance of lawyers and land agents, and with " gambling houses too numerous to mention." An actual count of the territory in 1857 showed 150,000 residents, which was an increase of 144,000 or 2400 per cent in the seven years since 1850. With the depression of 1857 the tide ebbed somewhat, and the census of 1860 showed 172,000.

Like other regions of the upper Mississippi Valley, Minnesota attracted considerable numbers of the foreign-born — particularly Danes, Swedes, Norwegians. Like Wisconsin before it, Minnesota gave official encouragement to such settlers from abroad. But the great impetus, as always, came from the letters of older immigrants to their friends at home. Their letters spoke glowingly of the lack of social classes and of the higher pay. They also advanced the remarkable claims that the United States was practically free of crime, drinking, profanity, and Sabbath-breaking. Fabulous stories were told of common pastures with cows that anyone could milk, of grass so high that it concealed all of the cattle but the horns, of freedom from taxes, and of rivers that ran syrup.

Minnesota had sufficient population by the middle '50s to warrant statehood, but the inhabitants were not anxious to change their status. They changed their minds when they realized that as a territory they could not borrow money to build railroads, but that as a state they could. Congress passed the enabling act in 1857. When a Minnesota constitutional convention assembled the Republicans and Democrats felt so bitter toward each other that they held separate meetings. Ultimately a compromise was effected by which both groups accepted the same constitution, which was then adopted by the people of the territory. Coming before Congress the southern members fought to exclude this new northern state but lost and Minnesota was admitted on May 11, 1858. Just as the admission of Wisconsin had left Minnesota dangling free, so the admission of Minnesota left unorganized the region between the western boundary of the state and the Missouri River ;

this district was finally included in Dakota Territory upon its organization in 1861.

The year 1861 saw all of the West, with the exception of present Oklahoma, divided into organized states and territories. Many of the territorial boundaries were to change in later years, but the way was opened for various developments, of which not the least was chartering and subsidizing transcontinental railroads. The change from the " permanent frontier " map of a quarter of a century earlier was notable. True, most of the land still remained under Indian control and contained no whites, but the handwriting was on the wall. Any intelligent man knew that in time white civilization would stretch completely across the continent.

GIFTS OF LAND BY CONGRESS

The same '40s and '50s which saw such an important change in the map of the West witnessed an equally important revolution in the laws concerned with the disposal of the public domain. Expanding settlement, with dozens of new states, brought substantial backing for any number of ingenious plans as to how the federal government could give away its land in desirable ways. And in truth the federal government, prodded by land-hungry westerners and by speculators from all over the country, was but mildly reluctant to accede to the demands, for here was an easy type of bounty that might be used for luring votes without increasing taxes. Best of all, one could always argue that the wealth and prosperity of the country were thereby enhanced.

One class of the population favored by the government was the soldiers, for Congress was both thankful for the services of its brave defenders and mindful of their votes. The soldiers of each major war were given land warrants, and in 1850 a general act included the Indian wars, so that any former soldier could obtain his 160 acres free. Then various near-soldiers, including teamsters and chaplains, were added (1855) and finally the navy (1857) was included. In the early years specific land had been set aside to fill these claims — first in Ohio and then in Michigan, Illinois, and other states — but eventually (1842) the claims could be located anywhere.

Military warrants were always the basis for a tremendous amount of speculation, even though legally they could not be transferred prior to the act of 1852. At all times they were sold freely and in large amounts; the common price in 1857 was about sixty cents an acre. One expert has estimated that not over one in five hundred of the warrants was actually located by the soldier or his heir. No new grants were made after 1855 since the next major war found land being given freely to everyone, but soldiers had special privileges such as being able to homestead 160 acres of the alternate sections of railroad grants, as compared to 80 acres for other people, and a shorter term of cultivation before the final title.

Education was likewise the occasion for munificent land grants. Starting with Ohio practically every state received gifts of land to aid all kinds of education, from primary through collegiate. In the early days this land could not be sold by the states, but from 1845 each state was permitted to dispose of its educational grant, although under some limitations. Aid to higher education was at first sporadic, but was later regularized in the Morrill Act of 1862; each state received land in proportion to its representation in Congress, with a maximum of 1,000,000 acres, of which the proceeds were to be used to establish and support agricultural and mechanical colleges. Money aid began in 1890.

A third important occasion for lavish gifts of land were internal improvements, particularly roads, canals, and railroads. Grants for specific improvements really became imposing after the Illinois Central grant of 1850 opened the way for large-scale giving. In addition to such specific gifts, certain other donations were expected to be used largely for public improvements. The preemption act gave 500,000 acres to each public land state. The swamp land act of 1850 gave outright to each state the swamp land within its borders; reputedly the land actually selected by the states was by no means always swampy. Some 80,000,000 acres were transferred under the terms of this act.

These and other magnificent gifts of the land heritage of the United States were justified publicly on the desirability of the national prosperity which they presumably advanced, but cynical commentators have long noted that speculators were active in the passage of the laws, harvested a considerable share of the land, and pocketed a goodly portion of the resulting profits. The work of early speculators such as Symmes was obvious. Quite clearly the military warrants were used primarily for speculative purposes, and there seems little doubt that Benton's graduation measure was most important for speculative purchases of large tracts. Railroad grants were frequently manipulated to the disadvantage of actual settlers. Educational grants were notoriously badly handled, soon appearing in private hands with little revenue to the state. Swamp lands were no better, since they also gravitated rapidly to the speculators, with little revenue to the state and no reclaiming of the swamps. All these gifts were at least disappointing, either in getting land directly to actual settlers or in providing revenue for public improvements. Whether they were dictated by the speculators or merely used by these gentry for their own advantage remains a subject for investigation, but the ultimate results are unquestioned.

HOMESTEAD ACT

The various grants, no matter how munificent, did not satisfy the West. What the West desired was free land for settlers, and this proposition it kept before Congress almost continuously throughout the '50s. The often repeated arguments in its favor were that such a measure would encourage the development of the United States by making it possible for every ambitious American to acquire a farm of his own, and that the increasing prosperity and taxes would more than compensate for any immediate loss of revenue from land sales. As time passed, free land seemed to become a natural right to which each American was entitled by the mere fact of being alive.

Western ambitions came closer and closer to realization as eastern conditions changed. Increased migration was taking care of the northern need for industrial labor, and Irish immigrants were more tractable than New England farm boys. Furthermore the frontier was becoming so remote in distance that it drew but little from the eastern seaboard; the new frontier of the '50s drew more from the farms of the Mississippi Valley than from those of New England. Not to be neglected was the desire of eastern manufacturers for markets even more than for labor, and the expanding West meant a vastly increased market.

The demand for free land was buttressed by the arguments of a growing labor and reform movement in the East. Led by such men as G. H. Evans and Horace Greeley numerous vocal minorities insisted that free land was one of the essentials for a rich and contented democracy. They argued not only for the general advantages of an expanding population, but that free land provided an outlet for the restless, the ambitious, the oppressed of the East. If industrialists offered low wages and bad working conditions, their employees could escape to the opportunities of the West. This argument was not validated by the facts — at least in short-range terms — but it had a considerable appeal.

Various homestead bills, designed to assure free or at least very cheap land, were considered by Congress during the '50s. Ultimately one of them passed both houses in 1860, only to be vetoed by Buchanan, who sympathized with the southern opposition. During the same year the Republicans linked free land with a high tariff to appeal to both East and West, and with the Republican victory free land was assured. President Lincoln finally signed a Homestead Act in 1862.

The Homestead Act of 1862 provided 160 acres of free land from the public domain for each American adult or head of a family; the only cost was a small fee of ten dollars. The one important qualification was that each settler had to prove five years of continuous residence and cultivation before receiving final title. After six months of residence he might commute his claim and obtain immediate ownership on the payment of $1.25 an acre. Although these provisions were modified slightly in the succeeding years, the law remained the basic feature of the American land system. It superseded but did not eliminate the preemption act, which was not repealed until 1891.

The Homestead Act was the best advertised of a great quantity of laws which threw the public domain open to land hungry Americans more freely than had ever been the case in the past. It and other laws for the benefit of individuals (see Chapter 37) and of railroad corporations insured that within the next generation the great bulk of agricultural land which did not need irrigation would go into private hands. The rapidity of the process exceeded anything that had preceded it; the second half of the continent was occupied, even though sparsely in many spots, in a tenth of the time that the first half had taken. Inevitably there was much selfish grabbing, fraud, and waste. Whether a more deliberate process would in the long run have brought more desirable conclusions is one of the historical queries which can never be answered satisfactorily.

READINGS

L. E. Atherton, *Main Street on the Middle Border* (1954), *The Pioneer Merchant* (1939); H. R. Austin, *The Milwaukee Story* (1946), chs. 9–12—episodical; P. Beckman, *The Catholic Church*

on the Kansas Frontier (1943), chs. 1, 2—monograph; W. W.
Belcher, *The Economic Rivalry Between St. Louis and Chicago,
1850–1880* (1947); M. W. Berthel, *Horns of Thunder* (1948)—
St. Paul; T. C. Blegen (ed.), *Frontier Parsonage* (1947)—Wis-
consin—*Grass Roots History* (1947)—Minnesota immigrants—
The Land Lies Open (1949), part 2, *Norwegian Migration to
America, 1825–1860* (1931), *Norwegian Migration* (1940); T. C.
Blegen and P. D. Jordan, *With Various Voices* (1949), chs. 3–9—
Minnesota; C. M. Brevard, *A History of Florida* (1925), chs. 4–
19; C. A. Clausen and A. Elviken, *A Chronicle of Old Muskego*
(1951)—Wisconsin; C. Cole, *Iowa Through the Years* (1940),
chs. 20–45; W. E. Connelley, *History of Kansas* (5 vols., 1928),
vol. 1, chs. 16–36, vol. 2, chs. 37–40; D. Dodd (ed.), *Florida
Becomes a State* (1945); W. W. Folwell, *A History of Minnesota*
(4 vols., 1921), vol. 1, chs. 8–15, vol. 2, ch. 1; P. W. Gates, *Fifty
Million Acres* (1954)—Kansas, *Frontier Landlords and Pioneer
Tenants* (1945)—Illinois; B. H. Hibbard, *A History of the Public
Land Policies* (1924), chs. 9–17; S. H. Holbrook, *The Yankee
Exodus* (1950), chs. 10, 12, 13; A. Howland, *Stephen A. Douglas*
(1920), chs. 9–12; M. E. Jarchow, *The Earth Brought Forth*
(1949)—Minnesota agriculture; A. Johnson, *Stephen A. Douglas*
(1918), chs. 11, 13, 15; S. A. Johnson, *The Battle Cry of Freedom*
(1954)—Emigrant Aid Company; A. J. Larsen (ed.), *Crusader
and Feminist* (1934)—Minnesota; R. L. Lokken, *Iowa Public
Land Disposal* (1942); T. H. McBride, *In Cabins and Sod Houses*
(1928)—Iowa; J. C. Malin, *Indian Policy and Westward Expansion* (1921), parts 2, 3, *John Brown and the Legend of Fifty-Six*
(1942), *The Nebraska Question, 1852–1854* (1953); S. W. Martin,
Florida During Territorial Days (1944), ch. 12; G. L. Nute, *Lake
Superior* (1944), ch. 12, *Rain River Country* (1950); W. J. Peterson, *Iowa* (1941); C. C. Qualey, *Norwegian Settlement* (1938),
chs. 3–6; W. F. Raney, *Wisconsin* (1940), chs. 5–7; I. Richman,
Ioway to Iowa (1931), pp. 149–344; R. M. Robbins, *Our Landed
Heritage* (1942), chs. 3–14; J. Schafer, *A History of Agriculture
in Wisconsin* (1922); M. Snyder, *The Chosen Valley* (1948)—
Minnesota; G. M. Stephenson, *The Political History of the Public
Lands from 1840 to 1862* (1917); B. Still, *Milwaukee* (1948),
chs. 4–9; R. G. Wellington, *The Political and Sectional Influence
of the Public Lands, 1828–1842* (1914); E. N. Wentworth, *America's Sheep Trails* (1948), chs. 8–25.

CHAPTER 28

FORTY-NINERS AND FIFTY-NINERS

PROSPECTORS and miners have always been among the more active elements pushing forward the white frontier. The searcher for mineral wealth has never been over-awed by wild aborigines or by the wilderness, even including mountains and deserts. The lure of great riches has blotted out dangers that otherwise might have been intimidating. Advancing white miners precipitated the removal of the southern Indians and played their part in the coming of the Black Hawk War.

The most exciting metal for whites to pursue has been gold, whether in the Indian country of Georgia or the snowy wastes of the Yukon. Gold has large value in small bulk and has been itself the standard of white values, but even more important it can be found uncombined in nature and hence presents opportunity to the poor prospector. Even the drugstore clerk or the dispossessed farmer has at least a chance for the lucky find that will make him independent for life.

IRON AND COPPER

And yet for a high-speed industrial civilization iron is more valu-able than gold, and copper than silver. Important discoveries of both of these base metals came during the 1840s. Most significant for the future were the findings by William A. Burt in 1844 of the Lake Superior iron deposits. By the end of the decade this ore had been carried to Pennsylvania to be married to Pennsylvania coal and the offspring of this union were to be important elements of American civilization. Large-scale operations did not come, how-ever, until the '80s.

The practical working of the Lake Superior copper mines dates from 1846, although their existence had long been known and some of the copper extracted earlier. Metal worth millions was removed before the Civil War, for the mines were of almost incredible richness. One miner in 1857 found a single lump of ore weighing 420 tons which yielded seventy-five per cent of refined copper. The famous Calumet & Hecla Consolidated Mining Company was formed in 1871 by the merger of companies which had started work in the '60s; by 1930 it had produced over 3,000,000,000 pounds of copper and had paid dividends of over $170,000,000. Operations of this kind of course needed considerable capital; a list of the stockholders of the Calumet & Hecla was full of the Boston socially elite.

CALIFORNIA GOLD RUSH

Michigan and Minnesota mineral discoveries were soon overshadowed by the most dramatic and best advertised mining boom in American history. The detonating spark came on January 24, 1848, when J. W. Marshall found traces of gold in the tailrace of a mill that he was erecting for J. A. Sutter on the south fork of the American River. Efforts by Sutter to keep the discovery a secret did not avert a mad mining rush during which sailors deserted their ships, cattle tenders left their herds, farmers abandoned their plows, and merchants closed their stores. All up and down the coast men were drawn by the lure of gold, while overland immigration was deflected from Oregon to California.

The gold fever infected the East late in the year and by 1849 thousands of ambitious young men were planning to seek the new El Dorado. Stores featured mining supplies ranging from picks and shovels to Spanish grammars. Frémont's reports received renewed circulation as travel guides. Potential miners swaggered in hip boots and talked of placers, fandangos, pound nuggets, and Spanish beauties. The expectation — seldom realized — was that a few months of mining would produce wealth sufficient for an eastern palace, blooded horses, and a trip to Europe.

Hopeful gold seekers streamed west during 1849, as individuals and in groups which were often organized elaborately under such names as Ophir or the California Mining Company. The organized group came usually from New England. It was founded on equal contributions and equal profits. With typical Puritan zeal and morality it had a full complement of officers and strict rules concerning such moral matters as swearing and Sabbath-breaking —

rules that lost force with the miles. The association was so popular that one was even formed for women. In sober fact, however, it must be admitted that aside from the wives who accompanied their husbands most of the women who went to California were anything but fit companions for God-fearing New England boys.

A large proportion of eastern migrants went to California by water. If by way of the Horn the tedious six-months' trip, with its monotonous diet of salt meat and hard bread, tended to fray the tempers of all but the least impatient of the young men. Even assiduous Bible reading, religious services and long hours communing with a diary did but little to alleviate the monotony. Reading, games, and music were possible, and ingenious souls spent countless hours inventing hundreds of variations to popular favorites:

> " I came from Salem City,
> With a washbowl on my knee,
> I'm going to California
> The gold dust for to see.
> It rained all night, the day I left,
> The weather it was dry,
> The sun so hot I froze to death,
> Oh! brothers, don't you cry.
>
> *Chorus*
>
> Oh! California,
> That's the land for me,
> I'm going to Sacramento
> With my washbowl on my knee."

The sea route could be made shorter but even more uncomfortable by crossing the Panama isthmus by land. The Pacific Mail Steamship Company had established water connections on both sides of the isthmus just before the gold rush, but its ships were crowded and expensive, while travel across the isthmus was difficult, dirty, and costly, with cholera, dysentery, and yellow fever rampant. The coast cities of Panama and Colon were so filthy that most miners rejected their dubious hospitality in favor of camping.

A variety of routes was possible through Mexico or the southern United States. Mexican routes were poor, in part because Mexicans remembered very vividly their late unpleasant experiences

with the United States. Various Texas routes generally drew together at El Paso and continued by way of the Gila. Farther north
another group of routes collected at Santa Fe, from which place
the traveler might either swing south or follow the Old Spanish
Trail.

The most popular overland route to the mines was the well-
known Platte River trail, which probably saw more traffic than
all other routes combined. Amateur travelers often suffered severely on the trip, so that soon the trail was marked by dead animals, jettisoned supplies, discarded furniture, and the graves of
the weak, the improvident, and the unlucky. West of the mountains various alternatives existed. Most migrants followed the
Humboldt River, which they might have reached by way of either
Fort Hall or Salt Lake; from the Humboldt there were several
possible choices, all poor, for crossing the Sierras. Many travelers
swung southwest from Salt Lake to Los Angeles, and a few of these
made the sad mistake of taking the unpleasant and highly dangerous route through Death Valley.

The great metropolis of the gold country was San Francisco
" the boisterous," where all sea traffic centered. Here the prospective miner waded through seas of mud or drifts of dust, garbage,
and filth. Saloons, gambling halls, and brothels in profusion welcomed the convivial, with a quarter the smallest coin in circulation
and gold dust the more usual medium of exchange. Prices left the
easterner popeyed, as he paid ten to twenty dollars a week for
a buggy bunk in a tent or two hundred and fifty dollars a month
for a room to himself.

A San Francisco filled with the young and footloose, not only
from the United States but from all over the world, with the riffraff of four continents from Valpariso to Hong Kong, and with
extraordinary amounts of loose gold, was bound to be rough and
rowdy. Between 1849 and 1856 there were a thousand homicides,
not to mention less spectacular crimes. A vigilance committee of
1849 soon " reformed " itself into a particularly vicious criminal
gang, while its successor of 1851 worked four years before it could
boast the suppression of the most violent and lawless.

The center of the gold fields was the scene of the first discoveries,
but from this point the miners spread in every direction. New
mining camps were established and died with bewildering rapidity. Poker Flat, Slumgullion, Delirium Tremens, Hell-out-for-
noon-City had their brief days.

> " Once more on Hanktown's hills we delve,
> On Murderer's Bar we mine,
> At Nigger's Tent and Boston Jim's,
> You Bet, Red Dog, Port Wine."

The early miners were seeking uncombined gold either as nuggets to be pried out of the rocks or as fine particles to be washed from the beds of the streams. Simplest of the methods of obtaining the smaller grains of gold was to rock a pan containing the gold, mud, sand, and water until only the gold and sand were left, whereupon the sand could be fanned off. Early improvements were merely in the size of the operations — a large cleated box replaced the pan and a sluice might provide the water; ordinarily mercury was used to catch the gold. As early as 1852 hydraulic mining still further dilated the process without changing it radically.

Crude mining methods were profitable only when gold was very plentiful. While California gold production increased to a peak of over $80,000,000 in 1852 and while stories were common of individual returns of as much as $1000 in a day, the average miner was lucky to make two dollars a day, which was far from a fortune in consideration of existing California prices; the real profiteers were the real estate men, the merchants, and the gamblers. As soon as easily worked deposits were exhausted the bulk of the miners left for more promising fields and the mining was taken over by companies which used stamp mills to crush the refractory ore and mercury to extract the gold. Even these processes, however, were not especially efficient.

LIFE OF THE MINERS

Save for the glamorous excitement of finding gold, the life of a miner was arduous and unpleasant. He lived in a crude tent or cabin, sat on a cracker box, darned his own socks, and ate a heavy and monotonous succession of simple meals prepared by himself from very expensive ingredients. Because of working in water much of the time, with bad diet and no doctors, the morbidity was high.

Since sheriffs did not keep pace with the mining camps, the miners had to provide their own law enforcement. Simple rules were soon adopted for making and holding claims, and these rules ultimately were written into the laws of the United States (1866). Crime was unusual in the early days, but increased rapidly as the scourings of the world poured into California. The usual camp then organized its own law enforcement in the form of a vigilance committee that used the primitive devices of whipping, exile, and death. Such a system was somewhat haphazard and not always just, but it provided a fair degree of order in an otherwise completely lawless community.

The recreations of the miners were necessarily circumscribed and tended toward the rough and crude. The absence of women was particularly deplored, with common stories that men would walk miles to see a grey-haired grandmother or even to see her clothes hanging on a line. The favorite center of entertainment was the saloon, where not only could the men drink themselves into a transient success, but could chance their earnings on roulette, faro, or poker, or sometimes dance with the girls provided by the house. Drinking and gambling were connected inseparably with mining life.

Wherever miners gathered there were songs to the accompaniment of a fiddle or flute, or even to beatings on tin cans and dishpans. Inevitable were such old and nostalgic favorites as " The Last Rose of Summer," but there were also innumerable varieties of such current favorites as " Joe Bowers from Pike."

> " My name it is Joe Bowers,
> I have a brother Ike ;
> I came from ol' Missouri —
> Came all the way from Pike."

The usual version had Joe kissing his girl goodbye, whereupon she married the red-haired butcher and had a red-headed baby.

The influx of miners strengthened the statehood movement, which had been active from the end of the Mexican War. For the time being a military governor headed a semicivil government, while Congress debated the disposition of the entire Southwest. As recounted in Chapter 27 California soon became impatient at Congressional deliberations and held a statehood convention in September 1849 ; the majority of its members were Anglo-American nonminers, but a respectable delegation of native Californians was included. A state constitution was ratified in November and the resulting state government put into operation. These developments were legalized the following year when California was admitted to the Union as one phase of the Compromise of 1850.

Hordes of hungry men prospecting for gold brought a tremendous demand for food of all kinds. Cattle and sheep men who here-tofore had had difficulty in obtaining sufficient funds to buy the gold braid for their jackets suddenly found themselves rolling in wealth. This new prosperity was unfortunately only temporary. The expansion of the eastern agricultural frontier and improved transportation made the California market more competitive, while bad times on the Coast, in particular the drought of 1863–64, sadly depleted the herds. But while the cattle boom was temporary, the expansion of agricultural crops proved permanent. Wheat produc-tion increased spectacularly through the '50s, with the utilization of such labor-saving machinery as the McCormick reaper, while the magnificently diversified California climate produced an un-usually wide variety of other crops.

Even though the mining industry of California declined both absolutely and relatively during the late '50s, it left a permanent imprint on the San Francisco area. As other mining booms de-veloped the natural metropolis for shipping and finance was San Francisco, which provided the main transportation and banking fa-cilities. In consequence San Francisco was not only the feverish center of trading in mining stocks, but the commercial center of the coast and the source of the financing which made possible much of the commercial enterprise of the Far West.

LATER GOLD RUSHES

The decline of California gold production, especially of placer production, meant that California had a large and exportable sur-plus of miners. Some of them returned East, others turned to ranching and farming, but many were held captive by the lure of the golden metal and wandered off to other promising regions. Cal-ifornia gold had been found in the streams, and the natural deduc-tions were that it might be found in other streams or in the moun-tainous areas from which the water had originated. Here were two clues that merited investigation.

As prospectors spread through the West there came rumors of rich finds here, there, and the other place. All the way from New Mexico to Washington, and even from far off Alaska came attrac-tive tales of rich and easily available deposits. Footloose miners rushed from one reported find to the next, with only a small por-tion either becoming rich and retiring or staying permanently in the new community. Gold hunting was a will-o'-the-wisp business that nearly always promised more than it paid.

As might have been expected, the first new finds came in the immediate vicinity of California. Wandering prospectors had discovered traces of gold in the present Nevada as early as 1849, and a handful of miners had been willing to forego the reported riches of California for the seemingly meager supply of Nevada gold. The peak of early placer mining in 1855 showed production of little over $110,000. A few miners recognized the existence of silver, but silver was less valuable and beyond the reach of the individual miner with his scant equipment and lack of capital. Gold remained king.

To the south, rumor had long indicated rich mines in New Mexico and Arizona, but the actuality of the '50s seemed disappointing. Most of the deposits were copper and silver, difficult metals to exploit at this time. A scattering of gold finds was reported, with the most important of them near the Colorado River in the '60s. The result was a sprinkling of mining communities, of which Tucson was the best known — " paradise of devils " — a title not lightly won in the mining West of the '50s. The main developments in the Southwest were to wait until after the Civil War.

To the north the most important find was at Colville, a Hudson's Bay post near the international boundary in present northeast Washington. The resulting small rush of 1855 soon expired but then came news of easily available wealth on the Fraser River in Canada, with a resulting stampede in 1858. A succession of later finds in the Far North culminated forty years later in the Yukon rush.

Many miners had hopes for the northern American Rockies, particularly along the Columbia, the Snake, and their tributaries. Their search in this region was aided by the construction of a road from the East across the mountains by way of Mullan Pass. Built between 1859 and 1863 at a cost of $230,000, this road made more accessible the entire area of the northern Rockies.

A succession of booms in the region of the Snake River started with discoveries on the Clearwater in 1860 and the establishment of Lewiston, Oro Fino, and Pierce City. Unfortunately this country had been guaranteed to the Nez Percè, a fact which was later to make much trouble for the United States. Following the Clearwater boom came a mad rush to the Salmon River (1861). The Territory of Idaho, including present Montana and Wyoming, was created to provide government for this district (1863).

Pushing east over the mountains the miners started a succes-

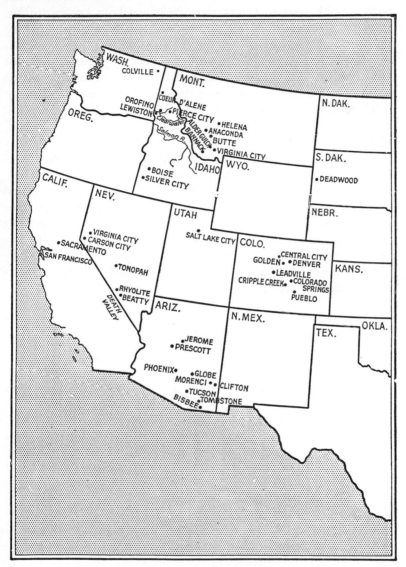

Mining Centers of the West

sion of booms in the Montana region. The existence of gold deposits in this part of the country had long been known to the
trappers, and definite mining operations had been prosecuted in
the '50s, but no great use of the information had been made at
this time. The first important work was done by James and Gran-
ville Stuart in 1862, and beginning with this year successive waves
of mining enthusiasm broke over the soil of Montana.

Three general regions in Montana, fairly close together, attracted the majority of interest. The Stuart discoveries were in the
vicinity of Bannock City. Next came the Alder Gulch and Virginia
region, which was opened in 1863. Finally in 1864 was opened Last
Chance Gulch, later to be given the more melodious name of Hel-
ena. The population which poured into these three districts again
made necessary a rearrangement of western territory, since the
government of Idaho could not care adequately for people across
the mountains near the head of the Missouri. Montana, with its
present boundaries, was made a territory in 1864, while at the
same time present Wyoming was again shifted, this time being
given back to Dakota.

COLORADO

The northern and southern gold rushes were cast into obscurity
by developments in the central area. In present Colorado gold had
long been known to exist, but discoveries of 1858 provided the
spark that started an avalanche of hopeful miners toward the land
of Pike's Peak. First arrivals came from nearby regions and tended
to collect in two main centers. The first was El Paso, near present
Colorado Springs. The second was at the junction of Cherry Creek
with the South Platte; a number of small villages — Montana,
Auraria, Highland, and St. Charles — soon coalesced to form Denver City.

The news of gold deposits near Pike's Peak was welcomed enthusiastically in the East. The panic of 1857 had produced thousands of men who were anxious to try new ways to better their
fortunes, and the new gold discoveries were more easily accessible
than previous opportunities of the same kind. The result was a
vast trek of fortune-hunting prospective miners in 1859. Estimates
have it that some 100,000 crossed Nebraska. The newcomers were
gambling with fortune and their frame of mind was expressed by
their most common slogan: " Pike's Peak or Bust! " In spite of
the nearness of Colorado the road was soon lined with mute evi-

dences of mistaken zeal, of inadequate knowledge, and of failures in judgment.

The Colorado mining boom produced a whole series of new towns such as Golden, Black Hawk, Central City, Idaho Springs, Georgetown, Pueblo, and Leadville, but the metropolis remained Denver, which boasted the *Rocky Mountain News* as early as 1859 and had its youthful cockiness enhanced by such distinguished visitors as Horace Greeley and Henry Villard. Government was a big problem in which Congress was not helpful. Big talk of statehood ultimately simmered down to the creation of the Territory of Jefferson (1859) without Congressional assistance. The Congressional debates on this self-invited, boisterous newcomer were confused by the slavery issue, so that it was not until 1861 that the Territory of Colorado came into existence with its boundaries the same as the present state. The Colorado boom proved of short duration, since the comparatively small quantity of free gold could not satisfy a horde of inexperienced miners. The quartz rock was rich in minerals of all kinds, but their extraction required expensive machinery. Many of the newcomers soon followed the lure of gold to other parts of the West. Others settled down to the safer but more prosaic business of farming or raising stock. Still others were completely disillusioned and returned East, their wagons bearing the significant motto: " Busted, by Gosh! "

A collapsed mining boom left Colorado in the economic doldrums, and population actually declined during the '60s. Late in that decade, however, better transportation gave renewed hope. Farmers began arriving in large numbers, including such organized group migrations as produced Greeley, Longmont, Evans, and Green City. More people brought greater prosperity and a renewal of interest in statehood. Colorado was admitted to the Union in 1876 as the centennial state.

NEVADA

The height of the Colorado gold boom coincided with the discovery of what was probably the richest ore-bearing region of the United States — the Comstock Lode of Nevada. The name came not from the discoverer but from one of the early claimants, who sold out his holdings within two months for $11,000. While Comstock threw away millions by this sale he was not acting stupidly; up to this time all mining had been of the placer variety and there was no knowledge of the vast store of wealth a few feet under-

ground. But by late 1859 it was discovered that a sample of the
" blue stuff " (quartz), hitherto disregarded as worthless, assayed
at $1595 in gold and $4791 in silver per ton. A new era had opened.

The first big rush to Nevada came from California late in 1859,
as thousands of the young and old, feeble and strong, men and
women, trudged across the high Sierras to the new El Dorado. Over
20,000 people arrived within a few months, with Virginia City
and Carson City the centers of their interest. For the first time
people had become silver crazy; the golden sun was sinking and
the silver moon was rising.

The search for silver posed many new and perplexing problems.
Everyone knew that silver could be found in quartz rock, but not
all quartz contained silver. Furthermore, quartz ledges ran in
seams, so that rich surface indications might disappear a little
farther down the seam, or a poor seam might develop into rich ore
under the surface. The result was that the miners dug exploratory
shafts all over the country. Enthusiastic miners might even start
digging in the street of a town or under a house, for no land was
sacred in the search for quick wealth.

Extensive prospecting by hit-or-miss methods produced much
waste and wild fluctuations in the prices of claims. Hundreds of
abandoned shafts gave proof of the days, weeks, or even months
of wasted labor. Mining claims, as represented by their stock, were
subject to vigorous speculation; they were sold and traded freely,
and even given away to friends. Every man could show a varied
assortment of from ten to a hundred different kinds of mining
stock. The prices of these securities fluctuated with tremendous
leaps. The shares of the Alpha mine, for example, which sold for
$1570 in February 1868, could find but few buyers at $33 in September of the same year.

The process of quartz mining which was typical of Nevada was
entirely different from the earlier gold operations in California.
The necessity for expensive machinery made the large companies
supreme. Individual miners had two possible options. They might
either spend their entire time in prospecting, and sell the resulting
claims to the larger companies, or else they might dig out the
quartz and then send it to the companies for smelting; in the latter
case they frequently paid an unreasonable fee for the service.

The income of some of the Nevada mines was little short of marvelous. The Gould and Curry mine took out $9,000,000 of ore in
the two years 1863 and 1864; the original investment in the mine

and buildings and machinery had been $200,000, and the dividends were $2,908,000. The Ophir mine extracted $15,000,000 of metal, although only $1,400,000 was returned in dividends. In the period of 1859–80 the total cost of operating all of the Nevada mines was $62,000,000; the bullion extracted had a value of $306,000,000; the dividends declared were $118,000,000.

Early mining life in Nevada had all the characteristics which distinguished every western mining rush. The men worked hard, lived poorly, and preserved their courage by exciting amusements and the hope of future wealth. Coarse, cheap, heavy clothing was the rule, with buttons reduced to the absolutely necessary minimum, and each man doing his own mending. Each man was his own cook, and on account of the scarcity of food the staples were flapjacks, beans, bacon, and coffee; the less said about their appetizing features the better. Housing long remained a difficult problem because of the lack of wood. In the early days wood was used only for cooking, and tents furnished the usual accommodations; in the winter many a man conserved fuel by living in a cave in the side of a hill.

As had been the case in California the chief forms of amusement were drinking and gambling. The best known saloon was the " Jones Canvas Hotel " at Virginia City, which was a tent of eighteen by forty feet; the bar was an old sluice box, the whiskey was contained in pitchers, and tin cups took the place of glasses. The gambling halls were well patronized, and could be recognized by the streams of profanity, shouting, and smoke which issued from their doors. The usual undesirable element put in its appearance with great rapidity — desperadoes, bad men, claim jumpers, gamblers, and prostitutes. A killer such as Sam Brown could stab a man in cold blood and then peacefully go to sleep on a convenient billiard table. Now and then came a group of wandering players, whose performance in some saloon or store was given a cordial reception. The first theatrical performance given in Virginia City was on September 29, 1860.

Prices in Nevada, as in other boom regions, were both high and fluctuating. Typical were brown sugar at fifty cents a pound, rice at forty-five cents, butter at a dollar, nails at a dollar, and whiskey at fifty cents a glass. The result was that a considerable part of the wealth of the mines went to the freighters, the storekeepers, and the gamblers. The usual wage of the miner who worked for one of the large companies was four dollars a day, and independent

prospectors did not average much better. The average income of
the man who worked for himself was little more than enough to
pay for the necessities of life, including the outfit for his next prospecting trip. Many of the miners could not even afford this minimum, and had to have their outfits advanced by silent partners
who were promised half of whatever finds were made. Such chances
rarely brought profit.

The search of the Nevada miner for paying ore was something
different from that of his predecessor who merely had looked for
free deposits of gold. His prospecting might take months and cover
hundreds of miles. Whenever he saw quartz that seemed promising
he examined it with a magnifying glass for possible specks of uncombined gold and silver. If this examination were satisfactory
he pulverized a specimen, washed the light matter away and dissolved the remainder in nitric acid. He then added salt of hydro-
chloric acid, which precipitated chloride of silver. This was dried
and then heated with a little soda in a hollowed piece of charcoal
by the flame of a candle. The result was a button of pure silver
which showed in a rough way the richness of the original specimen.
Sometimes, instead of following this process, the prospector only
collected samples and then carried them back to experts for assay-
ing. In any case if the prospects were good a claim was marked
and work started; if not, and this situation was more usual, the
prospecting expedition was continued.

Nevada was one of the few places where fortunes were made by
individual miners, although this happy result was by no means always due to the foresight and energy of the successful miner. Often
he might trade shares in his own mine for such attractive speculations as " Root Hog or Die," " Dry Up," " Grizzly Hill," " Wake
Up Jake," " Let Her Rip," " You Bet," or " Gouge Eye." If one
of these chances turned out to be rich he dug down into his box
of securities until he unearthed the right one, and then cashed in
on his good fortune.

Lucky miners who made their fortunes this way were notoriously easy to separate from their money. " Sandy " Bowers furnishes an excellent example. Bowers was an ordinary miner, married to a washerwoman, when he made a rich strike which netted
him more money than he had ever imagined existed in the world.
Immediately he built a house costing $407,000 and entertained lav-
ishly. Then he spent three years in Europe, during which time he
bought everything but the Tower of London. Upon his return to

Virginia City he hired a hotel and held open house for the entire town. When the mine's ore was finally exhausted (about 1868), Bowers was penniless and went back to prospecting. His wife told fortunes.

READINGS

P. Bailey, *Sam Brannan and the California Mormons* (1943); C. A. Barker (ed.), *Memoirs of Elisha Oscar Crosby* (1945)— gold rush; H. E. Briggs, *Frontiers of the Northwest* (1940), ch. 1; J. R. Browne, *A Dangerous Journey: California 1849* (1950); J. G. Bruff, *Gold Rush* (2 vols., 1944)—contemporary; F. A. Buck, *A Yankee Trader in the Gold Rush* (1930); J. W. Caughey, *California* (1953), ch. 16, *Gold Is the Cornerstone* (1948), *History of the Pacific Coast* (1933), chs. 18, 19, (ed.), *Rushing for Gold* (1949), (ed.), *Seeing the Elephant* (1951)—gold rush; R. G. Cleland, *The Cattle on a Thousand Hills* (1941), chs. 4–10, *A History of California* (1922), chs. 17–21, (ed.), *Apron Full of Gold* (1949)—woman '49er; C. Collins (ed.), *Sam Ward in the Gold Rush* (1949); O. C. Coy, *Gold Days* (1929), *The Great Trek* (1931)—routes to California; L. F. Crawford, *Rekindling Camp Fires* (1926); R. Eccleston, *Overland to California on the Southwestern Trail* (1950); G. W. B. Evans, *Mexican Gold Trail* (1945) —'49er; P. S. Fritz, *Colorado* (1941), chs. 6–10, 17; E. M. Gagey, *The San Francisco Stage* (1950), chs. 1–3; V. Geiger and W. Bryarly, *Trail to California* (1945)—diary; C. B. Glasscock, *The Big Bonanza* (1931), chs. 1–11—Nevada—*Lucky Baldwin* (1933)—San Francisco; L. R. Hafen, *Colorado* (1933), chs. 7–11, (ed.), *Colorado and Its People* (4 vols., 1948), vol. 1, chs. 10–15, (ed.), *Pike's Peak Gold Rush Guidebooks of 1859* (1941); I. Howbert, *Memories of a Lifetime in the Pike's Peak Region* (1925), chs. 1–5; O. T. Howe, *Argonauts of '49* (1923); A. B. Hulbert, *Forty-Niners* (1931)—synthetic diary; J. H. Jackson, *Anybody's Gold* (1941)—mining towns; D. C. Kemp, *Colorado's Little Kingdom* (1949)—good pictures; O. Lewis, *Sea Routes to the Gold Fields* (1949)—entertaining—*Silver Kings* (1947)— readable; C. Lindsay, *The Big Horn Basin* (1932), ch. 3; E. Lord, *Comstock Mining and Miners* (1883); G. D. Lyman, *The Saga of the Comstock* (1934); F. Marryat, *Mountains and Molehills* (1952)—California in 1850; J. Monaghan, *The Overland Trail* (1947), ch. 14; A. Murdoch, *Boom Copper* (1943), chs. 1–14; G. Nute, *Lake Superior* (1944), chs. 7, 11—iron, copper; E. Page,

Wagons West (1930) ; G. Paine, *Eilley Orum* (1929) ; R. W. Paul, *California Gold* (1947) ; J. E. Pomfret (ed.), *California Gold Rush Voyages, 1848–1849* (1954) ; G. C. Quiett, *Pay Dirt* (1936), chs. 1–7—gold; G. W. Read (ed.), *A Pioneer of 1850* (1927) ; G. W. Read and R. Gaines (eds.), *Gold Rush* (1943) ; W. W. Robinson, *Land In California* (1948) ; C. H. Shinn, *Mining Camps* (1948)—reprint of old book—*The Story of the Mine* (1906), chs. 1–5; W. J. Trimble, *The Mining Advance into the Inland Empire* (1914)—still good; S. E. White, *The Forty-Niners* (1920)— Chronicles of America; J. F. Willard (ed.), *The Union Colony at Greeley, Colorado* (1918) ; J. F. Willard and C. B. Goodykoontz (eds.), *Experiments in Colorado Colonization* (1926) ; M. F. Williams, *History of the San Francisco Committee of Vigilance of 1851* (1921) ; G. F. Willison, *Here They Dug the Gold* (1931), chs. 1–8; O. O. Winther, *The Great Northwest* (1947), ch. 14, *The Old Oregon Country* (1951), chs. 13, 14; R. K. Wyllys, *Arizona* (1950), chs. 6, 10; W. D. Wyman (ed.), *California Emigrant Letters* (1952)—letters of '49ers.

CHAPTER 29

THE
OVERLAND ROUTE

EARLY settlers in the Far West were practically isolated from their friends and relatives back East. The transmission of letters was a precarious business. Books, clothing, hardware, and other desirable elements of living were 3000 miles away, while markets for western products were equally remote. Such conditions were unpleasant even for the fortune seeker who expected soon to return to the East, but were intolerable for the man who had awakened to the realization that either because of desire or necessity his stay was to be much longer than he had originally planned.

COMMUNICATIONS WITH THE PACIFIC COAST

The best communication in the early days was by the ocean, even though no regular service existed. The shipper of goods or sender of letters had the trouble of finding a boat going to the general region in which he was interested and then of dickering with the captain for transportation. The journey around the Horn was time-consuming and the captain took little responsibility for deliveries; the letter might never reach the addressee, the goods might be dropped on the wharf to rot. Regardless of price, such service was unsatisfactory. The Pacific Coast seemed as isolated as Kamchatka or Capetown.

By land, transportation was even worse. Freight sent by wagon was slow, erratic, uncertain, and expensive. Rarely were goods of sufficient value to be worth shipment. For letters, it was necessary to find some person who was making the trip and then to rely on his kindness and memory. Here and there along the overland trails was a primitive " post office," usually a deserted cabin or the crotch of a tree, where letters and papers would be deposited in the hope that some future traveler would deliver them. No doubt some few were actually delivered, but the main profit was to passersby who could amuse themselves by reading the mail that had been deposited.

OCEAN MAIL CONTRACTS

Regularly scheduled communication depended largely on subsidies by the federal government. Regularity of operation was difficult and unnecessary unless mail was carried, and mail was profitable only with a government subsidy. The first mail contracts by the Panama route came in 1847. The men winning the concession from New York to Panama incorporated the United States Mail Steamship Company, while those who won the western contract from Panama to San Francisco chartered the Pacific Mail Steamship Company. Both groups started operations in 1849, with the western part of the trip the first to be opened. The first boat, the *California*, reached San Francisco along with the first big mining rush; all the crew deserted for the mines except the captain and one cabin boy. The original monthly mail service became semimonthly in 1851 with a government payment of $724,350 a year. The postage rate after 1855 was ten cents a half-ounce. Passenger rates were very high — a cabin all the way from New York to San Francisco in 1849 cost over $500, which of course was exclusive of the trip over the isthmus. Quite obviously the companies made large profits.

Big profits meant increased competition, and both the eastern and western companies occupied the whole route. This situation ended by an agreement (January 1851) for a division of territory. Even more important Cornelius Vanderbilt entered the fight with a complete service through Nicaragua in 1851, and his boats were more comfortable. While Vanderbilt was on a vacation in 1853 his associates double-crossed him and acquired control of his Accessory Transit Company, which handled the Nicaragua business. On his return, the three companies paid him a subsidy to keep his fingers out of the pie. The three companies alternately maintained rates and fought bitterly among themselves.

The Pacific Mail Steamship people took the initiative in remedying the very bad conditions on the Panama isthmus. In time (1853) they could sell through tickets from New York to San Francisco. The greatest improvement was the opening of the Panama Railroad in 1855 — forty-seven miles, for which the fare was twenty-five dollars; obviously it made large profits. The railroad gave a big advantage to the Pacific Mail Steamship Company, even after Vanderbilt reacquired control of the Accessory Transit Company (1856) and put up a fight. Vanderbilt had to battle Walker in Nicaragua as well as his steamship competitors, and for some years furnished no good service. Ultimately (1860) Vanderbilt got control of all the Atlantic business while the Pacific Mail got that of the Pacific, and rates went up. In time the transcontinental railroads were to bribe the steamships to avoid rate cutting.

Some efforts were also made to obtain mail service by the Tehuantepec route. An American concession, including the right to build a railroad, was given in 1853. Five years later came a mail contract at $250,000 a year, but the service was never satisfactory and was soon abandoned. Incidentally, while mail and passengers went through Central America, the great bulk of the freight continued to make the trip around the Horn.

LOOKING TOWARD OVERLAND MAIL ROUTES

The Panama route, while an improvement, left much to be desired. It was still long and slow, passed through foreign territory, required two reshipments, and was extremely circuitous for all points east of California. Westerners continued to agitate for more direct overland service, for which in general three routes were possible. Least desirable was the most northern by way of the Missouri and Columbia rivers. It was long, passed through few settlements, traversed the country of hostile Indians, and included bad mountain passes which were practically unusable in winter.

The central route had difficulties toward the west in dangerous deserts and mountains, but for most of its course was easy and well-marked, short, with few hostile Indians, and with the added advantage of passing the Mormon settlement. The southern route might follow either the 35th parallel from Santa Fe or the Gila River after the Gadsden Purchase. The most southerly of these options was the better, with few mountains and no winter snow, although it was long, and indirect, and crossed much desert country.

The beginning of overland mail service came in 1848, when a contract was awarded for the trip between Independence and Salt Lake City; the next year service was started to Santa Fe. Even these comparatively easy sections of the route proved difficult and deliveries were slow and uncertain. Provision was finally made (1851) for the western section of the central route, but two years later overwhelming difficulties led to moving the terminus from the San Francisco area to Los Angeles. Conditions remained unsatisfactory, however, partly because of the normal difficulties of travel and partly because the mule pack trains were at the best slow.

As western population increased the demand for coach service became greater and greater, while the more progressive citizens talked of railroads. A few ingenious persons considered another possibility. By common knowledge a considerable portion of the Southwest was a desert, so why not take a lesson from the Near East and use camels? The federal government was sufficiently impressed to detail an army officer to buy the necessary camels and seventy-five were delivered outside San Antonio in 1856. To the disappointment of lovers of the picturesque, camels did not prove practical in the " American desert."

Whatever the means of transportation, more adequate geographical knowledge was desirable. In spite of great amounts of earlier travel, including the Frémont expeditions of 1842, 1843, and 1845, doubts remained as to whether all available routes had been discovered and adequately surveyed. Between 1845 and 1853 at least twenty-five new expeditions were dispatched to less known parts of the West, while in addition there were thousands of reports from immigrants and other travelers.

The greatest single exploration of the West came in the years 1853 to 1855 under the orders of Secretary of War Jefferson Davis, with the primary objective of surveying all possible railroad routes. The explorations produced only the routes hitherto known: (1) the northern, between 47° and 49°; (2) the central, between 38° and 42°; (3) the southern, through Albuquerque and along the 35th parallel; (4) the southern along the 32nd parallel and following the Gila River. Davis was southern, and possibly for that reason concluded from the vast amount of evidence that one of the southern routes was to be preferred, but Congress failed to act upon his recommendations.

BUTTERFIELD

A speculative railroad to be built at some unspecified date in the future came far from satisfying the westerners who wanted immediate action. Their impatience produced results in 1857 when the Postmaster General called for bids on a fast and continuous service to the coast by road. The final contract was awarded to a group of men including John Butterfield who was one of the founders of the American Express Company, William C. Fargo of Wells, Fargo & Company, and William B. Dinsmore, later president of Adams Express Company. The payment was to be a federal subsidy of $600,000 a year for a semiweekly service taking not over twenty-five days for a single trip. As opened, the line started from both St. Louis and Memphis, converged at Little Rock, and then passed through Preston, El Paso, and Yuma on its way to San Francisco, 2795 miles distant.

Butterfield took a year to prepare for the opening of his line. The first stages left opposite ends in September 1858. The eastbound stage covered the distance in twenty days, eighteen hours, and sixteen minutes, which was well within the specified time limit. The Far West had now taken the first big step in acquiring rapid communication with the East.

The facilities of the Butterfield Overland Stage Company were of necessity elaborate and expensive, costing about a million dollars to install. Stages had to travel both night and day, which meant frequent changes of horses and drivers. " Swing stations " provided minimum care of the stock, while periodic larger " home stations " provided also company agents and meals for travelers. Stations were placed at intervals of between eight and twenty-five miles.

The coaches used in the traffic were of the Concord variety, so named from their birthplace of Concord, New Hampshire. Wide tires made the work of the horses less laborious on the sandy stretches. Leather straps served for springs, and leather curtains excluded a portion of the inclement weather. The three seats were built to accommodate nine passengers, although more were sometimes crowded into the space. The driver was perched on the top in front, and now and then a passenger or two rode alongside him. Mail and packages were put in the " boot " at the back, unless an overflow necessitated their taking passenger room. Mark Twain tells of a trip in which the mail was placed on the floor for the passengers to use as a bed. It was more usual in such cases, however, for the mail to be dumped in a pile beside the road to wait for an empty coach; passengers paid ready cash, while government mail was carried at a flat rate.

A trip on the overland stage was by no means a pleasure excursion. The passengers jolted steadily for over three weeks, day and night, on the most primitive of roads. Sleeping in a moving coach filled with passengers was done only in snatches. When the sun was shining the passengers roasted, and with rain they got wet, while in dry weather the dust was suffocating. Toilet facilities were nonexistent, so that bathing and shaving waited until the end of the trip. Little wonder that the passengers drank untold quantities of whiskey to keep up their courage. With little sleep, plenty of whiskey, and little water, travelers in the overland stage became a wild-looking aggregation before they arrived at the end of their trip.

One of the worst features of overland stage travel was the food. Of course each passenger might carry his own provisions, but food which could be carried in the hot sun for three weeks and then eaten without cooking was neither varied nor appetizing. The company furnished food only at the home stations, and even there it was far from luxuriant fare. The usual diet was rancid bacon, maggoty bread, and coffee that tasted like dishwater. The price for this unappetizing meal sometimes went as high as $1.50. The care of passengers was always secondary to the care of the livestock, for horses and mules were expensive to replace.

The drivers on the overland stages were sometimes drunk and always profane. The superintendents were even worse, although they had the virtue of being at least more thoroughgoing in their wickedness; frequently they were " bad men " making a little extra money when their own business was dull. The fare charged by the company varied with the amount of traffic and the business conditions of the country. A typical charge was that of 1859 — $200 for the trip west and $150 returning east; the difference between the two amounts represented the difference of the traffic in the two directions.

Butterfield did not confine his attention entirely to passenger and mail service, for along with them he promoted freighting activities. This portion of his traffic was in no way different from similar business carried on by other persons. The wagons, drawn by mules or oxen, lumbered across the plains just as they always had done, and made no particular effort to attain speed. There was no great rush to get freight across the continent, since time did not injure most articles; perishable commodities were not shipped. Many years were to pass before such products as fruits, vegetables, and dressed meats could be produced in the Far West for marketing in the East.

PONY EXPRESS

The passenger and freight business on the plains during the late '50s was not all carried by the Butterfield company, even though that organization was the largest in the field. Other companies appeared from time to time, some of them operating over long periods of years, and some having United States mail contracts. The most important of them was Russell, Majors & Waddell, which operated along the central route. Its organization was much the same as that of its southern competitor. Its most important division point was Julesburg (present Colorado), which was then the toughest town in the West.

It was the company of Russell, Majors & Waddell which added further to the speed of the trip across the plains by introducing the Pony Express. For some years Senator Gwin of California had urged upon William H. Russell the desirability of giving the people of California faster transportation, and had suggested the possibility of developing a sort of horse telegraph system. Not least among the advantages claimed for the plan was that it would advertise the central route, and might thus mean later mail contracts for Russell, Majors & Waddell. Russell was impressed by the idea. At first he attempted to obtain governmental assistance, but when he was unsuccessful in this effort decided to go ahead on his own resources. Stations were outfitted across the plains at ten-mile intervals, and Russell himself picked out hundreds of the fleetest horses and a highly selected group of riders.

Public announcement of the Pony Express created a great sensation. Russell advertised his willingness to transport letters between St. Joseph, Missouri, and Placerville, California, at $5.00 an ounce, and to do it in ten days, which was just half of Butterfield's best time. Later the rate declined to a dollar a half-ounce. Considerable doubt was expressed by many observers as to whether this speed were possible, particularly in winter. Leaving this doubt necessarily unresolved for the time being the route was opened on April 3, 1860, when the first rider left St. Joe; the next day another rider went out of Sacramento. The first trip was made in ten and a half days. The future was to show whether this time could be maintained, or possibly improved.

The practicability of the Pony Express rested primarily upon the ability and endurance of the riders. Care was taken to choose only light men and boys, and the weight of their clothes and equipment was reduced to the smallest possible minimum. The mail was wrapped in oiled silk to protect it from the weather. The burden carried on a trip was between forty and ninety letters, depending upon their bulk. Little wonder that the cost of the service was comparatively high.

The rider was expected to average nine miles an hour, day and night, with not over two minutes for changing horses. The usual "run" of a rider was between seventy-five and a hundred miles, with the round trip twice a week. Sometimes, due to sickness or accident, runs were increased; at one time "Pony Bob" Haslam covered 380 miles with but nine hours rest. It was a hard and dangerous life, and more than the usual amount of courage and stamina was required for the fast riding on bad roads in all kinds of weather, with perpetual danger from the Indians. The men received ordinarily about $125 a month for this work.

The real test of the Pony Express and of the route over which it operated came in the winter of 1860–61. The cold and snow resulted in perceptibly slower time, but still the men continued to ride through, and by the spring of 1861 they were averaging nine days for the trip. Even under extremely bad conditions, Lincoln's inaugural address was carried the 1600 miles between the ends of the telegraph line in seven days, seventeen hours.

The Pony Express attained its objective in proving that the central route was rapid and feasible for year round travel, but in the process of demonstrating this fact the firm of Russell, Majors & Waddell went bankrupt. The failure of the Pony Express to return profits was not unexpected, and the failure of the company which supported it was in part due to other causes. Of great importance in this connection was the completion of the first telegraph line across the plains in October 1861. No longer was there any real reason for the existence of a Pony Express, since the only type of message which could be sent by this means was delivered more rapidly and cheaply by the telegraph.

Even more disastrous to Russell's hopes was the failure of his company to benefit by expected government mail contracts. At the beginning of the Civil War the Confederates captured a portion of the route and property of the Butterfield company, which led Russell and his partners to expect that when the overland mail service was of necessity moved farther north they would get the contracts. Instead of this development taking place, Butterfield himself moved to the central route and continued operations until his contract expired in 1862. By that time Russell, Majors & Waddell had become bankrupt and had been forced to sell their interests (1862) to Ben Holladay, who was shortly to become dominant in overland transportation.

HOLLADAY

Ben Holladay was one of the best known figures on the plains during the '60s. Personally he was coarse, crude, uncouth, and lacking in education, but these less desirable qualities were offset by a keen mind, unusual foresightedness, and the supreme ability to organize and control men. Holladay was born in Kentucky and entered business at an early age, becoming a successful merchant in Missouri in the late '30s. His interest turned gradually to transportation, culminating in his purchase of Russell, Majors & Waddell in 1862. He expanded the business of the company rapidly until in 1866 he had over three thousand miles of stage line under his control. Probably his was the greatest one-man business in the United States. In addition to stage and freighting lines he had steamships running to Oregon, Panama, China, and Japan. Holladay spent most of his time in the East, where he had mansions in New York and Washington. During sessions of Congress he was generally to be found in Washington.

Ben Holladay's reputation throughout the United States was well illustrated in a story told by Mark Twain, and although there may be some doubts as to the exact truth of the incident, there is no doubt that the general point of view is accurate. According to the story a party of American tourists was visiting the Holy Land, and one of the boys of the group was being told impressively of how Moses had led the Israelites through three hundred miles of desert in forty years. He listened patiently for a while, but then could contain himself no longer: " Forty years? Only three hundred miles? Humph! Ben Holladay would have fetched them through in thirty-six hours."

Holladay's success was due in considerable part to his ability to organize his project satisfactorily. The main line of his overland route across the plains had three divisions, from Atchison to Denver, Denver to Salt Lake City, and Salt Lake City to Placerville. A superintendent had immediate supervision over each division. A conductor, or messenger, rode with each coach on the seat in front with the driver, his " beat " being about two hundred miles. The presence of this authorized representative of the company prevented many of the undesirable incidents which formerly had taken place on the Butterfield line.

The driver was the most interesting man in the employ of the company, since it was he who held the reins of power. His characteristics were somewhat different from those of his predecessor who drove for Butterfield. Usually he was a reticent, somewhat taciturn individual, who interrupted his driving only to chew and spit. Almost never did he use whiskey while on the job. When he was properly approached he told fascinating stories of holdups, accidents, and Indian attacks. With constant retelling these stories attained imposing proportions. The coach which the driver controlled was of the same type that had been driven on the plains for so many years. Each coach was drawn by four or six horses, which were picked for speed and endurance.

The stations along the Holladay route were very similar to those formerly maintained by Butterfield, and were placed at intervals of ten to fifteen miles. About every fifty miles was a home station, where the drivers were changed. Even the home station was exceedingly crude, the central building being constructed of rough logs and having a dirt floor. Ordinarily it included a blacksmith shop, living quarters for the drivers, and facilities for serving meals. All supplies used in the stations had to be hauled there by team. The worst element on the road was that of the stock tenders; most of them were undesirables and some had criminal records.

The price of the trip from the Missouri River to the Pacific varied widely because of the financial confusion of the period. Rates of travel advanced as the Civil War continued, paper depreciated, and other prices advanced. In 1863 the fare from Atchison to Denver was $75, to Salt Lake City $150, and to Placerville $225. In 1865 the cost of the trip to Denver was $175 and to Salt Lake City $350, while a little later prices were even higher.

The days of coach traffic across the plains were comparatively few, and the influence of the business on the era is remarkable in view of its brief existence. By the middle '60s farsighted men such as Holladay saw that the end was in view, for even then the Union Pacific was creeping across the plains. Holladay did not wait for the end, but sold out to Wells, Fargo & Company in 1866. The completion of the railroad three years later brought an end to the major portion of the transcontinental coaching traffic. It continued to exist for many years, however, in regions to which the railroad did not extend. The Deadwood stage of the '70s and '80s was famous, probably because of its use in Buffalo Bill's Wild West Show.

The stage portion of the traffic across the plains was much more picturesque than other forms of transportation, but it was no more important than the freighting which was done both by individuals and by large companies. The business was conducted ordinarily in covered wagons drawn by ox or mule teams. It was estimated that at one time Russell, Majors & Waddell had 6250 wagons and 75,000 oxen in use. A big wagon held three to five tons of freight, and a standard " train " included twenty-five freight wagons, together with a mess wagon, and extra animals and parts. Ordinarily oxen were the motive power, but sometimes mules were used. The usual six yoke of oxen per wagon was sometimes increased to ten or twelve under bad conditions. The " bull-whacker " or " mule-skinner " was particularly noted for his prowess with a thirty- to fifty-foot lash, which he could make snap like a pistol, and for his picturesquely profane vocabulary.

RAILROAD FINANCING

Coach travel was but a short episode in the life of the Far West. The successor of the coach was the railroad, which was adapted to conquer the long flat stretches of the plains. Not that the West had no problems to trouble the railroad — in fact there were many — but rather that the railroad offered by far the best solution to the special needs of the western farmer, stockman, and miner.

When the first trans-Mississippi railroads were constructed in the '50s American railroads were as yet in the first quarter-century of their history. Connections were just being made from the eastern seaboard to such middle western cities as Chicago, St. Louis, and Memphis. The first bridge across the Mississippi had just been built. Moreover population was scant and capital scarce; farmers were land poor, whether acting as individuals or as groups. The West lacked knowledge of the technical details of financing, construction, and operation, and was deficient in labor, skilled, unskilled, or managerial. It assumed the railroads would never compete effectively with good river transportation and hence could be used only as feeders; most westerners saw no reason for changing their minds even after the opening of the first bridge across the Mississippi in 1855.

The West was never long intimidated by obstacles, no matter how apparently overwhelming. During the late '40s and early '50s railroad enthusiasm was spurred by the camp meeting technique, with large and enthusiastic gatherings at such cities as Chicago, Iowa City, St. Louis, Little Rock, and Memphis. These meetings stressed plans for a railroad to the coast, but the resulting interest also spurred the construction of local lines. Congressmen were urged to work for federal aid and there was talk of state loans, county loans, city loans, town loans. Every possibility was canvassed hopefully.

Early western railroad projects, some going back to the '30s, were planned primarily as adjuncts to water transportation and only secondarily as the main means of transportation between the larger towns. Railroads were supported as public improvements, much like the parks and museums of a later day. Their backers were considered public-spirited citizens, acting in large part philanthropically. Not the railroad but the community was expected to profit. Costs of transportation would decline, property values would rise, profits of farmers would increase. The West would thus be able economically to raise itself by its own bootstraps.

The basic necessity if railroads were to be built was the collection of sufficient capital. The most obvious method of financing was to invite personal subscriptions, but while pledges were easy to obtain they were difficult to collect unless they were in land or labor. The West had little surplus capital; the great bulk of the funds had to come either directly or indirectly from the East or from Europe.

A second financial possibility was to utilize the credit of a small governmental unit, as that of a town, county, or city. A town, for example, would issue bonds to be exchanged for railroad stock or bonds. The town bonds would then be sold by the railroad in the East, usually at a large discount. To obtain such assistance, the railroad might play one town against another. Two or three routes might be surveyed, even if the final line had already been decided upon and the towns were encouraged to compete in offering assistance to obtain the road.

A third possibility of aid in financing was the state, which might use its bonds in the same way as the county or town. Missouri loaned some $19,000,000 in this way; the money was almost completely lost. Minnesota hurried her admission to the Union so she could loan $5,000,000 to prospective railroads. No railroads resulted, and ultimately Minnesota paid off her bonds at fifty cents on the dollar without providing for accrued interest. California gave some assistance to the Central Pacific. Texas had probably the best record, getting more railroads for her money than other states. In addition, Texas had her own land grant policy, for the state controlled her own public domain.

Both states and smaller political units found difficulty in paying their bonds, since many of the twenty-year issues fell due during the depression of the '70s. States were sovereign and hence could delay payment or repudiate. Towns and counties were less fortunate because the courts held such debts collectible, even though there had been minor irregularities in issuing the bonds. Most notorious was the hide-and-seek played by Yankton, South Dakota, officials to avoid payment. Conservative easterners were so aghast at this display of what they considered the western temperament that they argued against statehood for the Dakotas. Ultimately, of course, the bonds were paid.

The fourth possible source of railroad funds was the federal government, which had a precedent in its earlier aid of roads and canals. Loans would have been most delightful but were improbable. Land was different. The West held that land gifts would benefit the entire country by increasing western population and trade. Even the government would not lose, because alternate sections could be doubled in price, thus producing as much revenue as before. Congress remained reluctant because of sectional antagonisms until the Illinois Central grant of 1850 broke the jam. After 1850 all of the first tier of states west of the Mississippi were given railroad grants, while specific projects farther west were also aided.

The grants of the '50s were all similar in terms. The railroad was given alternate sections within six miles on each side of the road, and in case any of the land had already been settled, the railroad was allowed to make indemnity selections within fifteen miles. The grants were to revert to the public domain if the aided roads were not completed within ten years. After 1860 grants were made only to such strategic roads as the Union Pacific, Santa Fe, Northern Pacific, Texas & Pacific, and Atlantic & Pacific; their terms were usually somewhat more generous because the value of the lands farther west was less.

The administration of the railroad grants was in the hands of the General Land Office. As soon as a railroad filed its approximate route all of the land within the indemnity limits was withdrawn from sale, so that the settler might not occupy regions which might later be found to belong to the railroad. As fast as the road was located definitely land selections were made, final patents were issued, and the remainder of the land thrown back on the market.

The policy concerning railroad lands was a constant source of annoyance to prospective settlers. Large areas, frequently including much excellent land, were closed to settlement. The settler felt that he should have the right to take up unoccupied land at his own pleasure, and often proceeded to do so in spite of all restrictions. The situation was aggravated when the Supreme Court decided that the reversion clause of the grants did not work automatically, but needed special legislation by Congress. The result was that land grants were often kept out of the market for many years, even though the railroad gave no indication of building.

The last of the railroad grants was made in the early '70s, the end of the policy being due to a rising anti-railroad feeling which was evidenced also by the Granger movement. Approximately 180,000,000 acres of the public domain were actually received by the railroads. The total value of the gifts, at the prices for which the land was sold, amounted to possibly $500,000,000.

RAILROAD BUILDING

The railroad plans for which the West desired assistance in the '50s were of two general types, although in practice these two were often mixed. The first was the transcontinental project, which became somewhat more important a little later; many roads which today are of purely local significance at one time had plans for building across the continent. More important, the transcontinental projects aroused an enthusiasm which oftentimes advanced the construction of local lines.

The second type of western railroad project of the '50s was the one which was included in the plans of the various states for complete state transportational systems. In such plans each state considered primarily its own interests and paid but little attention to possible through connections with neighboring states. Minnesota proposed several lines running east and west across the state, and others centering in St. Paul. Almost every Iowa road was planned to run east and west. The Missouri system, with the exception of a northern road across the state, centered at St. Louis, Arkansas roads at Little Rock, and Texas roads at Galveston Bay.

The first feeble beginnings of actual construction occurred in these states during the '50s. Missouri, Iowa, and Texas acquired a few short, weak lines. Far west in California there was built a short mining road. These early efforts were ended by the panic of 1857, which in many ways was similar to the one of twenty years earlier, since both were caused largely by an excess of speculation in western internal improvements. Before the panic had receded and prosperity returned, the Civil War further disorganized the financial condition of the country.

Only two trans-Mississippi roads made important progress in the period immediately after the panic of 1857. The Hannibal and St. Joseph was completed in 1859 between the two cities named in its title, thus connecting the Mississippi and Missouri rivers north of St. Louis. The Missouri Pacific, after meeting many trials and tribulations, was finally finished from St. Louis to Kansas City in 1865.

The Civil War proved more destructive to the railroads of the Southwest than to those of the Northwest. Some of the lines in Missouri and Texas were used for military purposes, and upon various occasions portions of them were destroyed. When the war ended the South had less miles of railroad than it had possessed at the opening of hostilities. On the other hand the North continued to build, though more slowly, in part because of the necessity for finding a route which would replace the Mississippi in shipping goods to market. Such states as Wisconsin, Minnesota, and Iowa made reasonably satisfactory progress during the war period.

With the return of prosperity after the war, railroad plans and construction once more attained the center of the stage. The second bridge across the Mississippi (at Clinton, Iowa) was completed in 1865, and others followed. Excluding small projects, three main groups of lines, as classified by their objectives, were building. The first was the transcontinental group, exemplified by the Union Pacific, which was completed in 1869.

The second group, the so-called " granger " roads, was being built from Chicago and St. Louis to the Missouri River. The two Missouri roads have already been noted. The Chicago & Northwestern, crossing the Mississippi at Clinton, was finished to Council Bluffs in 1867. The Chicago & Rock Island, crossing the river at Rock Island, reached Council Bluffs in 1869. The Chicago, Burlington & Quincy, crossing at Burlington, also arrived at Council Bluffs in 1869. The Illinois Central, crossing at Dubuque, was opened to Sioux City in 1870. The Chicago, Milwaukee & St. Paul, the other important road of the group, did not attain its objective of the Missouri until the late '70s.

The third group of roads was being built to connect the Missouri River with the Gulf of Mexico. Two of the lines were completed in 1873. The Missouri, Kansas & Texas, commonly known as the " Katy," extended from the end of the Missouri Pacific at Kansas City south to Houston. The other line was really a combination of four roads which together joined St. Louis and Houston: the St. Louis, Iron Mountain & Southern in Missouri; the Cairo & Fulton in Missouri and Arkansas; the Texas & Pacific and the International & Great Northern in Texas.

It was also during the period immediately after the Civil War that the first important effort was made to build up a large and effective railroad system. Its sponsor was James F. Joy, a Detroit banker who was president of the Michigan Central and had an interest in the New York Central. Purchasing the Chicago, Burlington & Quincy he pushed it as far west as Fort Kearny by 1873. Then he added the Hannibal & St. Joseph, which he connected with the " Burlington " in the east, and from which he built branches in the west to Kansas City and Atchison. To these he added the Missouri River, Fort Scott & Gulf, with which he expected to make a connection with the Gulf, although he never succeeded in doing so. Joy's plans were widespread and magnificent, but he had expanded his interests too far for safety and when the panic of 1873 created a financial stringency the " Joy lines " collapsed with a resounding crash.

RAILROAD CONTROL

The attitude of the West toward its railroads, which had been so buoyantly optimistic during the '50s, underwent a radical revision in the early '70s. The first unbridled and rapturous enthusiasm cooled and finally turned to bitter opposition. The hoped-for prosperity had not arrived, while the railroad abuses which had appeared irritated farmers more and more as time passed. Railroad construction and finance had both been notoriously bad. The roads had been badly built, which meant poor service and many wrecks. Financial mismanagement was more common than its reverse. Many roads had been built entirely for the profits in their construction; the original owners juggled the construction accounts, voting themselves lucrative contracts, and finally decamping with all the cash proceeds, leaving the road in hopeless insolvency. Much of the money which had been thus misused had been borrowed from states, towns, and private individuals who could ill afford its loss. When the debts which they had contracted came due in the '70s they experienced a quick and glowing hatred of the railroads as the agency of their impoverishment.

Part of the reason for the reversal of feeling toward the railroads lay in a change in the railroads themselves. Frequently they had started business as small, struggling, local concerns, freighted with the hopes and desires of the community. Now they had grown into vast impersonal corporations; the Chicago roads were becoming dominant as they constructed western additions or bought and consolidated local projects. Most western roads had moved their headquarters, shops, and yards eastward. The executives frequently never saw the country through which their lines ran except through the windows of their private cars. A lack of contact and sympathy was the inevitable result. As expected, transportation charges had gone down, but unexpectedly market prices had also declined, and the farmer failed to benefit as he had hoped. The small producer actually suffered from the new conditions, since inequitable rates, rebates, and other special favors gave the large producer an even greater advantage than he had possessed before the railroad arrived.

The result of changing conditions was that the West's railroad enthusiasm began to abate and opposition to make its appearance. State aid came to an end. Constitutional prohibitions prevented local gifts. No more land grants were made. Regulatory legislation was debated in Congress and came near to passage, while particular states put such laws upon their statute books.

Railroad construction, however, experienced only a temporary cessation because of the panic of 1873. For half a dozen years all work was stopped, but then came a revival in the late '70s and early '80s which resulted in the largest amount of construction of any similar period in United States history. At its end the railroad net of the West was in the form which it was to retain permanently.

The change of the Far West from the stagecoach to the railroad did much more than increase the rapidity of the movement of passengers and freight. The whole concept of the West as a romantic Valhalla of romance was modified. Gone were the lumbering ox-cart, the covered wagon, the long dangerous trip across the plains, the nightly stop with its gleaming campfire. Gone were the jolting stage, the periodic station, the driver with his cracking whip. Gone were the trapper, the trader, the hunter, and the explorer. In their places appeared the modern and efficient, but impersonal, steam locomotive. The result was eventually a transformation in the characteristics and state of mind of the West.

READINGS

ROAD TRAVEL: W. and G. H. Banning, *Six Horses* (1930); L. Beebe and C. Clegg, *U. S. West* (1949)—Wells Fargo; G. D. Bradley, *The Story of the Pony Express* (1928); J. W. Caughey, *California* (1953), ch. 23; A. Chapman, *The Pony Express* (1932) —good; R. G. Cleland, *A History of California* (1922), ch. 24; W. F. Cody, *An Autobiography of Buffalo Bill* (1926), chs. 1, 2, 4; R. P. and M. B. Conkling, *The Butterfield Overland Mail* (3 vols., 1947)—detailed on route; E. Dick, *Vanguards of the Frontier* (1941), chs. 11–15; W. W. Folwell, *A History of Minnesota* (4 vols., 1921), vol. 1, ch. 12, vol. 2, ch. 2; H. D. Fowler, *Camels to California* (1950)—easy reading; J. V. Frederick, *Ben Holladay, the Stage Coach King* (1940)—scholarly; D. Gardiner, *West of the River* (1941), chs. 4, 9–13; L. R. Hafen, *The Overland Mail, 1849–1869* (1926)—scholarly; A. F. Harlow, *Old Post Bags* (1928), ch. 20, *Old Waybills* (1934), chs. 7–24; G. R. Hebard and E. A. Brininstool, *The Bozeman Trail* (2 vols., 1922), vol. 1, pp. 25–117; E. Hungerford, *Wells Fargo* (1949)—rather random account; W. T. Jackson, *Roads West: A Study of Federal Road Surveys and Construction in the Trans-Mississippi West, 1846–1869* (1952); C. Kelly, *Salt Desert Trails* (1930)—Great Salt Desert; J. H. Kemble, *The Panama Route, 1848–1869* (1943); W. C. Kennerly, *Persimmon Hill* (1948)—across the plains in '40s; J. R. Korns, *West from Fort Bridger: The Pioneering of the Immigrant Trail Across Utah, 1846–1850* (1951); L. B. Lesley (ed.), *Uncle Sam's Camels* (1929); J. Monaghan, *The Overland Trail* (1947), ch. 15—Pony Express; W. L. Ormsby, *The Butterfield Overland Mail* (1942); I. D. Paden, *The Wake of the Prairie Schooner* (1943)—finding the original trail to California; F. L. Paxson, *The Last American Frontier* (1915), ch. 11; C. C. Rister, *Southern Plainsmen* (1938), chs. 3, 4; F. A. Root and W. E. Connelley, *The Overland Stage to California* (1941)— a reprint; R. W. Settle (ed.), *The March of the Mounted Riflemen* (1940)—diary of 1849; R. W. and M. L. Settle, *Empire on Wheels* (1949)—Russell, Majors, and Waddell; A. W. Spring, *The Cheyenne and Black Hills Stage* (1949)—detailed; R. L.

Thompson, *Wiring a Continent* (1947), chs. 33–35—telegraph; H. W. Wheeler, *Buffalo Days* (1925); E. A. Wiltsee, *The Pioneer Miner and the Pack Mule Express* (1931); O. O. Winther, *Express and Stagecoach Days in California* (1936), *The Old Oregon Country* (1951), chs. 18, 19, *Via Western Express & Stagecoach* (1945).

RAILROADS: G. L. Allbright, *Official Explorations for Pacific Railroads, 1853–1855* (1921); H. G. Brownson, *History of the Illinois Central Railroad to 1870* (1915)—scholarly; F. A. Cleveland and F. W. Powell, *Railroad Promotion* (1909), chs. 8–15; C. J. Corliss, *Main Line of Mid-America* (1950), chs. 1–12—Illinois Central; P. Gates, *The Illinois Central and Its Colonization Work* (1934); L. H. Haney, *A Congressional History of Railways in the United States to 1850* (1908), chs. 1–13, *A Congressional History of Railways in the United States, 1850–1887* (1910), chs. 2, 3; A. Johnson, *Stephen A. Douglas* (1908), ch. 9; J. L. Kerr, *Missouri Pacific* (1928); A. C. Laut, *The Romance of the Rails* (2 vols., 1929), vol. 1; L. Lewis and S. Pargellis, *Granger Country* (1949)—pictures, C. B. & Q.; F. Merk, *Economic History of Wisconsin* (1916), chs. 9–13; H. G. Pearson, *An American Railroad Builder, John Murray Forbes* (1911)—includes C. B. & Q.; J. R. Perkins, *Trails, Rails and War* (1929), ch. 2; R. E. Riegel, *The Story of the Western Railroads* (1926), chs. 1–4; R. R. Russell, *Improvement of Communication with the Pacific Coast as an Issue in American Politics, 1783–1864* (1948); J. B. Sanborn, *Congressional Grants of Land in Aid of Railways* (1899); W. H. Stennett, *Yesterday and Today* (1910)—C. & N. W.; J. G. Van Deusen, *The Ante-Bellum Southern Commercial Conventions* (1926)—monograph; H. Wender, *Southern Commercial Conventions, 1837–1859* (1930)—monograph.

CHAPTER 30

WAR AND
THE UNION PACIFIC

THE increasingly rapid development of the trans-Mississippi West was retarded by the Civil War. Prospectors continued to make new finds and farmers continued to trickle onto the plains, but in diminishing numbers. The general confusion of the period prevented any new mass migrations to the area beyond the great bend of the Missouri River.

Western sympathies at the outbreak of the war were divided, for population movements had never been limited to the following of isothermic lines. Northerners could be found throughout the Southwest from Texas to California, while southerners might be found in the mines of Colorado or of Montana. As for the Mormons, they were quite content to mind their own business and hope they would be left alone. The greatest problems, however, materialized in the border and southern states; in the former because there was a real question as to the dominant sympathies and in the latter because the war found the North on the aggressive and invading the South.

CIVIL WAR IN THE WEST

Missouri was the most vital of the doubtful western states. Not only was it the most populous, but St. Louis was the greatest center of western trade and travel — a condition that was emphasized when the Butterfield route was moved north upon the outbreak of hostilities. Superficially Missouri was southern, with legalized slavery and a governor (C. F. Jackson) who was clearly southern in his sympathies. On the other hand Missouri actually had very few slaves and contained a large number of Unionists, notably among the antislavery Germans of St. Louis. This complexity explains why the state refused almost unanimously to secede (March 1, 1861) and yet Jackson refused flatly Lincoln's request for troops for the northern army.

Immediate and aggressive action by the wealthy and energetic Francis P. Blair made Missouri a Union state. St. Louis " home guards," mostly German, captured Jefferson City, put the state under martial law, and organized a loyal government. In reply, Jackson continued to insist he was the proper governer and in this capacity raised militia, called a state legislature into session, and had Missouri declared a free and independent state (August 6). With aid from outside the Jackson forces overran most of the southern part of the state and defeated the Union army at Wilson's Creek (August 10).

Command of the Western Department of the Union army was at this time most unfortunately in the hands of John C. Frémont, who at the least was dilatory and at the most was guilty of mismanagement, extravagence, favoritism, graft, and other sins. Moreover Frémont made the mistake of issuing a very drastic order (August 30) freeing all slaves and confiscating the property of all rebels. At a time when every effort was being made to win the sympathies of doubtful border areas, such an order was catastrophic. This situation gave Lincoln many bad moments. Investigations showed Frémont's administration bad and damaging to the Union cause, but Frémont refused to resign and had considerable personal popularity; after all he had been the first Republican Presidential nominee. Only after long hesitation was Lincoln willing to take the responsibility of removing Frémont (November 2).

Union forces took the offensive in 1862 and drove victoriously into Arkansas. For the remainder of the war Missouri was in general under the control of the northern forces. A southern raid in 1863 penetrated as far as Springfield and another in 1864 attained as far as Jefferson City, but neither had any real hope of adding the state to the Confederacy. Mainly they were bids for recruits, and here they failed most miserably, for Missouri members of the southern armies deserted much more numerously in order to go home than new recruits flocked to the colors.

Arkansas was of comparatively little importance in the war. She accepted secession, May 6, 1861, with but one dissenting vote. The military campaigns which touched Arkansas were concerned primarily with operations on the Mississippi or in Missouri or Texas. Arkansas had little strategic value for either side.

Texas was in some ways the reverse of Missouri, for in Texas the governor (Sam Houston) was Unionist and majority sentiment was southern. An irregular convention, boycotted by Union sympathizers, passed an ordinance of secession, February 1, 1861, by a vote of 167 to 7 and this action was legalized by the legislature over Houston's veto. Union property was confiscated and Union troops surrendered. A popular vote on secession late in February showed a three to one majority for secession. Under these circumstances Houston was forced out of office.

While Texas immediately took the offensive by sending expeditions north into Oklahoma and west into New Mexico and Arizona, these efforts were only temporarily successful. The Union forces made attempts during 1862 and 1863 to capture the Texan seacoast, but while such campaigns were technically successful the results did not pay for the expenditures of men and materials, and the troops were finally withdrawn. A new Union force in 1864 went up the Red River, but was repelled. Another finally was so overwhelming in size and power that the Texan army saw the wisdom of surrending early in 1865.

New Mexico and Arizona were generally southern in sympathy: Arizona voted for secession, New Mexico took no formal action. Texan troops overran the entire area during the winter of 1861–62, defeating their northern opponents. But then California troops arrived from the west and Colorado troops from the north, forcing by sheer weight of numbers the withdrawal of the Texan armies. The surviving half of the original Texan forces was back home by the summer of 1862. Here ended the war as far as New Mexico and Arizona were concerned.

California was also a doubtful state at the outbreak of the war. Many southerners talked vigorously of secession or even of an independent Pacific republic. But Union sentiment grew rapidly, and on May 17, 1861, the state declared its loyalty. The more doubtful southern part of the state was cowed by troops, and armies were dispatched eastward into Arizona; here they fought no more than rear guard actions with the outnumbered and retreating Texans.

The military operations in the Southwest were not in themselves impressive, but they indicated considerable disorder and confusion both at the scenes of the fighting and elsewhere. Troops used in such actions were not available for normal patrol activities. The resulting lack of strong governmental supervision gave the lawless more freedom than usual, and normally the West was not a region of complete peace and quiet.

The worst of the white disturbances came in the area centering in Kansas, for here was the scene of the violence of the '50s, and the Jawhawkers and border ruffians had found difficulty in returning to humdrum normal pursuits. Now with the war lawless bands roamed the countryside, stealing horses, cattle, and slaves, committing highway robbery, arson, and murder. Often such groups claimed loyalty to either North or South and occasionally they were commissioned units. Since the regular army also lived off the land it was sometimes difficult for the average citizen to distinguish between a regular army unit and a gang of bandits. These war guerrillas were the schoolmasters of such promising young desperadoes as the James and Younger brothers.

Most notorious of the Kansas guerrillas was William Clarke Quantrill, the bloody. Ambitious but lazy, Quantrill drifted from job to job until he ended ultimately in a life of theft. His sympathies in the Civil War seemed somewhat uncertain, but ultimately he threw his fortunes with the South and was at one time commissioned in the Confederate army. His presumed military operations consisted of more or less open banditry which included the looting of several towns, notably Lawrence in 1863. Outlawed by the Union forces, Quantrill came in time under Confederate suspicion and was arrested. He escaped to Texas and in 1865 evolved the fantastic plan of dressing his men as Union soldiers, making his way to Washington, and assassinating Lincoln. He created a trail of blood as far as Kentucky, where he was killed in a surprise attack.

INDIANS

The disorder and confusion of the whites in the West had repercussions among the Indians. The South made attempts to enlist the Five Civilized Tribes, and actually obtained several treaties of friendship. These treaties resulted in very little practical Indian help to the southern cause and there is no evidence to show that the South ever tried to instigate a general Indian war. At the end of hostilities, however, the Indians paid bitterly for their failure to remain completely loyal to the North.

All over the plains area the Indians recognized the opportunity afforded by division among the whites to advance their own interests. Attacks on the settlers in Minnesota or on the stages of the

Butterfield line were but illustrations of a general Indian unrest and an increasing aggressiveness. The effects of such outbreaks were of little long-run importance. A few troops were kept in the West that might otherwise have been used in the East. Basically, however, the Indian outbreaks were merely symptomatic of underlying frictions. The process of breaking Indian power which had been halted by the war was due to be carried to completion within a fairly short time after the end of that war.

NEW STATES AND TERRITORIES

While western troubles of the war period were highly visible, several outstanding gains were equally apparent to the observer. The withdrawal of the South from the Union had opened the way for much legislation, as that concerning land, tariff, and banking, desired by the North and West. The Republican party had every desire to maintain its working alliance between northern farmers and businessmen.

Among the political results of the war was a rapid increase in the number of organized states and territories of the West. In the past new western governments had been created slowly because of the sectional split in Congress. Now they came into existence rapidly, in part to please the area concerned and in part to gain additional Congressional strength. In some cases states were admitted long before the regions involved had sufficient population.

The states admitted during the war period were Kansas (1861) and Nevada (1864); Nebraska soon followed (1867). The Territories of Colorado (1861), Dakota (1861), Nevada (1861), Arizona (1863), Idaho (1863), and Montana (1864) were organized. As a result the West at the end of the war was approximately in the governmental form it was to retain permanently, except for the division between North and South Dakota.

EARLY TRANSCONTINENTAL RAILROAD PLANS

Very possibly the most important result of the war from the standpoint of the West was the clearing of the way for the construction of the first trancontinental railroad. Sectional disputes were no longer the decisive deterrent, and aid by the federal government became possible. The ultimate opening of the Union Pacific in 1869 may well have been the most important single event in western history. The railroad marked the beginning of the last stage of the American frontier.

The idea of a transcontinental railroad went back to the early '30s, although at that time it was chimerical. During the '40s the outstanding advocate was Asa Whitney, a New York merchant engaged in the China trade. Whitney favored the northern route from Lake Michigan to the coast, and after retiring from business in 1844 spent his entire time in trying to arouse interest in the project. Both Whitney and other promoters figured the cost of a transcontinental railroad at around $100,000,000, and the usual plan called for Congress to underwrite a considerable share of this large figure by an extensive grant of land.

Enthusiasm for a Pacific railroad increased notably during the late '40s and early '50s. Many conventions, as at Chicago (1847), St. Louis (1849), Memphis (1849), Philadelphia (1850), Iowa City (1851), New Orleans (1852), and Little Rock (1853), whipped up public interest. While such gatherings minimized the difficulties of the work, certain obstacles were decisive in this period. The lack of funds, the uncertainty of route, and the non-existence of eastern railroad connections debarred such a road for the time being.

During the '50s the technical possibilities of building the road improved but the actual chances of construction seemed to decline because of the increasing heat of sectional controversies. Northern interest favored a road from Chicago along the general route proposed by Whitney. Thomas Hart Benton visioned a " national " road from St. Louis. Jefferson Davis showed his sectional leanings when he favored a southern route in transmitting his report of the surveys of 1853–55. Senator Gwin of California preferred a southern route, with branches to St. Louis, Memphis, and New Orleans. Douglas tried to compromise with talk of three complete roads, but almost everyone else agreed that such extensive plans were impossible of realization.

CHARTERING THE UNION PACIFIC

With the withdrawal of the South from the Union, the southern routes were for the moment out of the competition, while at the same time Congress was unusually anxious to please the West. The result was the chartering of the first transcontinental railroad on July 1, 1862.

The building of the western part of the line was given to the Central Pacific Railroad, already chartered in California. The idea back of the Central Pacific was particularly the property of Theodore D. Judah, a young man who had worked on early eastern railroad construction before going to California in 1854 as chief engineer for a railroad in the Sacramento Valley. Judah had become enthusiastic about the possibility of railroad connections with the East and had made extensive surveys, ultimately interesting several moderately well-to-do Sacramento businessmen — Leland Stanford, Collis P. Huntington, Mark Hopkins, and Charles Crocker. These men chartered the Central Pacific (1861) with a nominal capitalization of $8,500,000. Judah made some field surveys for the company and then traveled east to Washington, where he was successful in obtaining the inclusion of the Central Pacific in the railroad plans being considered by Congress.

The eastern part of the new line was placed in the hands of a group called the Union Pacific Railroad. To compromise the pretensions of Chicago and St. Louis the eastern terminus of the main line was placed between the two cities and west of both of them — in central Nebraska on the 100th meridian; from that point to the west the road was to follow the old and well-known California trail. To the east, five branches were to radiate to Kansas City, to Leavenworth, to St. Joseph, to Sioux City, and to some unnamed place on the western boundary of Iowa. This last place was ultimately fixed as Council Bluffs, although in practice Omaha was the real terminus. This peculiar situation was evolved as a way of compromising sectional interests. The first four of the branches were given to companies already in existence, but none of the lines was built along the route specified in the original charter. The fifth branch was given to the Union Pacific itself and since it was the most direct route toward the East there can be no surprise that for practical purposes it became a part of the main line.

The aid granted by Congress to these new railroads was extremely generous. Each was to receive five odd sections of land on each side and within ten miles of the road, and also the right to use necessary building materials from the public domain. In addition, a government loan was provided on the basis of a mortgage on the roads. It was to be for $16,000 a mile over the greatest part of the route, $48,000 in the Rockies and Sierras, and $32,000 in the region between the two ranges. Finally the act made provision for organizing and financing the Union Pacific company, and provided that all of its property should revert to the government if the road were not completed by 1876.

By the terms of the original charter the building of the main line was to be the joint product of the work of two independent companies. The greater share was to be constructed by the Union Pacific, while the California portion was to be built by the Central Pacific. The connecting point was changed in 1866, at which time the Central Pacific was permitted to continue building eastward until it met the Union Pacific.

The chartering of the Union Pacific was an occasion of great rejoicing both inside and outside of Congress. As one prominent orator proclaimed grandiloquently: " It was said of the Nile that it was a god. I think that the Pacific railroad project comes nearer being the subject of deification than anything else I have ever heard in the Senate. Everyone is trying to show his zeal in worshiping the road." In truth the whole country was realizing a long-deferred hope and looking forward to the building and opening of the new line with eager expectation.

Unfortunately for railroad hopes, enthusiasm did not lay tracks. Public meetings, convincing perorations, and enthusiastic newspaper publicity failed to drive a single spike. The little surplus capital which existed during the war period could be invested more lucratively than in a wilderness railroad which might not pay dividends for many years. Almost as soon as the company was organized it petitioned Congress for more aid, and interested persons contributed $500,000 to a Washington " suspense account " to help persuade Congress to lend a favorable ear to their pleas. The result was satisfactory, for in 1864 Congress doubled its land grant and reduced its loan to the rank of a second mortgage, besides making certain desired minor changes.

BUILDING THE UNION PACIFIC

Actual construction was begun at Omaha in December 1863, but the early work progressed so slowly that only forty miles were built in the years 1864 and 1865. Labor and capital were both scarce, and the road could expect but little income since it traversed comparatively uninhabited portions of the country. Furthermore, the financial provisions of the incorporating act proved a hindrance. The company's stock which had to furnish the necessary working capital could be sold only at par and for cash. Almost as soon as it was put on the market it fell below par. Stock sales at par were a remote possibility when purchases might be made in the open market for less. Both stock sales and construction languished.

Just when conditions were most hopeless vice president T. C. Durant evolved a brilliant solution which would not only provide for the raising of the necessary capital, but would also allow the insiders to make their fortunes. Joining with his friends in the Union Pacific he bought a Pennsylvania corporation called the Credit Mobilier of America, which was particularly available because of the leniency of its charter provisions. The plan was then simple — at least after it was put into operation. Members of the Credit Mobilier, who also controlled the Union Pacific, voted construction contracts to dummies who transferred them to the Credit Mobilier. Construction contracts were paid by the Union Pacific in cash (actually by check), which was immediately returned to the railroad for its stocks and bonds at par. The Credit Mobilier then sold the stocks and bonds on the open market for whatever they would bring. The final receipts from these sales were the only real money that appeared in the transaction.

The Credit Mobilier was both ingenious and successful. It evaded legally the charter provisions which required the sale of Union Pacific securities at par for cash. It produced a goodly monetary return for the Union Pacific stockholders who were also members of the Credit Mobilier, for the construction contracts were lucrative. The parties who suffered were the small stockholders, the railroad itself, and ultimately the government: the railroad was bled white of both securities and cash, the smaller stockholders received no dividends, and their chance of realizing such income was postponed to the remote future. As for the members of the Credit Mobilier, they received an annual return of 100 per cent for the five years that the organization operated, estimating the percentage on the original capital of $3,750,000.

Immediately after the formation of the Credit Mobilier a factional fight occurred between Durant and the two Ames brothers, Oliver and Oakes, who were trying to obtain control of the Union Pacific. This quarrel was not settled until the summer of 1867, and consequently it was not until this time that construction began to move rapidly in the West. Oakes Ames, who was also a member of Congress, sought to aid the road by distributing Credit Mobilier stock to his Congressional friends with whom it would " do the most good." When this transaction later came to light Ames was censured by the House for his conduct.

The first forty miles of the Union Pacific, after being inspected, were accepted by the President of the United States on January

24, 1866. By July of the same year the road had been completed 305 miles west of Omaha and had forced the overland stage to move its eastern terminus to Fort Kearny. The summer of 1867, with the end of the Ames-Durant struggle and the completion of rail connections with the East, saw a still more rapid advance of construction.

This access of speed was by no means due entirely to the financial affairs of the company. The end of the Civil War produced an adequate labor force for the first time, since a financial depression in the East led many of the discharged soldiers to seek railroad work on the plains of Nebraska. Even the chief engineer, Colonel G. M. Dodge, was a former army officer; he possessed extensive knowledge of western railroading and an unusual aptitude for handling men.

The military training of many of the Union Pacific employees stood them in good stead, for the Indians were anything but pleased with the progress of the iron tracks, and engaged in continual and serious depredations. Sometimes the workers were protected by armed guards of United States troops, but more frequently they had to fend for themselves. Each man was ordinarily armed and the guns were stacked while work proceeded. If an alarm were given the boss called upon his men to " fall in," and defensive measures were begun at once. Isolated workers and men wandering off alone were always in danger of being ambushed and killed by hostile Indians. The building of the Union Pacific appeared at many times to be a good-sized Indian war.

Construction was carried on in hundred-mile stretches. The whole hundred miles was graded, and the bridges and fills put in place before any track was laid. This procedure increased the danger of Indian attack since the engineers, surveyors, graders, and bridge builders were always considerably in advance of the main construction crew.

Large fleets of wagons were necessary to haul materials and provisions. In the early days the necessary supplies had to be so transported for many miles since the Union Pacific made no connections in the East. This condition was remedied in 1867 with the completion of the " Northwestern," but even then it was still necessary to haul all the supplies for the crews working in advance of the track, and this haul might be as long as a hundred miles. A special difficulty was encountered in obtaining wood for ties, since there were but few trees on the western plains. This difficulty was lessened by the development of a method of hardening cottonwood so that it could be used.

The actual process of track-laying has been best described in an often quoted description by an eye witness: " Track-laying on the Union Pacific is a science, and we pundits of the Far East stood upon that embankment, only about a thousand miles this side of sunset, and backed westward before that hurrying corps of sturdy operatives with mingled feelings of amusement, curiosity, and profound respect. On they came. A light car, drawn by a single horse, gallops up to the front with its load of rails. Two men seize the end of a rail and start forward, the rest of the gang taking hold by twos until it is clear of the car. They come forward at a run. At the word of command, the rail is dropped in its place, right side up, with care, while the same process goes on at the other side of the car. Less than thirty seconds to a rail for each gang, and so four rails go down to the minute! Quick work, you say, but the fellows on the U. P. are tremendously in earnest. The moment the car is empty it is tipped over on the side of the track to let the next loaded car pass it, and then it is tipped back again; and it is a sight to see it go flying back for another load, propelled by a horse at full gallop at the end of 60 or 80 feet of rope, ridden by a young Jehu, who drives furiously. Close behind the first gang come the gaugers, spikers, and bolters, and a lively time they make of it. It is a grand Anvil Chorus that these sturdy sledges are playing across the plains. It is in a triple time, three strokes to a spike. There are ten spikes to a rail, four hundred rails to a mile, eighteen hundred miles to San Francisco. That's the sum, what is the quotient? Twenty-one-million times are those sledges to be swung — twenty-one million times are they to come down with their sharp punctuations, before the great work of modern America is complete! "

The men who built the Union Pacific lived in tent cities which moved west with the road. Whenever a stretch of track was completed all the equipment was moved to the next scene of operations. Rough streets were laid out, tents erected, and crude shacks built for the officers and the stores. To this hastily constructed town would come the usual camp following of land speculators, petty merchants, saloon keepers, gamblers, prostitutes. The bright lights of the saloons would gleam upon streets which were ankle deep in dust. The blare of cheap music and the allurements of the dancehall girls would furnish the laborer relief after his day's toil.

Drunkenness, profanity, immorality, and personal violence gave such towns the well-earned sobriquet of " Hell on wheels." More important cities would arise where work stopped during the coldest part of the winter. Julesburg, Cheyenne, and Laramie received their brief glory. In the spring the houses were torn down, the tents, supplies, and furniture packed, everything loaded on freight cars and moved to the next camp.

CENTRAL PACIFIC

While the Union Pacific gathered increasing momentum in its progress westward across the plains the Central Pacific was coming eastward with equal vigor. Actually the Central Pacific had to meet more difficulties than its eastern twin, since both money and labor were scarcer in the Far West than farther east. Chinese coolies had to be imported before a satisfactory laboring force could be collected. Even geography worked against the Central Pacific, for the Sierras interposed their snow-clad ranges to the first construction, whereas the first two thirds of the Union Pacific could be built on a beautifully level plain. The Central Pacific persisted in spite of its difficulties and by 1867 had succeeded in conquering its worst obstacles. Thereafter the building was rapid.

The Sacramento associates remained in control of the Central Pacific, although Judah had died in 1863. Huntington was the most important figure in his function of financial and purchasing agent; the thrifty Hopkins was treasurer and business manager; the optimistic and energetic Crocker was in charge of construction; Stanford, who had meantime been war governor of California, handled political problems within the state. This division of authority proved very happy, and affairs were handled with complete mutual confidence.

Actual building of the Central Pacific was done by construction companies — first Crocker & Company, and then the Contract & Finance Company. Both of these concerns were composed of the men who controlled the Central Pacific; use of the subsidiary company was an attempt to lessen public suspicion of the financial methods in vogue. The backers of the Central Pacific, just like those of the Union Pacific, had little idea that a transcontinental railroad would prove profitable to operate. They only hoped that by means of remunerative construction contracts they could corner all of the available cash, after which the road could be sold for whatever it would bring.

The methods of the Contract & Finance Company were similar to those of the Credit Mobilier, except that the western twin was so successful in muddling its accounts that no one has since been able to disentangle them. Huntington, Stanford, Crocker, and Hopkins held the capital stock, paying for it with their personal notes. Then in their capacity as controlling stockholders in the Central Pacific they voted themselves lucrative construction contracts. The money for the construction was advanced by each man as he had extra cash, and in every case the only record of the transaction was his own memorandum. Profits were either put back into the business or divided equally. This scheme of bookkeeping had wonderful possibilities in preventing a too close inquiry into the company's methods and accounts. The last dramatic bit of confusion was added with the " accidental " destruction of the company's books by fire in 1873 — a date suspiciously close to the Credit Mobilier scandal.

Both the Central Pacific and the Union Pacific were laying track at a phenomenal rate by 1868–69, and by the spring of 1869 the two construction crews came in sight of each other. Then it became evident that neither company was anxious to make connections with its competitor. The surveys began to parallel each other, and then the track followed suit. Inquiring people ran to their copies of the *Statutes at Large* and discovered that while the legislation assumed that the tracks would be joined, there was no mandatory provision to this effect. Why should not each line continue to build and thus increase the subsidies it might expect to receive from the government? Congress solved the difficulty by providing a meeting point at Promontory Summit, Utah, which was a little northwest of Ogden.

The final ceremony of connecting the rails took place on May 10, 1869. Governor Stanford of California represented the Central Pacific and president Sidney Dillon of the Union Pacific represented that road. Prayer was offered, congratulations exchanged, and the last spike driven home. All of the ceremony, including the taps of the sledge, was carried to the rest of the country by telegraph. Then followed celebrations throughout the nation. Bells were rung, whistles tooted, guns fired, processions formed, bunting hung, dinners held, toasts given. The great project was completed. The West was linked with the East, and the trade of the Orient lay ready for the taking. An epoch-making event had occurred.

THE PACIFIC RAILROAD AFTER ITS COMPLETION

The people of 1869 were right in feeling that the completion of the Union Pacific marked an epoch in the history of the United States, but they were wrong in expecting a vast increase in Far Eastern business, for such a result did not follow. What the event really marked was the definite beginning of the last stage of the frontier. An iron arrow had been shot into the heart of the Indian country — and other arrows soon followed — to result in the death and disintegration of that region as a home for redmen alone. The railroad brought population to the frontier faster than it had ever come before.

The building of the Union Pacific was an accomplishment deserving of great praise, but it included many factors which were highly undesirable; not everyone was pleased with the companies which had done the building. Minor stockholders protested that they had been defrauded. Users objected to the high rates and poor service. Communities which the railroad had missed felt aggrieved and disgruntled, and such cities as Denver and Salt Lake City found it necessary to work further to obtain satisfactory railroad connections. Other portions of the country, both north and south, counted the cost of the Union Pacific and felt resentful that this money had not been spent in roads which would be more directly useful to them. With the diminishing of the paean of praise, these protesting voices gradually came to be heard.

It soon became apparent to the practical eye that neither of the Pacific railroads had solved all of its financial difficulties when its line was completed. Both had sold large quantities of their capital stock at a heavy discount and were overcapitalized. Both had hurried construction regardless of cost with the result that they were heavily in debt. Both owed large sums to the government. Both had been poorly built and would soon need extensive repairs. Both traversed meagerly settled portions of the country and had to depend on their receipts from through business, which was a bad procedure for any railroad. Little wonder that the men who controlled the roads were anxious to retire before the crash came.

All of the early promoters of the Union Pacific except Ames soon disposed of their holdings. In 1871 the presidency went to Thomas Scott, who was vice president of the Pennsylvania Railroad and had extensive interests in other western railroad properties. Two years showed him he had picked the wrong horse and he sold out to Jay Gould, one of the shrewdest financiers of the period. Gould had a plan for the reorganization of the road, but when Congress failed to approve he abandoned it. A little later he acted as a railroad highwayman, placing a gun at the head of the Union Pacific and then rifling its pockets for whatever loose change remained. Jay Gould could never be accused of being tenderhearted in such matters.

The Central Pacific associates were also desirous of disposing of their holdings as soon as the road was completed. Their efforts in this direction finally proved unsuccessful because there was no Thomas Scott or Jay Gould who wanted to train the white elephant. Everyone, including the promoters, was sure that the Central Pacific was destined to be a losing proposition. The prosperity of the early '70s and the lack of purchasers finally led the associates to try to make California railroading pay. As they viewed the situation their only real opportunity lay in monopolizing the rail transportation of the state. Through fair means or otherwise they succeeded by 1873 in obtaining a complete control of the business of San Francisco; in this project the influence of ex-Governor Stanford was an important asset. They also bought the California & Oregon Railroad and started building north to forestall possible competition from that quarter.

The real danger to the Central Pacific's control of California lay in the possibility that some eastern road might enter the southern part of the state and build north. Here the associates were benefited by geography, for it was possible to cross the Colorado River only at Yuma and the Needles. Therefore the Southern Pacific of California (not to be confused with the later holding company of the same name which was incorporated in 1885) was organized and started to build south to head off possible competitors. By 1873 satisfactory progress was being made and the goal was in sight.

The panic of 1873 found the two parts of the transcontinental railroad in curiously different situations. The Union Pacific was weak and struggling, hardly able to remain solvent, and the plaything of ambitious financiers; not for a quarter of a century was it able to regain financial stability. The Central Pacific, on the other hand, was booming. Together with its associated roads it was dominant in California, controlling the railroad future of the state. During the next quarter century it was not only to maintain, but to improve and consolidate its position, both economically and politically.

READINGS

J. W. Caughey, *California* (1953), ch. 14—C. P.; G. T. Clark, *Leland Stanford* (1931), chs. 6–10—eulogistic; R. G. Cleland, *A History of California* (1922), chs. 25, 26; F. A. Cleveland and F. W. Powell, *Railway Promotion* (1909), ch. 16; C. Coan, *A History of New Mexico* (3 vols., 1925), vol. 1, ch. 21; W. E. Connelley, *Quantrill and the Border Wars* (1910); S. Daggett, *Chapters on the History of the Southern Pacific* (1922), chs. 1–7; G. M. Dodge, *How We Built the Union Pacific Railway* (1910); L. H. Haney, *Congressional History . . . to 1850* (1908), chs. 21–23, *Congressional History . . . 1850–1887* (1910), chs. 6–8; S. H. Holbrook, *The Story of American Railroads* (1947), ch. 14; A. Hunt, *The Army of the Pacific* (1951)—Civil War in West; C. S. Jackson, *Picture Maker of the Old West* (1947)—good pictures; A. C. Laut, *The Romance of the Rails* (2 vols., 1929), vol. 2, chs. 20–22; L. O. Leonard and J. T. Johnson, *A Railroad to the Sea* (1939)—U. P.; O. Lewis, *The Big Four* (1938)—C. P.; J. Monaghan, *The Overland Trail* (1947), ch. 17; J. Moody, *The Railroad Builders* (1919), ch. 6; F. L. Paxson, *The Last American Frontier* (1915), chs. 12, 13, 19; J. R. Perkins, *Trails, Rails and War* (1929), chs. 2, 4, 5, 9, 13, 14—Dodge and the U. P.; R. E. Riegel, *The Story of the Western Railroads* (1926), chs. 5, 6; E. L. Sabin, *Building the Pacific Railway* (1919); F. W. Seymour, *The Story of the Red Man* (1929), ch. 14; J. W. Starr, *One Hundred Years of American Railroading* (1928), ch. 15; N. Trottman, *History of the Union Pacific* (1923), chs. 1–4; N. C. Wilson and F. J. Taylor, *Southern Pacific* (1952)—short and eulogistic.

CHAPTER 31

THE
INDIAN AT BAY

THE construction of the Union Pacific was one of the many signs that all old " solutions " of the Indian problem were on the way to the discard and that a new formula must be evolved. The Indians could look back on a long succession of removals as they had been pushed aside to make way for white settlers. Many could remember the well-advertised " permanent frontier " of the '30s, which lasted scarcely more than a decade before new concessions were asked to provide for the changing conditions that were the only permanent factor in western history. Would the process never end?

The long series of treaties of the early '50s had the usual statements of eternal peace and friendship. They also made provision for white overland traffic. More important, they moved toward a new and supposedly more permanent solution of the Indian problem. The Indians were pushed back and tribal hunting grounds delimited as a step toward a future ultimate concentration into reservations, with the most populous to be located in the present South Dakota and Oklahoma. The long-range hope was that in time each Indian would be encouraged to settle on a farm of his own to practice the white man's kind of agriculture; the remainder of the land could then be distributed among land-hungry white settlers.

INDIAN TROUBLES OF THE '50S AND '60S

This new Indian policy seemed hopeful to the Indian Bureau, but would have been extremely unpalatable to the Indians if they had understood it, which they did not. At the moment the Indian mind was filled with bitter resentment at the arrival of caravans of immigrants, at the rumbling overland stages, at the dozens of exploring parties, at the railroad construction crews, and at the succession of military expeditions. Most aggravating of all the whites were the miners, who paid not the least attention to such scraps of paper as Indian treaties and international boundaries. Where gold beckoned they went. A boom occurred here one day and a thousand miles away the next, with any rush very possibly in the heart of the Indian country. Legally the miners had no right in any region reserved to the Indians, but the government seldom had either the troops or the desire to eject good white voters, no matter how turbulent; in fact it might well act for their protection in the very likely event of trouble with the Indians. Quite understandably the Indians resented such intrusions whole-heartedly.

Of even more vital importance to the Indians, white hunters were destroying the buffalo which was the economic basis of life for the plains Indian. Early hunters and travelers had been prodigal of buffalo life, but the fewness of the hunters and the vastness of the herds had made the slaughter relatively unimportant. Now plains travelers were increasing, and they were all hungry. Railroad construction crews depended on the buffalo for their meat supply, while by the late '60s special eastern excursions brought well-armed trainloads of men intent on the sport of shooting a few buffalo. The building of the Union Pacific denuded a fifty mile strip of all game, and the construction of other roads had similar results.

Even by the time of the Civil War the decrease of herds was evident, particularly in the Oklahoma area. After the war professional hunters armed with repeating rifles made the plains a slaughterhouse. Aided by the buffalo's stupidity the hunter might kill as many as a hundred at a single stand; the carnage might only be halted by overheated rifles or by the physical exhaustion of the two skinners who usually accompanied the hunter. By 1870 the buffalo were being killed at the rate of about a million a year, and by 1875 the southern herd had been virtually exterminated. The hunters then moved north, where they completed the total job by 1884. Two years later a representative of the Smithsonian Institution had difficulty in finding twenty-five specimens to preserve. Saddest of all, much of the slaughter was not even very profitable economically. Most of the meat was allowed to rot on the ground, while the plethora of buffalo robes caused their price to fall to unprofitable levels. In time a minor subsidiary occupation developed — gathering the tons of buffalo bones that lay over the plains. One wonders how many buffalo had died to bring five dollars for the ton of bones collected later.

The dwindling buffalo herds provided the handwriting on the wall for the old nomadic life of the plains Indian. The buffalo had provided food, clothing, tools, and weapons; its elimination made impossible the traditional life of the plains. Even without the many armed conflicts which were to occur before the end of the story, the fate of the Indian was inevitable. Some future day he must accept squaw's work — or rather, in more pleasant terms, he must practice the agriculture of the white farmer.

Many Indians were aware of the precariousness of their situation as early as the '6os. The old men shook their heads sadly and talked with regret of the good old days in which game had been plentiful and in which there had been no demoralization from the white man's whiskey and the white man's diseases. The young braves grew increasingly angry as they saw white encroachments and heard rumors of white atrocities. Every year more Indians came to believe that if their race were to avoid annihilation it must soon make a stand against white aggression.

For many Indians the confusion of the Civil War period offered a splendid opportunity for revenge against the conquering white. Not that the Indian had any general plan or ultimate goal, but rather that he was taking advantage of the remarkable and suggestive sight of white men fighting each other, while in addition the normally small policing force for the western plains was further reduced in size. Here was glowing and unmistakable opportunity for Indian malcontents.

CONTROL OF THE INDIANS

The possibility of Indian outbreaks was increased by the inadequate policing of the plains both in war and peace times. Seldom were more than two thousand soldiers available to control the vast reaches of the West and to man the scattering of forts. Even with the ending of the Civil War the number of western troops remained pitifully small, although the quality of the commanding officers improved as such able men as Sheridan, Miles, and Howard were sent to the plains. But even with better superiors, the possibility that the average army officer would be a good disciplinarian, an able tactician, a first-rate diplomat, a practicing psychologist, and something of a philanthropist at one and the same time was fairly remote.

In theory the Indian Bureau of the Department of the Interior had control of the Indians under normal conditions and merely called in the army when its wards got out of hand, but actually there was much overlapping jurisdiction and conflict between the two organizations. The army did not become invisible or attain a state of suspended animation in time of peace nor did the Indian agents evaporate when conditions became troubled. Although the two groups depended on each other and were supposed to act in harmony, in sober fact they were anything but " two minds with a single thought."

In general the Indian Bureau tried to be kind and beneficent, distributing goods, arms, and money, and settling Indian disputes in the hope that by kind treatment the Indian might be persuaded to be docile and peace-loving. This policy irritated the War Department, which felt certain that the correct attitude toward the savages was a stern fairness, made effective by the frequent display of large and heavily armed forces and severe punishment of any Indian who transgressed the white code of conduct.

Extremely controversial was the matter of arming the Indians. The Indian Bureau insisted that the Indian needed guns and ammunition to kill the game necessary for his subsistence. But the army became vigorously profane when these same guns were turned against the troops — and it was particularly irritated when the guns of the Indians were better than those of the soldiers. In behalf of the Indian Bureau it should be added that comparatively few of the plains Indians ever had guns and that the bulk of their few repeating rifles came from white traders rather than Indian agents.

The friction between Indian Bureau and War Department was further increased by indefensible acts by representatives of each. Certain Indian agents were notoriously inefficient and corrupt, lining their pockets with the gains from distributing shoddy clothing and blankets, moldy bread, and spoiled meat. Each unscrupulous agent was creating potential trouble for the army. On the other hand the military sometimes interfered improperly — often with such highhanded and dictatorial methods that peaceful agreement was impossible. Military expeditions sometimes created more trouble than they allayed, and an undiplomatic army officer could destroy within a few hours the effects of years of painstaking work by a good Indian agent.

Differences between the War and Interior Departments reflected the national lack of any commonly accepted program. Many Americans agreed with the War Department that the only possible way to keep the Indians in order was to administer frequent and severe chastisement, while the average westerner still clung to the belief that the only good Indian was one who had joined his fathers in the happy hunting ground. On the other hand a considerable portion of the East sympathized with the Interior Department's rule of love and reason. Many easterners with humanitarian propensities and who had never seen a live Indian except in a museum, pictured the red man as a noble figure compounded of all human virtues and fighting bravely against great odds to avoid extermination. In fact, of course, Indians were a composite of virtues and defects, just like the whites.

SIOUX OUTBREAK IN MINNESOTA

The result of Indian resentment combined with white division and lack of a definite policy was inevitable trouble. The first serious outbreak of the '60s occurred among the Sioux in Minnesota, and was the result of the same kind of frontier misunderstandings which had made Indian-white relations so unstable in the past. Its background included the underlying Indian resentment against white expansion, the sharp dealing of the traders, the seduction of Indian girls by unprincipled white men, and the inspiration of overly large doses of the white man's " fire water."

On August 18, 1862, six whites were murdered by a small Sioux party near New Ulm, Minnesota. The murders were unpremeditated and represented no general Indian attack, but whites became panic-stricken and fled to New Ulm, spreading exaggerated stories of a widespread Indian uprising. Most of the Sioux seem to have been almost equally thunderstruck at the news of the murders. Knowing the ways of the whites they concluded that they must either fight or flee toward the west. To remain peacefully in their lodges was to invite slaughter. In consequence of this reasoning part of the Indians prepared for war while the remainder packed their belongings and started west.

The band that remained to fight was led by Little Crow and included some thirteen hundred warriors. Not waiting for a white attack it immediately began offensive operations against the outlying settlers in the Minnesota River Valley. Men, women, and children were killed to the number of 737, barns and houses were burned, and the frontier was thrown into a fever of apprehension. The young state government called out the militia and asked for United States troops. Actually the federal troops proved unnecessary, for after a brief campaign the militia defeated Little Crow decisively, taking over two thousand prisoners.

The Indian prisoners were taken to St. Paul where four hundred of them were placed on trial. The temper of Minnesota was shown by an unsuccessful effort to lynch the whole group. As a result of the trial 303 of the defendants were found guilty of murder, rape, and arson, and sentenced to hanging. Most of these were pardoned by President Lincoln, but thirty-eight remained to be hanged on a single scaffold at Mankato on December 26, 1862 — a rather ironic sequel to the celebration of the birthday of the Prince of Peace.

The punishment of the Sioux had been swift and terrible, but more was to come. In 1863 a punitive military expedition was sent through Minnesota and to the west, where it defeated the remainder of Little Crow's warriors. In the same year Congress confiscated all the Sioux land in Minnesota, and during the following year the dispossessed Indians were sent to Dakota, where they arrived too late to raise corn. Government supplies were few and poor, which meant a year of misery, with cold, disease, poverty, and starvation. If punishment could ever prevent further crime, then no new outbreak should have occurred after the disaster to the Sioux of Minnesota.

NORTHERN PLAINS

Unfortunately for the usual white theory of penology, the harsh treatment accorded the Minnesota Sioux did not serve to intimidate their western relatives, but rather to make them more resentful and more warlike. As stories of the Minnesota troubles spread over the northern plains the Indians became more sure than ever that the day of their inevitable clash with the whites was drawing closer. When new treaties were presented for their signature in 1865 only a few were willing to sign, even though the terms were the same as those of the treaty of 1851, and the great majority of the Sioux never felt bound. The portents of trouble were clearly visible for even the most oblivious believer in peace and light.

While the Fort Sully Treaty was being considered in the summer of 1865 General P. E. Connor was leading a three-pronged expedition designed to overawe the Indians by operations concentrating in the Yellowstone region. The result has been called the greatest fiasco in American military history. Even the main column moving north under General Connor, and guided by old Jim Bridger, was far from successful. The expedition returned without having accomplished anything of importance except to demonstrate that the Sioux were thoroughly hostile and that future expeditions must be prepared to fight every step of their way.

The next year (1866) a new and smaller expedition of 640 men was sent north under Colonel H. B. Carrington. Its objective was also to open the Bozeman trail, which included the establishment of the forts necessary for its protection. It built Fort Reno on the Powder River, Fort Phil Kearney just east of the northern Bighorn Mountains, and between the two Pineys, and Fort C. F. Smith on the Bighorn River. It was hampered continually by the hostile actions of both Sioux and Cheyenne. Any small party, including even a wood-gathering detail, was liable to attack, which meant that the smallest detachment had to have the protection of at least thirty fighting men. Carrington protested time and time again to his superiors that his force was insufficient for erecting and manning forts, protecting communications, and doing the necessary incidental work; he maintained that positive and aggressive action would require a much larger army.

The truth of Carrington's lamentations was made evident in late December 1866. News had come to Fort Phil Kearney that a wood train had been attacked and needed relief. The rescue party was under the command of Brevet Lieutenant-Colonel W. J. Fetterman, who was cockily certain that "with eighty men I can ride through the whole Sioux nation." Eighty-one men marched out of the fort with Fetterman. Their mutilated bodies were later recovered for burial. Fetterman's rashness in pursuing Indian decoys led by Crazy Horse had involved the whole command in a traditional Indian ambush. The Indians had killed the whites at leisure — except for possibly Fetterman himself and one or two others who may have committed suicide.

The Fetterman massacre raised a terrific outcry in the East, where it seemed evident that Indian affairs on the western plains were being mismanaged. Regardless of the comparative merits of the conflicting policies of the War and Interior Departments, the obvious fact was apparent that the Indians were becoming increasingly restive and hostile. And when the army took the field, incompetence brought such disasters as the Fetterman massacre. Both inside and outside Congress arose loud demands for a more effective policy.

CENTRAL PLAINS

The great tribes of the central plains, the Arapaho and Cheyenne, were also troublesome during the '6os. The miners who had come to Colorado in hordes after 1858 aroused in the Indians a hot resentment which grew increasingly bitter as the miners invaded more and more territory. These newcomers had not the least legal justification since the entire region had been guaranteed to the Indians in 1851. The aborigines could hardly be blamed for viewing the incursions with hostility.

As in so many similar cases, the United States tried to settle the conflict between the two races by " buying " the disputed land from the Indians. The necessary treaty was signed in 1861 at Fort Wise (formerly Bent's Fort) on the Arkansas River. The new Indian home was to be a small tract of dry, sandy, almost gameless country on Sand Creek in southeastern Colorado. The only virtue of the new home was that it was so desolate and barren that it was unlikely to attract white cupidity.

The Treaty of Fort Wise made the Indians sullen and more resentful, and most of them refused to go to their new home. War parties ravaged outlying settlements, plundered travelers, and attacked the overland stage. Periods of ominous quiet were but uneasy interludes between frontier depredations. The patience of Governor John Evans of Colorado soon expired and in June 1864 he ordered all the plains Indians to report to Fort Lyon.

The immediate reaction of the Indians to the Evans order was an increased hostility. Murder, rape, and arson were widespread, and attacks on the whole of the Holladay stage line brought that enterprise to a halt. The militia prepared for action, and a first-class Indian war seemed to be in the making.

And then, whether because of sober second thought or because winter was approaching, the Indians began flocking to Fort Lyon on Sand Creek. Their move presented the possibility of a bad anticlimax to the white troops who were anticipating the excitement and the glory of slaughtering large numbers of Indians. Furthermore the whites had the uncomfortable feeling — coming from bitter experience — that while the Indians might live peacefully on government rations during the winter, the following spring would very possibly see more Indian parties on the warpath. The majority white reaction was expressed by Major-General S. R. Curtis, when he wrote from Fort Leavenworth: " I want no peace till the Indians suffer more."

Colonel J. M. Chivington and his 1000 militia echoed the Curtis sentiment and continued to move south. Chivington's subordinate Major Jacob Downing wrote: " I think and earnestly believe the Indians to be an obstacle to civilization, and should be exterminated." Meantime about five hundred Indians under Black Kettle had surrendered and were encamped at Sand Creek, under the impression that they had obeyed the governor's proclamation and were safe from harm. A white flag and an American flag were displayed to give evidence of their intentions.

Chivington and his troops reached Sand Creek late in November. Here they spied out the Indian village and prepared to win the glory for which they had armed. The attack of November 29, 1864, found the Indians completely surprised and unprepared. Their first reaction was to start to run, which gave the troops the opportunity to carry on the slaughter as they pleased. Both men and women were scalped, women were ripped up the body, children were brained, and every other conceivable mutilation was practiced. Here was Indian war at its worst. When the carnage ended the village had been destroyed and about a fifth of the inhabitants murdered. Black Kettle and the remainder had escaped.

The action near Fort Lyon has often been labeled either the " Chivington massacre " or the " Sand Creek massacre "; Colorado called it a punitive expedition and professed pleasure with the results. The immediate outcome was the signing of new treaties with the Apache, Kiowa, Comanche, Arapaho, and Cheyenne. These new treaties were completely satisfactory — to the whites — in that the Indians ceded their last bit of land, the Sand Creek reservation. For a time they wandered the plains without claim to any country they could call their own, but ultimately place was made for them in Indian Territory.

INDIAN TERRITORY

Conditions in Indian Territory had been far from idyllic during the Civil War, with both Indians and whites divided in their sympathies. The result had been an amazing confusion of efforts, with whites fighting whites, Indians fighting Indians, and Indians fighting whites. Furthermore the Indian country provided a haven for whites who desired Indian land and for outlaws who sought refuge from the better law machinery of neighboring states. Treaties of 1865 and 1867 brought little improvement even though they provided reservation space for the Kiowa and some portions of the Apache and Comanche. Probably most Indian signatures were obtained only by the bribery of gifts and annuities, with the signers never understanding the terms of the treaties.

An attempt to overawe the Indians came in 1867 under the orders of Major-General W. S. Hancock, who commanded the Department of Missouri. The expedition proved unable to engage in any hostilities because the Indians ran away to avoid another Sand Creek. The only result was to antagonize the Indians still further and to leave the entire plains in disorder and confusion.

A new effort to calm the region south of the Arkansas River came in 1868 under the command of General Sheridan. The original plans called for a three-pronged action, with columns from New Mexico, Colorado, and Kansas, but only the third of these finally saw action. The first fight was between George A. Custer and Alfred Sully for the top command — a dispute that was not ended until Sheridan arrived and sent Sully back home. Then Custer's Seventh Cavalry dawdled to await the arrival of a regiment of Kansas Volunteers commanded by the governor of the state. Their continued nonarrival finally exhausted Custer's patience and he started without them.

George Armstrong Custer, commanding the expedition of 1868, was probably the most picturesque and magnetic army officer of his day. Six feet tall, with the broad shoulders and narrow hips of the cavalryman, he wore his golden hair to his shoulders and moved with a swagger. Quite uniquely for the period he used neither liquor nor tobacco and swore but seldom and mildly. The great and abiding object of his life was glory, and in pursuit of this goal he was brave to the point of recklessness. His career had been brilliant but erratic. Graduating from West Point at the age of twenty-one, the Civil War had made him a brigadier-general of volunteers within two years and a major-general shortly later. As an Indian fighter in the '60s he was a lieutenant-colonel. His command was the Seventh Cavalry, which he had whipped into one of the best and certainly the most famous unit of its kind. Custer had that rare quality which, in spite of harsh discipline, attracted men who were willing to follow him to the death.

Custer left the rendezvous late in November to go in search of hostile Indians. Ultimately he stumbled on Black Kettle's camp of Arapaho and Cheyenne in the valley of the Washita near the Texas border — which meant that Black Kettle's bad luck pursued him to the end. The impetuous white charge struck a sleeping village drugged by the fatigue of ceremonial dances of the night before. Over a hundred Indians, including Black Kettle, were killed; others were captured and considerable amounts of provisions were taken.

Custer's victory was not without qualifications. The Black Kettle band had been small and as news of the action reached neighboring villages, hostiles began gathering in increasing numbers. Meantime Custer's ammunition was getting low, so after making a feint at other Indian villages he withdrew to the north. His moves were so rapid that he lost completely a detachment under Major G. H. Elliott; ultimately the mutilated bodies of this detail were found and buried by Sheridan, thus providing a somewhat inglorious end for the expedition. The sad fact was that the entire effect of the Custer campaign was not impressive, since no decisive defeat had been given the Indians. Parties of hostiles continued to ravage the frontier.

APACHE AND COMANCHE

Farther to the west, the Apache of Arizona were the chief white antagonists. More primitive than the plains Indians, the Apache were both proud and cruel, and adept at finding concealment in the Arizona country. Moreover they had extremely able leaders in Cochise and Mangas Coloradas. Cochise considered himself wrongly accused and betrayed, which led him to swear vengeance on the whites. The Apache felt contempt for the whites and showed this contempt by harrying the countryside. Isolated settlers were killed, improvements were burned, livestock driven off. For a time during the Civil War it seemed as though the whites of the region were to be eliminated and the country return entirely to Indian control. In fact the removal of troops during that war led the Indians to feel that they had won.

At the end of the Civil War more troops could be sent to Arizona, but their number was not sufficient to overawe the Indians. Numerous forts were constructed, but their influence was not great. Only in the immediate vicinity of a fort could a white settler feel comparatively secure.

CONGRESSIONAL INVESTIGATION

The troubled conditions of the plains naturally gave Congress concern, and particularly when the end of the Civil War allowed more time for such problems. Since most Congressmen were completely ignorant about Indian affairs and since the better informed members were as badly divided in opinion as the public at large, the first job seemed to be to collect information. A joint committee of seven was appointed in 1865 to investigate and to make necessary recommendations for legislation. The committee took its duties seriously and traveled widely over the plains, interviewing Indians, Indian agents, settlers, miners, army officers, in fact every available person with information or a grievance.

The report of the committee of seven was presented in January 1867. Its conclusions were that Indian troubles were caused by white aggression and the overly vigorous actions of the army, and that the Indians were dying off quite rapidly. The report suggested a small permanent committee to investigate further and to make specific recommendations to Congress. These rather modest proposals brought no action, but the investigations of the committee had provided a vast fund of information upon which future action could be based. In spite of the seemingly inconclusive results of the work of the committee, a more vigorous and better coordinated policy was just around the corner.

READINGS

J. Alter, *James Bridger* (1925), chs. 53–57; T. C. Blegen and P. D. Jordan, *With Various Voices* (1949)—contemporary on Sioux outbreak of 1862; W. M. Brackenridge, *Helldorado* (1928), ch. 3; E. D. Branch, *The Hunting of the Buffalo* (1929), chs. 7–12; H. E. Briggs, *Frontiers of the Northwest* (1940), ch. 2; M. S. Burt, *Powder River* (1938), chs. 12–20; P. E. Byrne, *Soldiers of the Plains* (1926), chs. 1, 2; W. Cody, *Autobiography of Buffalo Bill* (1920), chs. 3–8; E. E. Dale, *The Indians of the Southwest* (1949), chs. 1–9; E. E. Dale and M. L. Wardell, *History of Oklahoma* (1948), ch. 11; E. Dick, *Vanguards of the Frontier* (1941), ch. 19; F. Downey, *Indian-Fighting Army* (1941), chs. 1–6—easy reading; W. W. Folwell, *A History of Minnesota* (2 vols., 1921), vol. 2, chs. 5–10; G. Foreman, *A History of Oklahoma* (1942), chs. 10–15—detailed; G. A. Forsyth, *The Story of the Soldier* (1916), chs. 4–11; P. W. Gates, *Fifty Million Acres* (1954), chs.

1, 2, 6—Kansas; G. B. Grinnell, *The Fighting Cheyennes* (1915), chs. 9–24, *Two Great Scouts and Their Pawnee Battalion* (1928); L. R. Hafen (ed.), *Colorado and Its People* (4 vols., 1948), vol. 1, ch. 16; L. R. Hafen and F. M. Young, *Fort Laramie* (1938), pp. 303–362; G. R. Hebard and E. A. Brininstool, *The Bozeman Trail* (2 vols., 1922), vol. 1, pp. 119–346, vol. 2, pp. 15–204; A. W. Hooper, *Indian Affairs and Their Administration* (1932); I. Howbert, *Memories of a Lifetime* (1925), chs. 6–10, 11; F. C. Lockwood, *The Apache Indians* (1938), chs. 1–9; E. C. McReynolds, *Oklahoma* (1954), chs. 9, 10; W. S. Nye, *Carbine and Lance* (1937), chs. 1–5; F. L. Paxson, *The Last American Frontier* (1915), chs. 14–16, 18; R. N. Richardson, *The Comanche Barrier* (1933), pp. 15–321; C. C. Rister, *Border Command* (1944)— Sheridan, *The Southwestern Frontier* (1928), pp. 25–124; F. G. Roe, *The North American Buffalo* (1951)—detailed; M. Sandoz, *The Buffalo Hunters* (1954), *Crazy Horse* (1942), book 2; F. W. Seymour, *Indian Agents of the Old Frontier* (1941), *The Story of the Red Man* (1929), chs. 13, 15; D. L. Spotts, *Campaigning With Custer* (1928); A. W. Spring, *Casper Collins* (1927); P. R. de Trobriand, *Military Life in Dakota* (1951); F. F. Van de Water, *Glory Hunter* (1930), part 2—Custer; S. Vestal, *Sitting Bull* (1932), chs. 1–17, *Warpath* (1934); G. D. Wagner and W. A. Allen, *Blankets and Moccasins* (1936); P. I. Wellman, *The Indian Wars of the West* (1954)—reprint of popularly written book.

CHAPTER 32

"CUSTER'S LAST STAND"

THE inconclusive results of the investigation of 1865–67 led to the formation of a new commission composed of four civilians, including the Commissioner of Indian Affairs, and three generals. Congress stated its purpose as (1) the removal of causes of friction between the two races; (2) securing the safety of the overland routes; (3) discovering permanent homes for the Indians; and (4) finding ways of promoting Indian civilization without interfering with the rest of the United States. Moreover, the new commission was not limited to investigation and recommendations, but could negotiate any necessary treaties to put its program into effect.

PEACE COMMISSION

To carry out its stated program the commission visited the plains in 1867–68 and negotiated treaties with practically all tribes. These agreements provided for various reservations throughout the West. Most important was the Indian Territory, which was to contain all the tribes of the central plains, and South Dakota, which was given to the Sioux in the area west of the Missouri River. Forts Phil Kearney and C. F. Smith were to be removed.

The final report of the so-called "peace commission" was sympathetic to the Indian, but recognized realistically that the Indians could not be permitted to roam freely over the plains, and that their concentration in reservations was necessary. The friction between the War and Interior Departments was noted, and the suggestion made that a new and independent Indian Department be created to eliminate the resulting difficulties. Soon after the report was made the troubles occurred that culminated in the

Custer campaign on the Washita, and the commission then decided that complete control by the War Department would be the
best solution. Neither suggestion was put into practice.

POLICY UNDER GRANT

When Grant came to the Presidency he moved toward a more
sympathetic and tolerant policy, designed to placate the Indians
and win their friendship. Positions in the Indian service were filled
on recommendations of the various churches, with the Quakers receiving a considerable proportion of the appointments. War and
intimidation had been tried. Now the arts of peace were to be given
opportunity to show their merit. A sad omen appeared immediately, however, in disputes between the sects and dissatisfaction
with the division of jobs. The Catholic Church especially resented
its small proportion of appointees and felt the new policy was anti-
Catholic.

Another development in Indian policy came with the law of
March 3, 1871, by which the United States finally abandoned the
fiction of the sovereignty of the various Indian tribes. Treaties on
the old plan were abolished. Agreements might still be made, but
they were to be ratified by the entire Congress rather than merely
by the Senate. The change was in the direction of political realism,
since the Indians had never been foreign nations in the usual sense
of the term, but in practice the only important effect was to give
the House a long-desired voice in any new Indian agreements.

Negotiating treaties for the creation of reservations was by no
means equivalent to getting the Indians on the selected land and
making farmers of them. Actually it was unlikely that the Indians
could be confined to the reservations as long as game was available
on the plains. In the north the Sioux continued to roam as their
desires dictated, with apparently not the least intention of migrating to their new home. In the Southwest the Apache was similarly
recalcitrant. In Indian Territory the Indians delighted in spending
the summers in hunting and war parties and then returning to the
reservation for winter rations.

While the Indian problem had obviously not been solved by the
mere creation of reservations, the temporary confusion and bloodshed should not be allowed to obscure the general trend of the
time. Expanding settlements, together with more forts and soldiers,
were pushing the Indians back inexorably toward their reservations; the day was coming when war and hunting parties would

find no place to go. Moreover, the disappearance of game on the plains was eliminating rapidly the possibility of nomadic wandering. Not many years were to elapse before an Indian could avoid starvation only by staying on the reservation — if not to farm, then at least to draw his rations from the government.

With these basic conditions in mind, the Indian troubles of the '70s decline in importance. True enough, Indian disturbances were depressingly common and full-scale wars were not unknown. And yet these were but the last gusts of wind before the hurricane subsided. The comparative isolation of the various Indian tribes averted any possible chance of a general Indian war, and assured the ultimate complete victory of the whites. The many commentators of the '70s who saw the approaching end of all Indian troubles were well justified in their optimism, even though their predictions seemed silly when made in the welter of bloodshed.

INDIAN TERRITORY

The troubled conditions of the Indian Territory in the early '70s were created largely by the restlessness of the Kiowa and Comanche. War parties raided into neighboring states, particularly Texas, during the summer and then came home with sufficient penitence to be forgiven and fed by the Indian agents. The Quaker agents continued to maintain their confidence in the reformative effects of love and kind treatment, to the utter disgust of the army. Ultimately even the agents agreed that kindness was not enough and the army was asked to take charge. Several military campaigns were climaxed in 1874, when the last considerable resistance was broken. Many of the worst offenders were shepherded east by R. H. Pratt, an army officer, to repent their sins at leisure at St. Augustine. Here ended the military operations in Indian Territory. Conditions still remained unsettled, however, and the progress of the Indians toward accepting a white civilization was slow and ragged.

SOUTHWEST

Farther west, a succession of commanders tried their hands at subduing the Apache. Their usual point of view was that expressed by General J. H. Carleton to Colonel Kit Carson in 1862: " All Indian men of that tribe are to be killed whenever and wherever you can find them." But the Apache did not make easy targets, having no desire for immediate immortality. In fact they fought back aggressively even after the death of Cochise, their ablest chief. What with the widespread depredations of the Apache and the bloodthirsty efforts of the whites to kill the Indians as though they were wild animals, the Arizona situation was a stench in the nostrils of the world.

The man who brought order out of this chaos was Major-General George Crook, who arrived in 1871. Crook was tall, slender, and muscular. He used neither liquor, tobacco, nor profanity. He was quiet and industrious, with great attention to detail, even to the proper method of packing mules. His first job was the transformation of his army into an efficient fighting organization. Then he ordered the Indians back to their reservations. He expressed his sympathy for the Indians and his desire for peace, but promised uncompromising war if the Indians did not obey his orders. Crook's words could be trusted completely, and when the Indians flouted his commands he took the field late in 1872. Dividing his army into comparatively small parties he harried the Indians continuously, killing ruthlessly. By April of 1873 the Apache were at his mercy. For the first time in 300 years Arizona knew peace from Indian depredations.

Unfortunately for both the Apache and Arizona, Crook was transferred north in 1875. His departure was followed by immediate trouble. The Indians did not like reservation life — especially when they found themselves going hungry as the lack of game emphasized the inadequacy of their all too meager rations. Well-armed bands under such leaders as Victorio and Geronimo raided the countryside; when Arizona became too hot they crossed the boundary into Mexico, only to raid back across the border. Military expeditions found themselves hampered by the international boundary as well as by the conditions of Apache warfare. Ultimately in 1880 Victorio was killed, but it was another six years before Geronimo was cornered and forced to surrender, ending anything like effective Indian resistance.

NORTHERN PLAINS

The various southern Indian troubles were but side shows to the main performance that was taking place on the northern plains during the '70s. The Sioux were the one important tribe which had never experienced a major defeat by the whites and which had won several minor victories. Moreover the Sioux had a multitude of grievances. The bad conditions on their Dakota reservation had reinforced their desire to roam the plains farther west, where they came into collision with miners, stockmen, and a scattering of settlers. More important, white miners had invaded country reserved to the Indian, particularly the Black Hills region, where rumor had it that there was " gold in the grass roots." Early prospectors were ejected by the army, but a new group tagged along after the Custer expedition of 1874, and very soon the entire United States army might have had trouble in freeing the country from white trespassers.

The Sioux exercised remarkable self-control in view of their many grievances, but resentment was great. When an agreement was proposed in 1875 to replace the treaty of 1868 that had been broken by the whites, only a few Indians could be found who would sign, and talk of war became more and more prevalent. By December 1875 the Indian agents had become sufficiently panicky to order all Indians back to the reservation by February 1, 1876. This order was physically impossible to obey even if the Indians had so desired, and consequently when the specified date arrived considerable bands of Indians were still roaming the country to the west.

The Indian Bureau labeled this nonobedience as defiance and turned over to the military the control of all Sioux and Cheyenne who were away from their reservations. A punitive expedition was planned immediately, aimed primarily at the Sioux. One column under General Crook was to move north from Wyoming, a second under Colonel John Gibbon east from Montana, and a third under General A. H. Terry west from Dakota. Terry disliked the assignment and planned to give control to Custer, but was prevented by orders from Grant, who had been angered by Custer's evidence in the Belknap case involving the President's relatives and friends.

Crook left Fort Fetterman, Wyoming, in March 1876. Being a thoroughly experienced and competent man he moved slowly to guard against a major surprise by the warriors of Crazy Horse, who harassed the column continuously. Eventually he reached and destroyed Crazy Horse's village on the Rosebud, but the succeeding battle was indecisive. By this time Crook felt himself so much weakened that he decided to return to his base camp (mid-June), where he enjoyed a mild vacation of fishing, hunting, and idling. Ultimately he was reinforced, after which he moved north to join Terry, but again was fought to a draw, and hence was out of the picture of the ensuing campaign.

Terry did not leave Fort Abraham Lincoln, Dakota, until the middle of May. The main element of his force was the Seventh Cavalry under the command of Custer. Late in the month he joined Gibbon on the Yellowstone at the mouth of the Powder. Here his scouts reported an Indian trail up the Rosebud. Terry at once sent Custer ahead to follow the trail, with orders which gave him considerable freedom of action, but which urged caution—largely to permit the deployment of the remainder of the army to cut off any Indian retreat; no one conceived of an Indian victory.

When Custer left on his last fateful march he was only thirty-seven years old, but his strenuous life had made him pessimistic and older than his years. His hope of great fame seemed to be growing dimmer and he was in the mood to wager everything on a single throw of the dice, with an impressive confidence that his Seventh Cavalry could beat all the Indians on the plains. Custer followed the Indians up the Rosebud, and then remained in close pursuit as they moved over to the Little Bighorn. His scouts reported large bodies of hostiles, but Custer himself probably underestimated grossly the number of his opponents. A more correct estimate, however, would probably have made no difference, since Custer was supremely certain that a large village was as easy to overwhelm as a small one. On June 25, 1876, he came upon the Indians and immediately charged. Outnumbered probably eight to one, and with no possibility of reinforcement, he was soon forced back. When "Custer's last stand" came to an end, the entire 225 men of the unit lay dead.

Custer's annihilation turned out to be relatively unimportant. Terry had been delayed but not stopped by Sitting Bull, the most important of the Indian chiefs. Continuing the campaign he defeated the hostile Indians and took back with him to Dakota all that he could find. A few under Sitting Bull escaped to Canada, but later returned, surrendered, and were pardoned.

CHIEF JOSEPH

Immediately following the Sioux war came the most spectacular of all Indian exploits — the retreat of Chief Joseph and the Nez Percé. The events which led to the retreat had followed a pattern that by this time was becoming monotonous in its regularity. The Nez Percé had been forced out of their original Oregon home by white desires, and then their new country on the Clearwater in Idaho had been invaded by white miners. Annuity payments had been poor and inadequate. Hotheads among the young braves had retaliated against the whites and the army had been called upon to " pacify " the hostiles.

Chief Joseph had always counseled peace, but now that he saw nemesis about to descend on his people he led them in a magnificent retreat toward the east (1877). With some two hundred warriors, but hampered by almost twice that number of women, children, and aged, he moved up the Clearwater, across the mountains, through Yellowstone Park, down the Bighorn, and across the Missouri. The pursuing General O. O. Howard covered 1321 miles in seventy days, but was outmaneuvered and outdistanced. Nelson A. Miles and Gibbon tried to head off Joseph; Miles was eluded and Gibbon was left " flat-footed." Colonel S. D. Sturgis and the Crow on Joseph's flank were defeated. The white generals later paid tribute to the brilliant strategy involved. And during the entire retreat Chief Joseph fought fairly according to white standards; there were no atrocities.

Ultimately Chief Joseph stopped to care for his sick and wounded. Probably he thought he had reached Canada. A surprise attack by Miles failed, but after a five-day siege during which the Indian food was exhausted, Joseph felt compelled to make peace. By this time he had less than fifty effective fighting men. Miles promised that the Indians would be returned to Idaho. Actually they were exiled to Indian Territory, where most of them died.

MESSIAH CRAZE

The Sioux War was the last important Indian resistance within the United States, and as the Indians realized their military impotence they began to turn increasingly to mysticism to recapture the faded glories of their past history. The mind replaced the body, as extroverts became introverts. Mentally at least they could restore dying Indian customs and power as against the all-conquering civilization of the whites.

Through all of Indian history certain individuals were thought to have peculiar and magical powers. Now, during and after the '70s, came the rumor among the plains tribes that there was at hand the coming of an Indian messiah who would eliminate the whites and unite the Indians, both living and dead, in an earthly paradise where disease would not exist and buffalo would be plentiful. Various prophets of the messiah, including Smohalla, Louis Yowaluch, and particularly Wovoka, were somewhat vague as to whether these idyllic conditions were to exist in actuality or only in the believer's mind and whether on this earth or only in a future life after death. Most of the Indians who accepted the beliefs thought of them as of immediate and concrete application. The usual date given for the coming of the messiah was the spring of 1891.

The " messiah craze " found its greatest enthusiasm among the Sioux, who had so recently been defeated by the whites. The Sioux were faring badly, with venal and inefficient agents, with crop failures and cattle disease, and with epidemics of measles, grippe, and whooping cough. Many of them acquired " ghost shirts," the symbol of the new religion; the ghost shirt, preferably made of leather, probably represented symbolically the old customs and manners to which its wearer wished to return. Wearing ghost shirts, the believers practiced a " ghost dance," accompanied by ceremonial fasting and sweat baths, that produced trances and visions and could work an entire group into an emotional frenzy.

The ghost-dance religion would probably have burned itself out had not the Indian agents become frightened and called in the army. Most of the Indians ran away. An effort to arrest Sitting Bull led to the killing of that old warrior in 1890. White soldiers followed the fleeing Indians and succeeded in slaughtering several hundred of both sexes and all ages at Wounded Knee Creek. After a few more skirmishes, accompanied by the inevitable tension along the frontier, the Indians realized the hopelessness of their situation and surrendered to General Miles, January 16, 1891.

CHANGING ATTITUDE TOWARD INDIANS

The crushing of hostile Indian tribes and their isolation on reservations were but the first steps in the solution of the Indian problem. To consider the Indians as wards of the nation, to be cared for and protected, was satisfactory only on the assumption that some day they would reach maturity and provide for themselves like other adult residents of the United States. Efforts to give the Indians the white type of education and teach them the trades of the whites had long been in existence, but the results had been entirely inadequate. The efforts of both the government and private philanthropic agencies to make the Indians over along a white pattern had made extremely small impression.

The desire to improve Indian conditions was demonstrated and reinforced about 1880 by the organization of several groups designed to study and assist the Indian — the Bureau of American Ethnology (1879), the Women's National Indian Association (1879), the Indian Rights Association (1882), the Lake Mohonk Conference (1883), and the National Indian Defense Association (1885). Not to be undervalued was the publication of Helen Hunt Jackson's books, *A Century of Dishonor* (1881) and *Ramona* (1884). The end of any real danger from the Indians had apparently inspired a more widespread tolerance and desire to help.

To advance the Indians along the paths of white civilization two developments seemed at the time to be necessary — proper education and the allocation of land to the Indians to be held individually rather than in a group. Which of these developments came first was immaterial. Each should reinforce the other.

EDUCATION

Indian schooling on the reservation was paid largely by the federal government. Adult education held little promise, but many hoped that influencing the children would produce a new kind of adults within a generation. Unfortunately only one child in twelve was attending school as late as 1880. Moreover, the influence of the home often seemed more effective than that of the school for those children who attended day schools in the centers of Indian population. In consequence there was developed the reservation boarding school which could isolate the child somewhat more from home influences. Even here, however, there was a considerable amount of failure as the boy or girl went home for vacations, found his new ways of life not in accord with the opinion of the home community, and hence relapsed into tribal customs.

A novel and more effective method of education was introduced by an army officer, Captain Richard H. Pratt. Pratt had been put in charge of Indian prisoners to be taken to St. Augustine in 1875. At St. Augustine he experimented with the idea of allowing his prisoners a measure of self-government and of encouraging them to undertake various kinds of work in the neighborhood. The results were so encouraging that Pratt was inspired to hope that if younger Indians could be taken from their homes and given good training at least for them the Indian problem would be solved. To realize this hope he persuaded some fifty children to go to the Negro school at Hampton, Virginia. Ultimately over a thousand Indian boys and girls attended Hampton, where they were quite successful in acquiring white customs.

But Pratt was not satisfied short of an independent Indian school. Having obtained the aid of Congress he toured the West and collected over a hundred children, with whom he started a new school in an old army barracks at Carlisle, Pa. (1879). The children divided their time between school and farm or shop; during vacations they worked in homes of the neighborhood. At first the school was handicapped by a lack of funds and by the homesickness of the children, but ultimately it was successful and led to the establishment of dozens of similar schools. Carlisle itself never went higher than junior high school, and was finally closed when the army needed the barracks during World War I.

Nonreservation schools were effective in educating the Indians, but their facilities were limited. The great bulk of Indian youth continued to attend reservation day schools, which improved notably after 1890. The Indians were also encouraged to attend near-by white schools, and in time about half took this option.

LAND ALLOTMENT

Just as important as the effort to educate the Indian was the drive toward making him a settled farmer. A nomadic, hunting Indian would never accept white ways — in fact he was due to starve as the game disappeared. Most whites felt that the way to encourage the Indian to become a farmer was to divide up the tribal domain and give each individual a piece of land which he could cultivate and improve. The idea of giving land in severalty was not new, but it had never been applied on a large scale. It was generally accepted by the late '70s as inevitable. The only real questions were when and how.

The great piece of land allotment legislation was the Dawes Act of 1887, which applied to almost all Indians except members of the Five Civilized Tribes, who were not forced into line until 1898. The President was allowed to allot land whenever he thought desirable. Provided that the land were sufficient in amount each head of a family was to receive 160 acres, while others were to receive less; the amount was changed later. The beneficiary was to be allowed to choose his own land, so that he might include any improvements that he had made. The selections were to be held in trust for twenty-five years before they were turned over absolutely to the Indian or his heirs; within this period the land could not be alienated. The Indian became a citizen as soon as the land was alloted and before the trust period. If any surplus land remained after allotment it was to be opened for white purchase, with the proceeds going to the Indians.

The Dawes Act was sponsored by friends of the Indians but it also received the support of white land grabbers, traders, farmers, and lumbermen. These latter groups had been able to enter Indian reservations only illegally. Under the Dawes Act they thought their opportunity would be greater, either to obtain land from the Indian allottee or from the surplus after allotment. Their hopes were justified as the first twenty years saw 50,000 allotments and in addition the opening of considerable surplus tracts for white occupancy, notably in Oklahoma.

From the standpoint of the Indian the Dawes Act did not work well. Often the wrong man received improved land, for Indian names were confusing to white clerks. Allottees were generally poor farmers and lived in poverty and filth, with no real preparation for complete ownership; the result was that with the final patents they either sold their land or lost it for debts — often fraudulent — and then became poverty-stricken dependents on charity. Furthermore, since the Indian attained citizenship with allotment, the courts held that he could buy liquor; the new citizen was then demoralized, while the liquor he brought back to the reservation spread the infection.

Modifications of the Dawes Act brought little improvement. The permission to lease (1891) meant that allottees rented their land in order to live in idleness — and usually in comparative poverty. In 1902 the Secretary of the Interior was permitted to shorten the trust period if he thought such action was wise, which meant that in many cases the Indian lost his land in less than the twenty-five years of the Dawes Act. The Burke Act of 1906 deferred citizenship until after a fee simple title had been granted, thus lessening the drink evil to some extent; otherwise, however, the Burke Act brought no improvement. Further legislation of 1907 and 1908 allowed the Indian to dispose of his allotment before the end of the trust period. Presumably such laws were approved by the whites who were impatient to acquire Indian land.

The process of allotment fluctuated in speed, but was particularly rapid after 1916. By 1920 something over half the Indians had received their allotments. In round numbers, 175,000 Indians had received 37,000,000 acres; of these allottees, 117,000 had obtained their final patents, with about 90 per cent of them in Oklahoma; 35,000,000 acres remained unallotted, the heritage of some

135,000 Indians. Presumably the end of the tribal system was in sight. In prospect of this conclusion, all Indians were made citizens in 1924.

While in theory the day was soon to come when the Indian would be a citizen and landowner according to white standards, conditions in the Indian country remained extremely bad. Division of the land was not producing economically independent farmers, for the Indian had not as yet achieved competence in farm management and was in consequence an ineffective competitor. The land soon went out of Indian hands and the Indian relapsed into poverty and squalor — the recipient of white charity. This increasing demoralization meant that the virtues of the old Indian culture were being replaced, not by a better white culture, but rather by the worst traits of the whites. All friends of the Indian were distressed.

WHEELER-HOWARD ACT

Ten years after the Indian citizenship law, a New Deal came for the Indians, with the most cataclysmic change in Indian legislation that had ever taken place. Under the Wheeler-Howard Act of 1934, as expanded in 1936, a strong effort was made to turn back the clock and utilize the better traits of Indian culture. Allotments were to cease and existing trust periods and other limits on alienation were to be continued indefinitely. So-called " surplus " land awaiting sale was to be restored to the reservations, and new lands acquired. The Indians were encouraged to continue their tribal organization — in fact to incorporate and hold land as a corporation.

The effects of the act of 1934 are as yet uncertain, but seemingly Indian conditions have improved. What the next step will be is impossible to predict. Presumably the Indian will some day be absorbed into white culture, even though by devious means. Tribal organization may well be a highly desirable method of bridging the gap between the primitive and the complex, but in the long run would seem unsatisfactory to both Indian and white. At the moment the Indian needs sympathetic and understanding help so that in time he may take his rightful place as one of the stronger elements of American society.

READINGS

E. A. Brininstool (ed.), *Crazy Horse* (1949) ; G. F. Brinlow, *Cavalryman Out of the West* (1944) ; M. S. Burt, *Powder River*

(1938), chs. 21–26; P. E. Byrne, *Soldiers of the Plains* (1926), chs. 3–22; W. Clum, *Apache Agent* (1936); J. H. Cook, *Fifty Years on the Old Frontier* (1923), part 3; F. Crawford, *Rekindling Camp Fires* (1926), chs. 23–29; E. E. Dale, *The Indians of the Southwest* (1949); B. Davis, *The Truth About Geronimo* (1929)—eye witness; A. Debo, *The Road to Disappearance* (1941), chs. 5–11, *And Still the Waters Run* (1940); F. Downey, *Indian-Fighting Army* (1941), chs. 7–16; E. G. Eastman, *Pratt* (1935)—Carlisle; R. Emmitt, *The Last War Trail* (1954)—Utes; C. A. Fee, *Chief Joseph* (1936); G. A. Forsyth, *The Story of the Soldier* (1916), chs. 12–15; G. W. Fuller, *The Inland Empire* (3 vols., 1928), vol. 2, chs. 19, 20, vol. 3, chs. 21–23; W. A. Graham, *The Custer Myth* (1953)—documents—*The Story of the Little Big Horn* (1926); G. B. Grinnell, *The Fighting Cheyennes* (1915), chs. 25–31; L. R. Hafen and F. M. Young, *Fort Laramie* (1938), pp. 363–382; H. Howard and D. L. McGrath, *War Chief Joseph* (1941); F. and R. Hunt, *I Fought With Custer* (1947); J. P. Kinney, *A Continent Lost—A Civilization Won* (1937)—detailed on Indian land holding; F. C. Lockwood, *The Apache Indians* (1938), chs. 10–15, *Pioneer Days in Arizona* (1932), ch. 8; J. McLaughlin, *My Friend the Indian* (1926); L. McFarland, *Exploring the Northern Plains* (1955), chs. 32–36; W. C. Macleod, *The American Indian Frontier* (1928), chs. 33–36; L. V. McWhorter, *Hear Me, My Chiefs!* (1952)—Nez Perce; T. B. Marquis, *A Warrior Who Fought Custer* (1931); M. Merington (ed.), *The Custer Story* (1950)—correspondence with wife; J. G. Neihardt, *Black Elk Speaks* (1932); B. Nelson, *Land of the Dacotahs* (1946), chs. 11, 14; W. S. Nye, *Carbine and Lance* (1937), chs. 6–17; R. Odell, *Helen Hunt Jackson* (1939); R. H. Ogle, *Federal Control of the Western Apaches, 1848–1886* (1940); L. B. Priest, *Uncle Sam's Stepchildren* (1942)—scholarly on Indian policy; R. N. Richardson, *Comanche Barrier* (1933), pp. 323–397; C. C. Rister, *The Southwestern Frontier* (1928), pp. 127–217; M. Sandoz, *Crazy Horse* (1942), part 3; R. Santee, *Apache Land* (1947); M. F. Schmidt (ed.), *General George Crook: His Autobiography* (1946), chs. 5–7; E. I. Stewart, *Custer's Luck* (1955)—very good; F. Van de Water, *Glory Hunter* (1934)—Custer; S. Vestal, *New Sources of Indian History* (1934), *Sitting Bull* (1932), *Warpath* (1934)—Sioux; P. I. Wellman, *The Indian Wars of the West* (1954), section 1, chs. 9–26, section 2, chs. 12–27; R. K. Wyllys, *Arizona* (1950), ch. 9.

CHAPTER 33

MINING ADVANCES

THROUGH the pattern of Indian affairs always ran the thread of the mining boom as it appeared first here and then there, violating Indian country and drawing trade and settlement which otherwise might not have come for many years. Without the miners the final troubles which beset the Indians during the 1870s might have been long delayed.

NEVADA AND SILVER

The turning point in western mining crazes was the exploitation of the Comstock Lode in Nevada. Heretofore every mining boom of the Far West had revolved around the finding of gold — at first the free gold of the placer mine and then the gold bearing rock which the stamp mills had to crush. But with the profitable mining of silver in Nevada the number of desirable metals began to enlarge and the field of search to widen. Later rushes were to be concerned as frequently with silver or copper as with gold.

As for Nevada itself, the original discoveries seemed to have been exhausted by the late '60s. Adolph Sutro still had faith and was digging his famous tunnel to free the lower levels of the mines from water, but most people were pessimistic. Then came new finds, bigger and richer than anything which had preceded them — the " big bonanza." Within another twenty-two years two of the largest mines extracted some $150,000,000 in metal, of which over half was returned as dividends to the lucky owners.

The history of the big bonanza is in large part the biography of a Scotsman and three Irishmen — James G. Fair, John W. Mackay, James C. Flood, and William S. O'Brien. The first two had been prospectors, which led them later to acknowledge that they were mining experts. The other two had run a saloon in San Francisco,

506

with a little of the usual mining stock speculation on the side. Flood was later to be considered the financier of the group, while O'Brien goes down in history as the silent partner. At the very nadir of Nevada production the four men showed their confidence in the future of the region by joining forces in an informal agreement for the purchase of mining properties as fast as funds were available.

The four partners rode the crest of the boom of the 1870s, with each man becoming many times a millionaire. Their two largest companies, the Consolidated Virginia and the California were united in 1884 as the Consolidated California & Virginia Mining Company. Their spectacular rise to wealth may be followed in the great surge upward of the value of their companies. The Virginia, which had sold for $1 a share in 1870, reached $700 in 1875. The California made the almost unbelievable jump of from $37 in September 1874 to $780 in January 1875.

The Nevada mines brought serious engineering problems for a young industry. Immense amounts of wood had to be hauled to feed the necessary fires and support the mine shafts. When haulage became impossibly expensive huge flumes were constructed down the mountainsides and across the ravines to wash the logs to the mines. Since the veins which were being worked often widened into large lodes, a new method had to be devised for supporting the roof and the walls. Best-known of the engineering innovations, however, was the Sutro tunnel, completed in 1878. An impressive project constructed in the face of great obstacles, it permitted the draining of water even from the lower levels and at the same time provided for the transportation of the ore.

BLACK HILLS

Just about the time that the Nevada boom of the '70s was at its peak an equally impressive rush of miners struck a thousand miles to the east, in the Black Hills region of the present southwestern South Dakota. Miners had followed on the heels of the Custer expedition of 1874 and their good luck had brought others by the thousands, with the peak of the early boom coming in 1876. The most profitable single location was the Homestake Mine of George Hearst. The Homestake was able to claim a total production of some $250,000,000 by 1931.

The center of the excitement was Deadwood, which in its heyday served as a magnet for a very large share of the floating population of the West. Deadwood came into existence by the accident of gold discovery and grew haphazardly. The main street meandered along a gulch, to the sides of which houses clung precariously. The lower part of the town was sacred to the gambler and the prostitute, with no pretensions of even the little law and order that prevailed in the rest of the town.

The main street of Deadwood was jammed with the usual array of booted miners, cowboys, gamblers, storekeepers, and casual visitors. Long ox-teams further increased the congestion, with the usual equipage consisting of ten oxen and three wagons hitched together; the snap of the driver's 100-foot leather thong was hardly to be distinguished from the crack of the six-shooter which meant one more addition to the long list of homicides. Twice a month the steel-lined treasure chest of Wells, Fargo & Company pulled out of town with as much as $350,000 in bullion. Altogether it carried some $60,000,000 before it was replaced by the railroad.

The amusements of Deadwood were rough and rowdy, but a trifle more sophisticated than those of earlier camps. A theater like the Gem presented an impressive variety of plays and vaudeville acts; the " Mikado " had a remarkable run of 130 nights. After the theatrical performance the floor was cleared, a bar opened at one end of the theater, a band installed at the other end, and dancing begun. The ladies of the cast acted as hostesses. At the end of each dance the man was expected to order drinks, from which the girl received a rakeoff. Further income might be derived from ventures into commercialized vice. The girls were encouraged in such ventures by the use of curtained boxes.

The most conspicuous members of the Deadwood community were its ministers and gamblers, two classes which unexpectedly had much in common. Both idled when other men worked, both wore good clothes, both were highly self-controlled, and both had better than average manners. Moreover, both had approximately the same clientele. The miner who lost his money at poker or roulette on Saturday night might well appear on Sunday morning to attend Methodist, Congregational, or Catholic services; all three were available by 1877.

COLORADO

Even as Deadwood was booming, Leadville, Colorado was revived with a bang. Here was one of the many places where early prospectors had found gold, only to have it soon exhausted. Now in 1875 a trained metallurgist, in looking over the abandoned mines, discovered ore that was rich in silver and lead. His staking of claims precipitated a rush which produced the usual crop of new millionaires and the larger but equally usual crop of broke miners. Leadville itself was organized in January 1878 by the consolidation of two towns, and had the customary jam of miners, teamsters, gamblers, traders, and prostitutes. An unusual fillip was added with the battle of the Santa Fe and the Denver & Rio Grande to obtain control of the single practical railroad route up the gorge of the Arkansas and thereby to monopolize the wealth of Leadville.

ARIZONA

Deadwood and Leadville found competition in Arizona for the attention of the foot-loose, for again at approximately the same time came a silver rush to Arizona. Arizona's mineral richness had long been known; in fact various mines had been worked even in Spanish times. Wandering prospectors had turned up new finds in the '50s and '60s, producing a series of small booms, with most of the resulting business going to Tucson, Tubac, and Prescott, and to the towns on the Colorado River. The lack of large scale exploitation was due partly to the fact that the early prospectors were looking only for gold and their discoveries were soon exhausted. A more important deterrent, however, was the hostile Apache. A lone prospector was looking for trouble as well as for gold, while even larger mining parties were in imminent danger of Indian attacks.

With the temporary quieting of the Apache by Crook in the early '70s miners were able to ply their trade in greater safety, and the immediate result was more mineral discoveries. Outstanding were the numerous finds in the neighborhood of Globe. The rich Silver King claim was discovered in 1875; rumor had it that some of the ore assayed as high as an almost fabulous $1000 a ton in silver.

Most famous of the Arizona boom towns of the late '70s was Tombstone, in the southeastern part of the state and not far from Bisbee. Its origin traced to a silver find by Edward Schieffelin in 1877, and for a few years Tombstone was the roughest, the toughest, the most wide-open town in the West. Old yellowed files of the Tombstone *Epitaph* recall but faintly the turbulent days when the Earps, " Doc " Holladay, Billy the Kid, and other exponents of the Wild West tradition played their rough games. The Tombstone deposits were exhausted within a few years, and today one passes a country pock-marked with abandoned shafts to enter one of the most notable of the West's ghost towns. Rows of deserted houses and stores and saloons attest its once numerous population, while an imposing boot cemetery gives mute evidence of the frequent use of the " six-gun " in a long-departed past.

More important in the long run to Arizona than silver was copper, and then lately rarer metals. The Cornelia mine in southwestern Arizona had been worked inefficiently but more or less continuously since the '50s, but rich new finds were made in other parts of the state during the '70s. Work in the Morenci area of east central Arizona began in 1871 and provided an inspiration and model for other copper districts such as near-by Clifton. Copper mining had all of the usual difficulties with transportation, water, and supplies, but in addition had imposing technical problems to solve in extracting the copper. The Bisbee and Jerome regions were both opened in 1877, while in time the mines near Globe came to be concerned predominately with copper; the first copper was extracted at Globe in 1878. Since copper mining required large amounts of capital it was particularly the domain of the large company. By the '80s such organizations as the Calumet & Arizona Mining Company and Phelps, Dodge & Company were preeminent in copper production.

MONTANA

The trend of events in Arizona furnished a pattern very similar to that of the more northerly Rockies. Early prospecting in Idaho and Montana in the '50s and '60s had been for deposits of free gold, of which many had been found. During the '70s and '80s interest turned first to silver and then to copper. The specific areas which loomed largest in the public mind were those near Butte, Montana, and near Coeur d'Alene, Idaho.

The boisterous Butte was described as " an island of easy money entirely surrounded by whiskey." To this vigorous community came William A. Clark in 1872. The little, precise, parsimonious, and ambitious Scotch-Irish Clark came as a merchant and banker, from which occupations it was a natural shift into mine operator. His great competitor was Marcus Daly, short, stocky, ruddy Irish immigrant. Daly arrived in 1876 as a mining expert interested in silver, but transferred his attention to copper. Backed by the capital of George Hearst he bought the Anaconda mines, and eventually by the 1880s transformed the major industry of the region to copper production.

The fight between Clark and Daly was one of the epic struggles of the day. Clark was in control at Butte and advanced the fortunes of that young metropolis; his newspaper sneered at the pretensions of Daly. Daly was boss at his own new town of Anaconda, where his rival paper returned with interest all the jeers that were thrown in his direction. Ultimately both men spent money freely in a struggle for political control of the state.

Clark's great ambition was to become United States Senator, and in 1899 he spent some half a million persuading the state legislature of his merits. The ensuing scandal was so great that he resigned just before a Senate committee reported that he should not be seated. His seat then being vacant, he was appointed by the Lieutenant Governor, but the appointment was canceled by the Governor. Clark obtained his heart's desire in 1900, and sat in the Senate for six undistinguished years.

At about the close of the century Standard Oil money entered the copper industry and combined many of the mines, including the Anaconda, into the Amalgamated Copper Company, which later took the name of the Anaconda Mining Company. The Amalgamated made efforts to monopolize the copper business, but ultimately failed because of the power of Calumet & Hecla. It did manage, however, to play a dominant role in the affairs of the state of Montana. The cattle people were never able to compete effectively against the copper people.

IDAHO

The first big Coeur d'Alene boom came in 1883, when rumors of gold brought the usual motley crowd of miners, their suppliers, and their parasites. Dozens of new towns such as Eagle City, Delta, Murray, and Myrtle had their evanescent moments of glory before free gold disappeared. The really big find (1885) was the Bunker Hill lode of silver and lead. The Bunker Hill and Sullivan mine in time paid some $50,000,000 in dividends. This and other mines have seemingly inexhaustible supplies of silver, lead, and zinc.

The Coeur d'Alene mines attained something like national notoriety because of their labor troubles, particularly in the '90s and later. Mining was a dangerous and arduous occupation. Both operators and laborers were rough and tough, with neither willing to make concessions. Labor troubles meant armed forces on each side, shafts and buildings dynamited, pitched battles, and sudden death. Here it was that both William Borah and " Big Bill " Haywood began their national careers. Here it was also that the Western Federation of Miners, with its Local Number 1 at Butte, had its baptism of fire and created the ideology that a little later produced the Industrial Workers of the World.

By the late '80s the day of the gold rush, with fortunes for poor and independent prospectors, seemed over. No conclusion could have been less justified, for a whole new series of booms took place in the next two decades. Notable were the Cripple Creek discoveries. Here as in so many places there had been earlier mines which had been worked out. Now the new finds revealed wealth for the taking, and attracted a motley array of carpenters, schoolteachers, prospectors, and farmers, of whom the usual lucky few made fortunes. By 1897 production had reached $1,000,000 a month, while four years later this amount had doubled. But then came a decline beginning in 1904 which was halted only by the New Deal silver purchase program.

THE YUKON AND ALASKA

The late '90s saw the seekers of quick wealth depart for the Far North, with their usual disregard for international boundaries. The existence of gold in western Canada had been known as early as the '30s, and gold rushes had occurred from the '50s. Now came the biggest of them all as news arrived in 1897 of rich finds near Dawson, in the Yukon. Men came back to the States with tangible evidence in the form of nuggets and dust, and within a year the population of Dawson grew to 40,000, with other thousands spread over the claims of the surrounding region.

The frozen North presented new problems which were extraordinarily difficult for the flood of farmers and clerks who made up such a large part of the multitude seeking easy wealth. The early part of the trip to the new El Dorado was easy enough, with the inland passage providing a comfortable trip past Juneau, where gold also had been found. The real troubles started at Skagway, for most men preferred the overland trip to the longer sea and river route. Six hundred miles of frozen waste, precipitous and ice-covered mountains, and boiling rivers had to be crossed before the newcomer attained his goal of Dawson. Not least of his troubles was the cloud of man-eating mosquitoes, which surpassed the best the United States could boast. Moreover each man had to carry a year's supply of food, not only from necessity but because otherwise the Canadian police would not let him enter the Yukon country.

While the deposits near Dawson were sufficiently rich to produce many fortunes, the hazards were equally great. During the winter the men were forced to thaw out the gravel before it could be dug, and then pile it for later working since the use of water was impossible. The common rule was that if the mercury froze, the weather was too cold to work outside. Piling the gravel meant that the miner was not sure he had any gold until summer, so that he might have lost his entire winter's work. During the short warm period the gravel was panned for gold, much of which went to the businesses of Dawson — not only for the high-priced food and clothes, but for the saloons, gambling halls, and houses of prostitution.

Dawson was inevitably one of the wide-open towns of the West, and yet it had certain distinction. The Northwest Mounted Police were effective in preventing the worst disorder and loss of life that appeared south of the border. Moreover Dawson contained an unusual proportion of famous men, as for example Robert W. Service, Rex Beach, and Jack London; all three were to exploit in literary fashion the material they gathered in the Yukon.

The riffraff of the Yukon gold rush, such as the gang headed by the suave Jefferson R. (" Soapy ") Smith, gathered mainly at the last American town of Skagway. One would like to believe that this concentration merely meant that the hoodlums were unwilling to make the long and severe trip to Dawson. But unfortunately the Skagway situation was repeated in later American boom towns farther north, as in Nome, in Fairbanks, and then in others. The answer seems to be that the Northwest Mounted was a much more efficient organization than the marshal and his deputies on which the United States depended.

LATER RUSHES

The last important series of gold rushes hit the region of Death Valley and to the north and east in Nevada. Here again the search was not new. Ever since a few of the '49ers had made the mistake of crossing Death Valley a scattering of prospectors was lured into the grimness of that desert spot. Rumors of discoveries came from time to time, but no real boom developed until the '70s. Then the town of Panamint had a brief but wild orgy during the middle of the decade, to be followed by a similar boom at Darwin. Neither lasted long, but the collapses were not due primarily to a lack of good ore. The main difficulty was the extremely large cost of transportation which made any but the richest ore unprofitable to mine. Senators J. P. Jones and W. M. Stewart, whose Panamint Mining Company was the big organization of the earlier boom, were rumored to have lost $2,000,000 on the venture.

Sporadic later rushes have hit Death Valley, with numerous claims staked and even worked for a time, but the costs of transportation have continued to remain decisive. The real Death Valley fortune came from borax, which was discovered in 1880; F. M. Smith made the fortune and at the same time gave national fame to the twenty-mule teams that hauled the borax across a hundred and fifty miles of desert.

One other possible Death Valley fortune was that of Walter Scott, commonly known as Death Valley Scotty. Scotty lived in a two-million dollar house with electricity, paneled rooms, a pipe organ costing a quarter of a million, a glass swimming pool, and other things in proportion. From time to time he traveled East, where he was very successful in obtaining newspaper publicity, as by throwing money out of his hotel window. At his death the secret gold mine turned out to be a complete mirage.

A new center of excitement appeared at Tonopah, Nevada, in 1900, with millions of dollars of metal being mined — mostly gold but also some silver. For a short time Tonopah could boast of plate glass windows, the latest of French fashions, and dinners which included champagne, caviar, and oysters.

Tonopah was followed in 1903 by Goldfield, which had originally borne the name of Grandpa. Here again millions were wrenched from the earth, with a single mine making the record extraction of $4,500,000 in sixteen weeks. One George Wingfield, a gambler who speculated in mining claims, was reputed to have attained a fortune of $2,000,000 by the age of twenty-seven. Here came another gambler, Tex Rickard, who had earlier followed the Alaskan rush. Rickard ran a popular saloon and gambling hall, where stakes at times exceeded $10,000. In 1906 he promoted a boxing match between Joe Gans and Battling Nelson, and this adventure in ballyhoo undoubtedly gave him much valuable ex perience for his later work as a sports promoter.

New booms followed one another in rapid succession — Amargosa City, Bonanza, Bullfrog, Beatty. The year 1905 saw the construction of the model town of Rhyolite with concrete buildings, modern schools, attractive stores, three-story office buildings, electric lights, paved streets. At the time the town seemed permanent, for one mine alone had some $5,000,000 of ore in sight. The permanence was an illusion, for the boom collapsed with great suddenness, and by the end of 1908 the town was dead — one of the most impressive of many such corpses in the West.

EFFECTS OF MINING

The long succession of western mining booms brought into sharp focus many picturesque persons and institutions as miners flocked from one rumored find to the next. Each boom town was like every other boom town, with congested living quarters, astronomic prices, and an imposing boot cemetery. Traders, gamblers, and prostitutes trailed after the horde of predominantly young and vigorous men. With each find a few men made their fortunes, others missed by an eyelash, while the majority soon moved to greener fields. The color, movement, boisterousness, and virility are obvious and spectacular.

And yet the phenomena of western mining booms meant a good deal more than the provision of picturesque episodes which later would furnish good material for novels and scenarios. The men who were searching for wealth actually produced large quantities of real minerals and these minerals had important effects on the industrial life of the United States. Certain obvious results come quickly to mind, as the effect of vast new supplies of copper at a time when American streets were being transformed into mazes of telegraph and electric wires.

Most important was the effect of new supplies of the precious metals on the total economy of the United States. American industrialization was expanding impressively during the late nineteenth century, which meant that the number of business transactions was increasing in proportion. The result was a vastly stimulated need for money — a need which the banking system of the day could not satisfy. The result would normally have been deflation, that is a fall in prices. This fall actually occurred, but it was tempered by the vast new flow of precious metals from the West. Without the addition of this gold and silver the depressions of 1873 and 1893 might have been longer and more severe.

The greatly increased production of silver had its first effect in destroying the old ratio between the value of silver and gold. A sixteen-to-one ratio, which had at least been within hailing distance of the facts for the previous century now became ridiculously untrue. The immediate consequence was that when the farmers wanted inflation they talked of the " crime of '73 " and wanted free coinage of silver. Apparently, however, the flow of new money had caught up with business transactions so that prices began to rise from about the late '90s. This rise in prices produced a death blow to the demand for free coinage of silver — at least for the time being.

For the West itself, the mining rushes also had important implications. The movement of large numbers of miners into the Indian country precipitated final red-white conflicts somewhat sooner than might otherwise have been the case. Each new boom meant new towns with commercial opportunities attractive to storekeepers, bankers, artisans, labor, and railroad men, and these new residents in turn provided opportunities for still other people, including farmers and stockmen. When the " St. Paul " or the " Northwestern " went into the Black Hills or the Denver & Rio Grande followed the mining booms into central Colorado, not only did transportation improve for the mines, but for everyone else. The farmer or the cattle grower was attracted to the area served by the railroad, and the result was more and faster western settlement than would otherwise have occurred, and often in more or less isolated spots. Comparatively early statehood for Nevada, Idaho, and Montana, for example, must be credited largely to the mining industry.

The chaotic conditions of frontier mining have largely disappeared. Most mines have become stable enterprises, run much like factories, and surrounded by prosperous and orderly towns. And yet mining continues to remain more hazardous than most industries. A mine may be exhausted, but much more likely is a slight fall in the price of the metal, making operations unprofitable. Moreover, there is always the chance of new and more profitable discoveries. While almost all of the country has been prospected, there are few who would not admit the possibility of rich deposits as yet unknown. One wonders where the next mining rushes will take place.

READINGS

R. G. Athearn, *Westward the Briton* (1953)—views of travelers; E. Bennett, *Old Deadwood Days* (1928); J. Brown and A. M. Willard, *The Black Hills Trails* (1924); W. N. Burns, *Tombstone* (1927); R. G. Cleland, *A History of Phelps Dodge* (1952), chs. 5–8; E. Fergusson, *New Mexico* (1951), ch. 21; G. W. Fuller, *The Inland Empire* (3 vols., 1928), vol. 3, chs. 24, 25; C. B. Glasscock, *The Big Bonanza* (1931), chs. 12–21, *Gold in Them Hills* (1932), *The War of the Copper Kings* (1935); L. R. Hafen (ed.), *Colorado and Its People* (4 vols., 1948), vol. 1, ch. 24; J. K. Howard, *Montana* (1943), chs. 5–10; B. Lee, *Death Valley* (1930); O. Lewis, *Silver Kings* (1947)—Nevada; R. G. Lillard, *Desert Challenge* (1942), ch. 4—Nevada; F. Lockwood, *Pioneer Days in Arizona* (1932), ch. 9; E. M. Mack, *Nevada* (1936), pp. 437–460—not inspired; A. Murdoch, *Boom Copper* (1943), chs. 15, 16; J. M. Myers, *The Last Chance* (1950)— Tombstone; B. Nelson, *Land of the Dacotahs* (1946), ch. 10; W. Ogilvie, *Early Days on the Yukon* (1913); G. C. Quiett, *Pay Dirt* (1936), chs. 7–19; T. A. Rickard, *A History of American Mining* (1932), chs. 5, 8, 9, 11, 12, 14–16; C. H. Shinn, *The Story of the Mine* (1906), chs. 16–22; M. Sprague, *Money Mountain* (1953)—Cripple Creek; A. W. Spring, *The Cheyenne and Black Hills Stage & Express Routes* (1949); W. C. Stoll, *Silver Strike* (1932); G. F. Willison, *Here They Dug the Gold* (1931), chs. 9–14; N. C. Wilson, *Silver Stampede* (1937).

CHAPTER 34

THE
CATTLE COUNTRY

THE best advertised feature of the life of the post-Civil War West was the cattle business. A host of authors from Theodore Roosevelt and Andy Adams to Zane Grey, James Oliver Curwood, and the authoritative writers for the pulp magazines have given it a species of immortality. Painters such as Frederick Remington and Charles Russell have made it only slightly less vivid than did Buffalo Bill in his Wild West show of a previous generation. The movies in their turn have made the " horse opera " a staple of American entertainment. All this in spite of the fact that the cattle business has never been of overwhelming importance and that in the distinctive form which included the long drive it lasted less than two decades.

The raising of cattle has always been an industry distinctive of the frontier. When surplus grain is fed to cattle it is transformed into beef which can move to market under its own power — a real advantage with the usual poor transportation of the frontier. During the early nineteenth century the big cattle areas were Ohio and Kentucky, and the stock was driven across the mountains to market. As transportation improved and land became more expensive, the large herds migrated to Indiana, to Illinois, to Missouri, and to Iowa. This movement eventually reached the Great Plains. Older parts of the West continued to fatten and market cattle, but the main growing areas were always where population was scarce.

While the center of cattle population continued to move west, the cattle themselves did not necessarily participate in the movement. In both California and Texas existed millions of head which were increasing some 25 per cent a year. Here, and particularly in Texas, was the source of the western herds. Before the Civil War these western herds had been almost profitless because of the lack of an available market. The California rancher could sell a limited amount of hides and tallow to the New England trader. The Texan cattleman now and then pickled some of the meat for export, and occasionally drove a few animals as far as New Orleans or even St. Louis, but such incidents were rare.

Following the Civil War conditions changed radically for the western cattleman. The expanding railroad network bit into the western plains and provided transportation to the growing cities farther east. The development during the '70s of the tin can and of artificial refrigeration, both by railroad and by boat, sounded the death knell of the local butcher, who could no longer live up to his name. The big packers began to dominate the national market, which in turn meant that the advantage held by locally grown and slaughtered livestock tended to disappear. Cheap western herds, fattened on the grass of the public domain, could outcompete the better but more expensive animals grown farther east.

Texas cattlemen viewed the expanding railroads with hope, and in 1866 sent their first important herds over the long trail to the northern railroads. Unfortunately the first big drive was not very successful. Unfamiliarity with conditions of the trail led to the loss of an important fraction of the quarter-million animals that started the trip. The resulting discouragement of the dealers meant a slower development of the business than might otherwise have been the case.

ABILENE AND OTHER COW TOWNS

The man who saw most clearly the possibilities of the plains cattle business was Joseph G. McCoy, an Illinois stockman. Looking at the five-dollar price of cattle in Texas and the fifty dollars paid for a similar animal in the East, profits seemed there for the taking. Carrying his idea to the railroads, he persuaded them to give him special rates and then searched for a plains town that would meet his needs. The town he picked was Abilene, Kansas, to which the Kansas Pacific was due to be completed by 1867. Energetic advertising in Texas persuaded ranchers to overlook their failure of the previous year and again send cattle north. During the first year (1867) McCoy received only 35,000 head, but the number grew steadily.

Abilene created the pattern which later cow towns were to follow.

The economic heart of the town comprised the stock pens and railroad loading facilities, together with the three-story " Drovers' Cottage " and other hotels and boardinghouses necessary to entertain visiting cattlemen. Almost equally necessary were the amusements for the hundreds of cowboys who arrived from their long and tiring weeks in the saddle with a craving for bright lights and excitement and with several months' pay in their pockets. For them the lights glittered in the saloons such as the Bull's Head and the Alamo, for them the balls of the roulette wheel clicked and the cards fell in the gambling parlors, for them the Novelty Theater offered its tawdry entertainment, and for them the " Devil's Half-acre " on the other side of the tracks offered its castoffs of the river traffic to furnish a pathetic substitute for authentic romance. Drunkards and homicides were no news in Abilene in spite of sporadic and valiant efforts at law enforcement.

While the lights of Abilene beckoned invitingly for the cowboy with money to spend, the prospect was not so pleasing for more permanent residents, who saw their surroundings in the cold light of day and during the bleak winters. Stocktenders, railroad employees, businessmen, farmers and artisans, schoolteachers and ministers regretted the streets ankle deep in mud or dust, the rough wooden sidewalks, the shabby storefronts, the drunkenness, the personal violence, and the prostitution. In time their protests were effective; a better police force was installed and a farmers' protective association limited the ranging of the herds. By 1872 Abilene was no longer important as a cow town.

Not least in importance of the supporters of the new order were the hardworking wives of Abilene citizens. Such a woman must have had many pangs as the sun and wind of the plains dried out her skin and as hard work and excessive childbearing made her old before her time. There must have been days when she could have cried bitterly as she saw the few obvious pleasures monopolized by the young and the immoral. Understandable is the difficulty of choice when her husband died and her only possible occupations were boardinghouse keeper or prostitute. Every fiber of her being called for a new and better social order where the usual social values were respected and where children could be reared without contamination from a crude and lawless society.

Abilene was but the first of a long succession of towns that utilized their railroad facilities to capture the cattle business of the plains. While Wes Hardin, who was an expert on the subject, has been quoted as saying of Abilene (1871) : " I have seen many fast towns, but I think Abilene beats them all," even Wes may have changed his mind as he saw Ellsworth, Newton, Julesburg, Wichita, Hays City, Ogallala, and other plains settlements take their turn at attracting the cows and wickedness of the West.

Best known of all the cow towns was Dodge City on the Santa Fe, which ruled supreme as the " cowboy capital " in the decade from 1875 to 1885. During the height of its reign a quarter of a million cattle arrived each year ; in 1884 alone it shipped 3648 cars of beeves to Kansas City and Chicago. Along with the cattle came the usual horde of reckless cowboys who filled the tills of the saloons, supported the gamblers in ease, patronized the disreputable houses south of the tracks, and filled the well-populated Boot Hill Cemetery. In its moment of glory Dodge City was better known than Denver or St. Paul or Kansas City.

The cow towns existed only because of the peculiar nature of the western cattle business as it existed from the late '60s through the early '80s. Each spring saw vast herds collected in Texas and driven north over the public domain, living on the free grass of the government. Most of the cattle, exclusive of those used to stock northern ranches, were shipped east from such centers as Abilene and Dodge City. A few were fattened on Middle West farms before they were marketed. Others were wintered on the northern plains and then sent to market the following year. Conservative estimates have it that some 6,000,000 animals were driven north during the twenty years following the Civil War.

These Texas cattle that flooded northern markets produced nothing like the prime beef that the modern citizen enjoys. Texas cattle were long-horned and muscular. They were able to fight their own battles and to survive under bad conditions. No modern fat stock-show prize cattle could have existed under plains' conditions. The result was that the meat was tough and stringy, and could be sold only because the price was low.

Sooner or later almost all Texas cattle ended at the large packing houses of Chicago, St. Louis, Kansas City, and Omaha. Of these centers, Chicago was clearly dominant. Such men as Armour and Swift had based their fortunes on the lucrative contracts of the war period. By the '70s they were cooperating to dominate the market and, hence fix prices. The western cattlemen acting individually had no possible chance of fighting effectively against the packers acting in common.

THE COWBOY

The central figure of the western cattle business was the cowboy, who has frequently been considered picturesque because of his unusual clothes. Actually his apparel was designed with the idea of utility uppermost. Loose, heavy, woolen trousers were covered with " chaps " for protection against brush. A woolen shirt was worn open at the throat, with bright red or blue sleeve garters to make it manageable. A coat was unusual because it bound the arms and retained perspiration which might become dangerous with the sudden changes of temperature on the plains; in its place an unbuttoned vest provided a receptacle for watch, tobacco, cigaret papers, and matches. A large gray or brown Stetson, with a leather thong to keep the brim straight, had a variety of uses beyond protection against sun, rain, snow, sleet, and wind: folded it made a pillow; in time of necessity it could be used to carry food or water. A bright handkerchief knotted around the neck also had its utility as a protection against cold and wind.

The cowboy took great pride in his gloves, boots, and saddle. Gloves were gauntlets of the best buckskin, usually embroidered. They were worn all year round, more as protection against rope burns than against cold. Boots were black, tight, high-topped, and high-heeled. A cowboy was vain of his feet, even though he was shod in such a fashion that when put afoot he hobbled painfully. As for a gun, the usual cowboy found such hardware a nuisance, particularly since he was not a good shot. He would wear a gun only when one was really needed or when he dressed up to go to town. Then when he called on his lady friend or attended a dance he was likely to remove his gun and retain his hat.

The cowboy's saddle was designed not for speed but for comfort on long rides and to provide a stable seat for roping. It was large, broad, and heavy, weighing some thirty pounds. The stirrups were so long that the rider almost stood upright. Each man owned his own saddle, which might be highly ornamented, and in which he had great pride. For a man to sell his saddle meant that he was dead broke and had lost a measure of his self-respect. A cowboy's whip, called a quirt, had lashes of twelve inches or more and was carried by a thong around the wrist. His lasso (or lariat or rope) was an eighteen-foot, loose-running coil with which he was adept. Seldom did a man practice fancy roping. Every cow pony was taught to brace itself for a jerk as soon as a rope was thrown.

The cowboy's long solitary hours in the saddle may have been responsible for his quietness, which at times approached taciturnity. He seldom expressed his deeper emotions, and certainly never to strangers. Even in the bunkhouse among companions of long and tried friendship he was not likely to become loquacious. Typical is the story of the dude who turned to Reddy to verify a long-winded tale of adventure. Reddy responded: " All that mought be so. But the true facts was. The bar there. The dude he stepped on a stick. Skidoo."

The cowboy's limited conversation was couched in a vocabulary that was at once picturesque, profane, and obscene. After all, he was usually very poorly educated. " Damn " was only an adjective and not an expletive. Language was rich in the metaphor of the plains. " ' Bring me a rib steak about an inch thick,' I says to the waiter, ' Don't cook it too much, but just cripple the critter and drag 'er in.' " Or a man might be described as the surest shot " since a horse pistol was raised from a Colt." Or, describing a spree, one man contended that " I was so drunk I couldn't hit the ground with my hat in three throws."

The ordinary life of the cowboy was reasonably dull. Riding herd by himself was not an exciting occupation. The exclusively male companionship of the bunkhouse was not soul-thrilling. Possibly here lies the explanation of the cowboy's exaggerated courtesy toward the women he so rarely saw. To him a woman was either all good or all bad, and toward the " good " woman he was almost unbelievably respectful. Even the most attractive of the opposite sex could travel the plains unescorted in much greater safety than she could walk the streets of New York, Philadelphia, or Chicago. Any bad treatment of a woman might bring vindictively cruel punishment to the perpetrator.

Most cowboys were young and vigorous, since a ranch was hardly a convalescent home for the old and sick. Being young and strong, the cowboy's ordinary ailments were seldom more than stomachaches or sore throats, which was lucky in view of the lack of provision against illness. The ordinary medical treatment was a dose of some patent medicine — " cholera cure," " pain killer," " Universal Liver Remedy," or even diluted horse liniment. An aching tooth was removed by the blacksmith. Surgical treatment could be received only at the nearest settlement.

The amusements of the cowboy on the ranch were necessarily limited. Horse races, roping contests, and bull dogging combined business with pleasure. Any athletic contests on foot were pretty well excluded by high-heeled boots and the bowed legs that came from many hours of straddling a horse. The library of the ranch was confined to a few patent medicine almanacs, mail-order catalogues, saddle makers' catalogues, and some old newspapers of various dates and places, with possibly a few novels or books of travel. The cowboy ordinarily did his only reading either when he was extremely hard pressed for amusement or when he wanted to order a new suit or Stetson from Montgomery, Ward & Company.

In the evening in the bunkhouse, when he got tired of slapping down greasy, dog-eared cards, the cowboy might be moved to express his soul in harmony. A banjo or fiddle would be dug out of hiding and everyone would join in the singing with enthusiasm. High notes received lingering and sickening vibratos, while " barber shop chords " were dwelt upon lovingly. Included in the repertoire would always be such syrupy, sentimental ballads as " Rosalie the prairie flower " and " Annie Laurie." Home and death ditties expressed sentiments impossible of ordinary statement — " I'm a poor lonesome cowboy," " The dying cowboy," " The night my mother passed away."

Most interesting of the cowboy songs were those which were indigenous to the cattle business and which used local settings and vernacular.

> " Whoopee, ti yi yo, git along, little dogies!
> It's your misfortune and none of my own.
> Whoopee, ti yi yo, git along, little dogies,
> For you know Wyoming will be your new home! "

Many of such songs of unknown authorship were extremely pathetic and had to be rendered with long-drawn misery:

> " Oh, bury me not on the lone prairie,
> Where the wild coyotes will howl o'er me;
> Where the rattlesnakes hiss and the wind blows free,
> Oh, bury me not on the lone prairie! "

Unfortunately the poor cowboy's prayer was not answered, and " his bones now rot on the lone prairie."

When the cowboy made his infrequent trip to town he tried to squeeze into a short time all the amusements that he had missed most of the year. Poker, seven-up, faro, and keno brought the thrill of risking more money than he could afford to lose. Whiskey brought exhilaration up to the moment when the cowboy slid under the table. Prostitutes provided a synthetic and commercialized romance. Such a town spree, coming after pay day or when cattle were being sold, afforded a much needed relaxation from the usual humdrum life of the ranch. True the cowboy drank to excess and lost his money at cards, but he was young and vigorous, and recuperated rapidly. A good night's sleep brought him back to work little the worse for his experience. The worst effects were on the towns he visited and on his own reputation.

While most of a cowboy's life was spent in such dull occupations as riding range, caring for animals in trouble, mending fences, and repairing harness, certain outstanding events of the year broke the monotony. In the spring, the horses had to be " broken " or " gentled " for the year's work. " Breaking " was a descriptive word, since the refractory 20 per cent of the horses actually had their spirits broken. The usual method was to snub, blindfold, saddle, and mount the horse. Then the blindfold was removed and the rider tried to keep his seat until the horse gave up the struggle. The occasion was something of a sporting event as the cowboys gathered around to see the fun. If the rider " grabbed leather " (the pommel) his reputation suffered and hence he frequently held his hat in his hand to demonstrate his mastery. To be thrown was unpleasant in several ways, but was certainly completely honorable in the rare event that the horse rolled over. Possibly one in a hundred horses never was broken to the saddle, and many remained sufficiently wild that they bucked every time riders straddled their backs.

Even with the small horses of the plains, their control was hard on the men and helps to explain why the average life of a cowboy was estimated at seven years. Enough horses had to be broken to give each man a " string " of six to ten, to be ridden successively and changed from time to time. Only rarely did a cowboy have special affection for some particular horse. A good cow pony was trained to respond to the pressure of the knees rather than the pull of the reins, to cut a steer out of the herd, and to brace itself on its haunches whenever its rider threw his rope.

THE ROUNDUP

Most important in the cattleman's year was the roundup. The spring roundup was common throughout the country as a means of identifying and marking calves while they were still with their mothers. In Texas, cattle for the drive north were segregated at this time. A fall roundup was less frequent in the South than in the North, where cattle were selected for market in the autumn. With the unfenced country of the early days the herds were badly mixed and a roundup was a cooperative venture, with crews from the various ranches dividing the territory and driving the cattle to some central spot. If this spot were open country the cattle were held together by being made to " mill " (move in circles).

The real work of the roundup was the branding of the calves. Each calf had to be cut from the herd, roped, thrown, tied, and dragged to the fire. Cowboys sat on its head and feet while it was branded with a hot iron and sometimes had its ears notched. A tally man kept count for all ranches. Then the calf was freed and ran back, bawling and frightened, to its mother. The whole operation seemed to be one of the utmost confusion. The calves bawled and their mothers bellowed; dust billowed as the herd milled; the horses ran and the calves were dragged; the fire gave a fierce heat, the counters shouted, and the cowboys perspired and cursed. But underneath this confusing surface the work actually proceeded rapidly and methodically.

Cattle brands were at first simple markings developed at the pleasure of the owners, but with the vast increase of both herds and owners the system became complicated. To avoid confusion and duplication the stockmen formed associations which kept elaborate records. Certain markings were outlawed, as for example the " frying pan " brand, which could be used to obliterate earlier markings. Common types of brands included the 4 — 28, called the four bar twenty-eight; the A2 or big A two; ⊴ or lazy M bar; Ⓖ or circle G; ◈ or diamond S; ∽9∽ or flying nine. In addition some owners used various kinds of ear slits.

Many a western herd's birth was marked by the bar sinister. Always on the plains were a certain number of unmarked " mavericks " which became the property of the finder. Since a maverick was ordinarily the progeny of some cow which had met an untimely end there was a tremendous temptation to the ambitious cowboy to help nature make orphans. Having started a herd this way he might later be among the most ardent supporters of law and order. If he entered upon cattle stealing as a profession he became an artist with a piece of hot wire. ⊔ (flying U) was not hard to alter to ⊍ (Seven Up), while E (big E) was easy to convert to —E (pitchfork). The early defense against such marauders was a vigilance committee, a dark night, a tree, and a coil of rope. Later the stockmen's associations hired detectives and depended more on the enforcement of regular processes of law.

THE LONG DRIVE

The other outstanding event of a cowboy's life in the '70s and early '80s was the " long drive " from Texas to the northern plains or to a shipping point in Kansas or Nebraska. While the number of men engaged in the long drive was not large, their influence in breaking down sectional prejudices was great. The drive started in the spring, immediately after the roundup. The most efficient size for the herd was some 2500, with a dozen men and the necessary horses, mules, and " chuck-wagon." After a few days in which the herd was acclimated to the trail, the cattle moved at the rate of some ten to fifteen miles a day, which meant 300 to 500 miles a month. At this rate the cattle could gain flesh on the grass of the public domain.

A caravan on the long drive was headed by the foreman, who was followed by the cook with the chuck-wagon. Then trailed the herd, with the more experienced hands on each side to keep the animals from straying and to avoid collision with other herds. Also on one side was the horse wrangler with the spare mounts. In the rear came the remainder of the cowboys, who had the unpleasant job of swallowing the billowing dust from the herd so that they could round up any stragglers. All in all the work was hard, dusty, and monotonous. It did bring, however, a splendid appetite for the bacon, flapjacks, and coffee that the " old lady " dished out at the end of the day. After supper the cowboy unfortunately could not smoke his cigaret and roll into his blankets for a good night's sleep, for then he had to stand one of the three watches which prevented the herd from roaming during the night.

Numerous dangers confronted the men on the long drive. Cattle thieves and wild animals were always possibilities. Swimming a river was dangerous since the cattle were stupid and would crowd enough to cause many deaths unless they were well handled. Worst of all was a stampede, which might be produced by any startling incident such as the shot of a gun or a flash of lightning. Cattle were easily frightened, which was one of the reasons the cowboy so frequently sang while he was riding herd. Once a herd stampeded, the panic-stricken animals dashed wildly away from the object of their fears. If they came to a cliff they fell to their death, if to a river they drowned, if to a mountain side they trampled each other fatally. The only hope of the cowboy was that by hard riding he might head them off and cause them to mill. With this object in mind he took desperate chances, and not infrequently was trampled to death for his pains.

PERMANENT RANCHES

The striking character of the long drive tended to obscure the development of a more permanent and more important type of western cattle business all the way from Texas to Montana and as far west as California and Oregon. As much as three-quarters of the drive from Texas has been estimated to have been used for stocking the northern plains, which in turn had a large increase of their own. The result was that during the '70s the cattle of Kansas and Nebraska increased from 500,000 to 2,500,000; of Montana from 36,000 to 430,000; of Wyoming from 11,000 to 520,000; of Colorado from 71,000 to 791,000. During these same years Henry Miller was constructing his cattle empire farther west in California and Oregon.

A cattle boom on the western plains was evident by the late '70s. Even with increasing herds the price of beef continued to advance with American prosperity. By 1882 the price of beef in Chicago had hit $9.00 a cwt., which meant that a steer on a Texas ranch, worth not over five or six dollars in 1865, would bring around thirty-five dollars. Rumors were circulated of profits that amounted to 50 per cent or more in a single year.

The boom of the late '70s and early '80s attracted large amounts of speculative capital, not only from the United States but also from abroad, primarily from England and Scotland. The individual stockraiser of the past tended to be replaced by the corporation which raised its original capital from hundreds of small subscribers. Mammoth companies became frequent. The Prairie Land & Cattle Company, with ranches in Texas, Oklahoma, and New Mexico, could boast 7900 square miles of land and 140,000 head of stock. The Swan Land & Cattle Company of Wyoming, largely Scottish, held half a million acres of land and had an investment of some $3,000,000. The J A ranch of Charles Goodnight in the Texas Panhandle comprised over a million acres. Big business had reached the plains.

The ranches of the period began to exhibit new and changed characteristics. Above all, the rapidly growing herds were crowding the available land, so that no longer did there seem to be a limitless public domain where any man's cows might find sufficient grass. The result was a mad scramble to perfect control of the available land, and particularly that part of it which contained water. Land without water was useless and there was always a lack of water. Many and bitter were the struggles to control springs and creeks.

Various stratagems were necessary to acquire large parcels of land, since most of it remained part of the public domain and the entire development of the land system had been in the direction of small farms for settlers. Railroad land could sometimes be obtained. Homesteaders could be bought out; in fact many men entered homestead claims in several names so that they could sell to the cattle companies. Cowboys were encouraged to acquire land by homesteading, preemption, or timber culture and then assign it to their bosses. Of course such transactions were technically illegal, but punishment was highly unlikely. Only in Texas, which controlled its own land, could a large quantity be obtained legally from the government. The result was the Capitol Freehold Company, which in 1879 received a huge tract in the Panhandle in return for the promise to build a state capitol. The X I T brand soon appeared on some 160,000 cattle ranging 3,050,000 acres which were enclosed in 1500 miles of fence. Here was probably the world's largest ranch.

When all other methods failed, the cattleman merely fenced the needed land, regardless of ownership. The checkerboard of railroad sections might be so fenced that the alternate sections of public land were included. Fences might be strung up over land to which the grower had no possible claim, even crossing roads so that the traveler had to cut the strands to continue his journey. This kind of illegal fencing amounted to a national scandal during the late '70s and the '80s. An attempt to stop it came with the law of 1885, which provided severe penalties. Under Cleveland a considerable effort was made to enforce the law.

A permanent and fenced ranch, representing a large capital investment, inspired greater efforts for better beef production. Texas longhorns were small and scrawny, which meant low market value. Hence the desire to improve the breed by adding such blooded stock as Shorthorn, Hereford, Polled Angus, and Galloway. Better stock meant more care, since the better the beef the more helpless the animal and the greater the loss if it died. Water supplies were husbanded carefully and natural running water was supplemented by dug wells. Hay was grown and the barns necessary for its protection were built, even though the cowboy was far from enthusiastic about spending his time digging post holes, watering stock, running a mowing machine, and pitching hay.

More competition for land and water brought a need for cooperative action by the growers. The result was the formation of cattlemen's associations, of which the most important probably was the Wyoming Stock Growers' Association, founded in 1873. In time it operated in five states and controlled some 2,000,000 head of cattle. Such groups soon were created throughout the cattle country. They recorded the brands of their members, hired detectives to find cattle thieves, supervised roundups, settled conflicting claims, obtained railroad rebates, and did lobbying in both state and national legislatures. In time their various regulations were given legal authority by the several states.

The western cattle business underwent considerable changes during the middle '80s. Most obvious to the casual observer was the end of the long drive. The railroads which had made the drive possible now made it impossible by bringing thousands of farmers to the plains. These farmers quite naturally objected to the passage of cattle which broke their fences and trampled their grain, while local ranchers opposed outside competition. Since these farmers and ranchers were permanent residents the states could be persuaded by 1885 to pass a series of acts designed ostensibly to bar diseased cattle but aimed really at barring all cattle on the hoof. In consequence the long drive was at an end. The talk of a national cattle trail on the public domain never came to the point of action. In the future cattle were to be born, raised, and shipped from their home ranches.

The omen of an even greater change came in 1883, when American beef exports dropped 50 per cent. The next year saw a drop in the domestic prices, which by 1887 descended to $2.50 a cwt. One drovers' magazine urged that " If you have steers to shed, prepare to shed them now." To make the stockman even more unhappy the year of 1885 was hard on the cattle and 1886 was even worse; a hot summer was followed by a very cold winter, and during 1886–87 the cattle died by the thousand. Some herds lost as much as 90 per cent. The cattle boom was dead and the cattlemen, along with most of the West, tightened their belts and tried to hold out during the bad times of the late '80s and early '90s.

The collapse of the fever for cattle meant that many investors lost their money. The mortality among the large companies was notable, with a tendency for the smaller individual owners to come back to their own. Expenditures could no longer be on the lavish scale of the past, and the ranchers had to find cheaper and more efficient methods of operation. The tendency was to sell the animals younger, since it was too expensive to feed them until maturity. Many of the animals were sent to the corn belt for fattening before they made their appearance in the Chicago stock yards.

SHEEP

The same land that was fitted for grazing cattle could also be used for sheep, and as eastern land became more expensive, the tendency was for an increasing proportion of American sheep to be raised in the Far West. Even before the Civil War large flocks had grazed the land of California and New Mexico, and after the war there was great expansion to the north and east. These sheep were driven east to be fattened for market in Kansas and Nebraska. The height of the drive was between 1865 and 1885, and it has been estimated that some 15,000,000 animals were driven between 1870 and 1900. Mostly ewes were driven before 1880; later it was wethers. The trip took normally over seven months, with a day's trip of about eight to ten miles. Sheep were more docile than cattle, with the main hazard being that they might wander away and get lost.

Sheep trails, like cattle trails, were gradually closed by state action. Starting with Kansas in the mid-'80s all states acted by 1900, with the result that sheep had to be raised without the aid of free public grass. The greatest concentration of the industry came to be in the mountain and coast states, with the plains east of the mountains dominated by cattle. By the end of the century such states as Wyoming, Montana, Colorado, Utah, California, New Mexico, and even Texas found sheep in the majority. Wyoming, the traditional home of the little dogie, found that while it could boast in 1886 that cattle outnumbered sheep three to one, that in 1900 sheep outnumbered cattle by an impressive ratio of eight to one.

The main activities of the sheep business were driving the flocks to good pastures, protecting them from wild animals and other dangers, caring for new-born lambs, dipping, and shearing.

Shearing was done once a year and hence was a seasonal occupation, much like threshing; shearing crews worked north from early spring until late June. Ordinarily the sheep was dipped before and after shearing. The wool was the only important product, since mutton was hardly worth shipping until the twentieth century.

The sheepherder contrasted unfavorably with the cowboy. No one thought of the herder as a man of romance and excitement. He lived a life of solitude, except for his dog and his flock. If lucky, he might have a permanent cabin, but more frequently he followed his flocks with a bedroll on his back, or possibly with a covered wagon if his employer were generous. Daily association with sheep was reported to make a man queer—or possibly, said some, the occupation attracted the odd personality. When in the cattle country you called a man a sheepherder, it was well to be prepared to reach fast for your gun.

Cattlemen and sheepmen never wasted love on each other, since they competed for the same range. The cattleman insisted that sheep cropped the grass too close and ruined the range with their sharp hooves so that no self-respecting cow would graze on land formerly used by sheep—a proposition that was not true. Moreover, the cowboy looked down with disgust and contempt on the lowly, unmounted, and usually unarmed sheepherder with his dirty, smelly woolies, while in return the sheepmen resented bitterly the arrogance of the cowboy. Bitter feuds resulted, with the greater numbers and mobility of the cowboys permitting them ordinarily to take the offensive, although the sheepmen could hire gunmen to make the odds more even. Outstanding examples were the Tonti Basin War in Arizona in 1887, and the struggle in the Green River country of Wyoming in 1901. Thousands of sheep were clubbed, dynamited, driven over cliffs, fed poisoned grain, or given saltpeter, which was fatal to them but did not hurt cattle; shooting was considered too expensive. At times the herders fought back by cutting fences and slaughtering cattle, while personal physical combat was far from unknown.

Vengeful clashes were not to last forever. By the 1900s the general place of cattle and sheep in the national economy had been fixed, and the days of violence were mostly past. In spite of the cattlemen's opposition to the introduction of sheep, many a rancher had actually himself changed from cattle to sheep. In the long run, economic forces had won over sentiment.

READINGS

A. Adams, *The Log of a Cowboy* (1903); E. D. Branch, *The Cowboy* (1926); H. E. Briggs, *Frontiers of the Northwest* (1940), chs. 3, 4; D. Brown, *Trail Driving Days* (1952); M. S. Burt, *Powder River* (1938), chs. 27–47; H. Call, *The Golden Fleece* (1942)—reminiscences; J. Clay, *My Life on the Range* (1924); R. A. Clemen, *The American Livestock and Meat Industry* (1923), chs. 2–11; J. H. Cook, *Fifty Years on the Old Frontier* (1923), part 1; E. E. Dale, *Cow Country* (1942), *The Range Cattle Industry* (1930); E. E. Dale and M. L. Wardell, *History of Oklahoma* (1948), ch. 11; A. Debo (ed.), *The Cowman's Southwest* (1953); E. Dick, *Vanguards of the Frontier* (1941), chs. 20–22; C. Emmitt, *Shanghai Pierce* (1953)—Texas; E. Fergusson, *New Mexico* (1951), ch. 22; W. Gard, *The Chisholm Trail* (1954); J. E. Haley, *Charles Goodnight* (1936), *The XIT Ranch* (1953); F. Harris, *My Reminiscences as a Cowboy* (1930); J. A. J. Hopkins, *Economic History of the Production of Beef Cattle in Iowa* (1928); J. K. Howard, *Montana* (1943), chs. 11–15; W. James, *American Cowboy* (1942), *Cowboys North and South* (1924), *The Drifting Cowboy* (1926), *Lone Cowboy* (1930); V. Johnson, *Heaven's Tableland* (1947), chs. 3, 4; F. M. King, *Wranglin' the Past* (1946); W. Kupper, *The Golden Hoof* (1945)—sheep; C. Lindsay, *The Big Horn Basin* (1932), ch. 4; J. A. Lomax, *Cowboy Songs* (1924), *Songs of the Cattle Trail* (1920); J. McCarty, *Maverick Town* (1946)—Texas; J. E. Mc-Cauley, *A Stove-Up Cowboy's Story* (1943); J. G. McCoy, *Historic Sketches of the Cattle Trade* (1940)—reprint of classic; B. Nelson, *Land of the Dacotahs* (1946), chs. 12, 13; E. S. Osgood, *The Day of the Cattleman* (1929); O. B. Peake, *The Colorado Range Cattle Industry* (1937); L. Pelzer, *The Cattlemen's Frontier* (1936); W. M. Raine and W. C. Barnes, *Cattle* (1930); R. N. Richardson, *Texas* (1943), ch. 14; C. C. Rister, *No Man's Land* (1948), ch. 4; P. A. Rollins, *The Cowboy* (1936); F. A. Shannon, *The Farmer's Last Frontier* (1945), chs. 9, 10; C. A. Siringo, *Riata and Spurs* (1927); F. B. Streeter, *Prairie Trails and Cow Towns* (1936); G. Sykes, *A Westerly Friend* (1944), chs. 9–11; C. W. Towne and E. N. Wentworth, *Shepherd's Empire* (1945); E. F. Treadwell, *The Cattle King* (1931); P. I. Wellman, *The Trampling Herd* (1939); E. N. Wentworth, *America's Sheep Trails* (1948), chs. 8–15; C. P. Westermeier, *Trailing the Cowboy* (1955); R. K. Wyllys, *Arizona* (1950), ch. 11.

CHAPTER 35

SIX-SHOOTER EXPERTS

THE West of the long drive and of the mining booms was likewise the West of the most spectacular and dangerous of a long line of killers. Dozens of men such as Wild Bill Hickok, Billy the Kid, Bat Masterson, Wyatt Earp, Henry Plummer, and Jesse James come to mind with the greatest of ease. Some were on the right side of the law and some were not. Such are the injustices of history that the most dangerous are the best remembered. Mankind's memory keeps green the name of a Jesse James or a Billy the Kid while overlooking such eminent personages as Presidential candidates or even Vice Presidents. The record of many a sadistic killer who met an untimely death with his boots on has survived while hundreds of admirable and law-abiding citizens who could boast long lives of good deeds have passed into oblivion.

Violent men of direct action, on either side of the law, have been a deeply ingrained American tradition. Whether at the " Boston tea party " or in the snowy wastes of Alaska, Americans have seldom been docile conformists. When conditions seemed to them bad they acted directly and vigorously — if on the right side of the law, then well and good, but the mere existence of law has never been an effective deterrent. State after state constructed and put into operation its own extralegal government when the federal Congress failed to act. Settlers gathered into claims' clubs to protect what they considered their rights, regardless of the state of the law. Americans have never been passive in their desires.

Nothing was more natural than that the West should have more than its fair share of violent action. United States marshals and their posses were inadequate in number to police the large areas under their supervision, and in addition were limited by political boundaries. Even the normally law-abiding citizen accepted the necessity of fighting his own battles rather than running to a policeman for protection. As for the criminal, he found a haven of refuge in the West when the law breathed a little too hotly on his neck in the East. " Gone to Texas " was a current expression which was understandable to everyone. Little wonder that throughout its history the West contained a large number of antisocial persons. In an earlier day one found a Harpe, a Murrell, or a Jean Lafitte; in a later day it was a Joaquin Murietta, a Sam Bass, or a Bob Younger.

If the western gunman is considered as the lineal forebear of the modern gangster the reality has been missed completely. The present distinction between the lawful and the unlawful killer was not drawn so clearly in the old West. Some of the best and most efficient gun wielders, like Earp, were law enforcement officers. Others, like Hardin, were outside the law. But consider a man like Hickok, who by common knowledge was a professional gambler and a persistent murderer, and yet served at various times as an effective law enforcement officer. Quite clearly he wandered from one side of the law to the other without the West finding this mixture of good and bad particularly unusual.

The truth was that the western line between the law-abiding citizen and the criminal was not hard and fast. Many a cowboy lapsed now and again into cattle stealing, while not a few were involved in holdups as the men with the handkerchiefs in front of their faces. Even well-known killers were allowed to roam freely, since the western code of ethics did not always coincide with statute law. Generally speaking, if one killer beat another killer to the draw, the bystanders merely nodded approval. If nonprofessionals were included in the slaughter, the reaction might become a decided disapproval which eventuated in an equally illegal lynching.

Any frontier town was an attractive rendezvous for men who depended on their guns for a living, but the mining and cattle towns offered special opportunities. Each was a predominately male community filled with foot-loose and reckless men. Each was turbulent and unruly. Each emphasized the more boisterous amusements. Each had a plentiful supply of wealth that might be corralled without the usual legal niceties. Here congregated the riffraff of the West to give a proper setting for the man highly skilled in the use of the six-shooter.

CALIFORNIA

The course of events in early San Francisco furnished a pattern that later reappeared throughout the West with but minor variations. The seemingly inevitable disorder was met by the formation of a vigilance committee, which soon degenerated into a criminal gang, and ultimately was dispersed by a later vigilance committee. Incidentally, the usual vigilance committee was composed of the more orderly citizens who saw no way of obtaining order except by violence. Usually they provided some sort of trial, which might at times be quite elaborate, for the accused. Sentences were ordinarily exile or death, and were executed immediately. Of course the vigilance committee was as illegal as the criminal gang, but Americans were the legitimate heirs of the tradition of the Declaration of Independence and believed that when conditions became insufferable, men were justified in taking the law into their own hands.

Out of the California mines came one of the most picturesque of the earlier bandits, Joaquin Murietta. Like most such men, his background and accomplishments have been so embellished by generations of rumors that fact is difficult to separate from fiction. The usual and rather hazily romantic version is that he was born in Mexico and in time fell in love with Rosita Carmel Feliz, whose parents were pressing her to marry a rich old man. The young couple fled to the California gold mines, where five American miners reputedly coveted both Joaquin's mine and his wife. Attacking Murietta they beat him to a pulp and then raped his wife. When Rosita died from the treatment she received from the miners, Murietta swore vengeance on all white miners. Then usually follow stories in the best Robin Hood tradition, of how Murietta stole only from the rich, helped the poor and weak, was loyal to his friends, brave, chivalrous, and altogether admirable.

While most of the Murietta legends are of doubtful authenticity, there is no doubt that from late in 1850 to the middle of 1853 the gang which he led terrorized considerable portions of California. Possibly the group numbered as many as a hundred men engaged primarily in highway robbery, with homicide as a by-product. Ultimately a large reward was offered for the capture of Murietta and a special force of rangers was created by the state for his apprehension. The rangers completed their job on July 25, 1853, by killing Murietta while he was resisting arrest. At this time he was twenty-three years old. As so frequently happened in such cases, periodic rumors appeared for many years that Murietta was still alive and was raiding the highways.

NORTHERN MINES

Outstanding in the northern mines was the notorious Henry Plummer, slender, graceful, well-dressed, and attractive. This quiet, courteous, blue-eyed man was attractive to both men and women, to the ultimate distress of both. Men would find themselves betrayed and robbed, while women found themselves involved in relations that often became embarrassingly unpleasant, especially if the woman had a husband. Plummer's first brush with the law came in California when he shot and killed a husband who resented the affair between Plummer and his wife. The result of the shooting was a ten-year prison sentence, but the governor was induced to grant a pardon on the plea that Plummer had tuberculosis. Released from prison the Plummer trail can be followed through California, Washington, and Idaho by a series of love affairs, holdups, and brawls.

Ultimately Plummer arrived in Bannock, Montana, in the early '60s, having outdistanced his reputation. Here his personal charm and quickness with a gun obtained him the job of sheriff. Later he moved to Virginia City, where he was also sheriff — a prominent and superficially a respected citizen. In this role he married a local girl, but apparently her eyes were soon opened for after ten weeks of married life she deserted him.

Plummer's real activities were criminal as the head of a gang of holdup men. As sheriff, with three or four of his cronies as deputies, he had unusual facilities for obtaining information as to when and where gold was to be shipped. In the event that he furnished the guards for such a shipment their resistance to bandits was entirely formal, and then somehow the ensuing search never discovered the criminals. Altogether it was a beautiful racket until various citizens added two and two and produced the inevitable four. A vigilance committee began rounding up the criminals, and ultimately the trail led to Plummer, whose activities came to an abrupt conclusion at the end of a rope on January 10, 1864.

CATTLE TOWNS

The better known of western gun wielders were the men who congregated in the cattle towns from Arizona to the Dakotas.

Today they continue to remain better known, not because of intrinsic merit, but because their exploits were embedded in such literary masterpieces as the numbers of the Beadle Dime Novel series. Writers like Ned Buntline can be credited with having given them immortality. In quite a number of cases the stories of their lives were completely fictitious, and in any event the fictional element bulked large, so that accurately documented statements are extraordinarily difficult to make.

The " prince of pistoleers," according to his biographer, was James Butler (" Wild Bill ") Hickok, professional gambler and revolver wielder extraordinary. If the stories about him were true he could drive a cork into a bottle without breaking the neck, could hit a knot on a telegraph pole with all six shots as he galloped past on horseback, could cut the stem of an apple with the gun in his left hand and hit the apple with a shot from his other gun before it touched the ground. Such stories should of course be accepted with caution. For example, the six shots into the telegraph pole is clearly an exaggeration. Any gunman equipped his gun with a hair trigger, and then for his own safety allowed the hammer to rest on an empty chamber. In consequence he never had but five shots.

Regardless of exaggeration, a man with the reputation of Wild Bill definitely had to be a cool customer with great manual dexterity. Reputation with a gun was bought dearly, for there was always someone to challenge it, and a single mistake would be both the first and the last. A man who lived by his gun practiced incessantly for both speed and accuracy, and such practice was too expensive for the average westerner. For example, hold a poker chip in your right hand extended straight out from your shoulder. Drop the chip and try to get out your gun and fire two or three shots before the chip hits the ground. A good operator could do this stunt.

Pulling a gun fast was of great value, but it assumed secondary importance to accuracy of aim. What value drawing and emptying your gun unless you hit something? Many stories testified to the value of holding fire until the results were certain, even though the other man emptied his gun first. Incidentally, a good gunman almost never " fanned " his gun, which produced inaccuracy, and seldom shot with his left hand, preferring to transfer his second gun to his right hand after he had emptied the first.

Hickok was a native of Illinois, and reputedly had been educated for the ministry. Drifting west, he had worked on a canal and on the overland stage, and had proved himself a rough and rowdy fighter. Rumor of his prowess began to spread — witness the tale of his fighting and killing ten men in one general holocaust; unfortunately for this story, recent skeptical historians have dehydrated it. Ultimately he quieted in manner and improved in appearance. At the height of his fame he was tall (over six feet), broad-shouldered, blondly handsome, mild-mannered and sad-faced. His Prince Albert coat and immaculate linen proclaimed the professional gambler. At various times he was marshal of Hays City, of Fort Riley, and of Abilene, where his reputation with a gun produced a perceptible decrease in violence by other would-be bad men. He also appeared briefly (1873) behind the footlights with Buffalo Bill.

In 1876 Hickok drifted with the gold rush to Deadwood. There he spent most of his time playing poker, at which his particular qualities of mind and body were useful. Unfortunately he one day forgot the habits created through a lifetime of caution and sat with his back toward a doorway. This first mistake was his last, for he was shot through the heart from behind. The rapidity of his re-actions received eloquent testimony in that in spite of his almost instantaneous death, he had his gun halfway out of the holster before he went down.

Linked in popular stories with Wild Bill during his last days — and linked incorrectly — was the best-known woman of the plains, Martha Jane Canary, commonly known as Calamity Jane. Big, coarse, strong, vulgar, lewd, promiscuous, she wore men's clothes, could swear with the best, chew a sizable cud of tobacco, and drink most men under the table. Possibly she once drove a mule team for Russell, Majors & Waddell, but stories of her riding for the Pony Express and of doing army scouting are more difficult to credit. The tales of her tender care for lonely miners oppressed by sickness or other bad luck are probably at least exaggerated.

Martha Jane's affections were exceedingly variable, which meant a succession of lovers and at least one illegitimate child. Apparently there was always a very good chance that sudden death would overtake her current paramour, and under mysterious circumstances. Hence the name " Calamity." Of course no gentleman would question a lady very closely after such an unfortunate incident, even though that lady was known to be an exceedingly bad woman when she was drunk. Calamity Jane lived until 1903, at which time she was an old, haggard drunk. Upon her death she was buried in the Deadwood cemetery beside Wild Bill — undoubtedly an implied libel on the character of that "prince of pistoleers."

TEXAS AND OKLAHOMA

Calamity Jane's chief feminine rival for unsavory reputation was Belle Starr, whom the *Police Gazette* provided with the attractive sobriquet of "the bandit queen." Belle Starr grew up in the same Missouri that hatched the Younger, the Dalton, and the James brothers. In fact she was probably related distantly to these outlaws, and presumably had a child by Cole Younger. Involved in holdups in Missouri she moved to Dallas, Texas, in 1867. Here she flaunted her immorality in the faces of law-abiding citizens to the delight of the more sporting. Dressed in clinging black velvet and with a gun on each hip she made a spectacular figure on the streets of Dallas. Whether or not to her credit, there is no record that she ever shot at anyone, much less killed him.

Belle's active mind and strong will were responsible for the collection of a gang of holdup men and horse thieves in northern Texas. When this country became too hot for the gang, the headquarters were moved to the more lawless Indian Territory. Here Belle's home, with its succession of male "heads," became a hospitable center for many bandits, including at one time Jesse James. Rather ignominiously, Belle was in time (1883) convicted of horse stealing and sentenced to a short term in federal prison. Ultimately (1889) she was shot and killed; the best guess at the identity of the murderer places the blame on her son.

Belle Starr was but one of numerous outlaws infesting the entire Southwest from Texas and Indian Territory to California. Vast, sparsely populated areas provided plenty of scope for the lawless, with Mexican sanctuary within easy riding distance. Mexico offered not only refuge but also a market for stolen cattle and horses. What with hundreds of wanted men, both American and Mexican, and with hostile Indians, the Southwest was a dangerous region for men not prepared to defend themselves by force.

The plethora of Texas gun fighters defies the historian in his attempts to discriminate. J. K. ("King") Fisher, handsome and debonair, headed a notable gang of thieves. Ben Thompson, rowdy gambler and drunken prankster, was at various times proprietor of an Abilene saloon and city marshal at Austin, Texas. Fisher and Thompson were linked in death, since both were killed in a Texas barroom brawl in 1884. Another noted Texas gun wielder was John Wesley Hardin, son of a minister and named for another divine. Hardin apparently enjoyed killing for its own sake and reputedly might murder a man for no better reason than not liking his snores. He had been credited with the deaths of thirty-nine men by the time he was old enough to vote in 1874. Convicted of murder he spent some seventeen years in prison; shortly after his release his life was ended by assassination at El Paso in 1895.

The prevalence of outlawry in Texas, and particularly in southwestern Texas, led the state to revise the corps of Rangers that had originated at the time of the Texas revolution. Reconstituted in 1874 under Captain L. H. McNelly it performed noble service in bringing law and order to the wilder parts of Texas. The Rangers were effective, knew it, and were proud of it. The usual rule was one Ranger to one riot.

Among the more notable exploits of the Rangers was breaking up the Sam Bass gang of train and bank robbers. Bass had led a humdrum early life as farmhand and teamster, but had in time become a saloon addict with an aversion to manual labor. By gradual stages he drifted to the wrong side of the law — first cattle thieving and then holdups. His biggest feat was the robbing of a Union Pacific train at Big Springs, Nebraska, in 1877. Back in Texas he robbed four trains within fifty days, and all within twenty miles of Dallas. By this time the Rangers were on his trail, and his last job was the robbing of a bank in 1878. Shortly afterward the Rangers caught up with him and he died of the wounds received in the ensuing gun battle. The well-known poem of his life paints him in undeservedly eulogistic terms. It starts:

" Sam Bass was born in Indiana which was his native home,
Before he reached young manhood, the boy began to roam.
He first came out to Texas, a cowboy for to be —
A better hearted fellow you scarce could hope to see."

NEW MEXICO AND ARIZONA

West of Texas conditions were little better, even though the boast of Roy Bean that he was " all the law west of the Pecos " was hardly justified. Notable as a center for gun fighters was the Tombstone of the late '70s and early '80s. Here was Old Man Clanton and his son, Doc Holliday, Frank Stilwell, and other notorious characters. Here also was the best known peace officer of his day, Wyatt Earp, cool and efficient, together with his three brothers. Wyatt had been marshal at Ellsworth, Wichita, and Dodge City during their boisterous days. After a brief interlude at Deadwood he turned up at Tombstone, where he ultimately became deputy United States marshal.

Earp's record at Tombstone has been the subject of much debate, ranging around both his integrity and his effectiveness, but the consensus of opinion seems to be that he did a good job under trying conditions. After Tombstone died he followed various gold rushes, including the one to Alaska. In 1896 he refereed the Bob Fitzimmons–Tom Sharkey fight at San Francisco. His later years were spent in California, where he had the remarkable record of dying peacefully in his bed (1929) at a ripe old age.

The southwestern bad man whose name has collected the richest deposit of legends was William H. Bonney, known commonly as Billy the Kid. In the best outlaw tradition, Billy was said to have placed himself outside the law at the age of twelve by stabbing to death a man who had insulted his widowed mother. Admirers have called him quiet-spoken, courteous, given to laughter, lithe and sinewy, extraordinarily brave, and a favorite with the ladies. Tales of his generosity, his miraculous escapes from prison, his heroism, and his quickness on the draw are legion.

The real Billy the Kid was not as attractive as his press notices would indicate. The one remaining picture of Billy shows a slight, rough-looking, and unprepossessing lad, quite clearly adenoidal. As a boy in Silver City, New Mexico, he haunted the saloons, where he picked up the vices of the period, including the technique of the card sharp. Apparently he had good muscular coordination, since he had greater than average ability to handle either cards or a gun. Running away from home he drifted back and forth across the Mexican border as need arose, making a living from cards and cattle thefts. He was one of the hired gunmen in the Lincoln County War of the late '70s — ostensibly a fight between the big and little cattle owners. On several occasions he was arrested but escaped.

Billy the Kid's nemesis was the sheriff Pat Garrett, who cornered and shot him to death in a dark room in July 1881. At this date Billy was just a little over twenty-one, and boasted that he had killed twenty-one men, not counting Mexicans and Indians. Possibly he was truthful. The inevitable poem about Billy was not as worshipful as it might have been. In fact it tended toward the humorous:

> " Billy was a bad man,
> And carried a big gun,
> He was always after greasers,
> And kept 'em on the run.
>
> * * *
>
> " But one day he met a man
> Who was a whole lot badder
> And now he's dead,
> And we ain't none the sadder."

JAMES AND YOUNGER BROTHERS

Not to be forgotten among the outlaws of the '70s and '80s were the men trained in the school of Quantrill — notably the James brothers and the Younger brothers. Both families lived in Missouri and had members who had served under Quantrill. Both were demoralized by the fighting of the Civil War and found themselves emotionally unable to settle down to farming. Their release came in a series of bank robberies in western Missouri, starting with a $60,000 job at Liberty early in 1866. As these holdups became epidemic they were all credited popularly to the James and Younger brothers, but whether correctly or not is a trifle uncertain. The perpetrators were not likely to provide carefully documented accounts of their misdeeds.

The James brothers reputedly invented the new crime of train robbery. On July 21, 1873, a rail on a sharp curve of the " Rock Island " near Adair, Iowa, was unspiked and a rope attached. When the train approached, the rope was pulled and the engine wrecked, killing the engineer. The train was then looted of some $3000. While the idea was good (from the bandit's standpoint), the timing was poor. An express train with some $75,000 came twelve hours later. The gang had miscalculated the schedule.

Then followed more train and bank robberies, with an ever-increasing hue and cry against the criminals. Not only the police but also numerous Pinkerton detectives engaged in the man hunt, which if successful would have meant reaping large rewards. At times the pursuers got close and there were skirmishes and even pitched battles. Some of the gang were killed, but always the James and Younger brothers seemed to bear charmed lives.

The charm was finally dissipated in a spectacular raid on the First National Bank of Northfield, Minnesota. The two James brothers, the three Younger brothers, and three others rode into Northfield on September 7, 1876. Unfortunately for the holdup men, they failed to open the safe and were consequently delayed in their departure. Meantime the citizens of Northfield, unintimidated by the reputation of the Missouri bad men, started taking pot shots at the party. In the general street fighting two of the gang were killed and one was wounded. The six survivors fled, pursued by every able-bodied man in the vicinity — possibly a thousand in all. The two James boys, posing as their own pursuers, finally escaped. Of the other four, three were killed, while Bob Younger was badly wounded, captured and jailed; later Bob recovered and was freed.

After the Northfield raid Jesse apparently settled down to farming at various places and under different names. Several crimes were placed to his credit, but with dubious accuracy. He tried to resurrect his Missouri gang in 1879, but the effort failed. Then he retired to St. Joseph with his wife and family, living under the name of Howard. Here he was shot and killed on April 3, 1882, by Robert Ford for the reward which had been offered for his capture.

None of the western outlaws has been glamorized more than Jesse James. The result has been a sort of American Robin Hood legend, in which a much-wronged man became a modern knight errant, relieving the rich of some of their ill-gotten gains in order to bestow them upon the worthy poor. Traditionally he was quiet, soft-spoken, kind-hearted, religious, a model family man; presumably he embodied all human virtues. The actuality was of course far different, but the facts seemed unimportant to the builders of the legend. Now his memory is kept green by a song published shortly after his death — a song which glorified Jesse James and provided the well-known chorus:

" Poor Jesse left a wife to mourn all her life,
   His children three were brave,
But the dirty little coward that shot Mr. Howard,
   He laid Jesse James in his grave."

Later road agents and stick-up men never replaced Jesse James in popular estimation. Most noted were the five Dalton brothers, related to both the James and Younger brothers, who operated in

Indian Territory in the early '90s. They made at least a valiant effort to keep the heroic traditions of outlawry alive. Emmet Dalton spent fifteen years in Leavenworth prison, after which he gave his name to a book of the Dalton adventures. The book is probably ghost written and certainly highly fictional. The Daltons were succeeded by Al and Frank Jennings in the late '90s, but the Jennings holdups were almost farcical. Of four attempts, one fizzled completely; in two the Jennings got cold feet and ran away; in the fourth they obtained sixty dollars apiece and one watch.

CHARACTERISTICS OF THE GUNMAN

The heyday of the gun-toting western bad man was clearly the 1870's. He had numerous predecessors and a certain number of later disciples, but at no other period did he loom so large in the life of the nation. Every western sheriff had on hand the names and descriptions of thousands of men wanted for murder, arson, highway robbery, horse and cattle stealing, and other crimes. Misdemeanors were hardly worth consideration, although a particular sheriff might find his life healthier if he confined his attention to drunks and petty thieves.

Widespread lawlessness implied conditions which favored it. A considerable share of the bad men would probably have been law-abiding and respected citizens if they had lived at a different time and in a different place. Some, such as Bass and Billy the Kid, might well have been at least worthless if not criminal at any time, others like Hardin were psychologically queer, but men like Emmet Dalton, Jesse James, and Bob Younger were more victims of their environment.

The so-called bad man frequently had many redeeming traits. In fact he was almost forced to have certain positive virtues if he were to remain long at the top of his hazardous profession. Unceasing gun practice and vigilance were necessary. Cool nerves, great muscular coordination, clear vision were equally basic. Such qualities necessitated a temperate life. Plenty of would-be bad men drank and caroused to excess, but only the rare top-flight professional could maintain his superiority with a gun under such conditions. Sooner or later he met an equally proficient man who was not suffering from a hangover.

The idea that the western gunman spent all his spare moments in devilment came partly from the credulous easterners who visited the West more or less casually. Almost any saloon would produce a would-be bad man who boasted loudly of imaginary deeds of valor: " I'm the toughest, wildest killer in the West. When I'm hungry I bite off the noses of living grizzly bars. I live in a box canyon, where everybody is wild, and shoots so much they fill the ar plum full of lead, so there ain't no ar to breathe. The further up the canyon you goes, the wilder the people gets, and I live at the very top end. Whoop! "

The real killer did not need to boast. He could speak softly and count on his reputation and his gun to do all the necessary orating. Many a gun-wielding outlaw or sheriff was proud that he never pulled a gun unless it was absolutely necessary. But in such circumstances he used it immediately and drastically. The most outstanding exhibition was the cowing of an armed man or crowd without the use of a pistol. Such an action required steady nerves, absolute confidence, and almost incredible bravery.

For every reputable gun wielder, if that phrase is permissible, there was a rigid code of conduct. The gunman obeyed this code because he was proud of his reputation. He never shot a man in the back or from ambush. He never shot an unarmed man. Most of his killings were of men who had reached for their guns, and consequently could be labeled justifiable homicide. No one could take pride in lying in wait for an enemy and shooting him when he was not looking. But one could take pride in insulting that enemy to his face until his hand went for his gun, and then beating him to the draw.

For gunmen outside the law, one can only regret the waste of manpower. For gunmen supporting the law, appreciation must be given to their valor and yeoman service in providing at least the semblance of order under the most trying conditions. Wyatt Earp, Billy Tilghman, Bat Masterson, Mysterious Dave Matthers, and dozens of others lived dangerously, providing targets for every incipient gunman with a reputation to make. While many times they failed to quell the riotous communities over which they were supposed to preside, they did represent the most advanced pioneers on the frontier of law and order.

Law and order appeared quite normally with the advance of the farming frontier. An Abilene of cattle days defied the efforts of a city marshal and his one or two deputies, but as more settlers came and the long drive disappeared disorder was reduced to manageable proportions. True enough the saloons and the red light district hung on, but the maximum disturbance was ordinarily a fist fight that could be quelled by a policeman with a club. The law-abiding citizens, whose majority had been tenuous in the old days, now found themselves dominant, and their code of morality was necessarily accepted. The boom mining towns and the border areas were slower in reformation, but ultimately a stable and orderly population suppressed the more boisterous. Vigilance committees were never long necessary, for once the law officers obtained control the lawless were defeated. The newer gunman was to be the spawn of the city streets, for the cities offered more liquid wealth and greater anonymity than did the country. If statistics have any meaning, then the well-settled farming districts and small towns are the poorest breeding grounds for crime.

READINGS

D. Aikman, *Calamity Jane* (1927); H. Birney, *Vigilantes* (1929); W. M. Breckenridge, *Helldorado* (1928); W. N. Burns, *The Robin Hood of Eldorado* (1932), *The Saga of Billy the Kid* (1926); S. A. Coblentz, *Villains and Vigilantes* (1936); W. E. Connelley, *Wild Bill and His Era* (1933)—detailed; H. Croy, *He Hanged Them High* (1952); E. Cunningham, *Triggernometry* (1934); E. Dalton, *When the Daltons Rode* (1931); E. R. Forrest and E. B. Hill, *Lone War Trail of Apache Kid* (1947); M. G. Fulton (ed.), *Pat F. Garrett's Authentic Life of Billy the Kid* (1927); W. Gard, *Frontier Justice* (1949); J. B. Gillett, *Six Years with the Texas Rangers* (1925); J. K. Greer (ed.), *A Texas Ranger* (1932); J. E. Haley, *Jeff Milton* (1948); F. H. Harrington, *Hanging Judge* (1951); H. F. Hoyt, *A Frontier Doctor* (1929); S. N. Lake, *Wyatt Earp* (1931); N. P. Langford, *Vigilante Days and Ways* (1912); R. Love, *The Rise and Fall of Jesse James* (1926); M. A. Otero, *The Real Billy the Kid* (1936); W. M. Raine, *Famous Sheriffs and Western Outlaws* (1929), *45-Caliber Law* (1941), *Guns of the Frontier* (1946); B. Rascoe, *Belle Starr* (1941); T. H. Rynning, *Gun Notches* (1931); L. Sage, *The Last Rustler* (1930); C. L. Sonnichsen, *Roy Bean* (1943); Z. A. Tilghman, *Marshall of the Last Frontier* (1949); W. P. Webb, *The Texas Rangers* (1935); F. J. Wilstach, *Wild Bill Hickok* (1926).

CHAPTER 36

TRANSCONTINENTAL RAILROADS

INCREASING traffic on the western plains can be credited in some part to the constantly opening mines, which appeared here and there like corn popping in a hot skillet. Additional credit can go to the cattle business, the sheep business, and the other opportunities that lured men to the wilderness. And yet the major single influence in permitting and encouraging permanent settlement west of the great bend of the Missouri was the railroad. Without the railroad vast reaches of the West would have remained sparsely populated; the orderly countryside and towns of the present day would have been impossible.

The railroads not only provided for already existing business but themselves brought new business. American railroads in the West were in large part built ahead of settlement. Even their prospective appearance helped to produce a country of farms to replace the old cattle country. Enterprising American businessmen turned visionary in dreaming of prosperous farms and booming cities at places monopolized by the coyote. Being " practical visionaries " they worked to make their dreams come true. Long streamers of iron were shot into a wilderness which was soon to become populated. The railroads not only furnished transportation but provided the arguments to induce the settlers to come. The settling of the trans-Mississippi West was to a great extent a railroad accomplishment.

Railroads can usually be built only in times of prosperity, when men of capital feel optimistic. After the Civil War, a boom was killed by the panic of '73, which in turn gave way to prosperity by the latter part of the decade. Railroad construction followed this pattern. Expanding after the Civil War, it stopped in 1873, then revived and came to a crescendo of activity during the early '80s. The greatest single decade of American railroad building was 1878–88, and the bulk of the construction was on the western plains.

The outstanding accomplishment of railroad construction was the completion of a half-dozen transcontinental projects during the early '80s. The bridging of 2000 miles of plains, desert, and mountain was an accomplishment which overshadowed the more humdrum business of lacing steel fingers over the plains. But both actions were necessary and interrelated. The long roads needed many feeders for profitable operation, while the short lines depended on the longer connections to be really useful. When both were completed the frontier was a thing of the past.

The origin of all the transcontinental projects can be traced back to the two or three decades before the Civil War. At that time any construction was almost purely speculative and so the thinker could imagine a road wherever it would best please him. The result was that every possible route found at least a few ardent admirers who thought it would be best for railroad purposes. The opening of the Civil War provided the opportunity for the concentration upon one road, which eventually was built, and the construction of that line opened the way for others. During and immediately after the Civil War Congress chartered and aided with land grants all the important routes to the Far West. The Northern Pacific (1864) was to occupy the northern route from Lake Superior to Puget Sound. The Union Pacific, chartered the earliest, controlled the central route. The Atlantic & Pacific (1866) was to build along the 35th parallel from Springfield, Missouri, through Albuquerque to the Pacific. The Texas & Pacific (1871) was to run from Marshall, Texas, along the 32nd parallel to San Diego.

In addition to the major projects that were chartered and aided by Congress were a considerable number of other lines which had imposing aspirations. Any road could build across the continent if it were able to raise the money, and certain ones such as the Southern Pacific, the Great Northern, and the Chicago, Milwaukee & St. Paul succeeded in doing so. Still other roads, such as the Atchison, Topeka & Santa Fe, received aid for portions of their lines and had to raise their own funds for the remainder of the distance.

The building of the transcontinental roads fell into two distinct periods. Construction began on all of them during or immediately after the Civil War, but none except the Union Pacific attained completion in this period. Then came the gap caused by the panic of 1873, which was to be followed by more construction and ultimate success.

CONSTRUCTION BEFORE 1873

The first of the roads in this group to complete any important construction, although it never succeeded in crossing the continent, was the Kansas Pacific. Its original name had been the Leavenworth, Pawnee & Western, and it had been given federal assistance as one of the branches of the Union Pacific. Work was started near Kansas City in September 1863, even before similar operations were begun on the main line of the Union Pacific. Construction moved slowly in the succeeding half-dozen years in spite of the energy of John C. Frémont, who was one of the owners. Renewed interest was obtained when a change in route was permitted. Ever since the Union Pacific had decided not to build through Denver the people of that city had been anxious to have a direct railroad connection of their own. Congress finally listened to their lament and in 1866 authorized the Kansas Pacific to expand its main line so that it would pass through Denver. Construction then proceeded so rapidly that the road was completed from Kansas City through Denver to Cheyenne in 1871.

The other Kansas road to have great aspirations was the Atchison, Topeka & Santa Fe, which had been chartered by Cyrus Holliday in 1859 to connect the towns of Atchison and Topeka. Holliday had personal dreams that one day the road would expand to take advantage of the Santa Fe trade, but his friends laughed good-naturedly at such a ridiculous idea. Not until the late '60s was it possible to start real work, and by that time Mr. Holliday had lost control to a group of men from Vermont. By 1873 the Santa Fe had advanced as far west as Granada, Colorado, and in the succeeding years it was one of the few roads to continue building in spite of the panic.

The construction of the Santa Fe produced another crisis at Denver, which had just been congratulating itself on its success in obtaining the Kansas Pacific to replace the lost Union Pacific. Now the Santa Fe threatened to draw all southern Colorado business away from Denver. To combat this menace Denver chartered the narrow-gauge Denver & Rio Grande (1870) to build south and head off the Santa Fe. The Rio Grande reached Pueblo in 1873, and then planned to extend southward to attract the business of

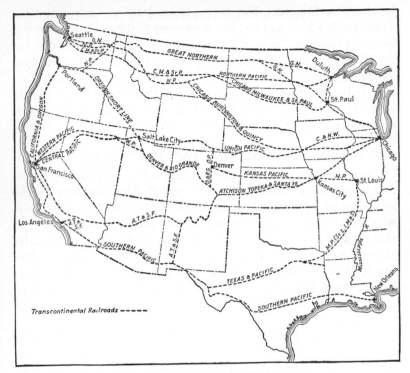

Transcontinental Railroads

the Southwest, and westward to control the rich mining areas near Leadville.

Farther to the south, and also building during this same period prior to 1873, lay the Atlantic & Pacific on the 35th parallel route. Here also Frémont was in control, with prospects of making a gigantic success. The Atlantic & Pacific was chartered only from Springfield and thus depended for its eastern connections on the state-aided roads of Missouri. This connection was made certain and satisfactory by the purchase of the Missouri Pacific. Construction was also started toward the west, so that by 1873 the line reached a junction with the Missouri, Kansas & Texas at Vinita, Indian Territory. Unfortunately for the Atlantic & Pacific its expansion had been too rapid for its financial resources, and consequently it suffered keenly from the panic of 1873. Its control of the Missouri Pacific was lost and its further expansion to the west postponed indefinitely.

The Texas & Pacific, which was the most southerly project to be aided by Congress, had been preceded by a number of local Texas roads which had already done some building. It was the pet idea of president Thomas Scott, who was also vice president of the Pennsylvania Railroad. Scott succeeded in building as far west as Dallas by 1873, and three years later the terminus was Fort Worth. He was especially anxious to continue construction so that he might receive the benefit of the Congressional land grant, which only started on the western border of Texas.

NORTHERN PACIFIC AND PANIC OF 1873

The most northern transcontinental project also carried on its first construction work in the same period. The Northern Pacific was accorded particular interest because of its advantages for trade with the Orient. Its terminus in the East was on Lake Superior, so that it could draw on all the lake business, while its western outlet afforded a shorter route to the Far East than did the ports farther south. In consequence the Northern Pacific was unusually attractive to businessmen interested in Far Eastern trade and received more attention from the public at large than did any road except the Union Pacific.

The Northern Pacific considered itself fortunate in having as its financial representative the famous Philadelphia firm of Jay Cooke & Company, which was well and widely known through its connection with governmental financing of the Civil War. Jay Cooke had considerable experience with financing railroads and was also interested in western lands, notably in Minnesota. His attitude toward the Northern Pacific had originally been skeptical, and he had refused several offers to take care of the financing. Ultimately he changed his mind, partly because of the favorable terms of the contract that he signed in 1870. Cooke obligated himself to sell $100,000,000 of first mortgage bonds within thirty years, to pay the costs of selling the bonds, and personally to advance up to half a million if necessary. In return he was to receive the bonds at 88, which meant that whatever he received above this amount was profit, and the interest on the bonds was an attractive 7.3 per cent. In addition he was to get about two-thirds of the Northern Pacific stock, which would have given him control. Subject only to selling expenses, he stood to make a good profit with apparently but little risk.

Once Cooke entered Northern Pacific affairs he read and talked extensively about all phases of western development, and apparently was utterly convinced that the Northern Pacific was a sound venture destined for a brilliant future. His enthusiasm for the land through which the road passed led that area to be given the name of " Jay Cooke's Banana Belt "; the name was well-chosen, since the literature which Cooke distributed was designed to give the reader the impression that Minnesota and the Dakotas were almost tropical in the luxuriance of their vegetation.

The construction of the Northern Pacific was begun in 1870 at Pacific Junction, so named because it was the prospective meeting point for lines from St. Paul and Duluth. Three years later the road had reached Bismarck, North Dakota, a new town which had been named after the German chancellor. Unfortunately this construction exhausted all available funds. United States investors had proved unexpectedly timid in supporting the project. Foreign sales had almost ended with the outbreak of the Franco-Prussian War. Construction and management accounts had been padded lavishly, and advertising had been excessively costly. The result was that Jay Cooke was forced to accept the inevitable and admit that he was at the end of his resources. The doors of Jay Cooke & Company closed on September 18, 1873, although it should be said that the company had sufficient securities to meet its obligations, and was merely hampered by a lack of ready cash.

The closing of the house of Jay Cooke & Company precipitated one of the worst financial panics in the history of the United States. Cooke had innumerable connections and ramifications, and when he admitted his inability to pay his debts other businesses suffered. More important, other firms were also overloaded with speculative paper, and the failure of Cooke created a wave of suspicion and doubt. More banking houses closed, and commercial concerns all over the country had to follow suit. Business throughout the country was prostrated. Western railroads, being profitable only in times of great prosperity, collapsed with great unanimity, and consequently all building stopped.

REVIVAL AFTER PANIC OF 1873

There was but little railroad construction in the West for the half-dozen years after the panic of 1873, but then came the revival. For the first time the plains were able to furnish enough traffic to make railroading profitable. The cattle business had continued to expand. Mining had become a stable year-round industry with the greater part of the work being done by large companies which extracted all of the metals and not only gold and silver; by 1880 the single town of Leadville, Colorado, was shipping a million dollars worth of minerals every month. Wheat growing was being introduced on a large scale in the Northwest. Towns such as Minneapolis, St. Paul, Sioux City, Omaha, Council Bluffs, and Kansas City were becoming important shipping and distributing centers. Furthermore the railroads were beginning to learn how to eliminate violent and disastrous fluctuations of rates by cooperation. The " Omaha pool " of 1870 was succeeded by numerous similar organizations which were at least partially successful in producing peace and prosperity — for the railroads.

Perhaps more important in the railroad construction after 1873 was the character of the men who dominated it. Western railroads were huge undertakings and required capable and energetic men for their construction and operation. Railroad building which was done by the thousand-miles, and strategy which involved half a continent brought forth bold, striking personalities — men who could lead, who could fight, and who had vision. Sometimes they were good and sometimes they were bad, sometimes they benefited the nation and sometimes they injured it, but no one can deny their capacity and genius.

GOULD LINES

Always outstanding is the shrewd, capable, cruel figure of Jay Gould. Primarily a Wall Street operator, he had little interest in railroads as living and operating organisms, but rather looked upon them as instruments with which to play, and traps with which to catch the unwary. Gould never allowed sentiment to influence the business of making money. He played the game of finance to win, and was not deterred by friendship or by pleas for mercy.

Gould entered the western railroad field with the purchase of the control of the Union Pacific in the early '70s. He had hopes of increasing rapidly the price of the stock by establishing a sinking fund. The plan did not materialize because of President Grant's opposition, and so Gould sold the majority of his stock — of course at a profit. He continued, however, to keep an eye on the Union Pacific and its affairs.

Gould saw another and more splendid opportunity in the late '70s. He speculated that if he bought the Kansas Pacific he could hold the club of competition over the Union Pacific and then dictate his own terms. The project looked well enough on paper, but as it happened the Union Pacific refused to be threatened. Gould then decided that the only trouble with his plan was that it had not been sufficiently comprehensive. Making one of his infrequent trips to the West he bought half a dozen other roads — the Missouri Pacific, the St. Joseph & Denver, the Kansas Central, the Central Branch Union Pacific, the Missouri, Kansas & Texas, the Texas & Pacific, the Denver & Rio Grande, and the Denver, South Park & Pacific. It was certainly a promising collection, particularly since it would be closely linked with Vanderbilt's New York Central, giving a desirable connection with the eastern seaboard. With this new and large gun Gould again held up the Union Pacific with the threat of paralleling its roadbed mile for mile. This time he was successful. The Union Pacific was forced to consolidate with the Kansas Pacific and its subsidiary the Denver Pacific on terms of equality (1880). Kansas Pacific stock, being less in value, rose in price, whereupon Gould sold out.

At the end of Gould's speculations he was left with a handsome profit, but also with a number of fairly useless western railroads. When he considered what might be done with them he saw two main possibilities. The first was to monopolize the traffic of the Southwest, and the second was to manipulate the securities of certain of the roads for his own benefit. He decided to develop both of these possibilities, and so he disposed of the Colorado roads, which had no value to him. Undoubtedly he was correct in his estimate of the financial possibilities of the western railroads of the period.

The cornerstone upon which Gould built his southwestern railroad system was the Missouri Pacific — a potentially strong road which had but little stock outstanding and thus could be held with a comparatively small investment. To it were added, by complicated leasing arrangements, the Texas & Pacific, the Missouri, Kansas & Texas, the St. Louis, Iron Mountain & Southern, the International & Great Northern, the Galveston, Houston & Henderson, and the Wabash. This group of lines made connections as far east as Buffalo, and in the West entered Chicago, St. Louis, Omaha, Kansas City, Galveston, and most of the other important towns of the region. A bitter struggle with the Chicago, Burlington & Quincy led the latter road to complete its extension to Denver in 1882.

Gould was never interested in giving good railroad service to the West, and consequently became one of the most hated men of the time. He was disliked both by those who worked for him and by those whom he served. Labor troubles (notably in 1885 and 1886) were frequent and severe. Gould devoted most of his energies to manipulating the securities of his roads — an occupation at which he was an adept. When most of them went bankrupt in the middle '80s it was found that his holdings had been reduced to the vanishing point.

SOUTHERN PACIFIC

Gould's connection with transcontinental communication came mostly in his holding of the Texas & Pacific. That road had earlier, under the leadership of Scott, made tremendous efforts to secure its completion in order to obtain the promised federal land grant. Not only did the Texas & Pacific fear the loss of its grant, but it was threatened by the Huntington forces, which were building south on the other side of the continent to head off outside competition. Since the Southern Pacific of California had the lesser amount of road to build it arrived at Yuma, on the eastern border of California, when the Texas & Pacific was still on the plains of Texas.

The Southern Pacific was by no means satisfied when it arrived at Yuma, even though it had thereby checked the possible expansion of the Texas & Pacific. The Colorado River had only two available crossings — at Yuma and the Needles; since the route of the Texas & Pacific was specified in its charter, that road had been thoroughly blocked by holding the Yuma crossing. On the other hand the California road was of little value unless it continued its construction farther east, and for this project it was desirous of federal aid. Huntington was sent East to see what he could do along this line. While in Washington he wrote that " more work [has been] done since Congress adjourned for the Texas & Pacific than was ever done in the whole history of the country." Presumably he himself was not idle.

Scott also sought further Congressional aid, because his own funds were exhausted. The result was a battle royal between the two men. Congress was loath to send good money after bad, but also objected to aiding two lines which were controlled by the same company (everyone knew that the Southern Pacific was controlled by the Central Pacific associates), so did nothing. When it seemed certain that Congress would take no action, the Southern Pacific took matters into its own hands. Without authority it crossed the Colorado and the Yuma Indian reservation; then it obtained Arizona and New Mexico charters and continued building east. Scott tried to stop its crossing of the river and reservation, but failed. Then he knew that he was beaten, and was glad of the opportunity to dispose of his stock to Jay Gould.

Gould was no Don Quixote to tilt at windmills. He immediately drew up an agreement with Huntington by which the two lines were to be joined near El Paso, the traffic prorated, and the Texas & Pacific land grant transferred to the Southern Pacific. The junction occurred in 1882, but Congress refused to sanction the transfer of the land. The joint line which was thus produced was entirely satisfactory to Gould, but it did not realize the ambitions of the Southern Pacific, which wanted its own complete road to New Orleans. Continuing work east from El Paso, and ultilizing those Texas roads already constructed, the Southern Pacific was able to run its through trains over its own tracks from San Francisco to New Orleans late in 1882.

ATCHISON, TOPEKA & SANTA FE

When the Texas & Pacific was eliminated from the transcontinental building competition (for it was never completed beyond El Paso) its place was taken by the Atchison, Topeka & Santa Fe. The Santa Fe had entered Colorado in 1873 and had then continued to build slowly but steadily southward toward New Mexico. Its most important competitor, the Denver & Rio Grande, was struggling to attain the same objective. For both roads the one desirable entrance to New Mexico was the Raton Pass, and so both sent their engineering crews to occupy this strategic point. The Santa Fe crew arrived first, and was able to hold the pass. Construction followed in 1878 and 1879. The Denver & Rio Grande, having been blocked in the south, confined its attention to the Colorado district.

The two roads soon found themselves in conflict again — this time in Colorado over a right of way. The Rio Grande had been built from Pueblo to Canon City in the direction of Leadville, but then work had stopped during the trouble in the south. Now in 1878 came the big boom in Leadville, and both roads saw the desirability of tapping the new mining area. Speed was essential, since just beyond Canon City was a narrow gorge through which only one railroad track could be laid. Both companies rushed crews of men to occupy the canyon and hold it at all hazards. Again the Santa Fe group arrived first, receiving support from the citizens of Leadville, who were angry that the Rio Grande had not built earlier. When the Rio Grande group arrived it found the canyon occupied by a mob of armed citizens and Santa Fe employees, and there was nothing to do but withdraw.

The Santa Fe at once made sure of its victory by laying its track in the disputed passage. All supplies had to be hauled from Pueblo by wagon, for the intervening gap had not as yet been filled. The Denver & Rio Grande resorted to the courts, where it lost its first battles, but appealed. The Santa Fe then carried the struggle to the heart of the enemy territory by threatening to parallel the entire line of the narrow-gauge road with a standard-gauge line to Denver. At this point the Rio Grande seemed hopelessly de-- feated, and was forced to surrender by leasing its entire line to the Santa Fe.

The old Rio Grande management continued the fight, however, and suddenly and unexpectedly in 1879 it attained successes all along the line. The Supreme Court, on appeal, overturned earlier decisions, and gave the Denver road the prior right to build in the Leadville canyon. Armed crews of the Rio Grande attacked the Santa Fe operatives and obtained control of the physical properties in dispute; the struggle was so severe that it was given the name of the " Rio Grande war," and the governor threatened to call out the state militia. Furthermore the Rio Grande obtained an injunction prohibiting a Kansas corporation from operating a Colorado railroad.

The final result of the struggle between the two roads was a compromise. The lease of the Rio Grande was repudiated. The Rio Grande was to pay for the construction which had been done in the Leadville canyon, and to agree not to do competitive building to the south. The Santa Fe promised not to parallel any of the tracks of its rival, but in return received the right to run its trains directly into Denver. Half of the through business of the Rio Grande was to go east by way of Santa Fe.

The agreement between the Santa Fe and the Rio Grande made certain the direction of future expansion of the two roads. The Rio Grande expanded in Colorado and built directly west, being completed to Salt Lake City in 1883; it was then able to compete for the entire haul of the Union Pacific by using the Santa Fe, the Burlington, or the Kansas Pacific for its eastern connection. As for the Santa Fe, its exclusion from Colorado led it to turn its at-

tention entirely to the south and west. Continued construction
enabled it to join its tracks with those of the Southern Pacific at
Deming, New Mexico, in 1881, thus completing the first transcontinental route to be opened after the construction of the Union
Pacific. While this junction was significant in the history of the
transcontinental routes, it was only incidental to the expansion
of the Santa Fe, whose main object was to obtain a through line
of its own to the coast; dependence upon the Southern Pacific
was viewed at most as only a temporary situation.

While the Santa Fe surveyed the possibilities for building to
the coast it could not avoid considering the situation of the Atlantic & Pacific, which had been chartered and given a land grant
over the very route which was most desirable for the Santa Fe.
It so happened that the Atlantic & Pacific was in bad financial
circumstances, and its construction had stopped, seemingly permanently, at Vinita. During the latter '70s it was owned by the
St. Louis & San Francisco, but the " Frisco " was not rich, and
listened eagerly to the overtures of the Santa Fe. In the final agreement (1880) the two roads decided to build jointly the western
part of the line of the Atlantic & Pacific, which meant a continuation of the existing Santa Fe line. Furthermore, the eastern parts
of the Santa Fe and Frisco were to be joined by a short link from
Pierce City to Wichita, thus furnishing through western connections for the Frisco and an entrance to St. Louis for the Santa Fe.

While the Santa Fe was moving toward the west, the Southern
Pacific was evolving defensive measures to maintain its control
of California. First it built to the Needles, which was the only remaining available crossing of the Colorado River. Then it joined
with Gould in buying control of the St. Louis & San Francisco,
thus giving the allies a half-interest in the Atlantic & Pacific. Of
course the Santa Fe retained the other half and the building contract, but it was obvious that the future existence of the western
part of its line would be made miserable. Both Gould and Huntington had been benefited. Gould had acquired another southwestern
road to add to his system, while Huntington obtained control of
all of the transcontinental routes except that of the Northern
Pacific.

For the moment the Santa Fe seemed to have given up its dream
of an independent line to the coast. It built to the Colorado River
and there joined its track to that of the Southern Pacific. The
whole line was completed in August 1883 except the bridge over

the Colorado which was not finished until the following year. But soon it was evident that the acquiescence of the Santa Fe to domination by the Southern Pacific was more apparent than real, for it started to rush construction on a line that would pass through Mexico and afford a Pacific outlet on the Gulf of California. Here was a new threat to the Southern Pacific, and this time the California road had to admit defeat. In the resulting agreement the Santa Fe obtained a controlling interest in the Atlantic & Pacific, a half-interest and lease of the line from the Colorado River to Mojave, and trackage rights to San Francisco. The first big inroad had been made on the Southern Pacific's control of California. Subsequently the Santa Fe built other lines in southern California. It also made connections with Galveston (1887), Denver (its own line in 1887), Chicago (1888), and thus by the end of the '80s was one of the strongest roads in the West.

NORTHERN PACIFIC

Even before these southern lines completed their through connections, the Northern Pacific was revived. Its prostration with the panic of 1873 had lasted throughout the '70s, but new life appeared with the presidency of Frederick Billings in 1880. Its development after 1880 was closely connected with the history of the Oregon Steam Navigation Company, which must be understood to make the story clear.

The Oregon Steam Navigation Company had been chartered in the '60s to improve navigation of the Columbia River, which it did by introducing steamboats on the navigable portions of the river and installing short railroad lines to cover the rest of the distance. It thus became the most eligible connection for any eastern road desiring to enter Portland. This availability was so evident that when Jay Cooke controlled the fortunes of the Northern Pacific he bought a majority interest in the Portland company. His failure caused control to revert to the West.

The Oregon Steam Navigation Company was badly affected by the panic of 1873, and since many of its bonds were held in Germany, the bondholders sent Henry Villard to investigate the situation and protect their interests. Villard was impressed by railroad possibilities in the Northwest, and began to acquire stock in those companies which he thought to be potentially important. Since he was not wealthy he was continually hampered by lack of funds and approached Jay Gould for assistance at the time when Gould controlled the Union Pacific. His plan was to interest Gould in the possibility of joining the tracks of the Union Pacific and the Oregon Steam Navigation Company along the general route of the old Oregon trail, and thus give the Union Pacific a line to the coast which would not be dominated by the Huntington associates. Gould was interested and agreed to the plan, but he soon retired from Union Pacific affairs, whereupon the proposal was dropped.

Having failed to obtain aid from Gould, Villard went ahead on his own initiative. Chartering the Oregon Railway & Navigation Company (1879) to combine the Oregon Steam Navigation Company and the Oregon Steamship Company, he started to build east. At about the same time the Union Pacific started to build northwest. The two roads finally came to an agreement by which their tracks were joined at Huntington in 1884. A new transcontinental connection had been added.

Just as Villard began to feel that he had the situation well in hand he received a shock in the information that the Northern Pacific had recommenced construction. Its completion to the coast would create a new and shorter line which would offer bitter competition for much of the traffic hitherto handled by the Oregon Railway & Navigation Company. Villard's first reaction was to try to induce Billings to agree to use the Portland road for his western connection, but Billings refused to make a definite promise. Then Villard conceived the boldest stroke of all. On the basis of no tangible security he advertised for subscriptions to a " blind pool," which he could spend as he pleased. The required $8,000,000 was oversubscribed at once.

Villard used the proceeds of his " blind pool " to charter the Oregon & Transcontinental Company, which took over Villard's old roads and also bought control of the Northern Pacific. The work on the Northern Pacific was continued, the last spike being driven in September 1883. The completion of the main line to Seattle occurred in 1887.

OTHER LINES

North of the United States a Canadian road was completed during the same period, and one has to marvel at the persistence and energy required to build a railroad across the wide, uninhabited spaces of that country. The project of the Canadian Pacific had taken form during the '70s, and construction was started in

1880. Certain American bankers such as Kuhn, Loeb & Company and J. P. Morgan had a hand in the undertaking. The last spike was driven on November 7, 1885.

The above roads were all the transcontinental projects completed by the end of the '80s. A few others were added later. The Great Northern was completed in 1893 under the guiding genius of James J. Hill. The Chicago & Northwestern attained a junction with the Northern Pacific in Montana in 1894. The San Pedro, Los Angeles & Salt Lake City was opened between Los Angeles and Salt Lake City in 1905. The Chicago, Milwaukee & St. Paul finished its road to Seattle in 1909, and was particularly notable for its long electrified section across the mountains. The Western Pacific was completed in 1911 as one of the links in the dream of George J. Gould for a railroad from ocean to ocean. The outstanding characteristic of this later period was the struggles between such men as Hill and Harriman and Gould, who treated railroad systems as toys, juggling them from one hand to the other. Their efforts to control the western railroad net were both interesting and important, but in constructing mileage they added little to the picture of the western railroads as it had been drawn by the late '80s.

The transcontinental lines completed by the middle '80s can be summarized briefly. First (1869) the Union Pacific-Central Pacific over the central route. Second (1881) the Santa Fe-Southern Pacific combination. Third (1882) the Texas & Pacific-Southern Pacific combination. Fourth (1882) the through line of the Southern Pacific. Fifth (1883) the complete Santa Fe line. Sixth (1883) the Northern Pacific. Seventh (1885) the Canadian Pacific. In addition there were the important fragments of the Kansas Pacific (1871), the Denver & Rio Grande (1883) and the Oregon Railway & Navigation Company (1884), to say nothing of the thousands of miles of connecting and tributary links. Forty thousand miles of railroad had been built in the West within a decade.

The immediate and inevitable result of the building of the railroads was the annihilation of the frontier. Population was strewn broadcast over the prairies, actually going farther into the Dakotas, Kansas, and Nebraska than the average annual rainfall warranted, and forming islands of settlement wherever the land was available farther west. The frontier which had moved so steadily across the continent was no longer to be visible when a new population map appeared with the census of 1890.

READINGS

H. O. Brayer, *William Blackmore* (2 vols., 1949), vol. 2—
D. & R. G.; G. D. Bradley, *The Story of the Santa Fe* (1920),
chs. 2–11; S. Daggett, *Chapters on the History of the Southern
Pacific* (1922); F. P. Donovan, *Mileposts on the Prairies* (1950)
—M. & St. L.; E. Gillette, *Locating the Iron Trail* (1925); S. H.
Holbrook, *The Story of American Railroads* (1947), chs. 15–18;
H. A. Innis, *A History of the Canadian Pacific Railway* (1923),
chs. 2, 3; G. Kennan, *E. H. Harriman* (2 vols., 1922); H. M.
Larson, *Jay Cooke* (1936), chs. 13–20; A. Laut, *The Romance of
the Rails* (2 vols., 1929), vol. 2, chs. 14–17; J. Marshall, *Santa
Fe: the Railroad That Built an Empire* (1945); V. V. Masterson,
The Katy Railroad and the Last Frontier (1952); J. Moody,
The Railroad Builders (1919), chs. 7–10; B. Nelson, *Land of the
Dacotahs* (1946), ch. 16—Hill; E. P. Oberholtzer, *Jay Cooke*
(2 vols., 1907), vol. 2, chs. 14–18; R. C. Overton, *Gulf to Rockies*
(1953); F. L. Paxson, *The Last American Frontier* (1915), ch.
22; J. G. Pyle, *The Life of James J. Hill* (2 vols., 1917); G. C.
Quiett, *They Built the West* (1934); R. E. Riegel, *The Story of
the Western Railroads* (1926), chs. 8, 10–18, 20; J. W. Starr, Jr.,
One Hundred Years of American Railroading (1928), chs. 16, 17;
N. Trottman, *History of the Union Pacific* (1923), chs. 5–10;
H. Villard, *Early History of Transportation in Oregon* (1944)—
contemporary; L. L. Waters, *Steel Rails to Santa Fe* (1950);
O. O. Winther, *The Great Northwest* (1947), ch. 16.

CHAPTER 37

THE
GREAT PLAINS

T HE westward surge of the agricultural frontier seemed to have come to an almost complete stop in the generation after the panic of 1837. The population map of 1840 had shown settlement as far west as the great bend of the Missouri River, and this point seemed the limit of the white advance. For thirty years restless farmers remained east of the Missouri, filling the more thinly populated states such as Wisconsin, Iowa, and Minnesota. A few made the long trek to the Pacific Coast, but the Great Plains west of 98° continued as the domain of the buffalo and the Indian. The only white intruders were travelers, soldiers, and cattlemen.

PRAIRIES AND PLAINS

The absence of white farmers on the western plains was not the result of a vigorous enforcement of the policy of a permanent Indian frontier by the federal government. Rather it meant that white farmers had looked upon the plains and had found them uninviting. The most obvious necessity for the frontier farmer was fertile land, and his easiest test was existing vegetation. As the easterner looked upon the prairie he saw only coarse grass. His conclusion was immediate — this part of the West was unfit for white habitation. Here, in the words of the average school geography, was the Great American Desert.

The reactions of early travelers to the Great Plains are understandable, even though the vast area from Montana and the Dakotas south into Texas has since become the national granary. This vast region of rolling high plains, bearing only sparse vegetation, lacking water, and harassed by perpetual winds appeared intimidating to the farmer from east of the Mississippi. His response was of long standing, since even farther east he had skipped the prairies of Indiana and Illinois to occupy the wooded areas along the streams.

Through the eyes of the land-hungry frontiersman, here was a lack of almost everything he considered necessary to support life. Farther east, the Ohio River had carried him well on his way to his new home. Now the rivers ran the wrong way to aid settlement, and with the exception of the Missouri did not even provide avenues of transportation for goods being carried to market. Farther east, the ever-present forests had necessitated great labor in their clearing, but in return had provided materials for homes and fences, furniture, utensils, railroad ties, and fires. Now the settler was at a loss for these basic essentials of life. He might for a time burn buffalo chips or twisted hay, but what would he do for a house and for protection against the herds of the long drive?

Moreover, the pioneer farther east had depended on small game to eke out his food supply of the first few years. On the plains the buffalo was truly a magnificent animal and a grand source of food, but unfortunately he was also exceedingly stupid so that his own elimination was extremely rapid. When the buffalo disappeared there remained for the most part only coyotes and jack rabbits, neither a tremendous source of food. All in all, the pioneer cannot be blamed for hesitating a generation before the open expanses of the plains. Their one apparent advantage was that they did not need clearing before the first planting, but even here there were troubles, since a special plow drawn by eight or ten oxen was necessary to break the tough prairie sod.

The settlement of the plains depended upon the solution of the various problems posed by the new conditions, and in time the solutions were found, even though a particular solution might at the best be only partial; for example, a lack of water always remained a lack of water, no matter how ingenious the settler became. The generation after the Civil War saw enough developments to permit settlement of the western plains, and in the process of this settlement there came into existence a new frontier process and a new frontiersman.

WATER

Undoubtedly the basic plains' trouble was a lack of water, and no help seemed to come from such easily conceived solutions as firing cannon into the air or appealing to the Deity for aid. Rainfall throughout the region was less than that of the East, and in the western part of the plains contracted to a pitiful ten to twenty inches a year. Furthermore, the rivers varied between poor and bad. In the spring they were vast, raging torrents carrying away barns, houses, and livestock. By midsummer they had died away to thin trickles or less. Any utilization of their water was at best difficult.

Three general approaches to the problem of aridity were developed. The first was to try in some way to get along with less water. While every growing plant needs moisture, some are more voracious than others. Special varieties of wheat, oats, barley, rye, and corn were discovered that could thrive on limited amounts of water. Moreover, new methods of cultivation were introduced. Deep plowing, sparse planting, frequent cultivation to keep down weeds, allowing land to lie fallow part of the time, all helped to preserve the limited moisture. Such " dry farming " permitted the cultivation of land that otherwise would have remained only pasture for cattle, but even at the best was hazardous. Too little rainfall meant ruin to even the hardiest food crop.

The second possible solution of the water problem was the utilization of the long known fact that underneath the plains was a great deal of water which with the necessary labor could be brought to the surface. And yet, even with this knowledge, many troubles remained. A man could dig a twenty- or thirty-foot well with a pick and shovel, but what of a hundred-foot or even a five-hundred-foot well? The solution was the use of drills, which came into popularity during the '70s. Well drilling crews toured the country, since the operation necessitated expensive equipment and specialized knowledge.

Once the well was drilled, there still remained the problem of raising the water. At fifty feet or more a bucket was practically impossible, while a hand pump was so inefficient that immense effort was necessary to produce even a thin trickle of water. Good pumping equipment was an unattainable luxury. The answer was to harness the indefatigable wind, thus giving it one desirable function. Again it was during the '70s that windmills were put into large-scale production. Their first western use was by stockmen and by the railroads, but by the '90s they dotted the entire countryside. For the traveler, a single mill marked one farmhouse, while a group marked a town.

The windmill had limited functions. It could supply water for household use and possibly for a vegetable garden. In time of trouble it might help water the stock. But as a real solution for deficient rainfall it was a total loss. Not even the most optimistic farmer ever considered cultivating 160 acres of farm land entirely on the basis of water from a windmill.

The third possibility of providing against deficient rainfall was the use of irrigation, and again the solution was of limited applicability. Irrigation depends upon river water, which in turn has come in most part from rain or snow. Irrigation can hold that water and use it through the drier seasons, but it cannot supply the rainfall. The best estimates indicate that possibly a sixteenth of the dry land of the West could be irrigated if every available drop of water were used. No such utilization is even now probable, and was certainly quite out of the picture in the 1870s and 1880s.

Irrigation had been practiced at certain Spanish missions and by the Indians of the Southwest and then not again until the Mormons used it in Utah. For non-Mormons, irrigation was not introduced until after the Civil War, and then dependence was placed on private initiative, which did not rise to meet the confidence. Practically no farmer had the money to invest in an irrigation project, while men who had the money were ordinarily skeptical of the possibility of profits. When a tract actually was irrigated by a private company — and the cases were few — the price of the water was placed so high that farming became unprofitable.

As in other times of trouble, the farmer looked to the government for relief. And then, in accordance with nineteenth century tradition, the federal government searched for some person or group that could be persuaded by subsidization to do the job. The first legislation was the Carey Act, passed in 1894, at a time when the well-watered part of the public domain had long been exhausted. Under this law proceeds from the sales of arid lands in several western states were to go to those states to be used for irrigation projects. The results were negligible. The funds were not large and the states were dilatory, no doubt in part because many of the better projects were interstate in character.

The really important law for irrigation was the Newlands Act of 1902. The federal government was itself to build irrigation projects from money paid for land in the arid states. The costs of such construction were to be met in time by the users of the water, and then the money paid out for further projects. By 1920 some

20,000,000 acres had been irrigated under this program, and considerable tracts were added later. Few of the projects touched the Great Plains, however, and all told they served only a small part of the region deficient in rainfall.

A part of the whole water problem was the disposition to be made of streams throughout the West. Should neighboring cattlemen and farmers be permitted to use the water, and to what extent? Under the English common law, as commonly accepted throughout the United States, the riparian owner could use all the water he desired as long as he did not pollute the stream or perceptibly lessen its flow. With western watercourses, such a rule was folly. The water was small in amount. Anyone who used it reduced its flow perceptibly. If applied literally, the common law rule would mean that no one could use the water, and hence instead of being of limited benefit it would be of no use whatever.

Western reaction was to change the common law. The arid states ruled that anyone on a stream could use all the water he pleased, unless he had forfeited the right by a considerable period of nonuse. In some ways such a regulation was disastrous. Men down the stream could expect that for a good part of the year they would be without water. On the other hand, however, there seemed considerable virtue in allowing someone rather than no one to benefit. The immediate result quite naturally was a rush to control the sources of the streams, particularly when a stream rose from a spring.

TRANSPORTATION

Next to water, the greatest problem of the plains was transportation. Rivers were unavailable most of the year, particularly in the fall when goods were marketed. Dirt roads were impassable bogs in wet weather, so that a horse might find himself laboring hard to walk, even without a load. Real road improvements seemed impossibly utopian, since most of the plains had no rock, and improved roads without the use of rock would have been next door to a miracle. Canals were equally impossible because of the lack of water.

The solution of the transportation difficulty was the railroad, which benefited from the flatness of the plains. Engineering difficulties were small and many roads were built at the rate of five to ten miles a day. All of which does not mean that railroad construction was effortless. Funds were hard to raise in a sparsely settled area, and eastern capitalists had to be persuaded of the potential profits of a line that at the time was a streak on a map which failed to show towns. Furthermore, the lack of stone and wood also hampered the railroads. Stone had to be hauled for considerable distances. Wood also had to be hauled, with the alternative here and there of treating the native cottonwood to retard its rotting.

FENCES

A problem of less importance, but also necessary of solution, was the building of fences with inadequate supplies of wood. Unfenced, the farmer's cattle trampled his corn unless perchance the herds being driven north got there first. Building wood fences, largely with wood from farther east, was estimated to cost about $500 for a quarter section — a price that was altogether too large for the pocketbook of the homesteader, or even for that of the large farmer or cattle grower with his thousands of acres. Various alternatives to wood were impossible. In a few places, as in certain parts of Texas, stone could be used. Hedges were tried, but their lives were precarious and cattle failed to give proper respect to them. Wire was likewise unsatisfactory. The cattle soon learned that it was harmless and that a hard push would topple over the entire fence.

The solution of the fence problem came with the marketing of good barbed wire, starting in 1874. The rapidity of the introduction of barbed wire was little short of amazing. In 1874 only 10,000 lbs. were sold at $20 a cwt. In 1884 the sales passed the 80,000,000 mark and the price had been cut in half. This rapid introduction does not mean that every farmer accepted barbed wire immediately and enthusiastically. Some men were just naturally conservative, others had extremely unpleasant experiences in trying to untangle and string badly rolled wire, while in many cases a farmer cursed feelingly as his valuable stock ran into the wire and cut itself unmercifully. Ultimately the enthusiasm for barbed wire passed reasonable bounds and men strung it not only over their own land but over railroad and government land and even over public highways.

REPLACING WOOD

One other great problem was the necessity for the pioneer to find some replacement for wood in constructing, lighting, and heating his house. The lighting was the easiest part of the job, since the rise of the oil industry brought cheap kerosene in the generation after the Civil War. Heating was not so simple, and heat was essential for cooking as well as for warmth. Buffalo chips were soon exhausted, and wood was expensive because of hauling charges. The two easily available fuels were sunflowers or straw, but straw burned out in one grand flare, so that baking bread or cake was a losing speculation. In time there was invented a new type of stove which used twisted hay as fuel, but to say that it was entirely satisfactory would be a gross exaggeration.

As for houses, early settlers dug into the sides of hills or bought wood, but the first was definitely unpleasant and the second was expensive. Native ingenuity finally hit upon the use of sod for construction. Pieces of sod were cut and laid much like oversize bricks, with wood used only for door and window cases and for rafters. The inside of the house might be whitewashed, and the whole structure, while not beautiful, kept out most of the weather and was at least moderately cool in the summer. Many such a home backed into the side of a hill, and it was not unknown to have the family cow wander onto the roof and come crashing into the house. Moreover, a strong rain might ruin the toughest prairie sod, while a prolonged drought did not prevent some of the houses from being damp.

The frontier of the sod house was comparatively short in time. Americans were not satisfied with dirt houses and as quickly as possible used other materials. Even in the heart of the plains country the settler soon scraped together the necessary funds to obtain lumber. While the sod house was outstanding as both picturesque and dirty, it had no permanent importance.

PROGRESS OF SETTLEMENT

Prairie settlements had come in the 1850s — largely in Kansas — but an invasion of the great plains waited until after the Civil War, when an increasing number of migrants entered the central area of Kansas and Nebraska. This particular boom stopped with the panic of 1873, but a new flood came in the late '70s and early '80s, occupying the country from the Dakotas south into Texas, where settlement before this time had stayed in the timbered areas. These pioneers of the plains owed their continued existence to the changes described earlier in this chapter. Many of them went too far west, being lured by the comparatively good rainfall of the early '80s. When the drier years of the late '80s and early '90s arrived, thousands of them were driven out of their new homes by the stark specter of hunger.

Even more on the plains than on earlier frontiers, the first arrivals were speculators looking for fertile land, for mill sites, for future town locations. This group had produced the original Kansas boom, and then had looked farther afield, south toward the Indian Territory and the plains of Texas, and north toward the Dakotas and Montana. For twenty years after the Civil War the first conquest of the plains was by groups of speculators generally looking for potential cities.

As soon as a speculator picked a good location he tried to acquire the land — legally if possible, but otherwise by fraudulent homesteading or by sheer appropriation. Having acquired a thousand acres or more he had the land surveyed and laid out future streets and building lots. By this time a name was necessary, and something impressive like Eureka or Garden City was preferred to a more prosaic title.

A speculative plains town desired publicity above all. Imaginative lithographic posters depicted impressive buildings, busy streets, and a river front crowded with boats, even though the actual stream was no greater than the Republican. A weekly newspaper would sound the clarion call for a new western metropolis, the natural center for all transcontinental railroads. A few lots might be given away as bait, as to the first woman or to the first child. If the idea caught hold the promoter made his fortune. If not, he tried to borrow enough money to try again. Hope might wither, but it did not die.

The speculator may well be considered an economic parasite, but he did encourage migration to the plains and hence must be credited as one of the agencies which produced the boom of the late '70s and early '80s. The states and territories were also interested, and practically every state and territory had a publicity agent or bureau to sing of the attractions of that region; their influence was felt as far away as Europe. The railroads were even more active, since they wanted to sell their lands and at the same time attract future traffic. Widespread publicity was buttressed by favorable installment terms on the land, while railroad agents carefully shepherded foreign groups all the way to their destination lest some rival railroad divert them. Special rates were offered, sometimes free seeds provided, and even temporary living quarters were arranged.

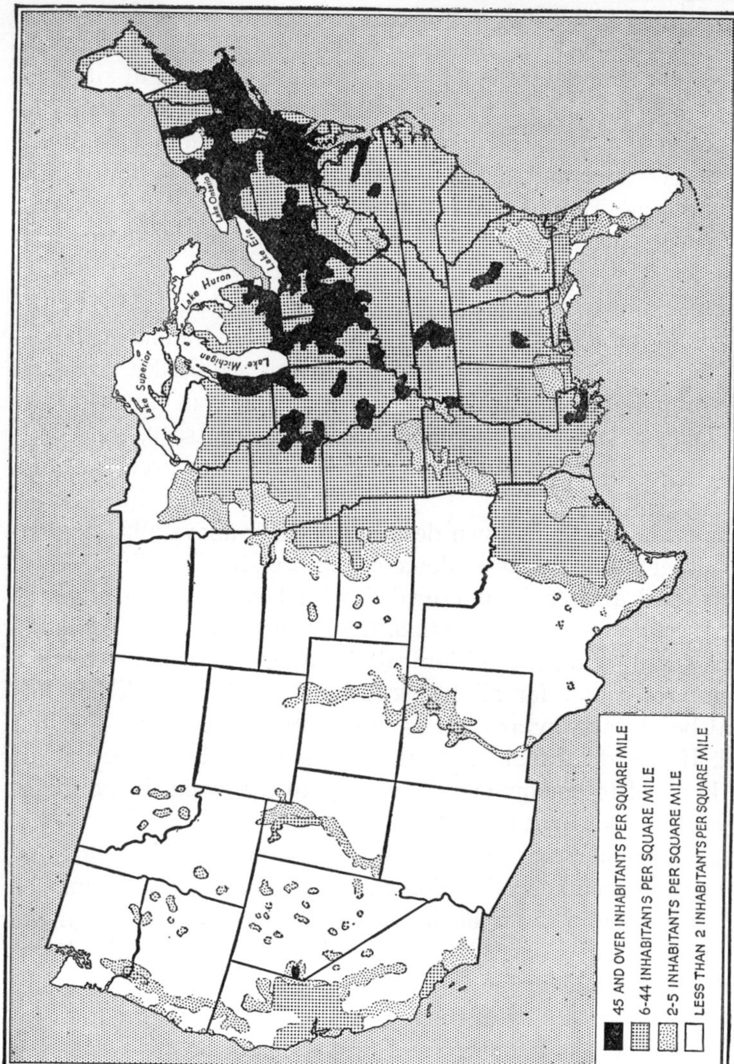

Population Density of 1870

45 AND OVER INHABITANTS PER SQUARE MILE

6-44 INHABITANTS PER SQUARE MILE

2-5 INHABITANTS PER SQUARE MILE

LESS THAN 2 INHABITANTS PER SQUARE MILE

Lake Erie

Lake Ontario

Lake Huron

Lake Michigan

Lake Superior

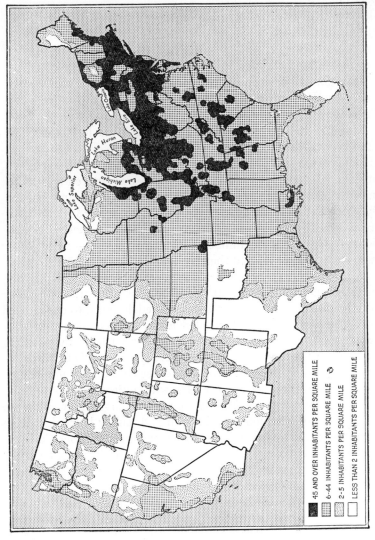

Population Density of 1890

45 AND OVER INHABITANTS PER SQUARE MILE

6 - 44 INHABITANTS PER SQUARE MILE

2 - 5 INHABITANTS PER SQUARE MILE

LESS THAN 2 INHABITANTS PER SQUARE MILE

Lake Ontario

Lake Erie

Lake Huron

Lake Michigan

Lake Superior

LAND LAWS

The prevalance of speculation on the western plains made difficulties for the man who really wanted to do farming. In theory he might homestead 160 acres, but in cold fact he usually found all available land claimed in any section of the plains blessed by fair transportation, even though that transportation was merely prospective. His only real option then was to buy either from the railroad or from an earlier arrival. In neither case was the land anything like the free homestead about which our legislators had talked in such glowing terms.

The sad truth was that the vast bulk of western land was never homesteaded, and that the part of it which was entered under the homestead act was seldom farmed by the original entrant. In fact only about a third of the homestead entries between 1862 and 1882 were ever made final. Presumably many entries were made solely to hold the land until the lumber could be removed — as in Wisconsin or Minnesota — and then the land relinquished. How many of the completed claims were fraudulent is anyone's guess, although no one can doubt that the number was great.

The land laws of the '70s and '80s seemed designed to encourage fraud. The Homestead Act needed a close supervision that the small Land Office could not afford. Men " settled " by placing four stones at the corners of a prospective house, and " cultivated " by running a short furrow. With less conscience a man might use a toy house on wheels or erect a stick with a piece of glass to represent a wall and window. If he were really immoral he would not even be this conscientious. If the man had money he could get a preemption claim and then add a tract under the Timber Culture Act of 1873, probably neglecting to plant the required trees. Or he might get 640 acres under the rather ridiculous Desert Land Act of 1877, of course neglecting to provide the water required under the law. In addition to these limited amounts, a man could obtain as many acres as he could afford by public auction in many states and territories during the years after 1860.

Illegal entries were a public scandal, especially during the '80s. Secretaries of the Interior asked continuously and fruitlessly for a larger force of inspectors, and pleaded for at least the proper classification of the public domain. Not until 1890 did Congress take any action. In that year it passed a railroad land grant forfeiture act which had but little effect. The next year (1891) it obliged with a general reform act, which included among its notable provisions the repealing of the timber culture and preemption acts, the modifying of the desert land act and the commutation provision of the homestead act, and the authorizing of forest reserves. Unfortunately these long-needed reforms came so late that most of their utility was lost.

The government land available for homesteading was estimated at 600,000,000 acres in 1894, but because most of it was undesirable for general farming, many people thought that homesteading was largely a thing of the past. But land-hungry Americans were not easily discouraged, and particularly when they were tempted by attractive advertising of railroads with land to sell. Montana alone saw 93,000,000 acres filed between 1910 and 1922. Much of this land was in regions of deficient rainfall, and the settlers soon went bankrupt. In the process, however, the public domain was further reduced so that by 1929 less than 200,000,000 acres were available for homesteading. Practically all of this land needed irrigation.

The government recognized the difficulties of homesteading by acts of 1909 and 1912 which increased homestead claims to 320 acres and decreased the time of cultivation to three years. The results were not good. As one man put it: " The government bets title to 320 acres against your filing fee that you'll starve before proving up — and the government usually wins." The truth was that the small farmer merely destroyed the good range grass and encouraged dust storms, while the cattleman had no way of obtaining adequate amounts of land from the government even by leasing. Very belatedly the Taylor Grazing Act (1934) improved the situation a trifle.

As long ago as 1878 John Wesley Powell, director of the United States Geological Survey, had made a report which if put into practice would have avoided most of the later troubles of plains farmers. He insisted that no average rainfall of less than twenty inches a year would support general farming and located the exact areas of inadequate rainfall. For drier land he held grazing to be the proper use, and suggested ranches of a minimum of 2560 acres. Only by long and bitter experience did the nation discover that Powell was right.

Powell also was interested in conserving the natural resources of the West, but not until after 1890 did the conservation movement gain any considerable acceptance. Even then the West was generally opposed. Each succeeding President added more and more land to the forest reserves and to the national parks. Various irrigation projects redeemed much land that otherwise would have remained useless. All these efforts are fine, but one can hardly avoid viewing with regret the gutting of a magnificent public domain, in spite of recent efforts to save a few of the odds and ends.

For the settler of the '70s and '80s the land problem was real and personal. With luck he might join the jam at a land office and get a free homestead. More likely he bought as best he could from an earlier arrival, and then faced his major problems of obtaining shelter, starting cultivation, and managing to exist until his first crop was harvested. These problems were essentially the same as had been faced by his more easterly predecessor, even though their exact solutions might be different.

FINANCES

In at least one respect the plainsman had the advantage over the earlier frontiersman. He found money much easier to borrow. After the Civil War the increasing prosperity of the East produced surplus funds for investment in the West, and a people nurtured on eastern farms saw farm mortgages as the safest possible place for investing their money. Much of this money was handled through mortgage companies, but whether loaned by a company or by an individual the rates were high, with four to six per cent a month not unusual. This availability of money encouraged an unusual flow of people to the plains and meant that for most of them the first " improvement " was a mortgage. Together with the number of speculative holdings, there resulted a tremendous amount of tenancy in time. Whether such mortgages and tenancy were in general steps up or down the economic ladder of success is arguable.

The westerner tended to consider the easterner who held his mortgage as a bloated capitalist living by the work of others. In some cases this accusation was justified but in other cases the shoe was on the other foot. Numerous westerners made only the pretext of farming, got their mortgage money and then decamped, leaving the lender with a tract of virgin prairie of no particular value. Many a frugal New Englander saw the plains drink up his life savings as thirstily as they absorbed the inadequate rainfall.

HOMES

The first home of the pioneer might be a cave in a convenient hillside or a rough board shack covered with tar paper. Sometimes

it was a sod house, utilizing half an acre of prairie sod. In this
event wood was necessary for window frame, door frame, and roof,
even though the wood might be covered in turn by more sod, so
that dandelions bloomed on the roof. At times the sod was used
only as a facing for a frame shack. The inside of the house might
be plastered roughly, but at best the interior remained dark. Pieces
of mud might drop on the dining table for several days after a
heavy rain, and sometimes the wall weakened so that the roof
timbers slid and the roof collapsed. No family expected to live in
a sod house permanently, and hoped at least to have a real frame
house by the time the mud one wore out in half a dozen years.

The furnishings of the plains house were much the same simple
rough trappings customary for a century and more. Crude beds,
tables, and chairs served until the family was more prosperous. Possibly a favored rocking chair or cherry table reminded one of eastern comfort. Even the old-fashioned fireplace was continued wherever possible. If wood were burned, it often was hauled twenty
miles or more — quite a morning chore. Otherwise corn cobs or
stalks would be used, and quite frequently the cooking was done on
a cook stove which burned corn cobs, and which was the center of
family life. A new development was a stove that burned cylinders
of pressed straw, with a new cylinder replacing each old one as
it was emptied.

The water supply of the earliest settlers was surface water, which
not only was polluted by the cattle but tended to be entirely inadequate or completely lacking at certain times of the year. Dug
wells were the obvious solution, with rich rewards for the man
who could sense the presence of water. Now and then it was possible to drive a pipe into the soil, but ultimately most wells were
drilled, with the pumping done by windmill. The cost of drilling
came to be about a dollar a foot, and Fairbanks & Morse were
the most important windmill makers.

FARMING ON THE PLAINS

Plains agriculture in the early years was concerned primarily
with the same grains that had followed the frontier west, but had
several unusually difficult problems to meet. The tough prairie
sod required a steel plow and at least three yoke of oxen, but probably remained cheaper in human energy for its original planting
than the forests farther east which required herculean chopping,
clearing, and grubbing out roots. Fencing was in time done with

barbed wire. The lack of rainfall in some years meant bankruptcy for thousands of farmers, with the late '80s and early '90s particularly bad. Prairie fires were a continual hazard.

The peculiar pest of both the prairies and plains was the grasshopper, which was notably bad in 1874 and the succeeding years. Grasshoppers filled the air like snowflakes and ate all plants except native grass and a few trees. Still hungry, they consumed such spare objects as clothes on the line. Moreover chickens became sick from overeating them, while livestock refused, except under extreme provocation, to drink the water they polluted. Even trains were brought to a halt by the carpet of grasshoppers.

The open plains country presented an excellent opportunity for large-scale farming, where operations were mechanized much as in a factory. The farm machinery invented by ingenious Americans before the Civil War was improved, supplemented, and put into use on a large scale. The harvester attracted a self-binder which used wire and then twine by the early '80s, while by this later period threshing was done by means of a straw-burning engine. The " combine " was the invention of a Michigan man, Hiram Moore, and the twine binder was the idea of a Wisconsin resident, J. F. Appleby. Planting was by machine instead of by hand. The early steel plow was developed into a plow capable of turning four furrows at once and into a disk gang plow. A corn cultivator appeared before 1860 and a self-dump rake during the '80s.

While large portions of the plains were fitted for large-scale farming, the greatest concentration was in the Red River Valley of the Dakotas. During the '80s over two hundred farms in this district contained 1000 acres or more apiece, and were highly mechanized. Such a large farm might have an absentee owner or owners and a resident manager. It hired its labor just like a city factory. Impressive pictures appeared of half a dozen huge harvesters in operation at one time on such a farm. Actually, the advantages of such large-scale production were not great, since most farmers could use approximately the same machinery if they worked co-operatively, and there were certain inherent inefficiencies in absentee ownership. A large share of the big farms failed to weather the hard times of the late '80s and early'90s.

DAILY LIFE

The daily life of the average pioneer prairie farmer was not far different from that of his eastern predecessor. His clothing continued to be homemade, although from homespun (wool) more frequently than from linsey-woolsey. The cold of the northern plains made clothes somewhat more bulky. His wife commonly wore calico, including a calico sunbonnet. Her dress was high necked, long skirted and shapeless, with some ten yards or more of cloth draped over four or five petticoats. Her labors in making the family clothing were somewhat lightened, however, by the use of the sewing machine which became fairly common by the '80s. Shoes continued to be made at home at times, and the family went barefoot whenever it could to save leather and labor. Food continued to emphasize pork and corn, with the traditional surplus of grease in its cooking.

Poor food, bad cooking, improper sanitation, and hard work all resulted in an excess of sickness, which included notably dysentery, ague, cholera, smallpox, and typhoid. Frequently in the more isolated districts no doctor was available and dependence was of necessity placed on home remedies, patent medicines, and prayer. Such doctors as could be called were altogether too frequently badly trained and overworked. Dentists were rare and little consulted.

While the life of the frontier farmer was difficult, special sympathy should go to his wife. Laboring to the limit of her strength from the time she arose until the time she went to bed, she was perpetually tired — a condition not improved by a succession of children, born usually without benefit of a doctor. Her entire life was spent in a bare shack, without a tree, a flower, or even a blade of grass, and the house was infested by flies, gnats, fleas, and vermin. The work, the hard water, the heat, and the perpetual wind combined to dry out her skin and often make her look old by thirty. Months on end she might not even see her closest neighbor. Little wonder that many a pioneer wife sat down and cried bitterly at the thoughts of the lost eastern life of her girlhood days.

Religious observance tended to become less as population became sparser, even though such churches as the Methodist, Christian, Presbyterian, Congregational, Catholic, and Episcopal followed the frontier quite closely. Communities were often rough and crude, with a high proportion of the ungodly. It was said commonly in Kansas that " There is no Sunday west of Junction City and no God west of Salina." The arrival of a church was important not only for bringing religious consolation to men confronted by a stern nature but also for bringing a moderate amount of social contact in such forms as church suppers and church "sociables" to people greatly in need of relaxation.

Education centered in the typical one-room ungraded school, built and supported by private funds. Not until after the frontier period did the government find itself able to take over the educational function. Texas was the first of the states to give state aid to education, but actually the Texan educational system was slow of growth, largely because of the war experience. A sprinkling of secondary schools and colleges gave evidence of a firm belief in the values of education, even though the training they offered was anything but first-rate.

No one could work every waking hour, and the farmer was no exception. Church suppers, dinners, bees, square dances, poker and other card games, spelling matches, visiting, reading, candy pulls, picnics, barbecues, and buggy rides were among the lighter occupations. Even such current fads as croquet and bicycling struck the plains. Unfortunately some of the sports were not so innocent. On his visit to town the farmer's interest was not confined to the handful of poor stores, the tawdry traveling show, or the lyceum lecture. Saloons, gambling halls, and brothels, established mainly for the cowboy trade, proved not without attraction to the farmer.

NEW STATES

The settlement of the western plains made necessary further governmental changes. When Colorado became the centennial state in 1876, the greater share of the vast region beyond Missouri remained in territorial status, and there was not sufficient population to merit any drastic change. While mining rushes had brought pockets of people here and there, while the Union Pacific had inspired a few towns such as Cheyenne and Laramie, and while a few settlers had pushed elsewhere as into southeastern Dakota, population remained in general sparse.

By 1880 conditions had changed. Washington, bristling with large hopes which included the coming of the Northern Pacific, had sufficient people for statehood, as had Dakota. But Congress failed to act. The new areas were supposed to be Republican in leanings, and for years the Republicans were not able to control the Presidency and both houses of Congress at the same time. The Democrats felt little glow of pleasure at the prospect of increasing their own handicaps. Furthermore, all conservative easterners were alarmed at the repudiation sentiment in the West.

Early in 1889, in prospect of a complete Republican control of both houses, Congress passed an omnibus bill to enable North and South Dakota, Montana, and Washington to form state constitutions preparatory to admission to the Union. All four states were admitted before the end of the same year. While these events were occurring, Wyoming and Idaho could see no good reason why they too should not become states, and so they followed their neighbors' example in adopting state constitutions, although of course without Congressional permission. Wyoming was unusual in providing for woman suffrage. When these two new constitutions were presented to Congress, that body was not loath to acquire more Republican members, and so the two states were admitted in 1890.

After 1890 only four potential states remained in continental United States exclusive of Alaska—Utah, Indian Territory and Oklahoma, New Mexico, and Arizona. Utah had for some time had the necessary population and was held back only by the polygamy controversy. When that situation was solved in the early '90s, statehood was only a matter of time. The necessary enabling act was passed in 1894, and the new state was admitted two years later.

Indian Territory presented a much more confused case. Presumably it was the exclusive domain of the Indians, but as other parts of the West were filled with white farmers, men began to look longingly at the sparsely settled Indian country. White cattlemen entered the country by leasing grazing land — a process of doubtful legality but highly acceptable to the Indians. Other whites married Indian girls, and apparently with some thought of the land which they might thereby obtain. Unauthorized traders slipped into the territory, while a few settlers edged past the army posts.

The prince of the Indian Territory " boomers " was David L. Payne, six foot four, handsome, jovial, and aggressive. While Payne had had but little luck at farming in Kansas, his personal popularity had sent him to the state legislature and had then obtained him the job of assistant doorkeeper for the federal House of Representatives. Forming a " Colonization Association " in 1879, and undeterred by President Hayes' threat to eject any white trespassers, he planned to lead a body of settlers into the Indian country. Whether he really thought himself legally justified or whether he was only the paid creature of the railroads may still be argued. In any case, each year found him heading a body of settlers which would elude the soldiers for a time, only to be surrounded and ejected, after which Payne yelled persecution and planned a new party. At his death in 1884 W. L. Couch continued his work.

A new factor appeared in 1887 with the passage of the Dawes Act. While this law was conceived by men who had the best interests of the Indians at heart, it was supported by more selfish individuals whose eyes were focused on the fact that after allotment there would be surplus land available to the whites. The first opening of such land came on April 22, 1889. At least 100,000 people lined up ready for the gun which marked the opening. Then came the mad rush by carriage, horseback, train, and even on foot. Towns such as Guthrie and Oklahoma City grew up over night. Inevitably a few " sooners " had beaten the rush and picked out favorable tracts, while many of the " boomers " never did get Oklahoma land. The Territory of Oklahoma was created in 1890.

The first land opening was followed by others and the white population of Oklahoma grew, even though the Five Civilized Tribes opposed allotments sufficiently to prevent the division of any of their land until the late '90s. By 1910 the allotments had been practically completed, although no one could say that whites and Indians had been amalgamated into a unified and homogeneous society. Governmental progress continued as the territory of Oklahoma expanded, largely on the desire of the whites, in spite of the continuance of multitudinous difficulties in the relations of the two races. An Enabling Act of 1906 inspired a constitution and the state of Oklahoma was admitted to the Union in 1907.

The last two states were New Mexico and Arizona. This entire area had been included (1850) in the Territory of New Mexico, a union which became increasingly obnoxious to the people of Arizona as their numbers grew. Arizonans were far distant from the towns of the Rio Grande and were vastly outnumbered. The movement for an independent territorial status came to fruition in 1863, and was succeeded by movements in both Arizona and New Mexico for statehood. Both regions were supposed to be Democratic, but the Democrats were practically never in control of all branches of the government and Arizona had insufficient population. When the Omnibus Bill of 1889 was passed the Democrats tried to include New Mexico but failed.

Matters dawdled along for another decade, with statehood seemingly delayed indefinitely as the Republicans held control of Congress. In 1906 there was talk of joint statehood, but while this proposition was acceptable to New Mexico it was rejected by Arizona. Ultimately separate statehood was accepted by Congress, and the two states were finally admitted to the Union in 1912, with Arizona the forty-eighth state.

READINGS

Settlement: M. D. Beale, *A History of Southwestern Idaho* (1942), chs. 17, 18; B. B. Chapman, *The Founding of Stillwater* (1949)—Oklahoma; C. D. Clark and R. L. Roberts, *People of Kansas* (1936)—detailed; C. Coan, *A History of New Mexico* (3 vols., 1925), vol. 1, chs. 22, 23—detailed; E. E. Dale and M. L. Wardell, *History of Oklahoma* (1948), chs. 11–15; A. Debo, *Oklahoma* (1949), *Prairie City* (1944), *Tulsa* (1943); E. Dick, *The Sod House Frontier* (1937)—excellent; G. Foreman, *A History of Oklahoma* (1942), chs. 17–23; M. L. Hansen and J. B. Brebner, *The Mingling of the Canadian and American Peoples* (1940), ch. 9; V. E. Harlow, *Oklahoma* (1935), chs. 37–53; J. K. Howard, *Montana* (1943), chs. 4, 16–23, (ed.), *Montana Margins* (1946); S. K. Humphrey, *Following the Prairie Frontier* (1931); J. Ise, *Sod and Stubble* (1936)—Kansas; M. E. Jarchow, *The Earth Brought Forth* (1949)—Minnesota; V. Johnson, *Heaven's Tableland* (1947), ch. 5—Texas and Oklahoma; E. C. Reynolds, *Oklahoma* (1954), ch. 12; J. C. Malin, *Winter Wheat* (1944); B. Nelson, *Land of the Dacotahs* (1946), chs. 8, 9, 12—South Dakota; A. Raaen, *Grass of the Earth* (1950)—Dakotas; R. N. Richardson, *Texas* (1943), ch. 17; R. N. Richardson and C. C. Rister, *The Greater Southwest* (1934), chs. 20–23; C. C. Rister, *Land Hunger* (1942)—Oklahoma, *No Man's Land* (1948), chs. 6–14—Oklahoma—*Southern Plainsmen* (1938); M. Sandoz, *Old Jules* (1935)—Nebraska; F. A. Shannon, *The Farmer's Last Frontier* (1945), chs. 2, 3, 6–9; E. V. Sutton, *A Life Worth Living* (1948)—Minnesota and Dakotas; A. E. Towne, *Old Prairie Days* (1941); S. Vestal, *Short Grass Country* (1945); W. P. Webb, *The Great Plains* (1931)—pioneering work.

Land: W. C. Darrah, *Powell of the Colorado* (1951); H. H. Dunham, *Government Handout* (1941)—public lands; P. W. Gates, *Fifty Million Acres* (1954), chs. 4, 5, 7, 8, *The Wisconsin Pine Lands of Cornell University* (1943); W. S. Greeves, *Arid Domain* (1954)—Santa Fe land grant; J. B. Hedges, *Henry Villard and the Railways of the Northwest* (1930); R. C. Overton, *Burlington West: A Colonization History of the Burlington Railroad* (1941); E. L. Peffer, *The Closing of the Public Domain* (1951); R. M. Robbins, *Our Landed Heritage* (1942), chs. 14–20; W. Stegner, *Beyond the Hundredth Meridian* (1954)—Powell.

CHAPTER 38

THE GOLDEN WEST

AMERICANS of the 1850s thought of the Pacific Coast area almost entirely in terms of the sweat and roistering of gold miners, including periodic sprees in the boisterous San Francisco, where reputedly vice was rampant and human life was cheap. In more sober fact, gold mining was confined to a relatively small part of the country west of the mountains, and the really pregnant developments were those in agriculture and the other more humdrum occupations. All the way from San Diego to Puget Sound an increasing flow of farmers, speculators, and businessmen was laying the foundations of the permanent prosperity of the Coast. In the long run the gold that was dug from the hills was less important than the gold of the expanding wheat fields. The outline of the future became moderately clear in the years between 1850 and 1900 even though the twentieth century was to see even vaster developments.

LAND TITLES

A special problem for California, as for all of the Southwest, was that of land titles. Ownership of much of the arable land from San Diego to the Sacramento valley was in the hands of some five hundred ranchers, who derived their titles from Spain or Mexico, and the United States had guaranteed these titles under the terms of the treaty of Guadalupe Hidalgo. In accordance with this commitment, Congress had the situation surveyed carefully by William Carey Jones, a son-in-law of Senator Benton. On the basis of his report was enacted the Gwin Law of 1851, which provided a commission of three to investigate all claims.

The commission started its work at San Francisco early in 1852, and for five years labored diligently and honestly to clear up the situation. It listened to over eight hundred cases, giving judgments in favor of the existing holders in over six hundred. In spite of this diligence, the results were often far from good. The law placed the burden of proof on the claimant, who had lived in careless comfort with little attention to bookkeeping and records, and who had almost no surplus funds to hire lawyers. When he hunted for papers in the attic he frequently found they had been mislaid or destroyed by fire. When he searched for witnesses he often found them either widely dispersed or dead. When he hired a lawyer it was not rare that he had to sell part of his land to pay the fees. Almost as costly and exasperating, he usually traveled long distances to collect evidence and to attend hearings; southerners were in particular distress because all of the meetings of the commission, with the exception of one short session at Los Angeles, were held at San Francisco. Moreover, the claimant's troubles seldom ended with the commission hearings. All but nineteen of the cases were appealed to the higher courts, either by the claimant or by a defeated rival. Our best authority on the subject has figured that the average case took seventeen years to reach a final decision, and that during these protracted and expensive proceedings many a claimant went bankrupt or was forced to sell out to speculators.

The aggressive American frontiersmen seeking a new El Dorado in California were by no means always willing to wait patiently until the courts made final disposals of the land-grant cases. Following good American tradition they saw no valid reason why they should not occupy idle lands. If the claimant were Mexican the new settler was certain that no full-blooded American should stand aside for the member of a group which had just been defeated in war, but even non-Mexicans were treated with scant consideration, and violence and bloodshed were far from unknown. Examples were the Fremont grant at Mariposa and the validated Sutter grant at Sacramento; in some cases, as that of John Bidwell, the owner found that expediency dictated the buying out of the squatters. The violence that was so frequent in the thirty years between 1850 and 1880 occurred not only on private claims but also on railroad grants, which comprised over 11 per cent of the state's acreage, including frequently the better land. Not exempt were municipal holdings, with San Francisco most distressed as its grant was overrun with squatters; ultimately it saved at least enough for the Golden Gate Park.

Since the squatters had more votes than the landowners, the state legislature was sympathetic to their point of view. One law was passed which held that all lands were open to private entry until ownership was proved, but the Supreme Court disallowed it. The courts also helped the landowners by refusing to permit the reopening of cases which once had been decided. Apparently certain squatters had tried blackmail by threatening to prove defective title unless they were given land; if such harassing suits had been permitted, presumably even the last surviving grant holders would have gone to the wall.

Washington and Oregon had no similar land problems. The one unusual feature was a Donation Land Law of 1850, designed to take care of early settlers. It provided that each adult who was a citizen or who had announced his intention of becoming one by December 1, 1851, was to receive 320 acres—a sort of early homestead act. The great bulk of the land, however, was distributed under the normal land legislation.

FARMING

The floods of gold miners descending upon California provided a real bonanza for the farmers and cattlemen who were in a position to supply these foot-loose and hungry seekers after liquid wealth. Greatest profit went to the cattlemen, since cattle could transport themselves to market. Whereas cattle had gone begging at five dollars a head before the gold rush, they soared to an astronomical five hundred dollars at Sacramento in 1849. Naturally such highly inflated prices did not last permanently, but profits still remained sufficiently high to attract herds from Texas and from the Mississippi valley, and to inspire California growers to occupy much of the state, including the San Joaquin and Sacramento valleys.

Unfortunately for the cattlemen, they were soon beset by major difficulties. The great drought of 1863–64 evaporated the herds almost as rapidly as the surface water, and before its end the ranchers were glad to sell their cattle for the prices of the skins. Estimates are that Los Angeles County lost up to three-quarters of its stock, while for the entire state the cattle population declined 46 per cent between 1860 and 1870. Of even more permanent importance was the fact that the farmers, and particularly the wheat growers, were flooding into the great interior valleys, and that regular farming could outcompete cattle growing. In addition, farmers outnumbered cattlemen and were able to persuade the legislature in the 1870s to transfer the responsibility and hence the cost of fence building to their rivals. The result was that cattle were driven to the hillier country, particularly to the northern part of the state and across the border into Oregon and Idaho; the height of the Oregon business came about 1880. The displacement of the cattle was never, of course, really complete; for example, the great firm of Miller and Lux continued to occupy large tracts of the San Joaquin valley as well as areas farther north.

The changing cattle business followed the eastern pattern with the introduction of blooded stock to provide better beef than the old scrawny Spanish animals, and this development necessitated more careful handling. All the way from San Diego to Puget Sound appeared such breeds as Devon, Durham, and Aberdeen-Angus. A further development was the growth of the dairy business, which had been so infinitesimal that milk had brought as much as 50¢ a quart in 1850. Now the expansion of cities and the provision of transportation changed the picture. While numerous interior cities, such as Sacramento and Stockton, provided promising markets the most lucrative possibility was the bay area, particularly San Francisco, so that there can be no surprise that the greatest dairy business developed in Marin County, just north of San Francisco.

To some extent the declining cattle herds were replaced by sheep, which were brought in large numbers from New Mexico and from the Mississippi valley. As early as 1860 a California Sheep Growers' Association was formed to present a solid front against the buyers. The height of the sheep industry came during the 1870s in California and somewhat later in Oregon and Washington, with Oregon much more important than Washington. Sheep were raised almost entirely for their wool, since Americans preferred beef to mutton, and the yield was increased by the introduction of blooded stock. Even as early as the 1870s most of the flocks throughout the entire trans-mountain region had assumed a distinctively merino appearance. The shearing was done in large part by peripatetic Mexican labor which was paid by the sheep rather than by the hour. The decline of sheep grazing was the result of factors similar to those which had hurt the cattle business. The great drought of 1876–77 killed thousands of sheep and led many owners to sell for whatever they could get, which meant prices of 25¢ a sheep and 50¢ a dressed carcass. At the same time farmers were pushing into the large fertile valleys, driving the sheepmen to the uplands, both in California and to the north.

While the advent of the farmer spelled the decline of the cattle and the sheep businesses, the transformation was not complete until the railroad furnished adequate transportation. The 1870s saw the blossoming of interior California valleys, such as the Sacramento and San Joaquin, with the coming of the railroad, but in Oregon and Washington the important agricultural areas continued to cling to water available for transportation—Puget Sound, the Willamette River, and the Columbia River east of the Cascade Mountains; the greater rainfall of these areas was of course also a factor. Farther eastern areas which later became important wheat producers, such as the Pendleton-Walla Walla district, did not expand greatly until the railroad construction of the 1880s.

The most important early crop was wheat, even though barley had the lead for a short period during the 1850s. Even as far north as the Willamette valley, early farmers devoted their primary attention to wheat. The top wheat-producing state of the '80s was California, which seemed to contemporaries to provide almost ideal growing conditions. The growing season was long, with no danger of frost. Harvesting came after the rains had stopped, so that the grain could be allowed to lie in the fields. The flat, open land permitted the extensive use of machinery, such as the gang plow, end-gate seeder, disc cultivator, and combine, of which many were altered to meet local conditions. Steam power became common by the '80s. Visitors were vastly impressed by furrows of a mile or more in length, and say ten eight-horse teams following each other with gang plows. Moreover, California wheat found a ready European market, particularly at Liverpool. The resulting conditions were those described by Frank Norris in *The Octopus*.

The growing of wheat by no means lacked problems. The absence of rain was fine for harvesting, but when it started too soon it brought bankruptcy. The wheat farmer was reluctant to undergo the expenses of irrigation, and this reluctance increased with the latitude since the amount of rain increased. A certain number of the farmers of the San Joaquin valley were driven to providing their own water in the late nineteenth century, but those from the

Sacramento valley north through Oregon and Washington generally held out until after 1900. In addition to the difficulties with water, the wheat farmer was faced with the competition for land by the grower of fruits and vegetables. Just as wheat replaced livestock on economic grounds, fruit and vegetables replaced wheat.

The fruit grown most commonly in early California, and particularly in the Los Angeles district, was the grape. Its primacy rested heavily on the fact that grapes were generally made into wine and hence could be transported without most of the problems that faced more perishable products. As early as 1862 the California Wine Growers' Association was formed to set standards for the industry. Whether or not the California wines measured up to world standards received varying testimony, but by the end of the century California dominated domestic wine production, with 80 per cent of the total output. The other great use of grapes was for raisins, and the raisin industry boomed largely during the 1870s; by 1900 some 43 per cent of all California grapes were being transformed into raisins. Here again the lack of rainfall was an advantage, since drying could be done in the fields.

Citrus fruits were entirely confined to California because of the climate. Most important were oranges, which had their first real start with the work of William Wolfskill in Los Angeles during the 1840s. Early development was small, partly because of the lack of necessary technical information, but even more because of the absence of the transportation so vital for marketing; the number of producing orange trees in 1860 was only 4,000, and by 1870 no more than 40,000. The greatest relative expansion came during the 1870s along with the railroad construction of the decade; the first carload lot was shipped east in 1877. It was also during this decade that the Washington navel orange was introduced. It came from Bahia, Brazil, via a missionary and the Department of Agriculture. The most serious insect pest was brought under control in the late '80s by the introduction of the ladybird from Australia, and oil heaters were in use by the late '90s. While the industry tended to concentrate in southern California it had spread as far north as the Sacramento valley by the '70s. The present Sunkist Fruit Growers' Exchange, designed to promote uniform sorting, packing, grading, and promoting, came into existence under a different title in the '90s.

Other fruits such as apples, pears, peaches, and cherries were widely grown all the way from the Mexican to the Canadian border. California fruit was notably large and attractive, although some detractors objected that its taste was not as good as the advance notice. Oregon was also early in the field, with the farmers of the Willamette valley strongly joined in the 1870s by the growers of the Umpqua and Rogue river valleys in the southwestern part of the state. Particularly noted were the Black Republican and Bing cherries, first grown in the Willamette valley during the '60s. The Fruitgrowers' Association of Oregon (1858) has been advertised as the first state organization of its type. The importance of the fruit of Washington came a trifle later; the first commercial shipment of apples, for example, did not occur until 1900.

Many other agricultural crops were tried with greater or less success, particularly in California where the warmness of the climate inspired experimentation. Most successful was the production of sugar beets, which began during the 1870s. An olive boom of the mid-'80s soon collapsed and then later was revived. Both figs and avocados had little importance until after 1900. Cotton booms occurred periodically but unsuccessfully from the 1840s to 1900. Tobacco was a plant of major interest during the early 1870s, but apparently the curing process was a failure. Just as in other areas, the silk mania held periodic sway. The greatest California craze came in the 1860s, with the legislature offering bounties under an act of 1864. Ten million mulberry trees were reported being grown in 1869, but the industry failed to attain permanent success.

WATER

No problem has been more persistently troublesome to the Pacific states, and particularly to California, than that of water. Generally deficient rainfall, except on the northwest coast, has been varied from time to time with floods that have carried away farms and inundated cities. In the early days city water came from local streams which were usually polluted and which at times died away to small trickles. Real improvement was slow to come to California, mainly because the large cities tended to be on the coast and the best drinking water remotely in the Sierras. Not until after 1900 were the engineering and financial problems sufficiently overcome to permit long water hauls. The Owen River project of Los Angeles was completed in 1913, and the Hetch-Hetchy valley project of San Francisco was started the next year.

Irrigation of farm land started in primitive fashion even before American acquisition of the coast area, and then was continued and expanded in southern California by the newcomers. Not only did individuals dig their own ditches, but at times ranch owners were forced to make provision for water in order to sell their land. Here and there appeared cooperative colonies; an example of the last was the Anaheim colony, organized in 1857 to provide its members with twenty-acre fruit farms. During the '60s and '70s the amount of irrigation increased, particularly in southern California and the San Joaquin valley, but also north into Oregon and Washington. Quite obviously any large-scale irrigation project was impossible for the individual farmer, with the result that large projects were initiated either by groups of farmers or by outside capitalists. The most important of the California companies was the "76 Land & Water Company," which constructed an irrigation canal in the San Joaquin valley in the early '80s, partly to water its own land but also to sell water to the farmers of the area. North of California the largest project was the Sunnyside Canal, built in the 1890s with Northern Pacific money.

Private irrigation encountered many troubles, of which the most obvious was the raising of funds. In any particular area certain farmers for one reason or another refused to participate, with many wheat farmers in particular preferring to take a chance on the rainfall; the Sacramento valley, for instance, obtained no large-scale irrigation until after 1900. Moreover there were considerable legal problems involved in the utilization of any particular stream. Could an irrigation company draw off sufficient water that men farther down the stream were handicapped? And suppose a new irrigation company then tapped the stream above the old one? Such problems represented stumbling blocks in the way of extensive irrigation.

The natural answer for the irrigation problem was the use of governmental authority. The California legislature made an effort in 1875 by authorizing a West Side Irrigation District which could issue bonds for the construction of a canal in the lower San Joaquin valley, but the courts threw out the plan as unconstitutional. The great landmark in such legislation was the Wright Law of 1887, which authorized the formation of water districts with elected officers and with power to issue bonds and to levy taxes. The act was not immediately successful, partly because of practical difficulties such as fights between large and small farm owners and between old and new projects, and partly because of the many years of legal battles before the law was judged constitutional; of the fifty districts originally formed under the law only four were successful. But in time the idea was accepted, became successful, and was copied by other dry states. The contribution of the federal government before 1900 was approximately nothing. While the Carey Act of 1894 applied to the Pacific Northwest, no practical accomplishments resulted until after the passage of the Newlands Act in 1902.

The most spectacular of the irrigation projects was probably the transformation of the Colorado Desert into the Imperial valley. Ingenious men were impressed in the 1890s with the fact that the Colorado River was higher than the desert and that the land was first rate if only water could be supplied. Why not, said they, scrape a canal and let gravity provide the moisture to make the desert bloom? The first water arrived in 1901, along with a flood of opportunity-seeking farmers; the most optimistic hopes of the promoters were realized, and the Imperial valley became one of the garden spots of the nation. Unfortunately the river failed to cooperate with proper docility, but in the years 1905–06 shifted its channel, with the threat of wiping out the entire improvements of the valley. A two-year fight, with E. H. Harriman of the Southern Pacific furnishing most of the financial ammunition, was necessary before the river was confined to its present channel. The newer, All-American Canal, was opened in 1941.

Probably the water problem of the Far West will never be solved with complete satisfaction. For certain areas water is either nonexistent or too far distant to be practical to use, and conditions tend to deteriorate with the rapid growth of population. At times even normal supplies of water disappear, with tragic results. A possible option has been the supplying of water from wells—more possible in California than in Washington or Oregon. Power for the pumping was furnished at first by windmills, and then successively by steam, gasoline, and electricity. The use of such water has been overenthusiastic, with the water table dropping rapidly; in fact recent years have seen some of the wells drawing salt water, which certainly is the beginning of the end.

INDUSTRIAL GROWTH AND THE CITIES

Expanding farm communities naturally demanded manufactured goods, and with the long hauls necessary from either the

East or Europe the result was a development of Far Western urban centers and manufacturing. The distinctive industries of any frontier area, such as sawmills, distilleries, tanneries, and flour mills, were as apparent as elsewhere, but soon others also appeared. The magnificent forests of northern California and Oregon, including notably the impressive redwoods, were exploited to furnish wagons and furniture, even before the Civil War. The great flocks of sheep inspired textile mills, with one opened at even as remote a place as Salem, Oregon, as early as 1858. Salmon canneries appeared in the Far Northwest, starting in the early '70s. Sugar refineries accompanied the introduction of sugar beets. The brief flurry of interest in tobacco brought cigar factories, particularly in San Francisco. The refining of various ores became at least in part city occupations; for example, the refining of borax from Death Valley came to be centered in San Francisco by the late '80s. Oil refining increased at an irregular rate, for while oil seepage had been observed in California as early as the 1840s, and while a refinery had been opened near Los Angeles in 1865, the development of the business continued to remain sporadic until after 1900.

The growth of manufacturing on the Pacific Coast was faced with several imposing obstacles, of which not the least was transportation. The very difficulties of travel which encouraged the beginnings of Far West manufacturing also limited its growth. Most favorably located was the San Francisco bay region, which had the advantage of much navigable inland water as well as of early railroad building. Farther north, Portland was best located because of its dominance over the Columbia River. But in many places, shipments had to depend on very primitive facilities; for example, northern California and southern Oregon were limited for many years to a combination of mule back or wagon and ocean freighters. The result was that most manufacturing establishments remained small until after the railroad construction of the 1880s. The census of 1860 showed the average California manufacturing establishment as employing 4.4 workers, while twenty years later the number had risen to only 7.4.

Another major manufacturing difficulty was the lack of capital. Much of the local speculative money went into mining, while eastern investors were somewhat loath to risk their capital in such a remote place. The financial center of the West Coast was San Francisco, but even here interest rates were little short of fantastic; as late as 1870 the normal charge was between 1½ and 4 per cent a month, with higher rates quite common. And then the depression of 1873 made conditions definitely worse, with the hardest single blow the failure of the important Bank of America in 1875.

The labor problem presented at least equal difficulties, since most men preferred to try their fortunes at mining, farming, or trading rather than to work for wages. The result was a labor scarcity in early years, with consequent high wages and at least equally high prices for finished products. Conditions changed radically with the depression of 1873, for whereas in early years jobs had been plentiful and wages high, now wages dropped and unemployment was prevalent. The first important labor reaction was to blame the troubles on the Chinese who had been brought to America to supply the labor deficit. The Chinese were an easy target because of their distinctive appearance, their strange-appearing food and customs, and their docility as workers. Moreover they had long been the subjects of suspicion and discrimination, even to the extent of physical violence, as in the holocaust at Los Angeles in the late '60s. Now leather-lunged and incendiary speakers, highlighted by the dynamic, rabble-rousing Dennis Kearney, went up and down the coast reiterating raucously the slogan "the Chinese must go." While Kearney and his kind insisted that they did not advocate violence, their speeches sounded that way to their auditors, and inspired mob action all the way from Puget Sound to San Diego. Possibly most drastic were the San Francisco riots, which included the looting of the Chinese district, and the actions of a Tacoma mob in expelling the entire Chinese population from that city.

But the unrest of the 1870s was a good deal more than a fight for the elimination of the Chinese. The Kearney groups, under the title of the Workingmen's Party of California, proposed "to wrest the government from the hands of the rich and place it in those of the people where it properly belongs." Among the desired reforms were more democracy in government, the end of land monopoly, the elimination of great wealth by taxation, and the regulation of big business. The growth of the party was spectacular, and it could have controlled completely the Constitutional Convention of 1878 if only it had not lost force by a split within its ranks. It did succeed, however, in having adopted such measures as new tax provisions, a railroad commission, banking control, an eight-hour day on public works, and restriction of the Chinese. For various reasons these ideas proved much less effective in action than they had loomed in Kearney's oratory.

The growth of industry and of a labor movement implied the development of cities, with the largest being along the coast. The top metropolis of the entire period was San Francisco, which started with the tremendous natural advantages of a magnificent harbor and of good interior water connections, particularly with the Sacramento and San Joaquin valleys. The first railroad building of the state centered in the bay area, and the masters of the all-powerful Southern Pacific, with their luxurious palaces on Nob Hill, worked hard and successfully to maintain the dominance of San Francisco. Starting with the earliest gold rushes, which were not far from the back door of the city at the Golden Gate, San Francisco maintained itself as the leading commercial, financial, manufacturing, and cultural center of the Pacific Coast.

The obvious location for the greatest city of southern California was at San Diego, where there existed the only good natural harbor south of the Golden Gate, but unfortunately for the hopes of San Diego, the main railroad lines preferred Los Angeles, even though the choice necessitated the construction of a completely artificial harbor at San Pedro. The immediate results of the completion of the Southern Pacific to Los Angeles in the '70s were not impressive, since southern California traffic to the East had to be routed through Oakland, but conditions changed during the '80s when not only did the Southern Pacific make connections with the East by the southern route, but also the Santa Fe reached the Coast. With these developments Los Angeles not only had a direct haul east, but also could benefit from the competition of two major railroad systems.

Railroad building co-ordinated with a tremendous land boom in southern California, particularly in the years 1886–88. Economically this boom was accompanied most visibly by a tremendous expansion of the citrus fruit industry, but in fact its basic cause was the glory of the southern California climate. Health seekers and others who disliked the rigors of particular more easterly areas were lured in tremendous numbers to what was advertised as the nearest approach to the Garden of Eden since the beginning of the world. Floods of hopeful migrants inundated the streets of Los Angeles, trading enthusiastically the city's newly opened lots, and in many cases soon claiming large wealth, at least on paper.

Suburban areas were expanded rapidly, with the Pasadena enthusiasm rivaling that of Los Angeles; when Azusa was opened eager buyers stood in line all the preceding night, and it was reported that the second in line refused a thousand dollars for his place. Burbank, San Bernardino, Santa Barbara, and dozens of other towns participated in the general excitement, even though some of them such as Sunset, Gladstone, Chicago Park, and La Ballona failed to remain for posterity. While this particular boom soon collapsed, the total growth of the area continued, and in time with greater and greater acceleration.

Leadership among the coast cities north of California went to Portland, which benefitted by its natural control of the trade of the Columbia valley; theoretically it should have been an important ocean port, but actually it was greatly handicapped by the sand bars at the mouth of the river. Farther north, on Puget Sound, were notably Tacoma, which advertised itself as "The Second Greater New York," and Seattle, whose exact location was apparently something of an accident. All the northern cities grew rapidly with the completion of the Northern Pacific and the Great Northern. All of them also had great hopes of trade with the Far East, since they were closer to Asiatic ports than San Francisco, but these hopes were never realized completely.

CULTURAL DEVELOPMENTS

The Pacific Coast passed through the same cultural developments which other farther eastern frontiers had experienced. The log cabin, home-made furniture, candles, and horse transport were just as typical of frontier Oregon as of early Ohio. Frontier Pacific towns, like their eastern predecessors, were characterized by unpaved streets, wooden sidewalks, hitching posts for the horses, inadequate and polluted water, improper disposal of sewage, and periodic epidemics, particularly smallpox. Saloons, gambling halls, and brothels lined the streets, while their denizens made street travel distasteful for the more sober citizens. Every man went armed, and life was held cheaply, with only the most cursory efforts at law enforcement. Just as farther east, conditions gradually changed, and in due course there appeared paved streets, sewage disposal, better water systems, street cars, telephones, and electric lights.

Rather less to be expected in a generally new and rough society, there were always groups in every area that made real efforts to enforce the highest Victorian standards of morality. The more courteous and conservative citizenry insisted upon as rigid conduct as would have been characteristic of a Back Bay Bostonian. Balls and dinner parties were conducted with elaborate politeness, plays and books with suggestive contents were taboo, and the gentleman escorted his lady with the same manners that would have befitted a New York or Philadelphia young man of breeding. No surprise need be felt at the long arguments as to how a lady might avoid compromising her modesty when crossing puddles of water in the street, or at the vitriolic outburst of a frontier Olympia newspaper editor as he protested the conduct of a woman who rode a horse astride and thereby caused "the blush of shame to mantle even the cheek of manhood." People of this frame of mind treated the widespread and highly visible vice by ignoring it— an attitude that became particularly difficult when a "gentleman" was observed staggering out of a saloon or a brothel.

The Pacific Coast was like other frontier areas in having a vast preponderance of men over women, and this situation lasted in many areas until late in the century. One result was that women had a scarcity value, and were often treated with exaggerated respect and courtesy—with the exception, of course, of the women of the painted faces, the low-cut gowns, and the blonde-dyed hair. Whether or not certain foreign visitors were correct in thinking that women were too much pampered and hence became headstrong and domineering, the fair sex was certainly given early privileges, as in education and voting. The best-advertised effort to supply the feminine shortage was undertaken by Asa S. Mercer, who brought parties of New England girls to Oregon in 1864 and 1866. These "Mercer girls" came as teachers, but probably not entirely to their surprise they turned out to be in even greater demand as wives. Unfortunately their number was not sufficient to supply even a perceptible part of the western demand.

Among the first cultural institutions carried west of the mountains was the printing press. The famous *Alta California* started publication in San Francisco in 1849, although rather surprisingly the first trans-montane newspaper was the *Oregon Spectator,* which began its short life at Oregon City in 1846. Magazines came fairly early, including the outstanding *Golden Era* (1852), a news weekly which also printed fiction, including some by Bret Harte and Mark Twain. Best known was the *Overland Monthly* (1868), which emphasized western material and which was particularly good under the editorship of Bret Harte. The coast has claimed a considerable number of outstanding literary figures, although in some cases their stay in the area was relatively brief. Among them may be mentioned Bret Harte, Mark Twain, Joaquin Miller, and Helen Hunt Jackson. Other arts were less practiced but far from unknown. For example, a Philharmonic Society appeared in Portland as early as 1859, and a California Art Association made its bow at San Francisco in 1871.

Amusements on the Pacific Coast were amazingly varied, being by no means limited to drinking, gambling, and horse racing. Everything from sewing bees and circuses to chautauquas and concert artists competed for public attention. Not least important was a rather impressive theatrical display, which in the early years supplemented but did not replace the attractions of the saloons and brothels. The first buildings designed primarily as theaters were the results of the gold rush—at Sacramento in 1849 and San Francisco in 1850. While some of the plays were pretty flimsy, a surprising proportion came from the pens of such classic playwrights as Shakespeare, Knowles, Bulwer-Lytton, and Payne. The quality of the acting remains a trifle dubious, but the current starring system permitted the appearance of such outstanding performers as Edwin Booth, James M. Hackett, Caroline Chapman, and Ellen Tree. Among performers particularly identified with the Far West were Adah Isaac Mencken, Lotta Crabtree, who started her professional career as a child prodigy in California, and the notorious and fascinating Lola Montez. Most of the Far West never saw dramatic performances because of the difficulties of transportation, and even the regular theaters of the larger towns of southern California, Oregon, and Washington were scantily used. Not until the '80s and later did the more southerly and northerly areas receive their proper shares of theatrical performances.

The religion which was practically universal in California at the time of the gold rush was Roman Catholicism, but the Protestant sects advanced rapidly with the American invasion. Soon the Far West was dotted with Protestant churches, particularly Washington and Oregon, which were settled largely from the Ohio valley and the Northeast. Home missionary societies carried on a considerable part of the effort, with the Presbyterians particularly active. Quite obviously the American frontiersmen carried their religion with them as they did other institutions.

Closely connected with religion was education, for many of the secondary schools and colleges were established under religious auspices. All three states of Washington, Oregon, and California made early provisions for universal elementary education, but in each case the lack of available wealth made the results somewhat pathetic in terms of the original blueprints. Private schools did much of the job for many years until the government took over. Much of the secondary education was also given by private academies, which emphasized the traditional classical training. Public high schools originated as early as 1856 in San Francisco, but at first expanded but slowly; toward the end of the century, however, they were obviously displacing the private institutions. Schools of higher education traced back in many cases to the 1850s, but actually the "colleges" of this period tended usually to be mainly secondary schools. Rather surprisingly the first of the state universities was that of Washington, which opened at Seattle in 1861. The University of California admitted its first students in 1869, and four years later moved its campus from Oakland to Berkeley; its second president was Daniel Coit Gilman. The University of Oregon opened at Eugene in 1876, and was kept alive in its early years by the gifts of Henry Villard.

In many ways the settlement and development of the Pacific Coast were typical of all frontier settlement, with the usual succession of stock growing, wheat raising, diversified farming, manufacturing, and the growth of cities. In several respects, however, the area was more or less unique. The character of the original California population, the mining boom, the attractive qualities of the climate, and the importance of irrigation were at least far from universal. Even more significant, the farthest western point of American continental expansion had been reached. True that much interior land remained to be exploited, and true also that much of American pioneering energy was to be devoted to the expansion of the economic system, but still the question was to be raised increasingly as to the form which future American expansion would assume and the place where it would occur.

READINGS

C. A. Barker, *Henry George* (1955), part 1; A. Binns, *Northwest Gateway* (1941)—popular on Seattle; C. H. Carey, *History of Oregon* (1922), chs. 35–41—plods; J. W. Caughey, *California* (1953), chs. 17, 20, 22, 25–28—good, *History of the Pacific Coast*

(1932), chs. 21, 24; R. G. Cleland, *The Cattle on a Thousand Hills* (1951), chs. 3–11—southern California; R. G. Cleland and O. Hardy, *March of Industry* (1929), chs. 2–8—economic history of California; J. Dana, *The Sacramento* (1939), ch. 4—thin; G. S. Dumbe, *The Boom of the Eighties in Southern California* (1944); A. B. Fisher, *The Salinas* (1945), chs. 7–11; G. W. Fuller, *A History of the Pacific Northwest* (1931), chs. 11, 16–19, *The Inland Empire* (3 vols., 1928), vol. 3, chs. 25–31; C. B. Hutchison (ed.), *California Agriculture* (1946), ch. 1; G. R. MacMinn, *The Theater of the Golden Era in California* (1941)—scholarly; P. Maddox, *City on the Willamette* (1952), chs. 1–10—miscellaneous material on Portland; E. S. Meany, *History of the State of Washington* (1909), chs. 17–31—scrappy; R. A. Nadeau, *The Water Seekers* (1952)—irrigation, but mostly after 1900; G. C. Quiett, *They Built the West* (1934), chs. 9–16—effects of railroads; M. B. Ritter, *More Than Gold in California* (1933), chs. 1–18—reminiscences of woman physician; W. W. Robinson, *Land in California* (1948)—scholarly; R. A. Rydell, *Cape Horn to the Pacific* (1952), ch. 9—ocean business of Pacific Coast; W. Smith, *Garden of the Sun* (1939), chs. 9–20—good on San Joaquin valley; F. Walker, *A Literary History of Southern California* (1950), chs. 1–7—detailed; S. Warren, *Farthest Frontier* (1949), chs. 5–16—stresses picturesque on Pacific Northwest; O. O. Winther, *The Great Northwest* (1947), chs. 11, 13, 17, 20.

CHAPTER 39

WESTERN PANACEAS

Any man who moved to the western frontier was something of a gambler, with an aggressive desire to improve himself. Typically he was loudly democratic, a strong nationalist, and a believer in direct and drastic action. He knew what he wanted and stated his desires in no uncertain terms. If he could attain them by individual action, so much the better; but if community or national efforts through governmental action were necessary, he allowed no abstract theory of individualism to halt him short of his goal.

Inevitably some of the western desires could be attained only through political action, and so the West became politically minded. In national politics the West always exercised considerable power because of its size. Western Senators were comparatively numerous, even though Representatives were not. The consequence was that the West played an important part in such movements as the establishment of Jeffersonian democracy, the declaration of the War of 1812, the development of Jacksonian democracy, the " manifest destiny " drive, the encouragement of internal improvements, and the changing of land legislation. Even without a legislative majority, the West could in many cases find a sufficient number of allies to gain its point.

The years after the Civil War saw the West develop several important political movements based primarily on economic desires. The average westerner had been working hard to make his fortune. A few had succeeded but many had failed, and it was hard to believe that such failure was due to personal inadequacies. A more palatable theory was that the rules of the game were wrong and that if the necessary changes were made by law everything would be rosy. Quite naturally such political protest movements drew their greatest strength in times of depression, when the number of unsuccessful was greatest.

Western reform movements were based fundamentally on two factors — that the West was an agricultural region and that it was in debt. Throughout its history the West has been predominantly an area of farmers, which has meant that its major interest has been in farm production and prices. A tendency has existed for older areas to become industrialized and change their point of view as the frontier continued to move, but this process was much slower when the frontier struck the region of the Great Plains. Cities developed with their factories, but the dominant major interest remained agriculture, which meant that possibly ten to twenty states could be counted upon as having Senators favorable to a farm program.

Of course the West was by no means the only farming area of the United States. Every state had important agricultural interests, and in the South and in parts of New England these interests might be supreme, at least in relation to particular issues. In consequence the West might hope for considerable sympathy and support from other sections of the country. Or possibly a fairer statement would be that the West had a high concentration of the very widespread industry of American agriculture.

The second basic factor was that the West, much like any other agricultural region, was consistently a debtor area. Few rich people moved to the frontier, and the meager capital of the West was strained to the limit to buy new land, stock, and machinery. Additional funds were obtained by wholesale mortgaging which appeared in such forms as state and municipal debts for public improvements, railroad bonds, and private mortgages. In consequence the West was interested in proposals which would benefit not only the farmer, but rather the farmer who was in debt.

GRANGERS

The first organization to arouse enthusiasm in the West after the Civil War was the Patrons of Husbandry, organized in 1867 by a clerk in the Department of Agriculture. At the beginning it was secret in nature, with a ritual modeled along the lines of the Masons and Odd Fellows. It was nonpolitical, and proposed aiding the farmers by encouraging cooperative buying of such articles as farm machinery and groceries. In its first few years of life it made but little progress, and its membership remained negligible.

The Patrons of Husbandry benefited by the financial reverses which led to the panic of 1873; as with other similar movements, it seemed more attractive with the arrival of hard times. The membership figures leaped skyward during the years 1872 and 1873, so that at the height of the movement over a million and a half were enrolled. The local unit of the organization was known as the grange, and so the entire activities of the members of the association were described popularly as the " granger movement." The center of granger influence was the upper Mississippi Valley, principally Illinois, Wisconsin, Minnesota, Iowa, and Missouri. The organization was also active elsewhere, however, and even to-day it is possible to see frequent grange halls as far distant as New England.

Partly by accident the development of the granger movement coincided with the revulsion of feeling against the railroads. The farmers who composed the grangers were the same men who were certain that the depression of the '70s had been caused by the high rates and favoritism of the railroads, and consequently the grangers became active in advocating some effective curb of the railroads. The most favored proposal was that governmental agencies control rates and prevent unfair railroad practices.

The granges soon found that their old idea of not entering politics was inapplicable if immediate results were to be attained. The consequence was the formation of small political parties under such names as Independent, Reform, or Anti-Monopoly. These groups, depending mainly on the granges for their support, developed in eleven western states. Usually they cooperated with one of the older and larger parties, attempting to act only as a sort of balance of power. United States Senators having granger sympathies were elected in Illinois, Kansas, and California, while lesser victories occurred elsewhere.

The most important result of the granger activities was a series of state railroad regulation acts passed between the years 1871 and 1878. During this period such legislation was enacted by Illinois, Wisconsin, Minnesota, Missouri, California, and Iowa; other states followed at a later date. The laws had two general types of provisions. A schedule of the maximum rates which the railroads of the state could charge was inserted in every law except that of California. Every state provided furthermore for a commission to inspect the roads of the state, prosecute violators of the law, and report needed legislation to the government; only

Missouri gave the commission power to adjust the rates which had been specified in the original law. In addition to these main provisions, there was ordinarily a prohibition of specified forms of discrimination practiced by the railroads in the past.

The railroads naturally opposed this regulation — not so much because of its immediate effect as because it might open the way for later and more drastic measures. Some of the larger roads made their rate structures as ridiculous and unjust as the law permitted, to show how foolish it was for legislatures to meddle with the practical business of running a railroad. Lobbying efforts aimed at the repeal of the laws. Cases were taken to the courts on the plea that property was being confiscated without " due process of law " and that only Congress had the power to regulate business which was primarily interstate in character. The Supreme Court of the United States, however, came to the conclusion in several cases of 1876, notably *Munn v. Illinois* and *Peik v. Chicago and Northwestern Railroad,* that the states had a regulatory power, even over rates on goods shipped across state lines.

No one realized better than the farmers that though the state laws were constitutional, they did not provide adequate regulation. The most important hauls were between East and West, and even at the best they could be regulated only partially by individual western states. Furthermore most of the railroad companies were foreign corporations (incorporated in some other state), and it was difficult to make them produce accounts and records which would have any meaning to local officials. Confusion also resulted from varying state regulations; for example, a railroad might be required to change its type of headlight three or four times in a single run. It was therefore recognized as early as the '70s that federal action was necessary to supplement and make effective local regulation.

Congress considered possible railroad regulation at great length during the period, but finally did nothing. The Windom report (1874), the Reagan report (1878), and the discussion of a multitude of bills presented the situation very fully, but the majority of the members of Congress felt that railroad regulation should be entirely a state matter. This attitude was made untenable in 1886, when the Supreme Court in the Wabash case somewhat changed its former attitude, and placed rather narrow limits on the power of the states. The following year Congress enacted the important Interstate Commerce Act, which together with many later amendments eventually resulted in making the Interstate Commerce Commission the most important regulatory body in the United States.

GREENBACK MOVEMENT

The granger movement, which had played such an important part in the origin of these developments, began to decline during the late '70s. Its decreasing importance was due in part to an increasing prosperity which made the people forget the sins of the railroads, and in part to the disastrous failure of the grange cooperative enterprises. During its later years it shared the center of the stage with another reform movement — the demand for large issues of paper money to help the debtor portions of the community. At a still later date popular esteem went to silver rather than to paper, but the general aim was the same. The greenback movement developed as the influence of the granges declined. The only tangible connections between the two were that large numbers of one group supported the program of the other, and that the leaders of one tended to shift to the other with the veering of popular support.

The greenback movement was based in theory on a demand for a " managed currency." Greenbackers pointed to the decline in the per capita amount of money in circulation and to the corresponding decline in prices. They held that an increase of paper money would be desirable in restoring prices to what they considered a proper level. In the future prices might be stabilized by proper manipulation of the nation's circulating medium.

The average western Greenbacker was not a profound theorist on monetary matters but he realized that large issues of paper money were good for debtors, and that the West was largely a debtor community. An increase of cheap currency tended, according to Gresham's law, to drive out the more expensive medium, in this case gold, for no one would spend gold when the cheaper paper money did as well. The paper money tended to drop in value because of its very profusion; in practice this meant that prices rose, which amounted to the same thing. The consequence was that any given amount of money would be worth progressively less and less in real goods because of the rise in prices. This situation would be to the advantage of the debtors, who could sell their products at the higher prices and then pay their debts more easily than before the additional paper currency had been issued.

The most considerable inflation of the currency of the United States had come during the Civil War, when large quantities of irredeemable greenbacks were printed and put into circulation. Prices rose rapidly, which was excellent for the debtor, and put the burden on the creditor. After the war an attempt was made to restore the parity of paper and specie. To do this, the government felt that some of the greenbacks should be retired at once, so that when the final resumption occurred the Treasury would not be swamped by the demands made upon it for gold. The necessary authorization was provided by the act of 1866, which called for retirement of $4,000,000 of the greenbacks each month. Immediately mutterings were heard throughout the country, for the debtors disliked looking forward to deflation and resumption. The result of these protests was the repeal of the act of 1866 two years later, at which time there were over $356,000,000 of greenbacks still in circulation.

The problem of the resumption of specie payments continued to agitate the public mind in the years after 1866. In the Presidential campaign of 1868 the Republican party was generally understood to favor resumption and the Democratic party to oppose it, although the Democratic candidate Seymour did not agree with this principle of his party. In spite of the Republican victory no resumption act was passed until 1875, and then it was not to go into force for another four years. As the time for resumption approached the price of greenbacks gradually rose, until at the date set for the change they had attained par and consequently there was no rush to the Treasury to exchange them for gold.

As paper money rose in price the mutterings of the debtor class became a loud roar. Prices descended, with the result that the farmer was receiving less money with which to meet the debts he had contracted in a time of high prices. Protesting groups held meetings all over the country, while larger conventions gave vocal expression to the existing dissatisfaction. Out of this rising wave of feeling came the call for a national convention to represent all of the people who wanted more paper money. When it met in 1876 it took the name of the National Independent party, but by popular consent the group was more ordinarily called the Greenback, or Greenback Labor, party.

This convention of 1876 was held at Indianapolis and was composed of 240 delegates, representing eighteen states and the District of Columbia. After a long debate in which everyone had an opportunity to free his mind of his own pet grievances, a vigorous and oratorical platform was adopted. Then Peter Cooper of New York was nominated for the office of President of the United States. Mr. Cooper was a picturesque and appealing figure. He had made a fortune in iron, first at Baltimore and then at Trenton, and had retired to New York to use his money for philanthropy. His greatest achievement was the establishment of Cooper Institute (to which he gave a total of $800,000) which was designed to aid working men by providing a free library and reading room, and by giving regular night classes. In spite of Mr. Cooper's benevolences, however, it still seemed somewhat strange to see this rich elderly philanthropist as the leader of a movement for more paper money.

The Greenbackers were particularly fortunate in their choice of a man to organize clubs throughout the country. Being cognizant of the value of advertising they picked Marcus M. (" Brick ") Pomeroy, who was a journalist by profession. According to his own claims he organized 4000 clubs, and even allowing a modest 50 per cent of error, the figures are impressive. In addition he found time to write many propaganda tracts under such appealing titles as " Meat for Men " and " Hot Drops."

The election of 1876 did not prove satisfactory to the new Greenback party, which received only 80,000 of a total of 8,000,000 votes. Its principal support in the West came from Illinois, Indiana, and Michigan, and in the East from Massachusetts. The Greenbackers were not discouraged by this failure, for they realized that the party was still young. Additional work brought new recruits until by the local elections of 1878 the party was able to cast a million votes. As later events showed, this election was the high point of the numerical strength of the movement. In 1880 General James B. Weaver of Iowa was nominated for the Presidency, but polled only the disappointing total of 308,000 votes. In 1884 the Greenbackers joined the Anti-Monopoly party in nominating General Benjamin F. Butler of Massachusetts who, needless to say, did not win the election.

THE POPULISTS

The early '80s proved to be a wonderful period of prosperity for everyone, with the consequence that the granger and greenback movements disappeared. Labor found the unusual situation of rising wages and falling prices. The farmers had bumper crops and consequently profited in spite of a decline of prices; their income increased and the cost of the articles they purchased declined. No considerable reform movement could live under such conditions because there was nothing which any considerable number of people wanted to reform. A party of protest was an anachronism.

Small and fairly isolated groups continued to struggle along the path of reform, for under no conceivable situation could everyone be entirely satisfied. Labor groups such as the Union Labor party and the United Labor party maintained at least a nominal existence. Farmer groups, many of them nonpolitical, did likewise; some of the more important were the National Farmers' Alliance and Industrial Union, the National Farmers' Alliance, the Agricultural Wheel, and the Farmers' Mutual Benefit Association. While wielding little influence they at least had organizations which were in a position to take advantage of any period of depression that might occur.

Economic conditions became steadily worse during the late '80s. Wages began to decline; crops failed in the West, especially in western Kansas, Nebraska, and the Dakotas. The result was new adherents for some of the protesting groups. Here and there were fusions of the smaller groups to gain increased strength. The organizations which obtained the most profit, both by new members and by the absorption of other groups, were the Farmers' Alliances, of which there were two, " Northern " and " Southern." Both were nonpolitical, and threw their support to whichever candidate most represented their views, in the same way as does the American Federation of Labor today. This policy produced a considerable number of local successes by 1891.

With the development of the protest movements about 1890, various leaders saw the possibility of combining them all into one great political party which might have a chance to win a national election. The main difficulty in this procedure was to find a program which was sufficiently broad to include all reform elements and yet would not antagonize any. There were obvious and huge difficulties in reconciling such divergent elements as those favoring easy money, antimonopoly, labor legislation, woman suffrage, single tax, and socialism — to name only a few.

The most important problem in making such a combination, then as today, was to reconcile the opposing viewpoints of the farmer and the industrial laborer. Labor desired high wages and low prices. The farmer, on the contrary, wanted high prices except for the goods he bought, and preferred all prices high rather than none.

Furthermore the farmer was glad to have a low wage scale, since he was also an employer of labor. In point of fact the two groups had little in common except their objections to the existing economic system in a time of depression.

The Farmers' Alliance was willing to attempt to unite all protesting groups, and at a meeting at Ocala, Florida, in December 1890 it called for a convention of all dissatisfied minorities to convene at Cincinnati the following year. The convention met as scheduled, with 1400 delegates present. The great variety of groups gave the meeting the nickname of the " conglomerate conference." Its chances of success were distinctly reduced, however, by the absence of some of the most important groups, the rival farmers' organizations and labor, notably the Knights of Labor.

The platform adopted at Cincinnati showed the nature of the reform elements which were represented. It advocated a reduction of taxes, a request which was by no means novel. It asked for government ownership of railroads, telegraphs, and telephones, which seemed a natural step after the development of the granger movement. Alien ownership of land was to be prohibited and no land was to be held speculatively; both of these demands illustrated vividly the disappearance of the good land of the public domain. The circulating medium was to be plentiful, both in paper and silver, and silver was to be coined freely at a ratio with gold of sixteen to one. This last plank was a logical result of the greenback agitation, the only difference being in the increased emphasis on silver rather than on paper.

Minor provisions of the platform of 1891 were not without their interest. The national currency of the United States was to be loaned liberally at an interest rate of 2 per cent. A graduated income tax, postal savings banks, the Australian (secret) ballot, liberal pensions, the eight-hour day, and the initiative and referendum were to be introduced. The President of the United States was to be allowed only a single term. United States Senators were to be elected by direct vote of the people.

The platform was obviously the combination of many proposals. Read in the light of the present day few of its demands seem unusual; many of them have been put into practice. At the time it was adopted, however, it seemed very radical, not to say revolutionary. The more conservative elements of the population were so alarmed as to appear panic-stricken. They shook their heads dolefully and uttered loud lamentations as to the degeneracy o the times. Everything was " going to the dogs." The Constitution was being undermined. Such a program, if adopted, would destroy the civilization which had been constructed so laboriously. Particularly dangerous were the proposals to put the government into business and thus reduce that competition which was " the life of trade." Dire calamities were predicted if even the least of the proposed reforms were put into practice.

By the time the new party held its most important convention at Omaha in 1892 it had achieved the name of the People's party, and its members were called Populists. Thirteen hundred and sixty-six delegates were present at this convention of 1892, and General James B. Weaver of Iowa was nominated for President amid scenes of the wildest confusion. The spirit of the body was well expressed by the preamble of the platform which it adopted : " We meet in the midst of a nation brought to the verge of moral, political, and material ruin. Corruption dominates the ballot box, the legislatures, the Congress, and even touches the ermine on the bench. The people are demoralized. The newspapers are largely subsidized or muzzled, public opinion silenced, business prostrated, our homes covered with mortgages, labor impoverished, and the land concentrated in the hands of the capitalists. Urban workmen are denied the right of organizing ; imported pauperized labor reduces their wages, while a hireling army shoots them down. The toils of the millions are stolen to build up colossal fortunes. From the prolific womb of governmental injustice we breed the two great classes — tramps and millionaires. . . . Wealth belongs to him who creates it, and every dollar taken from industry is robbery."

On the basis of this platform, which in its phraseology is very reminiscent of Marxian socialism, Weaver waged a vigorous campaign. When the votes were counted the Populists had a total of 1,041,577, compared to approximately 5,000,000 each for Cleveland and Harrison. As was to be expected, most of this support came from the South and West. From every viewpoint the campaign was a success. A million votes was a tremendously encouraging start for a new party.

CAMPAIGN OF 1896

As has so often happened, the new party had the ground cut from under its feet by the adoption of much of its program by one of its larger rivals. When the Democratic convention met in 1896 a considerable element favored the Populist views, and many of the ideas were inserted in the platform in an effort to draw the million Populist votes. The greatest fight of the convention was over the Populist demand for the free coinage of silver. Here the Democrats seemed hopelessly split. The western members favored the measure while the eastern members opposed. The resulting debate was long and heated. Unity was desirable, but at the same time free silver was necessary to draw Populist support.

It was at this dramatic moment that the stage of national politics received a new actor — William Jennings Bryan, a young lawyer from Nebraska. The " boy orator of the Platte " delivered the closing speech in the debate upon the platform, and ended it with the most famous utterance of his career: " We care not upon what lines the battle is fought. If they say bimetallism is good, but that we cannot have it until other nations help us, we reply that, instead of having a gold standard because England has, we will restore bimetallism, and then let England have bimetallism because the United States has it. If they dare to come out in the open field and defend the gold standard as a good thing we will fight them to the uttermost. Having behind us the producing masses of this nation and the world, supported by the commercial interests, and the toilers everywhere, we will answer their demand for a gold standard by saying to them: You shall not press down upon the brow of labor this crown of thorns, you shall not crucify mankind upon a cross of gold."

At the conclusion of the " cross of gold " speech pandemonium broke loose. Everywhere there was wild enthusiasm. Men stood on chairs, stamped, waved, whistled, and shouted. The silver plank and the entire platform was adopted with a rush, and Bryan himself was nominated for the Presidency. Incidentally the Bryan speech killed the Populist party, for its chief appeal was gone. The only possible thing it could do was to support Bryan.

The campaign of '96 was a spirited contest, during which Bryan performed prodigious feats in the miles traveled, the number of speeches made, and the hands shaken. McKinley remained more dignified, conducting his side of the campaign from his own porch at Canton, Ohio. For some unascertained reason " the producing masses of this nation," to say nothing of the world, failed to see that their hope of economic salvation lay in the Democratic party. Great numbers of them voted for the many minor parties in the field or for McKinley, who won easily.

As prosperity returned Populism disappeared, and the demand for free coinage of silver passed to the limbo of forgotten things. When Bryan ran for the Presidency twice later he still believed in free silver, but he listened to councils of discretion and placed a continually decreasing emphasis on this issue, not even mentioning it in 1908.

JAMES BAIRD WEAVER

The political movements furthered by the West during the late nineteenth century overlapped and dovetailed. Underlying all of them were several main desires — for greater political democracy, for control of large aggregations of wealth, and for more plentiful and hence cheaper currency. Specific party names and programs might fluctuate, but the core of ideas remained the same. All of which meant that the same people might graduate from one party to the next and find the same leaders, who had been carried along with the tide. No single man illustrated this constant shifting and overlapping better than James Baird Weaver, who twice ran for the Presidency, and each time under a different party banner.

James Baird Weaver came of a typical family which had followed the push of the frontier to the West. When James was born in 1833 the family resided at Dayton, Ohio; in 1835 it moved to Michigan, and in 1842 to Iowa. A brother went to California in 1849. James also wanted to go to the Far West, and finally obtained his parents' consent in 1853; he did not like it, and soon returned. He then took up the study of law, graduating from the Cincinnati Law School in 1856.

Weaver's first political allegiance was Democratic — which was not conducive to a happy state of existence in Iowa before the Civil War. By diligent reading of the New York *Tribune* and *Uncle Tom's Cabin* he was converted to Free Soil principles in 1857. Next he fell in with the new Republican party, making speeches for it throughout the state. During the war he served in the army, and when he returned to Iowa he continued as a Republican, thus remaining loyal to one set of political principles for an unusually long period.

Then along came the Greenbackers, so in 1877 Weaver joined the new party. An increased personal following was shown by his election to Congress in 1879. He was nominated for the Presidency as a Greenbacker in 1880, and made an impressive campaign of 100 days, in which he delivered over a hundred speeches. He traveled 20,000 miles, shook hands with 30,000, and addressed a total of 500,000 people. Apparently he did not convince everyone to whom he talked, for his total vote was only 308,578. After the election he returned to Iowa, was elected to the House of Representatives, and spent most of the '80s in Congress as a Greenbacker.

When a new movement, with new powers of attraction, came to the front about 1890, Weaver became a Populist. In 1892 he was nominated at Omaha for the Presidency, and again made an extensive tour of the country. This time he received 1,027,329 votes, which was a decided improvement; if he could only have run often enough. In 1896 he supported Bryan and a fusion with the Democrats. From that time until his death in 1912 he remained a staunch Democrat. His record typified that of many of his associates and contemporaries.

WESTERN POLITICAL INFLUENCE

Western political influence did not stop with the Populist movement. Such democratic measures as woman suffrage, direct primary, direct election of Senators, the initiative, referendum, and recall made better progress in the West than in the East. As expressed by Theodore Roosevelt in his " progressive " movement of 1912 they received much western support. Moreover the Wilson nomination of 1912 depended in part on the influence of a westerner, William Jennings Bryan, and the West was an influential factor in the elections of 1912 and 1916. The National Non-Partisan League (formed in 1915) was western, while the La Follette campaign of 1924 looked largely toward western support. Other illustrations merely reinforce the obvious statement of western influence in national elections.

More important in the long run to the West than its influence on national elections has been its importance in Congress. Due to the Constitutional provision that each state shall have two Senators, the less populated agricultural states have always had important voices in the Senate, and these voices have been heard loudly in favor of the farmers. Even during the " business man government " of the 1920s the farm bloc was able to obtain concessions, while with the coming of the New Deal its power was vastly increased. The AAA, with its preference for single-crop farmers, has been one of the results of this political power.

To speak of the political power of the farmer as being a manifestation of the West is technically correct, but at the same time misleading, for it implies strong frontier connections with the measures supported. The result is to think of Illinois as a frontier state in the 1870s because it had an influential granger movement. In no reasonable sense were many of the granger states of the '70s frontier states. The mere fact that they had many railroads to regulate would preclude that possibility. Equally difficult is the picture of the Wisconsin of Robert La Follette as a frontier state or of William Jennings Bryan as a later Daniel Boone.

The proper statement about western political sentiment seems to be that it has been and still is the sentiment of an area that is primarily agricultural. The important fact is that the major economic group is that of the farmer and not that the region is geographically western. Large sections of the South and certain portions of the Northeast will also support an agricultural program. A typically western complexion comes from the fact that the Middle West includes many states that are heavily agricultural, while the South had forfeited much national influence by being too closely associated with one political party.

In only one sense have western reform movements of the past three-quarters of a century had a frontier interpretation. The frontier was composed predominantly of farmers who believed in political democracy and hence their desires were similar in many respects to those of farmers any place and any time. Quite possibly the fairest point of view would be to consider the frontier farmer as one specialized case of the universal farmer. But the caboose does not push the train. Rather, any farmer is confronted with certain conditions that almost inevitably produce certain responses. The important fact is that farmers occupied the frontier and not that a few farmers were at one time frontiersmen.

READINGS

W. J. Bryan, *The First Battle* (1896); S. J. Buck, *The Agrarian Crusade* (1920), *The Granger Movement* (1913)—the classic account; C. J. Bullock, *Essays on the Monetary History of the United States* (1900), part 1, chs. 7, 8; C. McA. Destler, *American Radicalism, 1865–1901* (1946); W. W. Folwell, *A History of Minnesota* (4 vols., 1921), vol. 3, ch. 2; F. E. Haynes, *James Baird Weaver* (1919), *Third Party Movements Since the Civil*

War (1916); A. B. Hepburn, *A History of the Currency* (1915), chs. 12–21; J. D. Hicks, *The Populist Revolt* (1931)—excellent; J. Moody, *The Railroad Builders* (1919), ch. 12; R. B. Nye, *Midwestern Progressive Politics* (1951), chs. 1–3; R. E. Riegel, *The Story of the Western Railroads* (1926), ch. 9; T. Saloutos and J. D. Hicks, *Agricultural Discontent in the Middle West* (1951), chs. 1, 2; F. A. Shannon, *The Farmer's Last Frontier* (1945), chs. 13, 14.

CHAPTER 40

THE WEST
IS FICTIONALIZED

THE West has furnished a tremendous store of material for the men and women who earn their bread and butter by writing. That western plots and incidents should be used in novels, plays, and paintings is not remarkable. The really remarkable circumstance was that frontier themes should appear so late and then in such small variety and with such a paucity of imagination.

The one frontier theme which appealed to the writers of the early nineteenth century was the conflict between the Indian and the white. Here obviously was high adventure. The Indian might be pictured as anything from a cruel and bloodthirsty savage who held back the progress of civilization to a brave, noble, and virtuous primitive man who fought against overwhelming odds to protect his family and friends. Here and there a novelist saw interesting material in other frontier topics such as banditry, but practically none saw opportunity in the ordinary struggle of the farmer to subdue the wilderness. Conflict between men seemed exciting, but conflict between man and nature seemed dull unless it involved great feats of exploration.

Early American novels were copied in both contents and style from European models. Not until the frontier was well past the Appalachians did frontier stories make an appearance. A frontier at your own backdoor was visibly dirty, uncouth, vermin-ridden, and dominated by dull and back-breaking labor. A frontier became romantic and colorful only in the hazy distance where unsavory and often disgusting details were obscured or even completely invisible. The hardships appeared no longer as only unpleasant experiences but rather as obstacles to be overcome by brave men and

616

women. Day-by-day monotony was forgotten. What emerged was the picturesque incident, the heroic episode.

By the time the frontier attained the Great Plains there existed east of the Mississippi a large book-buying public to whom the West was remote, colorful, and exciting. To the average eastern factory worker or farmer the West had become a magic word with which to conjure alluring pictures of an open, wind-swept plain over which roamed bold and romantic riders. With the background of a daily round of farm chores or of tending a machine, the West appeared a land of freedom, where a man was his own master, bold and self-reliant, meeting human and physical hazards with heroic bravery.

And in truth the Far West had certain elements of color that the more eastern frontier had possessed only to a lesser degree. The 2000-mile trek of covered wagons inspired the imagination more than did the floating of flatboats down the Ohio. The mad rush to gold fields hundreds of miles from civilization was clearly more spectacular than the exploitation of the Georgia gold deposits or of the lead country of Illinois and Wisconsin. Custer and Chief Joseph seemed more exciting than had Harrison and Tecumseh. The cowboy had had no eastern peer. The Pony Express and the Overland Stage cast the traffic of the National Road into the shade, while the construction of the Union Pacific outclassed the building of the Ohio Canal in its appeal to American imagination.

POST-CIVIL WAR AUTHORS

A romantic West was particularly attractive to the authors of the generation after the Civil War, since the current literary trend was to exploit the local color of special sections of the country. Naturally there appeared men who saw opportunity in frontier short stories and novels. Ordinarily such writers were natives of the regions they described, but there were few cases in which the writers had been associated with frontier conditions personally. Typical of the group were Edward Eggleston and George Washington Cable. Eggleston wrote sketches of pioneer life in southern Indiana. His best known book *The Hoosier Schoolmaster* is not great literature, but it is an attractive account of small-town life in pioneer Indiana. Cable wrote quaint and charming accounts of early New Orleans and of other parts of Louisiana. Such books as *Old Creole Days* still retain a piquant charm that keeps them a living part of American literature.

Standing head and shoulders above all other men who wrote about the West in the generation after the Civil War was Samuel L. Clemens, better know by his pen name of Mark Twain. Not only was Clemens foremost in his own generation, but his fame seems to have become permanent. By many people he is included among the literary great of all time.

As a boy Clemens lived in a small Missouri town on the Mississippi and was steeped in the life and traditions of the river, while as a young man he worked for some years as a pilot. The pen name which he adopted was a call of the man who used the lead to plumb the depth of the river. Clemens' first experience with the Far West came when he accompanied his brother to Nevada in 1862. Engaging both there and elsewhere in newspaper work he attained national reputation with his jumping frog story, which was probably a revision of similar stories published earlier by others. Journalistic success brought requests to do lecturing, at which Clemens was effective, so that soon he had acquired international reputation as author and speaker. Clemens' angular body and eccentric habits soon became an American landmark, and more so after his red hair had changed to a beautiful thatch of white. Even his innate pessimism did him no harm, which was somewhat surprising in view of the childish optimism of the American public.

Clemens' one book on the Far West was *Roughing It* (1872), which was concerned largely with the mining boom in Nevada. Its humor was typically American and typically western, depending largely on exaggeration and unusual juxtapositions. Such incidents as the author's dinner with Brigham Young and his family, and the effort of a rough miner to persuade a recent theological school graduate to preach the obsequies of a pal, are in the best Twain tradition, and remain as funny today as when they were written. If allowance is made for exaggeration, *Roughing It* is a fine description of mining life in Nevada during the 1860s.

The major claim of Samuel Clemens to literary immortality rests on his charming descriptions of the life of a small boy along the Mississippi. The series started with *Tom Sawyer* (1876) and ended with *The Tragedy of Pudd'nhead Wilson* (1894). Here in Clemens' inimitable style is the true flavor of the river imbedded in a delicate, penetrating analysis of boyhood life. Charming when they were published, and with equally vital life today, they have not seriously been challenged in their own field. Long after such a serious work as *The Gilded Age* is forgotten, Tom Sawyer and

Huckleberry Finn will remain vitally and lovably alive for all Americans.

Ranking well behind Mark Twain, but at the same time with a considerable claim to fame, comes Bret Harte. Harte was born and educated in the East, where he was something of an infant prodigy with a yearning toward writing. His father died when Bret was nine, and in time his mother journeyed to California to re-marry, taking her family along. On the coast, Harte tried various jobs, but gravitated toward journalism, attaining something of a local reputation. In 1868 he became editor of the *Overland Monthly,* in which appeared some of his best stories such as " The Luck of Roaring Camp " and " The Outcasts of Poker Flat."

Growing fame drew Harte to the East in 1871, where he was re-ceived with enthusiasm; the *Atlantic Monthly* offered him $10,000 for anything he might produce within a year. Unfortunately, suc-cess affected Harte very badly. His work declined both in quantity and quality. Ultimately he moved to England, where in time he became little more than a hack writer, living in poverty. His death in 1902 came as a shock to most Americans because his productive period was so far in the past that they had thought him long dead.

Harte's fame rests on his short stories of the West, which are masterpieces of artful craftsmanship, the results of years of pains-taking experimentation. Typically they deal with human paradoxes — the self-sacrificing gambler, the crude miner with the soul of a child, the prostitute who is filled with mother love. Equally in-evitable, the climax comes in some curious twist of fate. For some readers, these stories are exaggerated and artificial. For others they represent a peak in the art of short story writing. Their permanent place in literature remains to be fixed.

DIME NOVELS

Artistic literary descriptions of the West found a good American market, but the real bonanza remained to be exploited by the west-ern thriller. Increasing masses of people were now being taught to read but the majority of them were not thrilled by the *Atlantic Monthly* nor were they sufficiently rich to be able to afford a cloth-bound volume that might cost two days' pay. For them a cheaper and more sensational type of writing was desirable. The man first to exploit this profitable possibility as it related to the West was Edward Zane Carroll Judson, who wrote under the pen name of Ned Buntline.

Judson wrote from the background of a personal experience that was both varied and exciting. He had served as a common sailor, he had been a soldier in the Seminole War, he had traveled up the Yellowstone for a fur company, he had fought and been imprisoned in the Civil War, he had lectured extensively on temperance — on delirium tremens that he had known. Just prior to the Civil War he had written for the New York *Mercury,* a four-penny thriller, and had established his weekly *Ned Buntline's Own.* In both these sheets he had exploited " thrilling " material, particularly that related to the West. While in prison during the war he had used his spare moments to write three blood-and-thunder novels. All of these activities failed to make Judson wealthy, but they demonstrated the existence of a wide market for rapid action stories, and especially for those of the West.

The man who profited by the Judson idea was Erastus Beadle, proprietor of America's most famous series of " dime novels." Rather surprisingly the first of the series (1860) was from the pen of Mrs. Ann S. Stephens, a well-known editor and a novelist of some reputation. She called her book *Malaeska, the Indian Wife of the White Hunter.* Laid along the Hudson in the early days of Dutch settlement it was the pathetic story of the disastrous effects of an Indian-white marriage. Ultimately the son of the marriage commits suicide, while his bride-to-be remains in lifetime celibacy and Malaeska herself fades away to a lonely grave. In spite of the sadness of the novel it had a notable sale of some 65,000 copies. The way was opened for later books of the series.

During and immediately after the Civil War Beadle disposed of his dime, half dime, and quarter series literally by the million. They were more truly a gold mine than anything that had been discovered in the West. The type of books which they contained is indicated but feebly by a few of the titles — *Carson the Guide, California Joe, Arizona Joe, Bigfoot Wallace, The King of the Lariat, Deadly Eye and the Prairie Rover.* In the main they were written, or at least signed, by men who could claim competence in the subjects which they handled. Among the authors were such well-known westerners as W. F. Cody, Captain " Bruin " Adams, Major St. Vrain and Captain Jack Crawford.

The Beadle novels were read by soldiers in the army, small boys in the woodshed, and by everyone else who was in search of a vicarious thrill. In general they were considered somewhat immoral and reprehensible — at least for others to read. Parents used a hickory stick or the flat of the hand to persuade their progeny of the error of their ways. As a matter of fact they were not at all immoral, if that term is used in any ordinary sense. Rather they were violently and blatantly self-righteous. No expressions occurred which might shock even the most modest or prudish. The hero was always everything that a hero should be, and the unbelievably bad villain was always confounded in the end. The vogue of the Beadle novels gradually declined during the '90s, and the last one was published in 1897. The later ones dealt less frequently with the West, and were more likely to describe the exploits of detectives and train robbers.

The place of the Beadle novel has been filled in more recent years by the western story magazine. Purely at random may be taken such titles as *Frontier Stories, West, Pioneer Tales, Western Story Magazine,* and *Cowboy Stories.* In recent years there have been literally hundreds of them, and they have vied with the " art " and " movie " magazines for popular favor. Interestingly enough they have sold extremely well in such industrial regions as New England. If their publishers are to be believed, a considerable share of their readers are not virile, red-blooded " he-men," but members of the opposite sex.

The western story magazine is devoted exclusively to tales of rapid action, with a little sex interest to add spice to the story. Guns spit fire and redskins drop. Bloodstained fists crunch against yielding flesh. Wild rides through storm and danger bring rescue just in time. Desperate bands of cattle thieves are defeated by the forces of right in the last paragraph. The hero is brave, keen, farsighted, strong, and loyal. The villain is black-hearted, mean, cruel, and entirely despicable. The heroine is brave, beautiful, pure, and strong, but entirely feminine. Wickedness is always crushed in the last moment, right is triumphant, and the hero and heroine fall into each other's arms to live happily ever after. No wicked sex tangles or marital problems mar the pure and simple heroicism of these tales.

WESTERN PLAYS

In addition to the literary expression which has been given the West, it also has received dramatic interpretation. Here again the real story in its relation to the present begins with the versatile E. Z. C. Judson, whose interests included the drama. A play," Buffalo Bill, the King of the Border Men," which was founded on a

Judson story, was produced successfully in New York in 1872. While it was playing it was visited by no less a person than Buffalo Bill himself. Cody had a touch of childish naïveté, a love of admiration, and a keen sense of the dramatic, so he found the play immensely pleasing. He was persuaded to go upon the stage and be introduced to the audience, which received him with a great ovation. The result was that Buffalo Bill was violently attracted to stage life and wanted to be an actor.

Judson realized the financial advantages which would result from personal appearances of Buffalo Bill and other noted plains characters, and so he quickly utilized Cody's aspirations. It is said that he wrote the entire manuscript of " The Scout of the Plains " at Chicago in one evening, and that story seems by no means unlikely considering the nature of the play and Judson's facility with the pen. The cast of characters included Buffalo Bill, Texas Jack Omohundro, and a group of " Indians " gathered from the streets of Chicago. If the personnel was any criterion the play was to be truly western in tone.

Within a year " The Scout of the Plains " was revised as " Scouts of the Plains," Buffalo Bill acquired a stage presence, Wild Bill Hickok was added to the cast, Judson was dropped, and New York crowds were receiving the presentation enthusiastically. Indians were killed wholesale, and the heroes and beautiful heroine were rescued from all kinds of terrifying situations. Wild Bill's opening speech, as he galloped on the stage shooting a few Indians, ran: " Fear not, fair maid; by heavens, you are safe at last with Wild Bill, who is ever ready to risk his life and die if need be in defense of weak and helpless womanhood." In addition to certain fairly obvious flaws in the realism of this form of address, it should be noted that the speech represented the beginning of the play and not the final dramatic incident.

Buffalo Bill thoroughly enjoyed his work on the stage, since he liked the footlights, the posing, and the applause. Wild Bill Hickok, on the other hand, longed for the West. Many stories are told of how he failed to appear various times and how he shot out the spotlight. Within a short time he left the show and drifted to Deadwood, where he met his death.

This early effort to put the Far West before the public in dramatic form had at least two immediate and important results. The first was the opening of a real dramatic field, which probably reached its highest point in " The Girl of the Golden West," but this phase of the story will have to be omitted. The other was the development of the picturesque Wild West show, with which the name of Buffalo Bill is so inextricably linked.

WILD WEST SHOW

The meteoric rise of Buffalo Bill to national prominence was due primarily to the work of his devoted friend and press agent Major John M. Burke, and secondarily to the writings of that dime novel expert Prentiss Ingraham. Between these two men Buffalo Bill was made one of the best known men of the world. The idea of the Wild West show probably did not originate with Cody. P. T. Barnum had a similar idea as early as 1860. The immediate formation of the show was due in large part to the enthusiasm of the actor Nate Salsbury, who later became Cody's partner. After the dramatic season of 1882–83 Cody went back to the plains and gathered large numbers of cowboys, Indians, ponies, buffalo, and other paraphernalia of the West. With this equipment he opened his first outdoor show at the Omaha fair grounds on May 17, 1883, calling it " The Wild West, Rocky Mountain and Prairie Exhibition." For a time the show was in perpetual danger of financial failure, largely because Cody was always a much better showman than business manager. Salsbury furnished most of the funds and financial judgment. Cody was frequently drunk in the early years, was lavish with relatives and old friends, and embarked on numerous outside, and expensive, ventures. No matter how much the show paid, Cody was always in debt.

After 1885 Buffalo Bill's Wild West show was secure as a brilliant success. It played in England in 1887, which was the year of Queen Victoria's Jubilee, and made an instantaneous hit. Two command performances were given for the Queen. Other royalty attended. The Prince of Wales rode on the Deadwood stage, and Buffalo Bill was presented to the Queen. For the time the Wild West was the fashion in England. Two years later the show toured the continent, and again was acclaimed. In 1893 Buffalo Bill set up his show opposite the main entrance of the Chicago Fair and rivaled the fair itself in drawing power.

A good share of the Wild West show's attractiveness lay in the fact that it exploited for the first time a new and fresh phase of American life. At first it was purely western, with pony races, Indian dances and battles, bucking bronchos, steer roping, the pony express, and the attack on the Deadwood stage; the stress was on riding and shooting. By the early '90s it had become a " Congress of Rough Riders of the World " and included Indians, cowboys, Mexicans, German Uhlans, French chasseurs, British lancers, American cavalrymen, Cossacks, Gauchos, and Arabs. By the late '90s it had added the regular circus side-show attractions — snake charmers, sword swallowers, midgets, giants, mind readers, magicians, fire eaters, jugglers, and the rest. In 1908 it was combined with " Pawnee Bill's Far East," and shortly thereafter became less profitable ; the last good season was 1910. Buffalo Bill lost everything in bad investments and was poverty stricken when he died in 1917.

One of Buffalo Bill's chief drawing cards was the exhibition of wonderful shooting, both by himself and others. His own most admired shooting was from horseback. His protégé, Johnny Baker, was a boy prodigy. Best known and most admired, however, was Annie Oakley. In reality Annie was not herself a westerner, having been born and raised in Ohio, when the frontier had long passed that region. Dressed in a buckskin suit, however, she was able to pass as the real article. Personally she was a fine, modest woman, well-liked by the other performers. Her death occurred as recently as 1926. The reputation of Annie Oakley was so widespread that a punched ticket became known popularly as an " Annie Oakley " because of its similarity to the appearance of a card at which the lady herself had shot.

In spite of Buffalo Bill's excessive use of liquor, his lack of business judgment, and his exaggerated reputation based largely on press agent publicity, he remained an outstanding and picturesque figure. Anyone who was born too late to see Buffalo Bill ride his white charger at the head of the procession, with his dramatic movements and great shock of snowy white hair, has missed one of the great thrills that should be in the life of every child. Always somewhere in the program was the exciting Indian attack upon the Deadwood stage. As Buffalo Bill grew older his marksmanship declined, but even in the last of his " farewell tours " he was as impressive and picturesque as ever.

MOVING PICTURES

The year 1910 saw the arrival of a new dramatic possibility in the moving picture. It was in this year that Goldberg made his magic lantern slides of Buffalo Bill, that Powers took his moving pictures of Buffalo Bill and that the Essanay Company started its weekly Saturday one-reel releases of " Broncho Billy." As the motion picture developed it carried the western story along in its progress, until such great spectacles were produced as " The Toll of the Desert," " The Taming of Texas Pete," " The Iron Horse," and " North of 36." Names like those of Tom Mix, William S. Hart, Hoot Gibson, and Harry Carey became known to every small boy in the country — to say nothing of his parents. The western movie has seemingly become a staple amusement in the life of the nation.

Recent moving pictures on the West have included notable efforts at realistic background, as in the building of the Union Pacific or the migration of the Mormons. Others have created a new and idyllic West. Beautiful and well-dressed ranchers' daughters seem to live at every farmhouse; their nails are manicured, their hair curled, and their speech well-chosen. A handsome hero seems to exist for each lovely heroine; the hero is of course good-looking, an excellent horseman, a first-rate shot, careless of personal danger, clever with his fists, and has the cat's proverbial nine lives, for no western hero, as far as the records go, has ever died. The idyllic peace of the beautiful West is marred only by the villain — an evil, ill-favored, sardonic chap, who spends all his time concocting criminal plans for stealing the old ranch or waylaying the hero. No single relieving kindly trait connects the villain and his evil gang with the ordinary everyday world.

The West of the movies is at least fascinating. Each cowboy has a bright and shining gun, which he carries continually and uses on the slightest provocation. Also he always has a favorite horse to which he is passionately devoted. Indians are perpetually giving war dances, preparatory to attacking settlers. A continual series of overwhelming and seemingly inescapable dangers are followed by an equal series of hairbreadth escapes. Right is always triumphant eventually and villainy crushed to earth. And so the younger generation is encouraged to build a beautiful and heroic myth of the West. Rather curiously, parents do not seem to object as strenuously to these vivid dramas as they did to the dime thrillers.

COWBOY LITERATURE

The more lurid types of western magazines and movies had their counterpart in the cloth-backed novels, for around 1900 more and more people were able to afford the books which their fathers had found too expensive. One of the earliest in the field was Emerson

Hough, who in 1895 published his descriptive book *The Story of the Cowboy,* a reasonably interesting picture of certain phases of the cattle business. More typical of Mr. Hough's work was *North of 36* (1923), which cannot be criticized for being dull. Mr. Hough was exceedingly impressed with the heroic nature of the western experience, and viewed with nostalgic sadness the passing of the good old days.

Owen Wister was responsible for one of the better of the western novels of the early twentieth century with *The Virginian* (1902). Mr. Wister was born and reared in the East, graduating from Harvard in 1885. He visited Wyoming for his health, and became so enthusiastic about the western country that he returned several times and talked about it incessantly. Although his business was the practice of law in Philadelphia, he affected loose-tied bow ties, short sleeves, and western stories. In fact he came to feel that he had a mission to bring the West into American literature. In *The Virginian* he describes interestingly life in Wyoming in the late '70s and the '80s. The Virginian himself is a cowboy of somewhat unusual characteristics, but the atmosphere and most of the incidents are admirable.

Other popular writers on western themes have been legion. Most of their work has been ephemeral. As one man passes from the scene another takes his place. Jack London had great popularity for a time with his epic tales of raw passion in the frozen North. Harold Bell Wright depicted western scenes in such books as *When a Man's a Man,* and profited thereby. B. M. Bowers (Bertha M. Sinclair) has contributed the enjoyable Flying U stories, such as *Chip of the Flying U,* while C. E. Mulford has created the unforgettable character of Hop-a-long Cassidy.

Two exceptional men, Andy Adams and Will James, both former cowboys, have recreated the cattle country in a series of semi-autobiographical descriptive books. Adams wrote as he talked, with an inimitable slang and a trick of vivid presentation. His best work is probably the *Log of a Cowboy,* although other volumes are about equally good. Will James has done similar work in his *Cowboys North and South* and *Cow Country,* and his books are illustrated by his own excellent action drawings. Unfortunately the public taste in western literature had become pretty standardized before Adams and James appeared on the scene, which meant that their sales have not been as great as their works merit.

Adams and James belong to the small group of westerners who

grew up in the West of the frontier and managed with a minimum of formal training to produce work which was acceptable in a literary sense. The list which their names head is short. Possibly the California poet Joaquin Miller should be included. More certainly the Montana cowboy painter Charlie Russell deserves a place. With only slight allowance for an absence of formal instruction, the work of Russell can be compared to that of his better known contemporary Frederic Remington.

Undoubtedly the best of all spinners of western yarns — if popularity be granted as a proper test — has been Zane Grey. Mr. Grey was educated as a dentist, receiving his D.D.S. from Pennsylvania in 1896, and then began practice in New York City. His literary labor began in 1904 and found immediate popular favor. In time he became convinced that the public would always recognize and buy a good book with a strong appeal — to wit, his own. His novels, according to a recent commentator, are grim stories of sadists who are supermen, and of strongly sexed, but virginal women. The reading of Zane Grey is an experience which should not be missed. Any book will do, since it is hard to distinguish one from another. A copy is easy to obtain, since in his heyday Mr. Grey was producing about one a year.

REALISM

The West has furnished material for hundreds of books of action and romance, but perhaps more important to the literary historian have been the efforts to depict the farming West with greater accuracy. The great landmark of western realism was E. W. Howe's *The Story of a Country Town* (1883) which describes the less pleasant aspects of life in a small town in the wheat country of Kansas. Four years later Joseph Kirkland, the son of Caroline Kirkland, published his *Zury,* which did a similar job for frontier Illinois.

Howe and Kirkland started a trend, but the popularizer was Hamlin Garland, who was born (1860) and reared in the upper Mississippi Valley at a time when that area was not far removed from frontier conditions. Garland worked long and hard as a farm boy and succeeded in obtaining an education only in the face of severe handicaps. Little wonder that in time he became active in the Populist movement. A radical and introspective young man with literary aspirations naturally evolved a philosophy of life to apply to his writing. In his own words, he developed " two great literary concepts — that truth was a higher quality than beauty, and that to spread the reign of justice should everywhere be the design and intent of the artist."

Garland's first book was *Main Traveled Roads* (1891), but his best known works have been the various semi-autobiographical *Middle Border* books which tell of the pioneering of his own family. Garland tells here of the dirt and vermin and fleas, of the monotonous and back-breaking drudgery, of the drabness and meanness of western life, but he also tells of hilarious parties, of gorgeous sunrises, and of the smell of sizzling sausage on a cold morning. Because of these latter more pleasant incidents, certain literary highbrows profess to feel that he was really a romantic at heart.

Garland expressed a point of view which was important, but he did not himself exemplify that point of view in his fiction. Thin love stories like *The Spirit of the Sweetwater* and *Her Mountain Lover* were anything but realistic, and yet Garland's influence was important. He recognized the literary and dramatic values of a fight for existence by the frontier farmer, as he pitted his brain and brawn and his endurance against the forces of a reluctant nature. Moreover he influenced and assisted young writers such as Stephen Crane and Frank Norris. Crane was not concerned with western themes, but Norris was.

Frank Norris was more versatile than Hamlin Garland, but less intimately associated with the West, even though part of his education was obtained at the University of California. Just before his death he was engaged in writing what was to be a trilogy on wheat. *The Octopus* (1901) presented the conflict between the California growers and the railroad. *The Pit* (1903) was the story of the Chicago grain exchange. *The Wolf*, never written, was expected to use the wheat to stop a European famine. Of the two published volumes, *The Pit* had the better sale because of its dominant love story, but for this very reason accomplished Norris' objectives less well than did *The Octopus*, which depicted the growing and shipping of wheat on such a large canvas that the individual characters were dwarfed by the immensity and power of the inanimate grain.

After 1900 there was a notable increase in the novelists who tried with greater or less success to use western themes with attention not only to accuracy of detail but to the larger truths. Among the better productions may be mentioned Herbert Quick, *Vande-*

mark's Folly; Mari Sandoz, *Old Jules*; Willa Cather, *My Ántonia*; A. B. Guthrie, *The Big Sky*; H. L. Davis, *Honey in the Horn*; V. Fisher, *City of Illusion*; W. V. Clark, *The Ox-Bow Incident*. Certainly high on any list of realistic novelists should be the Norwegian born O. E. Rolvaag. His first and best novel *Giants in the Earth* (1927) has for its main character and central theme the prairies, which dominated the lives of Per Hansa, his wife Beret, and their children. When the prairies smiled, life was happy and prodigal. When the locusts came or the snow descended, the prairies became malevolent, seeking whom they could destroy. The book ends as Per Hansa, traveling in the middle of winter to get a minister for a dying man, loses his way in the snow and freezes to death. The last chapter is titled: "The Great Plains Drinks the Blood of Christian Men and Is Satisfied."

A slightly different type of work should be noted in passing, largely because of its unusual character. John G. Neihardt has picked the 1820s for his epic of the plains and the Indian wars. A trilogy of three long poems, *The Song of Hugh Glass* (1915), *The Song of Three Friends* (1919), and *The Song of the Indian Wars* (1925) is based on detailed and accurate research. Mr. Neihardt has not disdained prose, and his *The Splendid Wayfaring* (1920) has a lyric swing which makes it not inferior to the poetry. The last-named book is an account of the travels of Jedediah Smith.

The widening use of authentic western material by the novelists is a happy augury for the future. And yet the subject matter as yet unutilized is tremendous. Material concerning mining, land speculation, cattle raising, and other occupations of the West is as yet largely unexplored. Greatest enthusiasm has been shown for semi-fictionalized and heroic sagas of such heroes as Daniel Boone and Davy Crockett, whether in novels or on radio or television. Certainly there still remains an almost inexhaustible supply of the necessary raw material for whatever kind of tale the writer desires, from blood-and-thunder action stories to subtle analyses of human emotions. And equally certainly the most distinctive of American experiences deserves a greater number of honest and penetrating treatments than have as yet been accorded it.

READINGS

R. F. Adams and H. E. Britzman, *Charles M. Russell* (1948)— beautiful job; R. G. Athearn, *Westward the Briton* (1953), ch.

1- interesting on British travelers; P. H. Boynton, *The Redis-covery of the Frontier* (1931)—literature; E. D. Branch, *The Cowboy and His Interpreters* (1926), chs. 11–16; T. D. Clark, *The Rampaging Frontier* (1939)—humor; C. R. Cooper, *Annie Oakley* (1927); L. J. Davidson and F. Blake (eds.), *Rocky Mountain Tales* (1947); B. De Voto, *Mark Twain's America* (1935); D. A. Dondore, *The Prairie and the Making of Middle America* (1926), pp. 305–344, chs. 7, 8—scholarly; D. Emrich, *It's An Old Western Custom* (1949); C. J. Finger, *Frontier Ballads* (1927); J. T. Flanagan (ed.), *America Is West* (1945)—anthology; W. S. Hart, *My Life East and West* (1929)—movies; W. Havighurst, *Annie Oakley* (1954); L. L. Hazard, *The Frontier in American Literature* (1927), pp. 126–137, ch. 5—scholarly; I. H. Herron, *The Small Town in American Literature* (1939), chs. 6, 8; J. A. Lomax, *Cowboy Songs* (1924), *Songs of the Cattle Trail and Cow Camp* (1920); E. M. Mack, *Mark Twain in Nevada* (1947); J. R. Masterson, *Tall Tales of Arkansaw* (1943); J. Monaghan, *The Overland Trail* (1947), ch. 16—Mark Twain; E. Pearson, *Dime Novels* (1929); F. E. Pond, *Life & Adventures of "Ned Bunt-line"* (1919); C. Rourke, *Trouper of the Gold Coast* (1928)— Lotta Crabtree; R. E. Spiller and others, *Literary History of the United States* (3 vols., 1948), vol. 2, ch. 53; G. R. Stewart, Jr., *Bret Harte* (1931); E. Wagenknecht, *Mark Twain* (1935); F. Walker, *San Francisco Literary Frontier* (1939); R. J. Walsh, *The Making of Buffalo Bill* (1928), chs. 14–28; see also the works of the authors mentioned in the chapter.

CHAPTER 41

THE HISTORIAN DISCOVERS THE WEST

HISTORIANS are a conservative species. Not until the frontier had disappeared did they accord it recognition as an important factor in American life. Quite typically, the epochal volumes of George Bancroft were concerned with the West only in connection with such notable legislation as the Northwest Ordinance. Francis Parkman wrote of the West, but only as the scene of the struggle of rival European empires. Our first important graduate school, that of Johns Hopkins University, was overwhelmingly concerned with the Germanic origins of Anglo-Saxon political institutions.

The lack of interest in the West merely illustrates the obvious fact that historians, like other men, are influenced by their environment. Early historical writers were almost entirely eastern in birth and training, with more connections east of the Atlantic than west of the Appalachians. They were more conversant with Charlemagne than with Lewis and Clark. They wrote in praise of a democratic government and a free people from the point of view of their own section. For the majority of them New England was the most important part of the country and Boston the hub of American culture. In consequence they neglected the middle states, the southern states, and the West.

EARLY INTEREST IN WESTERN HISTORY

But historians over the course of the years did not remain exclusively New Englanders, nor even entirely easterners. Other sections produced competent workmen with their own local interests and pride. In time these backlanders were to express their basic interests and loyalties and thereby to broaden immensely the scope of written American history. Their break with the past came slowly, however, because professional education in graduate school continued to be dominated by the older traditions. Only within comparatively recent years have earnest and able students felt that they could get their entire training in the schools of the Middle or Far West and still be able to look their eastern contemporaries in the eye without cringing.

Not to be ignored in the expansion of the concepts of American history was the work of an ever increasing horde of local historical societies devoted to preserving and publishing the histories of their particular localities. Every county, city, or state takes pride in its own past — a pride which is attested by the sale of thousands of volumes of local history, with their subsidized pictures and sketches of prominent residents. Such local historical societies increased rapidly in number from about the middle of the nineteenth century, so that some two hundred were in existence when the American Historical Association was formed in 1884. Of them, the state societies were most important, since they collected avidly the raw material for the historian, often provided mediums of publication, and always pushed local history enthusiastically. For each state the period of frontier origins was of first interest, and for the Far West that period was so close that original material was comparatively easy to obtain.

The beginnings of a new trend in the writing of history became visible during the 1880s, and especially with the work of H. H. Bancroft and of Theodore Roosevelt. H. H. Bancroft was one of America's most diligent collectors, scouring the Far West to acquire thousands of letters, diaries, and other documents that probably would otherwise have disappeared. In this work he was doing privately what Lyman Draper was doing for the Wisconsin Historical Society. Between 1874 and 1890 Bancroft signed his name to some forty volumes of Far Western history, while his documentary collections in time furnished a seemingly inexhaustible source for later publications. H. H. Bancroft was primarily a regional historian. He made little effort to relate the West to the rest of the nation or to find the basic significances of the western experience.

Of greater national popularity than Bancroft's rather dull writings were the volumes of Theodore Roosevelt, which were published between 1889 and 1896 under the title *The Winning of the West*. Roosevelt had gone West in 1884 to avoid the unpleasant necessity of supporting Blaine in the Presidential campaign of that year. He was fascinated by western life and in time produced several books about it. *The Winning of the West* was concerned with the early trans-Appalachian frontier, and was confined largely to the description of such dramatic incidents as Indian fights and the Revolution. While Roosevelt contributed largely to an interest in western history he was little concerned with the peculiar contributions of the West, if any, to national culture, and of course he described only a single frontier, limited in both time and space.

FREDERICK JACKSON TURNER

The real beginning of the modern history of the West came with the reading of a short paper by Frederick Jackson Turner in 1893 at a small meeting of historians convening at the World's Columbian Exposition in Chicago. The very descriptive title was " The Significance of the Frontier in American History." Not by accident did Turner hail from Wisconsin, where the files of the Wisconsin Historical Society, as collected by Lyman Draper and Reuben Gold Thwaites, were the best in the West. Turner had found inspiration in the western material around him and in current speculation about population, so that when the census of 1890 showed for the first time no clear population frontier he was ready to indicate what he considered the importance of the frontier in American history.

The influence of Turner grew rapidly, so that within a generation the Turner ideas had become thoroughly embedded, not only in historical writing, but in other fields of research and even in general literature. And yet this effect came as the result of comparatively little writing. Much more it was based on the enthusiastic championship of the Turner concepts by hundreds of students at Wisconsin, and later at Harvard. Above all Turner was a teacher who had the gift of inspiring his students with a deep love both for himself and for the subject he taught. These students in turn carried the torch to all parts of the country and transmitted the Turner theses, even though diluted and modified, to their own students.

Turner's general theories were almost all advanced in his first paper. Later publications restated but did not change the idea significantly. In fact, when the original essay was republished in 1920, Turner saw no reason for changing as much as a footnote in what he had written twenty-seven years earlier. Presumably the ideas which he had first expressed somewhat tentatively had turned out, in his judgment, to be accurate and sufficiently complete.

For Turner " the existence of an area of free land, its continuous recession, and the advance of American settlement westward, explain American development." The influence of the frontier has been the decisive factor in welding an American nation and in making it different from other nations. The seeds of American ideals may have existed in Europe or on the Atlantic seaboard, but without the environment of the frontier they could not have developed into full-blown plants.

The frontier of which Turner spoke began with the Atlantic Coast and ended with the Pacific, but he noted specifically that only " from the time the mountains rose between the pioneer and the seaboard, a new order of Americanism arose." Then for the first time the pioneers were thrown completely on their own resources to develop distinctively western traits. Of the vast area west of the Appalachians, Turner stressed the log-cabin frontier of the Old Northwest, although he by no means omitted other regions completely.

The frontier meant to Turner a region of sparse settlement, " the meeting point between savagery and civilization," although now and then he spoke of the frontier as a line or as a process of change or even as a state of mind. The important attractive power was cheap land, with freedom as a secondary objective. The great conditioning factor was the richness of that land. Comparatively little emphasis was placed on minerals, climate, rainfall, and other material factors.

The process of settlement was almost entirely economic to Turner. Each new region was recapitulating the general growth of society as well as the experiences of former frontiers. First came the hunter and trapper, then the trader, the rancher, the pioneer farmer, the specialized farmer, the manufacturer. The frontier stage ended with the pioneer farmer. Little attention was paid to artistic, educational, and intellectual factors. For example, Turner never spoke of a literary frontier or an educational frontier.

The traits which Turner saw as characteristic of the frontier were democracy, individualism, freedom, coarseness, strength, acuteness, inquisitiveness, materialism, exuberance, laxness of business morals. The West was a region of great individualism — " society became atomic " — even though westerners cooperated effectively for the things they wanted. Westerners were impatient of restraint, even though they developed and were willing to follow strong leadership. Being inquisitive and meeting new conditions they were ingenious innovators in material things and radicals in social and political thought. They were optimistic and nationalistic, believing in the manifest destiny of the American nation.

As to the importance of the West — or of the frontier, since Turner never distinguished the two terms clearly — in the history of the United States, above all it created and established firmly American democracy. By democracy Turner meant not only certain political forms but also a consideration for the rights of the common man, which implied programs of social amelioration. Westerners were fairly equal in wealth and social status, and hence believed in political equality and in programs to assist the average citizen. Democracy came not from the *Mayflower* but " from the forest."

Along with democracy went individualism and freedom of opportunity. The frontier prevented the development of class lines by providing opportunity for the ambitious who felt circumscribed by European or eastern conditions. It was " a safety valve of abundant resources open to him who would take."

Moreover the frontier was the region which effectively took various European stocks and welded them into one nation. The wilderness stripped the European of his customary clothes and habits, and forced him to adopt the garments and the usages of the frontier if he were to survive. In time he became entirely American, which meant not only that he adopted American habits but that he became an ardent patriot.

The frontier for Turner produced an aggressive nationalism as the pioneers dreamed of new frontiers and sought to attain them. It favored more lenient land legislation, internal improvements at federal expense, a protective tariff, all of which meant a loose construction of the Constitution and hence were factors assisting the growth of the power of the federal government. The West was but little interested in European conditions. Quite typically it backed the purchase of Louisiana and the War of 1812, thus indicating the expansionist tendencies in its nationalism.

When Turner said in 1893 that " the frontier is gone," he spoke partly in regret, for instead of the sectional struggles of the past in which the West in general supported true Americanism, he envisaged an increasingly bitter class struggle. And yet he was basically optimistic, for he felt that the frontier ideals as they were retained in the Middle West could be the salvation of the nation. To accomplish this end the individualistic drive must be sacrificed at least in part to uphold the democratic tradition of the rights of the common man as against the power of the large corporations. The great task of the future is to adjust democracy to an industrial nation, and here the Mississippi Valley will be decisive. " The social destiny of this Valley will be the social destiny, and will mark the place in history, of the United States."

CRITICISMS OF TURNER IDEAS

Within recent years the Turner ideas have been subjected to increasing criticism and have also been defended vigorously. The controversy tends at times to become vitriolic, largely because friends and students of Turner are often involved emotionally even more than intellectually. At times the Turner admirers insist that his ideas are above discussion. One recent enthusiastic supporter of eminent professorial dignity has even asserted as to the Turner thesis, that " its soundness . . . must in large measure be gauged by its effect on the men of its generation." This idea of estimating truth on the basis of contemporary agreement is at least novel.

Criticism of the Turner ideas starts frequently with questions as to Turner's use of the term " frontier." At various times he considers it as a line, an area, a process, a state of mind. In his justification it may be said that each statement is moderately clear, but on the other hand the serious investigator would find helpful a more consistent use of the term. Somewhat more confusing is Turner's interchangeable use of " frontier " and " West." While the frontier was always to the west of something or other, anything that can be termed West was not always frontier, and particularly since Turner's West was anything from Plymouth Rock to the Golden Gate.

Turner's concept of the frontier has been challenged as being too limited in time, place, and content to merit any important generalizations. Can general conclusions as to frontier influences be drawn from a single nation? Would the Turner frontier traits be shown in Canada or in Brazil or in Russia, to name only a few frontier countries? Moreover, would a United States frontier be even consistent within itself if it pushed overseas, as to Hawaii? The answer to each of these questions is certainly not an easy " yes."

Turner was preoccupied with the frontier of the pioneer farmer, which meant that he spoke little of the land speculator, the miller, the artisan, the mill owner, and other varied westerners. Likewise he devoted almost no attention to the rise of towns and cities. Even more important he minimized such developments as of the arts, education, amusements. His critics insist that these segments of life are of importance comparable to the growing of hogs and corn, and that no analysis of the frontier which omits them can be valid.

Several modern writers have speculated that the physical frontier was merely one outlet for the ambitious of humankind. An energetic man of 1830 might have migrated to Illinois, but also he might have entered a textile mill at Lawrence, or even experimented with rubber or engaged in the temperance movement. A century later he could not have acquired cheap western land, but he might have entered the airplane industry in California, obtained a job with Standard Oil in Chile, or crusaded for the teaching of more American history in the public schools. Rather fascinating is the game of imagining possible moral equivalents for the physical frontier.

Turner has also encountered criticism for his analysis of the reasons why men went West. When he described the " westward marching army of individualistic liberty-loving democratic backwoodsmen " he has been accused of misemphasis on the ground that the desire for liberty, if it existed, was infinitesimal in comparison to the desire for wealth. Except for the outer fringe of settlement, comprising but few persons, most settlers were merely taking new farms in less settled areas. Essentially they were doing the same kind of work they had left in the East, but under more difficult conditions. Their possible reward for these hardships was more wealth. The freedom to work harder so that prosperity and release from labor would later be possible was certainly not the kind of liberty which Turner had in mind.

Practically no critic has had the temerity to express doubts that the frontier was crude, materialistic, unlettered, exuberant, and lacking in artistic development. But some doubts have been expressed that these and other traits applied exclusively to the frontier. The East was never completely out of sight of the West. Very possibly the western characteristics were only a slightly more primitive reflection of the culture prevailing in the East at any specific period.

The proposition that the West was a great innovator of both material things and of social ideas — a " region of revolt " — has met great opposition. Comparatively few inventions came from the West, even though a list can be compiled which would include notably certain farm machinery, the typewriter, and the solar compass, and almost no novel political, economic, or social ideas. The usual westerner was striving to obtain his fortune so that he might enjoy the good things of life. He had neither time, strength, nor desire for anything strange and new. Social uniformity was as great in the West as in the East, with no remarkable difference in the styles either of politics or of women's clothes. So-called radical desires, as for cheaper money, have long been traditional with agricultural groups and represented no distinctive frontier contributions.

Turner's greatest point that democracy was a product of the forest has been discarded entirely by his critics. They point out that democracy for Turner was a vague term, including at least such diverse elements as the beliefs of Jefferson and Theodore Roosevelt. They insist that the frontier was in many respects not highly democratic — that, for example, until near its end it never gave the suffrage to women, to Indians, to Negroes. Turner himself held that southern expansion was the influence that fixed the slave system securely in the South. Slavery and democracy are not highly compatible bedfellows. The critics are insistent that democracy is an idea of long development, with roots deep in European history and that even such specific devices as woman suffrage were European in origin.

Democracy in the sense of helping the common man, state the critics, was primarily eastern. Whether it was the antislavery movement, missionary enterprise, railroad control, or prison reform, the West copied the East, which in most cases had taken the idea from Europe. From this point of view the West produced no new trends in social reform, in literary endeavors, in religious beliefs. The only way in which the West might be considered radical is that it was enamored of certain political-economic concepts such as the free coinage of silver which seemed desirable to an agricultural population.

Individualism, to the man who views Turner skeptically, was no more western than steamboats. As one writer has said, the West contained many individuals but very little individualism. The average westerner conformed to the general ideas of his time, which included a minimum of social control over private enterprise — a product of the industrial revolution. In fact, the West was quite ready to encourage government interference whenever the government could help — as in the building of canals and railroads, the establishment of banks, the control of railroads. Westerners were close to their governments and had no objection to utilizing them, although their ingenuity in such use was to increase with the years.

Regarding the Americanizing influence of the frontier, several objections have been raised. Comparatively few immigrants went to the raw frontier, which was occupied mainly by American farmers. Turner specifically and correctly repudiates the leap-frog process of settlement in which each frontier was settled by a new group of frontiersmen from the East or from Europe. Once on the frontier, the immigrant was not always Americanized rapidly. German and Scandinavian customs were slow in being displaced. Moreover the frontier did not produce a uniform culture. For example, the Anglo-Saxon and German frontiers were quite different in appearance. Some question is thus raised as to whether the more eastern states did not modify European customs more rapidly than did the West.

The critics do accept the Turner statement that the frontier produced the most vigorous of American expansionist sentiment, but add the corollary that such sentiment was almost entirely continental — stretching no farther than the West Indies. The forces favoring overseas expansion in the '90s and later were very little western, not to say frontier. The Middle West has contributed notably to isolation sentiment during the past half century. Nationalism did not, however, imply necessarily loose construction of the Constitution. True, Clay wanted his American system. But Jackson, at least as good a westerner, opposed the bank and vetoed the Maysville bill. And upon what evidence is the West depicted as giving strong support to a protective tariff?

Possibly the most debated of Turner's points has been the suggestion that the frontier has been a " safety valve of discontent." He made this type of statement several times, but never elaborated it and apparently did not consider it of first-rate importance. His exact meaning is therefore doubtful. As near as can be ascertained he was contending that the opportunities afforded by cheap western land averted severe class conflicts in the United States because the discontented could find outlets for their dissatisfaction and aspirations without trying to overthrow existing institutions. Unhappy easterners became happy westerners, not bitter reformers.

As expanded by other men, this safety-valve concept has come to mean not only that dissatisfied easterners moved west, but that they moved in the periods of their greatest dissatisfaction. The result has been a picture of the westward tide rising during periods of depression and embracing notably unemployed factory workers. In this form, the idea is demonstrably false. The West was settled primarily by farmers moving in times of prosperity.

No reasonable doubt exists that western migrants were predominantly eastern farmers. Detailed studies have been made of specific areas, both urban and rural, at different times. The conclusion is always the same. Farmers and not industrial laborers moved to the frontier. Artisans attracted by western high wages were fewer in number and factory workers were almost entirely missing. An unemployed factory worker on the frontier was a candidate for either charity or starvation.

Even less doubt exists that the westward movement was greatest in prosperous times. Census figures, including special state enumerations, bear out the contention. The dates of the admissions of new states were concentrated toward the ends of periods of prosperity. Land sales reached their peaks just before our various panics, and again the evidence is suggestive, even after making allowances for the difference between settlement and land sales. Finally, all accounts by people who witnessed the migration agree that its peaks came in periods of prosperity, as just before the panics of 1819, 1837, 1857, 1873, and during the good times of the early '80s.

More drastic critics of the safety valve theory insist that there has never been such a safety valve either in short-run or in long-run terms. Such attackers argue that the westward movement could only lessen eastern difficulties if there remained a real labor scarcity in the East and consequently labor prices increased. But migration merely produced a vacuum which attracted immigrants and women. True enough, wages were higher in America than in Europe, but this situation was more the result of American ingenuity and cheap raw materials than of a scarcity of labor. Hence the so-called safety valve was at best no more than a suction pump to attract labor to replace what had moved. Professor Fred A. Shannon has suggested that the real American safety valve has been the city, which has furnished an outlet for rural discontent.

The Turner critics have had an extremely useful function in raising doubts about generalizations that most people were beginning to accept without adequate consideration. Only by questioning and continual testing can progress be made. An idea which cannot bear examination in the light of new facts is of dubious validity. On the other hand, of course, questions may become completely irresponsible, cynical, contentious — producing heat but no light. Criticism may be bad-tempered and bad-intentioned, shaking the foundations of perfectly valid ideas by innuendos and suggestions that have little if any merit.

In the case of the Turner writings, the criticisms are now becoming so widespread that many people are throwing out all that Turner wrote, the good with the bad, the baby with the bath. In some instances the critics would seem to be more interested in supporting the pretensions of their own sections against Turner's Middle West than in finding the truth. All told, there seems to be a trend toward developing the thesis that the frontier had *no* significant influence, which is ridiculous. No one of intelligence can really believe that the conquering of three thousand miles of wilderness did not leave some stamp on American history and on the American character.

CHARACTERISTICS OF THE WEST

The frontier clearly attracted some people and not others. The economically successful easterner seldom moved west. The migrant must have been economically, socially, or emotionally unhappy, and in addition he must have been superior in energy and initiative to break home ties and start a new life in the wilderness. In intelligence he probably represented a cross section of American life, but in aggressiveness he was above average — which implied holdup men as well as solid, substantial, law-abiding citizens. Basically these men and women were choosing between trying their fortunes in the West or in the factories of the growing eastern cities.

The characteristics of the West of the nineteenth century, with which this book has been largely concerned, vary somewhat with time and place. For the outer fringe of the frontier, including explorers, traders, trappers, miners, and the earliest speculators and farmers, the westerners included a high proportion of vigorous young men. Of necessity they were hardy and brave. No others could have survived. They made great contributions in leading the way for permanent occupation, but their influence on the ways of life of the entire United States was small. In consequence, the main significance of the frontier experience must depend on the characteristics of the great body of migrants who occupied the more sparsely settled areas to the east of the outer edge of the frontier.

For the average migrant to the West — and by West is meant the sections of lesser population — life was above all a continuous round of hard work, with a minimum of conveniences. The average man was a farmer fighting against a reluctant nature, and suffering from lack of quantity and variety of food, flood, drought, locusts, vermin of all kinds. Lice and bedbugs were more prevalent than feats of valor. He seldom saw an Indian, although now and then the frontier was ravaged by Indian raids. He seldom performed any heroic exploit, unless washing in ice water could be put in that category. His health was not good, for he was scourged by ague, malaria, typhoid, and other ills to which the flesh is heir.

The West then cannot be considered as a region in which guns flashed, redskins bit the dust, and fair maidens were rescued from a fate worse than death. Such incidents were rare, and seldom affected the average farmer-settler. But on the other hand, the heroism of meeting adverse conditions week after week without complaint, of taking hardships and monotonous routine as part of life, should not be underestimated. Starting life anew in the West was a tremendous gamble, greater the farther behind one left his home. The gamble might well fail, forcing the gambler to either try again or return to his more eastern friends and relatives as a failure. Greater virtue may inhere in the ceaseless effort to overcome large hardships than in the more dramatic willingness to sell life dearly on the Little Big Horn. Forty years of drudgery to provide increased comfort for one's family may be more admirable than forty days of heroic exploration.

Western life was supportable only to people who were basically optimistic. Men moved west because they were hopeful of the future, and that hope sustained them throughout life. The men who planned a New Buffalo as the metropolis of the Middle West were typical of the hopefulness of the frontier. And for each such optimist, exaggeration was as natural as breathing. Western stories were taller than eastern — some people unkindly called them lies. As it appeared in literary form, the humorous tale of exaggeration probably originated in frontier Maine and attained its peak in the work of Mark Twain. Neither optimism nor exaggeration can be labeled as exclusively western, but the West certainly gave them a favorable environment.

Optimism had its corollary in aggressive nationalism. The emphasis should be on the aggressiveness even more than on the nationalism. Westerners gave little respect to Indians, Spaniards, or Mexicans when they desired new land, and they always desired new land, even when the necessity was very remote. Generally the westerner was a patriot and linked his expansionist sentiment with his patriotism, but there were exceptions. Separatist sentiment all the way from Vermont to California was a well-known trait.

Western expansion sentiment was limited to the continent of North America and its adjacent islands, for the West was concerned primarily with agriculture, mining, and stock raising. Missionary opportunity in Hawaii or textile markets in the Far East were more an eastern than a western interest. Obtaining profits for eastern businessmen was never a major ambition of the West.

The very motives of western migration guaranteed that the West would be highly concerned with the more material factors of life. Men moved west to make their fortunes and not to obtain themes for novels or to educate their children. Success was measured in acres, in buildings, in cash. The materialistic measure of life was common throughout the United States, and the West did no more than to underline a trait which every foreign visitor observed as common to Americans.

The emphasis on materialism meant less attention to noneconomic activities. The West had neither time nor money for inconsequential pursuits such as landscape painting. And yet this frame of mind should not be overstated. A visitor to a log cabin might find the owner immersed in Bancroft's history of the United States and anxious to discuss the latest European scientific discoveries. Parents wanted their children educated. A primitive St. Paul could boast a theater, and a cotillion party was not unknown in the cruder sections of the West. All that can be said is that the West was somewhat behind the East in the noneconomic interests of life — not that the two sections were utterly different. Presumably the West exercised some sort of retarding influence on the cultural advance of the United States.

Viewed as an individualist, the westerner was not perceptibly different from his eastern contemporary. There were but few Daniel Boones who continued to move in search of elbow room. Roads, canals, railroads, banks, steamboats, and stores were possible only as group activities. So also were theaters and Paris fashions. The westerner was no hermit, but a sociable creature who wanted the good things of life. He gave a vague support to laissez faire, as did all other Americans, and objected strenuously when the government balked him in his desires. Who did not? But when the government could help him he was wholeheartedly enthusiastic for the assistance.

The frontier may be considered individualistic in its willingness to use personal force, whether in a gouging match or in a vigilance committee. Yet this trait has been visible throughout American history in all parts of the country. The American Revolution is possibly the most striking example, but the long continued practice of dueling or the violence in labor disputes are equally typical. The West was somewhat more vigorous than the East because of the lack of policemen. Basically the sections were not vastly different.

Socially the westerner was a conformist. Generally he lived in a farming community or in a small town where everyone knew and was interested in his neighbors, and where standards of acceptable conduct were fairly rigid. Western communities should not be considered as lacking in class distinctions, for the wife of the village banker hardly exchanged calls with the wife of the livery stable handyman, but the gulf was by no means impassable. The clerk of one day might be the proprietor of the next. A common code of conduct and a common test of success produced a general spirit of uniformity.

Politically and economically the westerner was likewise not radical. His criterion of individual wealth as the measure of success agreed with the ideals of the easterner, and hence his political and economic thinking was not original. In general the West functioned inside the traditional two-party system. As a predominantly agricultural area it had certain desires which were sometimes labeled as radical by their opponents, although by the time the West supported the Populist movement and such radical innovations as the direct election of Senators, some question may be raised as to whether any important frontier influence was represented. The Wisconsin of La Follette had little in common with the Kansas of Wild Bill Hickok.

Much more important than any specific political, economic, or social program was the basic desire of all westerners to attain the values which were held in esteem farther east. An Ohio farmer who moved to Iowa had no idea of creating a new and glittering utopia. Rather did he desire heartily to attain as commodious a house as his richer Ohio neighbor, as smart a horse and carriage, as good clothes for his wife and children. Western culture was imitative, as is apparent after moderate reflection.

IMPORTANCE OF THE FRONTIER

The importance of the frontier in American history has been great. Most obviously, the frontier was the first step in our occupation of a continent. Without the exploration and the occupation of the continent we would presumably today all still be in Europe — or Africa or Asia. The energy and aggressiveness that carried Americans across the continent are living parts of the American tradition. Whether they make the United States unduly cocky and self-righteous as a nation had probably better be left in the realm of speculation.

Frontier expansion meant that until late in the nineteenth century the major part of American energy and wealth was devoted to internal development. Not until well toward the end of the century did the United States have important amounts of capital or manufactured goods to export. The lateness of American interest in overseas expansion and in world politics must be credited largely to the frontier — a point which is emphasized by the long continued isolationism of the Middle West as compared to the Atlantic Coast.

Not only did the existence of the frontier lessen American world interests, but it also slowed down the industrial developments on which such interests are based. If the United States had been confined east of the Appalachians, the magnificent birth rate, irrespective of immigration, would soon have brought a population density that would have produced a mechanical development similar to that of England. With a slower industrialization, the attendant problems, such as those of labor, were naturally delayed.

An expanding frontier meant a deficit of workers in terms of available resources. The obvious indication of this situation was the high American wage-scale. High pay attracted immigrants, which meant a yearly crop of new citizens which had to be absorbed. Without a frontier the increase of population would have come largely from the domestic birth rate, which would have eliminated the necessity for Americanizing new arrivals. Consequently the frontier may be said to have slowed the process of producing a unified American culture. Presumably the new stocks have been a source of strength to the United States.

In so far as the frontier slowed industrialization, it delayed the development of class warfare — particularly between capital and labor. American society was slow in solidifying. Its fluidity was based on great opportunity of all kinds, notably agricultural and industrial. While there was no safety valve in the sense of an outlet for the industrial unemployed in time of depression, there was a real western safety valve operating indirectly over a long period of time. Migration to the West reduced eastern concentration of labor which in turn kept wages high as compared to Europe and reduced industrial discontent. Wages of the nineteenth century depended heavily on labor competition and but little on other factors.

A preoccupation with material development slowed the progress of other developments. In this respect the West merely reinforced a trend existing throughout the nation. Americans have never been impressed with the virtues of starving in an attic for the love of art. A man's first job has been to make a comfortable home for his family. The body must be fed before the soul is free. The West clearly emphasized, even though it did not create, this point of view.

In the long run, the frontier produced at least a few effects on noneconomic culture. No student of American literature can fail to note the varied use of frontier themes, and in particular the development of realistic writing in connection with western material. Exaggeration as a literary device has a definite western tang. In education, the increase of coeducation had western, and even frontier, implications. Singing schools, barn dances, quilting parties, and many other long-followed American customs retained popularity partly from the influence of the frontier.

Politically, the frontier influence is linked inextricably with the economic. The frontier produced a large and long-continued agricultural area which has entrenched itself through the American system of representation. Farmers have been capitalists, but also debtors. On the one side they are interested in moderate wages and high prices — for farm products. On the other side they believe in the control of large aggregations of capital in manufacturing, distribution, and transportation, and in low and easy terms on loans. Traditionally, the satisfaction of their desires was forwarded by having more and more people voting, and hence the desire for an expanded suffrage, direct elections, and similar democratic measures. Within recent years, with a larger laboring class, increased democracy is less appealing.

The political influence of the frontier has in consequence been indirect. An expanding frontier meant a predominantly agricultural nation, which gave importance to the viewpoint of the farmer. Hence the result was the stressing of a particular economic class. The more unique desires of the frontier, such as protection against the Indians, have had relatively little long-term significance.

Any generalizations as to the importance of the frontier should be considered as largely tentative. The mass of data on which they are based has filtered through the minds of their authors, and must inevitably have been influenced by their personalities and points of view. To state the results dogmatically as true requires a positive and intolerant state of mind that should be foreign to the historian. In general, the frontier seems to have had its greatest importance not in originating new trends, but in throwing its weight in one direction or another. From this point of view, however, the frontier has been of great importance in the development of the distinctive culture of the United States, and its influence is bound to continue into the remote future.

READINGS

J. D. Barnhart, *Valley of Democracy* (1953)—supports Turner ideas for Ohio valley; J. W. Caughey, *Hubert Howe Bancroft* (1946); A. Craven, "Frederick Jackson Turner," in W. T. Hutchisson (ed.), *Marcus W. Jernegan Essays* (1937)—friendly; M. E. Curti, *Frederick Jackson Turner* (1949)—excellent, "The Section and the Frontier in American History: The Methodological Concepts of Frederick Jackson Turner," in S. A. Rice (ed.), *Method in Social Science* (1931), pp. 353–367; E. E. Edwards, "References on the Significance of the Frontier in American History," in *Biographical Collections* of the United States Department of Agriculture Library (1935); D. R. Fox (ed.), *Sources of Culture in the Middle West* (1934)—critical of Turner; L. M. Larson, *The Changing West* (1937); J. C. Malin, *The Grassland of North America* (1947), *Grassland Historical Studies* (1950); F. Mood, *The Early Writings of Frederick Jackson Turner* (1938)—includes a biography; J. P. Nichols and J. G. Randall (eds.), *Democracy in the Middle West* (1941); J. C. Parish, *The Persistence of the Westward Movement* (1943); F. L. Paxson, *When the West Is Gone* (1930); H. N. Smith, *Virgin Land* (1950)—interesting in-

terpretations; G. R. Taylor (ed.), *The Turner Thesis* (1949);
F. J. Turner, *The Frontier in American History* (1920)—essays,
The Significance of Sections in American History (1932), *The
United States 1830–1850* (1935); W. P. Webb, *The Great Frontier*
(1952)—expands Turner thesis to the world stage; the periodical
literature on the Turner ideas has become so vast as to be un-
manageable.

INDEX

UNITED STATES
1850

"Aye, do you chop wood or what?"

Lop Ear was too disgusted to reply at once, and Charlie, lest Robert should offend him, hurriedly uttered a rebuke. "I'm surprised at you, Darkie," he said, "insulting Lop Ear after all he has done for us. Asking him if he worked! You see," he continued, turning to Lop Ear, "the sort of chap he is—always thinking about work! Overlook it, Loppy!"

"But how do you contrive to get all that meat if you don't do anything for it?" Robert persisted.

"I esk for it!" said Lop Ear with dignity. "I just esk for it!"

"And they give it to you?"

"Most always!"

"The people of this country must be kind-hearted!"

That had not occurred to Lop Ear. "Why shouldn't they give it to me!" he demanded. "There's plenty, ain't there? I gave youse two a share of my food when you esked for it, an' I didn't insult you by eskin' you to do no work for it! I had the food an' youse two needed it! There didn't seem no need to say no more!"

He looked about him to see that no suspicious official was listening near them, and then asked them to follow him. "There's a car in a side track there! I esked a switchman about it an' he told me all about it. It's goin' west an' I guess that's good enough for youse!"

They stole down to the siding in the dusk, and, after walking a little way by the side of the freight train, came to the empty car of which Lop Ear had spoken. They climbed into it and lay down on the floor, while Lop Ear disburdened himself of some of his stores. Presently he thrust food into their hands and, as best they could in the dark, they ate it. In a little while they heard the noise of the engine being coupled to the train which, after some harsh jolting, began to move out of the depot. They lay still for a few moments after they had finished their food, and then they fell asleep. They were awakened by a light flashing in their faces. A man in uniform was standing in the door of the car looking at them. There was a star on his breast. "Come on, boys!" he said, "you'll be welcome at the old home!"

Robert rubbed his eyes, while Charlie sat blinking in the light. The man with the lantern swung it round in the car. "Lop Ear!" he exclaimed joyfully. "Well, ain't that just fine. I'm genuinely glad to see you. I thought we wasn't going to entertain you no more." Lop Ear smiled amiably and yawned, and the policeman, turning the lantern on to Robert and Charlie, asked, "These guys friends of yours, Lop Ear?"

"Yeah," said Lop Ear, still yawning.

"Well, I'm glad to see any friends of yourn, an' I guess there's a few in the jail that'll be glad to see them, too!"

Robert jumped. "Jail!" he shouted.

"Yeah, the county jail!" the policeman continued. "We ain't been doin' well lately. Youse three'll be a God-send to us! How long'll you an' your friends stop with us, Lop Ear? A coupla months!"

"Coupla hell," Lop Ear replied. "I don't stay no more'n thirty days!"

"All right, Lop Ear, all right! We'd rather you stayed longer, but thirty days'll do. Now, come along, boys, I wanna get home quick!"

Robert could not speak. A terrible fear was forming in his mind, but he did not dare to think about it.

To Anita, M

You always liked Aquariums
This book should be
helpful & possibly be
interestering to you.
I hope you have a
garden pond, they can
be very interesting. You
used to have a tub
on penn St.
　　I hope you enjoy
this book as I have.
　　　　Love, Ron

9 Oct. 2018

Encyclopedia of Reptiles and Amphibians

By John F. Breen

Distributed in the U.S.A. by T.F.H. Publications, Inc., 211 West Sylvania Avenue, P.O. Box 27, Neptune City, N.J. 07753; in England by T.F.H. (Gt. Britain) Ltd., 13 Nutley Lane, Reigate, Surrey; in Canada to the book store and library trade by Clarke, Irwin & Company, Clarwin House, 791 St. Clair Avenue West, Toronto 10, Ontario; in Canada to the pet trade by Rolf C. Hagen Ltd., 3225 Sartelon Street, Montreal 382, Quebec; in Southeast Asia by Y.W. Ong, 9 Lorong 36 Geylang, Singapore 14; in Australia and the south Pacific by Pet Imports Pty. Ltd., P.O. Box 149, Brookvale 2100, N.S.W., Australia. Published by T.F.H. Publications, Inc. Ltd., The British Crown Colony of Hong Kong.

Frontispiece:

African treefrog, *Hyperolius* sp., a member of the large African and Asian family Rhacophoridae, related to the ranids. Photo by Van Raam.

ISBN 0-8766-220-3

TO

MARY E. DONOVAN

Contents

Preface

In the past two decades the interest in reptiles and amphibians has increased tremendously. The literature relating to the natural history and care of these fascinating creatures has hardly kept pace with the quest for knowledge. In 1967 alone, according to U.S. Fish and Wildlife Service figures, the United States imported 405,134 reptiles and 137,697 amphibians. Additional millions of individuals of native species were bought and sold. Specific information on the various individual reptile and amphibian species has been scattered, and in the past it has often been necessary to consult many books and pamphlets in order to acquire some piece of basic information. Clearly, there existed the need to bring under one cover a complete account of the many reptiles and amphibians that are commonly available.

The primary function of this book is to give the reader the necessary knowledge for the keeping of reptiles and amphibians alive and in good health in captivity. Secondarily, it is a general survey of the herptiles of the world that should prove useful to those who do not keep live specimens but nevertheless have a desire to learn more about them.

I would like to take this opportunity to thank the many workers in the field of herpetology who have gladly shared their experiences with me. Thanks are due S. N. F. Sanford and Alice Kendall for their valuable counseling. A special note of thanks to Glen G. Gowen, a keen young herpetologist who has assisted in many ways. Finally, I want to thank my mother, who withstood the growing pains of an aspiring herpetologist, and my wife, who many times set aside personal interests to further the present study.

John F. Breen

CLASSIFICATION OF THE
LIVING REPTILES AND AMPHIBIANS

according to Mertens, 1960.

AMPHIBIA
Caudata; Newts and Salamanders

1. Hynobiidae.
2. Cryptobranchidae.
3. Ambystomatidae.
4. Salamandridae.
5. Plethodontidae.
6. Amphiumidae
7. Proteidae.
8. Sirenidae.

Salientia; Frogs and Toads

1. Ascaphidae.
2. Discoglossidae.
3. Pipidae.
4. Pelobatidae.
5. Leptodactylidae.
6. Bufonidae.
7. Rhinophrynidae.
8. Brachycephalidae.
9. Hylidae.
10. Ranidae.
11. Rhacophoridae.
12. Microhylidae.

Gymnophiona; Caecilians
1. Caeciliidae.

REPTILIA
Testudines; Turtles and Tortoises

1. Cheloniidae.
2. Dermochelyidae.
3. Chelydridae.
4. Kinosternidae.
5. Platysternidae.
6. Dermatemydidae.
7. Emydidae.
8. Testudinidae.
9. Carettochelyidae.
10. Trionychidae.
11. Pelomedusidae.
12. Chelidae.

Crocodylia; Alligators and Crocodiles

1. Alligatoridae.
2. Crocodylidae.

3. Gavialidae.

Rhynchocephalia; Tuataras

1. Sphenodontidae.

Sauria; Lizards

1. Gekkonidae.
2. Pygopodidae.
3. Agamidae.
4. Chamaeleonidae.
5. Iguanidae.
6. Xantusiidac.
7. Cordylidae.
8. Teiidae.
9. Lacertidae.

10. Scincidae.
11. Dibamidae.
12. Anguidae.
13. Anniellidae.
14. Xenosauridae.
15. Helodermatidae.
16. Varanidae.
17. Lanthanotidae.
18. Amphisbaenidae.

Serpentes; Snakes

1. Typhlopidae.
2. Leptotyphlopidae.
3. Aniliidae.
4. Uropeltidae.
5. Xenopeltidae.
6. Boidae.

7. Acrochordidae.
8. Colubridae.
9. Elapidae.
10. Hydrophiidae.
11. Viperidae.
12. Crotalidae.

I

Turtles Common and Rare

TURTLES IN GENERAL

The herptile neophyte may occasionally mistake a salamander for a lizard, a legless lizard for a snake, or even an aquatic snake for an eel. But there is no possibility of mistaking a turtle or tortoise for anything else we know. All turtles and tortoises possess a shell of sorts. It may be very rudimentary, as in the ocean-dwelling leatherback, or quite highly developed, as in our common box turtles, but it is always present and serves to unite all the diverse species into the order Chelonia. Turtles and tortoises of all kinds are commonly referred to collectively as chelonians. The name "terrapin" is sometimes encountered in our reading, but it has little scientific significance and if used at all should perhaps be confined to the diamondbacks—salt- or brackish-water species of the genus *Malaclemys*.

Of all the herptiles, turtles are the ones most commonly under observation in the home. When I was about six years old, an aunt returning from a trip to a distant city presented me with two baby turtles as souvenirs of her trip. I knew little about reptiles at the time, but the quaint little creatures captivated me at once, and I spent most of my after-school hours watching them. Considering what little I knew of their requirements, it seems remarkable to me that they survived for many months. Soon after their arrival, other baby turtles were purchased locally from time to time. I could not differentiate one species from another, but I would try to pick out individuals having different markings. Thus was initiated a lifelong interest in reptiles and amphibians. Many herpetologists, both amateur and professional, will no doubt be able to recall a similar initiation into their field of study.

13

Students of animal behavior regard chelonians, especially the land-dwelling forms (the tortoises), as the most intelligent of reptiles. Tortoises seem more intelligent than their aquatic relatives, and those turtles that leave the water frequently to dwell on land seem more intelligent than the strictly aquatic types. None of our so-called intelligence tests is fool-proof, but in such common laboratory test problems as finding their way out of a maze, tortoises have fared as well as rats. We must always be mindful that instinctual behavior can be confused with intelligence. As an example, we place a turtle and a tortoise on a table or elevated platform and leave the room. Very often, when we return, we find that the turtle will have managed to fall off the table while the tortoise has warily inspected the drop to the floor and has decided to stay put. Before we rush to the conclusion that the tortoise is the more intelligent of the two, we must remember that in the natural state the turtle suns on rocks and logs and is accustomed to dropping safely from a height into the water below while the tortoise does not do so. A tortoise does not appear very intelligent in a watery environment, and here the results of any test we might devise would weigh heavily in the turtle's favor. A true test of intelligence would involve two reptiles of the same species, age, sex and conditioning, but this would only tell us what we already know—that in every species of vertebrate animals, including human beings, some individuals are brighter than others!

Turtles and tortoises, for the most part, adapt readily to conditions of captivity. As a result of this, they frequently breed in confinement. In most species the sexes may be separated quite readily by the difference in tail length and thickness. The male has the longer, thicker tail. In addition, males often have a concave lower shell. Also, there may be differences in color between the sexes. Courtship performances may be quite elaborate; the mating itself may take place in the water or on land, depending on the species. The normal hatching time runs from two to three months, but in some cases the baby turtle may· spend the winter within the egg and come out in the spring. If a female of one of the aquatic types deposits her eggs in the water because she cannot find a suitable nesting site on land, the eggs will quickly drown and become useless for hatching purposes. If deposited on land in a location lacking adequate moisture, they will spoil by drying out. Sometimes eggs will be trampled or broken by the turtles if not taken out of the enclosure at once. In

A box turtle hatchling.

Notice the large umbilicus on the hatchling below. Photos by R. J. Church.

Hermann's tortoise, *Testudo hermanni*, depositing an egg in her nest. Photo by O. Stemmler.

any given batch of eggs from the same female, some may be fertile while some are not. A female may lay fertile eggs from a mating which took place quite some time back. It is not unusual for a female to lay fertile eggs when she has had no contact with a male for two years. Eggs are best hatched in a sterile environment. A gallon jug having a wide mouth is good for a small number of eggs. The cover may be perforated to admit some air, and paper towels may be used as the hatching medium. Under natural conditions the eggs may adhere to each other, but under artificial incubation they are best separated. Damp paper towels may be crumpled and placed under and above the eggs to provide a duplication of the soil in which the eggs would naturally develop. A temperature range of 65 to 80° F. is desirable during the incubation period, and a slight night-to-day temperature fluctuation is considered by some to be beneficial. Alternate methods for the successful incubation of turtles' eggs are available; any method that controls the critical factors of heat and humidity is likely to be successful.

Chelonians have become adapted to many kinds of environments. Some never leave the water, whereas others never go near it. The majority of the 250-odd species of chelonians reside in the vicinity of a body of water but spend much of their time sunning out of the water. In captivity, the different species present quite distinct problems in their care, and chelonians of various families cannot be indiscriminately mixed with any degree of success unless a large outdoor enclosure is available. In general, turtles and tortoises are peaceful animals, although males of some species may fiercely combat each other during the breeding season. We do not know how prevalent this fighting is among chelonians in the wild state, but it has been repeatedly observed among such different captive species as the common snapping turtle, *Chelydra s. serpentina*, and eastern box turtle, *Terrapene c. carolina*.

Baby turtles are sold by the hundreds of thousands each year, and this has been going on for decades. They are the most popular of the herptiles bought for the home vivarium. Some are captured wild, but many are raised under semi-natural conditions on the so-called turtle farms of the southeastern United States. Of late, these farms have been forced to meet exacting standards of cleanliness, and this has resulted in a low production of baby turtles. As a result, certain very common foreign turtles have come to take the place of native American turtles in pet shops and department stores. At the present time, the South American slider, *Pseudemys scripta callirostris*, is the foreign turtle most frequently seen in the tanks of dealers.

The red-ear turtle, *Pseudemys scripta elegans*, is the most popular American turtle. Photo by R. J. Church.

17

Some species of baby turtles are easy to raise and quite undemanding, but others are very delicate and will tax the skill of their keeper to the fullest. Once the critical first year in the turtle's life has passed, it seems much better equipped to cope with the limitations imposed upon it by conditions of captivity.

Some baby turtles are very rarely met with in the wild state, possibly because of their extreme secretiveness during this stage of their lives. Baby box turtles are seldom found, baby wood turtles are real rarities, and even baby spotted turtles are not often collected, even where most common. Juveniles often present problems in identification, though nothing like the ones posed by larval frogs and salamanders. Once in a while one may buy or find a baby turtle that does not fit the description of any known species. I have such a specimen in my collection at the present time. It has traveled many miles to the offices of turtle specialists in an attempt to find a name—all without result. One can only guess that it is either an extreme aberrant of some known species or a hybrid resulting from the interbreeding of different species. It is an extremely beautiful little creature, now in its third year. It has been greatly outstripped in growth by the other turtles with which it is being raised, and I can only conjecture that its slow growth is in some way connected with its uncertain parentage. Such are the rarities which the turtle hobbyist seeks out. Occasionally a two-headed turtle is found, and amazingly, may pass through a number of hands before it is finally recognized. Often such a freak will have internal abnormalities prejudicial to its continued existence, though a few have been kept alive for several years. The most recent example to come to my attention was a hatchling southern painted turtle, *Chrysemys picta dorsalis*. It changed hands several times at a profit to each previous owner, in terms of dollars. This particular species is not an easy one to bring out of babyhood, and I would consider the several months that the two-headed individual survived to be about the average for a more normal specimen under anything but the most exceptional care.

Turtles and tortoises are perhaps the longest-lived of all backboned animals. A properly-cared-for specimen may well outlive several owners. No really short-lived species is known, and representatives of some species have been known to live a hundred years or more. Because of their long natural life and their general hardiness when out of the baby stage, the turtles that a herptile hobbyist

Baby box turtles (above) are very different in appearance from their parents, but the stinkpot, *Sternotherus odoratus* (below), is simply a miniature version of its elders. Photos by R. J. Church.

One advantage of baby turtles in the apartment is their ability to thrive in small, simple containers. Photo by R. J. Church.

acquires are likely to become permanent fixtures in any general collection of reptiles and amphibians. One may still walk into a pet store and purchase a baby turtle for less than a dollar, but anything that is at all uncommon on the turtle market will command a good price.

Because nearly all species of turtles are declining in numbers, some seeming almost at the point of disappearing in the wild state, it is most heartening to learn of the successful propagation of the rarer kinds in captivity. Even such unlikely places as New York apartments have become successful breeding plants for our rarest turtles. Luckily, a baby turtle given good care will mature rapidly and may become capable of reproduction before the end of its third year. The interest in chelonians has continued unabated for very many years and has today reached its highest state of sophistication.

Turtles are the oldest of our living reptiles; on the basis of fossil records, the basic chelonian stock has been practically unchanged for at least 200,000,000 years. The turtle of today looks very much the same as it did long ago. In the line of evolution the tortoises or land-dwelling forms were derived from those which live mostly in or near water. All turtles, even the marine types, lay eggs and must come ashore to do so; thus, no turtle species could survive very long without a beach or land area in which to deposit its eggs, nor could any turtle exist long in a place which has permanently frozen soil.

Like all other reptiles, chelonians reach the height of their abundance in the warmer regions of the world. The life history of many species is very incompletely known, and even their classification remains the subject of argument by taxonomists. Some taxonomists place all our turtles and tortoises in the order Testudinata, rather than Chelonia. Whatever their scientific designation, the turtles and tortoises, in their limited number of something over 200 species, form a conveniently circumscribed group for study in captivity. It is possible for a private collector to assemble a reasonably complete gathering of the world's chelonians, at least as regards the representation of the major families.

All sea turtles, even the gigantic leatherback, *Dermochelys coriacea*, must come ashore to lay their eggs. Photo by Malay Information Service.

SNAPPING TURTLES

If the snapping turtle, *Chelydra serpentina*, were a rarity, it would be much-sought-after by zoos and private individuals. Because it is common and familiar to nearly everyone, however, few stop to consider what a really curious turtle the snapper is. With its huge head, ungainly build, outsized tail, and vicious disposition, it presents a memorable picture when stranded out of its watery home. Snapping turtles are thoroughly aquatic animals, seldom voluntarily leaving the water except to deposit their eggs, which may number about 25. The eggs are round in shape and have been likened to ping-pong balls. They normally require about three months to hatch, but there have been cases in which the babies have spent the winter within

Common snapping turtle, *Chelydra serpentina*. Photo by R. J. Church.

their eggs and emerged during the spring. Babies measure a little over an inch in shell length and adapt themselves readily to an aquarium arrangement with a few inches of water and a couple of rocks. The snapper is neither a swift nor graceful swimmer—it is primarily a bottom-walking species—and will make use of the rocks to protrude its head occasionally to obtain air and survey its surroundings. It is said that snappers eat vegetable matter, but I have never seen one—and I have kept many—that did not prefer a diet of meat and fish. If kept on a well-balanced diet, the snapper does not require sunlight or any substitute for it. Fairly cool water, 65 to 70 degrees, seems to suit it best; it is one of the hardiest turtles in captivity.

The alligator snapping turtle, *Macrochelys temmincki*, is one of the largest fresh-water turtles in existence. A fully grown specimen may have a shell length of over two feet and reach a weight in excess of 200 pounds. Both the common and the alligator snappers are ready biters when out of water and are able to inflict considerable damage with their strong jaws. The alligator snapper is not as agile as the common snapper and shows little of the aggressiveness of that species. Either species may be safely handled by its long tail, held well away from one's body. No very large snapper should be lifted by the tail, however, because any damage to the tail vertebrae is likely to prove fatal ultimately. Large snapping turtles of either species are very predaceous creatures, and no other animal is safe in an enclosure with them. At the same time, baby snappers may have their very long tails injured or even bitten off by aquatic turtles of other kinds. Both kinds of snappers become quite tame in an aquarium and will grow rapidly if cared for properly. Whole or chopped raw fish is the best food for the alligator snapper; the shell quickly softens if the animal does not receive an adequate intake of calcium. Though shy by nature, alligator snappers in aquariums will learn to compete with other turtles for proferred bits of food. The ideal arrangement for a snapper is, however, an aquarium or outdoor pool of its own. The two species of snapping turtles resemble each other in appearance, but each is quite distinct and there is no interbreeding in areas where their ranges overlap. Together they make up the family Chelydridae and range from Canada to northern South America.

PLATELESS RIVER TURTLE

Whenever I visit the reptile house of the Bronx Zoo (New York Zoological Gardens) in New York, my first stop is in front of the large tank housing a single specimen of the plateless river turtle, *Carettochelys insculpta*. The front limbs of this strange turtle are developed for use as paddles, like those of the marine turtles, while its shell is covered with a layer of skin instead of horny plates. As the droll creature flippers lazily from one end of its tank to the other I pause to wonder how many herpetologists have, or will have, the opportunity to see a living specimen of this rare New Guinean turtle. Its range is limited to the southern part of the island, and there is very little in the literature of herpetology to tell us much about it. It is said to favor the brackish water of its island home.

Big-headed turtle, *Platysternon megacephalum*. Photo by G. Marcuse.

BIG-HEADED TURTLE

Another turtle oddity is being imported in some numbers. This is the big-headed turtle of southeastern Asia, *Platysternon mega-cephalum*. Superficially resembling our snapping turtles, the present species is in a family all by itself. It frequents mountain streams that are cool and in captivity does best in water between 65 and 70 degrees. Meat and fish form the bulk of its diet. It is a good climber and leaves the water frequently to sun itself on overhanging branches. Many of the specimens reaching this country are between six and seven inches in shell-length and have a tail about as long as the shell. Some examples are quite willing to bite when handled. Not much has been learned of this turtle's habits; it is said to deposit only two eggs at a time and captives occasionally emit a kitten-like mew. Two sub-species have been named: *megacephalum* from China, the rarer form, and *peguense* from Burma, Thailand, and Vietnam.

MEXICAN RIVER TURTLE

Some of the herptiles which are regarded as being very rare are, in fact, quite common in the areas where they are found but are seldom exported. The Mexican river turtle, *Dermatemys mawi*, may fall into this category. Having no close relatives, it currently enjoys sole occupancy of the family Dermatemyidae. A coastal river turtle, this species may feel at home in slightly brackish water. In southern Mexico it is sold in the market places and is also eaten by the natives of British Honduras and Guatemala. Very few specimens appear on the price lists of herptile dealers.

MUSK AND MUD TURTLES

The family Kinosternidae embraces a group of aquatic turtles known as musk and mud turtles. The common musk turtle, *Sternotherus odoratus*, is well known in the eastern United States, where in many places it is the commonest reptile. It is one of our smallest turtles, and an adult will seldom measure more than four inches in carapace length. In color, the musk turtle well matches the muddy ponds, ditches, and generally stagnant water that it inhabits, the

Mexican river turtle, *Dermatemys mawi*. Photo by J. Alan Holman.

only relief from its drab brown being the two light stripes on the head and neck. Mainly carnivorous, musk turtles forage by night and day and will devour nearly anything in the way of animal matter that they may find. They come out of the water to bask only rarely and under aquarium conditions will do well without any means of leaving the water. I have kept musk turtles in shoreless aquariums for periods of up to four years. I know of no hardier turtle, nor of any whose appetite is easier to please. Musk turtles seem very resistant to the illnesses which occasionally plague the semi-aquatic and terrestrial chelonians, and sunlight is not a requisite in their care. When first caught, a musk turtle will try to bite and will exude a musky secretion; it is surprisingly difficult to hold one without being bitten, for a musk turtle has a short tail, quite unlike the snappers', and the shell is often slippery and algae-covered. The half-dozen or fewer hard-shelled eggs of this species are often deposited in a seemingly careless situation, sometimes not even covered with soil or leaves.

Mud turtles, genus *Kinosternon* and related forms, are closely allied to the musk turtles, differing from them in having lower shells which are hinged to the extent which permits some species to close up as completely as a box turtle. Generally, mud turtles frequent shallow water; only rarely may an individual be found wandering about on land outside the egg-laying times. Olive, brown, and black are the predominate colors of the numerous species of the genus which, in one form or another, ranges throughout North and Central America and northern South America. Under captive conditions mud turtles are active and seem always on the look-out for food. An adult or baby will thrive in a straight-sided aquarium without means of leaving the water, but the depth of the water should be adjusted to the size of the individual so that it may obtain air at the surface without swimming. Babies, as well as adults, are voracious feeders on meat and fish and if mixed with other baby turtles are likely to obtain much of the food supply. While it is possible and often pleasing to mix various species of chelonians in the same cage, in my opinion the individuals should at least be of the same family. The mud turtle is a rugged animal and can be expected to live many years under captive conditions. Some twenty species and subspecies of mud turtles are recognized, and only a real turtle expert could identify all of the known forms without recourse to formal keys and technical descriptions.

Big-headed mud turtle, *Claudius angustatus*. Photo by J. Alan Holman.

Two genera of the family Kinosternidae are seldom seen in captivity, although they are common in the market places of the cities of southern Mexico, where they are sold for human consumption. These are *Claudius* and *Staurotypus*. The big-headed mud turtle, *Claudius angustatus*, has a greatly reduced lower shell which is not movable to any extent. The guau turtle, *Staurotypus triporcatus*, is a really huge member of the musk and mud turtle family, attaining a shell length of at least fifteen inches. Its disposition is fully as irascible as our diminutive musk turtle's, and its huge size renders it an adversary to be reckoned with at close quarters. A third species, *Staurotypus salvini*, of southern Mexico, is sometimes called the crucilla turtle. All three species could well be termed giant musk turtles; their habits appear very similar to those of our more familiar types.

EMYDID TURTLES

The largest group of turtles, in terms of number of species, is the Emydidae. This family contains most of the pet trade turtles and those for biological laboratory study. Some of the most beautiful

Blanding's turtle, *Emydoidea blandingi*. Photo by Dr. Herbert R. Axelrod.

turtles in the world are members of this family. Because of their diversification of coloring and habits there is little monotony in a study of the group, of which there are over 130 species and subspecies. An account of all of the emydid turtles is much beyond the scope of a book of this type. Besides, there are very many about which very little is known. Importations from Asia are supplying us with species which have been little known heretofore and, hopefully, observations of private collectors, as well as aquarium and zoo staff members, will supply us with good published accounts and pictures of the less familiar emydid turtles.

The painted turtles, *Chrysemys picta*, are beautiful, alert, quick-diving denizens of practically all sizable bodies of water in the eastern United States. In its four subspecies, *Chrysemys picta* presents a most attractive blending of black or olive, red, and yellow stripings and blotches. The most familiar of the painted turtles to the pet trade is the southern painted turtle, *Chrysemys picta dorsalis*, which comes from Louisiana and bordering states. In this form, the brilliant orange-yellow stripe running the length of the black upper shell is characteristic and is carried into adulthood. Grown painted turtles do well in captivity, but the babies are delicate little creatures, requiring a great deal of sunlight and a nourishing diet high in calcium and vitamin content and presented to them in finely ground form. They do not compete well with the more robust babies of other species of turtles and are best kept segregated for rearing purposes. All painted turtles, whether young or adult, are much given to sun-basking and must be provided with a suitable land area for this purpose. The males are readily distinguishable by their possession of long claws on the forefeet.

Blanding's turtle, *Emydoidea blandingi*, most common in the states bordering the Great Lakes, is a moderately large species which may measure eight inches or more in shell length when fully grown. It is an omnivorous creature but in captivity, at least, seems to prefer a meat diet. The Blanding's turtles that I have owned have all become amazingly tame; if they have any drawback as members of a turtle collection, it is in the tremendous appetite they display. The males seem ready to mate at all seasons, and perhaps the species is one which might be raised in quantities under favorable conditions. A bright yellow chin and throat impart a relief to the otherwise sober coloration. Blanding's is one of the emydid turtles whose babies are seldom found.

The European pond turtle, *Emys orbicularis*, is considered a close relative of Blanding's turtle and, like the latter, can eat either in or out of water. It lives well in captivity and becomes tame. Because of their large adult size, both the European pond turtle and Blanding's should have a good-sized water area in which to exercise. Pond turtles are said to over-winter in their eggs and emerge in the spring. Both species prefer to hibernate under water, buried in mud, but in neither is this rest period essential for longevity.

"Terrapin" is a name that is commonly applied to those fresh and brackish-water turtles that are of some importance economically because of the palatability of their flesh. In the present writing, we will confine the name to the diamondback terrapin, *Malaclemys terrapin*, a resident of eastern United States coastal marshes and other tidal waters from Massachusetts to Florida, then west to the Gulf coast of Texas and Mexico. The diamondbacks are confined to salt and brackish water in the natural state, and there is a difference of opinion among turtle keepers as to whether the salt content of their water is an important factor in maintaining them in captivity. My own opinion is that it is very necessary to provide brackish water for these handsome terrapins if they are to be kept over a long period; this is especially important if the other conditions of their environment are less than ideal. At least a tablespoonful of ordinary salt to a gallon of water provides the salinity these turtles require to prevent skin troubles from arising. Among the diamondbacks, of which there are seven subspecies currently recognized, the female attains a shell length nearly double that of her mate. The species has acquired its name from the distinctively sculptured shell, each plate of which is raised in concentric rings. A really beautiful turtle is Florida's west coast variety, the ornate diamondback terrapin, *Malaclemys terrapin macrospilota*. These turtles will learn to accept food items quite different from anything they might find in their native marshes, but an occasional feeding of molluscs is desirable.

The map and sawback turtles, genus *Graptemys*, are an interesting complex of nine currently recognized species confined to North America. Like the diamondbacks, to which they are closely related, the turtles of this genus show great disparity in size between the sexes, the female being much the larger. As a group, they are deep-water, diving turtles, and the adults are wary and very difficult to net. Some of the species have pronounced serrations along the keels of their carapaces and from this may be recognized at a distance. Sunning turtles all, they require in captivity a recognition of their individual needs and will fail to thrive unless these are met. The adult females of some species develop enormous heads and jaws, presumably to cope with the hard-shelled molluscs to which they seem partial. The Mississippi map turtle, *Graptemys kohni*, is the

Sabine map turtle, *Graptemys pseudogeographica sabinensis*, Louisiana-Texas border. Photo by J. G. Walls.

Spanish turtle, *Mauremys leprosa*. This turtle is often included in the genus *Clemmys*. Photo by G. Marcuse.

European pond turtle, *Emys orbicularis*. Photo by G. Marcuse.

species most often sold in pet stores. Generally considered delicate, the young can be raised successfully on chopped raw fish supplemented with lettuce leaves. Among the more beautiful members of the genus are the ringed sawback turtle, *Graptemys oculifera*, and the yellow-blotched sawback turtle, *Graptemys flavimaculata*. The map and sawback turtles do not enter the brackish water frequented by diamondbacks.

The spotted turtle, *Clemmys guttata*, is familiar to most residents of the eastern United States. Their small adult size of about four inches and the bold yellow speckling of their carapaces lead to their ready identification. Small, shallow bodies of water are a frequent abode, and often the turtles may be caught by hand in large numbers. Turtles which are abundant in the spring and early summer may disappear when the weather becomes hot, and it is believed that the species may aestivate. Baby spotted turtles are not common in collections; like many other baby turtles they are highly secretive until well grown. The sexes of the spotted turtle may be distinguished at once by anyone who has had much experience with the species. The male's head is less ornately adorned than the female's, his plastron is decidedly concave, and his tail is longer and thicker. There is not much difference in size between the sexes. Like all other members of the genus *Clemmys*, the spotted turtle makes a good adjustment to confinement and becomes very tame. A diet of meat and fish is preferred.

Many writers about reptiles have commented on the desirability of the wood turtle, *Clemmys insculpta*, for collections. Lacking the brilliant markings of some emydid turtles, the wood turtle is, nevertheless, a quietly handsome member of the family. Its shell is roughened, each scute set apart from the others, and its fleshy parts are adorned with brick red or, more rarely, yellow. Wood turtles are able to live on land or in the water and are practically omnivorous. The best arrangement for them is a large land area and a spacious pool to satisfy their occasional inclination to enter the water. Berries of several kinds, strawberries in particular, are relished by captives. Unfortunately, this desirable turtle does not appear on the price lists of dealers as frequently as it once did. Turtle collectors and collections are on the increase, and I do not know whether this has played a significant role in the lessening numbers of wood turtles.

Alligator snapping turtle, *Macrochelys temminckii.* Photo by Dr. Herbert R. Axelrod.

Common snapping turtle, *Chelydra serpentina.* Photo by Dr. Herbert R. Axelrod.

Spotted turtle, *Clemmys guttata*. Photo by. R. J. Church.

Clemmys nigricans, northern China. Photo by G. Marcuse.

The bog turtle, *Clemmys muhlenbergi*, once fairly common in favorable localities, has become so rare and sporadic in occurrence that it is possible that some readers may never see a live one. We do have the encouraging information that a few are being bred and raised in captivity, and it seems possible at present that such colonies may exist long after the species has vanished from its native haunts. I have a single adult male from Chatham, New Jersey in my collection. He was captured in the typical meadow stream habitat of the species, and I would judge from his appearance that he is quite old. In the six years he has been with me he has remained very timid, in distinct contrast to the other *Clemmys* turtles I have. He will leave the water and scamper toward my hand to take food, but he always pauses while still a few inches away, seemingly unable to work up the courage to take the proferred morsels from my fingers. When I withdraw my hand, leaving the food behind, the pieces of meat are grasped and taken into the water for swallowing—he will never eat anything while out of the water. When handled, as during the periodic cleaning of his shell, he will remain withdrawn in his shell indefinitely. Any kind of rock in his pool seems to terrorize him, and he will ceaselessly seek escape while it is present. The requirement of a dry area has been solved by gently sloping the aquarium by propping one end on a block of wood. This set-up provides a water depth of about two inches and a dry area covering one-third of the container. Most nights are spent out of water. Over the years, my specimen has been kept in good health on a diet of lean raw beef chopped into small pieces and supplemented frequently with a few mealworms or a nightcrawler. To discourage the possibility of fungus development, a small amount of vinegar is added to the water occasionally, after cleaning. In keeping with his distinction as a rarity and to minimize his chances of contracting a disease, he is kept isolated from other turtles. He receives no sunlight, except that filtered through ordinary window glass, and this seems to be not an essential requirement for the successful maintenance of most adult turtles.

The west coast pond turtle, *Clemmys marmorata*, in its two sub-species, ranges from British Columbia southward to northern Baja, California, and may reach a carapace length of over seven inches. It is very aquatic in its habits and sometimes enters brackish water; large colonies may sometimes be found confined to small areas.

Plateless river turtle, *Carettochelys insculpta.* Photo by P. C. H. Pritchard.

Mexican river turtle, *Dermatemys mawi.* Photo by P. C. H. Pritchard.

Common musk turtle, *Sternotherus odoratus*. Photo by P. C. H. Pritchard.

Eastern mud turtle, *Kinosternon subrubrum subrubrum*, eastern United States. Photo by P. C. H. Pritchard.

Pseudemys is the genus which supplies so many of the small turtles used for the pet trade and in research. Its various species and sub-species have a wide distribution in the western hemisphere, and most are very attractive turtles and eminently suitable members of the private collection. The red-eared turtle is the one seen most often in the aquariums of pet dealers where, unfortunately, their care is often not of the very best. There seems to be a prevailing idea that these small creatures can best be kept in good health, while awaiting buyers, in dry or nearly dry tanks. This is not so. True, when a large number of turtles are confined, they present less of a cleaning problem in the absence of water. But under such conditions these small turtles do not feed and the mortality resultant from desiccation and starvation must surely offset whatever small advantage accrues from not having to feed them and provide a change of water daily. All of the pseudemid turtles are sun-loving creatures and are at their best in an aquarium which provides a large, rounded rock or dry shore for sunning or at least drying out occasionally. Feeding habits within the genus are varied—some species seem omnivorous and quite willing to eat most anything, while others exhibit a preference for either vegetable matter or meat. From personal experience I can attest that the growth of these babies can be phenomenally rapid under favorable conditions in captivity. A hatchling the size of a quarter may in a couple of years become the size of a small saucer.

The red-bellied turtles, *Pseudemys nelsoni* and *Pseudemys rubri-ventris*, with their coral plastrons, are bright and hardy members of the family. The adult females may reach a length of nearly fifteen inches; the males are smaller and have the long foreclaws which distinguish the males of many emydid species. Red-bellies have a curious distribution, consisting of at least four distinct populations, the most perplexing of which is the isolated colony in Plymouth County, Massachusetts. One expects to find large basking turtles in some places, but their presence in New England is surprising and they seem, somehow, out of place.

In our southern states the cooters and sliders, *Pseudemys floridana* and *Pseudemys concinna*, are common and very familiar animals. There is a bewildering array of variation among them, and even the student who specializes in the study of turtles will find it difficult to attach with certainty a subspecific designation to some individuals of the group. Mostly, they reach a large adult size and do well in captivity. Babies enter the pet trade, to some extent, and enjoy a varied diet. These turtles, in their two species and some eight sub-species, intermingle freely in the wild state, and this habit is carried over into captivity. The subject of hybridization is a fascinating one, and in the literature one finds records and photographs of the curious creatures that have resulted from the union of two quite different animals. Experiments of this kind have been taking place for some time; the San Diego Zoo, which has produced a wealth of information about reptiles through the activities of the reptile men connected in one way or another with it, has succeeded in hybridizing rattlesnakes—animals which normally do not adjust to captivity to the extent of breeding, even within their own species! What brings all this to mind is the attempt on the part of some of my male sliders to court a much larger yellow-spotted Amazon turtle, *Podocnemis unifilis*, female that is temporarily caged with them. This turtle and the sliders are so far removed from each other on the turtles' phylogenetic tree that they have been placed in different suborders. With our ever-increasing knowledge of how to make herptiles feel at home in captivity and with the maturing of artificial insemination experiments, who can say what future investigation along these lines may reveal?

The red-eared turtle, *Pseudemys scripta elegans*, has long been the reptile most widely kept as a pet in the United States, even though reduced numbers are causing it to be supplanted, to a degree, by the very common South American slider. Red-eared turtles are the first reptiles acquired by many reptile admirers, and their pretty colors and good disposition combine to make a favorable introduction to the world of reptiles. A close relative of the red-eared turtle is the yellow-bellied turtle, *Pseudemys scripta scripta*, of the southeastern United States.

Northern South America is the home of a common and beautiful turtle that is imported in large numbers. The South American slider, *Pseudemys scripta callirostris*, delicate of form and coloring, is a tropical turtle and is best kept at a temperature of not less than 78–80 degrees.

The chicken turtle, *Deirochelys reticularia*, is, for a turtle, a graceful and streamlined inhabitant of that region—the southeastern United States—which is the home of so many species found nowhere else.

Guau turtle, *Staurotypus triporcatus.* Photo by P. C. H. Pritchard.

Western painted turtle, *Chrysemys picta belli.* Photo by Dr. Herbert R. Axelrod.

Southern painted turtle, *Chrysemys picta dorsalis.* Photo by Dr. Herbert R. Axelrod.

Blanding's turtle, *Emydoidea blandingi.* Photo by Dr. Herbert R. Axelrod.

The extremely long neck of this species is reminiscent of the Australian and South American snake-necked turtles, but actually chicken turtles are not closely related to the snakenecks. An inhabitant of ponds and other quiet waters, the chicken turtle is mainly carnivorous. I would call the species a difficult one to raise from babyhood but quite hardy as an adult of four to six inches. The olive-brown carapace is finely lined with yellow—reticulated—whence the species has received its specific name.

Conspicuous and unique in the turtle fauna of the United States and Mexico is the box turtle in its several species. The eastern box turtle, *Terrapene carolina carolina*, may be taken as representative of the species. The highly domed carapace and the hinged plastron will at once serve to distinguish this turtle from other chelonians of the areas it inhabits, as will its habitually terrestrial mode of living. All of the box turtles have brown or blackish shells, adorned in some cases with yellow radiating lines. Males of the eastern species are among the handsomest turtles of the North American continent; they often have bright red eyes and seem to attain a larger average size than their mates, sometimes reaching a carapace length of six inches.

Box turtles are long-lived reptiles. With whatever skepticism we may view published records of longevity in turtles, there seems little doubt that box turtles may, on rare occasions, live a century. Sometimes very old-looking individuals may be found, but they are not common; to my way of thinking, this fact lends considerable credibility to the tales of longevity we read about. Box turtles resemble the true tortoises in their way of life, but are more closely related to the aquatic and semi-aquatic species mentioned in the foregoing paragraphs. After a rain they may be found wandering about in abundance in some places; in hot, dry weather they go into seclusion. Specimens in captivity do best under dry conditions, with periodic soakings in water. In a well-regulated household a bathtub may not be considered the ideal place for turtles, but I know of one specimen that has for years been doing well in such a situation. She is thoroughly soaked with a bathspray each day and about once a week allowed to wallow about in water of two-inch depth. It is at such times that she seems to drink. Her diet consists almost solely of hamburger, and she is not interested in less than the best grade. No amount of teasing will cause her to close her lower shell. She was picked up

Comparison of the single hinge of a box turtle (above) and the double hinge of a mud turtle (below). Photos by G. Marcuse.

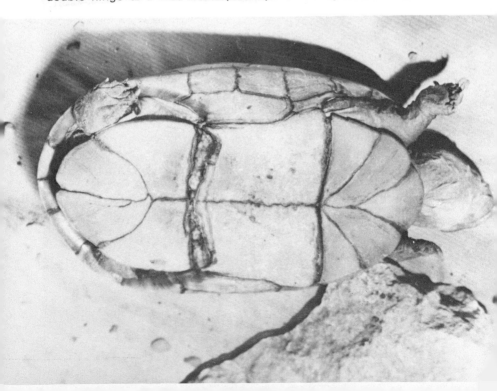

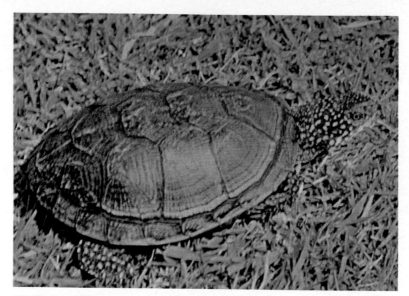

European pond turtle, *Emys orbicularis*. Photo by P. C. H. Pritchard.

Diamondback terrapin, *Malaclemys terrapin*. Photo by Dr. Herbert R. Axelrod.

Florida diamondback terrapin, *Malaclemys terrapin macrospilota.*
Photo by P. C. H. Pritchard.

Mississippi map turtle, *Graptemys kohni.* Photo by Dr. Herbert R.
Axelrod.

wandering along a busy street of a large city, apparently an escaped pet, since from the very first she has displayed no timidity.

Baby box turtles are not found with any degree of frequency. They require more moisture than their elders and more attention to their dietary requirements. Often they feed readily and voraciously and prefer a meat diet. I have kept many juvenile box turtles of different subspecies and cannot recall of any that would partake of vegetable or fruit offerings. The baby Gulf Coast box turtle, *Terrapene carolina major*, is sometimes represented by an individual or two in the large batches of turtles which originate in Louisiana. It has distinctly aquatic proclivities and, in general, is a more difficult animal to raise than the young of the Florida box turtle, *Terrapene carolina bauri*, and the ornate box turtle, *Terrapene ornata*. The last two do well as babies and will often live, but they show hardly any growth if their diet is lacking in the essential vitamins and minerals. Adult box turtles can be called omnivorous, and the types of food they accept would form a long list. Whole or chopped earthworms are greedily accepted by most individuals, but box turtles display a great deal of individuality. Nearly all adults make a quick and good adjustment to cage life, but rarely one is found that day after day and month after month will do little besides seek escape. Such individuals feed sparingly, which reflects itself in a rapid loss of weight. There is little point in keeping such an animal.

Florida box turtle, *Terrapene carolina bauri*. Photo by Dr. Herbert R. Axelrod.

Fat-necked turtle, *Siebenrockiella crassicollis*, Southeast Asia.
Photo by M. F. Roberts.

Box turtles can be tethered out-of-doors by means of a small hole drilled in the posterior margins of their carapaces. This should be done only in places where they will be free from attack by dogs or other predaceous animals. Water should be available constantly, as should a means of getting out of the sun. If more than one turtle is kept, they should be separated to avoid entanglement of their restraining lines. In a fenced yard they may be allowed to roam freely and will seldom make an attempt to dig out. However, despite their clumsy build, they can and do climb; if the fence is low it should be fitted with an overhang to prevent this means of escape. In general, box turtles can be expected to do well in captivity and often become the favorites of a collection.

Mexico is a vast area, and inhabiting its varied terrain are many creatures of great zoological interest. Four, possibly more, box turtle species are found here but, like so many Mexican reptiles, they seldom reach zoos or private collections, so we know little of their habits.

Of the various Asiatic species of emydid turtles, the batagur turtle, *Batagur baska,* is one of the largest, having a shell length of two feet or more. This very common chelonian is herbivorous and, as can be imagined, consumes great amounts of plants, its saw-edged jaws

Yellow-blotched sawback, *Graptemys flavimaculata*. Photo by P. C. H. Pritchard.

Spotted turtle, *Clemmys guttata*. Photo by P. C. H. Pritchard.

Bog turtle, *Clemmys muhlenbergi.* Photo by P. C. H. Pritchard.

Wood turtle, *Clemmys insculpta.* Photo by P. C. H. Pritchard.

Reeves' turtle, *Chinemys reevesi*. Photo by G. Marcuse.

enabling it to make clean cuts with a minimum of effort. Good eating, it is hunted locally, and its eggs are collected in large numbers for human consumption. The batagur is not one of the really handsome emydids, but males of the species are said to assume a nuptial dress, something not common among turtles. The batagur frequents brackish water, and captives will benefit from the addition of salt to their water. Batagur turtles deposit large numbers of eggs on the beach at a point beyond tidal influence. The oval eggs are three inches in length and require over two months to hatch. The adults are wary reptiles, fast runners and strong swimmers. The usual method of capture is by means of a trap. Neither babies nor adults are commonly exported.

The three-striped batagur turtle, *Callagur borneoensis*, also an Asiatic species, though commonly regarded as a fresh-water species, is actually a frequenter of coastal waters and is a plant-eater.

Reeves' turtle, *Chinemys reevesi*, is a member of a genus containing three species. A common and small species of China and Japan, Reeves' turtle is a dull-brownish little animal that is not often more than four inches in shell length. Hardy and long-lived, they spend most of their time under water, where they will voraciously eat meat,

50

worms, and fish. I once acquired a number of hatchlings and will always remember them for their continual fighting with each other. They were well fed, so their squabbles were not prompted by hunger. Little harm resulted from their disharmony.

The Spanish turtle, *Mauremys leprosa*, and the Caspian turtle, *Mauremys caspica*, are commonly imported. The Spanish turtle often arrives with its shell in a deplorable condition, said to be caused by the seasonal drying-up and stagnating of the ponds it inhabits. As a species it does well in captivity, as does the Caspian turtle. Many kinds of turtles, especially those of the tropics, have had their shells devastated by erosion by the time they are collected. The etiology of these conditions is probably varied. Some respond well to treatment while others are resistant. I do not think it is wise to introduce a turtle with a bad shell to one's collection; in the case of valuable exotic specimens that cannot be seen before purchase, it is worth the price of a telephone call to the dealer to ascertain their true condition before they are shipped.

The Asiatic box turtles of the genus *Cuora* have recently become popular among herptile keepers. The Malayan box turtle, *Cuora amboinensis*, is the species most often available. It rather closely resembles our native box turtles. Like them, it has the ability to close the lobes of the plastron. *Cuora trifasciata* (three-lined box turtle) is, to me, an exquisitely beautiful turtle whose delicate shadings of color show off to great advantage under good lighting. There is nothing gaudy about it, yet the contrasts of brown, yellow, and red and the dark band on its head impart an out-of-the-ordinary appearance. The care of captives is not difficult; perhaps the best arrangement is one which provides equal land and water areas, with the water depth proportioned to the sizes of the turtles. Like other turtles native to the warmer regions of the world, the members of this genus should never be subjected to low temperatures. I would regard 75 to 80 degrees an ideal temperature range. It is fortunate that we are today able to procure from reptile dealers at a relatively low price so many kinds of reptiles which not long ago could be obtained only with considerable difficulty and after lengthy correspondence. The Asiatic box turtles fall into this category. Although the older books on reptiles hardly mention them, no doubt our knowledge of the *Cuora* species and others will keep pace with the influx of live material.

Red-bellied turtle, *Pseudemys nelsoni.* Photo by P. C. H. Pritchard.

West coast pond turtle, *Clemmys marmorata.* Photo by C. M. Bogert.

Cooter, *Pseudemys floridana*. Photo by Dr. Herbert R. Axelrod.

Slider, *Pseudemys concinna*. Photo by P. C. H. Pritchard.

Three-lined box turtle, *Cuora trifasciatus*, above; Malayan box turtle, *Cuora amboinensis*, below. Photos by G. Marcuse.

Confronted by so many desirable reptiles offered by dealers, the collector must exert will power to keep a private collection within reasonable bounds. Each additional specimen will mean additional work, and work is pleasurable to a point only. Certainly the care and feeding of any private collection should never be allowed to become burdensome. Most herptiles will live for a long time if properly cared for, and one of the purposes of this book is to enable a beginner to lay out a plan for a collection. He may wish to specialize in one kind of reptile or another or to have a collection that represents a cross-section of the reptile and amphibian worlds. Whatever the choice, it is important to impose limitations on the numbers of individuals and not purchase any herptile simply because it is available at the moment. There is fun in waiting, and although the particular species you want may take time to obtain, its value will be enhanced when you finally obtain it.

Thurj's turtle, *Hardella thurji*, is a large, thoroughly aquatic species from India and Pakistan. The shell of a fully grown female may be 20 inches in length. It feeds mostly on plants and is best kept at a temperature not lower than 75 degrees. The temple turtle, *Hieremys annandalei*, is similar in size and habits and is likewise Asiatic in origin.

The roofed turtles, genus *Kachuga*, are represented by six species, some quite attractive in their color and markings. Their shells are prominently keeled along the top and, viewed from the front, are rather tent-like in conformation. Roofed turtles do not appear to be built for swimming, but I would call them diving turtles. They are thoroughly at home in an aquarium that provides only a small island for leaving the water. As captives they feed incessantly upon lettuce leaves and other green matter; they do not show any interest in meat.

Southeast Asia provides us with the snail-eating turtle, *Malayemys subtrijuga*, a species closely resembling our native musk turtles in gross appearance. Turtles of this species do best in fairly shallow water that does not force them to swim to the surface to take air. Captives will seldom leave the water, and it is questionable whether a landing-place lends anything to their comfort. This rather somber little turtle may feed largely upon molluscs in its native habitat, but my records show that the ones I have had have readily accepted pieces of raw beef as a substitute for their natural diet. Snail-eating turtles are a common species, and a single shipment arriving in the United States may contain several hundred specimens.

Yellow-bellied turtle, *Pseudemys scripta scripta.* Photo by P. C. H. Pritchard.

Red-eared turtle, *Pseudemys scripta elegans.* Photo by Dr. Herbert R. Axelrod.

South American slider, *Pseudemys scripta callirostris*. Photo by Dr. Herbert R. Axelrod.

Chicken turtle, *Deirochelys reticularia*. Photo by P. C. H. Pritchard.

Kachuga smithi, Pakistan and northern India. Photo by G. Marcuse.

Thurg's turtle, *Hardella thurgi*. Photo by G. Marcuse.

Snail-eating turtle, *Malayemys subtrijuga.* Photo by G. Marcuse.

Gulf coast box turtle, *Terrapene carolina major*. Photo by P. C. H. Pritchard.

Eastern box turtle, *Terrepene carolina carolina*. Photo by M. F. Roberts.

Florida box turtle, *Terrapene carolina bauri*. Photo by Dr. Herbert R. Axelrod.

Three-toed box turtle, *Terrapene carolina triunguis*, Mississippi to Texas. Photo by P. C. H. Pritchard.

Three-keeled turtle, *Geoemyda trijuga.* Adult above, juvenile below. Photos by G. Marcuse.

The flat-shelled turtle, *Notochelys platynota*, is a vegetarian, feeding mostly on berries and greens. It comes on the turtle market once in a while and is native to Vietnam, Burma, Sumatra, and Borneo.

Turtles of the genus *Geoemyda* are found in the tropical Americas and Asia. Some are semi-aquatic, while others dwell mostly on land. There is great diversification in appearance among the related forms, a few possessing a bizarre shell development in their early years. They are not the easiest of turtles to pinpoint as to species and subspecies and, like other difficult groups, are occasionally misidentified. A clue to the habits of any turtle may be had by noting whether the hind feet are webbed and, if they are, how extensively. Most, if not all, chelonians have good olfactory powers; the more terrestrial *Geoemyda* species seem to have their sense of smell especially well developed. Their keen investigation of other turtles and foreign objects gives an impression of intelligence.

Geoemyda grandis, Southeast Asia. Photo by M. F. Roberts.

Caspian turtle, *Mauremys caspica*. Photo by P. C. H. Pritchard.

Reeves' turtle, *Chinemys reevesi*. Photo by Dr. Herbert R. Axelrod.

Spanish turtle, *Mauremys leprosa*. Photo by G. Marcuse.

Malayan box turtle, *Cuora amboinensis*. Photo by P. C. H. Pritchard.

Rough turtle, *Geoemyda punctularia*. Photo by R. J. Church.

All *Geoemyda* species should have both land and water areas in their cages. Individuals will soon show their preference, and the proportions of dry and wet areas may be adjusted accordingly. Some commonly imported turtles of this group are the furrowed land turtle, *Geoemyda areolata*, the rough turtle, *Geoemyda punctularia*, and the three-keeled turtle, *Geoemyda trijuga*. All *Geoemyda* species should be kept warm. In most of their forms they represent a sort of transition from aquatic to terrestrial habits, and turtles of this type seem admirably adapted to confinement. An example is our North American wood turtle, *Clemmys insculpta*.

II

Other Turtles and the Tortoises

SOFT-SHELLED TURTLES

The numerous soft-shelled turtles form a thoroughly aquatic family: the Trionychidae. With their flexible, leathery shells and elongated snouts, no one acquainted with turtles is likely to mistake these curious animals for anything else. Some writers have called these turtles the most aquatic of freshwater species, but I would hesitate to apply this designation to them. In the wild state, they may once in a while be seen basking on a floating log or sandy beach. Such species as our common snapper seem much more independent of land, though not the efficient swimmers the soft-shells are. Soft-shelled turtles, especially juveniles, become tame enough to greedily snatch food from one's fingers. The adults are sometimes morose and resent familiarity by biting viciously when handled. It is difficult to avoid the serpentine thrusts of their heads, and the best way to handle a large specimen is by the rear of the carapace. The eastern spiny soft-shelled turtle, *Trionyx spiniferus spiniferus*, is fairly typical of the group. It is a difficult turtle to catch with a net. For an animal whose entire structure is modified to suit the needs of an aquatic existence, its ability to run quickly on land is amazing.

Soft-shells should not be allowed to crawl on hard or rough surfaces, because they lack the bony armor of other turtles and may easily injure their tender plastrons. I consider it neither necessary nor desirable to provide their aquariums with landing places. Best suited to their needs is an aquarium with several inches of very fine sand on the bottom. The sand should be covered with water to a

Three-banded box turtle, *Cuora trifasciata*. Photo by P. C. H. Pritchard.

Thurg's turtle, *Hardella thurgi*. Photo by G. Marcuse.

Snail-eating turtle, *Malayemys subtrijuga.* Photo by Dr. Herbert R. Axelrod.

Roofed turtle, *Kachuga smithi,* India and Pakistan. Photo by S. Minton.

Spiny soft-shell turtle, *Trionyx spiniferus*. Photo by Dr. Herbert R. Axelrod.

depth not too great to prevent the turtles from extending their long necks to the surface without leaving their hiding places under the sand. It should not be inferred from this that soft-shells remain habitually buried in an aquarium. Tame ones are quite vivacious and spend much time exploring the confines of their home. Soft-shells should not be mixed with other, less fragile types of turtles, for they are easily injured by bites and scratches from other turtles. The soft, proboscis-like extension of their snouts can easily be amputated in a dispute over a morsel of food. Kept alone, with a minimum of handling, soft-shells do well. The babies of some species are adorned with attractive markings; young Florida soft-shelled turtles, *Trionyx ferox*, are especially attractive. Some species, like the giant soft-shelled turtle of southeast Asia, *Pelochelys bibroni*, grow to a shell-length of over three feet. Soft-shells are primarily carnivorous; none of the number of species that I have kept would show any interest in lettuce or other vegetable matter. North America, Asia, and Africa all have indigenous soft-shelled turtles.

SEA TURTLES

The true sea turtles have been placed in two families. The lone member of the first family is the huge leatherback turtle, *Dermochelys coriacea*, of the family Dermochelyidae. Attaining a shell-length of over five feet and weight approaching a ton, the leatherback has rarely been kept in captivity. Like other marine turtles, the leatherback has huge flippers instead of the usual turtle forelimbs. This may be the heaviest of our living reptiles, and a verbal description hardly does justice to the immensity of a fully adult living specimen. Imagine a turtle whose flippers may span 12 feet! The lack of a horny, plated shell is one of the more obvious features that separate this turtle from other sea turtles which are, outwardly, of similar form and habits. Babies, measuring three inches at hatching, are brightly spotted and covered with small scales. As the reptile grows, the scales are lost and replaced with the leathery skin of the adult, dark brown or black in color. The dissection of leatherbacks discloses omnivorous feeding habits.

The family Cheloniidae includes our more familiar sea turtles like the loggerhead, *Caretta caretta*, hawksbill, *Eretmochelys imbricata*, ridleys, *Lepidochelys* species, and green turtles, *Chelonia mydas*. Sea

Pacific ridley turtle, *Lepidochelys olivacea*. Photo by P. C. H. Pritchard.

71

Rough turtle, *Geoemyda punctularia*. Photo by Dr. Herbert R. Axelrod.

Furrowed land turtle, *Geoemyda areolata*. Photo by P. C. H. Pritchard.

Florida soft-shelled turtle, *Trionyx ferox*. Photo by P. C. H. Pritchard.

Three-keeled turtle, *Geoemyda trijuga*. Photo by P. C. H. Pritchard.

turtles are among those marine animals that adapt readily to a synthetic oceanic medium if it even grossly approaches their natural water in its principal salts content. Aquarists who keep marine fishes have long been familiar with the packaged chemical compounds which, when dissolved in fresh water, create an approximation of natural ocean water. These complicated compounds are very necessary in the keeping of most fish species, but hardly so in regard to marine turtles, which have survived over long periods in ordinary tap water to which enough table salt has been added to lend a brackish taste. Natural sea water can be used for sea turtles, but in some ways the artificial product is better, lacking, as it does, the many microorganisms which die off and start to alter the nature of sea water when it is placed in an aquarium.

Baby sea turtles are often encountered in large numbers when they have broken out of their shells and are crawling toward the shallow waters that will harbor them in their infancy. A single specimen may be confined in a five-gallon aquarium but can be expected to grow rapidly and will soon require a much larger aquarium. Clean and sterile conditions are desirable, as with the keeping of all reptiles, and this can be best accomplished if the turtle is fed in a basin or other container separate from the dwelling unit. This method of feeding will not allow decaying food particles to foul the water of the turtles' permanent homes. Since only the adults come out on land, and they only for egg-laying, it is not necessary to provide any land area in the aquarium housing small sea turtles. In the early stages of their lives, when first hatched, ocean turtles will thrive in shallow water only a few inches deep. This, unfortunately, does not show off to any great extent their graceful swimming motions which are so attractive in deeper water. Food will consist of fish, molluscs, and water plants mostly; experimentation will quickly show what is preferred. Though rarely available commercially, baby sea turtles may be acquired through purchase or exchange with a collector who has the opportunity to catch them near their nesting sites.

SIDE-NECKED TURTLES

If this book were to make an attempt to present information about reptiles in the strict order of their taxonomic classification, the side-necked turtles of the families Chelidae and Pelomedusidae would have to be put into a section by themselves. All of the turtles we have

Helmeted turtle, *Pelomedusa subrufa.* Photo by P. C. H. Pritchard.

so far discussed draw their heads into their shells by a vertical bending process. With the present group, however, the neck is bent under the shell sideways. This difference in the way the neck is bent is considered a very fundamental one, so much so that the side-necks have been put into a separate suborder. All side-necks are fresh-water turtles; some are thoroughly aquatic, others less so, but there are no marine or strictly terrestrial species among them.

The matamata turtle, *Chelys fimbriata,* is a sidenecked species and one of the most bizarre reptiles in the world. Its grotesquely flattened head terminates in a projecting snout and is covered with filamentous protuberances which may be an aid in detecting the aquatic creatures upon which it feeds. The mouth is very large and the jaws are fleshy, rather than hard and sharp. When it feeds, the matamata simply opens its mouth and sucks in the fish or other small animal that unwarily approaches too close. The shell is odd in that each shield is. elevated to a point. In fact, there is little about the matamata that is not curious. Compared with other turtles, its features seem an accentuation and combination of the more unusual features of other genera of chelonians.

Leatherback turtle, *Dermochelys coriacea*. Photo by P. C. H. Pritchard.

Loggerhead turtle, *Caretta caretta*. Photo by D. Faulkner.

Atlantic ridley, *Lepidochelys kempi*. Photo by P. C. H. Pritchard.

Hawksbill turtle, *Eretmochelys imbricata*. Photo by P. C. H. Pritchard.

Matamata, *Chelys fimbriata*. Photo by Dr. Herbert R. Axelrod.

Green turtle, *Chelonia mydas*. Photo by P. C. H. Pritchard.

Argentine snake-necked turtle, *Hydromedusa tectifer*. Photo by P. C. H. Pritchard.

Toad-headed turtle, *Batrachemys nasuta.* Photo by P. C. H. Pritchard.

By no means so exclusively aquatic is the yellow-spotted Amazon turtle, *Podocnemis unifilis*, of South America. Until recently, babies of this species were imported in great numbers. With proper care, they live well and grow rapidly. Specimens in my collection have been omnivorous, eating with equal relish such varied items as canned dog food, bits of raw beef, chopped whole fish, and lettuce and other greens. They seem to have more intelligence than the semi-aquatic emydid turtles. Sun-lovers, they will frequently usurp the available land-area of their aquarium and bite other turtles which attempt to dislodge them. Likewise, they will gain possession of rocks or other sunning places by harmlessly nipping other basking turtles. Very sensitive to chilling, these turtles should be kept at a temperature of about 75 degrees, and this must not be allowed to drop at night. Like many other tropical reptiles, *P. unifilis* can be killed by a single chilling. The six-tubercled greaved turtle, *Podocnemis sextuberculata*, is another species frequently imported. It does well if kept warm. It does not often leave the water and is mainly, if not wholly, carnivorous. The arrau turtle, *Podocnemis expansa*, is the largest of the genus; its shell may measure over two feet. It is an important food animal in northern South America.

TORTOISES

The true tortoises of the family Testudinidae are the favorite group of many amateur and professional herpetologists. They range in size from diminutive forms to the gigantic tortoises of the islands of the Aldabra and Galapagos groups. Some are somberly hued, while others must be classed among the most beautiful of the world's reptiles. Over sixty species and subspecies have been named, but of this number about one-fourth are the aforementioned giants which can rarely be procured or seen outside zoos. Tortoises are highly responsive reptiles and have long been regarded as the most intelligent of reptiles, but we cannot be sure whether this is true. Mostly creatures of warm and dry places, few will long survive captivity if kept in dampness or allowed to become chilled. They are the most docile of the reptile groups in their general demeanor and can seldom be induced to bite. Of the continents, only Australia is without tortoises. Africa has the greatest number of species. If we examine the hind foot of a tortoise we see that it is without webs; these reptiles are completely adapted to a terrestrial existence, and

Yellow-spotted Amazon, *Podocnemis unifilis.* Photo by R. J. Church.

Toad-headed turtle, *Batrachemys nasuta.* Photo by G. Marcuse.

Flat-headed turtle, *Platemys platycephala*. Photo by Dr. Herbert R. Axelrod.

Common snake-neck, *Chelodina longicollis*. Photo by G. Marcuse.

Broad-shelled snake-neck, *Chelodina expansa*. Photo by C. M. Bogert.

Emydura kreffti, Australia. Photo by C. M. Bogert.

Texas tortoise, *Gopherus berlandieri*. Photo by R. J. Church.

Bowsprit tortoise, *Chersina angulata*, South Africa. Photo by R. J. Church.

most kinds will not voluntarily enter water. Most subsist on vegetable matter, although a few will take meat from time to time. All should have fresh drinking water available in a low-walled container which cannot be easily tipped.

Four kinds of tortoises are found in North America. The gopher tortoise, *Gopherus polyphemus*, is familiar to residents of the southeastern United States. Gopher tortoises' long burrows, with a mound of sand at the entrance, are in evidence wherever the terrain is suitable. The Texas tortoise, *Gopherus berlandieri*, takes the place of the gopher in that state, while further west the desert tortoise, *Gopherus agassizi*, prevails. The Mexican giant gopher tortoise, *Gopherus flavomarginatus*, is found in the northern part of that country and has recently come on the animal market in some numbers. These tortoises may require some moisture in the early stages of their development, but the adults thrive best in a warm and dry environment. Vegetables and fruits make up the bulk of their diet.

The genus *Testudo* is made up of five species which are further divided into a number of subspecies. All are very much alike in outward appearance and habits, but the tortoise specialist nevertheless takes special delight in identifying them right down to subspecies.

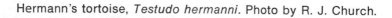

Hermann's tortoise, *Testudo hermanni*. Photo by R. J. Church.

African mud turtle, *Pelusios subniger*. Photo by Dr. Herbert R. Axelrod.

Yellow-spotted Amazon, *Podocnemis unifilis*. Photo by Dr. Herbert R. Axelrod.

Gopher tortoise, *Gopherus polyphemus.* Photo by P. C. H. Pritchard.

Texas tortoise, *Gopherus berlandieri.* Photo by P. C. H. Pritchard.

Two of the most commonly kept kinds are Hermann's tortoise, *Testudo hermanni,* and the spur-thighed tortoise, *Testudo graeca.* Imported specimens commonly measure about six inches, and specimens of this size are frequently kept outdoors, in an enclosed yard or garden. Succulent fruits and vegetables are their choice of foods, and a specimen in good condition will consume a surprisingly large amount. If in perfect health, they may be permitted to hibernate, but any tortoise which is not of normal weight and vigor is not likely to survive such a period of rest. Certainly hibernation is not essential to their well-being, and if kept warm most specimens show little inclination to dig in for the winter. Though land animals in every sense of the word, Hermann's tortoise and the spur-thighed tortoise will enter a shallow container of water and seemingly benefit from such a bath. It cannot be emphasized too strongly, however, that these reptiles are extremely sensitive and are not able to withstand chilling, especially if it is combined with dampness. They are quick to contract respiratory disorders, a common manifestation of which is a wheezing cough.

One of the most beautiful members of the tortoise family is the Indian starred tortoise, *Geochelone elegans.* Of moderate size, this species has each shield of its shell raised in a concentrically ridged cone. Radiating lines of bright yellow symmetrically arranged on a field of black present a striking picture of this Asiatic species. Closely related and hardly less handsome is the leopard tortoise, *Geochelone pardalis,* of Africa, which sometimes will weigh eighty pounds when fully grown. Lately this species has become familiar, as large numbers are imported and sold to private collectors and zoos. There are two varieties, the commoner being the eastern leopard tortoise, *Geochelone pardalis babcocki.* In contrast to most tortoises, one South American kind is noted for its partiality to a humid forest environment. The South American forest tortoise and the red-foot tortoise, *Geochelone denticulata* and *Geochelone carbonaria,* are very much alike and were long considered a single species. Commonly imported, they are among the least expensive of exotic chelonians and do not demand the arid conditions upon which so many kinds of tortoises are dependent. They should be kept warm, 75 to 85 degrees, and fed abundantly on soft fruits and vegetables.

The real giants among the tortoises are, curiously, confined to small islands—the Galapagos Islands off western Ecuador and the

Seychelles Islands and Aldabra Islands off the east coast of Africa. Two species of giant tortoises are recognized, one from the Galapagos, *Geochelone elephantopus*, and one from the Aldabra group, *Geochelone gigantea*. Both species have subspecies. In the case of *G. elephantopus*, there are very many subspecies—each island having, it seems, a distinct form of tortoise. Giant tortoises have been known to exceed a shell length of four feet and a weight of 400 pounds. Despite the tight restrictions governing their export, quite a few Galapagos tortoises somehow get out of the islands. Grey or black in color, they would be even more startling to behold if they matched in gaudiness some of their smaller relatives. The giant tortoises live well over a hundred years and may even exceed two hundred. They grow quickly at first, then much more slowly. They are being propagated in small numbers in the United States.

The pancake tortoise, *Malacochersus tornieri*, is a frequent arrival from East Africa. This agile reptile has a very soft and flexible shell which enables it to squeeze into rock crevices in time of danger. An adult will have a shell about six inches long and only an inch high, presenting a very flattened appearance. In breeding habits the species is unusual in depositing only a single egg in July or August, the baby emerging in the fall. In captivity, pancake tortoises can be made to feel at ease by the provision of a hiding place to imitate the narrow rock crevices of their natural habitat. Whether a box or some other arrangement is made, it should have a roof only slightly higher than the tortoises' shells.

Among the more commonly imported African tortoises are the hinged tortoises, *Kinixys erosa*, *K. homeana*, and *K. belliana*. These are curious in the structure of their carapaces, being able to bring the rear portion down to meet the lower shell, affording the animal good protection from predatory creatures. Some dwell in damp places and are said to pursue and devour aquatic animals as well as the vegetables and fruits which form, at least in captivity, their more usual diet. Other, more obscure forms of African tortoises are those of the genera *Psammobates* and *Homopus*. The former genus has several small, rather bizarre little species that are confined to South Africa and are not commonly imported. They are among the smallest of the tortoise group. Madagascar has the spider tortoise, *Pyxis arachnoides*, perhaps the smallest tortoise.

Giant gopher tortoise, *Gopherus flavomarginatus*. Photo by P. C. H. Pritchard.

Desert tortoise, *Gopherus agassizi*. Photo by C. M. Bogert.

Hermann's tortoise, *Testudo hermanni.* Photo by P. C. H. Pritchard.

Indian starred tortoise, *Geochelone elegans.* Photo by P. C. H. Pritchard.

Hinged tortoise, *Kinixys homeana*. Photo by G. Marcuse.

TURTLE CARE

The care of turtles can be as simple or as complicated as one wishes to make it. Beginning turtle keepers are advised to start with inexpensive, easily procured types and, when the successful care of these has been mastered, graduate to the exotic or rarer kinds of native turtles. It should be understood that while baby turtles are very appealing, their care presents more problems than that of their more adaptable adults. Because they will readily consume many kinds of foods that are deficient in the vitamins and minerals which are essential to growth and health, many baby turtles in captivity appear to be doing well for a short time, only to fall eventually into a state of poor health which can be reversed only with great difficulty, if at all. It would be senseless and needlessly repetitive to list under the heading of each species all the foods that that particular kind of turtle can be fed.

Generally speaking, aquatic turtles are largely carnivorous, semi-aquatic types both carnivorous and herbivorous, and the tortoises largely herbivorous. This is not an infallible way of defining feeding habits, but it will apply in a general way. I have found it easy to bring babies of the aquatic types out of their critical period of infancy with finely chopped whole fish of the various kinds sold as bait for fresh and salt-water anglers. These bait fish seem to contain all the really essential ingredients for the promotion of normal growth, and may be varied with chopped worms, freeze-dried and live tubifex worms, enchytrae, crushed snails, and other small aquatic animals. The packaged ant-egg products sold so widely as food for baby turtles are all but useless in the care of baby turtles and should have no place in their diet. If a baby turtle is well nourished, an occasional feeding of finely ground lean raw beef seems to do little harm, and a few of the really hardy types of small turtles can even be maintained indefinitely on a diet of this sort, although they will seldom show normal growth. Vionate and bone meal, mixed in small amounts with a chopped beef diet, will help prevent vitamin deficiency conditions. Canned dog foods of the better grades are well fortified with vitamins and minerals and can be used with success when the infancy stage has been outgrown. From the standpoint of the keeper, it certainly is a convenient food to feed sub-adult and grown turtles.

Baby turtles such as the chicken, painted, and European pond turtles are difficult to raise and must be provided with food closely approximating that which they would find in the wild state. Freeze-dried and live tubifex worms, varied with ground pond snails, form a good starting diet for hatchlings. Marine turtles, babies especially, will do well on chopped fish and molluscs. In the early stage of my reptile-keeping, I maintained a baby snapping turtle on a diet of nothing but finely cut raw beef. It was about two inches long when I obtained it and after a year still appeared in excellent condition, with no shell-softening, but neither had it shown any noticeable growth during this time. I now realize that if it had been given more nourishing food it would have shown much growth. The snapper is a notably hardy turtle, and I doubt whether many other turtles could be successfully maintained over a long period of time on such a deficient

Forest tortoise, *Geochelone denticulata.* Photo by P. C. H. Pritchard.

Leopard tortoise, *Geochelone pardalis.* Photo by Dr. Herbert R. Axelrod.

Red-footed tortoise, *Geochelone carbonaria*. Photo by H. Schultz.

Galapagos giant tortoise, *Geochelone elephantopus*. Photo by P. C. H. Pritchard.

diet. A similar experiment with a baby alligator snapper terminated with great shell-softening and early demise. In connection with this experience with the baby alligator snapper, it will be of interest to note that it is the only turtle in my experience which will develop the symptoms of vitamin deficiency, such as soft-shell, and yet continue to grow several inches before succumbing. The thoroughly aquatic baby turtles will generally ignore lettuce leaves or other vegetable matter; the semi-aquatic, basking types of the family Emydidae will often avidly devour such matter thrown into their water. The terrestrial emydids such as the wood, box, and Blanding's turtles can and do eat on land, but their babies are best fed in very shallow water. Only a very few kinds of adult turtles resemble the true tortoises in being able to eat on land.

Poor nutrition early in life can lead to dwarfing. This two-inch turtle is a three-year-old diamondback. Photo by R. J. Church.

In the case of turtles beyond their third year, much less attention needs to be given to diet. While babies are best kept on a daily small feeding, most adults will do well on a liberal meal twice a week. The bone-hardening process seems to be completed during the first years of a turtle's life, and I cannot recall a case of shell-softening in an adult turtle, though other debilities can develop through improper feeding. For the reasons given above, it is obvious that a half-grown or adult turtle is easier to care for than a juvenile. I consider the box turtle an ideal species to begin with—but only if well grown.

Baby tortoises are, if anything, even more difficult to raise than their aquatic and semi-aquatic relatives. For the most part herbivorous, it is essential that the crushed fruits and vegetables given them be well mixed with powdered vitamins and calcium. They should have drinking water available at all times, for creatures of small bulk will desiccate much more rapidly than larger ones. Some of the fruits and vegetables which may be offered tortoises are lettuce, bananas, pears, berries, and chopped carrots; hard-boiled eggs with crushed shells and canned dog food may be offered. Some baby tortoises will take earthworms. Their drinking water should contain copper—a penny will do—and a piece of slowly dissolving calcium block in the water will be of benefit, too. These should be placed in the swimming-water of baby aquatic and semi-aquatic turtles, also. Caring for baby turtles and tortoises requires something of the gardener's "green thumb." Some persons have had remarkable success in raising them but in such cases a great deal of patience has played a major role. Collectors with little time for the sympathetic care required by most baby chelonians will find half-grown or adult specimens more accommodating in their requirements.

The matter of providing correct air and water temperatures for turtles and tortoises is a very important one, as it is for nearly all other reptiles. Some writers attempt to describe what they consider optimum temperatures for various chelonians. Such information seems somewhat overdone; all turtles and tortoises are warmth-loving animals, with the possible exception of the Asiatic big-headed turtle and certain very aquatic native species. I consider a temperature range of 78 to 83 degrees quite satisfactory for the great majority of turtles and tortoises. Tropical tortoises, particularly, are apt to fall into serious trouble if the air temperature falls below 70 degrees. With these, even cold drinking water may prove detrimental. At 90

Hinged tortoise, *Kinixys belliana*. Photo by Dr. Herbert R. Axelrod.

Aldabra giant tortoise, *Geochelone gigantea*. Photo by P. C. H. Pritchard.

Parrot-beaked tortoise, *Homopus areolatus*. Photo by M. F. Roberts.

False gavial, *Tomistoma schlegeli*. Photo by H. Hansen, Aquarium Berlin.

degrees many turtles show evidence of distress. This is especially true of those species which may normally aestivate in the wild state during hot weather, and of the aquatic species which may enter deeper water at such times. At the upper limit of the desirable temperature range, there is increased activity and a need for larger and more frequent feedings.

Tied in closely with the subject of feeding captive turtles is the matter of cleanliness. It is rather startling to read, as I have recently, in a supposedly erudite publication, that cleanliness is not important in keeping chelonians. Anyone who has kept large numbers of turtles and tortoises will know the detrimental effects that a sustained state of fouled water can have. I consider it a good idea to feed aquatic and semi-aquatic turtles in a container other than their permanent home. Few keepers of turtles have the facilities for installing the complicated plumbing which will permit large aquariums to be easily drained and refilled with fresh water. The excreta of turtles has far

Example of a well-planned but simple aquarium for water turtles. Photo by R. J. Chuch.

Terrariums for tortoises need not be complicated to be attractive. Photo by R. J. Church.

less of a polluting effect on their water than decaying bits of fish or meat. The plastic basins sold in department and variety stores are light and easy to handle, and may be bought cheaply. They are ideal feeding places for turtles of small to medium size. Water used in these basins should be near the temperature of the permanent home. Incidentally, when large numbers of baby turtles are being reared, these plastic containers can be utilized as nurseries. The cleanliness of the turtles themselves should be given some thought. Algae are often found on the shells of wild turtles, often to the degree of completely obscuring their shell markings. I do not think that captives should be compelled to have their beauty so concealed, and I use ordinary household vinegar and a soft cloth to periodically clean the shells of my turtles. A brush would be more effective, but experience has shown that even a soft-bristled brush will greatly agitate turtles, sensitive as they are to any tactile stimuli of their shells.

The pH factor in water has undergone considerable study by aquarists who keep and breed fishes. They have found that it may be critically important in the propagation of certain fish species. The

Young caiman, *Caiman yacare*. Photo by H. Hansen, Aquarium Berlin.

Gavial, *Gavialis gangeticus*. Photo by K. Alexander.

Spectacled caiman, *Caiman crocodilus*. Photo by M. F. Roberts.

Desert iguana, *Dipsosaurus dorsalis*. Photo by J. K. Langhammer.

matter is little understood as it relates to turtle husbandry, but we do know that fungus infections can often be cleared up when there is a drastic reduction in the alkalinity of the water. Monobasic sodium phosphate can be added to water to bring it to the desired pH. Vinegar can be added to achieve the same result. Kits for the simple testing of pH content can be bought in most pet shops. A slightly acid water may be best for most turtles—a reading of pH 6.6 or 6.8. With continued experiments in the breeding of chelonians in captivity, it would not be surprising to find that pH is a factor of some consequence.

Sunlight is very important to most turtles and tortoises and is essential in the raising of some species. The ordinary high-walled aquarium will filter out most of the beneficial rays, as will ordinary window glass. For this reason, low-sided aquariums are best for turtles. These can be placed in open windows, preferably with a southern exposure; so placed, they will allow the inmates a natural sunbath. Of course, this can be done only in warm weather. During our northern winters, turtles which have hatched in the fall can be brought through the difficult months with the use of one of the many sun lamps on the market. These lamps vary considerably in the intensity of their ultraviolet ray output and lacking, as we do, specific information pertaining to the effect of long exposure of turtles and tortoises under these lamps, it is best to limit their use to the time specified for humans. Such directions accompany these lamps, some of which may be purchased for as little as ten dollars.

Most turtles will feed readily in confinement, although some are excessively shy when first caught and may refuse to eat the first week or two. If a turtle is being kept under good conditions and refuses to eat over a long period, there can be any one of several distinct causes. First of all, the food itself may be at fault. Most turtles' feeding habits are not specialized to the extent that they will accept no substitute for the food they are accustomed to taking in the wild state. I have, however, noted that certain of the mollusc-devouring species which develop enormous heads in the adult stage will often refuse any substitute for their natural fare. This condition may prevail in adults of certain map turtles and musk turtles. Snail-eating turtles of the genus *Malayemys* are said to feed on little else, but in an aquarium they will readily accept a substitute diet. A turtle which naturally hibernates in cold weather may be disinclined to partake of food during this period, but this is not usual; such a specimen will continue to feed, at least sparingly, as a rule. A turtle in really poor health will not eat, and a variety of conditions may be responsible. The turtle's illness will generally manifest itself in other recognizable ways.

BUYING TURTLES

The illnesses to which captive chelonians are susceptible may be traced mostly to the lack of proper care. Once a turtle is sick, a spontaneous recovery is very rare; definite measures must be taken to reverse the conditions which brought about the illness. Before taking up what we know about turtle ailments, let us discuss the methods whereby we may at least assure ourselves that the specimen we are about to acquire is in good condition to begin with. Sick turtles, or other herptiles, for that matter, are seldom found in the wild. Nature is no respecter of ill health or old age, and no creature survives long when it has become infirm. We may therefore assume that a turtle we have captured ourselves is in good condition. A turtle purchased from a dealer, on the other hand, may have been subjected to gross mistreatment from the time of its capture.

I would not buy a turtle that has been kept under filthy conditions, allowed to go without water over a long period, or that is in contact with other turtles that seem in bad condition. It is better to patronize those dealers who care enough about the welfare of their live wares to assure them conditions of reasonable comfort while awaiting a sale. Perhaps the first and easiest thing to assess, in the case of a juvenile chelonian, is the hardness of its shell. A few turtles and tortoises have a naturally soft shell. This is true of the pancake tortoises and the aptly named soft-shelled turtles. Other turtles should have a reasonably hard, firm shell. The eyes should be bright and alert, without a trace of film or exudate of any kind. The area about the nostrils should be free of any discharge. The shell should be without eroded or eaten-out spots. The weight should be good, and this can be readily determined by anyone who has had some little experience with turtles. Normally, a turtle or tortoise feels quite heavy for its bulk. The head, neck, and limbs should be checked for the presence of whitish spots that may indicate a fungus infection. It should be without lumps or sores. Finally, it should be placed in several inches of water, if an aquatic or semi-aquatic

Chuckwalla, *Sauromalus obesus*. Photo by J. K. Langhammer.

Earless lizard, *Holbookia maculata*. Photo by F. J. Dodd, Jr.

Collared lizard, *Crotaphytus collaris.*

Zebra-tailed lizard, *Callisaurus draconoides.* Photo by F. J. Dodd, Jr.

Green anole, *Anolis carolinensis*. Photo by G. Marcuse.

Leopard lizard, *Crotaphytus wislizenii*. Photo by J. K. Langhammer.

Clark's spiny lizard, *Sceloporus clarki.* Photo by F. J. Dodd, Jr.

Spiny lizard, *Sceloporus nelsoni,* Mexico. Photo by F. J. Dodd, Jr.

can range in price from a couple of dollars to well over a hundred dollars, and herptile hobbyists do not differ from others in continually seeking bargains. Take the "odd" one home and have fun identifying it in your leisure time.

All crocodilians lay eggs; the eggs are laid on land, in a situation which will provide the necessary heat and moisture for their development. Some species remain near their nests to protect the eggs from the predations of creatures which consider them a delicacy. Would-be hunters of crocodilian nests had best keep this in mind. Nests may be elaborate or simple, depending on the species. A baby crocodilian is among the most engaging of baby reptiles and from the very first will display all the characteristics of adult members of its kind. If treated properly, however, it will soon grow to a size that is not easily accommodated in the average private collection. A curious thing that I have not seen mentioned elsewhere is that under certain circumstances a baby crocodilian that is kept warm and fed well, but kept in a small cage, will have its growth limited by the area of its surroundings. I have seen this happen in the case of an American alligator which occupied for over ten years a cage about the size of a twenty-gallon aquarium. It was about a foot long when obtained and took perhaps two years to reach a length of two feet. Beyond this point, it did not grow but remained vigorous and in apparently the best of health. It was kept at a constant temperature of eighty degrees and fed exclusively on goldfish and other aquatic animals. It became very tame—a veritable pet—and assumed the heavy body build of an adult, but remained adjusted in size to the aquarium it occupied. It had a bathing pool sunk in a floor of gravel, but entered it only at feeding times. It received sunlight only in the filtered form, through two thicknesses of glass. Whether such dwarfing of a specimen is always possible—or desirable—I do not know, but mention it only as an aside to the usual experience of having a young croc outgrow one cage after another. It would seem that spaciousness of surroundings, in addition to all the other factors of caring for a young crocodilian, plays an important part in the growth process.

Crocodilians of all sizes are well-equipped for defense, and even very small ones are best held just behind the head to prevent scratches from their sharp teeth and strong jaws. Specimens of three feet are best handled with thick leather gloves. Some crocodilians have an unvarying aggressiveness and remain vicious even after a long period of confinement. In the wild state a crocodilian will overpower and eat animals of large size. The man-eating propensities of a few kinds are well authenticated. Food may be seized on the land or in the water, but is always devoured in the latter element. Here the croc is perfectly at home, and I do not think many creatures have lived to tell the tale of an engagement with a large crocodilian. Crocodilians' jaws are very powerful in regard to biting pressure, but this power, strangely, cannot be exerted to open the mouth. It is possible for the average person to hold the mouth of a large crocodilian shut with only his hands. This may be witnessed in the alligator-wrestling shows.

Crocodilians display great agility—in and out of water. An effective means of defense and offense is provided by their powerful tails. This is swung with great swiftness and can easily topple a man if the blow comes from a large specimen. With its muscular tail the crocodilian swims gracefully and well. Some species enter the ocean and swim far from shore. Crocodilians run well out of the water and do so with the body well raised from the ground. They seem incapable of sustaining this means of locomotion over a long period, however. Some of the larger types are genuinely dangerous animals and will kill and eat a man as they would any other mammal of similar size. Even such good-dispositioned species as our American alligator will sometimes display suspicious activity in this respect, especially in those places where it is under legal protection and has come to the state of contempt bred by familiarity and non-molestation.

All crocodilians are completely carnivorous. To sustain good health, they must receive an adequate intake of vitamins and minerals. I consider small fishes, fed whole or chopped, the best food for juveniles. Larger specimens may be fed mice and rats, as well as other vertebrate animals. Their calcium requirements are high and adequate portions must be provided if normal health and growth are to be ensured. Sunlight is a great asset if judiciously provided and the animals are not allowed to become overheated. All species do best in a temperature of 80 to 85 degrees. Whether kept in a large aquarium or other type of cage, they must be provided with water in which they can completely submerge, but must also be provided with a land area for completely drying out, as they would on the banks of their native rivers. They seem to be subject to fewer diseases than lizards, turtles, or snakes. Rickets will develop in malnourished captives; with the

Tree lizard, *Urosaurus ornatus,* southwestern U.S. Photo by F. J. Dodd, Jr.

Brown-shouldered lizard, *Uta stansburiana,* southwestern U.S. Photo by F. J. Dodd, Jr.

Texas horned lizard, *Phrynosoma cornutum*. Photo by J. K. Langhammer.

Short-horned lizard, *Phrynosoma douglassi*, western U.S. Photo by J. K. Langhammer.

long, slender-snouted crocs, rickets can result in gross deformity. Crocodilians live to a great age—possibly approaching that of some turtles. They grow rapidly and are likely to add a foot or more to their length each year under especially favorable conditions.

Crocodiles and alligators should not be mixed with other reptiles or amphibians, nor should they be mixed in sizes among themselves. Cuts and bruises are frequent from fights and these can be swabbed with iodine and will usually heal without complications. Baby crocodiles should have their mouths examined periodically. Their teeth should be clean and if encrusted, as seldom happens, can be brushed with very soft bristles. This will seldom be found necessary if the animals are housed in clean and well-kept cages and liberally supplied with the right foods. Such an examination of the teeth and mouth can be made while the reptile is basking with its mouth open. In their first months of captivity, crocodilians sometimes void large numbers of intestinal worms. These become fewer in number as time goes on and often disappear entirely. They appear to be of little consequence to their hosts.

Young crocodilians are often considered to be delicate, but they will do well if fed often on the right foods and given enough heat. Photo by M. F. Roberts.

Crocodilians from temperate regions hibernate in the natural state during the cooler months, while those of some tropical areas may estivate. Either of these inclinations may be carried over into captivity and cause an apparently quite healthy reptile to go off feed for a period of time. In anticipation of such a fast, the keeper of crocodilians should make every attempt to keep his specimens well nourished. They will thus have the weight to carry them through several weeks or even months of abstention from food. I would recommend that a baby crocodilian be fed not less often than every other day. This will mean a considerable amount of cleaning, as it is essential that a young crocodilian's water be kept free from pollution. Generally, it will not be practicable to remove a croc from its permanent home for feeding—a system often used with turtles. Many baby crocodilians will not feed in unfamiliar surroundings.

Crocodiles and alligators are subject to fewer disease conditions than other reptiles. Sometimes, however, there appears a cracking and sloughing of the outer epidermis, a condition which is probably related to excessive dryness. It can be alleviated by massaging with pure petroleum jelly. Crocodiles and alligators continually lose and replace teeth in the wild, but in captivity they may lose this capacity because of poor feeding habits. Once again, it is essential to provide the baby crocodilian with its natural food supplemented with small amounts of vitamins and minerals.

I do not think that any private collector has anything like a complete collection of the crocodilians of the world; the rarity of many species and the rapid growth of the animals themselves form an effective barrier to the formation of such a collection without unlimited financial resources. Since they are so alike in habits and general appearance, a young specimen or two will well represent this entire order of living fossils.

GAVIAL

The most curious of the living crocodilians is the gavial, *Gavialis gangeticus*, the single member of its family, Gavialidae. Though growing to a huge size, more than twenty feet, it is not considered a dangerous species in its native haunts—the great river systems of India. It has greatly attenuated jaws that are studded with a massive array of closely interlocking teeth. Despite the great bulk of a fully grown specimen, its diet consists entirely of fishes, and its slender

Regal horned lizard, *Phrynosoma solare*. Photo by J. K. Langhammer.

Yucca night lizard, *Xantusia vigilis*. Photo by F. J. Dodd, Jr.

Broad-headed skink, *Eumeces laticeps.* Photo by F. J. Dodd, Jr.

Arizona alligator lizard, *Gerrhonotus kingi.* Photo by F. J. Dodd, Jr.

Indian gavial, *Gavialis gangeticus*. Photo by G. Marcuse.

snout seems an adaptation to this diet. The gavial is one crocodilian which must be handled with the best of care in captivity. Special attention should be given its diet, which should consist entirely of fish. These may be fortified with additional calcium and vitamins before they are tendered the animal. Though formidably arrayed with teeth, the jaws of a gavial look, and are, very fragile and easily broken. More than one gavial is today surviving in a zoo minus a portion of its snout—the result of a quarrel over food with a species of more robustness. Common in India, gavials are rarely imported and are among the most expensive crocodilians.

AMERICAN ALLIGATORS

The American alligator, *Alligator mississipiensis*, was once the most readily procurable crocodilian, but it is now rigidly protected throughout the southern United States. Dealers are no longer allowed to handle this animal.

If the mass commercial traffic in alligator skins and baby specimens for souvenirs had not been halted, this creature might today be on the list of those close to extinction. When any animal is threatened with extermination, generally the larger individuals disappear first. It is said that American alligators once abounded as twenty-foot monsters, but now any individual over twelve feet must be considered very large. Baby alligators are among the more handsome members of the crocodilian tribe, being jet black in ground color and crossbanded the length of the back and tail with bright yellow. They are somewhat hardier than many exotic crocodilians and can withstand lower temperatures, but this is not said with the intention of easing caution in the matter of providing a warm environment. Alligators hibernate in the winter but in captivity should be kept constantly in an environmental heat of 75 to 90 degrees, and this applies to air as well as water. Bits of lean raw beef and liver will be greedily devoured but do not constitute a complete diet; insects, earthworms, and fishes and other small vertebrates are needed. Easily-tamed, the alligator can often be handled easily even when fully grown—this in distinct contrast to many of the foreign crocodilians.

Adult alligators have dens to which they regularly retire. These dens are holes in river banks, and it is in them that the cooler months are weathered. Males grow larger than females and, except at breeding time, are likely to lead a solitary existence, driving off smaller reptiles and even devouring their own young when they are encountered. Courtship and mating take place in the water, and the

American alligator, *Alligator mississipiensis.* Photo by Wathen.

Gila monster, *Heloderma suspectum.* Photo by H. Hansen, Aquarium Berlin.

Island glass lizard, *Ophisaurus compressus*. Photo by F. J. Dodd, Jr.

Gecko, *Peropus mutilatus*. Photo by F. J. Dodd, Jr.

female constructs a rather elaborate nest for eggs. The nest consists of a mound of debris several feet in width and height. The eggs, numbering up to almost 75, are deposited in a central hollow which is then smoothed over. Two to three months are required for incubation; during this time the female remains close by. When the babies are ready to emerge she assists them by opening the nest with her jaws—the same manner in which she constructed it. Baby alligators have many enemies besides man, so probably only a few reach maturity. The cottonmouth moccasin may play an important part in keeping a population balance.

Baby alligators give voice to grunts in recognition of their keepers as providers of food. These noises become deeper as the young reptiles mature; in adult males, the grunts assume the proportions of a resounding roar which can be heard for great distances in the stillness of a bayou night. Baby alligators get accustomed to handling. In common with some other reptiles and amphibians, notably certain lizards and toads, they can be pacified by being laid on their backs and gently massaged on the stomach area.

CHINESE ALLIGATOR

The Chinese alligator, *Alligator sinensis*, is a close relative of the American alligator but is very much separated geographically, being found in eastern China. It is a small species, seldom growing to more than six feet. It is considered a rare animal and is seldom offered for sale by dealers. Together with the American alligator and the South American caimans it makes up the family Alligatoridae.

CAIMANS

The caimans are the crocodilians most commonly sold by pet dealers these days. They are imported from South America in immense numbers and have all but taken over the unenviable position once held by the American alligator in the pet trade. The little creatures most commonly seen are varieties of the widely-distributed spectacled caiman, *Caiman crocodilus*. Bony ridges in front of and around the eyes are responsible for the common name of these reptiles. All of the caimans are tropical reptiles, and this above all else should be kept in mind when one purchases a baby. They have a maximum length of about eight feet and show rapid growth under good conditions. Like other crocodilians, they are

The crocodiles (family Crocodylidae) differ visibly from the alligators and caimans (family Alligatoridae) by having the fourth tooth in the lower jaw visible when the mouth is closed; it is hidden in a pocket in the upper jaw in alligators. Photo by G. Marcuse of a young alligator.

entirely carnivorous and can be fed snails, earthworms, minnows, frogs, and other small animals. Their usual diet, unfortunately, is a much less nourishing one, consisting for the most part of scraps of raw beef and liver. Caimans generally will not take any spiced or cured meat or salted fish. If fed on bits of lean beef, this should be sprinkled with bone meal and a vitamin compound. Hamburger is not a good food, because it falls apart easily, and much of it is left to foul the water of the reptile's cage. Hatchlings of eight to ten inches can readily swallow whole pieces of meat the size of an almond nut. As with all of the crocodilians, some sunlight is a very great aid in promoting the health of captive caimans, especially during their first year. The aquarium or cage for caimans should be about equally divided between land and water, the latter being of about four inches in depth. In selecting a caiman from the aquarium of a dealer, pick the liveliest of the group—one that is ready to bite when picked up.

Tokay gecko, *Gekko gecko*. Photos by H. Hansen, Aquarium Berlin.

Madagascar day gecko, *Phelsuma madagascariensis*. Photo by H. Hansen, Aquarium Berlin.

Many of the specimens we find have been poorly conditioned and are quite thin. Apathetic toward their surroundings, they lie limply about, awaiting an early end. Freshly caught specimens are vigorous little animals, bright and strong, and will remain so if handled correctly. They tame after a while, but remain voracious and will leap from the water to grasp a piece of food offered to them. Caimans are today the least expensive of the crocodilians. It remains to be seen how long their tropical jungle homes will be able to supply the large numbers being sold as pets, not to mention the demands of the leather trade for the hides of grown specimens.

The largest living member of the caiman and alligator family is the black caiman, *Melanosuchus niger*, of South America (20-foot American alligators are no longer found). Its maximum length may be about fifteen feet, but few specimens of this size are captured alive. Babies of this species resemble small American alligators very much. Like other caimans, they do well if kept warm and provided with a nourishing diet.

I recommend a constant temperature range of 78 to 85 degrees for all crocodilians. They succumb almost at once to a really bad chilling. The critical low for the various crocodilians had not been established, but I would suspect that it might be surprisingly high. Undoubtedly, the most tolerant of the crocodilians in regard to temperature drops is the American alligator, but even this species must be kept very warm. Other kinds of caimans which are imported from time to time are the dwarf caiman, *Paleosuchus palpebrosus*, and the smooth-fronted caiman, *Paleosuchus trigonatus*, of the Amazon Basin. These are really small crocodilians, averaging around four feet.

CROCODILES

The family Crocodylidae contains the true stars of the world of crocodilians. Ranging in size from four-foot dwarfs to twenty-five-foot giants, the members of this family flourish throughout the New and Old World tropics. Zoo curators and keepers have long been aware of the differences in temperament among the various species of crocodilians. Among the present group we find some truly dangerous animals—feared in their native haunts and best handled with extreme caution in captivity. In comparison with alligators and caimans, the true crocodiles appear formidable, and their looks are hardly belied by their dispositions. The true crocodiles provide the only authenticated instances of habitual reptilian predation upon human beings. Few private collectors will have the inclination or means of keeping adult crocodiles in captivity, and even very few zoos are equipped to handle really large specimens. Babies are often offered for sale and, during their first two or three years, make interesting occupants of a collection. A fully-grown crocodile of one of the larger kinds may exceed a ton in weight. By comparison, a giant python may weigh in the neighborhood of 250 pounds.

The American crocodile, *Crocodylus acutus*, is the only one of its family which is found in the United States. In extreme southern Florida it frequents brackish coastal waters in small numbers. In Central America, Mexico, the West Indies, and South America it is an abundant reptile. Young specimens are olive-tan, with dark cross-striping along the back and tail; as the animal grows these markings become obscure and finally are lost entirely, leaving a plain dark brown or black animal. I had owned many alligators before I acquired my first crocodile, and it presented an interesting contrast in behavior to the former. It would bask in the sun for hours at a

American crocodile, *Crocodylus acutus*. Photo by G. Marcuse.

Day gecko, *Phelsuma* sp. Photo by H. Hansen, Aquarium Berlin.

Leopard gecko, *Eublepharis macularius.* Photo by H. Hansen, Aquarium Berlin.

Tree lizard, *Calotes calotes*. Photo by H. Hansen, Aquarium Berlin.

time with its jaws agape—a habit I have not observed among alligators. It would occasionally utter a long, drawn-out grunt—this with open mouth—which was very different from the noises made by the baby alligators. It was an agile creature, and though slender in comparison with alligators of the same length, it seemed more powerfully muscled. It became very tame, but its strenuous twisting made it always a difficult animal to pick up and hold for long. In connection with the handling of crocodilians it should be advised that they never be picked up or allowed to hang by the tail. The proper grasp is a firm one just behind the head, the other hand supporting and restraining the rear portions of the reptile. Freshly-caught crocodiles may have leeches attached to them, mostly about their legs. These are easily removed with forceps.

Nile crocodile, *Crocodylus niloticus*. Photo by L. E. Perkins.

Close-up of the head of a crocodile, *Crocodylus* species. Photo by G. Marcuse.

The Nile crocodile, *Crocodylus niloticus*, is a species which is greatly feared by the natives of African villages. A sixteen-foot example can easily kill a man. In the taking of any prey species, the crocodile's mode is to seize the victim and bring it to deep water, where it can be held until it drowns. Unable to swallow massive objects, the crocodile reduces its victims to manageable pieces by twisting and tearing the bodies in its powerful jaws, which are equipped with long, sharp teeth. If two crocodiles seize the same animal, they will fold their limbs and twirl about in opposite directions, tearing their victim apart. Crocodiles fight among themselves, especially when hungry, and serious injury or death may be the result of such quarrels. Alligators and caimans cannot match the dental equipment of the true crocodiles and are likely to come out the worse in any dispute with their vicious relatives. The situation was once reversed at Ross Allen's Reptile Institute in Florida, when a huge crocodile somehow managed to thrust its head into a pen containing a large alligator. The latter seized the crocodile's head and went into the characteristic rolling. The injuries inflicted proved fatal.

Another of the man-eaters is the salt-water crocodile, *Crocodylus porosus*, of Asia and Australia, which may reach twenty feet in length. Even as babies these reptiles show a great exhibition of temper and for a while some may not feed in captivity. It frequents estuaries

Tree lizard, *Calotes versicolor,* Afganistan to southern China. Photo by H. Hansen, Aquarium Berlin.

Frilled lizard, *Chlamydosaurus kingi.* Photo by G. Marcuse.

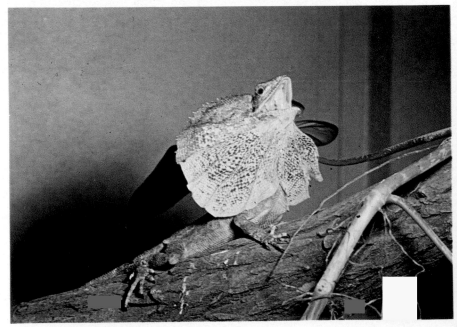

Household agama, *Agama agama,* Africa. Photo by Dr. Otto Klee.

mostly but has been seen far offshore in salt water. Crocodiles of this and other kinds may be successfully force-fed, but force-feeding should be resorted to only when the animal has fasted for some time and there seems little likelihood of its taming sufficiently to partake voluntarily of food. Fresh whole fish are best used for force-feeding; the fish should be inserted head-first into the reptile's throat and placed as far back as possible. Wooden blunt-tipped forceps may be used to minimize damage to the angry reptile's teeth and mouth when it clamps shut. Most crocodiles will eat after they have been in captivity for a short time, and it is not desirable to maintain a specimen of any herptile which does not feed voluntarily.

Muggers are Asiatic crocodiles known scientifically as *Crocodylus palustris.* Widespread and very abundant, they are timid animals and somewhat alligator-like in disposition. Like alligators, they have broad and massive heads. Occasional examples have become predaceous upon humans, but with this species the rule is here excepted. In India, muggers are often corraled in a semi-domesticated state; they are said to breed well under such conditions. Muggers have an average length of about twelve feet. An example of this size would require about twelve pounds of meat a week to keep it in good condition.

Two species of dwarf crocodiles are recognized. One, the Congo dwarf crocodile, *Osteolaemus osborni*, is considered the smallest living crocodilian, with an adult length of about four feet. The other, the West African dwarf crocodile, *Osteolaemus tetraspis*, is but slightly larger. Little is known of the habits of either of these rare reptiles.

The false gavial, *Tomistoma schlegeli*, stands in a genus of its own. It is the most slender-snouted of the true crocodiles and superficially resembles the true Indian gavial. False gavials are found on the Malay Peninsula, Sumatra, and Borneo. Like all other crocodilian species with excessively slender snouts, false gavials can be quickly and permanently deformed if fed on the wrong kinds of foods during their early years. Fish constitute the main fare of these animals in the wild state and must be provided in captivity. If a young false gavial is fed on meat, the snout will not lengthen in natural conformity with the growth of the infant, but instead will hook upward, with the teeth growing in every which way. If natural sunlight or the substitute of a sun lamp is not available, it is especially important to

False gavial, *Tomistoma schlegeli,* in top and side views. Photos by
G. Marcuse.

Water lizard, *Physignathus cocincinus,* southern Asia. Photo by H. Hansen, Aquarium Berlin.

Water lizard, *Physignathus lesueuri*, Photo by H. Hansen, Aquarium Berlin.

to make sure that all baby crocodilians receive vitamin and mineral supplements to their regular diets.

Frequently the reptile man is asked to explain the difference between an alligator and a crocodile. The question is asked, generally, by someone who thinks that the names denote quite different animals. This is not so. The alligators, caimans, crocodiles, and gavial are very closely related, more so than the members of other orders of herptiles. It is true that the animals we know as crocodiles are usually more vicious and harder to tame, but even in this matter of temperament there are exceptions. Muggers, which are true crocodiles, tame readily in captivity, whereas caimans of some kinds are often hard to handle and resemble the worst of the crocodiles in this respect. A simple answer to the question of the difference between an alligator and a crocodile must revert to details of dentition. Simply put, with the crocodiles the fourth tooth of the lower jaw remains visible when the mouth of the reptile is closed. With the alligators and caimans, this tooth fits into a socket in the upper jaw and is thus not to be seen when the mouth is closed. Some of the caimans are very like crocodiles in appearance, and this matter of tooth difference can serve to enable anyone to determine whether a questionable specimen is a caiman or a crocodile.

Crocodiles in general, no matter how abundant they may be in their Old World jungle homes, will command a better price than the more common caimans. Persons engaged in the selling of reptiles are almost always aware of the identity and true value of their wares. The American crocodile is usually the only true crocodile which can be purchased for a moderate sum.

IV

Native American Lizards

The lizards of the United States are a fascinatingly varied group of reptiles that will well repay the effort expended on their behalf in providing suitable conditions for them in captivity. None grows to a really large size, and most are readily procurable.

Unlike the snakes and other reptiles which often make a quick and good adjustment to cage life, lizards are a bit more demanding in their requirements. Also, they usually don't live as long as other captive reptiles. This may be due to the fact that many of the smaller kinds are naturally short-lived, as many of the smaller snakes are believed to be. This may not be the whole story, however, for in exceptional cases even the smallest lizards have lived for very long periods. It is a very rewarding accomplishment to maintain a varied group of lizards in good health.

Lizards belong to the suborder Sauria and are often referred to, collectively, as saurians. They are quite closely related to snakes; the latter have, in fact, been derived from them. The smaller lizards, especially the secretive kinds, are often mistakenly identified as salamanders—even by herpetologists in the field, where a snap judgment of a scurrying creature has to be made! All lizards differ from salamanders in having a scaly, usually dry skin; salamanders have a moist, scaleless skin which feels clammy and often sticky to the touch. Some lizards have no legs; the legless lizards are few in number in the United States, and where they are found they are commonly regarded by local residents as snakes. Like most other lizards, they have eyelids and external ear openings that immediately separate them from the snakes, which have neither. The Southwest

Sail-tailed water lizard, *Hydrosaurus amboinensis.* Photo by H. Hansen, Aquarium Berlin.

Knight anole, *Anolis equestris.* Photo by G. Marcuse.

Spiny iguana, *Ctenosaura hemilopha*, Mexico. Photo by F. J. Dodd, Jr.

is the stronghold of the lizards in the United States, followed by the Southeast. As one proceeds toward the North, the numbers and kinds of these sprightly forms diminish, because lizards are warmth-loving animals; most of the 3000 lizard species live in the tropics. In New England, for instance, any lizard is an exceptionally rare find.

Lizards live in trees, on the ground, and in subterranean tunnels. Matters of habitat and moisture requirements must be taken into account if they are to be kept in health. Most lizards in this country are diurnal, but there are a few kinds which are active by night. Lizards are among the cleanest of animals in captivity and, once set up in an appropriate cage, require but little attention. Like snakes and turtles, they are quiet animals and not likely to disturb their neighbors, in this respect, at least. Many species have a fragile tail, and no lizard should ever be handled by its caudal appendage. In most species, the tail is likely to break under the slightest stress, while those species that have a more durable tail can suffer a vertebral injury if allowed to twist about or hang by this member. With the single exception of the Gila monster, the lizards of the United States are harmless to man; most can inflict no more than an inconsequential nip. Many of the more active types become very tame, readily accepting food from the hand. If several lizards are kept in a cage, there is likely to be a great deal of activity, especially if conditions are to their liking. Some will breed and produce fertile eggs. Others produce living young. Some lizards of the United States rival the most beautiful exotic forms in their coloration and markings. There are few handsomer saurians than the male collared lizard in his breeding adornment.

AMERICAN GECKOS

The family Gekkonidae has only a few representatives in this country, of which the most familiar and best adaptable to vivarium life is the banded gecko, *Coleonyx variegatus*. This delicate little three-inch lizard of the southwestern deserts is yellowish with a series of dark bands across its back. Like most geckos, it is nocturnal and issues from rock crevices at dusk to prowl and search for food in the form of small insects. Its wanderings during the night may take it a considerable distance from its home, and it may be encountered on highways after dark. When caught it will attempt to bite and may emit a squeal. During the spring the species deposits two eggs. Banded geckos are accomplished climbers, the adhesive qualities of their toes enabling them to scale the smoothest surfaces and even walk across ceilings. In captivity, banded geckos should be provided with pieces of bark or rocky caverns in which to pass the daylight hours.

Similar in size to the banded gecko is the Mediterranean gecko, *Hemidactylus turcicus*, an Old World gecko that has become well established at various places in the southern United States. Geckos in general seem little afraid of humans, and *H. turcicus* is among those which readily take up an abode in or near houses. Insects are attracted to light, and where geckos are common a good place to look for them at night is on the window screens of dwellings.

DESERT IGUANA

Few lizards have been as widely kept as pets as the members of the family Iguanidae. Typically Western Hemisphere inhabitants, the members of this family are known collectively as iguanids. A rather large denizen of our southwestern deserts is the desert iguana, *Dipsosaurus dorsalis*. Growing to a foot or more in total length, this lizard inhabits some of the hottest and dryest country and can be found actively foraging during daylight hours when the temperature may be well over 100 degrees. Like that of many desert reptiles, the

Banded gecko, *Coleonyx variegatus*. Photo courtesy American Museum of Natural History.

Common iguana, *Iguana iguana*. Photo by H. Hansen, Aquarium Berlin.

Rhinoceros iguana, *Cyclura cornuta*. Photo by H. Hansen, Aquarium Berlin.

true beauty of this lizard can be appreciated only at close range. In a vivarium, under good lighting, its delicate shadings of gray and brown, reticulated with lines and striations, produce a uniquely handsome animal. The species is an active one and will readily part with its tail. Eggs may number from two to eight and are deposited in the summer, the babies emerging late in that season or in the early fall. Young and adults feed on insects and tender foliage, usually the buds and blossoms of desert plants. Clover blossoms are relished by captives. I would consider a temperature of 95 degrees to be ideal for this species in captivity.

CHUCKWALLA

If the sunshine and constant dry heat they require can be provided, certain desert lizards make very attractive additions to a collection. One of these is the chuckwalla, *Sauromalus obesus*. Dull brown, olive, or even black, the mature chuckwalla is a heavy-bodied lizard but one which can sprint away at great speed when it feels itself in danger. Its habit is to dash into a rock crevice and then inflate its body if attempts at removal are made. The skin is rough and granular, making it almost impossible to extract the lizard without injury when it is pressed tightly against the walls of a crevice. Chuckwallas

Chuckwalla, *Sauromalus obesus*. Photo by L. van der Meid.

Earless lizard, *Holbrookia maculata.* From Van Denburgh.

are very tame in captivity and will feed on succulent greens. A wide variety of fruits, flowers, and leaves should be offered. These may be difficult to provide, especially during the cooler months, and this is just one of the difficulties of keeping these fine lizards alive over a long period. Another is their constant demand for heat and sunshine. Perhaps *Sauromalus* is one of those few reptiles which will do best only in their native regions. The species lays eggs, and the young present a rather startling contrast in color to their parents, being mottled and crossbanded.

EARLESS LIZARDS, ZEBRA-TAILED LIZARD, FRINGE-TOED LIZARD

Several rather nondescript little lizards inhabit the desert wastes of our southwestern states. Two of these, *Holbrookia maculata* and *Holbrookia texana*, called earless lizards, are readily identified by the absence of an external ear opening. Small and fast, they are active during the day and are insectivorous. When running they curl their tails upward, presenting the vividly-barred undersurface.

A similar species is the zebra-tailed lizard, *Callisaurus draconoides*, notable for the fact that it is one of our fastest lizards, having been clocked at 18 miles per hour. At top speed it will rear upon its hind legs and progress in this fashion, a habit common to certain other lizards. Its food requirements are blossoms, tender leaves, and insects.

151

Island iguana, *Cyclura baelopha*, West Indies. Photo by H. Hansen, Aquarium Berlin.

Basilisk, *Basiliscus basiliscus.* Photo by H. Hansen, Aquarium Berlin.

Curly-tailed lizard, *Leiocephalus carinatus,* West Indies. Photo by H. Hansen, Aquarium Berlin.

Zebra-tailed lizard, *Callisaurus draconoides*. From Van Denburgh.

Fringe-toed lizard, *Uma notata*. From Van Denburgh.

The fringe-toed lizards of the genus *Uma* form another group of desert species noted for their alacrity when pursued over desert dunes and their habit of disappearing suddenly into the fine sand. In captivity these lizards will devour insects and also smaller lizards— a fact to be kept in mind. All require a great deal of heat and sunshine, but they also require shady places to which they may retire. Perhaps most reptile collectors will tend to regard these small desert lizards chiefly from the standpoint of food for certain desert snakes. For this purpose they can, if necessary, be killed and kept frozen until needed. Each, however, has a life history of its own, and with the majority this has been little studied. Observation in captivity under favorable conditions could provide us with much information about these smaller desert lizards.

COLLARED LIZARD

The collared lizard, *Crotaphytus collaris*, is an outstanding species among our native lizards. A foot long and of robust build, it is an abundant inhabitant of rocky desert terrain. The color patterns of the male and the female are quite different, but both have the characteristic and vivid double black collar. Females are generally fawn colored or gray, taking on a speckling of red during the breeding season. The males are truly handsome animals, especially in some of their racial variants. Bright green is the predominant color, but over-laying this is a profuse spotting of white, yellow, or red. The throat is washed with a deep orange. For a desert lizard, the present species may be considered fairly hardy in captivity. A dry, warm cage is essential; either natural sunlight or a substitute must be provided or these bright and energetic little animals soon fall into a state of indifference, ceasing to feed and soon succumbing, one by one. The collared lizard furnishes us with an example of the many beautiful reptiles that have requirements that cannot easily be met, particularly in northern latitudes. Because of their beauty and interesting habits, lizards of this kind are much in demand, but unless careful thought is given to their needs, few will survive for any length of time in captivity. Vitamin and mineral compounds intended for human consumption flood the market these days. Mixed with such food as these desert species normally eat, they can be of assistance in maintaining difficult species. Collared lizards are largely carnivorous, but most individuals will take lettuce leaves and other plant material as

Keel-tailed lizard, *Tropidurus torquatus*, South America. Photo by G. Marcuse.

Helmeted iguana, *Corythophanes cristatus,* Central America. Photo by H. Hansen, Aquarium Berlin.

Collared lizard, *Crotaphytus collaris*. From Van Denburgh.

well. Anyone who has caged these aggressive lizards with smaller animals has probably had the sad experience of learning, first-hand, how pugnacious they are. They will unhesitatingly devour any such small vertebrates that they can overcome, including other lizards and snakes. The collared lizard is an oviparous species and deposits up to a dozen eggs in early summer. The eggs hatch about ten weeks later, producing charming little editions of the adults.

LEOPARD LIZARD

The leopard lizard, *Crotaphytus wislizenii*, is a close ally of the collared lizard and, like it, a ferocious predator. Reddish-brown in general color, with numerous spots covering the body and legs, it does not have the huge head of the latter, but it seems not in the least handicapped by this deficiency, for it, too, feeds upon almost any other reptile that can be swallowed and even some that can't. More than one leopard lizard has been found choked to death by the size of the prey it had attempted to swallow. It is a fast-running, diurnal lizard which, because of its extreme wariness, is not easily noosed.

ANOLE

The green anole or American "chameleon," *Anolis carolinensis*, has probably found its way into more homes in this country than any other lizard. It is a member of a genus of over 300 species and

Leopard lizard, *Crotaphytus wislizenii*. From Van Denburgh.

Green anole, *Anolis carolinensis*. Photo by M. F. Roberts.

Common chameleon, *Chamaeleo chamaeleon*. Photo by H. Hansen, Aquarium Berlin.

Crested chameleon, *Chamaeleo cristatus*. Photo. by Dr. Otto Klee.

Jackson's chameleon, *Chamaeleo jacksoni*. Photo by K. Alexander.

subspecies, all very much alike in body configuration and habits, common throughout the tropical and subtropical portions of the Americas. The species under consideration is the only true native of the United States, but several other species have been introduced and apparently are successfully colonizing. Though not closely related to the geckos, anoles have a toe development which enables them to climb smooth surfaces with much the same facility of the latter. The true chameleons are Old World reptiles and have little in common with our anoles except the ability to change color. In our green anole, the change from brown to green is caused by alteration of the pigment cells of the skin and may be the response to various stimuli such as temperature, light, and emotion. A resting anole is usually brown during the day, turning green at night, but fright and other stimuli will cause it to turn green at any time.

Another curious feature of the anole is the possession of a throat fan which can be distended at will. Anoles are lizards with territorial convictions, which can be readily observed in a cage containing a number of specimens. Males will distend the pink throat fan and bob the head to warn off other males from their territory. A six-inch anole is fully grown and makes a hardy and vivacious inmate of a collection of reptiles. It should be provided with a fairly humid cage; the foliage should be sprinkled from time to time, because it is from hanging drops of water that the lizards will obtain their liquid nourishment. Captives can be maintained over long periods on a diet of mealworms, but a varied diet of flies and other insects is to be preferred. Anoles' tails are very fragile and readily lost. If the break is incomplete, with part of the original tail left in place, a new tail may form beside the old one, causing the lizard to have two tails. A specimen with this deformity came into my possession recently, and it seemed in no way handicapped by the extra tail. This habit of parting with the tail is common to many families of lizards. The new tail will seldom resemble the original one and it is possible to tell at a glance whether a lizard has its original tail or a regenerated one, since the latter is usually shorter and of different scalation from the original. Under conditions of repeated partial breaking, it is possible to produce lizards with three or more tails. These freaks are curious to the layman but of little interest to the herpetologist. Among the reptiles, only the lizards—and not all of them—are able to regenerate lost tails.

It is interesting to establish a colony of, say, a dozen anoles in a large aquarium or other cage. Abundant foliage should be supplied, and the cage should be well lighted. If possible, it should be provided with some sunlight for at least part of each day. Under such conditions, these vivacious little lizards will follow much the same activity as they would in their natural haunts. Territories will be established, and breeding may take place, the tiny eggs being deposited at intervals under bark or rocks in a moist situation. Anole babies, like most other infant reptiles, receive no parental care and are soon stalking their own food supplies in the form of small insects. Growth is quite rapid, and the species may equal or exceed what would probably be its natural life span in captivity.

Despite the large number sold as pets, the anole is still a very familiar reptile throughout the South, where it frequents trees, shrubs, vines, and the environs of old houses. Large numbers may be caught at night with the aid of a flashlight. It is far too abundant in its native haunts to warrant any "farming" by the wholesale suppliers of this little lizard. It is about the least expensive lizard that may be bought by the private collector.

SPINY LIZARDS

The spiny lizards, often called "swifts," form another group of very common lizards which are admirably suited to life in a vivarium. Mostly creatures of dry regions, they abound in some places but are difficult to catch because of their speed and cunning maneuvers when being pursued. Like squirrels, they attempt to keep rocks or tree trunks between themselves and their would-be captors. Two persons working together from opposite sides of a fallen tree or boulder will have better luck than one. Like many other lizards, spiny lizards will quickly part with their tails. None grows to a very large size—even the biggest western species attain a total length of about a foot. It is useless to provide any of the spiny lizards with a container of drinking water. Their habit is to lap drops of water from foliage or rocks. They are active by day and retire to favorite hiding places at dusk.

The eastern fence lizard, *Sceloporus undulatus*, is fairly typical of its genus, bristling, as it does, with coarse, sharply-tipped scales. Males may be easily distinguished from females by the bright bluish-green blotches on their stomachs and throats. This species deposits eggs, but some others produce living young. A very dry cage, liber-

Girdle-tailed lizard, *Cordylus warreni,* southern Africa. Photo by H. Hansen, Aquarium Berlin.

Parson's chameleon, *Chamaeleo parsonii,* Africa. Photo by Dr. Otto Klee.

Girdle-tailed lizard, *Cordylus cordylus,* southern Africa. Photo by G. Marcuse.

Western fence lizard, *Sceloporus occidentalis*, west of Rocky Mountains. Photo by Muller-Schmida.

ally furnished with pieces of bark and a few stones, forms an ideal home for several lizards. They become quite tame and will readily accept mealworms and other insects from one's fingers, with a studied care not to bite the hand that is feeding them. Their sharp claws enable these agile lizards to run rapidly over any surface which is rough in the slightest degree. Unlike geckos, they cannot walk up the straight sides of an aquarium; they are, however, fair jumpers and their cages are best kept covered. Sunlight or a substitute is a requisite for the successful keeping of spiny lizards. They show little of their normal vivacity in a dark cage. Eastern fence lizards have several subspecies which extend the range from the South well into the West. In the east, the New Jersey pine barrens are the northernmost limit of the species.

Some of the western spiny lizards are especially attractive. One of these is the rock crevice spiny lizard, *Sceloporus poinsetti*, of New Mexico and Texas. With its jet-black collar and vividly banded tail, one of these lizards can be seen at a distance. But one seen is by no means one caught, for these beautiful lizards move quickly among the rocks and boulders of their habitat and will usually succeed in eluding any would-be captor. Insects make up the bulk of the diet of the rock crevice spiny lizard, but buds and leaves are occasionally eaten. Several live young are born in the spring and are miniatures of their parents, although they have a more distinct pattern of banding on their bodies. A temperature of 80 to 85 degrees is recommended for this species.

Clark's spiny lizard, *Sceloporus clarki*, is another fine species and one of the largest found in the United States. In general, the larger spiny lizards are hardier in captivity than their smaller cousins. These lizards reach the height of their colors and activity when the sun is high; on cloudy days they may remain concealed and will seldom show any interest in food at such times. I suppose that everyone who has kept lizards has his favorite kinds; of our native lizards I would consider the spiny lizards among the best for pets or exhibition purposes.

The spiny lizards have a number of small relatives which have been placed in the genera *Uta*, *Urosaurus*, and *Streptosaurus*. They are mostly tree- and rock-dwelling lizards of arid and semi-arid regions. They are easy to care for but perhaps not as captivating as their larger relatives.

HORNED LIZARDS

Probably there are not many people who do not have at least a passing acquaintance with the horned lizards. Formerly called "horned toads," these lizards are among the herptiles frequently

Rock lizard, *Streptosaurus mearnsi.* From Van Denburgh.

Red tegu, *Tupinambis rufescens.* Photo by H. Hansen, Aquarium Berlin.

Caiman lizard, *Dracaena guianensis.* Photo by H. Hansen, Aquarium Berlin.

brought home as souvenirs from the West. Placed in unnatural surroundings with insufficient heat, they rarely live as long as six months in the average household. Even under really good conditions, with an adequate supply of unfiltered sunshine and a cage temperature of around 85 degrees, few horned lizards live more than a year or two. Wild horned lizards are believed to feed chiefly upon ants, and a diet of this sort cannot be readily provided in captivity. In the absence of their natural food, various other kinds of insects may be given. Mealworms will be taken but do not constitute a proper diet.

The Texas horned lizard, *Phrynosoma cornutum*, abounds in some areas and is the species very often brought home by travelers. Like most other horned lizards, the present species is adorned with a crown of prominent spines on its head. It has a squat body, short legs and tail, and obviously is not built for a great deal of running. Horned lizards are active during the hottest part of the day and at night bury themselves in sand. The last item is a very important one to consider in providing a home for these quaint little lizards. A four-inch bed of very fine, dry sand should cover the bottom of their cage. Horned lizards do not normally nose about seeking escape, thus scraping and bruising their snouts. Therefore, a cage of all-screen construction is suitable and will provide the dryness and ventilation they require.

Coast horned lizard, *Phrynosoma coronatum*. From Van Denburgh.

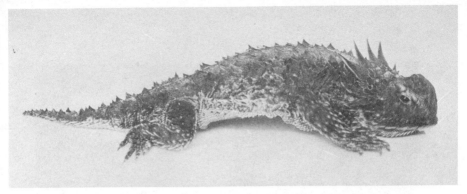

Regal horned lizard, *Phrynosoma solare*. From Van Denburgh.

An interesting feat performed by some individuals is the squirting of streams of blood from the corners of their eyes. This usually occurs only when the reptile is roughly handled or badly frightened. We do not know for sure whether the horned lizard does this voluntarily or not. Some specimens feign death when first captured.

A species of our westernmost coastal region is the coast horned lizard, *Phrynosoma coronatum*. Somewhat more elongated of body than the preceding species, this one presents an even more bristling appearance. It does quite well in captivity if kept dry and very warm. Drinking water for this and other horned lizards can be presented once in a while on a lettuce or cabbage leaf. A fine, mistlike spray of water from an atomizer can be squirted occasionally on the lizards themselves, but this should be done only when the sand of their cage is sure to dry out quickly. No horned lizard is able to tolerate prolonged dampness. An adult may measure in excess of six inches from snout to tail tip. The short tail of this species and others of the genus does not break and regenerate like that of many other lizards. One would think that the horny armament of these creatures would deter any creature from attempting to make a meal of them. Such is not the case, for certain desert snakes eat them quite regularly.

The beautiful regal horned lizard, *Phrynosoma solare*, is one of the largest and finest species. In the United States it is confined to Arizona and is protected by the laws of that state, so is not often to be

Ameiva, *Ameiva ameiva.* Photo by Dr. Herbert R. Axelrod.

Sand lizard, *Psammodromus algirus,* northern Africa. Photo by H. Hansen, Aquarium Berlin.

Wall lizard, *Lacerta muralis*. Photo by H. Hansen, Aquarium Berlin.

had from dealers. The head spines reach a magnificent development in this species, forming a circlet about the head. These may be employed defensively by the twisting and turning of a newly-captured specimen but, for the most part, this and the other horned lizards are among the most inoffensive of reptiles and are a charming part of our desert wildernesses.

NIGHT LIZARDS

The night lizards of the family Xantusidae are secretive and nocturnal animals which were once considered rare. Two genera and four species are found in the Southwest and are among the commonest lizards. The yucca night lizard, *Xantusia vigilis*, fully-grown at four inches or less, resembles the snakes in lacking functional

Granite night lizard, *Xantusia henshawi.* From Van Denburgh.

eyelids. The vertical pupil of its eye is clearly an adaptation to night-prowling habits, though an occasional individual may be found abroad in hours of daylight. The usual hiding places are crevices among rocks and among the leaves of plants. Species of the United States bring forth their young alive—usually in the number of one to three. Night lizards feed upon insects and other arthropods. One kind, the island night lizard, *Klauberina riversiana,* grows to the tremendous size—for a night lizard—of eight inches and is confined to the islands off the coast of southern California. It is frequently seen during the day and is said to include in its diet the leaves, blossoms, and seeds of plants. In captivity all night lizards should be given ample hiding places in a dry cage.

Island night lizard, *Klauberina riversiana*. From Van Denburgh.

SKINKS

Cosmopolitan in distribution and well represented in the United States are members of the family Scincidae, commonly known as skinks. Skinks of this country are smooth, shiny lizards of secretive habits. Herptile hunters make it a point to overturn rocks and strip the bark from fallen trees along their routes of travel. If skinks are at all common, a number of them will certainly be uncovered in this way. The slippery surface of a skink's skin makes it difficult to hold, and skinks have a way of nosing themselves out of one's grasp. Their tails are fragile and easily broken. Although short-limbed, skinks can make good progress over favorable terrain, so collecting them in numbers is no easy task. Because they are generally found in damp areas, their cages should have both moisture and dryness in equal proportions. Skinks will sometimes mate in captivity under very favorable conditions and produce fertile eggs which are sometimes guarded by the female. Some natural sunlight is undoubtedly beneficial, but skinks can apparently do without it if other conditions are right. Most species will find and drink from a small water dish. Insects and other invertebrates are eaten, and the larger species will not hesitate to devour baby mice.

175

Brueggemann's wall lizard, *Lacerta muralis brueggemanni.* Photo by
H. Hansen, Aquarium Berlin.

Sand lizard, *Lacerta agilis*. Photo by H. Hansen, Aquarium Berlin.

The small ground skink, *Lygosoma laterale*, abounds in some areas of the Southeast. Brown above and light below, this lizard may be considered fully grown when only four inches long. It is quite salamander-like in configuration and frequents damp places that are the favorite haunts of insects and other small invertebrates upon which it feeds. Eggs numbering one to five are deposited in such situations and require about two months to hatch. The ground skink is one of the many herptiles of whose life history we know little.

An attractive addition to any collection of herptiles is the five-lined skink, *Eumeces fasciatus*, of the south-eastern states. In the past there has been much confusion in the naming of skinks, and with the present species the young are so much different from the adults that they were long considered a distinct species! When it breaks free of the egg the tiny five-lined skink is a vividly marked animal. The ground color is black and the stripes which run the length of the back are yellow or white. The tail is blue. As the reptile grows toward its adult length of nearly eight inches, the colors become more and more obscure, leaving a plain brown lizard. The adult female retains faint stripes and does not grow as large as the male, which loses all trace of stripes and develops a widely-swollen reddish head. In the rural South these large, vicious-looking males are called "scorpions."

Efforts to collect this and other skinks with a noose are usually fruitless. They do not permit close approach and even if the collector succeeds in getting the noose over the lizard's head the smooth, shiny creature will, likely as not, manage to slip out of it and scurry off to cover. Possibly the best method of capturing these skinks and other diurnal lizards is by stripping the bark from fallen and decaying trees in the early spring and at night. During such collecting ventures it should be carried in mind that one is likely to encounter other and somewhat less pleasant creatures in company with the lizards. Many skinks will try to bite when first captured, and the larger specimens, especially the heavy-jowled males, can inflict a painful squeeze and tend to hang on. Their highly-polished bodies make them rather difficult to hold, and the tail will break readily. Five-lined skinks like a moist environment but also like to sun in a dry place, so any cage for them should provide both damp and dry places, as well as hiding places such as slabs of bark or small houses. Insects and spiders are eaten, but some skinks will accept a beaten egg and shredded raw beef mixture that is placed in a shallow dish. This greatly simplifies

Southeastern five-lined skink, *Eumeces inexpectatus*. Photo by F. J. Dodd, Jr.

feeding them when insects are not abundant. If necessary, vitamin drops may be added to this diet. Skinks may not look like good climbers, but they are, and in some portions of their range they are to be found well up in trees. Mating takes place in the spring when the lizards have emerged from their winter quarters and the eggs are deposited in wood pulp in mid-summer. Skinks are among the few reptiles which exhibit any parental solicitude toward the developing babies. A female will remain coiled about her eggs during the incubation period of about six weeks, but she shows no interest in the babies after they have emerged from their shells. A temperature range of 78 to 85 degrees is ideal for any of our North American skinks.

Likely to be confused with the five-lined skink because of their similar coloring and habits are the broad-headed skink, *Eumeces laticeps*, and the southeastern five-lined skink, *Eumeces inexpectatus*. Differences in scalation cause the demarcation of the three forms. The broad-headed skink reaches the impressive length of over twelve inches. All three species are found in the same broad geographical range.

Green lacerta, *Lacerta viridis.* Photo by H. Hansen, Aquarium Berlin.

Eyed lizard, *Lacerta lepida.* Photo by H. Hansen, Aquarium Berlin.

Sand skink, *Neoseps reynoldsi.* Photo by F. J. Dodd, Jr.

Glass lizard, *Ophisaurus ventralis.* Photo courtesy American Museum of Natural History.

The Great Plains skink, *Eumeces obsoletus*, is another large species. Like the previously-mentioned skinks, this species undergoes a color transition from the young to the adult stage. Tan or light grey, the mature animal is rather attractive. This species, like many other North American skinks, would make an ideal lizard for study if it were not for its secretive habits. Deprived of hiding places, these lizards do not thrive.

Many other kinds of skinks are found throughout the United States. One of these is the small sand skink, *Neoseps reynoldsi*, of Florida, a species which is believed to be in the evolutionary process of losing its limbs. These are of little use to the reptile in its subterranean abode. Whether this is truly a rare lizard, or simply one which is not seen often, is not known. Very little is available concerning the sand skink's life history. Most specimens are taken in relatively dry situations.

WHIPTAILS AND RACERUNNERS

Lizards of the family Teiidae are commonly called whiptails and racerunners. Long-tailed and fast runners, either of these names well describes *Cnemidophorus*, the genus to which all the teiids of the United States belong. The six-lined racerunner, *Cnemidophorus sexlineatus*, bears a superficial resemblance to the striped skinks but has a proportionately much longer tail and is never shiny. Racerunners live in dry, rather open areas and are strictly diurnal. They

Racerunner, *Cnemidophorus gularis*. From Van Denburgh.

183

Striped lizard, *Lacerta trilineata,* Balkans to Asia. Photo by H. Hansen, Aquarium Berlin.

Yellow-throated plated lizard, *Gerrhosaurus flavigularis.* Photo by G. Marcuse.

Red ground skink, *Lygosoma fernandi,* Africa. Photo by J. K. Langhammer.

live entirely on the ground, actively hunting insects, and taking quick flight if approached closely. The western whiptail, *Cnemidophorus tigris*, is found in one or another of its varieties over much of the Southwest. It is like the racerunner in size and habits, flicking its tongue out and in as it progresses over the ground in search of food. Although some of these lizards reach a fair size—over twelve inches—none of the kinds found in this country is able to bite with any effectiveness. Their skin has a dry, soft texture; this makes the lizards easy to hold, once they have been caught—a feat requiring no mean ability on the part of the captor. These lizards will do well only if kept very dry and warm. Mealworms and other insects will be eaten and some individuals will partake of a meat and egg mixture. Handling one of these slender and fragile-looking lizards, it is hard to imagine that it is a close relative of the strong and robust tegus of South America.

ALLIGATOR AND GLASS LIZARDS

Lizards, as a group, are harder to keep alive over long periods than most members of the other major reptile groups. One family, however, produces species which make a quick and satisfactory adjustment to captive conditions. This is the family Anguidae, represented in this country by the alligator lizards and the glass lizards. The southern alligator lizard, *Gerrhonotus multicarinatus*, sometimes called the plated lizard, will live for years in a dry cage that has a sand base and contains rocks and pieces of bark for hiding. Curiously enough for a terrestrial lizard, it seems unwilling, at times, to drink from a low water container and must be provided with sprinkled leaves. Serpentine of body, with rather short legs and a very long tail, its actions when moving along in search of food remind one of a snake. The impression is enhanced by the continual flicking of the lizard's tongue as it explores holes and crevices. *G. multicarinatus* and the other alligator lizards have strongly keeled scales along the back, and each flank has a fold of skin running from the ear to the tail, giving them an emaciated appearance. Alligator lizards differ from species to species in their breeding habits, some laying eggs while others produce living young. The present species deposits up to twenty eggs during June, July, or August. Hatching takes place nearly two months later, and the babies shift for themselves as soon as they are free of the eggs. They measure three to four inches in

Southern alligator lizard, *Gerrhonotus multicarinatus*. From Van Denburgh.

over-all length at time of hatching and can reach an adult length of twenty inches. An example this long is so slender, however, that it could hardly be regarded as a large lizard. Many lizards will part with their tails if handled or grasped by that appendage; the present lizard goes a step further, having the ability to voluntarily throw off the tail and leave it writhing violently to decoy its pursuer.

The northern alligator lizard, *Gerrhonotus coeruleus*, is a smaller species than the preceding and differs from it in having its babies born alive in late summer. A brood will often consist of six or seven baby lizards. None of the alligator lizards could be called really beautiful, but those from Arizona, *Gerrhonotus kingi*, have a more boldly defined pattern of crossbands than the others of this country and their upper jaws are adorned with black and white spots. Alligator lizards can and will devour nearly any small living creature, including spiders and scorpions, that they can swallow. They should not be mixed with other lizards in a cage because of this propensity. Western lizards all, the members of this genus can be found in many habitats, but perhaps the best place to look for them is along the course of streams or in other places where there is some moisture.

Blue-tongued skink, *Tiliqua nigrolutea*. Photo by H. Hansen, Aquarium Berlin.

Striped mabuya, *Mabuya striata,* southern Africa. Photo by H. Hansen, Aquarium Berlin.

Northern alligator lizard, *Gerrhonotus coeruleus*. From Van Denburgh.

In the East the family of anguids is represented by the glass lizard,
Ophisaurus ventralis, and its allies. Because of the absence of legs,
these lizards are often mistaken for snakes. Eyelids and external ear
openings are features which will readily separate these or other
legless lizards from the snakes. Usually some shade of black, olive,
or brown, glass lizards are not colorful, but their adaptability to cage
life more than makes up for this. Glass lizards have smooth and shiny
scales which permit them to make good progress when underground,
where they seem to spend much of their time. They are entirely
carnivorous and in addition to the insects they encounter they readily
consume birds' eggs, other lizards, small snakes, and earthworms. In
captivity they will take an egg and chopped raw beef mixture. It is not
essential to provide them with soil in which to burrow—a piece of
bark or small house will meet the requirement of a place to retire.
Our native glass lizards attain a length in excess of three feet and in a
lizard of this size the tail will account for more than two feet! Despite
their streamlined build, the glass snakes project a clumsy image when
they attempt to slither away. They lack the graceful motions of a
typical serpent and, in fact, even feel quite different when handled.
Most will attempt to bite when first caught, but as a rule they tame
readily and are soon feeding from their keeper's fingers. The island
glass lizard, *Ophisaurus compressus*, and the slender glass lizard,
Ophisaurus attenuatus, are the two other species found in the United
States. All three differ little in habits.

BURROWING LIZARDS

Like the snakes, the lizards have many species which spend virtually all of their time underground. One of these is the worm lizard, *Rhineura floridana*, of the family Amphisbaenidae. Confined to Florida, this lizard has no eyes and no external ear openings. When grown it may measure a foot in length and greatly resembles a large earthworm. It frequents areas of well-drained soil and feeds upon insect larvae and earthworms. Specimens may be found by raking through leaf-mold; after a heavy rain they may be found on the surface. Coloration is usually a delicate shade of pink or lavender. The young are hatched and are surprisingly large—about four inches. An aquarium makes a good home for worm lizards if the bottom is covered with several inches of sandy soil, topped with an inch-deep layer of leaf mold. A moderate humidity may be obtained and sustained by periodic spraying. Burrowing lizards of this family require no sunlight.

Another of our burrowing lizards is the California legless lizard, *Anniella pulchra*, the sole native member of the family Anniellidae. The present lizard is a silvery gray in color and reaches a length of nine inches. In general structure the species is similar to the worm lizard, but it has tiny eyes with functional eyelids. Babies numbering

California legless lizard, *Anniella pulchra.* From Van Denburgh.

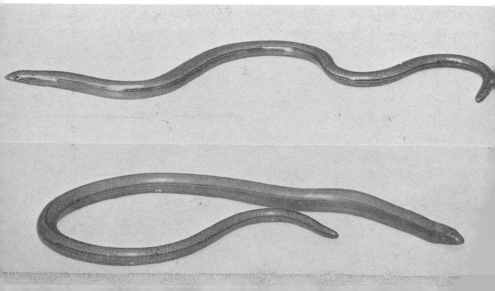

Gidgee skink, *Egernia stokesii,* Australia. Photo by H. Hansen, Aquarium Berlin.

Cunningham's skink, *Egernia cunninghami.* Photo by Dr. Otto Klee.

Sand skink, *Eumeces schneideri*, western Asia to northern Africa. Photo by H. Hansen, Aquarium Berlin.

European glass "snake", *Ophisaurus apodus*. Photo by J. K. Langhammer.

two to four, usually, though rarely a single baby, are born alive in the fall. This lizard requires an aquarium set-up similar to that described for the worm lizard. Excessive dampness is harmful and hardly less so is complete dryness. A happy medium must be reached and therein lies the key to the successful keeping of these secretive lizards. Temperature should be maintained at about eighty degrees. Burrowing lizards of this and the preceding family are rarely to be seen in any cage which provides the correct conditions for then. Keeping them in captivity is a little like keeping a cage full of invisible lizards.

POISONOUS LIZARDS

The family Helodermatidae contains one genus and two species of poisonous lizards. Our native species is the famous Gila monster, *Heloderma suspectum*. Large in size, bizarre in coloration, and grotesque of form, in many ways this lizard is the most interesting one we have. The scales of the Gila monster are very beadlike in character on the back, sides, head, and tail. Each one is rounded and set in relief—the total effect produced is like that of a piece of Indian beadwork. Black and pink prevail as the colors, and no two of these lizards are exactly alike. The head is blunt and swollen and so is the tail, which becomes very heavy in a well-fed lizard but diminishes markedly in size during times when its owner is not eating regularly.

Captive Gila monsters will live for years on a diet of beaten eggs and raw meat. In the wild state, small mammals as well as bird and reptile eggs are eaten. Captives generally show little interest in any other reptiles which may be caged with them. Several specimens may be fed in a low dish containing the semi-liquid mixture of eggs and meat. It is interesting to watch them slowly lap up the contents, periodically raising their heads to allow it to flow down their throats. One egg and a teaspoonful of minced raw beef each week will keep an adult in fine condition.

Gila monsters escape the worst of the desert heat by remaining in burrows during the day. At dusk and during part of the night they may be met prowling in brushy country or even crossing highways. As the reptiles slowly crawl about, they constantly flick out their forked tongues, in this manner picking up scents which are conveyed to paired orifices in the roof of the mouth. These tell the animal what is edible and what is not. Provided with sharply clawed and strong feet, the Gila is well equipped to unearth the eggs of tortoises, lizards, and snakes. If interfered with, a wild Gila monster can move with surprising alacrity and is quite ready to defend itself. Its jaws are large and powerful; once they have fastened on something, it is most difficult to break the hold. Grooved teeth channel the lizard's venom into the bitten object. Some human fatalities from the bite of *Heloderma* are on record. Even without the presence of venom the jaws would be capable of inflicting a most painful injury. There is no specific serum for the treatment of a Gila monster bite.

Captive Gila monsters that are kept indoors soon abandon all inclinations to defend themselves by biting and settle down to a phlegmatic existence, showing no nervous reactions toward humans. They do best in a plain cage which can be easily cleaned. Though true desert reptiles, captives will enter a low dish of water and soak for long periods. Unlike other desert lizards, they do not require sunlight for their well-being. A large Gila may measure two feet in length and makes a spectacular exhibit, but should never be handled carelessly, despite its apparent docility. Females deposit their large

Gila monster, *Heloderma suspectum*. Photo by G. Marcuse.

Papuan monitor, *Varanus salvadorii*, Papua New Guinea. Photo by Dr. Otto Klee.

Sand monitor, *Varanus gouldii*. Photo by Dr. Otto Klee.

Head of a Gila monster, showing poison gland on lower jaw. From Van Denburgh.

eggs, numbering usually five or six, in mid-summer. The four-inch-long babies hatch about a month later.

In this country, Arizona is the stronghold of the Gila monster, and for over fifteen years it has been protected by the laws of that state. It is our only poisonous reptile that enjoys such protection and this was brought about in consideration of the diminishing numbers of the animals in their natural haunts. The species ranges into northern Mexico. Fine specimens could once be purchased for as little as five dollars; now one can expect to pay ten times this amount for one of the few specimens which come on the animal market. The Mexican beaded lizard, *Heloderma horridum*, is the only close relative of the Gila monster and, like it, is poisonous. Its care in captivity is basically the same as that recommended for the Gila, but since it is a larger reptile it requires more commodious quarters. A temperature range of 75 to 80 degrees is ideal for both members of the genus.

V

Exotic Lizards and the Tuatara

FAMILY GEKKONIDAE

In tropical and semi-tropical regions the variety of lizards increases greatly. Lizards, in one form or another, seem to be everywhere—by day and by night. The small lizards of the family Gekkonidae, the geckos, are mostly nocturnal creatures. When the multitude of sun-worshipping lizards have retired for the day, an army of geckos emerges to enliven the night. It is not alone in their night-time activities that these lizards stand apart from most others; they are different in other ways, too. Most geckos' eyes lack movable lids and have the unblinking stare of snakes; their toes are equipped with clinging pads which enable their owners to run quietly over walls and even ceilings; some have a loud call which is used frequently. There are many genera and species of geckos, all of them interesting, and most are adaptable to life in a vivarium.

TOKAY GECKO

The tokay gecko, *Gekko gecko*, is one of the largest species and is imported more frequently and in greater numbers than the others. Fully grown at twelve to fourteen inches, the tokay is usually gray, liberally sprinkled with red dots. As with other geckos, the colors may darken or lighten from time to time. The massive head of this lizard is equipped with a cavernous mouth. A large specimen in my collection would readily devour any smaller lizard, as well as small mice and all kinds of insects. Tokays have good appetites and probably thrive best on small daily feedings. Imported specimens

Yellow monitor, *Varanus flavescens*. Photo by H. Hansen, Aquarium Berlin.

Steppes monitor, *Varanus exanthematicus,* southern Africa. Photo by H. Hansen, Aquarium Berlin.

have frequently been without food or water for some time and are quite emaciated when they reach the cages of retailers, but a tokay in good health has a well-rounded appearance. Many geckos voluntarily

Wall gecko, *Tarentola mauritanica*, Mediterranean area. Photo by G. Marcuse.

take up their abode in human dwellings—the tokay is one of these and so should not feel too much out of place in an apartment!

The tokay gecko's voice is quite loud, and the sound is the one from which the animal gets its common name: "to-kay." It is not a harsh or altogether unpleasant sound, though I imagine that a number of specimens could create quite a din. Mine would usually start calling at 3 o'clock in the morning and stop at 4:30—a rather early alarm clock!

Geckos like the present species should be kept in glass-fronted wooden cages of the type used for the larger snakes. They remain lethargic and inactive during the daylight hours, clinging to the top and sides. At dusk they awaken and spend most of the evening hours scampering about in search of food. No smaller animal of any kind should ever be housed with geckos. The temperature range should be 70 to 85 degrees. Water should be provided by the liberal sprinkling of a piece of bark or some very sturdy foliage plant; this should be done each evening. All geckos can bite and many are quite ready to. They should be lightly but firmly grasped just behind the head when it is necessary to handle them. Like other lizards, and reptiles in general, they do best with a minimum of handling. They may be allowed the run of a reptile room, providing no small animals in uncovered cages are exposed to their predations.

MADAGASCAR DAY GECKO

Tastes differ, and perhaps no two herpetologists would agree in their choices of the world's most beautiful lizard. My own vote would be for the Madagascar day gecko, *Phelsuma madagascariensis*. There are many green lizards in the world, some with subtle shadings and others with handsome patterns, but the day geckos stand alone in the intensity of their color. Scattered over the green body color are streaks and spots of scarlet. There is nothing garish about the creature, yet the simple colors combine to produce an effect which looks positively artificial, especially when the lizards are housed under good lighting. They are not very sociable animals, and if several are kept together in a large cage they usually remain well separated.

Madagascar day gecko, *Phelsuma madagascariensis.* Photo by G. Marcuse.

Girdle-lizard, *Platysaurus* sp., family Cordylidae. Photo by H. Hansen, Aquarium Berlin.

Dull monitor, *Varanus* sp., northern Africa to southwestern Asia. Photo by G. Marcuse.

An unidentified *Platysaurus*. Photo by H. Hansen, Aquarium Berlin.

These and the other day geckos are, as their name implies, diurnal creatures which enjoy sunlight in moderate amounts and a cage that provides some humidity. A small limb with branches attached will help to make these tree-dwellers feel at home. Unlike the majority of geckos, the *Phelsuma* species have round pupils, and this imparts a benevolent expression quite unlike that of their slit-eyed nocturnal relatives. None of the day geckos grows to a large size, seven inches being about average for an adult *P. madagascariensis.*

The geckos are commonly thought of as climbing forest lizards, but some live in areas of great drought and could properly be called desert lizards. Oddly, the body forms of the many species are similar; it is in the tails and feet that differences show up. Nearly all geckos reproduce by means of eggs, though a few live-bearing forms are known from New Zealand. Two, but sometimes only one, eggs constitute the mode for the family. So close has the association of some species with humans become that the eggs are often deposited behind the shutters of houses. More usual places are under stones and beneath the rotten bark of fallen trees.

Leopard gecko, *Eublepharis macularius.* Photo by G. Marcuse.

Brook's gecko, *Hemidactylus brooki*, Africa. Photo courtesy American Museum of Natural History.

Saddle-backed gecko, *Hemidactylus triedus.* Photo by R. Pawley.

Eastern garter snake, *Thamnophis sirtalis sirtalis.* Photo by J. K. Langhammer.

Rosy boa, *Lichanura trivirgata.* Photo by F. J. Dodd, Jr.

Washington garter snake, *Thamnophis sirtalis pickeringii.* Photo by J. K. Langhammer.

Eastern ribbon snake, *Thamnophis sauritus.* Photo by J. K. Langhammer.

Turkish gecko, *Hemidactylus turcicus.* Photo by F. J. Dodd, Jr.

Sand gecko, *Teratoscincus scincus.* Photo by G. Marcuse.

An unusual variant of the leopard gecko, *Eublepharis macularius*. Photo by R. Pawley.

LEOPARD GECKO

The attractive leopard gecko, *Eublepharis macularius*, reaches the fair size of about eight inches and is one of the fat-tailed species, living on the ground among rocks and doing well in a semi-desert type of vivarium. This species, unlike the great majority of geckos, has movable eyelids. Another desert form is the sand gecko, *Teratoscincus scincus*, an animal whose skin has smooth scales, quite unlike the wart-like scalation of most geckos. The saddle-backed blotched gecko, *Hemidactylus triedus*, is a member of a genus that is world-wide in its distribution. Many of its forms are very tiny creatures which require sympathetic care on the part of their keeper, particularly in regard to feeding. Others, like the robust Turkish gecko, *Hemidactylus turcicus*, and the house gecko, *Hemidactylus frenatus*, are larger and easier to care for.

Northern water snake, *Natrix sipedon sipedon.* Photo by F. J. Dodd, Jr.

Northern brown snake, *Storeria dekayi.* Photo by J. K. Langhammer.

Flat-tailed water snake, *Natrix sipedon compressicauda,* two color phases, Florida. Photos by F. J. Dodd, Jr.

FAMILY PYGOPODIDAE
SNAKE LIZARDS

The Pygopodidae, a family of limbless lizards confined mostly to Australia, is a group about which little has been learned. Like many Australian reptiles, they come on the animal market very rarely, and most zoos do not have them. Lacking limbs in most of their species, they glide about like snakes and like snakes have lidless eyes which they clean by means of their tongues. Some give voice to various sounds, like the geckos, to which these strange creatures seem most closely related. The species about which we know a little deposit eggs and are carnivorous: lizards and grubs have been taken by captives. There are some twenty species, a few of which are distinctly burrowing animals. Collectively they are known as snake lizards. One of the better known of them is the attractive Burton's snake lizard, *Lialis burtonii*, of Australia and New Guinea.

FAMILY AGAMIDAE

Some of the most attractive vivarium animals are supplied by the lizards of the family Agamidae. These lizards which make up this family are the Old World counterparts of the more familiar iguanid lizards of the New World. Like the latter, they are strong and active animals which forage by day. In captivity, few will do well unless given sunlight in which to bask. No agamid grows to a really large size, but some are thickset and, though only three feet in length, require large cages if their normal activity is to be seen. Some show rather elaborate courtship displays, and nearly all reproduce by means of eggs.

FLYING LIZARDS

Southeastern Asia and the East Indies are the native lands of the numerous small saurians which have long been called "flying" lizards—something of a misnomer, for the fragile little creatures never actually fly but are able to make extended glides from tree to tree by means of folds of skin which can be distended to support the light body. The "wings" are supported by elongated ribs, much like an umbrella, and the lizard is able to land gracefully quite some distance from its take-off point. In some species, the wings are brilliantly colored. *Draco* is the name of the genus of flying lizards; many species are recognized. They are tree lizards and few ever descend to the ground except to deposit their eggs, which may number from three to five or more. Average length for the various members of the group is ten to eighteen inches. A well-heated cage provided with many branches and twigs can be used to keep captives, but they are delicate lizards, none having lived very long in captivity. Lizards that feed largely upon ants, as the flying lizards do, are very difficult to keep over long periods. Other types of insects do not seem to form a satisfactory substitute. What little we know about the flying lizards indicates that the animals feed largely upon ants in the wild state.

TREE LIZARDS (CALOTES)

One of the difficulties we encounter in writing a non-technical account of the smaller tropical lizards is in the matter of names. In many, the scientific name seems absurd when translated, and often the species do not have native names, or, when they do, the names

Smooth-scaled agamid, *Leiolepis belliana*. Photo by G. Marcuse.

Kirtland's water snake, *Clonophis kirtlandi* (sometimes placed in the genus *Natrix*), north-central U.S. Photo by J. K. Langhammer.

Juvenile **racer**, *Coluber constrictor.* Photo by J. K. Langhammer.

Blue racer, *Coluber constrictor*, color pattern found in central U.S. Photo by J. K. Langhammer.

Striped whipsnake, *Masticophis lateralis*. Photo by F. J. Dodd, Jr.

relate to some imagined characteristic that the species in question do not really possess. *Calotes* is a widespread and abundant genus of lizards which lack a good common name. Let us call them variable tree lizards, for such they truly are or, perhaps more simply, calotes. They are Asiatic in origin and may number in excess of twenty distinct species, most of which are small, slender tree-dwelling forms that are noted for their rapid changes of color, particularly about the head. *Calotes calotes* is a slender and active tree lizard that can be kept alive in captivity over long periods under the best of conditions in regard to sunlight, heat, and abundant insect food. The species has a beautifully colored head of orange, red, yellow, and green—these colors suffusing into a bright red when the lizard is excited. The body is green and the tail is long and whiplike. Their pretty colors show off best in a warm cage, 75 to 80 degrees, that permits the normal running and jumping that these creatures enjoy.

SMOOTH-SCALED AGAMID

The smooth-scaled agamid, *Leiolepis belliana*, is one of the ground-dwelling members of its family, living in burrows and including vegetation in its diet. It grows to about eighteen inches. Its back is olive or brown with a speckling of yellow; this coloration gives way on the flanks to vivid bars of black and orange, while the belly is orange or red. Captives are not secretive, and the males do much harmless fighting among themselves. They should be kept warm and dry, their cage-floor covered with fine sand or dry soil.

TOAD-HEADED AGAMIDS

The toad-headed agamids (*Phrynocephalus neydensis* and related species) are hot country animals which will not tolerate any degree of dampness in their cages. Some possess the ability to threaten enemies by opening the mouth and expanding flaps of skin on either side of the head. These threats may be backed with a sharp bite. Insects are their principal food and, like other strong-jawed agamids, they can easily crush the hardest beetles. Water should be given to them only in the form of drops on a leaf. These small lizards can jump well and often bury themselves in the sand.

Toad-headed agamid, *Phrynocephalus neydensis.* Photo by G. Marcuse.

WATER LIZARD

Many of the agamid lizards run to a certain monotony in form and habits, much the same as our iguanid lizards of southwestern United States. As among the latter group, however, certain forms stand out because of size, appearance, or unusual habits. Among the agamids, one of these is the water lizard, *Physignathus lesueri*, of Australia and New Guinea. This handsome lizard is one of the finest to be seen i captivity. It grows to a length of over three feet, much of this tak

Corn snake, *Elaphe guttata.* Photo by Dr. K. Knaack.

Western patch-nosed snake, *Salvadora hexalepis.* Photo by F. J. Dodd, Jr.

Glossy snake, *Arizona elegans,* western United States. Photo by J. K. Langhammer.

Rat snake, *Elaphe obsoleta.* Photo by F. J. Dodd, Jr.

up by the long, flattened tail. Olives and browns predominate as the colors on the back, but stripes and bands stand out in contrast. The neck is crested with spines and a wide, dark band extends from the eye backward. The belly is red. I think that one of the handsomest exhibits of reptiles I have seen featured examples of these large, semi-aquatic reptiles. The cage, really a huge aquarium, was about ten feet in length and had a water depth of eighteen inches. Running the length of the rear wall was a land area of sand, rocks, and stones which dropped abruptly at the water's edge. A background resembling a jungle river bank added a feature which would transpose the onlooker from an artificially heated reptile house of a modern zoo to the sluggish water's edge of a New Guinea river. Protruding from the water and overhanging its shore was part of a large tree, and reclining on this were several of the most beautiful lizards I had ever seen. This was my first acquaintance with the water lizards, which have remained my favorites among the agamids.

Water lizards will not do well in a small vivarium—they need space, lots of it. They are powerful runners on land, often using a bipedal locomotion, and equally at home in the water. A temperature of 80 degrees is suitable. In general, water lizards can be expected to accept as food any small invertebrates or vertebrates that are placed in their cage. Mice and birds are eaten readily. The species deposits its eggs in tunnels close to water.

FRILLED LIZARD

Sometimes imported from Australia and New Guinea is the frilled lizard, *Chlamydosaurus kingi*, a small species that would tend to pass unnoticed if it were not for its habit of expanding a wide frill about the head when the creature is alarmed. Small and slender, the present animal is likely to startle one who is unfamiliar with its ways. Normally, as when at rest, the reptile's wide collar lies folded inconspicuously against its sides, but a sudden fright throws the frilled lizard on the defensive. The mouth is opened and simultaneously the wide, nearly circular expanse of skin is erected, forming a collar which may be ten inches in diameter and having the flashing brilliance of coloring often seen in really dangerous animals. Captives become tame and spend most of their time on trees and branches, feeding readily on insects and small vertebrates; they soon lose all inclination to expand the frill.

Frilled lizard, *Chlamydosaurus kingi.* Photo by G. Marcuse.

Bullsnake, *Pituophis melanoleucus sayi*. Photo by H. Hansen, Aquarium Berlin.

Florida kingsnake, *Lampropeltis getulus floridana*. Photo by G. Marcuse.

California kingsnake, *Lampropeltis getulus californiae*. Photo by F. J. Dodd, Jr.

Bearded lizard,
Amphibolurus barbatus.
Photo by Muller-Schmida.

Water lizard, *Physignathus lesueuri.* Photo by H. Hansen, Aquarium Berlin.

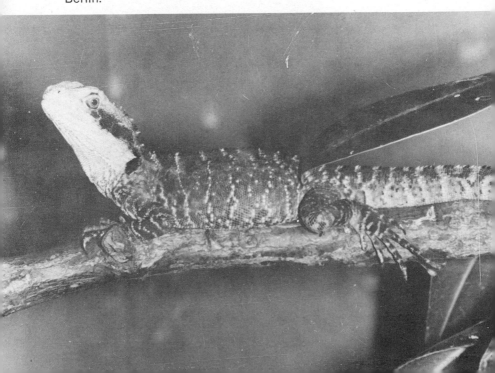

BEARDED LIZARD

Rather similar to the frilled lizard in the method of its bluff is the bearded lizard, *Amphibolurus barbatus*, also from Australia and New Guinea. Desert-inhabiting reptiles, bearded lizards should be kept warm and dry. Insects and occasional vegetable matter are eaten. This spiny 18-inch lizard lives well if properly cared for.

SAIL-TAILED WATER LIZARD

The sail-tailed water lizard is a very large agamid. Known to science as *Hydrosaurus amboinensis*, it attains a length in excess of three feet. The males have a large and showy tail crest. Though strongly built and quite ferocious looking, these semi-aquatic lizards feed to some extent, at least, on the tender leaves of waterside plants. They take to the water when alarmed and are strong swimmers. Only a very large enclosure is suitable for water lizards of this kind.

SPINY-TAILED AGAMAS

The spiny-tailed agamas (genus *Uromastix*) are often imported but seldom do well unless their requirements for heat and a dry atmosphere are provided. The black spiny-tail, *Uromastix acanthinurus*, is representative of the group and, like the others, is a desert dweller which subsists mostly on plant life and is much given to burrowing in the wild state. Young specimens will sometimes take insects. None of the spiny-tailed agamas is brightly colored...the principal adornment of these blunt-snouted desert-dwellers is their large, heavily armored tail, which can be used quite effectively for defensive purposes. Desert lizards of many kinds can do without drinking water if they are sprayed occasionally. They seem able to absorb liquid nourishment through the skin. Their cages must be kept very dry, however. A high temperature range is required and good ventilation is a necessity in maintaining these lizards. They show normal vivacity at 85 to 90 degrees.

THORNY LIZARD (MOLOCH)

Without doubt, one of the strangest-looking lizards in the world is the thorny lizard, *Moloch horridus*, of Australia. Most of us have seen horned lizards of the southwestern United States—some kinds are quite bristly and nearly all have prominent spines, especially around the head. The moloch appears as a gross exaggeration of

Longnosed snake, *Rhinocheilus lecontei*, western United States. Photo by J. K. Langhammer.

Milk snake, *Lampropeltis triangulum*. Photo by F. J. Dodd, Jr.

Great Plains ringneck snake, *Diadophis punctatus edwardsi*. Photo by J. K. Langhammer.

Eastern hognose snake, *Heterodon platyrhinos*. Photo by J. K. Langhammer.

Hardwick's spiny-tail, *Uromastix hardwicki.* Photo by G. Marcuse.

horned lizard. Like the latter, it lives in dry, sandy places and seems to subsist mainly on ants and termites. For this reason, they are impossible to keep in an average collection for any length of time, since 1,000 or more ants may be eaten at a single meal. Moloch lizards deposit their eggs in January; the eggs hatch in February or March, the six to eight young being spiniferous replicas of their parents.

FAMILY IGUANIDAE

The family Iguanidae, like the family Agamidae, is a huge one, having some 700 species which are confined mostly to the New World. Among the many forms one finds a multitude of species which seem to have counterparts among the agamids. Parallelism of development, this is sometimes called. Indeed, the two families have been separated mainly on the basis of dental structure, and without reference to such detail most herpetologists would be hard put to distinguish the less-well-known iguanids from the agamids.

KNIGHT ANOLE

When we think of anoles usually it is in terms of the charming little lizards so well represented by our native species, but there are over 150 other species of anoles found throughout the warmer portions of Central and South America. Most, like *A. carolinensis,* are small lizards not exceeding six or eight inches in length, although certain very large species inhabit the islands of the West Indies. One of these is the knight anole, *Anolis equestris*, of Cuba, a species which commonly measures eighteen inches. Knight anoles are handsome reptiles, mostly green with a network of white markings. Their eyes are circled with blue and the distensible throat fan of the males is pale pink. Like their smaller relatives, they do well in a cage that is supplied with branches, where the anoles will spend much of their time. A damp cage is not suitable, nor is one which is completely dry. Anoles of all kinds must have careful attention paid to their moisture requirements. They require water, which must be provided in the form of drops hanging from foliage. They will not make use of a drinking dish. In the past, the larger species particularly have been considered delicate animals, but many will live a long time if kept warm, fed well on insects other than mealworms, and supplied liberally with water on leaves of plants. The knight anole is large enough to eat mice and small birds. Other giant anoles are found on Puerto Rico, Jamaica, and Hispaniola.

Knight anole, *Anolis equestris*. Photo by G. Marcuse.

Western ringneck snake, *Diadophis punctatus regalis*. Photo by J. K. Langhammer.

Spotted night snake, *Hypsiglena torquata*, western United States and Mexico. Photo by J. K. Langhammer.

Reticulate python, *Python reticulatus*. Photo by H. Hansen, Aquarium Berlin.

Blood python, *Python curtus*. Photo by J. K. Langhammer.

IGUANAS

The common iguana, *Iguana iguana*, is a large arboreal lizard that is imported in great numbers for the pet trade. The pretty green babies one sees in such large numbers are often hatchlings that have been so weakened by lack of food during the most critical period of their lives that there is little hope of bringing them back to health. Iguanas in good condition are lively and vivacious lizards, most often a clear, bright green in color. Specimens that are mottled or that appear emaciated should be avoided. Perhaps it is best to buy a specimen that is out of the infant stage, say 15 to 18 inches long. These will cost a little more but are far more likely to do well in the home. The species grows to six feet and is eaten to some extent by the natives of the tropical areas where it occurs.

All iguanas should have roomy cages with plenty of stout branches for climbing and resting. They need abundant light, and some natural sunlight each day is very beneficial. The adults have the habit of resting on tree limbs overhanging water. When frightened they will drop off and swim away with great speed. Despite this, iguanas could not be described as aquatic lizards. I have never known any that would accept food in the water, and they seem content with just a small dish for drinking. The adults are chiefly vegetarian, but the young will accept animal matter as well as plants. Powdered calcium and a multi-vitamin should be mixed with the chopped fruits and vegetables that are offered. Bananas, pears, cabbage, clover leaves and blossoms, lettuce, and mealworms and other insects are among the many things appreciated by the growing iguana. Some specimens will become accustomed to feeding on the better kinds of canned dog food, which forms a readily procurable and nourishing diet, especially if vitamin drops and bone meal are added. Baby iguanas become very tame and show little of the nervousness exhibited by some lizards. Specimens that are kept alone seem to adjust more quickly than those kept in groups. This is true of nearly all herptiles, with the possible exception of certain turtles. One should never forget that iguanas are tropical lizards that require a great deal of heat—a temperature of 80 degrees suits them fine; their cage should be well ventilated. Artificial lighting is better than none and a bulb may be left burning overhead continuously during the day when an abundant supply of natural light is not available.

Other iguanas become commercially available from time to time. One of the rarest of these imports is the Fiji Island iguana, *Brachylophus fasciatus*, a handsome animal about three feet long which lives entirely on vegetation. The rhinoceros iguana, *Cyclura cornuta*, is a heavy-bodied, dull-colored member of the family. A fully grown male rhinoceros iguana is an impressive animal. The snout is provided with three horns and the stout body is crested with a row of spines. The legs are robust and the habit of the reptile is to walk about with its body well elevated from the ground. One must have a very large cage or outdoor enclosure to properly care for these huge ground lizards. They feed on vegetable and animal matter and become very tame in captivity, though fierce when first caught. A high temperature, at least 80 degrees, is required for them.

Cayman Islands rhinoceros iguana, *Cyclura caymanensis*. Photo by Muller-Schmida.

Rock python, *Python sebae.* Photo by J. K. Langhammer.

Boa constrictor, *Boa constrictor.* Photo by J. K. Langhammer.

Rainbow boa, *Epicrates cenchris*. Photo by G. Marcuse.

Brown sand boa, *Eryx johni*. Photo by G. Marcuse.

The South American iguanids of the genus *Polychrus* are interesting little arboreal lizards that are quite like chameleons in a few respects. Their bodies are highly arched and flattened from side to side, as in most tree lizards, while the toes of their feet are opposable to allow a firm grasp on the branch of a tree. The eyes are rather bulbous and the tail partly prehensile; in addition, the lizards are able to change color to a considerable degree. They feed chiefly on insects. *Polychrus acutirostris* and *Polychrus marmoratus* are the species most frequently imported.

BASILISKS

The basilisks (genus *Basiliscus*) form a small group of tropical American iguanids that have long been favorites in reptile collections. The males are adorned with crests along their backs and tails, while

Basilisk, *Basiliscus basiliscus*. Photo by G. Marcuse.

the females lack these and are more ordinary-looking. Large specimens may reach the length of three feet, of which much is taken up by the long tail. Basilisks live near water and are noted for their ability to run for short distances across the surface of water. Primarily lizards of the trees, they do well in the type of cage recommended for anoles. Some will eat pieces of soft fruit, but in general the several species are carnivorous and in addition to insects will take small mammals and birds. Because of their bizarre adornment, males cost more than females. If possible, the basilisks' cage should have a sizeable container of water. A temperature of 75 to 82 degrees is recommended.

Spiny-tail iguana, *Ctenosaura acanthura*, Central America. Photo by G. Marcuse.

Curly-tailed lizard, *Leiocephalus carinatus*, West Indies. Photo by G. Marcuse.

Green tree boa, *Corallus canina*, orange young. Photo by J. K. Langhammer.

Green tree boa, *Corallus canina*, adult. Photo by H. Hansen, Aquarium Berlin.

Keel-tailed lizard, *Tropidurus semitaeniatus*, South America. Photo by G. Marcuse.

Marine iguana, *Amblyrhynchus cristatus*, Galapagos Islands. Photo by G. Marcuse.

MISCELLANEOUS IGUANIDS

Tropical America has dozens of genera of small iguanid lizards that can be kept over long periods in captivity. Specimens of the genera *Corythophanes*, *Leiocephalus*, and *Tropidurus* are a few of the kinds imported. Many do not have common English names. The appearance of a lizard can often provide clues to its habits. Species with flattened bodies are generally ground dwellers, while those in which the body is compressed from side to side generally live in trees or bushes. Prehensile tails indicate arboreal habitats, while a flattened tail may indicate that its bearer is at least semi-aquatic.

Mountain chameleon, *Chamaeleo montium*, Cameroons. Photo by Dr. Otto Klee.

FAMILY CHAMAELEONIDAE

True chameleons of the family Chamaeleonidae are found only in the Old World.

Africa and Madagascar are the homes of these lizards, only a few of the eighty or more species entering Europe and Asia. Chameleons are among the most highly specialized groups of reptiles, and numbered among them are some whose grotesqueness defies adequate verbal description. In size they range from pygmy species of two inches to giants of two feet or more. As a group they are admirably adapted to the life they lead. Slow-moving and flat-bodied, they

Diced water snake, *Natrix tessellata*. Photo by H. Hansen, Aquarium Berlin.

Checkered water snake, *Natrix piscator*. Photo by H. Hansen, Aquarium Berlin.

blend beautifully with the foliage of the trees and bushes that they seldom leave. Their feet have opposable toes which afford a sure grip on the branch of a tree. The tail is prehensile and is used effectively to anchor the lizard to its perch. From the blunt head project bulging eyes which are moved independently of each other, enabling their owner to concentrate on two or more widely separated objects. The tongue is extremely long and thickened at its terminal portion, like a club. When an insect or other small creature arouses a hungry chameleon's attention, the tongue is shot out in a motion too quick for the eye to follow. The sticky tip nearly always finds its mark and returns the hapless victim to the lizard's mouth. Chameleons are capable of rapid and drastic changes of color, and these can be brought about by any of a large number of factors—psychological and physical.

Chameleons have never had the reputation of being hardy or long-lived in captivity. Six months was once considered a good record of longevity. With the advancing of our knowledge concerning reptiles in general, however, the care we are able to provide has become more sophisticated. Lives of captives can now be measured in years rather

Flap-necked chameleon, *Chamaeleo dilepis*. Photo by G. Marcuse.

Meller's chameleon, *Chamaeleo melleri*. Photo by G. Marcuse.

than months, though they must still be considered among the more delicate of lizards. Possibly, as a group, the chameleons are naturally short-lived.

The common chameleon, *Chamaeleo chamaeleon*, is found from Palestine eastward along coastal North Africa to southern Europe. It measures about ten inches in length and is at home among thick branches in a good-sized aquarium or other cage. Chameleons are not sociable and a single one does quite well if a temperature of 75 degrees is maintained for it. Like other lizards, it will benefit from brief exposures to natural sunlight. Water must be provided by spraying the foliage of the lizard's cage, but this should be done lightly and in one section only, so that a situation of continual dampness does not obtain. Mealworms, flies, and spiders will be accepted; a daily feeding is recommended. The common chameleon, like most of its clan, deposits eggs.

Meller's chameleon, *Chamaeleo melleri*, is one of the largest members of the family. Fully grown individuals will eat small birds and mice and require a great amount of food to keep them in health. Jackson's chameleon, *Chamaeleo jacksoni*, is adorned with long projections resembling horns, as are several other species. The

Oriental rat snake, *Ptyas mucosus*. Photo by H. Hansen, Aquarium Berlin.

Black and yellow rat snake, *Spilotes pullatus*. Photo by H. Hansen, Aquarium Berlin.

African flap-necked chameleon, *Chamaeleo dilepis*, is commonly imported and lives fairly well, as do some of the dwarf chameleons. Some chameleons, especially among the smaller species and those from mountainous regions, give birth to living young.

FAMILY CORDYLIDAE

Some of the lizards of the family Cordylidae are known as sun-gazers or girdle-tails. The first name comes from their habit of squatting in a frog-like position with the forepart of their bodies raised; the other name comes from their sharply pointed scales, which reach the height of their prominence on the tail. These lizards are among the most heavily armored of reptiles; despite their small size—most are only twelve to fifteen inches in length—they are able to deal telling blows with their tails. They inhabit desert areas where there are outcroppings of rocks. Here they find a haven when danger threatens, their spiny bodies pressed closely to the sides of the recesses among the rocks. For desert lizards, the cordylids are particularly hardy in captivity, feeding well on arthropods and small

Giant girdle-tailed lizard, *Cordylus giganteus*. Photo by G. Marcuse.

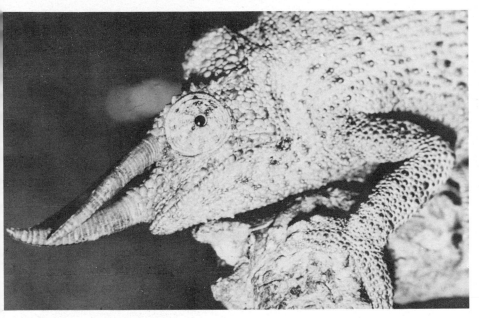

Jackson's chameleon, *Chamaeleo jacksoni*. Photo by Muller-Schmida.

Crested chameleon, *Chamaeleo cristatus*. Photo by Dr. Otto Klee.

Mussurana, *Clelia clelia.* Photo by G. Marcuse.

Coluber species. Photo by G. Marcuse.

Cuban racer, *Alsophis angulifer,* Cuba. Photo by H. Hansen, Aquarium Berlin.

Leopard snake, *Elaphe situla,* southern Europe and western Asia. Photo by Dr. K. Knaack.

Smooth girdle-tailed lizard, *Cordylus coeruleopuretatus*, southern Africa. Photo by G. Marcuse.

vertebrate animals. They should be kept at a temperature of 80 degrees. They are not brightly colored lizards, being mostly brownish or yellowish. The giant girdle-tailed lizard, *Cordylus giganteus*, is the largest of the more familiar members of the family, reaching a length of eighteen inches in exceptional cases. All cordylids produce their babies alive.

FAMILY TEIIDAE

The tropical lizards known variously as tegus, caiman lizards, and rainbow lizards are members of the family Teiidae. There are a great number of species in this family, but only a few are really well known. The common tegu, *Tupinambis teguixin*, is a large species and is attractively marked with white on a shiny black dorsal surface. The species may reach a length of four feet; old males tend to develop enormous heads and powerful jaws. The similar golden tegu, *Tupinambis nigropunctatus*, is also a very large species. Its appearance is quite shiny, the yellow markings standing out in contrast to the black body. The red tegu, *Tupinambis rufescens*, is an attractive animal that is not as readily available as the other two. The tegus are tropical American lizards and should be kept at a temperature of 80 to 85 degrees. They are ferocious creatures when first caught and can inflict considerable damage with their strong jaws. They tame readily, however, and may then be handled without show of bad temper. As is the case with many tropical reptiles, a single chill can kill a tegu without its showing any signs of ill health beforehand. Reptiles of temperate climates tend to develop symptoms of respiratory malfunction when they have been chilled. With tegus and other tropical forms death may ensue before there are any observable symptoms of bad health. In captivity tegus can be maintained indefinitely on a diet of raw meat and eggs. Mice, other reptiles, and small birds will provide some variety in their diet. Normally they are active lizards, but tame captives tend to move about little and rapidly gain weight under favorable circumstances.

The caiman lizard, *Dracaena guianensis*, is a teiid which looks much like its namesake. It frequents marshes and feeds mostly on molluscs. Nearly four feet when fully grown, it should have a large cage with a capacious container of water. The smaller teiids are often called rainbow lizards on the price lists of dealers in tropical reptiles. Mostly, they belong to the genus *Ameiva* and are closely related to our own racerunners, but more beautifully colored. All are carnivorous and reach an average size considerably inferior to that of the tegus.

Common tegu, *Tupinambis teguixin*. Photo by H. Schultz.

Green tree snake, *Leptophis ahaetulla*. Photo by G. Marcuse.

Green vine snake, *Oxybelis fulgidus* (top) and brown vine snake, *Oxybelis aeneus* (bottom). Photo by G. Marcuse.

Long-nosed tree snake, *Dryophis* sp. Photo by G. Marcuse.

Golden tree snake, *Chrysopelia ornata.* Photo by G. Marcuse.

Caiman lizard, *Dracaena guianensis*. Photo by G. Marcuse.

FAMILY LACERTIDAE

In Europe any mention of lizards is likely to bring to mind those kinds belonging to the family Lacertidae. These are the typical lizards of the Old World; the family is made up of a number of genera, *Lacerta* being the largest. Members of the family are found in Europe, Asia, and Africa and are among the commonest reptiles of these continents. Such familiar forms as the wall lizard, *Lacerta muralis*, the sand lizard, *Lacerta agilis*, and the viviparous lizard, *Lacerta vivipara*, adapt quite well to confinement in a suitable terrarium. The various species may be mixed providing there is no great disparity in size among them. The green lacerta, *Lacerta viridis*, is an attractive species, as is the eyed lizard, *Lacerta lepida*. Both of these will depart from the usual insect diet of the smaller lacertas and take a meat and raw egg mixture from a dish. Larger specimens will even devour mice and other small vertebrate animals. Occasionally lacertids will mate and produce fertile eggs in captivity. They should have a sandy cage that is provided with rocks and a spacious water dish. In a well-lighted cage there are few vivarium animals more attractive than an adult male eyed lizard. Lizards of the genus *Psammodromus* are closely related to those of the genus *Lacerta* but should have drier surroundings.

AFRICAN PUFF ADDER

Writers who attempt to evaluate the deadliness of the world's snakes with "the ten most" lists always include the forbidding-appearing African puff adder, *Bitis arietans*. There is little likelihood that anyone would mistake a puff adder for a harmless snake; everything about the reptile bespeaks sinister intent with capability to match. Five feet seems to be the greatest length attained by puff adders, and a specimen of this size is tremendously heavy-bodied. The yellowish-brown skin has interspersed over its surface a series of broad and much darker chevrons which are accentuated by light borders. There is some variation among specimens from different regions. Those from the drier areas tend to be lighter colored. Puff adders are difficult to see in their natural habitat and many accidents result from stepping on them. They are very common snakes and probably bite more people than any other African snake. In captivity puff adders do well, and large ones make sensational exhibits. Rodents, which often die within seconds after being bitten, are the preferred food. Young specimens are easily reared and are able to swallow small mice from the moment of birth, though some show a preference for tree frogs. Broods often number twelve or fewer babies. I mentioned earlier that I prefer to house only one poisonous snake in a cage, primarily for reasons of safety during cage-cleaning. Another reason is that if live mice or rats are fed to captive viperine snakes, the snakes may strike wildly and cause severe mechanical injuries to each other with their long fangs, though the various species are immune to the poison of their own kind. The fangs of a viper or large rattlesnake may be nearly an inch in length; with a few species this length is well exceeded. Any accidental penetration of the spinal area by one of these instruments, as has happened when two or more specimens were confined to the same cage, is certain to cause the death of the specimen so injured.

GABOON VIPER, RHINOCEROS VIPER

The Gaboon viper, *Bitis gabonica*, and the rhinoceros viper, *Bitis nasicornis*, are large and very beautiful relatives of the puff adder. The former may reach a length of six feet, while the latter is smaller. Rhinoceros vipers have horn-like appendages on their snouts and a beautifully-interwoven color pattern. Blue is not a common color among snakes, but it figures prominently on the head and back of

Gaboon viper, *Bitis gabonica.* Photo by G. Marcuse.

B. nasicornis, in combination with yellow, black, red, and brown. All of the African vipers of the genus *Bitis* require warm and dry quarters. A temperature of 78 to 85 degrees seems to suit them well. They are not active snakes but because of their huge bulk they should have a good sized cage. They seek to intimidate the observer by hissing loudly. Their strike is delivered with great swiftness, however, and is impossible to avoid if one is within range—a distance of perhaps a third the length of a coiled reptile.

HORNED ADDERS AND VIPERS

Bitis caudalis and *Bitis cornuta* are African desert species which possess enlarged and pointed scales over their eyes. These resemble horns and give these desert reptiles their popular name of horned adders. Their cage should have a sand covering on its floor, to the depth of several inches, and it is necessary to keep the temperature no lower than 78 degrees. The horned vipers, *Cerastes cerastes* and *Cerastes cornutus*, are also desert creatures, only about two feet when fully-grown. They spend much of their time buried in sand, with only their heads visible. None of these desert viperines has been kept over a very long period in captivity. The provision of natural sunlight or the substitute rays of an ultraviolet lamp is beneficial to them.

NIGHT ADDER

The night adder, *Causus rhombeatus*, of tropical and South Africa is a true viper but differs in many ways from most other African types. For one thing, it lays eggs, often in September, and its food consists mostly of frogs and toads—in contrast to the warm-blooded prey preferred by other vipers, especially forest species. Enormously developed venom glands are carried from the head well back into

Horned viper, *Cerastes cerastes*. Photo by G. Marcuse.

the body of these snakes; the purpose of this is not known. Night adders do not have the marked enlargement of head that is prevalent among viperine snakes and, adding to their innocuous appearance, are round pupils, though the reptiles are nocturnal to a large extent. Two to three feet is the average length of an adult, which is grayish-green and prettily blotched with dark rhombs along the back and stripes on the sides and head. An arrow-like design, its point toward the snout of the snake, is very prominent.

SAW-SCALED VIPER

Another curious little viper, *Echis carinatus*, has a wide range in Africa and Asia. Known as the saw-scaled viper, it is able to produce rather loud rasping noises by rubbing together loops of its body. Large examples are only two feet long and will eat insects in addition to the more usual viper fare of mice and small birds. Babies are easy to rear on a diet of small lizards. The species, like other African and Asian reptiles, requires a fairly high temperature, 78 to 85 degrees. Saw-scaled vipers are irascible in temperament and, as with all poisonous snakes, great care should be used in working with them.

COMMON ADDER

A common poisonous snake of Europe and the only one found in the British Isles is the common adder, *Vipera berus*. Curiously for a reptile from temperate regions, this species needs to be kept warm or it will not live in captivity. Even under the best of conditions, it is delicate and not easy to induce to feed. It is thus at variance with some of its very close relatives from warmer climates. These often thrive for years under careful management. Some writers have suggested that the common adder lives best if allowed to hibernate during the cold months. If this is true, it is not so of other snakes which normally hibernate but are not allowed to do so in captivity. Captive adders will sometimes accept mice, lizards, or fledgling birds; babies, which are born alive, show a preference for very small lizards.

EUROPEAN ASP, SAND ADDER

The European asp, *Vipera aspis*, is closely related to the common adder but can be distinguished from it by a slightly upturned snout. A further development of this feature is found in the sand adder,

Saw-scaled viper, *Echis carinatus.* Photos by G. Marcuse.

Sand adder, *Vipera ammodytes.*

Common adder, *Vipera berus.* Photo by H. Hansen, Aquarium Berlin.

Vipera ammodytes, a species that grows to the moderate length of about three feet and has the zigzag line down its back—a feature common to many of the European vipers. In captivity the present species flourishes indefinitely, but only if kept both warm and dry. In their manner of caring for reptiles, European herpetologists tend to favor semi-natural settings in their cages. These are very necessary in the cases of types which spend much of their lives underground, or those which live in trees. Most terrestrial snakes, however, will do better in cages which can be easily cleaned and do not hold dampness.

KUFI

Vipera lebetina is one of the largest species of the genus and is found in portions of three continents. Adults reach a length of five feet and are able to consume rats as well as smaller rodents. Its large size and the proportionate quantity of venom it is able to inject make the kufi, as this snake is sometimes called, a very dangerous one. Mem-

Kufi, *Vipera lebetina.* Photo by G. Marcuse.

bers of the genus *Vipera* are characteristically snakes which produce small to very large broods of living babies. The present species follows this mode of reproduction in some portions of its range, while in others it deposits eggs. An inconsistency of this type has been noted with some other serpents, though it is not a common phenomenon.

RUSSELL'S VIPER

The most formidable of its group is the large and handsome Russell's viper, *Vipera russelli*, of Asia. Its color pattern is quite distinctive, consisting of three rows of large spots which are reddish-brown and outlined with black and white. These stand out vividly on a background of light brown. Russell's viper is one of the most dangerous of the Asian snakes and each year takes many lives. It is a very common reptile in some areas, a fact which may be accounted for by the huge broods it sometimes produces. In exceptional cases a female may give birth to five dozen babies. Adult vipers of this kind are really large reptiles and should not be cramped in small quarters. They feed well upon rodents; younger specimens will take frogs and lizards.

Russell's viper, *Vipera russelli*. Photo by G. Marcuse.

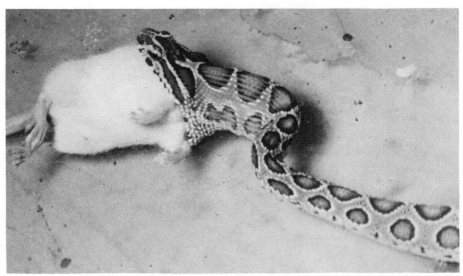

FAMILY CROTALIDAE

The pit vipers are closely related to the true vipers of the Old World, but most herpetologists accord them full family recognition under the family designation Crotalidae. One feature immediately identifies any member of this group: the presence of an orifice on either side of the head, between the eye and the nostril. This is a sensory organ and is believed to be used primarily for heat perception. Since many pit vipers feed exclusively upon warm-blooded animals, its usefulness in dealing with such prey at close range may be surmised. Serpents often seem unable to accurately direct their strikes at moving targets; the presence of heat detectors may assist in this as well as other ways. The larger pit vipers have an unsavory reputation and one which is well deserved, for they are among the most dangerous snakes.

TRIMERESURUS

Trimeresurus is a genus of tropical pit vipers of the Asian mainland and Pacific islands. They differ little from the tropical American *Bothrops*, and some herpetologists combine the many species under a single generic heading. The scientific listings of herptiles and other animals are in a constant state of change. This is often troublesome to the neophyte who wishes to look up a specimen in various books, but a closer familiarity with the subject soon acquaints the student with the synonyms that are used in describing species. In this book, snakes of these related genera are placed under separate headings: *Bothrops* for the New World species, *Trimeresurus* for those of the Old World.

Asian pit vipers, especially the island forms, once were difficult to come by. For a number of years now they have been imported in some numbers, though certain species are rarely to be found even in the preserved collections of the larger museums. Mainly, they are terrestrial snakes, although there are some kinds which have pre-hensile tails and spend most of their time in trees and bushes. One of these is the bamboo viper, *Trimeresurus gramineus*, a green snake of small size that makes a decorative exhibit in a cage containing branches. It feeds on frogs and small birds, sometimes descending from its arboreal perch to hunt along streams. A similar species is *Trimeresurus stejnegeri*, which grows to only two feet and adapts fairly well to cage life. The more terrestrial members of the genus

Bamboo viper, *Trimeresurus gramineus*. Photo by G. Marcuse.

are typified by the habu, *Trimeresurus mucrosquamatus*, a brown reptile with a series of darker blotches along its back and sides. A length of four feet is attained and food consists of birds and mammals. In its nocturnal search for rodents the habu has been known to enter human dwellings. The yellow-green habu, *Trimeresurus flavoviridis*, and the purple-spotted pit viper, *Trimeresurus purpureo-maculata*, are occasionally available. Generally speaking, poisonous snakes of these and other kinds are more expensive to buy than the equally-common harmless types from the same areas. This is understandable, in view of the risk that is involved in their capture and transportation.

BOTHROPS

The jumping viper, *Bothrops nummifera*, is a thick-bodied and very pugnacious little snake of Central America. So much energy is expended in the strike of a three-foot reptile that it may actually leave the ground. Coloration is brownish, with dark rhomboidal spots along the back. The fer-de-lance, *Bothrops atrox*, is a greatly-feared snake of Central and South America. Specimens vary a great deal in color, but usually some shade of gray or brown prevails as the ground color and this is overlaid with light-edged triangles along the sides. These meet in the middle of the back, and the effect produced is that of a diamond-backed serpent. In some areas the fer-de-lance seems to grow not more than four feet, while in others specimens eight feet long have been found. Large litters are produced, four or five dozen being common. In captivity the fer-de-lance is a quiet snake in its demeanor; occasionally an individual will feed well and live for a long time. This is not the usual experience, however, for the majority of fer-de-lances are not as adaptable as the pit vipers of North America. Perhaps some of the trouble is concerned with the shock to the reptile of being captured. I have noted repeatedly that snakes which are incorrectly noosed or pinned with force to the ground during capture are much less likely to feed subsequently than those which are taken with a minimum of such disturbance. The jararaca, *Bothrops jararaca*; the urutu, *Bothrops neuwiedi*; and the jararacucu, *Bothrops jararacussu*, are allied to the fer-de-lance and some are very beautiful in their colors and markings. The palm vipers, *Bothrops schlegeli* and *Bothrops nigroviridis*, are slender greenish snakes which have taken up life in the trees. Some have horn-like developments over their eyes.

BUSHMASTER

The bushmaster, *Lachesis muta*, of the American tropics sometimes attains a length of twelve feet or more and is the largest viper in the world, from the standpoint of length. Specimens present a vivid and startling combination of pink and black when freshly shed. With fangs in excess of an inch in length and venom glands of huge capacity, the bushmaster is probably the most dangerous of the New World snakes. The bushmaster seems to be a rather uncommon species. The Instituto Butantan, a government agency of Sao Paulo, Brazil annually receives thousands of snakes. From these the venom is extracted and used in the production of sera for the treatment of snakebite. It is of interest to note that in a 62-year period of operation, the institute received nearly 800,000 snakes, both poisonous and nonpoisonous. Of this number, only 49 were bushmasters. Non-poisonous snakes numbered some 183,000, while poisonous snakes totalled over 590,000. This reflects a curious fact: although non-poisonous are found in greater numbers than poisonous snakes (the ratio being about five to one), the latter are more easily captured because of their tendency to stand their ground and actively defend themselves. A large crotaline snake is a very difficult animal to capture unhurt, especially in a jungle area. Noosed specimens struggle violently, and many undoubtedly incur internal injuries, particularly of the spine, during the process of capture. I believe that this may be a reason why the larger poisonous snakes of the tropics often fail to thrive in captivity. Unlike most American pit vipers, bushmasters lay eggs; reports have it that in some instances, at least, the eggs may be guarded by the female. Mammals and birds are eaten. Unlike most tropical snakes, bushmasters should be kept at the relatively low temperature of 70°. This is because they normally inhabit a very cool micro-habitat.

AGKISTRODON

Eastern Europe, Asia, and North and Central America have a variety of pit vipers, some very beautiful and interesting, belonging to the genus *Agkistrodon*. Some of the species bear living young; others lay eggs, which in some cases are brooded by the mother snake. About five feet when fully-grown, the hundred pace snake, *Agkistrodon acutus*, is a handsome species. It has a sharply-pointed, upturned snout and smooth scales. Triangular side blotches, quietly blended with dorsal rhombs, present a multicoloring of red, gray, brown, and black. Like many other snakes, it is very difficult to see when coiled among leaves. The Malayan pit viper, *Agkistrodon rhodostoma*, is another very pretty reptile, smaller than the preceding species and with keeled scales. It lays eggs that take only about a month and a half to hatch. Both the hundred pace snake and the Malayan pit viper are deceptively docile in captivity and will eat small mammals and birds.

In the United States, one of the better-known poisonous snakes is the copperhead, *Agkistrodon contortrix*. A good-sized snake of this species is about three feet in length. Tan is the prevailing ground

Copperhead, *Agkistrodon contortrix*. Photo by G. Marcuse.

color, and along the sides are triangular blotches of a deep chestnut color. These meet on the back, sometimes converging and forming an hourglass pattern. Copperheads are usually found in wooded, hilly areas that are broken up by expanses of rocky ledges. These are the hibernating places of the reptiles, where they may be found in large numbers in the spring and in the autumn, before they retire for the winter months. In the summer they disperse and may be found nearly anywhere, a favorite lurking place being old stone walls. Copperheads account for many bites among humans, but few if any of these terminate fatally, for the venom is not injected in a large quantity and is not very potent—compared, say, with that of the timber rattlesnake, a species of similar range and habits. Copperheads will eat both cold-blooded and warm-blooded animals and often show a preference for birds in the spring. In the summer many specimens will take only mice, while in the autumn the food of choice consists of frogs. These feeding idiosyncrasies are not invariable but nevertheless prevail among the majority of captives.

The water moccasin, *Agkistrodon piscivorus,* of the southeastern United States is a familiar reptile of swamps and river courses. Exceptionally, a six-foot specimen is found, but the majority of moccasins are about four feet. Those of the Carolinas and Georgia

Water moccasin, *Agkistrodon piscivorus.* Photo by F. J. Dodd, Jr.

are larger than the moccasins from Louisiana. "Cottonmouth" is the name often applied to these snakes because of their habit of posing with jaws widely agape before striking. Even the most ardent snake admirer would not call the water moccasin a pretty reptile; it is a dingy brown with obscure crossbands that may become visible only when the snake is wet. Babies are more brightly colored and bear a resemblance to copperheads in the boldness of their blotching. Of all the venomous snakes, perhaps there is none which makes a better adjustment to a life of confinement than the moccasin. Freshly-caught, it is a vicious reptile, but this attitude quickly gives way to one of quiet docility. Captive moccasins will eat almost anything in the way of animal matter. Fishes, frogs, salamanders, lizards, birds, mammals, and even other snakes are eaten with equal relish. Babies can be successfully reared on a diet of fishes alone. Water moccasins, which are among the least nervous of poisonous snakes, should be kept in plain wooden cages without sand or other accessories. Water should be provided in a small dish which does not readily tip.

The cantil, *Agkistrodon bilineatus*, of Mexico and Central America is another semi-aquatic *Agkistrodon*. It is a pretty dark reddish-brown or black reptile, attractively embellished with white lines about the head and outlining obscure blotches along the back. It does not grow as large as the cottonmouth, from which it seems to differ little in habits, though it is less hardy in captivity.

RATTLESNAKES

Rattlesnakes are found only in the Americas. They range in size from tiny species only slightly over a foot in length, whose rattles can hardly be heard, to massive creatures of six feet or more in length, with a weight of over fifteen pounds. The rattle itself is a horny, segmented tail appendage which may produce anything from a few spasmodic clicks to a loud, sonorous buzz. Some species make little use of this member, even when freshly caught, and one kind, discovered and named in recent years, seems to have lost the rattle entirely. With the exception of this species, the rattle is a mark of sure identification. Babies are born with a "button"—to this is added a segment with each shedding of the skin. This occurs several times in the course of a year, so it is not possible to tell the age of a rattlesnake by the number of rattles it possesses. Rattles frequently

Red rattlesnake, *Crotalus ruber,* showing detail of the head and rattle. Photos by G. Marcuse.

break, and this fact further disqualifies any assumption as to the age of a snake. Really large adults are seldom found with complete rattles.

Mo

The pigmy rattlesnake, *Sistrurus miliaris*, is found in fair abundance over much of the southeastern United States. It is a dusky gray or brownish snake with a series of darker blotches running the length of its back. The slender tail of a two-foot adult terminates in a diminutive rattle that can scarcely be heard at a distance of six feet. Pigmy rattlers differ from members of the larger genus *Crotalus* in having the tops of their heads covered with plates rather than granular scalation. Generally they are to be found in damp or actually wet situations, where they feed upon mice, frogs, salamanders, lizards, and occasionally smaller snakes. Babies are produced alive in broods which commonly number less than a dozen. They are only about six inches long and are difficult to rear, even if an adequate supply of the tiniest foods is available. In connection with the raising of the present species, as well as babies of some of the other small rattlesnakes, it might be mentioned that the little reptiles will often accept portions of larger animals, such as the legs or tails of lizards. From the accounts of bites which have been sustained it appears that the venom of this small rattler is a very potent one. If it were not for its small size and the minute amount of venom it is able to deliver, the pigmy rattlesnake would be a very dangerous snake indeed.

Mo.

A larger relative of the pigmy rattler is the massasauga, *Sistrurus catenatus*, which (exceptionally) may reach a length of three feet. In one or another of its varieties this snake ranges over a wide belt from the Great Lakes area south to Texas and west to southeastern Arizona. The habits of the massasauga do not differ much from those of the pigmy rattler. In mixed collections of rattlers which I have received from various areas, I have noticed that the massasaugas are sometimes the most hostile, continually rattling when being transferred from cage to cage. They are also among the hardiest. I recall one shipment which arrived in the winter. It had been mishandled in transit and every rattler, with the exception of the massasauga, had contracted a respiratory illness to which it succumbed shortly. The massasauga was unaffected by the severe chilling.

Massasauga, *Sistrurus catenatus*. From Ditmars, *Reptiles of North America*.

Mo

In a large portion of the eastern United States, the timber rattlesnake, *Crotalus horridus horridus*, is the only poisonous snake, except where it may share its domain with copperheads. Mountain ledges are favorite haunts of the timber rattler, and portions of these ledges have deep crevices in which the species spends the winter months. In the spring, usually by the last week of April, the snakes emerge from their dens to bask in the sun. Often large numbers may be counted in a small area at this time. The reptiles mate, then each goes its own way in search of favorable feeding ground. In early fall there is a migration back to the dens, when they may again be found in numbers for a brief period before cold weather forces them to retire for the winter. Timber rattlers occasionally reach six feet, but three and a half is an average size. Two color phases occur—one a sulfur yellow with darker crossbands, the other brown, with more obscure markings. In some areas completely melanistic examples are not rare. Babies are always light in color; those of the darker phase start to change during their second summer, the process beginning at the head. In captivity timber rattlers survive over long periods. Mice are the favorite food and a rattler of average size can be kept in good health with a single large mouse each week.

The canebrake rattler, *Crotalus horridus atricaudatus*, is a handsome southern variety which grows to a larger average size than the timber. Some specimens are distinctly pinkish, with wavy crossbands of chocolate-brown. At present I have a specimen which was born in captivity and is growing rapidly. Though still less than three feet in length it is a fearless creature and quite remarkable in its aggressive disposition. In contrast to most rattlers, especially those born in captivity, this specimen has never tamed to the slightest degree. When the door of its cage is slid back, there is a quick rush to the point of disturbance—not the slow, sinuous glide of an animal interested only in food. If a dead mouse is offered with a pair of tongs, the mouse is bypassed by the snake in its attempt to imbed its fangs in the hand that is feeding it. For a snake with such a disposition it is unusual in that it feeds readily. No chances are taken with the reptile—I consider it one of the most dangerous poisonous snakes I have ever kept under observation.

The eastern diamondback rattlesnake, *Crotalus adamanteus*, and the western diamondback, *Crotalus atrox*, are formidable reptiles with long fangs and poison glands of large size. Both grow to huge size, over six feet, and the western species causes more deaths in the

A Timber rattle snake in Florida was 14ft long.

Timber rattlesnake, *Crotalus horridus horridus*. From Ditmars, *Reptiles of North America.*

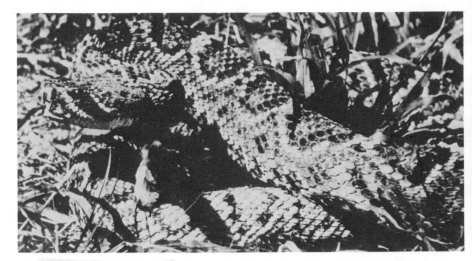

Eastern diamondback rattlesnake, *Crotalus adamanteus.* Photo by Ross Allen.

Tropical rattlesnake, *Crotalus durissus,* Central and South America. Photo by G. Marcuse.

Western diamondback rattlesnake, *Crotalus atrox.* From Van Denburgh.

United States than any other snake. With their handsome coloration and sullen demeanor, large specimens make spectacular exhibits, but often refuse to feed. It is best to acquire them as babies and raise them on a diet of mice, graduating to rats as the reptiles mature. These and other rattlers of North America do well if kept at a temperature of 75 to 80 degrees. When conditions are especially favorable rattlers will breed in captivity. Some have lived well over twenty years.

The hardiest rattlesnake and the one easiest to keep and feed is the prairie rattlesnake, *Crotalus viridis.* Several races, varying somewhat in size and color, occur throughout the West. They lack the beauty of some of the other species but more than make up for this in the ease with which they adjust to cage-life. Even fully-grown examples, captured but recently, seldom sound their rattles and feed without hesitancy upon mice.

Many other rattlers do fairly well in captivity. Especially attractive is the black-tailed rattler, *Crotalus molossus,* and the lighter phase of the red rattler, *Crotalus r. ruber.* Attempts to maintain the tiger rattler, *Crotalus tigris,* over long periods generally have met with little success. The same is true of the speckled rattlesnake, *Crotalus mitchelli.* All rattlesnakes give birth directly to their babies; babies are usually few in number, not over ten in the case of some species.

It is thought by some that rattlers can strike only from a coiled position. This is not true; rattlers can strike from nearly any position,

Prairie rattlesnake, *Crotalus viridis*. From Van Denburgh.

Black-tailed rattlesnake, *Crotalus molossus*. From Van Denburgh.

Red rattlesnake, *Crotalus ruber.* Photo by G. Marcuse.

Sidewinder, *Crotalus cerastes,* southwestern deserts. From Van Denburgh.

Willard's rattlesnake, *Crotalus willardi*, Arizona and adjacent Mexico.
From Van Denburgh.

even when crawling rectilinearly, though from this position the forward striking range would be but a few inches. How this is accomplished by an animal that is drawn nearly straight out, with no visible loop of neck or body, I am not able to say, but it can make exceedingly dangerous any attempt to hand-feed a supposedly tame specimen. Rattlers which have met death accidentally often retain reflexes which can cause the head to swing around and bite an object which touches the body of the expired reptile. Persons have been seriously poisoned in this way. Snakes which die from natural causes seem to lack this post-mortem reflexibility; nevertheless, caution is urged in handling even such specimens. Examining the head and mouthparts of a deceased snake should be a cautious procedure, for the fangs are needle-sharp and venom can be expressed from the glands with but slight pressure.

Some of the most experienced herpetologists and snake collectors have died from the bites of poisonous snakes. This chapter is best closed with the simple admonition: if you decide to keep one or more poisonous snakes, treat your material with the respect it deserves!

Newts, Salamanders and Caecilians

AMPHIBIANS IN GENERAL

The newts and salamanders, along with the frogs, toads, and caecilians, comprise a group of animals which are known as amphibians. Herpetologists, both professional and amateur, concern themselves with the study of amphibians as well as reptiles, though fundamentally the two classes of animals are quite distinct. The unity of the two classes as a scientific discipline contributed to the coinage of the term "herptile," a word used frequently in this book and others in referring collectively to amphibians and reptiles.

I have never seen a really representative living collection of the world's amphibians, even in the best zoos and aquariums. As a group, they have been sadly neglected. We have a thorough knowledge of the life histories of some of the very common species, but of the vast majority we know little. While it is quite simple to gather an assemblage of the more common amphibians found in one's own area, it is a very different matter to obtain desired species from other places. Only a few amphibians are regularly carried in the stocks of dealers. The individuals which come in with reptile importations are frequently offered to prospective buyers on an unidentified basis. The prices of such specimens are generally low, and with luck it is possible to acquire some uncommon specimens. Many faded specimens of once-gorgeous frogs and salamanders repose in the preserving jars of museum study collections. Looking at them, one wonders what fascinating details of life history they would reveal under vivarium conditions.

Amphibians have much to recommend them to the keeper of herptiles. They will nearly always feed readily under captive conditions and do not require the high temperatures so necessary for the well-being of many reptiles. Nearly all do best in a moderately cool environment. Being less highly evolved than reptiles, they show little of the individual variation in temperament of the latter. For instance, one can say with some assurance that spotted salamanders will adapt well to captivity if their basic needs are provided. This could hardly be predicted with equal assurance of many kinds of lizards and snakes. Most amphibians show a degree of responsiveness to kind treatment. They learn quickly to associate the presence of their owner with a supply of food and will focus their attention upon him in alert expectancy. They do not like to be handled, however, and even very tame ones will try to escape when picked up. Salamanders and frogs have moist, slippery skin, and this makes them quite difficult to hold. Toads and newts usually have a drier skin and are less likely to be harmed by handling. The slimy skin secretion of amphibians is a protective covering that is similar to that of fishes. Aquarists and anglers know that dry hands will cause this skin covering to rub off and allow the entrance of infection. It is best not to handle frogs and salamanders frequently; if they must be picked up it should be done with wet hands. This, incidentally, adds to the difficulty of maintaining a firm yet gentle grasp. Also, it is well to remember that the skin secretions of some amphibians are poisonous and the hands should be washed thoroughly after being used to hold a frog, toad, salamander, or newt.

The salamanders present quite a variety in forms, sizes, and colors, as well as habits. Some are thoroughly aquatic, rarely, if ever, voluntarily leaving the water. At the other extreme are a number of species which spend their lives on land and become aquatic during a brief period only, when courtship and the depositing of eggs takes place. Yet others live entirely on land and do not go to the water even to deposit their eggs. A few ascend trees; others seem to spend most of their lives in burrows underground.

Salamanders are sometimes confused with lizards but can at once be distinguished from these reptiles by their smooth, scaleless skin. Like the other classes of animals, salamanders show enough diversity to be split up into several families. Some salamanders make excellent terrarium or aquarium animals, thriving and even breeding in captivity. Among the larger species one, at least, has lived fifty years in captivity; even more surprising is the great age attained by some of the smaller types. Several have approached or exceeded the twenty-five-year mark under very ordinary cage conditions.

Dryness and excessive heat are the great enemies of newts and salamanders. The importance of the heat factor has been stressed many times in the chapters on reptiles; in the present chapter and the one on frogs and toads, the stress must be placed on coolness, rather than heat. Because of this fundamental difference in their requirements, it is not a really easy thing to combine successfully a collection of amphibians and reptiles, unless the more tolerant of each class are selected. If individual cage controls are available, it is another matter, but the average private collector will not have an elaborate system of this kind. City apartment dwellers will often find it easier to care for amphibians than reptiles. The former are able to withstand cool nightly temperatures while the latter fare poorly if there is a drop to below 65 degrees. In my own home I solve the problem by keeping all reptiles in a constantly heated room and scattering the amphibians throughout other rooms, where the temperature can be kept relatively cool and allowed to drop even further at night.

Aquariums make the best homes for newts and salamanders. By means of a glass cover, a good humidity control can be maintained. They do not require a lot of light; most species prefer subdued lighting, and no salamander regularly suns itself. Thus, in the keeping of newts and salamanders, the reptile keeper's problem of providing sunlight is absent. Food requirements for salamanders and newts are not complex; they will be discussed under the headings of the various species.

MUDPUPPY

The most commonly kept of the larger, thoroughly aquatic salamanders are those of the family Proteidae, of which the mudpuppy, *Necturus maculosus,* is a familiar form and one that is used extensively in biological study. A large example may measure nearly eighteen inches and will require an aquarium of between twenty and thirty gallons capacity, with a water depth of eight to ten or more inches. Mudpuppies breathe by means of the bushy gills situated on both sides of the head; their oxygen requirements seem quite high, and for this reason it is well to provide the aquarium with an aerating unit of the type used by fish enthusiasts. When a mudpuppy is not receiving sufficient oxygen, the gills expand into plumes; while this may present an interesting and attractive picture in an aquarium, it is not a desirable one. Normally, the gill structures will be folded back and inconspicuous. Plain brown, sometimes with a dark mottling, the mudpuppy is not a beautiful animal, but it is interesting and will live over a long period if properly cared for. Earthworms, pieces of raw beef, and small fishes will be taken by captives. Breeding takes place in the fall; the eggs are deposited under, or attached to the undersurface of, a submerged log or flat rock. The female guards the eggs until they hatch some two months later. Young, when hatched, measure about an inch in length. These salamanders can withstand a great drop in temperature and remain active and healthy. In the wild state, they are frequently to be seen crawling under the ice of frozen lakes. In an aquarium they should never be over-crowded—I would consider two foot-long specimens ideal for a

Olm, *Proteus anguinus*. Photo courtesy American Museum of Natural History.

twenty-gallon container. Babies, or individuals of small size, can be kept in a smaller container. The water surface should not be closer than six inches to the top frame of the aquarium, which is best covered with a slightly raised sheet of glass, for the animals are able to escape from an uncovered tank that is filled close to the top. The water should be changed after the salamanders have been fed, to minimize fouling, a condition which the aquatic salamanders particularly dislike. No aquarium plants should be used in the tank housing mudpuppies; a few rocks firmly set in place to form a natural cave in the background may be used if one wishes to add a decorative touch. Nor should sand or gravel be used as a floor covering, for these add nothing to the comfort of the animals and make cleaning the aquarium more difficult. Aquatic salamanders are able to withstand the amount of chlorine present in freshly-drawn tap water and except, perhaps, in a few areas of the country, this should not present a problem. I would regard a temperature range of 50 to 60 degrees as ideal.

OLM

Closely related to the mudpuppy is the ghostly-white olm, *Proteus anguinus*, an interesting foot-long salamander found in the caves of southern Europe. Like the mudpuppy, the olm has red gill structures, and these gills present a beautiful contrast to the pink-white of the creature's body. The eyes are hidden beneath the skin—a condition often noted among animals which dwell in total darkness—but the creature seems nonetheless aware of what is going on about it and will readily find and devour the small worms and crustaceans which make up its diet. Eggs are deposited on the underside of stones and take about three months to hatch. In rare instances the female retains the eggs within her body until hatching and produces babies alive! The babies are miniatures of their parents, but possess rudimentary eyes. They require cool water, preferably not higher than 50 degrees, and should be kept in a darkened place. This may be accomplished to a degree by painting three or even four sides of the aquarium on the outside, leaving a small area of the front pane of glass unpainted so the occupants may be seen. An aquarium reflector equipped with a red bulb will afford fair visibility and discomfort the olms less than ordinary white light. Olms once were fairly common on the animal market, but today they are seldom listed by dealers.

In general, their care does not differ greatly from that of the mud-puppy, but smaller foods, in smaller amounts, should be given to them. Tubifex worms are a favorite item in the diet of captive specimens. It is a curious fact that if olms are kept constantly exposed to strong light they eventually turn black. With this species, it is said to be the male, rather than the female, which guards the eggs.

AMPHIUMA

The southeastern United States is the home of a huge elongated salamander called the Amphiuma, *Amphiuma means*, a species that lacks a good common name. "Congo eel" is the appellation applied in some areas of the South. The Amphiuma has a brownish-black dorsal surface and a lighter belly; its eyes are rudimentary, as are its legs, which are reduced to useless appendages less than an inch long in the case of an adult measuring three feet. Lakes, ditches, bayous, and streams are frequented by these salamanders. They are quite adapted to life in the water and seldom leave it except during the breeding season. Captives do well in a shoreless aquarium and will

Amphiuma, *Amphiuma means*. Photo by F. J. Dodd, Jr.

live for many years on a diet of raw beef pieces placed in front of them. Their aquarium, depending on the size of the inmates, should have water of several inches to a foot or more in depth. They should be able to reach the surface without swimming. Eggs are deposited in fairly dry situations under logs and stones near water. They may number only 150 and are guarded by the female, who remains coiled about them. Aquarium specimens are uncomfortable in bright light and will bite viciously if handled. Few salamanders make any attempt to bite, and those which do can usually produce nothing more than a series of superficial scratches. My first experience with an Amphiuma, some years ago when there was little information about them available in print, was something less than an agreeable one. I carefully lifted a fifteen-inch specimen from its aquarium to place it in an adjoining container while its permanent home was being cleaned. During the process, it swung its head about and fastened its jaws on the ring finger of my left hand. The bite seemed no more painful than that which could be produced by a small harmless snake and I did not become aware of its severity until I closely examined the wound. The flesh had been incised as though by a razor and only a tight compress would stop the flow of blood. Eventually it healed but the scar remains to remind me of the incident. Amphiumas are best moved about with a deep net. The family Amphiumidae has only one genus.

SIRENS

The siren, *Siren lacertina,* of the family Sirenidae, is another large aquatic salamander of the quiet waters of the southeastern United States. In body form it is somewhat similar to the eel-like Amphiuma, but it has weakly developed forelimbs, while rear legs are lacking entirely. Gill tufts adorn each side of the siren's rather angular head, and the over-all color of the amphibian is gray or dark greenish. Three feet may be reached by a large adult but the average length is about a foot shorter. Crayfish and worms may be the principal foods in the natural state, but in captivity a diet of lean raw beef, cut into slender strips, will maintain specimens in health over long periods. A shoreless aquarium is recommended, and this should be perfectly plain—devoid of foliage or sand, to make easier the frequent cleaning that is necessary. Almost nothing is known of the breeding habits, except that the species deposits eggs. I have always preferred to keep the larger aquatic gilled salamanders in a tank of their own, without mixing species. Even among individuals of the same species there is some biting, which often results in the destruction of the plumelike gills which are the principal adornment of these rather drab animals.

A smaller relative of the siren is the species known as *Siren intermedia*. A really tiny member of the family is the dwarf siren, *Pseudobranchus striatus*, with an average length of only five or six inches. The dwarf siren's habits are similar to those of its large relative, but dwarfs may be kept in small aquariums and fed on tubifex and white worms, as well as tiny bits of meat. Members of both *Amphiuma* and *Siren* genera can tolerate a degree of heat which would distress many other salamanders, but I would recommend a temperature not higher than 70 degrees.

GIANT SALAMANDERS

The giant salamanders belong to the family Cryptobranchidae, which has as its North American representative the hellbender, *Cryptobranchus alleganiensis*, a thoroughly aquatic river and stream type which exceptionally may reach thirty inches in length. Grotesque in the extreme, the hellbender is a broadly-flattened, wide-headed salamander with loosely-hanging folds of skin along its side. Its limbs are short and chunky and its tail is much compressed. In every way, this salamander appeals to the imagination as a primitive one—and such it actually is. Its close relative of the Orient, the giant salamander of Japan, *Megalobatrachus japonicus*, may reach a length of five feet and a weight of close to a hundred pounds. Giant salamanders are long-lived amphibians, possibly exceeding in this respect any other amphibian species. They live well even in deep aquariums where they must swim periodically to the surface for air. They are awkward in swimming, however, and in a private aquarium should have water of about twelve to eighteen inches in depth. The water must be changed frequently, especially if the aquarium is not large. In spite of their large size and slippery skin, hellbenders and giant salamanders can be easily handled if grasped behind the head with the rest of the body supported by the other hand. Eggs of the hellbender are deposited in running water in late summer and are guarded by the male. Upon hatching two to three months later, the gilled larvae are a little over an inch in length. At six inches, a

Japanese giant salamander, *Megalobatrachus japonicus*. Photo above courtesy American Museum of Natural History; that below by G. Marcuse.

Hellbender, *Cryptobranchus alleganiensis.* Photo courtesy American Museum of Natural History.

length which may be attained in less than two years, they have lost their gills and are replicas of the adults. The American and Oriental giant salamanders are frequently taken on hook and line. Their food consists of aquatic animals of a multitude of forms; captives are easily kept on a meat and fish diet. A filtering system in an aquarium of twenty to thirty gallons is of little value because of the grossness of the feeding habits of these amphibians and the large amounts of food they require. A running water system is much better. Single specimens of small size can be kept in a relatively small aquarium if the water is changed frequently.

The kinds of salamanders so far discussed can be kept in an aquarium which provides no means of leaving the water.

SALAMANDRIDS

The family Salamandridae provides the herptile keeper with some of the most attractive and interesting of the smaller vivarium animals. The Old and New World newts are members of this family and so, too, is the European fire salamander. North American newts start their lives as gilled larvae. Some kinds, when they have reached the age of three months, lose their gills, and come ashore for an interlude of land existence which may last three years or more, then return to the water for the balance of their lives. During the land stage they are reddish-orange in color and can frequently be found wandering in damp woods in broad daylight. Other kinds remain completely aquatic from the time they hatch, while still others are largely terrestrial and enter the water only to breed. Salamandrids, as the newts and salamanders of the present family are properly referred to, occur in Europe, Africa, and Asia, as well as North America.

The newts of Europe have for a very long time been studied in laboratories and private collections. Some of the species most frequently available are the smooth newt, *Triturus vulgaris*; the crested newt, *Triturus cristatus*; and the Alpine newt, *Triturus alpestris*. Mostly small amphibians, the largest kinds reach a length of only about seven inches. In the spring, when they go to the water to breed, the males take on beautiful colors that rival those displayed by the most beautiful fishes. They develop a crest along the back and tail; this is lost when the breeding season is over. Mating is preceded by an elaborate courtship, after which the male deposits a sperm mass which is taken up by the female in her cloaca, where fertilization

Palmated newt, *Triturus helveticus*, male, western Europe. Photo by L. E. Perkins.

takes place. The eggs are then deposited on aquatic plant leaves and abandoned. Recently hatched larvae are tiny creatures with bushy growths of gills on both sides of the head. These shrink day by day;

Smooth newt, *Triturus vulgaris,* male above, female below. Photos by G. Marcuse.

Crested newt, *Triturus cristatus*, female above, male below. Photos by G. Marcuse.

Alpine newt, *Triturus alpestris,* male above, female below. Photos by G. Marcuse.

finally the front legs make their appearance as stubs, followed by the growth of the rear limbs. At this stage the tiny newt dashes to the surface of their water to obtain air—it has already begun to devour tiny worms and crustaceans. Enchytrae and tubifex worms are good foods during this early period of growth. Parent newts should be removed from the aquarium when the egglaying has been completed. Otherwise, if the eggs are not devoured, the newly-hatched larvae certainly will be. Baby newts are reared without difficulty. Adults in the aquatic stage will eat almost any animal matter that is dangled in front of them with forceps. Chopped earthworms form a very satisfactory diet, but even pieces of finely-shredded lean raw beef will be eaten with relish.

The European newts do best in a vivarium which is approximately evenly divided between land and water areas. Water should be of six to ten inches depth and the land portion of the container should have flat stones or pieces of bark under which the adults can hide when they decide to leave the water. All aquariums or other containers housing newts should be kept securely covered. This can be accomplished with a framework of screening or a sheet of glass. If glass is used, it should be in two sections, with an opening between the halves to admit air.

Adult newts are comparatively easy to maintain because of the wide range of foods which they'll accept; here an adult newt is swallowing a tadpole. Photo by H. Pfletschinger.

Like other herptiles, newts should never be crowded. It is often possible to obtain very large catches in the field, but only a selected few should be brought home. A five-gallon aquarium will comfortably house a pair of newts. If breeding is to be attempted, a larger size is preferable. Newts are perhaps the easiest of all herptiles to successfully breed and rear in captivity. An ideal water temperature for the European newts is one which does not go over 60 degrees. Temperatures much lower than this are tolerated without adverse results.

Notophthalmus viridescens, the common newt of the eastern half of the United States, has an adult length of about four inches. Greenish-brown in color, it is not as attractive as some of the exotic kinds, but is readily available and lives well in an aquarium under the conditions described for the European species. Like them, it will breed in an aquarium, which activity can take place during the fall, winter, or spring. Along the western coast of the United States are two large species known variously as rough-skinned newts, *Taricha granulosa*, and California newts, *Taricha torosa*. The various species and varieties have a dorsal surface that runs from reddish-brown to black, while the belly may be orange or yellow or, in one very attractive form, scarlet red. They are hardy amphibians which, in the natural state, spend much of their time on land in damp places under stones and logs. They can be caused to adopt a completely aquatic existence if deprived of a landing place in their aquarium; they are perhaps most interesting when maintained in this manner. Most learn to recognize their keeper and can be hand-fed on small pieces of meat and worms.

Though a member of the same family and closely related to the newts we have discussed, the fire salamander, *Salamandra salamandra*, is quite different in appearance, being robustly built and positively striking in its gorgeous livery of black and yellow. Most persons who keep herptiles have their favorites; among the tailed amphibians, this species is my favorite. A large fire salamander may be over six inches long, but it normally is not an active animal and will do well in a small terrarium which is kept moderately damp and provided with stones and pieces of bark. Not more than a pair should be kept together, for fire salamanders tend to congregate if kept in numbers, and this habit is believed to give rise to fungoid conditions of the skin. Kept alone, or with a single companion, a fire salamander will live for many years under the most simple of terrarium conditions. I once kept a specimen for five years in a two-

Fire salamander, *Salamandra salamandra.* Photo by G. Marcuse.

gallon aquarium which was provided with a base of damp sand. The
only other furnishings were a flat-topped rock over which was arranged a piece of bark, forming a hollow between it and the rock.
The cage was kept in the coolest part of the house and the salamander was hand-tendered a strip of lean raw beef once each week.
This was followed by a rinsing of the cage and gravel under cold
tap water. Covering the cage were two pieces of glass, separated in
the middle to form a quarter-inch opening to allow a circulation of
air. The handsome creature was discomforted by heat in excess of
65 degrees and at such times would prowl about. At other times it
would invariably be found in its resting place beneath the portion of
tree-bark. It became sort of a conversation piece; European visitors
would recognize the animal at once.

The breeding habits of the fire salamander are interesting. The
species normally gives birth to living young in shallow water some
ten months after the adults have mated on land in June or July.
The babies, numbering anywhere from a few to several dozens, have
gill structures and remain in the water until the gills are absorbed,
when they come ashore to assume a terrestrial life.

Other exotic salamandrids which are imported with some frequency are the colorful and voracious red-bellied newt, *Cynops pyrrhogaster*, of Japan, and the ribbed newt, *Pleurodeles waltl*, of Spain and North Africa. Red-bellied newts have a great tolerance of temperature changes and are among the easiest of the salamanders to keep. They are rather stout and chunky little creatures, when in good health, and squabble much among themselves over pieces of meat that are put into their aquarium. Their backs are very dark brown or black, while their stomachs are a bright red, in striking contrast. The ribbed newts live well also, with a minimum of care. One of their peculiarities is the tendency of the ribs to pierce their skin and protrude as tiny knobs along the sides of the adult specimens.

Ribbed newt, *Pleurodeles waltl*. Photo by G. Marcuse.

MOLE SALAMANDERS

North America has the distinction of being the home of more kinds of salamanders than any other continent. The family Ambystomidae, composed of the so-called mole salamanders, creatures resembling the fire salamander in the stoutness of their configuration and often of pretty coloration, is one of the largest. Mole salamanders are, for the most part, secretive amphibians which spend much of their lives underground. If they are seen at all it is likely to be at breeding time, when enormous numbers congregate in suitable ponds and other still waters for a brief period of courtship and the depositing of eggs. Unlike most burrowing animals, which only too often will sicken and die if not allowed to follow their natural habits, the mole salamanders will adapt to terrarium conditions which cater only in part to their tendencies to hide. This can be accomplished with a thin layer of aquarium gravel, rather than soil, for a floor covering, and the provision of hiding places in the form of propped-up flat stones and large segments of rotten tree bark. Of course, a more conventional terrarium set-up, with plants and soil, is suitable also, but it will be impossible at most times to observe the salamander inhabitants of such an arrangement. There seems little to be gained in the keeping of any animal which can never be seen.

Over the eastern half of the United States, the spotted salamander, *Ambystoma maculatum*, is a common amphibian. With its speckling of yellow on a blue-black ground color, it is a pretty denizen of the woods. Eight to nine inches is the size range of the largest adults. Spotted salamanders would be very conspicuous herptiles if it were not for their secretive habits. During warm, rainy nights in early spring they migrate to ponds in large numbers and may even cross highways in their march to a favored breeding pool. Eggs are deposited in large masses which measure about three inches in diameter and are attached to submerged twigs or plants. They hatch in three to six weeks, depending on the prevailing temperatures of the water. When the larvae hatch they are tiny gilled creatures, but growth is rapid and by fall their legs have developed and the gills have been lost. By this time the little salamanders will be over two inches in length and ready to take up a land existence, returning to the water in the second spring after their birth, when they will be young adults and ready themselves to carry on the reproductive process. During their larval stage the babies, like those of many

Spotted salamander, *Ambystoma maculatum.*

herptiles, seem to differ much in natural vitality; some grow quickly and prey upon their weaker members. This is a natural thing and little can be done to prevent it in an aquarium, though it can be minimized by the sorting of specimens by size. From a single egg mass which may contain a hundred or more eggs, normally only a small percentage of the salamanders will ever reach adulthood. Tubifex and white worms, as well as daphnia and other tiny crustaceans, form a convenient food upon which to raise the larvae. Transformed individuals feed readily upon earthworms and soft-bodied insects; those which I have kept would readily take meat from forceps or the tip of a straw when it was moved about directly in front of them. Like most other herptiles, these salamanders are able to go without food for long periods, but they become terribly emaciated during such prolonged fasts. Inadvertently, a small specimen was once left in a plastic collecting bag with moss and wood pulp for a period of several months. When discovered it was very thin, but active and in apparently fair health. It was carefully nursed along with tiny bits of raw beef and in the ensuing weeks regained the normally rotund appearance of the species.

Some of the other mole salamanders are very attractive herptiles. The marbled salamander, *Ambystoma opacum*, is a beautiful animal, black with white or silvery crossbands. It is fully grown when four to five inches long and differs from the spotted salamander in laying its eggs on land in the fall of the year. These are deposited singly, in a depression under a rock or fallen log, and the female stays with them during the period of incubation. In some cases, hatching may not occur until spring. The marbled salamander has much the same range as its spotted relative, but in contrast to the latter may often be found in fairly dry situations. It lives well in captivity, making a very decorative inmate of the terrarium.

Axolotls, *Ambystoma* sp. Photo by L. E. Perkins.

Crested newt, *Triturus cristatus.*

Alpine newt, *Triturus alpestris.* Photo by S. Frank.

Axolotl, *Ambystoma* sp., leucistic strain. Photo by L. E. Perkins.

Another familiar ambystomid is the tiger salamander, *Ambystoma tigrinum*, a large species that is widely distributed in North America and shows great variation of color and markings over its broad range. Under certain circumstances, the larvae of the tiger salamander, and other species as well, fail to lose the gills and remain permanently aquatic animals. In Mexico they are called axolotls, and this name has carried over into English usage. Axolotls may reach a very large size, corresponding with transformed individuals of the same age. A white or leucistic strain is frequently kept in aquariums and makes a quite handsome display animal.

There are many other kinds of mole salamanders, all of them interesting and attractive. The species I have kept have been uniformly hardy under terrarium conditions, and I would say that the mole salamanders are the most responsive and easily kept of the New World salamanders. Observation of captive individuals has extended over long periods, and the life span of mole salamanders may be in excess of twenty-five years. Included in the family group is the largest known land salamander in the world—the western giant salamander, *Dicamptodon ensatus*, a creature which reaches a length of at least twelve inches and is able to devour fair-sized vertebrate animals as well as insects and earthworms.

PLETHODONTIDS

The largest family of salamanders in the world is the Plethodontidae, a group of aquatic and terrestrial species which has its headquarters in the Appalachian Mountains of the eastern United States but has forms which extend the range to the western part of the country and tropical America. These salamanders have no lungs, respiration taking place through the delicate skin. Size range among the varied types runs from an inch to eight inches or slightly more. Most are very secretive and hide during the day, coming out at night to hunt for food. Like many of the lizards, the plethodontids have fragile tails, and this should be borne in mind when it is necessary to handle them. They do best if handled very little and kept in a cool environment. They are extremely dependent upon moisture, quickly dying from dessication in its absence. For this reason, specimens which escape from their cage seldom survive. Among such a large group there is, naturally, some diversification of habitat preference among the terrestrial kinds. But most will do well in a damp terrarium with an abundance of hiding places. Earthworms and insects constitute an adequate diet; in the case of very small salamanders, tubifex and white worms form an acceptable diet. A few climb to some extent while others spend their entire lives in underground streams. The majority make their homes close to brooks and ponds, or in swamps. In the eastern United States, an ideal place to look for these salamanders is under stones near swiftly-flowing mountain streams where there is a heavy overhang of tree cover. Such places are often cool on even the hottest days, and coolness is one of the determining factors in the abundance of these small animals in such areas.

The commonest herptile in many places is the red-backed salamander, *Plethodon cinereus*, a species which occurs in two color phases. One is plain black or gray, flecked with lighter markings, while the other has a broad red band the length of its back. Like most others of its family, this salamander is never found wandering about in the daytime. Sometimes six or more individuals will be uncovered when a log is overturned. In regard to its moisture requirements, the red-back is less fussy than most plethodontids and is sometimes found far from any permanent body of water, though never in any place which completely lacks moisture. Four to five ches is the average size of adults; the babies, which do not go

Marbled newt, *Triturus marmoratus,* southwestern Europe. Photo by J. K. Langhammer.

Common newt, *Notophthalmus viridescens,* eft. Photo by F. J. Dodd, Jr.

Broken striped newt, *Notophthalmus viridescens dorsalis*, Georgia and Florida. Photo by M. F. Roberts.

Rough-skinned newt, *Taricha granulosa*. Photo by H. Hansen, Aquarium Berlin.

Red-backed salamander, *Plethodon cinereus*. Photo by F. J. Dodd, Jr.

through a larval stage, hatch from eggs which are deposited in damp terrestrial situations. Captives live quite well in a terrarium and are able to tolerate more warmth than their relatives of mountain-brook habitats.

The prettily speckled slimy salamander, *Plethodon glutinosus*, grows to nearly eight inches and has acquired its common name from the skin secretion which rubs off when the animal is handled. Its habits are similar to those of its smaller cousin, the red-back, but because of its larger size the slimy salamander is not so likely to get lost in a large terrarium. Also, it is able to devour earthworms of fair size, which may simplify the feeding problem. In general, the salamanders of the genus *Plethodon* are less frightened by humans than the species which live in or near streams. Often they can be tempted to accept pieces of raw beef from the end of a straw. In the hand-feeding of salamanders and frogs a straw is to be preferred over forceps. There is a natural quivering at the tip which simulates the movement of an insect, and this quivering may prompt the appetite of an amphibian which would refuse a morsel offered with forceps. Another advantage to the use of a straw is the ease with which a bit of meat may be snapped up by a shy animal. If a piece of meat is offered with forceps and the animal is unable immediately to free it from the grip of the instrument, further interest may not be shown.

The lungless salamanders are mostly sleek and graceful amphibians, but rather plainly colored or obscurely striped. A few species, however, are strikingly beautiful. One of these is the red salamander, *Pseudotriton ruber*, of the eastern states, chiefly in mountainous areas. The species reaches a fair size, seven inches or slightly more, and is an over-all brilliant red with jet black spots profusely scattered over the back in vivid contrast. In my early collecting days one of my first big field discoveries was a colony of these handsome salamanders in a spring-fed swamp in New York. The owner of the land kindly lent me some hip-boots, and with these I was able to explore likely hiding places in the knee-deep moss and mud. A breeding congress

Red salamander, *Pseudotriton ruber.* Photo courtesy American Museum of Natural History.

Fire salamander, *Salamandra salamandra.* Photo by G. Marcuse.

Tiger salamander, *Ambystoma tigrinum*. Photo by H. Hansen, Aquarium Berlin.

Slimy salamander, *Plethodon glutinosus.* Photo by F. J. Dodd, Jr.

of garter snakes inhabited the area—this was exciting enough to a youthful herpetologist, but far more important was the discovery of several of these really gorgeous salamanders. Two were brought home and lived for some time. They would have survived longer, I realize now, if they had been kept cold and provided with moss and pieces of bark under which to hide.

Some salamanders move quickly when uncovered and are exceedingly difficult to catch and hold. The dusky salamander, *Desmognathus fuscus*, is one of these. A collector may work his way along a shaded mountain brook, turning over rocks and logs, and find perhaps fifty of the agile amphibians in a few hours. Generally, though, only a small percentage will find their way into the collecting bag. Dusky salamanders are mostly plain brown creatures with darker stripes and spots; there are many species and varieties in the genus and one kind, the black-bellied salamander of Georgia and the Carolinas, grows to the impressive length of eight inches. Known scientifically as *Desmognathus quadramaculatus*, the black-belly occasionally ventures into the open during daylight hours.

Mountain salamander, *Desmognathus ochrophaeus*, Allegheny Mountains. Photo courtesy American Museum of Natural History.

Spotted salamander, *Ambystoma maculatum*. Photo by J. K. Langhammer.

Dusky salamander, *Desmognathus fuscus*. Photo by F. J. Dodd, Jr.

Longtailed salamander, *Eurycea longicauda,* eastern United States.
Photo by J. K. Langhammer.

Cave salamander, *Eurycea lucifuga,* central United States. Photo by
J. K. Langhammer.

Western North America, particularly the coastal areas of Washington, Oregon, and California, has an interesting salamander fauna. The ensatina, *Ensatina eschscholtzi*, with its vividly blotched varieties, is a very handsome salamander, dark brown or black with stipplings of bright orange or yellow. Large specimens may run to six inches in length; they live well in a damp woodland terrarium but are not often available commercially because it is only rarely that they are found in any numbers.

The slender salamander, *Batrachoseps attenuatus*, and its relatives are diminutive kinds with elongated bodies and tiny legs. They rarely grow larger than four inches and are blackish, often with a lighter dorsal stripe. Eggs are deposited on land and the babies do not go through a larval stage.

Climbing salamanders (genus *Aneides*) are a small group of plethodontids, some species of which are noted for their inclination to climb trees. The arboreal salamander, *Aneides lugubris*, is often encountered in live oak trees at a great height. Most salamanders are voiceless, but members of the present group often emit a squeal when picked up. They have strong jaws and sharp teeth and do not hesitate to defend themselves by biting. Needless to say, with such a small creature—adults average only about four to five inches—only super-

Two-lined salamander, *Eurycea bislineata,* eastern United States. Photo courtesy American Museum of Natural History.

ficial scratches can be inflicted. Climbing salamanders are usually some shade of tan or dark brown. They have tails which are prehensile to a degree and, as might be imagined from their arboreal habits, require somewhat less moisture than the earth-bound plethodontids. A single species of the genus lives in the eastern part of the United States. This is the green salamander, *Aneides aeneus*, whose coloring is quite unique among the members of its family. It frequents the narrow crevices of cliff faces and a piece of wire or some other tool is often a necessary adjunct to the collecting of specimens.

The web-toed salamanders (genus *Hydromantes*) have a curious distribution, the several California forms having their nearest relatives in southern Europe. These salamanders have very long tongues which can be shot out to pick up the insects which come within range. Their webbed feet enable *Hydromantes* species to ascend steep rock surfaces of their mountain and cave homes. The Mount Lyell salamander, *Hydromantes platycephalus*, and its related species have very restricted ranges and habitat preferences. They are not likely to be encountered on any ordinary field trip, but if the prospective collector will learn all he can of their habits and locality records, and picks the right time of year for his search, he is more than likely to return with some specimens.

Italian cave salamander, *Hydromantes italicus*, Italy. Photo courtesy American Museum of Natural History.

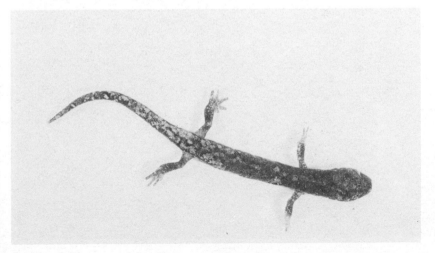

Clawed frog, *Xenopus laevis*. Photo by Dr. Herbert R. Axelrod.

Fire-bellied toad, *Bombina orientalis*. Photo by W. Mudrack.

Surinam toad, *Pipa pipa.* Photo by H. Schultz.

Fire-bellied toad, *Bombina orientalis.* Photo by W. Mudrack.

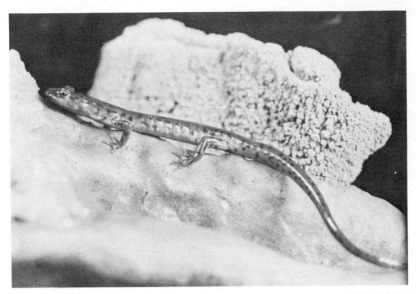

Cave salamander, *Eurycea lucifuga,* central United States. Photo courtesy American Museum of Natural History.

Georgia blind salamander, *Haideotriton wallacei,* Georgia and Florida. Photo by F. J. Dodd, Jr.

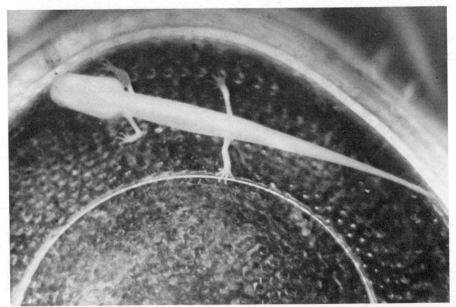

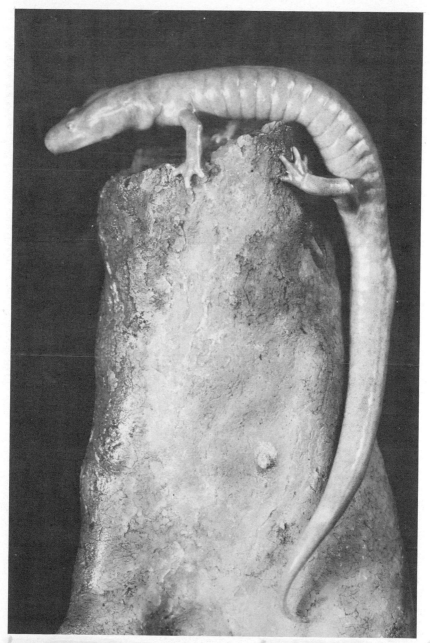

Grotto salamander, *Typhlotriton spelaeus,* Ozark Mountains. Photo courtesy American Museum of Natural History.

Couch's spadefoot, *Scaphiopus couchi,* southwestern U.S. and Mexico. Photo by F. J. Dodd, Jr.

Megophrys nasuta, southern Asia. Photo by J. K. Langhammer.

Western spadefoot, *Scaphiopus hammondi,* western United States. Photo by J. K. Langhammer.

There are many other salamanders which make excellent cage animals, but the habits of some are all but unknown. Careful observations of even the common species may enhance our knowledge. In general, it may be said that the smaller and more secretive the animal, the less we know of its life history. Since most salamanders fit very well the description of being both small and secretive, it is not surprising that there is much to be learned about them.

CAECILIANS

The caecilians of the order Gymnophiona, family Caeciliidae, form one of the strangest groups of amphibians. They are highly specialized, wormlike burrowers or aquatic creatures with no trace of limbs. As a group they are the least known of the amphibians. Some are known to be egg-layers while at least one form produces its young alive. The few caecilians which have been kept in captivity have done indifferently well in a burrowing medium of moss or soft soil. One genus, *Typhlonectes*, is believed to be thoroughly aquatic. Many of the terrestial forms coil about their eggs during the period of incubation. Some species have fed well under captive conditions upon earthworms. The group is one which is worthy of much study.

X

Frogs and Toads

ANURANS IN GENERAL

The frogs and toads of the world easily outnumber the salamanders and newts by more than ten to one. Each year some previously undescribed kinds are given technical names and placed in our checklists. Many species are known to us only from preserved specimens in museums. There are gaps in our knowledge of even the commoner species, and many of these gaps can be filled by the observations of keen herptile enthusiasts. None of the frogs and toads grows to really large size; even the giants of the group have a body length of less than a foot. Therefore, they do not present the housing difficulties which may be encountered in the keeping of the larger members of other groups of herptiles. When collecting in the field, one will often come across a frog or toad in a place that seems to support no other herptile life. As a group they have invaded even the Arctic Circle.

Collectively, the frogs and toads are often referred to as anurans. From the standpoint of the vivarium-keeper the various anurans can be conveniently grouped according to their habitat preferences. Such a way of splitting them up corresponds roughly with their technical family classifications, for the latter are based on structural details and these, in turn, are linked with modes of life. There are burrowing types which spend most of their lives underground, completely aquatic species which never leave the water, surface-dwelling forms which spend much of their time in or near water, terrestrial types which require some moisture but enter the water only to breed, and

South American bullfrog, *Leptodactylus pentadactylus*. Photo by van den Nieuwenhuizen.

Barking frog, *Eleutherodactylus sp.* Photo by F. J. Dodd, Jr.

Horned frog, *Ceratophrys cornuta*. Photo by Dr. Herbert R. Axelrod.

Horned frog, *Ceratophrys calacarata*. Photo by F. J. Dodd, Jr.

finally arboreal types which have varying degrees of specialization for life in trees and bushes. Few amphibians have successfully invaded the desert, and none lives in the sea. No frog or toad is known to have a poisonous bite, but the skin glands of many kinds produce exceedingly poisonous secretions. Examples are the poison arrow frogs and the giant toad. More than one dog has died from the effects of foolishly mouthing a giant toad. Certain South American frogs can bite painfully with large, tooth-studded jaws, but the vast majority of the tailless amphibians are harmless and beneficial animals, benevolent of mien and with dispositions matching their looks. Some of the tropical frogs have a beauty of coloring which rivals that of the butterflies and moths which flutter about them in their jungle homes.

AFRICAN CLAWED FROG

The very aquatic tongueless frogs of the family Pipidae are among the most familiar of the exotic amphibians which are offered for sale in pet stores and aquariums. A species often imported is the

Pair of dwarf water frogs, *Hymenochirus curtipes*, male at left. Photo by B. Haas.

Amplexus in *H. curtipes.* Photo by B. Haas.

Young larvae of *H. curtipes.* Photo by B. Haas.

American toad, *Bufo terrestris americanus;* mating (above), albino (below). Photos by J. K. Langhammer.

Colorado River toad, *Bufo alvarius*. Photo by J. K. Langhammer.

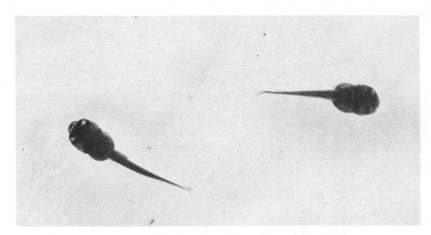

Tadpoles of *H. curtipes*. Photo by B. Haas.

Mother and young *H. curtipes*. Photo by B. Haas.

very small *Hymenochirus curtipes*. Several other very similar species are also often imported. They are gracefully-swimming little animals that can be kept in good health for years and even bred in a fairly large aquarium. The much larger *Xenopus*, often used medically for pregnancy tests, is also commonly available. Of the several species, *Xenopus laevis* is probably the most commonly imported. While specimens of *Hymenochirus* seldom greatly exceed one inch in length, adult *Xenopus* are commonly five or six inches long.

Clawed frogs are not colorful, but their interesting habits make them worthwhile additions to any herptile collection. Often these aquatic frogs are kept in rather deep aquariums, but a better arrangement is one where the depth of the water does not exceed four or five inches. A water temperature of 70 to 75 degrees is suitable, and food should consist of small animal matter such as white and tubifex worms, chopped earthworms, and even scraped lean beef. A layer of ordinary aquarium gravel makes a good floor covering for the tank housing clawed frogs—perhaps mud would be better, but it certainly would do little to enhance the appearance of the aquarium. The frogs spend much of their time swimming over the bottom, using their front feet to scoop into their mouths such edibles as may be found. Captives become quite tame and will swim to the surface of their tank and take food from one's fingers. Frequently, contented

Large clawed frog, *Xenopus laevis*. Photo by G. J. M. Timmerman.

Spiny toad, *Bufo spinulosus,* South America. Photo by H. Hansen, Aquarium Berlin.

Giant toad, *Bufo marinus.* Photo by Dr. Herbert R. Axelrod.

Common toad, *Bufo bufo*. Photo by H. Hansen, Aquarium Berlin.

Tadpole of *Xenopus laevis*. Photo by G. J. M. Timmerman.

specimens will protrude their heads from the water and chirp, especially in the evening. They never leave the water voluntarily and on land are all but helpless.

Clawed frogs often breed in aquariums, attaching their several hundred eggs to aquatic vegetation. If this happens, the adults should be removed at once to prevent them from devouring their eggs or offspring. The eggs normally hatch in less than a week; the tiny tadpoles will remain clinging to aquatic plants for a few days, absorbing the egg yolk. Shortly they become free-swimming and

Detail of foot of *Xenopus laevis*. Photo by G. J. M. Timmerman.

start feeding on protozoans. The large green algae masses found in stagnant waters will provide the growing creatures with a proper diet, but care must be taken not to introduce any predaceous insects. Perhaps a better aquarium diet is dried and powdered egg. Tadpoles normally swim in a head-downward position. From the time of hatching until metamorphosis into tiny froglets will take about two months. The tadpoles of *Xenopus* differ from those of *Hymenochirus* by having two long tentacles or antennae growing from the head.

SURINAM TOAD

A weird-looking member of the family to which the clawed frog belongs is the Surinam toad, *Pipa pipa*. The interchangeability of the terms "frog" and "toad" as parts of popular names should be noted here. Though they belong to the same family and are very closely related, *Xenopus* is commonly referred to as a frog, while *Pipa* is called a toad. Surinam toads grow to a larger size than clawed frogs and live equally well in aquariums, but do not often breed. Their appearance is bizarre in the extreme. A much-flattened body appears rectangular in outline when viewed from above; the head is triangular, terminating in a pointed snout. The hind feet are broadly webbed, while toes of the forefeet end in starlike tips. The South American rivers inhabited by Surinam toads are very muddy and the toe tips, as well as fleshy appendages about the mouth, doubtless prove of assistance in locating food. There is little need for eyes in such an environment, and the Surinam toad's eyes have been reduced to tiny dots. The female toad carries her eggs on her back, where they are placed by the male after fertilization. The entire larval development takes place on the back of the mother; when the babies are fully developed they emerge from the skin recesses in the back of the female, where they have been for several months, and swim off to live their own lives. Babies and adults alike are carnivorous and should have a water temperature of about 75 degrees.

DISCOGLOSSIDS

The fire-bellied toad, *Bombina bombina*, belongs to the family Discoglossidae, a small group of aquatic forms native to Europe and Asia. Fire-bellied toads have rather plain grayish backs, but their underparts are beautifully colored in red or orange. Stagnant pond and ditch waters are their usual habitats, and in captivity an aquarium

Crested toad, *Bufo superciliaris,* Africa. Photo by H. Hansen, Aquarium Berlin.

Atelopid, *Atelopus cruciger*, South America. Photo by J. K. Langhammer.

with a few inches of water and a large, very rounded stone which protrudes above the water surface are their essential requirements. Floating plants and a layer of sand on the bottom may be used, if desired. As a substitute for this kind of an arrangement an aquarium which is divided between water and land areas may be used. Fire-bellies spend much of their time floating leisurely in the water, with just their heads protruding, but these anurans do occasionally like to crawl out on land. They will accept earthworms, insects, and even pieces of raw beef.

The related yellow-bellied toad, *Bombina variegata,* has similar habits and is found in southern Europe. *Bombina orientalis* is a particularly beautiful mountain stream dweller of Asia. All of the *Bombina* species have a poisonous skin secretion which makes them immune to depredation by most animals. The well-known European midwife toad, *Alytes obstetricans,* is a discoglossid, but except in the matter of its breeding habits is not as colorful or interesting as the *Bombina* species. After mating on land, the male carries the eggs about, attached to the rear of his body, until they are ready to hatch. He then goes to the water, and the larvae emerge and fend for themselves.

Painted frog, *Discoglossus pictus,* southern Europe and northern Africa. Photo by G. Marcuse.

Midwife toad, *Alytes obstetricans*. Photo by W. Lierath.

SPADEFOOT TOADS

Pelobatidae is the name of the family to which the spadefoot toads and their relatives belong. Representatives of the family are found in Europe, Asia, Africa, and North America. The spadefoot toad of Europe, *Pelobates fuscus*, is strikingly reminiscent of the North American spadefoots (*Scaphiopus* species). The skin of spadefoot toads is much smoother than that of the more familiar garden toads of the genus *Bufo*. Their eyes are curious in that the pupils are vertically elliptical when exposed to light, but become round in the dark. If nothing was known of their habits it would be easy to guess, from their appearance, that they were nightroving amphibians. Even in places where they are common, however, it is not usual to find many about except during the breeding period, which in the United States follows warm rains in the spring and summer.

I have found spadefoots rather difficult to maintain satisfactorily in a terrarium. They fare poorly if kept without hiding places or earth in which to burrow. Yet if provided with such a duplication of their natural environment they remain out of sight and seldom show much interest in food. Such habits in captivity probably correspond

Spring peeper, *Hyla crucifer*. Photo by W. Mudrack.

Bell frog, *Hyla gratiosa,* spotted phase, southeastern United States. Photo by F. J. Dodd, Jr.

Poison arrow frog, family Dendrobatidae. Photo by W. Mudrack.

Megophrys nasuta, an unusual member of the family Pelobatidae from southern Asia. Photo by Dr. Otto Klee.

with those of wild specimens which may remain in underground burrows for weeks or months. In contrast, however, to the specimens which are dug out of their burrows in the wild state, captives become emaciated in a relatively short time. An aquarium with several inches of soil, a sunken water container, and a covering of moss or dead leaves and pieces of bark seems to make the best home for spadefoots. One has to rate the spadefoots among those frogs and toads that do not adapt well to artificial conditions. In their many species they are inconspicuously-colored little creatures, usually a shade of brown or gray, sometimes with darker markings on the back.

BARKING FROG

The family Leptodactylidae embraces a tremendous array of frogs whose headquarters are the American tropics. Curiously, in the Old World they are confined to Australia. Viewed as a group, their breeding habits are as varied as the animals themselves. Some lay their eggs in the water; others in frothy masses on land, from which the tadpoles are washed down into ponds by rain; other species lay on land and stay nearby until they hatch fully developed babies which have completed their metamorphosis within their eggs. The frogs of this family range in size from very tiny species to large ones.

South American bullfrog, *Leptodactylus pentadactylus*. Photo by G. Marcuse.

gratiosa, green phase, southeastern United States.

back.

460

Pine barrens tree frog, *Hyla andersoni,* New Jersey to northern Florida. Photo by J. K. Langhammer.

Eastern chorus frog, *Pseudacris triseriata.* Eastern United States. Photo by W. Mudrack.

The barking frog, *Eleutherodactylus latrans*, occurs in the southwestern United States and northern Mexico, where it frequents rocky areas. It is a secretive species and remains hidden in fissures and under rocks during the day, coming out at night, when its call, resembling the bark of a dog, can often be heard during rainstorms. Barking frogs reach a length of only about three inches and are grayish in color, often clouded with lighter or darker blotches. The breeding season of this species runs from late winter to May; the eggs, often numbering fifty, are laid on land, separated from each other, and are often if not invariably guarded by the male. Completely terrestrial, the barking frog should be kept in an aquarium with a damp sand base and a scattering of fair-sized rocks in the background. The rocks may be formed into a cavelike structure, care being taken that each rock is firmly placed and cannot be readily shifted. It is amusing to watch one of these frogs progress from one place to another in a curious and deliberate walk. The food of the barking frog consists mainly of insects and spiders.

SOUTH AMERICAN BULLFROG, MOUNTAIN CHICKEN

The South American bullfrog rivals or may even exceed our native bullfrogs in size. Its scientific name is *Leptodactylus pentadactylus* and it is one of the kinds which deposit their eggs on land, covered with foam. The larvae undergo part of their development within the frothy mass but complete it in the water. A large adult may measure nine inches and is colored handsomely in tan or brown, suffused with orange. Another beautiful though somewhat smaller leptodactylid species is called the mountain chicken, *Leptodactylus fallax*. Nearly all of the really large frogs will not hesitate to eat any smaller ones which may be confined in the same cage, including even those of their own species. It is important, therefore, not to mix frogs of very unequal sizes.

HORNED FROGS

The horned frogs of the genus *Ceratophrys*, in some of their forms, are beautifully adorned and highly aggressive creatures that make handsome vivarium inmates. Some grow to a length of eight inches and have an immense body bulk. All of the horned frogs have enormous mouths and are highly predatory, the food of some consisting almost solely of other frogs. Large specimens will attack anything which threatens them; they can inflict painful bites, holding on with bulldog tenacity. Even the tadpoles of the horned frogs are highly carnivorous. In our studies of herptiles we cannot fail to note the frequency with which a multiplicity of unusual characteristics occurs within a species or group. The horned frogs are outstanding in almost every respect. Some of the species are small, but several grow to huge size and have beautifully blended colorings of reds, tans, browns, greens, and blacks. On a plain background these frogs are most conspicuous, but on the jungle floor, among leaves and debris, they can hardly be seen. They move about but little, preferring to lie in ambush for the unwary snakes, lizards, mice, and other vertebrates which come within range of their powerful jaws. Some species have prominent hornlike developments over their eyes, adding further to their bizarre appearance. The horned frog of the Amazon, *Ceratophrys cornuta*, is one of the largest species; *Ceratophrys dorsata* of Brazil is another. The kind we find most often in dealers' cages is the Colombian horned frog, *Ceratophrys calcarata*, a rather quiet and demure species if, indeed, we can use these terms to describe any of the horned frogs. Forest frogs of this genus do not require a water pool in their cage. A sand or soil covering may be used for the floor, and this may be overlaid with moss and dead leaves. The *Ceratophrys* species described above and most other tropical species should be kept in a cage temperature range of 70 to 75 degrees. Lowland types require a higher temperature than those from elevated regions.

BUFONID TOADS

When one speaks of toads it is usually one species or another of the family Bufonidae that comes to mind. These are the common garden-variety toads that are so numerous nearly everywhere. Every continental land mass except Australia has native toads of this family. *Bufo* is the most important genus in the family, and it alone has more than 250 distinct kinds of toads. Though varying greatly in size from tiny species like the oak toad, *Bufo quercicus*, to huge ones like the giant toad, *Bufo marinus*, all of the *Bufo* species are very much alike in over-all appearance. They have heavy bodies and cannot make the long leaps of the more agile frogs. Their skins are dry and in many species very rough, giving the appearance of being wart-covered. Toads cannot, of course, cause warts if handled. But the skin glands do produce a poison which can be very irritating to mucous mem-

Hyla smithi. Photo by F. J. Dodd, Jr.

Dumpy green treefrog, *Hyla caerulea,* Australia. Photo by G. Marcuse.

Australasian green treefrog, *Hyla infrafrenata*. Photo by Dr. Otto Klee.

American toad, *Bufo terrestris*. Photo courtesy American Museum of Natural History.

branes and fatal if swallowed in sufficient amount. For this reason toads are molested only by animals which have special ways of dealing with them. The hognose snakes eat toads; in fact, these snakes feed upon little else, but most kinds of snakes which regularly eat frogs will ignore toads. Toads, like other amphibians, require moisture but will not dry out and die as quickly as most other amphibians if deprived of it. A moderately damp terrarium or box with a floor covering of soil will comfortably house one or more toads. If the animals and their surroundings are sprinkled daily with water it is not necessary to provide a pool. I believe, however, that it is better to have one in the cage, sunk flush with the soil or gravel. This enables the amphibians to absorb the proper amount of moisture. Except in the breeding season, toads of the genus *Bufo* are seldom found actually in water. They are terrestrial amphibians, and the members of the family which are aquatic or arboreal have been placed in other genera. The toads of North America and Europe are rather drab creatures when compared to some of their tropical relatives. Though no toad is as colorful as some of the more beautiful frogs, certain tropical species have handsome blends of tans, browns, and black.

Fowler's toad, *Bufo woodhousei fowleri*. Photo courtesy American Museum of Natural History.

Over the eastern half of the United States the American toad, *Bufo terrestris,* is perhaps the most often encountered herptile. In many books it is referred to as *Bufo americanus,* the name *terrestris* being reserved for the southern variety, which differs in minor details from the northern population. Currently, however, both southern and northern populations are regarded simply as geographical variations of a single species: *terrestris.* This is mentioned only to point out to the neophyte herpetologist the fact that scientific names change from time to time, as the study of relationships progresses. Serious students take such changes in stride, but they can be confusing to the beginner. Unless one has access to the latest technical writings in all of the major languages it is impossible to keep completely up-to-date. The habits of the American toad are similar to those of other species. It emerges from hibernation in early spring and travels by night to the pond where breeding will take place. The males arrive first and their trilling becomes a sound of the spring night. When the female arrive on the scene, mating and egg-laying take place. The eggs deposited in long strings and commonly number several thousa from a single female. Hatching takes place in about a week, and poles frequent the shallow shore waters in enormous numbers.

Marsupial frog, *Gastrotheca marsupiata.* Photo by Dr. Otto Klee.

Nesting treefrog, *Agalychnis dacnicolor,* Central America. Photo by J. K. Langhammer.

Burrowing treefrog, *Pternohyla fodiens*, Mexico. Photo by F. J. Dodd, Jr.

Mexican tree frog, *Smilisca baudini*, Central America. Photo by F. J. Dodd, Jr.

which survive the onslaught of predators transform into tiny toads in a few weeks and for awhile thereafter remain close to the pond where they were born. Eventually each goes its own way and reaches maturity in two to three years.

Nearly all of the many kinds of bufonid toads live well in captivity. Records of some that have survived twenty or more years are not uncommon. Toads, and other anurans as well, require food at more frequent intervals than most reptiles. Generally speaking, they will not accept other than living food, though pieces of meat which are put in motion before them will sometimes be accepted by specimens which are accustomed to vivarium life. An exception to the rule of feeding naturally only upon live creatures has been brought to light in a number of articles which state that wild *Bufo* specimens will sometimes recognize as food and devour such unlikely items as canned dog food. The veracity of these reports can hardly be questioned, but in the vivarium toads will not show any interest in nonmoving creatures or objects. It would, indeed, be convenient if we could feed them dog food, upon which many turtles seem to thrive. Toads which are accustomed to hibernating may stop eating in the fall. The instinct is so strong that even in a warm room they tend to remain in seclusion during the winter months, but usually they can be induced to accept worms or insects. An alternative can be had in allowing the creatures to go into actual hibernation. This can be accomplished if the animals have been well fed during the summer and have accumulated enough fat to carry them over a period of several months. Their cage should be filled nearly to the top with wood pulp, leaf mold, or moss and placed in a room or other situation where the temperature will remain around 40 degrees. The hibernating medium should be sprinkled occasionally but not allowed to become soggy. Some, though not much, ventilation is necessary. I have at times allowed herptiles to hibernate over the winter months but no longer make any attempt to do so, for I do not believe it will appreciably benefit the animals or increase their captive lifespan. This will be disputed by some vivarium keepers, who will insist that herptiles from cold winter climates do benefit by a period of rest in captivity. I can only answer that nearly all of the longevity records were established by herptiles which were not permitted to hibernate. Of course, if it is not possible to keep herptiles warmed during the winter, they must be allowed to go into hibernation. Any reptile or amphibian which has not been feeding regularly or is not in really top shape is unlikely to survive a period of hibernation. Toads' eggs can be hatched and the tadpoles brought through transformation in an aquarium. Perhaps the best way of doing this is by bringing a portion of the natural pond home, along with the eggs. This can be done with wide-mouthed glass or plastic gallon containers. Gently scoop up and place some of the eggs in one of the jugs which has been half-filled with surface water from the pond. In another jar place generous quantities of the leaves, twigs, and debris from the bottom of the pond. Fill the remaining containers with plain water. In an aquarium or other container at home, the process can be reversed. First add the water to a suitable depth,

Green toad, *Bufo viridis*. Photo by Van Raam.

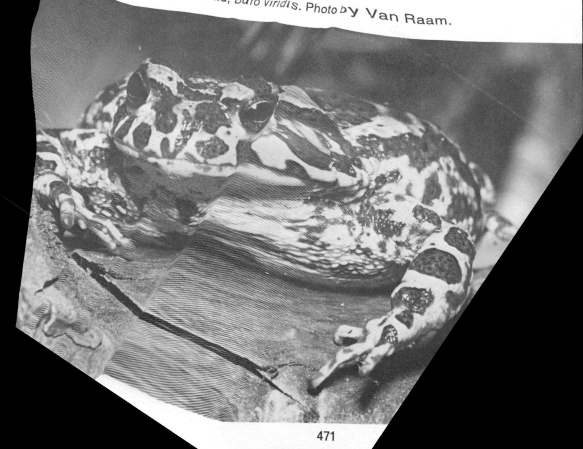

Arum frog, *Hyperolius horstockii*, southern Africa. Photo by W. Mudrack.

African treefrog, *Hyperolius fusciventris*, Africa. Photo by W. Mudrack.

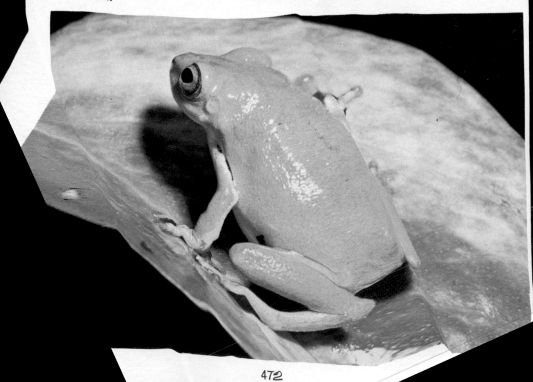

Golden mantella, *Mantella aurantiaca*, Madagascar. Photo by W. Mudrack.

Black-spined toad, *Bufo melanosticus,* Southeast Asia. Photo by G. Marcuse.

usually not more than six or eight inches. Introduce the bottom debris, including any slime-covered rocks, and allow the silt to settle. Then pour the eggs into the container. In the absence of pond water any soft or slightly acid water may be used. When the eggs have hatched, keep only a few of the larvae—they will have a much better chance of living if not overcrowded. The water must not be allowed to become contaminated; a frequent change may be necessary to avoid this, especially if the aquarium is a small one.

Most frog and toad tadpoles are herbivorous, while the larvae of salamanders are carnivorous. Suitable foods are such items as boiled lettuce leaves, spinach, pond algae, pieces of hard-boiled egg, dried daphnia, and small amounts of canned dog food. The diet of the babies should be varied to insure proper growth and a small daily feeding is much better than a larger one at less frequent intervals. Make sure the food is quickly cleaned up and not allowed to decompose.

Argentine toad, *Bufo arenarum*, South America. Photo by G. Marcuse.

Most tadpoles will transform into tiny frogs or toads in periods ranging, with the species, from a few weeks to a few months. First the back legs make their appearance, then the front ones. By this time the aquarium must have a shore or landing place where the baby amphibians can leave the water. Then comes the problem of supplying live food in sufficient quantities to satisfy the appetites of the youngsters. The white worms known as enchytrae can be used in part for this purpose, but even better are the multitudes of tiny creatures found in the lower leaf debris of damp woods. When a small amount of this is placed in the vivarium it can be confidently assumed that the tiny toads or frogs will find and devour whatever small livir creatures it may contain. Salamander larvae may be cared for much the same manner, the chief difference being that they require animal matter during their development. Brine shr finely-ground earthworms, crushed snails, canned dog food, fresh raw meat, and white worms are a few of the food items a

Leopard frog, *Rana pipiens*. Photo by F. J. Dodd, Jr.

Pustulose frog, *Rana pustulosa*, Central America. Photo by F. J. Dodd, Jr.

Burrowing frog, *Rana adspersus,* middle and southern Africa. Photo by J. K. Langhammer.

by developing salamanders, and also by spadefoot toad larvae and the young of certain other carnivorous baby anurans. Amphibian larvae have been little described and it is often next to impossible to determine what species of frog, toad, or salamander one has on hand until transformation takes place. Salamander larvae differ from those of the anurans in sprouting the front legs first.

The toads of the United States that are likely to be available are such species as Fowler's, *Bufo woodhousei fowleri*; Colorado River, *Bufo alvarius*; western, *Bufo boreas*; oak, *Bufo quercicus*; and the American green toads, *Bufo debilis* and *Bufo retiformis*. European species are the common toad, *Bufo bufo*; the European green toad, *Bufo viridis*; and the natterjack toad, *Bufo calamita*. The very large Blomberg's toad, *Bufo blombergi*, from South America is an especially handsome creature, reaching a length of eight to ten inches. Equally large, though not nearly so colorful, are the South American populations of the giant toad, *Bufo marinus*. The last species will devour nearly any living creature which it can cram into its capacious maw. This includes such vertebrates as mice, small rats, and sparrows. Occasionally some very attractive toads from Asia and Africa are

Blomberg's toad, *Bufo blombergi.* Photo by G. Marcuse.

imported. Generally the prices of imported toads are not high, and I have often thought that a good collection of the many different *Bufo* species would afford an interesting example of the variation in size and colors that may take place within a single genus of animals.

POISON ARROW FROGS

The extremely colorful and rather active little South American frogs of the family Dendrobatidae are often imported. The strawberry poison arrow frog, *Dendrobates pumilio*, is red and black; other species in the genus have vivid black and yellow markings. One to two inches represents the maximum growth attained by these decorative frogs. They are among the most handsome members of any collection of herptiles, and if they have a disadvantage it is in their feeding habits—they require the tiniest of insects, which may sometimes be hard to procure. A moss-covered terrarium with a few branches or strong-leaved plants makes a suitable home for *Dendrobates* and the related *Phyllobates*. They are forest frogs, rarely entering the water, but requiring humid surroundings and a temperature of 70 to 75 degrees. The male frog carries the eggs about on his back

Crested toad, *Bufo typhonius,* Brazil. Photo by H. Schultz.

Rana erythraea. Photo by Dr. Otto Klee.

Poison arrow frog, *Dendrobates* sp. Photo courtesy American Museum of Natural History.

until they have hatched and the larvae have reached a fairly advanced stage of development. He then enters the water, allowing the tadpoles to swim free and finally metamorphose. The poison arrow frogs, of some species at least, have a very toxic skin secretion which has long been used by the Indians in the poisoning of their arrows to produce quick death in a mammal or bird. Some care should be used to see that this skin secretion does not get into the eyes or mouth after handling a frog. The little frogs are so delicately formed and fragile that it is perhaps best not to handle them at all, except with a net when it is absolutely necessary. They live quite well in confinement if properly cared for but it is likely that they do not have a very long natural span of life.

TREEFROGS

I am not very much in favor of displaying herptiles in so-called "natural environment" arrangements if they will live just as well in simple cages with a minimum of accessories. Some herptiles, in fact, do very poorly in cages which attempt to duplicate the natural habitat of their inmates. Other herptiles demand an imitation of their natural home, to some degree at least, or they will fail to thrive. Or if

Gray treefrog, *Hyla versicolor*. From Dickerson, *The Frog Book*.

they do live they will show few of their characteristics. Such are the treefrogs of the family *Hylidae*. Treefrogs are agile and long-limbed; they have toe pads which enable them to ascend smooth vertical surfaces. Many have a pronounced ability to change color. They number in their clan some of the smallest frogs as well as species which reach a length of at least five inches. In their various greens and browns, many are delicately handsome and some do exceedingly well in captivity if provided with an adequate supply of insects and other small invertebrates. They are found on every continent but reach their maximum abundance in Central and South America. The United States has a fair number of species.

The gray treefrog, *Hyla versicolor*, is a widespread and fairly common species over much of the eastern half of the United States. It is about two inches when fully grown and may be brown, green, or gray—the color changing according to the mood of the animal and environmental factors. Usually this treefrog is found on the trunk or branches of trees which are close to water. In its grayish color phase it is almost impossible to see when clinging to the bark of a tree. The usual time for breeding and egg-laying is early June; the eggs are attached singly or in small groups to the stems of pond vegetation.

Phyllomedusa rohdei, Paraguay. Photo by Van Raam.

They hatch in a few days and the tadpoles are easy to identify because of their distinctive golden color and red tail. The change to the adult form occurs during the summer, at which time the half-inch froglets leave the pond and take up residence in trees and bushes. Gray treefrogs are hardy terrarium inmates and like other species of their kind can be made to feel at home in a well-planted terrarium with a floor covering of soil and moss, some hardy broad-leaved foliage, and perhaps a portion of a tree limb.

The green treefrog, *Hyla cinerea*, is another attractive species that is very streamlined in over-all appearance and has a somewhat pointed head. It occurs chiefly in the southeastern United States and the Mississippi Valley. The spring peeper, *Hyla crucifer*, is less than an inch in length when mature but does well in a damp terrarium if kept well supplied with tiny insects and worms. It is perhaps the most abundant treefrog over its wide range in the eastern United States. The European treefrog, *Hyla arborea*, is a chunky little species that is less active than many of its New World relatives. It has long been recognized as an excellent terrarium animal by European herpetologists; that is probably one of the reasons why we seldom find it offered for sale in the United States.

Spring peeper, *Hyla crucifer*. Photo courtesy American Museum of Natural History.

Pacific treefrog, *Hyla regilla,* Pacific coast of United States. Photo by L. Van der Meid.

European treefrog, *Hyla arborea.* Photo by Muller-Schmida.

Golden treefrog, *Hyla aurea,* Australia. Photo by G. Marcuse.

Tropical and semi-tropical regions have treefrogs of huge size and all the attractive coloration of their smaller cousins. The Australasian *Hyla infrafrenata* is a beautiful green species that reaches many times the size and bulk of our more familiar treefrogs of Europe and North America. Giant treefrogs of this and other species require sturdy foliage in their terrariums to support their considerable weight. One such giant, the Cuban treefrog, *Hyla septentrionalis,* is an immigrant which has become successfully established in Florida and the Keys. It may reach a length of five inches but lacks the beautiful coloring of some members of its family.

Some of the less well known members of the treefrog family are those of the genera *Phyllomedusa, Gastrotheca,* and *Agalychnis.* Some are most remarkable in appearance or habits. *Gastrotheca,* for example, carries her eggs on her back concealed in a sort of pouch, and members of this genus are often called marsupial frogs. Depending upon the species, the young may emerge from the pouch as tadpoles and finish their larval stage in water, or complete transformation may take place within the pouch.

Marsupial frog, *Gastrotheca marsupiata.* Photo by G. Marcuse.

Agalychnis dacnicolor, Central America. Photo by F. J. Dodd, Jr.

Flying frog, *Rhacophorus* sp., eastern Africa, family Rhacophoridae. Photo by G. Marcuse.

African treefrog, *Hyperolius* sp., a member of the large African and Asian family Rhacophoridae, related to the ranids. Photo by Van Raam.

TRUE FROGS

The true frogs of the family Ranidae are what we might call typical frogs; a description of them is hardly necessary. *Rana* is the largest genus of the family and contains over 250 species, distributed on every continent. It includes such familiar amphibians as the edible frog of Europe, *Rana esculenta*, and the bullfrog of North America. Mostly, the ranid frogs stay close to water; when alarmed, they plunge in and swim to the bottom, taking refuge among aquatic plants or bottom debris. Many are tremendous leapers and are able to cover great distances in a single jump. Though many are rather prettily marked, none shows the beauty of coloration found among members of certain other families of frogs. The typical frogs live quite well under terrarium conditions which allow them to enter or leave the water at will. They can be kept over long periods in shallow water without a landing place, but they cannot survive long in a situation where water is not abundantly available. Some of them remain very nervous for a time after capture and may injure their snouts severely in frantic leaps against the sides or covers of their cages. This wildness persists longer when numbers are housed

Golden mantella, *Mantella aurantiaca*, Madagascar, related to the ranids. Photo by Muller-Schmida.

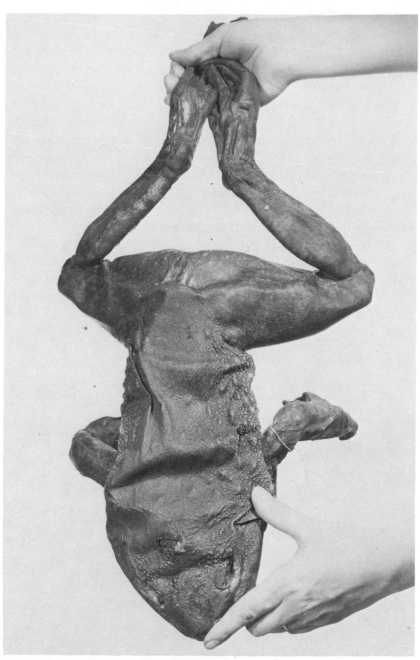

Goliath frog, *Gigantorana goliath,* preserved example to show size.
Photo courtesy American Museum of Natural History.

Burrowing frog, *Rana adspersa*, middle and southern Africa. Photo by G. Marcuse.

together. This may be a good time to mention that nearly all amphibians live better when kept alone or with just one or two others of their kind. Large frogs readily devour small ones and the bullfrog, particularly, is a notorious cannibal.

During the early days of their captivity, frogs should be disturbed as little as possible. Their cages may be partially covered to prevent outside disturbance at this time. They tame rather quickly if kept alone or in pairs and soon reach the point where they will accept food from the hand. Nearly all invertebrates of a suitable size fall prey to frogs, and even such vertebrates as mice and reptiles may be eaten by the larger species. The largest frog in the world belongs to this family. It is called *Gigantorana goliath* and is found in Africa. Large adults may be close to twelve inches in body length. Another unusual African species is the hairy frog, *Astylosternus robustus*, the males of which develop slender filaments of flesh resembling strands of hair along the sides of their bodies during the breeding season.

The North American bullfrog, *Rana catesbeiana*, is a common species and one which has been introduced into places where normally it would not occur. Its large size combined with the fact that it is edible have caused it to be hunted extensively, and in some areas its numbers have considerably diminished. This has brought about laws which regulate the capture or possession of the species in some states. Bullfrogs in their adult stage are rather solitary creatures and often a small pond will form the home area of only a single large adult. The sexes are easy to distinguish because the tympanum or ear opening of the male is much larger than that of its mate. With the latter, it may be about the same size as the eye, while in the male it considerably exceeds this organ in diameter. Nearly all frogs are vociferous, but the resounding boom of the bullfrog in a quiet woodland pond just before a shower or at breeding time in the spring or early summer is one of the noises the naturelover delights in. Egg masses of the bullfrog are deposited at the surface of quiet water, and a single laying may contain very many thousands of frogs-to-be. The tadpoles hatch in about a month and the babies may remain in the larval stage for two years and attain a length of six inches. When transformation finally takes place the babies are not the tiny creatures one might expect. Instead, they are nearly three inches in body length when the tail is finally lost and they take up a partial land existence. Because of their size and the wide variety of foods they will accept, baby bullfrogs are easily reared in a terrarium. Their life expectancy is well over ten years.

Bullfrog, *Rana catesbeiana*. Photo by G. Marcuse.

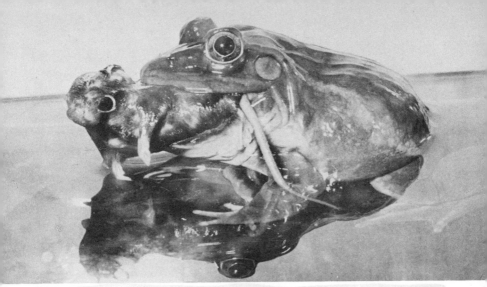

Large frogs, like this bullfrog, are often carnivorous. Photo by G. Marcuse.

Adult bullfrogs are extremely wary and are not often caught in the daytime. At night, in the beam of a flashlight, they seem unable to sense danger and are easily taken. Though bullfrogs may reach a very large size, they are completely inoffensive as far as humans are concerned. They never attempt to bite but will kick so vigorously that it is difficult to hold a large specimen. This is best accomplished by grasping the amphibian about its waist, with the legs extended. In this position even the largest specimen is helpless. A bullfrog is one of the best anurans to keep and study in a terrarium. It loses its natural shyness and a single individual of large size can be housed comfortably in an aquarium which measures eighteen inches in length. Bullfrogs and other species of its genus do well on a diet of earthworms.

The green frog, *Rana clamitans*, is often confused with the bullfrog but is a much smaller animal. It is closely related, however, and from a distance it is difficult to determine whether one is looking at a fully-grown green frog or a half-grown bullfrog. Both are greenish with lighter underparts, but the green frog has a fold of skin along its side, distinguishing it at once from its larger relative, whose sides are smooth. Its habits are similar but it is more gregarious than the bullfrog, and sometimes large numbers of green frogs may inhabit a pond.

493

Green frog, *Rana clamitans*. Photo by M. F. Roberts.

The pickerel frog, *Rana palustris*, is often found in great numbers in or near small bodies of water in the eastern United States. Tiny irrigation ditches are a common habitat, and though these frogs are quick to take alarm and dive to the bottom, they have little hope of escape, at least from humans, in such places. The species is attractively spotted and the undersurfaces of its rear limbs are orange-yellow in color. It is noted for its toxic skin secretion, which causes the species to be rejected by many frog-eating animals. It is not wise to house pickerel frogs with other animals. Even on collecting trips it is best to segregate these frogs from other species, because the other species are likely to succumb to the effects of the poison which the pickerel frog exudes.

Another spotted frog is the leopard frog, *Rana pipiens*. Superficially, it resembles the foregoing species, but has more rounded spots and its legs lack the bright orange coloration of the related species. Its range, in its many varieties, covers nearly the whole of the United States. It is the species often used as fish bait and in biology classrooms and can be purchased very cheaply from biological supply houses. In the terrarium it does well, but some individuals tend to retain an excitable disposition and dash themselves against the glass of their cages when disturbed. Though their ranges coincide in the East, on field trips I have not noted the leopard and pickerel frogs living together.

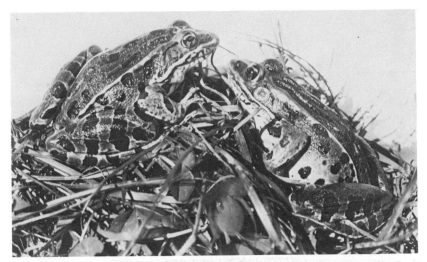

Leopard frog, *Rana pipiens.* Photo courtesy American Museum of Natural History.

Pickerel frog, *Rana palustris.* Photo courtesy American Museum of Natural History. *Toxic*

Indian bullfrog, *Rana tigrina*, southern Asia. Photo by L. E. Perkins.

Moor frog, *Rana arvalis*, north and central Europe, western Asia. Photo by G. Marcuse.

A pretty ranid frog is frequently found in damp woods, not close to any permanent water. It is the wood frog, *Rana sylvatica*, light tan in color with dark brown blotches behind the eyes. Wood frogs change color to a considerable extent and in places with a very dark ground cover the frogs themselves may be dark brown in over-all coloration. In length it does not often exceed three inches. A damp, not wet, terrarium makes a good home for one or more wood frogs. If kept moist with a fine spraying daily the species does not require a pool in its cage. Insects and earthworms are the principal fare of captives.

The red-legged frog, *Rana aurora*, is a species of our western coast and is the largest native frog of that area, growing to at least five inches. Rather pretty, this species usually has a reddish overcast to its skin; the undersides of its rear limbs are bright red. Unlike many of its relatives, the present species is somewhat delicate in confinement and offers interesting possibilities to those who would like to experiment with ways of maintaining it over long periods. Possibly a very cool environment is the answer to keeping red-legged frogs in good health. One specimen lived over ten years, but the majority do not live this many months.

Common frog, *Rana temporaria,* Eurasia. Photo by H. V. Lacey.

Many imported ranids live very well in terrariums, but are rarely available on the animal market. In nearly every country the larger species are sold as food and may be purchased in local market places. Ranid frogs will not withstand high temperatures, so the shipping of specimens from tropical places is more than likely to prove discouraging.

NARROW-MOUTHED TOADS

The narrow-mouthed toads of the family Microhylidae are mostly small and very secretive animals that live in nearly all the warmer portions of the globe where there is sufficient moisture. A few kinds are arboreal or terrestrial, but the majority seem to spend most of their lives in burrows or otherwise hidden from observation. As with the majority of anurans, we know little of their life histories. The eastern narrow-mouthed toad, *Gastrophryne carolinensis,* is a smooth-skinned, dark brown or gray amphibian with a markedly pointed snout. In a terrarium it seldom ventures into the open, and often an entire display will have to be torn apart to find a specimen that has burrowed deeply. Wild specimens are found with some frequency on rainy nights or, in dryer weather, under stones or logs

Eastern narrow-mouthed toad, *Gastrophryne carolinensis*. From Dickerson, *The Frog Book*.

Marsh frog, *Rana ridibunda*, central Europe to western Asia. Photo by G. Marcuse.

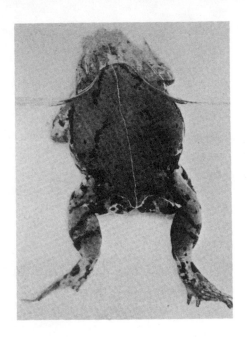

Sheep frog, *Hypopachus cuneus*, southern Texas to Mexico. From Dickerson, *The Frog Book*.

in damp places. These frogs feed on the tiniest of insects; some members of the family appear to eat nothing but termites and live within the nests of these insects. The African *Breviceps* species are members of this family; at least some among them deposit their eggs on land. The entire development of the larvae takes place before hatching. *Kaloula* of Asia is sometimes imported and seems a little less secretive than other narrow-mouthed anurans.

At one time or another I have kept representatives of the majority of families of frogs and toads. All were interesting and some lived for considerable periods. I do not think that any of the many kinds I have kept made better vivarium inmates than the toads of the genus *Bufo*. I would also rate the bullfrog highly in this respect. Some of the treefrogs are not unduly secretive and make decorative, interesting, and often long-lived terrarium inhabitants. Herpetologists, like other workers in scientific fields, have their specialties—favorite animals, if you will. Fewer seem to have studied the tailless amphibians than other kinds of herptiles and as a consequence we know next to nothing about the life histories of most species. Frogs and toads, as well as another amphibian group, the caecilians, offer an inviting field of study at professional or amateur level.

XI

Collecting Herptiles

Probably few herptile keepers confine their attention to a single animal. Most have several specimens and many have extensive collections. Some have only snakes or turtles, while others have a more varied assortment of the many types. There are living in the world today close to 10,000 recognized species of reptiles and amphibians. No one, in a single lifetime, could possibly hope to have under observation more than a tiny percentage of the living forms. Young people, in particular, tend to acquire and keep whatever comes along and learn as much as possible about the various class and family members. Often this type of interest gradually evolves into a specialty. There is little accounting for the likes and interests of humans, and the herptile collector may decide to concentrate on salamanders, or perhaps lizards, or even a single genus in some family. There is little doubt that at the present time more people keep turtles and tortoises than any other herptiles. This may be due, in part, to these reptiles' ready availability both in the wild state and in the cages of dealers.

Whether one decides to develop a specialty or maintain a general collection there is a word of advice which should be well-taken: limit the numbers of individuals in your collection to a reasonable figure. The care of a large collection of reptiles requires not only considerable expenditure of time and effort but also can be very expensive as well. The observation of a few individuals over a long period can be more rewarding than keeping a large collection whose members are suffering from varying degrees of neglect. My own special interest is snakes, and I try never to have more than a dozen individuals on hand at any given time. The cleaning and feeding of a collection of this scope can easily occupy one evening a week. Special problems arise from time to time, and they can occupy much of one's spare time.

BUYING HERPTILES

There are many dealers in the United States who offer herptiles for sale by mail order. With some, this is an adjunct to a bird, mammal, or aquarium fish business. Others make a specialty of local and imported herptiles and maintain fairly large stocks, especially during the warmer months of the year. Some issue monthly or bimonthly bulletins which describe what is on hand; the bulletins may be in addition to a printed listing of stock available at nearly all times. Often a price bulletin subscription service is offered; such a subscription will provide an influx of interesting mail for the herptile enthusiast. It is a way, too, of keeping abreast of the going prices on the commoner imported reptiles and amphibians.

Prices, particularly of imported specimens, may seem high to the novice herpetologist, but it must be recognized that the dealers suffer losses in the importation of herptiles as well as in their own compounds after arrival. Herptiles have to be fed and kept clean and, in cool climates, artificially heated. They have to be advertised or they will not be sold. Nearly all dealers guarantee the live delivery of the herptiles they sell by mail. All of these items affect the price tag on a reptile or amphibian. Like everything else we buy, the prices of herptiles have been rising steadily over the years, and there seems little likelihood that this trend will ever be reversed. It is amusing to compare a reptile price list of twenty years ago with those of today. The selling prices of many of our commoner native species have more than quadrupled. Dealers in reptiles may be honest or otherwise. Those who are "otherwise" commonly do not last long in the business because word of them soon gets around. Often a price list will describe an animal of particular interest, and the collector may wish to learn more about it before laying his money down. A telephone call to the dealer may be well worth its price to determine the actual condition of the animal, its sex, whether it is feeding, and so forth. Most dealers do not have the time, and many are ill-fitted temperamentally besides, to enter a mail correspondence about a reptile or amphibian.

The New York Zoological Park, Bronx, New York 10460 publishes a leaflet which gives the names and addresses of dealers in amphibians and reptiles. Inquiries should be sent to the Reptile Department. Another such list is published by Ross Allen's Reptile Institute, Silver Springs, Florida 32688. Many large pet shops now carry native and exotic reptiles, and even department stores frequently have them in stock. The advantages of buying locally when possible are obvious. The animals may cost more, but one can see what he is getting and often determine whether it is feeding, and there are no transportation expenses. In purchases by mail the last item is nearly always borne by the consumer.

There are many ways of getting in touch with other persons who are interested in herptiles, and often pleasant and mutually beneficial friendships develop. Herptile clubs that offer interesting possibilities for the exchange of ideas and specimens, as well as companionship on field trips, have been formed in many communities. Your nearest museum or zoo will often be able to provide the addresses of such clubs or put you in contact with individuals who have interests similar to your own.

On field trips you will occasionally encounter very large populations of herptiles. While the depletion of these populations by collecting is decidedly ill-advised, from the standpoint of conservation, there can be little objection to the taking of a few extra individuals for other herpetologists. The interest in herpetology would not be making the progress it is making it if were not for the availability of live material to study in private collections.

SHIPPING HERPTILES

Correspondence with collectors in other areas is another way of obtaining specimens not found locally. Mutually profitable exchanges may be made by mail or express. In the United States, post offices do not knowingly accept snakes for transportation through the mails, but other small herptiles may be sent in this manner. For the domestic shipment of snakes, as well as the larger lizards, turtles, and crocodilians, air express is generally used. Before packing any specimens for shipment it is well to obtain the advice of someone who has had experience in their shipment. Snakes are generally enclosed in bags, then packed loosely in wooden boxes with shredded newspapers. Cloth bags are better than plastic ones for reptiles, but in the case of amphibians plastic bags will conserve the needed moisture better than cloth ones. Air parcel post should be used for mail shipments if the distance is more than a few hundred miles. Fresh sphagnum moss makes an excellent packing material for the bags containing aquatic turtles, crocodilians, and all amphibians. Most snakes should be kept dry in transit. When you buy something from a dealer by mail, note carefully his packing methods. If shipments are carefully packed and plainly labelled as to contents, with the notation "Do not overheat or freeze," surprisingly few losses occur in transit. I am strongly opposed to the winter shipping of reptiles and amphibians, particularly tropical kinds, to or from cold climates. Chills almost inevitably occur, and the results of them may not become manifest for days or weeks after the specimens have arrived at their destination. Styrofoam shipping containers minimize the possibility of chills.

FIELD TRIPS

Herptile enthusiasts should at least occasionally take to the field for first-hand observation and collecting of reptiles and amphibians in their natural haunts. The equipment required for such excursions need not be elaborate or expensive. Nor are trips into remote heavily forested areas essential. As one travels along in a car, many likely spots at the side of the road may be spotted and investigated. Friends are often amazed by the few pieces of equipment I take into the woods on collecting forays. Generally, everything I need can be carried without creating even a bulge in my pockets.

Unless poisonous snakes are concerned, I rarely carry a stick or noosing pole. Except in the case of poisonous reptiles, the hands form the best collecting tools. Aquatic types may require the use of a net or seine, while poisonous kinds must be handled with staffs or tongs. Some lizard species are not readily caught without the aid of a noose. But the majority of all herptiles may be caught easily with the hands alone. In the United States, the poisonous snakes, Gila monster, large snapping and softshell turtles, and *Amphiuma* salamanders are the herptiles most capable of producing serious injuries to the collector; they have been listed in the order of importance in this regard. The many other species are capable of producing little more than superficial scratches with their jaws or teeth. (Probably few collectors will have the opportunity or inclination to capture the large sea turtles, which can produce injuries with both jaws and flippers.)

Dry, rocky terrain usually provides good habitat for many species of lizards, snakes and some tortoises. Photo by O. Stemmler.

The herpetologist soon becomes familiar with the herptile fauna of his own area and the places where certain species are most likely to be found. A number of pamphlets and books dealing with the herpetology of the individual states can be useful in collecting specimens in unfamiliar areas. Zoo and museum curators and their staffs, if convinced that the amateur is serious, can offer good clues to likely habitats of desired specimens. The preserved study collections of museums can offer valuable collecting data which can be put to use in the field.

Herptiles of various species have very specific habitat preferences, and a thorough knowledge of them is essential if there is to be any fruitful collecting. Nearly all reptiles and amphibians tend to form colonies: where one of a kind is found, there are likely to be more Only rarely does an individual turn up far removed from others of its

Southern bayous and other bodies of water are good collecting areas for many aquatic snakes and other species which like wet habitats. Photo by R. E. Watts.

Tropical habitats are many and varied, often within the distance of a few yards. Photo by Dr. Herbert R. Axelrod.

kind. Some herptiles are rated as being excessively rare, but this description is based on the scarcity of captured specimens. Excessive rarity is probably more often apparent than real, for no animal continues to perpetuate itself when its numbers have been reduced to a critical minimum. Many species once considered rare are now known to be very common, a fact discovered by the careful field study of habitat preferences. Reptiles and amphibians may or may not diminish in numbers in areas of heavy human population. In fact, people quite often will unwittingly bring about an increase in herptiles. The experienced collector knows that a trash heap will often reveal more reptile life than a similar spread of favorable rocks in a clean woodland. The polluted waters with which we are now so much concerned are another matter. Frogs and salamanders disappear from polluted waters first, being followed by the turtles and other aquatic reptiles.

Fortunately for the reptile hunter, he has few laws to contend with in the pursuit of his quarry. But there are some restrictions that must be observed if conflict with the law is to be avoided. It is well to familiarize oneself with local and state ordinances before embarking on a collecting trip. Marine turtles and crocodilians are under protection in some places, and the poisonous Gila monster is protected in Arizona, its area of principal abundance within the United

In areas which lack otherwise suitable habitat, amphibians are often abundant in or near small ponds or water tanks. Photo by Dr. Herbert R. Axelrod.

States. Horned lizards are also protected in Arizona and Texas. There are laws governing the capture of tortoises in Texas, and several states protect wood turtles, box turtles, sliders, and diamondback terrapins. Frogs used as food are protected in many states, at least during the breeding season. All animals, including herptiles, are protected in most state parks and in all national parks and monuments. Check with the ranger or security officer before collecting in these preserves. Salamanders are not specifically protected in any state, although several species and populations are included in recent lists of endangered wildlife; presumably such species will eventually have protective legislation. As a general rule, snakes are not protected even though they are certainly the most beneficial of all herptiles. Arizona is considering the protection of all its herptile fauna, however, and Florida has recently passed several restrictions on collecting. Mexico, once the week-end collecting utopia of many southwestern herpetologists, now has strict laws to protect all of its fauna.

Collecting on private or posted property is another matter to be considered. Many owners willingly grant permission for such activities; others will not. The more enlightened land owners may be aware of the value of snakes as rodent destroyers and accordingly be reluctant to have them removed from their property. Before collecting poisonous snakes it is well to be aware that accidents which may result, if due to the knowing and willful handling of such creatures, may not be covered by the terms of an insurance policy.

The element of luck seems to play a part in determining whether a field trip will prove productive. Under seemingly ideal weather conditions, at the best time of the year, one often searches in vain for herptiles which are known to be common in the vicinity. Then, on a day when everything seems wrong, a good catch will be made. The weather preceding the day of collecting may have a bearing on this. When large numbers of reptiles or amphibians are found, it is not a good policy to take more specimens than are required. Remember that herptiles do well if kept in pairs or trios but that they seldom thrive if large numbers are caged together. By taking only a few specimens and leaving the habitat as undisturbed as possible, the collector realizes that he has a good chance of finding others in the area at some future time, if they are needed. A day of careless collecting in a small area can all but destroy a colony of herptiles. For the same reason, careless dissemination of information as to the where-abouts of favorable collecting sites is not be to approved. For this reason, the novice may find it difficult to obtain information from zoo and museum curators, unless he can convince them that he is earnest in his study and will take only a limited number of specimens. Little reliance can be placed on the information given by rural residents. Names of herptiles may be inaccurate, descriptions vague, and estimates of numbers of individuals completely unreliable. There are some rather famous collecting sites in the United States, and during favorable times of the year they may attract herpetologists from far and near. In some of these places, the reptiles concerned are, at best, not abundant forms; how long they may be able to withstand such annual onslaughts is a matter for concern.

FIELD EQUIPMENT

The most essential items in the equipment of a field collector are a series of cloth and plastic bags. The bags may vary in size from about twelve by eighteen inches to the size of a large pillow case. The plastic ones should be capable of holding water, and the cloth ones should have seams which cannot be forced open under considerable pressure. All bags should be examined to make sure they are free of cuts or holes. When not in use these bags can be conveniently folded and put in pockets or under the collector's belt, leaving the hands free. Though these cloth and plastic bags are interchangeable in use, in general it will be found better to place the amphibians in the plastic bags and the reptiles in the cloth ones. When a capture is made the bag itself may be knotted at the top, though I prefer to carry short lengths of bell wire with which to secure the openings. Except in the case of very small specimens, I adhere to the rule of one specimen to each bag. Often, in the case of active herptiles, the introduction of a second specimen will allow the escape of the first.

Bags containing specimens must be kept out of the direct sun at all times. If it is necessary to leave occupied bags, in order that the hands may be free to effect further captures, be sure that a shady place is selected and remember that the sun shifts. The place where bags are temporarily deposited should be well marked so there is no difficulty in finding them when one returns. Bags containing poison-ous specimens should be boldly labelled as such. Since a collector may often not wish to retrace his steps in a collecting area, it is perhaps better to carry all captives along as one proceeds. The temporary deposit of bags is useful mostly in areas where the going is rough, as on mountain ledges. Bags containing small reptiles can be tucked under the belt; those containing poisonous snakes should be carried well away from the body. I use a hook at the end of the noosing pole to transport venomous snakes out of the collecting area and back to the car.

Knowledge of an animal's habits combined with the experience of having actually captured specimens combine to enable a good collector to find specimens where they could be easily overlooked. Thorough collecting is not easy work; it involves much lifting of rocks and turning of logs, probing of crevices and investigation of holes. Harmless snakes often fight furiously when captured—this may be especially true of such kinds as the larger water snakes and whipsnakes. Nevertheless, the use of one's hands alone is preferred over a noosing stick with these species. There is far less chance of injuring specimens. The injuries they are able to inflict with their teeth are inconsequential. Water snakes may lie out on bushes overhanging ponds and rivers and dive quickly into the water when approached. With them, the use of a long noosing pole may be essential if they are to be captured during daylight hours. They are easily taken at night with the use of a strong flashlight or headlamp.

Night collecting equipment should include a source of light (carbide lanterns and battery operated lamps are both good) and a net for capturing aquatic forms. Photo by R. E. Watts.

Bullfrogs and related species are most easily captured at night. Photo courtesy American Museum of Natural History.

NIGHT COLLECTING

Many reptiles and amphibians are nocturnal. Such species may remain far underground during the day, and even the most diligent search will fail to reveal their whereabouts. At dusk and during the night, however, they prowl on the surface and are easily captured. During really warm weather periods many reptiles are most active at night. In places where poisonous snakes are found, night collecting is an activity which must be pursued with great caution. These animals are naturally most alert and active in times of dusk and darkness and the danger involved in collecting and bagging them at such times is great. I do not think it is advisable for a field collector to work alone at night where there are dangerous snakes. Relatively few bites occur at night, but this is only because collectors are not usually active during the hours of darkness in places where broken, brushy terrain can conceal coiled forms. In some areas, the larger rat snakes regularly ascend trees, and collectors should develop the habit of looking upward, as well as under foot.

COLLECTING POISONOUS SNAKES

The capture of poisonous snakes involves special techniques, varying somewhat with the species involved. As with everything else, practice leads to perfection in the bagging of venomous snakes. The procedure cannot be separated from a degree of danger, and the first attempt of an inexperienced collector to capture alive and unharmed a poisonous snake of large size can be a breath-holding experience for the onlooker. There is little standardization of the equipment used to capture poisonous snakes: I know of no two field men who use identical equipment. I use a slim but strong dowel with a screw eye attached to one end. The pole is about four feet long and perhaps half an inch in diameter. The other end of the pole has an L-hook attached to it. A seven-foot-length of bell wire is bent double and threaded through the screw-eye opening; the terminal portion is spread to form an opening about six inches in diameter while the loose strands are held in the hand against the pole. When slipped over a coiled reptile's head, the noose is brought back to a point at least a foot behind the snake's neck before the noose is drawn tight. This method allows the escape of some specimens that could easily have been taken if the noose were drawn tight immediately behind the head. The reason for securing a hold farther back is to prevent injury to the snake's spine during its violent efforts to free itself from the noose. Rattlers which have been noosed and allowed to dangle by the neck often will not feed in captivity.

An opened bag must have been prepared beforehand. In brushy country this is quickly and easily accomplished with the use of safety pins and wire. Three of the pins have been fastened at regular intervals about the opening of the bag. Each pin has a twelve-inch length of wire attached. The affair is quickly attached to bushes with its mouth open in a triangular form and the bottom barely touching the ground. This operation takes but a few moments and is done after the quarry is sighted. Poisonous snakes often "freeze" when they first sense possible danger, and few will escape during the few moments it takes to fasten the bag in place. The noose is drawn securely but not too tightly about the snake's body and the struggling reptile is placed in the waiting receptacle. This is freed of the bushes and twisted several times to close the mouth, which is then bound tightly with wire in two places. The bags are carried from the place of capture hanging from the hook-end of the pole. Freshly caught

Catch Frogs

Collect Snakes

Common collecting implements. Top, Pilstrom tongs; center, noose; bottom, snake stick fashioned from hoe. From Smith, *Snakes as Pets*.

snakes bite through the bags in their efforts to escape, and the droplets of venom trickling down the sides of a collecting bag give mute testimony to what would happen if they were allowed to dangle carelessly at one's side.

There are many other ways of catching poisonous snakes; each collector seems to have his own method. Snakes may be pinned to the ground and grasped behind the head—this method I emphatically do not recommend, especially to the novice. Aluminum tongs are available commercially and are useful. They have a hand grip which operates the jaws by means of a spring and are especially good for dealing with coral snakes and *Amphiuma* salamanders. The huge diamondbacks are best captured without the use of restraint; this can be accomplished because the snakes often hold their ground when encountered, scorning the flight of their smaller relatives. They can be lifted from the ground and placed in a bag with a long pole having an angle iron on the end. Or they may be gradually backed into an open-mouthed bag that is attached to the frame of a large landing net that fishermen use.

The eastern diamondback is often found in the burrows of the gopher tortoise. A twenty-five-foot length of garden hose is ferreted into the burrow as far as it will go, and it is often possible to tell whether a rattler is present in the burrow by listening at the end of the hose. The rustling caused by shifting of the coils of a large rattler is easily distinguishable from the more ordinary noises of the other inhabitants of such a retreat. Or a snake may hiss or sound its rattle when prodded by the end of the hose. If the indications point to there being a rattler present, a small quantity of gasoline can be poured into the hose and results awaited. The fumes will usually cause snakes to make a quick exit. Refinements such as the addition of a furniture caster to the end of the hose will make it easier to get it to the end of the gopher burrow. Several small cuts can be made near the end to allow the escape of gasoline and a plastic funnel may be used over the ear to help detect sounds within the hole. Often a rattler will emerge from a gopher hole if the entrance is simply covered. A whole book could be filled with accounts of how to capture poisonous snakes and the successes—and failures—that have accompanied this precarious pastime.

Except, perhaps, in open places where every footfall can be studied with care, snakebite-proof boots should be worn in areas where poisonous snakes are numerous. Manufacturers produce knee-high leather boots which cannot be penetrated by even the largest rattler. Aluminum leggings with strap fasteners also can be obtained; they cost much less than the heavy leather boots. Ordinary wire screening, sewn into the leg bottoms of dungarees, affords some protection. Rubber overshoes and ordinary hunting boots will prevent many bites. In ledgy country it is difficult and dangerous to climb with leather-soled footwear. Ordinary rubbers, slipped on over whatever other footwear is being worn, will help to prevent falls.

Persons who engage more or less regularly in the hunting of poisonous snakes, or those who keep specimens in captivity, should not be without a supply of the sera used to counteract the effects of bites, since it sometimes is not quickly available when needed. It is rather expensive to buy but will maintain its strength for a number of years and should be a part of the equipment of anyone who handles the venomous crotaline snakes. If exotic elapines are to be handled it should be determined in advance where sera effective against their bites can be obtained in a hurry. Often this will be the nearest large zoo.

The bite of a poisonous snake, if an appreciable amount of venom has been injected, constitutes a medical emergency of the first order. Rightly, the treatment from the very start should be in the hands of a doctor who is qualified to assume the responsibility. In some areas, where not many bites occur, most doctors will not see a case of snakebite during their entire years of practice. Two booklets should be kept on hand by those who study or collect venomous snakes. One is published by the Wyeth, Inc. firm of Philadelphia, Pennsylvania and is titled *Antivenin*. The other is titled *Venomous Snakes of the United States and Treatment of Their Bites*, written by W. H. Stickel and published as Wildlife Leaflet Number 339, available from the U.S. Fish and Wildlife Service, Washington, D.C. Both are free and can be had by mail request. They are informative and well-illustrated publications that conveniently capsule the information required by a doctor who is treating a snakebite victim. Neither presupposes a previous knowledge of tropical medicine—the heading under which snakebite is placed.

Snakebite kits consisting of suctioning devices, tourniquets, and incising instruments are available commercially, cost very little, and are accompanied by instructions for their use. So many factors enter the problem of snakebite that it is presumptuous of one not in the medical profession to offer remedial suggestions; there are enough of these in the assorted literature, and I believe that often they have done more harm than good. The only advice of the present author is this: before doing anything, make sure that it is a poisonous snake that has bitten you. Books commonly state that a poisonous snake will leave one or two prominent punctures in the skin, while the bite of a harmless snake leaves a U-shaped series of small cuts. This can be misleading. If a harmless snake has the opportunity to seize and chew it will leave a series of lacerations, but from a strike and immediate withdrawal the resulting wound may consist of two punctures which precisely resemble those of a poisonous snake. Pain and swelling will quickly follow the bite of most poisonous snakes of the United States. When you are sure you have been bitten by a venomous snake, get to a hospital as quickly as your means will permit, but without undue exertion—in other words, walk, don't run. If the bite has occurred on the hand, remove rings at once, or the swelling following a bite will make it difficult to cut them off. Keep as calm as possible and remember that only a small percentage of bites are fatal, regardless of treatment. Provide the doctor-in-charge with the aforementioned booklets and the sera.

There is much lack of agreement as to the proper treatment of snakebite, but there is one thing that is generally agreed upon throughout the papers dealing with the subject. This is that the ingestion of alcohol in any amount can do nothing but worsen the condition of the patient. Snake handlers sometimes boast of the number of times they have been bitten. This is curious reasoning. To be intimately associated with poisonous snakes over a long period of time without being bitten is an admirable accomplishment and one that attests to the skill of the herpetologist. The capturing of poisonous snakes has been gone into in some detail because potentially the venture is a dynamite-laden one. Most herpetologists find it more pleasurable and interesting to collect the many beautiful and harmless herptiles that are found in forest and desert.

CAPTURING LIZARDS

Lizards can be caught in a variety of ways. Some can be approached closely enough to permit a quick grasp. Others flee with great alacrity when the collector approaches to within a few feet. These kinds can be noosed with a slender pole or a fishing rod. Fine copper wire, sewing thread, and fishing line have all been used with success. The noose should be one which will stay open, yet have a loosely-sliding knot. It is slowly worked into position just behind the unsuspecting reptile's head, then tightened with a quick upward pull. Lizards should never be grasped by the tail, for most will readily divest themselves of this member and leave it writhing in the hand of their would-be captor while they scurry off to safety. More than any other reptile, perhaps, the lizards are, typically, creatures of the sun.

Species which may be very difficult to capture during the day can often be taken readily after the sun has gone down or in the early dawn. Collecting of nocturnal lizards requires a knowledge of their retreats. Some hide among rocks or under the bark of fallen trees, while a few are quite specific in their plant associations, especially in tropical regions. Dogs are sometimes used to find and run down the really large tropical lizards. Generally, the herptile collector will find little use for a dog in the field, but it is interesting to note that hunting types can be trained to locate and point reptiles as well as birds and mammals.

COLLECTING TURTLES

A long-handled net is an essential item of equipment for the turtle collector. A boat, too, is useful, but many kinds can be taken from the shore by hand or with a net, particularly during the spring and fall, when they may congregate in shallow water. The larger diving species are easily among the most difficult of all reptiles to capture, but that their capture can be successfully done on a wholesale scale is attested to by the large numbers which are offered for sale in markets. Skin and scuba diving have been successfully employed in the capture of certain rare freshwater turtles of the larger types. When under water turtles seem to lose much of their natural caution and can be easily approached in their hiding places. In muddy or silt-laden waters this method is not effective. Small turtles often frequent shallows in large numbers and can be netted or seined without much difficulty, especially at night. Another favorite abode of baby turtles are the offshore masses of lily pads or water hyacinths. These, incidentally, are the favorite habitat of the more aquatic snakes and salamanders. A mass of hyacinths that is raked ashore or scooped into a boat will often reveal small aquatic herptiles of many kinds. The diminutive water snakes *Liodytes* and *Seminatrix* often abound in company with salamanders like *Amphiuma, Siren,* and *Pseudobranchus,* and baby turtles of the larger species.

Turtles can be successfully trapped in places where they are abundant. Turtle traps of various designs have been invented. One consists of a barrel or large wooden box with a ramp that is pivoted with just the right weight distribution to permit a turtle to ascend it in quest of the bait fish or meat, but will give way under the animal's weight when a certain point is reached, dumping the hapless reptile into the enclosure. A trap of this type may be weighted down with heavy stones and the water level should be kept low, to prevent the drowning of the less-aquatic types that may enter it. Like all traps, it should be visited frequently. A lot of time and money can be spent in the making of traps and the results they produce are hardly worth it from the standpoint of a private collector who wishes to obtain only small numbers of animals. Snakes have been taken in enormous numbers with funnel-like arrangements leading from their den openings in the spring. Pits dug in lizard areas will sometimes trap a few individuals. For the more secretive snakes and lizards, as well as salamanders, one of the best traps is a board or flattened cardboard box, placed strategically in their known haunts. It is particularly useful where natural cover is not abundant. In favorable places, such a simple trap will reveal specimens nearly every time it is visited.

COLLECTING AMPHIBIANS

Frogs and toads can be netted or caught by hand during the day but the best method of taking them is at night, when they appear stupefied by the glow of a headlamp or flashlight. Wading boots or waterproof overshoes are useful adjuncts to collecting in swampy areas or the shores of ponds and streams. It is best to segregate the species in bags of their own. Some frogs exude a poison which will quickly kill frogs of other kinds. As already noted in Chapter X, one such American species is the pickerel frog, an animal that should never be allowed close contact with other amphibians.

A simple turtle trap. From Fish and Wildlife Service *Circular 35.*

A boat makes it possible to easily collect sleeping turtles at night and on overcast days. Photo by D. W. Tinkle.

Standard procedure for the hunting of salamanders consists of turning over rocks and pieces of wood along the course of streams, both in the water and along the shore. Some of the aquatic species are exceedingly slippery, and the roughened-surface rubber gloves that are available can be very useful in collecting hellbenders, mud-puppies, and the like. In good spots, during the spring, one may be able to catch, literally, as many frogs, toads, and salamanders as he desires by night collecting. Be conservation-minded and capture only what you actually need for study.

MISCELLANEOUS

Night driving over little-used roads in suitable areas can be very productive. Road surfaces tend to retain heat for a longer period than the surrounding soil and air. Many nocturnal snakes, lizards, frogs and salamanders will come to rest on a road. The best ones are bordered by fairly heavy vegetation and have a dark top. Driving should be at the rate of 12 to 18 miles an hour for best results. This

519

improves the chance of sighting an animal and permits a quick stop to minimize the possibility of its crawling off after it has been sighted. The bagging of a venomous animal such as a Gila monster (where it is legal to capture them) or rattler is best accomplished under the illumination of the automobile headlamps.

Many of the methods of capturing herptiles described here are equally applicable to the collecting of exotic or tropical species. Because some of the latter may grow to huge size, two or three persons may be better than one. In the United States the spring and fall are the best seasons for collecting. In northern portions of the country herptile collecting comes to a halt in October and cannot be resumed until March, at least. In the South, collecting of some kinds of herptiles is possible throughout the year. All areas seem to produce a midsummer lull, when one may hunt for days without finding any individuals of even the commonest species. Some may actually aestivate at such times, while others may take to roaming mostly by night.

Collecting bags and jars for amphibians should be provided with moss to prevent the drying out of captured specimens. On a long automobile trip they may be stored in a styrofoam cooler to prevent losses from overheating. Bagged poisonous snakes should be enclosed in strong wooden boxes. Florida now has a law specifically governing the manner in which poisonous snakes may be transported and displayed.

Collecting reptiles in their natural haunts can be a rewarding and healthful pastime. A notebook should be used to record the names of specimens and the times and places of their capture. The information can then be transferred to a permanent record system which keeps a running account of the animals' activities in captivity, including such items as growth and feeding, breeding, etc. It is by such observations that we have acquired much of our knowledge about herptiles.

XII

Housing Herptiles

The housing of herptiles can be made as simple or as elaborate as one wishes. One often sees a beautiful and exquisitely detailed terrarium inhabited by herptiles in varying stages of decline, while the crudest of arrangements will often house a thriving colony. The amount of money and effort that one is willing to invest in a cage for herptiles is related only remotely to the ultimate welfare of the animals it will house. Often a simple cage which provides the correct degree of lighting, heat, and humidity will serve far more satisfactorily than an expensive one which fails to provide any of these important fundamentals.

The average herptile enthusiast starts off with a single cage. Others are added in time, and the end result is often a conglomeration of cages which vary much in size and design. There may be nothing basically wrong with such a display, but a much more appealing arrangement can be developed with careful thought beforehand. Different herptiles require quite different surroundings in captivity, but it is possible to maintain a certain uniformity that will not be disrupted by additions to the collection. Try to set aside a room, or a portion of one, and plan on paper how it will be developed into a small herpetarium. Think carefully about lighting and heating problems. Remember that cages have to be cleaned and their inmates fed, and make sure the cages you select provide for quick and easy accomplishment of these tasks.

CAGES

The most versatile of cages for herptiles is the ordinary aquarium that is equipped with a secure cover. Such a cage can comfortably house anything from a desert lizard to a thoroughly aquatic salamander. Aquariums are not expensive, and one or more can be arranged to enhance the decor of even the most tasteful living room. Try to settle on a size for your tanks, giving due thought to the

With the correct type of cover and substrate, an aquarium can be used as a cage for almost any type of herptile. Photo by M. F. Roberts.

cleaning problem. I do not believe that a size smaller than the standard ten-gallon aquarium is practical; the low silhouette twenty-gallon size is ideal for anything but the largest snakes, crocodilians, and lizards, for which special cages must be bought or built.

Despite their attractiveness and general usefulness, however, aquariums do have disadvantages. For the larger and less secretive snakes—those which do best without soil or plants in their cages—

aquariums are difficult to keep in sparkling-clean appearance because of the large amount of glass surface that is exposed. For the same reason they are not the perfect cages for such large lizards as tegus and Gila monsters. And I consider them totally unsuitable for the housing of any but the smallest poisonous snakes. Growing turtles and crocodilians, as well as newts and the larvae of salamanders and frogs, require frequent feedings and changes of water. Larger aquariums may present a problem in this respect unless the herptile keeper wants to go all out and install special plumbing that will permit the draining and refilling of aquariums without their being moved . . . or unless he's willing to purchase one of the power filters designed for effective filtration of large aquariums.

Theoretically, it might be thought that a captive herptile will prosper directly in proportion to the extent in which its natural environment is duplicated. This seems not to be the case with some species. First of all, it is next to impossible to completely duplicate a natural environment in a cage. The closest approach to this ideal would be to go into the field and select an area which encompasses the natural range of a group of herptiles, then erect an escape-proof barrier around the area. Even this plan would have many flaws, so intricate is the exchange between living organisms and their total environment. Many environmental factors are not critical ones for herptiles, and with each species it is our problem to determine just what the critical factors are; these factors can then be adjusted according to the requirements of the animals. Certain problems of light, heat, humidity, and food intake must be resolved. If any one of these is grossly distorted, the animal will certainly die. To successfully maintain herptiles, one must know something of their natural history. The present book and others fill this need.

BASIC VIVARIA TYPES

No matter how much thought is given to the subject, any indoor enclosure for herptiles will fall into one of five types. Even if the aquarium or other cage is very large it will tax one's skill to the utmost to successfully combine any two of these distinct types. Even zoos rarely attempt it. The word "terrarium" is, by definition, a place where land animals are kept. Some of our herptiles are completely aquatic and suitable homes for them would have to be called aquariums. The term "vivarium," though connoting, in its narrowest sense, an enclosure where there is at least a partial duplication of natural habitat, will be used in referring collectively to all of the enclosures used to house reptiles and amphibians. There follows a list of the five basic types of vivaria for herptiles, with mention of the animals that are commonly kept in them:

1. **The exhibition cage:** contains no furnishings other than a drinking dish or tree bough; papers or small rounded pebbles may be used as a floor covering. Used mainly for snakes of the larger, non-burrowing species but may be used also for tegus and other large lizards and some tortoises.

2. **The desert terrarium:** has several inches of fine sand on the bottom and is appropriately landscaped with potted cacti and other desert plants; may or may not have a water container. This type of vivarium is the only one in which certain desert animals will thrive. Included in this category are horned lizards and other desert species, some tortoises, and a few snakes.

3. **The woodland terrarium:** may represent a portion of a temperate forest or a piece of tropical jungle; humidity may be adjusted to the needs of its occupants and may range from quite low to very high; water pool is usually present; foliage may be dense or sparse. Useful for many of the smaller herptiles, particularly lizards, small snakes, and amphibians.

Herp cages can be as simple or complicated as desired, as long as the animal can adapt to it easily.

4. **The marsh-stream terrarium:** has approximately equal areas of land and water. Used extensively for semiaquatic reptiles and many amphibians.

5. **The aquarium:** may have a projecting rock or two but is used primarily for the thoroughly aquatic herptiles which seldom or never leave the water; may be fresh water, ocean water, or mildly saline. Used for the thoroughly aquatic herptiles, including such types as amphiumas, sirens, mudpuppies, mud and musk turtles, marine turtles, and snakes.

EXHIBITION CAGES

A series of exhibition cages, uniformly stacked or arranged in tiers, lighted from the inside or from without, can form an extremely attractive display of reptiles. A well-constructed wooden box can be converted into a suitable cage with a few tools and a little effort. The better method, however, is to plan on paper exactly what you want the finished product to look like, carefully note the measurements of the cage's components, then go to a lumber yard and select the wood. Ordinary commercial shelving is a little less than a foot wide and may be purchased in many grades. It is easily handled and will serve very well for the bottom, sides, and even top of the cage. Four pieces, cut to specified size, can be nailed together to form the framework. The back can consist of a section of pegboard, nailed securely to the four sides. In the front, two pieces of right-angle countertop, binding strips can be fastened to accept a sliding pane of glass which will open from either side. The floor of the cage may be covered with a strip of paper toweling, a water dish added, and one has an acceptable display case in which the majority of snakes will thrive for years.

The above instructions cover the construction of the simplest kind of cage, yet one which suits very well the needs of most snakes. All sorts of refinements and modifications can be made. Do not be afraid to use your imagination. I have studied the construction of snake exhibition cages in dozens of institutions and private collections and have yet to find the perfect one. The dimensions of the cage described will often be about two feet in length and a foot high. It provides good ventilation and can be easily and thoroughly cleaned; food can be introduced from either end, and the occupant is perfectly visible. One may wish to have a hinged cover of hardware cloth, or glass which slides up and down rather than sideways and can be

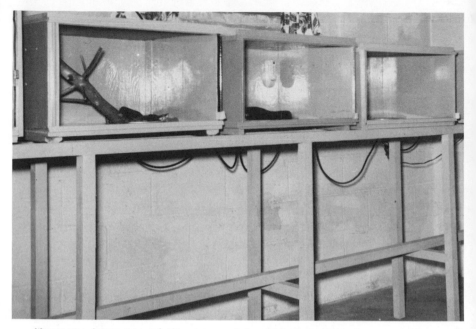

Home-made cages of the same style and size present a very neat and attractive appearance.

locked in place with an overhanging cover that is provided with a hasp. Cages can be painted or stained in any desired color and thoroughly waterproofed with a coat of clear shellac or varnish or one of the newer clear plastic sprays. A hoodlike arrangement over the top can be constructed to provide concealed lighting and some heat as well. Screening should not be used anywhere in the construction of a snake cage, for there are only a few snakes which will not rub their snouts raw in attempting to nose their way through it. Hardware cloth of suitable mesh size is better, but even this can cause damage; I prefer pegboard to other means of ventilation.

Exhibition cages should have no openings through which it is possible for a snake to gain exit. And be aware that captive snakes often give birth to babies that are able to squeeze through the smallest holes. For instance, a baby brown snake (*Storeria*) could easily squeeze through a pegboard hole, but snakes of this size are not ordinarily kept in exhibition cages. They do better under moderately dry woodland terrarium conditions.

Cages for poisonous snakes should have sliding partitions to permit the locking of the inmates in one side while the other side is being cleaned. They should be handled as little as possible, both as a safety precaution and because of the fact that most of them are very temperamental and are likely to go off their feed if unduly disturbed. If it is necessary to remove a specimen from its cage, do so with a snake hook—an angle iron or shelf bracket fastened to the end of a stick. Many books give the impression that a snake will wind itself about the end of such an implement and not attempt to escape or fall off. This cannot be depended upon. Snakes, especially juveniles, will often lose their balance and fall to the floor when being transferred with a hook. Such a fall, particularly in the case of a heavy-bodied snake, is likely to result in an injury which may not be apparent at once but is ultimately fatal. Because of this I long ago formed the habit of placing every cage housing poisonous snakes at floor level before attempting a transfer of the occupants. Most venomous snakes can be gently guided from one container to another without any physical restraint. I always take pride in being able to guide a rattler in and out of its cage without having the snake sound its warning. Harmless snakes may be placed in a bag during cage-cleaning; if they are large, they may be allowed to crawl about and get some exercise.

Ground-dwelling herps can be kept warm by using a perforated false bottom. Light bulbs placed under this bottom will provide sufficient heat. Photo by G. Marcuse.

527

The exhibition type of cage may or may not be provided with a small box which allows the occupant to remain out of sight when it desires seclusion. It is almost a necessity for a few of the more nervous species, but most can do without it. Any snake which remains perpetually hidden makes a poor subject for observation.

Exhibition cages must be provided with a container for drinking water; some species drink often, others only rarely. I have experimented with every conceivable type of dish and have found that nearly all have serious drawbacks. Either they can be entered by the snake and the water thus tracked about the cage, or they tip easily—with the same result. The one exception is the small glass dish that is sold in stationery stores as a sponge cup. It comes in straight-sided designs and with convex sides. Either type is good and cannot be tipped by any ordinary snake. I prefer the dish with the rounded form.

A rock to assist in skin shedding may be placed in an exhibition cage, and a single tree branch may be added for snakes which climb, but I would not advise the use of any other accessories. Exhibition cages can be constructed in any size desired. One that is three feet long and half as wide and high will house comfortably the largest snakes found in the United States. Their glass fronts may be cleaned easily, inside and out, by simply reversing the surfaces.

It is possible to set up elaborate thermostatically-controlled heating units in exhibition cages, but this is not done even in the better zoos. Hot water pipes can be diverted to heat reptile cages, but this has its drawbacks. By far the best heating arrangements for a collection of reptiles is a central one which can be controlled with a thermostat. A range of 70 to 85 degrees is suitable for nearly all snakes; many tropical kinds do best at the upper limit of this range. A nightly drop is permissible, but I would regard 65 degrees as a point of danger for non-hibernating snakes in captivity. Snakes may regularly encounter much lower temperatures in the natural state, without ill effect, but captives seem to lack the ability to do so, although otherwise very healthy. In the absence of a better heating method, strategically placed light bulbs of the appropriate wattage can be used to maintain suitable cage temperatures. Do not attempt to maintain a collection of reptiles without a good means of controlling temperature; serious exotic fish fanciers would not attempt to maintain their animals in a cold environment, and most reptiles are no better able to withstand chills than tropical fishes.

A simple but efficient desert terrarium. Photo by R. J. Church.

DESERT TERRARIUM

The desert terrarium is perhaps the easiest to set up and keep in good condition. In its simplest form, the desert terrarium has two to three inches of fine sand, a few potted cacti and stones in the background, and perhaps a weathered piece of wood. There is no drainage problem, for the idea is to keep the desert terrarium as dry as possible. What little moisture the potted plants require can be supplied to them directly, at their roots, without dampening the remainder of the cage. The cacti used should be kept in the soil in which they were found or purchased. If they were bought unpotted, a sandy loam mixture with a little slaked lime added makes a good potting medium.

The sand selected should be of a fine grade, not the coarse type sold for use in aquariums. It should be rinsed repeatedly to remove the dust, then thoroughly dried out before use. This can be accomplished quickly by heating in an oven. The potted cacti should be sunk in the sand to conceal their individual pots, and the sand gently sloped toward the front of the cage. Desert animals will rarely find or use a drinking dish, even if it is sunk level with the surface of the sand.

Water should be provided by a spray over the background rocks, or a lettuce leaf may be wetted and placed in the cage from time to time.

A constant dry heat is especially essential for the desert terrarium. An aquarium tank with a screen cover and a light reflector above makes a good desert terrarium. One with better ventilation can be made by fastening screening or hardware cloth to a wooden framework. Nearly all desert reptiles require natural sunlight or a substitute for it. Few thrive for any length of time in northern climates, though there are exceptions which do exceedingly well. Many desert reptiles will burrow into the sand at night.

WOODLAND TERRARIUM

The woodland terrarium, more than any other, will tax the artistry of the herptile enthusiast who contemplates it. Once again, an ordinary aquarium is probably the best container with which to start. Over the bottom, lay an inch-thick layer of charcoal and coarse gravel, well mixed. The charcoal and gravel will assist drainage and help keep the cage free of disagreeable odors caused by souring of the soil. Slope the floor covering from the rear to the front. The taller plants will be in the rear, and this is where the greatest depth will be required. Next, add about two inches of good soil—select this from a place where many and varied plants are growing in profusion. If you do not have the inclination to go out and dig in the woods, potting soil may be purchased in stores. An advantage to selecting the soil from a healthy natural woodland is that many of the plants and seedling trees may be picked up along with it and one can be sure that their soil will have the correct degree of acidity or alkalinity.

Aquarists have produced beautiful arrangements in the tanks of their exotic fishes, and it is no less possible to do the same with an artistic arrangement of forest plants. Try to visualize a piece of landscape with tall plants in the rear, shorter ones in front, a few moss-covered rocks and the decaying portion of a tree bark. Here we have all the ingredients of a beautiful design—it remains only to carefully pot the plants so as to appear natural, yet not hide the animal forms the vivarium will contain. A container of water should be sunk flush with the surrounding terrain near the front of the enclosure. Small stones imbedded in the soil about the perimeter of the pool will make easier the removal and occasional cleaning of it. If woodland plants are used they may be set directly into the soil of the

Toads and many small snakes and salamanders will survive in a simple woodland terrarium. A partial glass cover will help retain the high humidity required. Photo by M. F. Roberts.

terrarium. Potted plants that are bought in a store had best be left in their containers, which should be sunk flush with the surface of the surrounding soil. This type of terrarium should have at least a partial covering of glass and should be sprinkled frequently. Tree-climbing lizards will appreciate limbs over which to cavort—in fact, a terrarium of the woodland type can be heightened to provide a good home for arboreal as well as terrestrial and burrowing animals. Salamanders may peer from beneath pieces of bark while anoles chase each other over the branches. It is about the only kind of a set-up in which herptiles of very different types may be mixed—with due regard, of course, for the respective sizes of the animals.

Some care must be used in feeding terrarium inmates to make sure that a few do not get the entire food supply. If any small snakes are introduced, make sure they are of kinds which will not promptly devour the other animals in the cage. For instance, ringneck snakes (*Diadophis*) are handsome little creatures which do well in a moderately moist environment, like that of a woodland terrarium. Their drawback is that they will devour any of the equally attractive little salamanders that one may wish to keep. Brown snakes (*Storeria*),

531

while not as beautiful as the ringnecks, will confine their diet to slugs, earthworms, and insects. The growth or decline of the plants in a woodland terrarium is a good indication of whether the soil has a correct moisture content; spraying can be adjusted accordingly. In general, it is best to keep the bottom layer of gravel and charcoal quite wet. With the woodland terrarium it is possible to bring indoors for year-round enjoyment a small portion of the forest and its inhabitants.

MARSH-STREAM TERRARIUM

Many herptiles inhabit the shorelines of lakes, ponds, and streams. Some spend a portion of each day in the water and the rest of their time on land. Still others are aquatic at certain times of the year, but terrestrial for the remainder of the time. For most of these types, the marsh-stream terrarium is suitable. It is probably the type of terrarium that is used more frequently than any other, for the baby turtles and caimans that are sold in such large numbers find an ideal home in this type of cage. A terrarium of this type can be very simple in design. Starting with an aquarium which does not leak, we simply add a couple of inches of well-rinsed gravel and slope it at one end to form a land area. To reinforce the bank, we can add a row of small stones as a line of demarcation between water and shore. Water depth may be about two inches, and the dry area can rise another two inches above this. The whole set-up can be attractively lighted with an inexpensive aquarium reflector, which will also provide some heat. In a more elaborate form, the marsh-stream terrarium can be divided across the center, or diagonally, with a piece of glass or wood. The land area can be set up as in the woodland terrarium, but the plants chosen should be of kinds that can withstand a great deal of moisture. Bog plants are excellent for this purpose. The water area can have as its bottom a layer of gravel. The dividing wood or glass strip may be of any height desired, but the water level must be approximately equal, or the animals will not be able to go from one section to the other easily. An assist in this regard can be had by placing next to the shoreline a rock which slopes from the water to a level even with the bank of land area. Such a rock will also help to prevent the partition from shifting. In this connection, a diagonal dividing strip is better than one which goes from side to side, for it will be held in place by the corner angles of the aquarium. Still another variation of the marsh-stream terrarium can be made by using an island, sur-

The marsh-stream terrarium is easily constructed and will house a great variety of amphibians and reptiles. Photos by M. F. Roberts.

Small terraria or aquaria with shallow water may be heated by suspending an aquarium heater in a jar of water. Photo by M. F. Roberts.

rounded by water. This can be simply done by arranging a group of stones in the middle of the aquarium, or at its end, fitted together so as to allow no crevices between them. Turtles and small crocodilians are unappreciative of plant life and tend to trample the foliage in their cage. A plain rock shoreline fits their needs very well and permits the terrarium to be more easily cleaned than would be the case with a more elaborate set-up.

Another way of setting up a marsh-stream terrarium involves the use of a plastic basin, glass bowl, or metal tray. This is planted to simulate a small island, then placed in the aquarium while the water level is raised to a point just below the edge. When cleaning becomes necessary, the island is simply lifted out of the aquarium.

In any of these arrangements, an undergravel aquarium filter may be used to help keep the water clear and lessen the frequency with which it must be changed. In the water section, a few plants will add to the naturalness of the picture. These are useful chiefly where salamanders and frogs are concerned, for many turtles can be expected to devour aquatic plants. Generally speaking, the marsh-stream terrarium does not lend itself well to a company of mixed herptiles. Turtles tend to bite and harass other animals, while frogs will devour any salamanders that they can cram into their mouths. The woodland terrarium is by far the best if one desires a "happy family" grouping of herptiles, and even in this type of cage all of the inmates should be of approximately the same bulk.

AQUARIUM

The herpetologist finds a limited use for the true aquarium. Gilled amphibians, which derive their oxygen from the water, can be kept in an aquarium and if this is aerated, so much the better. Certain other herptiles, while finding it necessary to come to the surface for air, nevertheless spend most of their time underwater, either lying on the bottom or swimming about. The management of an aquarium for herptiles differs little from that in which fishes are kept. It can have a sand or gravel base, a filter, and an aerator, as well as an attractive arrangement of underwater plants. None of these is essential, however, and I am a great believer in simplicity of design when it comes to cages for animals. Often the presence of numerous accessories will have no bearing whatever upon the welfare of amphibians and reptiles. Or their effect may be deleterious if they interfere in any way with a state of total cleanliness in the tank. In most cases, the herptiles which can be kept in a shoreless aquarium will be comfortable in water of shallower depth than that which would be used for most fishes. Freshwater turtles should be able to reach the surface of the water without swimming, for even some of the very aquatic types will tire and drown, while others, like the soft-shells and marine turtles, find no inconvenience in periodically swimming to the surface for air.

MISCELLANEOUS EQUIPMENT

All containers for herptiles, even the true aquarium, should be kept covered with screening or glass. If the latter is used, provision must be made to allow a change of air within the cage. This can be accomplished by slightly elevating the glass at its corners, or using two pieces and separating them a bit in the middle. Condensation of moisture should not be allowed to become too great. If there is a dripping from the top or on the sides of the terrarium, the whole thing should be allowed to dry out for a day or so, during which time a screen cover may be used. Subsurface heating cables can be em-

Often a light bulb in a reflector unit is the simplest way to heat a terrarium or shallow aquarium. Photo by M. F. Roberts.

Some of the tools necessary to keep the marsh-stream terrarium or aquarium clean. Photo by M. F. Roberts.

ployed in terrariums, but I am not in favor of their use, for they do little to warm the air which the creatures breathe and thus only half-fulfill their purpose. Light bulbs in sufficient wattage will warm not only the air but the soil as well. In a cool room a good blanket will help to prevent too great a fall in temperature if the bulb is extinguished at night. A careful check with a thermometer should be maintained in all herptile vivaria.

In very large terrariums, an infrared lamp may be used for heating purposes. It may be alternated with one of the simpler sun lamps which screw into a regular socket. Spotlights, either within or outside large terrariums, can be used to create beautiful lighting effects. In addition to aquariums and wooden exhibition cages, many other containers can be utilized in the keeping of herptiles. In rearing large numbers of baby turtles or amphibian larvae, the plastic basins sold in department stores for household use are very good. They are light and can be cleaned frequently with a minimum of effort. Plastic baby baths and wading pools can be used with good results for some herptiles that are unable to climb a smooth wall.

OUTDOOR TERRARIUMS

The subject of outdoor pools is one upon which many books have dwelt at length. Details of their construction and maintenance are readily available. In warm climates, outdoor enclosures similar to the flight cages used by aviculturists are excellent for some of the larger reptiles. The present book is meant to stimulate the imagination and encourage the development of new ideas in the field of herptile husbandry. If the reader's experiments disclose a new or better way of keeping a certain species of herptile in health over long periods, the information will be gratefully received by herpetologists everywhere. I have long entertained the idea of turning an entire room into a sort of huge woodland or desert terrarium, where herptiles of suitable compatibility could lead their lives fairly naturally. It is a plan which requires considerable thought in advance, but has been accomplished successfully with birds—why not herptiles?

XIII

Feeding a Collection

Before any herptile is purchased, its food requirements should be given some consideration. When a specimen has been captured in the field and brought home, the problem becomes a ready-made one, if the creature is to be kept in health. Many herptiles can go without food for long periods—a year or more in some cases, if they have an abundant supply of water. The herptile menu is a very varied one; some species are extremely specialized in their requirements while others eat a wide variety of animal and vegetable substances. A good appetite is one of the surest signs that a reptile or amphibian is in good health. If there is anything radically wrong with the animal or its environment, it will generally refuse to eat. It will not always be possible to determine whether a snake, lizard, turtle, or salamander has been feeding before it is acquired. Some species lose weight rather quickly when they have been off-feed; others do so more gradually. Some can be brought back to a state of health after a very long fast, but others seem to reach a point of no return after fasting for a considerable time. If and when such kinds finally do start eating, the intake of food sometimes hastens their death. The herpetologist with a practiced eye can usually evaluate the condition of a specimen without trouble. The inexperienced person may find this more difficult. When the purchase of a specimen from a pet shop is contemplated, I do not think it is unreasonable to ask a dealer to demonstrate whether it will feed. Such a demonstration, if negative, cannot be accepted as conclusive, however, for some reptiles will feed in the dark when they will not do so under light, some require a minimum of disturbance while eating, and so forth. Personally, I would not own or keep in confinement any animal which refused to eat. When I acquire a herptile and find that it refuses to accept food when all conditions seem to be right, I persevere with numerous attempts with types of food that I believe approximate the natural diet of the animal. When signs of emaciation start to become manifest, I quickly dispose of the herptile—releasing it locally if it is a native species.

There are pros and cons to the subject of force-feeding. I would not force-feed any herptile unless it was extremely rare or valuable. With the smaller species, force-feeding will seldom meet with good results. It is the snakes and crocodilians which may benefit from force-feeding—the latter nearly always feed of their own accord when the temperature is right; snakes, on the other hand, sometimes refuse to feed under the most ideal conditions, though this is not usual if they are otherwise healthy.

Most herptiles in the adult stage are carnivorous animals; herbivorous species are to be found among lizards and chelonians, but among the former are rare and among the latter consist mainly of the land-dwelling tortoises. Few kinds exclude all animal matter from their diet. Terrestrial or semi-aquatic amphibians—the frogs and their relatives—generally recognize only live food, though individual specimens can be tempted with pieces of meat moved before them. Aquatic amphibians are a little less particular and will usually find and devour bits of meat placed in their aquarium. Snakes are entirely carnivorous; the rodent-eating kinds seem to prefer their food dead, but not decomposed. This greatly simplifies the matter of feeding them, for baby chicks and mice can be frozen and stored for later use. Lizards will accept both living and non-living food, though the smaller kinds are quite amphibian-like in their inability to see non-moving objects. Turtles and baby crocodilians present few problems in their feeding, but in the case of baby specimens, the food presented must be highly nutritive, which means that vitamins and minerals may have to be added.

Many herptiles can be provided for, in part at least, by the foods bought for human consumption, especially if these foods are enriched by the addition of powdered or liquid vitamins and minerals. With other species, the food must be purchased as needed, collected in the field at intervals, or raised in cages. The herpetologist who has only a few specimens may find it not worthwhile to raise their food, if it can be readily captured or purchased locally. Those having large collections may find it very necessary to raise their own herptile food, if a continuous supply is to be ensured at all times during the year.

Many of the snakes most favored for private collections live largely, if not exclusively, upon warm-blooded vertebrates. Most which feed upon mice and rats will also accept baby chickens; this may simplify the feeding problem, for chicks cost no more than mice, and those who would be averse to the storing of frozen mice in the home refrigerator may not offer the same objection to frozen chickens. Frozen animals should be thoroughly thawed before being offered to snakes or other reptiles. In the case of recalcitrant feeders, good results can often be had by slightly warming the preferred food. Once it was thought that snakes would accept only live food; curiously, this idea persisted for many years and was prevalent even among professional reptile keepers—those on the staffs of zoos, for instance. Experience has shown that snakes will often accept dead food more readily than that which is alive. Reptiles can be severely injured by the bites of rodents, and this possibility is eliminated with

Chickens, from chicks to adults, are useful foods for many constrictors and poisonous species. They are often easier to obtain than rats or mice. Photo by C. P. Fox.

Mice are an old standby for feeding snakes. Modern plastics make it possible to raise large numbers easily and with little of the smell associated with rodents. Photo by T. A. Mazzarello.

the use of dead food. Poisonous snakes will often approach and strike a dead animal just as they would a live one. It is a mistaken notion that poisonous snakes will strike only moving objects. The venom assists in the digestive process but is not essential to it. An animal that has been poisoned by a venomous snake can be fed to a harmless reptile without ill results. This is mentioned because sometimes a rattler or similar type of snake will envenom a live animal, then refuse to show further interest after it has expired.

RODENTS

Mice may be caught in large numbers in suitable places both in city and country. Ordinary snap traps may be used, or one may prefer to catch the mice alive with a simple box trap or one of the cage-like commercial products. Wild rodents are difficult to handle, and I can see little advantage to trapping them alive, particularly if ordinary snap traps can be set out in the evening and visited the next day. In hot weather an animal quickly decomposes and is attacked by hordes of carrion-eating insects. Wild reptiles have been seen feeding upon decomposed animals, but I do not recommend the feeding of such to captives. The mice and rats that are sold as pets can often be purchased at a special price if the herptile-owner will explain to the pet shop proprietor what they are needed for and how many will be bought each week. One of the quickest and least messy ways of killing one or several rodents that are to be used as reptile food is to enclose them in an airtight container of small size. I find a quart-size juice container with a screw top convenient for this purpose. Six adult mice will expire in a few minutes when confined together in a jar of this type. For a single mouse a smaller jar would be effective.

There is a wealth of information available in booklet form on the subject of raising mice, rats, hamsters, and other small mammals. If you wish to raise your own supply of mice or other rodents you can easily and inexpensively do so. I can offer a few suggestions on the raising of mice. To start your breeding colony, select mice which have a large average size and can be handled without biting. The progeny of such specimens are likely to inherit the disposition of their parents. White or albino mice may be the easiest to obtain for a start, but you may find that your breeding plant produces a surplus beyond what you need for your herptiles. If this happens you may wish to sell mice to local pet shops. White mice bring the minimal price; the so-called fancy varieties—blacks, blues, reds, tans, and so forth—can be sold at a higher price and the income from this source can help defray the cost of raising them. Standard wire cages with exercise wheels and watering bottles can be purchased in pet stores and are fairly satisfactory if they are protected from drafts. Perhaps better are simple wooden boxes of small size, equipped with hinged covers of hardware cloth. For the raising of mice on a wholesale scale, plastic basins of rectangular shape can be fitted with suitable covers and have the advantage of being easily washed from time to time. Nesting material may consist of wood shavings, shredded papers, or hay. In a cage which has only the top exposed to view, it is hardly necessary to provide nesting boxes. The female has a gestation period of twenty-one days and should be placed in a cage of her own when about to give birth. Mice of gentle, well-domesticated strains generally do not harm their babies, although nervous mice may eat them. Babies are weaned at three to five weeks and are mature at two months. Mice live up to four years, but their prolificacy diminishes long before this; in a breeding colony it is hardly worthwhile to maintain individuals over a year in age. An ideal temperature for breeding is 75 degrees. Sudden drops should be avoided, as with herptiles, and the temperature should never be allowed to go below 55 degrees. A wide variety of food is eaten. One very successful breeder uses a soft mash consisting of a mixture of dog food, chicken meal, bread, oats, and mixed grains. Sweet potatoes, apples, lettuce, nuts, and clean grass cuttings are offered sparingly. Rats and hamsters may be propagated with little more difficulty than mice, but they require larger quarters. If gently treated, rats can become extremely responsive pets, and the more tender-hearted herpetologist may find it difficult to feed them to his reptiles.

INSECTS

A collection of lizards or amphibians will require a steady supply of insects. These can often be netted or otherwise trapped during the summer, but such a supply is often abruptly terminated with the onset of cold weather. The meal worm (*Tenebrio*) has long been a stand-by of the vivarium keeper. A colony is easily started in a discarded aquarium or other smooth-sided, covered container. Wheat bran will form the burrowing and feeding medium for the "worms," which grow to about an inch in length, pupate, then become blackish beetles about half an inch in size. It should be about three inches in depth and covered with a piece or two of burlap that is kept moistened. Adult beetles will feed upon slices of apple or carrot. Worms

Mealworms are simple to maintain in many types of containers, as long as they are well fed and not allowed to become too moist. Photo by R. Gannon.

or larvae will tend to congregate in the folds of damp cloth from which they can be easily removed with forceps. A certain number of adult beetles may be removed from the colony, but enough should be left to ensure the deposit of large numbers of eggs. A temperature of 75 to 80 degrees is satisfactory, and breeding activity can be increased with the sparing addition of canned dog food. Before feeding them to one's herptiles, the worms may be allowed to crawl around in a saucer containing a few drops of a vitamin concentrate. Some of this will adhere to their bodies and the lizards will benefit from it. Mealworms should not be used continuously in the feeding of lizards or other small herptiles. They have a shell-like covering which gives rise to intestinal disturbances in animals which have been fed upon them exclusively. They should be varied with other kinds of insects and spiders.

A better insect food, particularly for the very small herptiles, will consist of newly-hatched praying mantids (*Mantis* and *Paratenodera*). The mantid's egg cases may be collected in large numbers in the autumn and if kept stored in a cool place will not hatch until needed. Normally, an egg case will contain more than a hundred small mantids, and hatching can be allowed to take place in the vivarium itself. The babies will emerge soon after the egg case is warmed and will for a time provide an abundant supply of food for small lizards. In the natural state, hatching does not occur until spring.

Although mealworms are a good occasional food, they are very hard-shelled, and continuous feeding may be harmful to herps. Photo by R. Gannon.

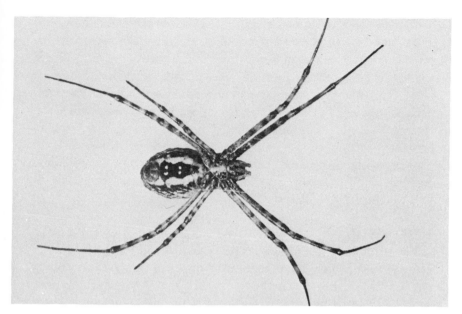

Spiders are good food for many amphibians and some lizards and snakes. They are easily collected in meadows by using a sweep net like that used in collecting insects. Photo by G. Marcuse.

Ants are good food for many lizards, but they are unfortunately difficult to raise in numbers. Dried pupae sold as "ant eggs" are not very nutritious. Photo courtesy American Museum of Natural History.

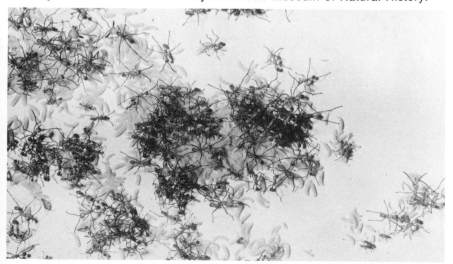

Crickets (*Gryllus*) are an excellent food for insect-eating herptiles. They may be raised in numbers in a terrarium-like set-up which provides an inch or two of loam spread over a base of gravel. Numerous hiding places in the form of pieces of cardboard should be provided. The colony may be started with a dozen or so adults. They will deposit their eggs in the soil, and soon the baby crickets will make their appearance. The adults should be removed at this time, to prevent the eating of the young, for crickets are cannibalistic. Food may consist of such items as oatmeal, lettuce leaves, raw apple, and dog biscuit. The colony should be lightly sprinkled from time to time; a temperature of about 75 degrees is adequate.

EARTHWORMS

The earthworm (*Lumbricus*) is particularly good for the feeding of many terrarium animals, though the majority of insect-eaters among the lizards will not touch them. Usually one may collect his own supply of worms by simply going out with a flashlight on a warm night when it is showering. They come to the surface at such a time

Earthworms are relished by many herptiles and are inexpensive; they can often be picked up after heavy rains. The smaller worms are usually taken more easily by many animals than are the larger ones. Photo by P. Imgrund.

and can be picked off lawns quite easily. If not overcrowded, worms can be stored in a cool place for long periods and will require little attention. Damp leaf mold, rather than soil, is preferred for the temporary storage of worms. If one wishes to carry a supply over the winter, a special box or other large container must be arranged to house them. Rich loam, mixed with rotted wood fragments and leaf mold, forms a good burrowing medium for the worms. Finely chopped raw potatoes and bread saturated with milk are good foods, but should be introduced in small quantities just below the surface; careful watch kept to make sure there is not excessive souring of the burrowing mixture. The mixture may be sprinkled from time to time to keep it moist, but not wet. A piece of burlap bag can be placed over the surface and the worms that are selected for food can be taken from under this, to avoid excessive spading or shovelling which will result in the injury and death of some worms, with consequent fouling of the soil mixture. The correct amount of moisture and a cool environment are the secrets of maintaining a good supply of worms over the winter months. Live bait dealers carry worms and these may be used to form the start of a colony, or they may be purchased in small quantities to meet actual weekly requirements of the herptiles. Unless, however, the vivarium keeper maintains a supply of his own, they will seldom be available in the winter.

WHITE WORMS

White worms, *Enchytraeus albidus*, are a nourishing food for newly-hatched turtles, the smaller salamanders and salamander larvae, and adults of the smaller kinds of frogs and toads. They remain alive and active for long periods in water, and this is an advantage to their use for aquatic herptiles. Inexpensive to buy, nearly any aquarium or pet store can provide a starting culture, along with a small amount of soil. To raise them in quantities, a well-constructed wooden box filled to a depth of six inches or more with garden soil and leaf mold or peat mixture will prove satisfactory. The worms should be separated into several groups and each buried under the soil at a depth of about two inches. Good foods for the worms are small portions of stale bread moistened with milk and cooked oatmeal. It is customary to lay a piece of glass over the soil to conserve moisture—it is necessary that the loam be kept damp but not actually wet. A temperature of 60 to 65 degrees gives best results.

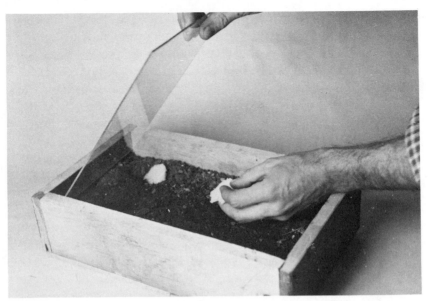

Although special raising containers are required, white worms are well worth the extra bother. Small amphibians love them. Photo by R. Gannon.

The worms will form masses, particularly where food has been introduced, and the required quantities can be picked out with forceps. If the soil should sour it will be necessary to start the colony anew with a fresh mixture of loam and dead leaves or leaf mold. The adult worms measure less than an inch in length and should be placed before the herptiles being fed in small masses, rather than individually.

TUBIFEX WORMS

Tubifex worms (*Tubifex, Limnodrilus*) are also useful in the rearing of some small herptiles and the feeding of adults of some larger species. They may be caught or purchased alive, or obtained in the freeze-dried form. The latter will serve most purposes as well as live worms. The worms themselves are tiny red creatures which inhabit muddy shallow waters. Their collection and storage presents some problems; for this reason the freeze-dried product is preferred over the natural one. The babies of the very small basking turtles—bog and spotted, for instance—are exceedingly difficult to bring to maturity without a highly nutritious diet that can be easily assimilated. Tubifex meet their requirements very well, but should be alternated with other nourishing items. They are not easily propagated under artificial conditions, but live worms can be stored over considerable periods in damp sand in a cool place.

OTHER FOODS

Various other small invertebrates can be raised with a degree of success as food for herptiles. Included are such forms as wax worms, flies, and fruit flies. Cockroaches make a fine food for many reptiles and amphibians, but most persons would find raising them for this purpose objectionable in the extreme. Be careful of feeding to

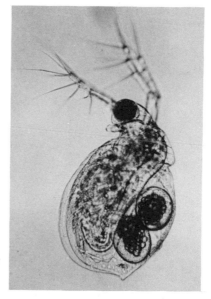

Daphnia and other small crustaceans are good as treats for salamanders, some frogs and some young water turtles. They are often difficult to culture, however. Photo by K. Lerch.

herptiles cockroaches captured in apartment houses and other places where measures for their control are being exercised. Some of the insects may be carrying poisonous substances.

Minnows of various kinds are among the best foods for small carnivorous turtles, crocodilians, certain lizards, and snakes, particularly garter and water types. One may seine them from ponds and streams, as well as saltwater inlets, but probably the easiest way to obtain a supply is from the dealer in live baits for fishermen. The latter often classify them according to type; such names as "shiners," "chubs," and "mummies" are common designations. The fish may be freshwater or saltwater kinds and will vary considerably in price. Saltwater types seem just as satisfactory as those from fresh water, from the standpoint of the vivarium keeper. They may be fed whole to animals like snakes and small monitors, or they may be finely chopped for feeding to turtles. They are so highly nutritious that it is possible to raise the commoner pet store turtles from infancy to adulthood on a diet of chopped fish alone. They can be kept frozen and used as needed during winter months when the live bait dealer may be out of them. Water snakes care little whether their fishes are alive or dead. Smelts, a fish-market item, will also prove useful in feeding herptiles. It is a good practice to rinse them thoroughly in fresh water before feeding them to terrarium animals.

Small fish, whether purchased goldfish or guppies, or collected minnows, are excellent food for many water turtles and water snakes. They will also be taken by some frogs and salamanders. Photo by L. E. Perkins.

An item used widely these days in the feeding of herptiles is canned dog food. Crocodilians, the larger aquatic salamanders, and many turtles will gustily devour spooned portions that are placed in their water. One of the better grades should be purchased and to each spoonful that is used a pinch of bone meal and vitamin concentrate may be added. On such a diet many captive herptiles will flourish for years. It is hardly necessary to list the many vegetables and fruits that are consumed by vegetarian herptiles. Specific food preferences are given in the accounts of the different species. In general, no vegetable substance that a reptile or amphibian will consume is likely to prove harmful to it. Some of the mushrooms which are very poisonous to humans are eaten by box turtles without ill effect. Tortoises and lizards may prefer vegetables which have been grated finely to those which are offered in larger pieces. With the former it is an easy matter to mix powdered vitamins and minerals when their use is indicated. Experiment with the foods bought for human consumption, both fresh and canned. Results will often surprise you—as when a favorite lizard that has been off its feed will perk up and show an interest in the white portion of a hard-boiled egg!

LACK OF APPETITE, FORCE-FEEDING

Herptiles occasionally stop eating for reasons that are not at once apparent. Species which are accustomed to hibernating may feed sparingly during the winter, even if kept warm. Prior to parturition, some reptiles fast and may continue to do so for a while after the eggs have been deposited or the young ones born. An incipient illness will cause a reptile or amphibian to stop eating. Severely chilled reptiles, in particular, often stop feeding before other symptoms of respiratory affliction are shown. Usually a snake stops eating for some days before shedding its skin. Some of the more nervous types of snakes will refuse to eat for long periods without apparent cause. A hiding box within their cage will often benefit such specimens. In fact, I think it is a good idea to provide all newly-captured reptiles with retreats in which they may feel themselves secure.

If all conditions of its environment seem correct and a herptile still shows no appetite after being tried with several kinds of natural foods over a period of a month or two, force-feeding may be considered, particularly if the specimen is a rare or exotic one. Force-feeding will not work well with amphibians or turtles; it can be

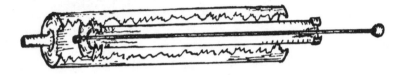

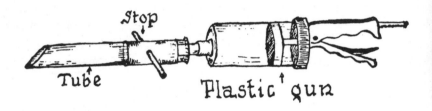

Various methods of force-feeding reptiles. From Smith, *Snakes as Pets*.

successfully used with crocodilians and the larger snakes and lizards. The force-feeding of a poisonous snake is not worth the risk involved.

In force-feeding a reptile an assistant should hold the animal still and in a straightened position while the operator administers the feeding. Slender and blunt-tipped forceps can be used to force some article of natural diet well into the throat of the reptile. The food should first have been lubricated with cod liver oil to facilitate its passage, at the same time lending additional nourishment to the meal. When the mouse, fish, or other item is pushed into the throat, the forceps should be carefully withdrawn. Often the meal will be swallowed at once, semi-voluntarily, one might say. In other cases,

Force-feeding large or dangerous species, such as this king cobra, is a job which should be undertaken only by experts. Photo by B. Haast.

however, it will be necessary to hold the reptile's mouth closed and gently massage the throat area to induce passage of the meal. After force-feeding, or natural feeding, for that matter, a reptile should not be handled for a while. After one or more forced meals, many reptiles begin to show a natural interest in food.

Instead of using a whole animal in force-feeding, some herpetologists prepare a special mixture with the idea of getting as much concentrated nourishment as possible into the animal. The following is a sample preparation for the force-feeding of a six-foot snake:

3 tablespoons of finely ground liver or lean raw beef

1 raw egg

4 drops liquid multivitamin preparation

Enough milk or water to bring the mixture to the consistency of a thick liquid

To the above, an antibiotic medication may be added in appropriate dosage, if required. Depending on the size of the reptile being fed, one may use a caulking gun, battery hydrometer, or ordinary hypodermic syringe. A rubber or plastic tubing of suitable diameter can be attached. The tube is inserted into the animal's mouth and slowly forced well into the gullet. Then the food mixture is forced through the tube. The size of the meal should be determined by the size of the reptile. With small specimens, a single tablespoonful or less may be suitable. Between forcefeedings, natural food should be offered. When it is necessary to continue the forced administration of food over an extended period, it may be done at intervals of a week or ten days.

Snakes, particularly those which are not feeding voluntarily, should have a plentiful supply of fresh drinking water available at all times. Water which has been contaminated from any cause should be removed at once from the cage. The tendency of rodents to urinate or defecate in a dish of water is another strong point against their use in the live state as food for snakes. A reptile may die from the effect of drinking contaminated water. Snakes can seldom be induced to drink milk voluntarily.

The appearance of a reptile or amphibian will reflect the attention that has been given to its diet. In nature, few species feed entirely upon a single substance. Snakes are rather more specialized in their feeding habits than most herptiles. The majority appreciate and benefit from some variety in their diet.

XIV

Illnesses and Other Problems

If carefully managed, herptiles do not present their keeper with many health problems. Ill reptiles and amphibians are rarely found in the wild state; many of the afflictions of captive specimens are traceable to mishandling at time of capture or thereafter. It is an unfortunate circumstance that some of the more important ailments of captive herptiles are contagious and will quickly spread from one animal to another if they are in contact. If there is one most important rule that should be observed by those who keep herptiles, it is this: isolate all new specimens for at least two weeks to determine their true state of health before they are brought into contact with the rest of the collection. Herptiles which appear healthy will once in a while be carrying an incipient illness. New specimens should not only be caged apart from the others but also should be kept in another room, if possible, until they have started to feed regularly, appear to be free of parasites, and present a generally healthy appearance. The introduction of a sick animal can throw an entire collection of similar types into poor health almost at once.

The herptile illnesses with which we are familiar are not known to be directly transmissible to humans. In fact, they are often highly selective to the animals themselves. There are few diseases which can be transmitted from amphibians to reptiles or vice versa, red-leg being one of the exceptions, unfortunately common. It is much easier to use common sense precutions to prevent illness than to cure it after it has arisen. Once an illness takes hold, only rarely is there a spontaneous remission—generally the cure of the afflicted creature will rest with the know-how of its owner. It can be a

Well-meaning people sometimes buy a nearly-dead specimen with the hope of reviving it. It would probably be more humane to let such specimens die or to kill them instead of prolonging their agony. Photo by M. F. Roberts.

most gratifying experience to bring a really sick herptile back to a state of health. Like the breeding of herptiles and the successful rearing of their babies, the curing of a sick animal is demonstrative of an expertise of which the herptile enthusiast may be justifiably proud. The specific illnesses of reptiles and amphibians have been less studied than those of many other animals. They therefore present an excellent field for experimentation. It should be remembered that even among humans some of the most important cures for common illnesses have been discovered quite by accident and sometimes by persons not in the medical profession!

TURTLE DISORDERS

Tortoises, even those from relatively cool natural environments, often contract a pneumonia-like respiratory condition when they have been chilled. Aureomycin can be useful in combating this. The tablets or capsules sold for use on birds may be dissolved in the afflicted reptile's drinking water or sprinkled on its food. Some veterinarians are qualified to treat sick reptiles and will inject an antibiotic.

Swellings on or about a turtle's head, or elsewhere, may be found occasionally. A bot fly is often responsible for these; its technical name is *Sarcophaga cistudinis*. Each lump may contain several maggots which will eventually emerge and fall off their host, pupate, then become adult flies. The condition may be cleared up by incising the lump carefully with a sharp razor or scalpel, forcing out the contained matter, then swabbing the affected area with an antibiotic emulsion. This will prevent an infection, a condition which often occurs even when the maggots emerge naturally. Sometimes, if deeply burrowed into the tissues of the turtle, they will prove fatal. Our box turtles are common hosts of these parasitic flies.

Eye disorders in turtles often produce total blindness and are usually accompanied by loss of appetite and general debility. Gantrisin is a product of promise in the treatment of eye troubles. The affected animal's eyes should be swabbed with soft, dry cotton tips to remove as much pus as possible. Then a drop of Gantrisin is placed on each eye. The condition usually clears up quickly. Terramycin or any of the fungicide remedies sold for aquarium use may prove effective, applied in the same manner.

Fungus infections are among the most serious with which a turtle keeper may contend. Some fungus afflictions remain confined to a small area indefinitely. We might call them non-malignant. Other types will spread rapidly. Turtles with fungus should be isolated at once in an easily-cleaned container. A high state of general cleanliness must be maintained and the animal must have a means of leaving the water to dry out completely, from time to time, during the course of treatment. A 5% iodine solution may be applied to the affected area, but never around the eyes. This is allowed to dry before the turtle is permitted to enter water. The treatment may have to be continued daily over an extended period. Vinegar has long been considered a good fungus cure and a badly affected turtle may, as a last measure, be placed in a very strong bath—say 50% vinegar and 50% water, and allowed to remain for a couple of days. Some zoos use this method of treating fungus to the exclusion of all others. Table salt is useful in the prevention, as well as cure, of some types of fungus. About three ounces to each five gallons of water does well. An abundance of sunlight will prove very helpful.

Often a liquid vitamin compound like Poly-Vi-Sol will help promote healing of injured skin and shell areas. This can be applied freely, then covered with vaseline to prevent washing away. Cuts may be swabbed with a $2\frac{1}{2}\%$ solution of mercurochrome, which should be allowed to dry before placing the animal back in its aquarium. A timid turtle may stay withdrawn into its shell while one attempts to treat conditions of the head, neck, or limbs. Such a reluctant patient can be made to extend its head and limbs by a gentle rasping of its shell or by holding the reptile in an upside-down position.

A few kinds of turtles have a naturally soft shell. With most, however, a soft shell is indicative of poor health. An abundance of vitamins and sunshine are the requisites for treatment. It seldom occurs in turtles which are beyond babyhood. In far-advanced cases the shell may become as soft as tissue paper and in my experience has been incurable by any means. Baby turtles that are fed nutritiously and given adequate sunshine or a substitute do not develop soft shell. Fortunately, the practice of painting turtles' shells to increase the saleability of the little reptiles is no longer a common one. If a turtle is acquired in this condition, the paint must be removed as promptly and thoroughly as possible. This is best accomplished by careful chipping with a sharp knife. Paint removers should not be used.

RICKETS

Crocodilians and lizards are sometimes afflicted with rickets, a condition caused by a lack of vitamins and sunshine. In the slender-snouted crocodilians, the jaws may become grossly deformed. In lizards, a common manifestation of the condition is a paralysis of the rear legs or weakness of the jaws. The condition can be cleared up by providing a good diet and plenty of sunshine. Multivitamin preparations will prove useful; if natural sunlight is not available, the use of an ultraviolet lamp will help. Rachitic animals commonly do not survive their early years, but even if the condition is arrested with proper care, the bone deformities will remain.

SNAKE AILMENTS

Snakes sometimes have difficulty in the shedding of their skins. Normally, when this process is about to take place the reptile's eyes will turn bluish-white and its body will lose much of its natural luster. Gradually, the eyes become clear again and the snake is about ready to shed. If this does not take place within a week after the eyes have cleared, it is well to apply assistive measures. The best I know is to

An improper diet early in life caused the humped back in this caiman. Although the animal may live, it will always be deformed. Photo by M. F. Roberts.

place the snake in a damp linen bag for about twenty-four hours. The shedding starts at the snout and if the rostral shield of the reptile has been damaged it will often prevent an effective sloughing of the old epidermis. An assist with fine-tipped tweezers to get the process started will often help in such cases. A snake may sometimes fail to shed several times, then relinquish two, three, or more old skins at once. This is not usual, however. Most snakes rapidly decline when they are unable to slough. A snake in the best of condition will be able to shed its skin even when there is no rock or other rough surface in its cage. A complete skin-shedding without assistive measures is another indication of good health among serpents.

Probably most snakes would have little difficulty in shedding if they were supplied with a container of water in which to immerse themselves. With most species, however, a bathing tank will be used to the extent where the continual wetness gives rise to blisters of the skin. These blisters are believed to be fungoid in origin. They spread and ultimately cause the death of the reptile. Strangely, snakes which are semi-aquatic in the wild state are as susceptible as others to this condition. Treatment consists of carefully slitting open the blisters, forcing out any liquid, and applying a solution of 50% ethyl alcohol. Sul-Met may be used instead of alcohol. Even the extremely aquatic snakes which spend nearly all of their time in the water can contract this condition. Its occurrence among them in an aquarium can be minimized by the use of water which is highly acid.

Respiratory illnesses among snakes seem to vary in their intensity, much as they do among humans. They run the gamut from simple colds which can be cleared up quickly by keeping the reptile warm and well fed to pneumonia-like conditions which are always fatal if broad-spectrum antibiotics are not applied. A snake with a cold will frequently cough or sneeze, much as a human does. When an infected snake is held in the hand, a peculiar rattling or disturbance of breathing will be noted. At the first sign of such trouble, isolate the affected reptile in a cage that is kept at a temperature of 80 degrees. Often the disturbance will clear up in a few days. More serious is the pneumonia-like condition brought about by severe chilling. A snake with this condition will refuse food and frequently raise its head and puff out its throat—an indication of labored breathing. The only cure for this condition is the injection of an antibiotic. It can reach epidemic proportions in a collection, either by direct contagion or the transference by mites, and can seldom be cured by home remedies. If the snake is highly valued, see a veterinarian. Otherwise, destroy the reptile when a puffing-out of the throat is first noted. If dissected, a snake with this pneumonia-like condition will show a bubbly congestion of the lung. I have had much personal experience with respiratory illnesses in snakes and can attest to the inadvisability of having reptiles shipped to cold climates by whatever means. Air transportation, even when the animals are picked up at the airport, does not solve the problem, for nearly always chills will occur. Perhaps the use of insulated shipping crates or styrofoam containers would minimize their incidence. If you insist upon receiving a snake in a cold climate during wintertime, keep the reptile isolated and in a warm situation until you are sure that it has not contracted a respiratory illness.

Mouth-rot is a disease about which much has been written. It occurs among snakes and lizards as well, but is perhaps most prevalent among the large constricting serpents. Its causes are obscure and among others have been suggested such things as long fasts, deprivation of drinking water, mouth injuries caused by biting or striking hard objects, and so forth. Most authorities agree that a bacillus is responsible for the onset of the condition. At first, the condition may manifest itself by only a small white spot in the mouth of the reptile. This rapidly enlarges and causes necrosis of tissues throughout the mouth. In extreme cases, the mouth itself may be much distorted by the masses of matter which develop. Mouthrot is very contagious, and a victim of it should be at once isolated from other reptiles. Fortunately, it is a curable condition. Any mild antiseptic, applied daily to the snake's mouth with a cotton swab, will prove beneficial; many severe cases have been cured in this way. Presently, the product of choice for the cure of mouth rot is Sul-Met, a $2\frac{1}{2}\%$ aqueous solution of sulfamethiazine, applied liberally and daily to the mouth of the affected reptile until the condition has cleared up. Snakes with mouth rot generally refuse to eat, and it may be necessary to force-feed them during the period of treatment. During this time loose teeth and decayed gum tissue should be removed from the reptile's mouth. Eventually, if the treatment is successful, the reptile will start eating of its own accord and may be considered cured when no evidences of oral lesions are present.

Ticks are a common malady of recently imported reptiles. The condition is easily cured and causes no lasting damage. Photo by G. Marcuse.

From the beginning of snake-keeping, parasites have been a problem. Serpents from the tropics and semi-tropics are often literally covered with parasites when captured. With such specimens they are often of little more discomfort than are fleas to a dog. But with captive snakes it is different. The smaller kinds spread quickly throughout a collection and may speedily prove fatal to the smaller snakes. There is evidence that they are able to transmit serious blood-poisoning among reptiles. Ticks are easily seen with the naked eye and can be pulled off the skin of a snake with tweezers. Perhaps a better method is to suffocate the parasite with a drop of oil or glycerin. It will then drop off and the danger of leaving its head imbedded in the skin of the reptile is eliminated. Mites pose a more difficult problem, for they are tiny and often multiply rapidly when conditions are favorable. A collector who has a large aggregation of specimens can be justifiably proud if no mites are present. To exclude them from a collection one must exercise the most meticulous quarantine measures for specimens coming in.

There are many ways of eliminating mites—nearly all are effective in some degree, but few seem to solve the problem completely once the pests have become firmly established. Snakes infested with mites may be placed in jars of water; this will drown most of the parasites in a short time. Those that crawl to the head may be eliminated with the application of olive oil. Cages must be thoroughly cleaned or a reinfestation of the reptiles will occur when they are placed back in them. Aquariums are easily cleaned with the use of ammonia and water. Wooden cages present more of a problem, for the tiny arachnids may hide in crevices, and nothing short of a complete repainting of the cage will eliminate them. Gradually, specifics for the cure of reptile maladies are being developed. In the case of mites, Dri-Die is one of these, and perhaps the best. It has long been used to eliminate mites among birds and is readily available commercially. Unlike many parasite killers, it does not contain DDT and is harmless to reptiles. Every new snake should be placed in a bag which has been liberally dusted with Dri-Die and allowed to remain there for an hour or more. When a general infestation of cages has taken place, the powder may be sprinkled into all corners and crevices. Almost any flea powder will help to eliminate the mite problem, but none containing DDT should ever be used. Water containers should be removed from the cages of specimens being treated for mites, since some mite-killing powders are very injurious to reptiles if swallowed. The manufacturers of insecticides sometimes change the ingredients of their preparations without changing the brand names. For this reason always check the label of every container purchased. Dri-Die, for instance, sometimes comes premixed with insecticides.

One of the most important considerations to be taken into account in the construction or purchase of a snake cage is whether it has any interior surface which could cause bruises to the reptile's snout if rubbed against. Wire screening, unlacquered wooden surfaces, and corner constructions are a few of the cage conditions which may cause severe bruising to the snout of a reptile which is continuously nosing about its cage. Snakes seem unmindful of the injuries caused to their snouts and consequently the rostral shield is often destroyed. This is less likely to happen with boas and pythons and the poisonous snakes than with the more nervous colubrine serpents. Snout

Various medications for the treatment of common ailments of turtles maintained in captivity are available at pet shops. Additionally, preventives in the form of food additives, especially vitamin-fortified preparations, are available. There are, however, very few commercial remedies specifically compounded for the treatment of ailments of other herptiles.

Turtles kept on concrete floors rub the plastron badly. This can be prevented by using smooth or soft flooring materials. Photo by M. F. Roberts.

destruction has been linked by some herpetologists to mouth rot. I have not seen evidence of this, but the destruction of a snake's snout may spoil an otherwise perfect specimen. Lizards can reproduce tails which have been lost, and among amphibians the replacement of lost limbs and other structures is commonplace. But I have not known of a snake to regrow the scalation on its snout when it had become damaged by abrasion against rough surfaces. Once a snake's snout has been damaged, if the nose shield has been completely destroyed, it will not be regenerated. A snake which has damaged its snout by probing can have the injured tissue swabbed with mercuro-chrome. It should be placed in a bag for several days to allow partial healing, then put into a cage where there is no possibility of further damage. The damaged area may heal over but will not assume its original coloration or surface tissue.

DISEASES OF AMPHIBIANS

Among amphibian diseases, the red-leg disease of frogs is one of the most commonly encountered. It is not only communicable from frog to frog, but may even be transmitted to salamanders and snakes. I have captured frogs which developed red-leg after a short period of confinement. The amphibian simply became badly bloated and a suffusion of red over the under-surface of the rear legs became apparent. These specimens ceased to feed but often lived for long periods. Their bodies appeared water-logged. Some references state that a protracted period of confinement at a low temperature will cure this ailment, but I have kept such specimens at temperatures of 40 to 50 degrees with no apparent improvement in their health. The disease is usually caused by the bacterium *Aeromonas hydrophila*, and should respond to antibiotics. The cure is so uncertain and the spread of the disease so swift that it is probably better to destroy infected specimens.

Fungus infections are not uncommon among captive newts and salamanders. Their development seems linked to overcrowding and temperatures which are too high. A lowered temperature will prolong the life of an amphibian which has fungus but, as with red leg, cure is evasive if possible at all and, once again, it is probably best to eliminate quickly diseased specimens, for fungus is very contagious. If one wishes to experiment in the matter of a cure, this had best be accomplished with the specimen in strict isolation from the rest of the collection. Some of the remedies used by aquarium fish hobbyists to combat fungus infections will benefit sick amphibians.

Unless every effort is made to prevent them, escapes are bound to occur in a collection of herptiles. Sometimes the animal is quickly recovered and seems none the worse for its experience. Rarely, its

With few exceptions, salamanders and frogs have very delicate skin, as shown by the exposed blood vessels of this newt. Desiccation leads to death; abrasion often leads to fungus. Photo by M. F. Roberts.

health may actually have improved during a period of freedom, even under seemingly adverse conditions. When an escaped specimen is caught, it is well to isolate it as one would a newly-received specimen, until it is certain that no ailment has been contracted. Amphibians particularly are likely to suffer skin abrasions after escape from their vivarium. These often form the planting ground for fungus infections.

When any reptile is placed in a bag, as during cage-cleaning, every care should be exercised to see that the animal does not fall from a table or chair. It is best to leave bagged animals on the floor, in a place where there is no danger that they will be stepped on. A fall from a height of several feet will almost never kill a reptile at once. However, spinal injuries are very frequent and these ultimately prove fatal. Often, after a fall, a specimen will stop eating and go into a slow decline. Reptiles have a delicate bone structure, and while the breaking or loss of the tail may be of little consequence, any injury, however slight, to the main portion of the spine will eventually cause the death of the animal.

Occasionally it may become necessary to destroy a sick animal. There are many ways of accomplishing this, for reptiles and amphibians are not as tenacious of life as commonly thought. I consider freezing the most humane method of killing a sick herptile. The specimen may be placed in a cloth or plastic bag and put into the household freezer. The struggles of animals so treated are half-hearted and quickly diminish, for cold takes an extremely rapid hold on reptiles particularly. Amphibians are a bit slower to succumb. It is doubtful whether any herptile suffers physically when this method of killing is employed.

SELECTED
BIBLIOGRAPHY

Anyone interested in herptiles should belong to at least one of the international organizations devoted to their study. Each of these groups publishes a journal which contains articles of interest to all herpetologists, whether taxonomists, ecologists or behaviorists.

The quarterly journal *Copeia* is published by the American Society of Ichthyologists and Herpetologists and contains articles on both fish and herptiles (about half-and-half). Generally speaking, it has a larger content of long articles than the other journals. If interested in membership, apply to Secretary, Division of Reptiles and Amphibians, U.S. National Museum, Washington, D.C. 20560.

The Herpetologists' League has published *Herpetologica* since 1936. This exclusively herpetological journal is smaller than *Copeia* and tends to have shorter articles; it is strong on taxonomic and North American subjects. Interested parties should contact Hobart E. Landreth, Okla. Zoo—U. of Okla., R.R. 1, Box 478, Oklahoma City, Okla. 73111.

The Society for the Study of Amphibians and Reptiles (formerly the Ohio Herpetological Society) publishes a journal which contains articles of varying size and content—both notes and monographic studies have been published. The Society also has a reprint program, providing reprints of major early herpetological work. Contact SSAR, c/o Zoology Department, Ohio State University, Athens, Ohio 45701.

Two books of importance to keepers of amphibians and reptiles are mentioned here to emphasize their value to terrarium keepers. One is John Van Denburgh's *Reptiles of Western North America* (California Academy of Science, 1922). Although this two-volume work is somewhat outdated taxonomically, it still contains a great deal of useful description of western lizards and snakes. The photographs are clear and very useful. The book is usually easily available from second-hand book dealers.

The popular *Field Guide to Reptiles and Amphibians* (of eastern North America) by Conant now has a western companion. It is Robert Stebbins' *Field Guide to Western Reptiles and Amphibians* (Houghton Mifflin, 1966). This small volume contains information on all the salamanders, frogs, toads, turtles, lizards and snakes found west of the Great Plains area. The plates are beautifully done, and the text contains a great deal of information on natural history as well as identification. The two field guides should be in the library of every keeper of herptiles.

Articles of interest to amateur herpetologists also appear occasionally in other journals, such as *The American Midland Naturalist* and *Southwestern Naturalist*. Most college libraries receive most or all of the above journals, so they should be available to interested parties.

The following is a list of some of the more significant English-language works on reptiles and amphibians. No strictly juvenile books have been included, nor have any purely technical treatises. The books listed vary in depth of their treatment of the subject matter; all are thoroughly readable and useful to students at every level of learning. Many older books, particularly those of that master writer-herpetologist, Raymond L. Ditmars, have much to offer but are now obsolete in some ways. Some of the books are no longer in print but may be available in libraries or used book stores.

Allen, E. Ross and Wilfred T. Neill, 1950. *Keep them alive*. Ross Allen's Reptile Institute, Silver Springs, Florida.

Bellairs, Angus de'A., 1957. *Reptiles*. Anchor Press, Ltd., Tiptree, Essex, England.

Bishop, Sherman C., 1943 (and later reprints). *Handbook of salamanders of the U.S. and Canada*. Comstock Publishing Co., Ithaca, N.Y.

Breen, John F., 1967. *Reptiles and amphibians in your home.* T.F.H. Publications, Inc., Neptune City, N.J.

Carr, Archie, 1952. *Handbook of turtles.* Cornell University Press, Ithaca, N.Y.

Clyne, Densey, 1969. *Australian frogs.* Periwinkle Books, Lansdowne Press, Melbourne, Australia.

Cochran, Doris M., 1961. *Living amphibians of the world.* Double-day & Co., Inc., Garden City, N.Y.

Cogger, Harold, 1967. *Australian reptiles in colour.* East-West Center Press, Honolulu, Hawaii.

Conant, Roger, 1958. *A field guide to reptiles and amphibians of the U.S. and Canada east of the 100th meridian.* Houghton Mifflin Co., Boston, Mass.

Curran, C. H. and Carl Kauffeld, 1937. *Snakes and their ways.* Harper Brothers, N.Y., N.Y.

Ditmars, Raymond L., 1908 (and later editions). *The reptile book.* Doubleday & Co., Inc., Garden City, N.Y.

——, 1931 (and later editions). *Snakes of the world.* Macmillan Co., N.Y., N.Y.

Fitzsimons, V. F. M., 1962. *Snakes of southern Africa.* Macdonald & Co., Ltd., London, England.

Isemonger, R. M., 1962. *Snakes of Africa.* Thos. Nelson & Sons, Johannesburg, South Africa.

Kauffeld, Carl, 1957. *Snakes and snake hunting.* Hanover House, Garden City, N.Y.

Klauber, L. M., 1956. *Rattlesnakes.* 2 vols. University of California Press, Berkeley, California.

Oliver, James A., 1955. *The natural history of North American amphibians and reptiles.* D. van Nostrand Co., Inc., Princeton, N.J.

Pope, Clifford H., 1939. *Turtles of the United States and Canada.* Alfred A. Knopf, N.Y., N.Y.

——, 1955. *The reptile world.* Alfred A. Knopf, N.Y., N.Y.

——, 1961. *Giant snakes.* Alfred A. Knopf, N.Y., N.Y.

Pritchard, Peter C. H., 1967. *Turtles of the world.* T.F.H. Publications, Inc., Neptune City, N.J.

Rose, Walter, 1950. *The reptiles and amphibians of southern Africa.* Maskew Miller, Ltd., Cape Town, Republic of South Africa.

Schmidt, Karl P. and Robert F. Inger, 1957. *Living reptiles of the world*. Hanover House, Garden City, N.Y.

Smith, Hobart M., 1946. *Handbook of lizards*. Comstock Publishing Co., Ithaca, N.Y.

——, 1965. *Snakes as pets*. T.F.H. Publications, Inc., Neptune City, N.J.

Stebbins, Robert C., 1954. *Amphibians and reptiles of western North America*. McGraw-Hill Book Co., Inc., N.Y., N.Y.

Worrell, Eric, 1963. *Reptiles of Australia*. Angus & Robertson, Ltd., Sidney, Australia.

Wright, A. H. and A. A. Wright, 1949. *Handbook of frogs and toads*. Comstock Publishing Co., Ithaca, N.Y.

——, 1957. *Handbook of snakes of the United States and Canada*. 2 vols. Cornell University Press, Ithaca, N.Y.

Zim, H. S. and H. M. Smith, 1953. *Reptiles and amphibians: A guide to familiar American species*. Simon & Schuster, N.Y., N.Y.

INDEX

574

575